HS92

£ 15.00

D0985070

THE WORLDS OF PATRICK GEDDES

THE WORLDS OF PATRICK GEDDES
Biologist, Town planner,
Re-educator, Peace-warrior

Philip Boardman

Routledge & Kegan Paul
London, Henley and Boston

First published in 1978
by Routledge & Kegan Paul Ltd
39 Store Street,
London WC1E 7DD,
Broadway House,
Newtown Road,
Henley-on-Thames,
Oxon RG9 1EN and
9 Park Street,
Boston, Mass. 02108, USA
Printed and bound in Great Britain by
Lowe & Brydone Printers Ltd,
Thetford, Norfolk

British Library Cataloguing in Publication Data

Boardman, Philip
  The worlds of Patrick Geddes.
  1. Geddes, *Sir* Patrick
  I. Title
  711'.092'4   HT166   77-30515

ISBN 0-7100-8548-6

CONTENTS

ACKNOWLEDGMENTS

To Patrick Geddes's daughter Norah and son Arthur I am indebted for
oral and written answers to sporadic questions from 1935 to 1944 and
to 1968, respectively.   Dr Arthur Geddes also allowed me, in 1968,
to record on tape both responses to questions and reminiscences
about his parents and home life.   His widow, Mrs Jeannie Geddes,
has kindly given me access to material in her possession and full
permission to use her copyrighted documents in the National Library
of Scotland.

I am especially grateful to the late Philip Mairet for permission to
quote widely from his biography, 'Pioneer of Sociology - The Life
and Letters of Patrick Geddes' (Lund Humphries, 1957), now out of
print.   Besides knowing Geddes for over twenty-five years, Mr
Mairet had close cooperation with Arthur and his book contains valuable information from family sources, as well as from certain documents no longer available.   Other excellent sources have been
Amelia Defries's 'The Interpreter Geddes' (Routledge, 1927) and
'Patrick Geddes in India' (Lund Humphries, 1947, edited by Jaqueline
Tyrwhitt).   Both publishers have graciously authorised much use of
these books.

The University of North Carolina Press has generously given me permission to utilise both printed and illustrative material from my
first biography, 'Patrick Geddes - Maker of the Future', 1944.   The
present book has, however, been completely rewritten with copious
additions from new sources, as well as with extensive deletions.

It is to Lewis Mumford that I am most indebted: first, for helping
explain Patrick Geddes to me ever since 1928 and, more recently, for
his catalysing persistence in starting me on this new biography.
He has patiently replied to scores of letters, contributed original
information, and made valuable suggestions on drafts of many chapters.   He has nevertheless largely refrained from appraisals,
placing ultimate responsibility for the book upon its writer.

I must not fail to thank Geddes himself who received me at his
College des Ecossais in Montpellier in 1929 and 1930 on a 'work

scholarship' which he really could not afford.   (I had come upon
him quite by chance in 1925-6 while studying in southern France on a
US Junior-Year-Abroad scholarship, and returned to him three years
later as an eye-strained and impecunious graduate.)

Acknowledgment of past kindnesses is also due his second wife,
Lilian Geddes, and younger colleagues Edward McGegan, T.R. Marr and
John Ross - all now departed.   The latter three helped me collect
material in Edinburgh, London and Montpellier used in a doctoral
thesis on 'L'Oeuvre éducatrice de Patrick Geddes' (University of
Montpellier, 1936);   while Paul Reclus, then Adviser of Studies at
the *Collège*, was a shrewdly helpful coach.   Their generous assistance made it possible to expand the French work a few years later
into 'Patrick Geddes - Maker of the Future'.

For recent, efficient help I am obliged to kind individuals at many
institutions: the National Library of Scotland Departments of Manuscripts and of Printed Books, and Map Room have given prompt and
interested service.   Let me thank personally Allan Bell, Elspeth
Yeo, Ann Young, A. Baillie and Sheila Gebbie;   the British Embassy
Information Service in Oslo, Deichmanske Library, Oslo;   the Universities of Dundee, Edinburgh and St Andrews, and especially the University of Keele Library where Victor Branford's manuscripts are
preserved.   At the University of Oslo I have received much assistance from its main Library, British Institute, and Photographic and
Reproduction Services, while colleagues at the International Summer
School have shown helpful understanding during my biographical tru-
ancies and otherwise.   In London, John Tandy has given friendly,
untiring assistance with a wide range of problems;   likewise, David
Lock has continued his help far beyond the skilful editing performed
in line of duty.

I wish to mention two of the younger generation of Geddes scholars,
Drs Helen Meller and John P. Reilly, thanking the latter for letting
me preview his thesis, 'The Early Social Thought of Patrick Geddes'
(Columbia University, 1971), and the former for some information on
Geddes in India which will be greatly extended in her coming book.
Further, I much appreciate Paddy Kitchen's permission to make use of
her recent book on Geddes: 'A Most Unsettling Person ...' (Gol-
lancz, 1975).   Specific credit is given in the text concerned.

Coming to personal indebtedness, I am grateful to my publisher
brother, Myron, for much encouragement and critical reading of typescripts, likewise to a person who wishes to remain anonymous, for a
subsidy-loan without which needed research and travel to Great
Britain could not have been accomplished.   Finally, I offer inadequate words of thanks, for season after season of patient and skilful retyping of impossible drafts, to my wife Aase.

P.B.
Asker, Norway

x

The author and publishers are grateful to the following individuals
and organisations to reproduce illustrative material:
    Jeannie Geddes
    Gladys Mayer
    André Schimmerling
    Sir Landsborough Thompson
    The Secretary, The University of Dundee
    The Trustees of the National Library of Scotland
    The Royal Society of Edinburgh
    The National Library of Norway
    The University of Keele Library
    The University of Strathclyde (Geddes Collection)
    The University of North Carolina Press
    Lund Humphries
    The *Builder*
    The *Survey Graphic*

It has proved difficult in certain cases to trace copyright owners
of illustrative material. However, all possible care has been taken
to trace ownership of the illustrations used and to make acknowledgment for their use.

INTRODUCTION

Patrick Geddes was active in so many apparently unrelated fields
that today most people who already know of him have confidently
labelled him as a biologist *or* town planner *or* sociologist *or*
educator. Those who hear about him for the first time may,
quite understandably, regard him as a dispersive jack-of-all
trades shuttling among jumbles of now academic, now practical
interests.

My hope in this book, however, is to present an unusually *complete*
man: one who delighted in escaping from all labels, pidgeon-
holes and compartments, be they of science or of action. Turn
by turn - and even simultaneously - he was a botanist, economist,
sociologist, producer of pageants, public lecturer, writer of
verse, art critic, publisher, civic reformer, town planner,
Victorian moralist, provocative agnostic and academic revolutionary. But in his own mind he was a 'comprehensive, synthe-
sising generalist' whose unswerving aim was to 'see life whole'.
To his own family he was both lovable and an unintentional
tyrant; to friends, colleagues and would-be disciples a source
of utter exasperation as well as vital inspiration.

His life spanned parts of two very different centuries, 1854 to
1932, yet his thoughts and deeds were not only divided among many
interests but in addition often so far ahead of contemporaries
that even his most practical object lessons have been ignored
for decades. Now, happily a Geddesian renaissance is setting
in; there is a scramble to republish his main works on town
planning with new prefaces and to mine articles and theses out
of his multitudinous notes, letters and diagrams, and his relatively sparse publications. New biographies are also on the
way for which there is more than enough unused material to go
around. Yet valuable though every detailed study of this or
that aspect of his thought may be, there are really only two
justifications for writing about Patrick Geddes. One is to
present him as, in most ways, a rare prototype of the whole man
who is needed now more than ever in civic life and industry as
well as in universities and churches. The other is to assess,

1

improve and apply his diagnoses and treatments of rural, urban
and international ills; and to bring the wisest and keenest of
his messages to present and future generations.

The 'Case of Patrick Geddes' contains many psychological enigmas
to which full answers may never be found either in the personal
documents that have escaped destruction (1) or in the recollections
of colleagues. His passion for seeing life whole he himself
ascribed to a happy childhood with a 'wise and gentle' father as
his first teacher, and to the harmoniously beautiful Perthshire
region in which he had the good fortune to grow up. But Patrick's
two elder brothers developed none of his 'Geddesian' traits, nor
did the boyhood friends who explored with him the same interwoven
pattern of town and countryside. Nevertheless, all of his
varied interests and activities of maturity can be traced back to
stimuli in an almost ideal childhood. 'The child is not only
father to the man', he wrote in a biography; (2) 'the child is
the man!'

Patrick's home was lacking in but one vital aspect, music. Both
parents were Free Kirk fundamentalists, and song and ornament in
church were against its principles. Yet, though even laughter
was forbidden on the silent Sabbath, the father read Old Testament
stories which both delighted the boy and cropped up later in the
grown-up town planner. At other times the father recited Highland
ballads with such fervour as to arouse an enduring love of dramatic
poetry and provide some of the emotional experience which music
might have given. Even so, Geddes would later confess to having
'Scottish repressions' and occasionally give witness that he was
at heart a poet, neglected and 'choked down'.

This conflict of interests and feelings reappeared in his own
family relationships. Patrick, the eye-minded natural scientist,
met a gifted musician, Anna Morton, and both fell deeply in love.
Their marriage was one of affectionate, yet intellectual and
moralistic, home life with three children who tried to combine
musical expression with early introduction to the father's world
of nature exploration, science and civic affairs. Neither parent
was happy when the other had to be away, yet Patrick never seemed
to turn down an opportunity to lecture, consult or just travel.
(He even went on a trip to Greece with a friend just after his
engagement to Anna!) Numerous love-letters have been preserved
from both of them, and this phrase in one of Patrick's is a true
expression of his feeling: 'The best of life for man is the
worship of woman.' At 50, Anna would still count the days until
his return from an absence, just as she had done in her engagement
love-letters to him.

Contrarywise, when writing to his daughter and two sons, Geddes
mixed one-fifth affectionate interest in their welfare with four-
fifths tutorial admonition and self-centred concern about their
preparation for helping him as junior colleagues. Upon Anna's
tragic death in India after thirty-one years of marriage, his
sorrow was increased by self-recrimination for neglecting her

health under his constant pressure of work and travel.   That same
year, 1917, the older and patently favourite son was killed in
France, and this double tragedy warped his own life and human contacts from then on.   He sought relief in even harder work 'as the
only anodyne', and increased his injunctions and pleas for collaboration to the remaining son and daughter.   Occasionally there
was a desperate plea for them to realise that he really loved them
and was *not* the 'spiritual tyrant' they alleged him to be.   At the
same time his search for the perfect disciple became more and more
intense, just as an increasing yen for optimal evaluation of past
accomplishments and current projects played a more noticeable part
in his relations with others.   Whereas this trait had usually
confined itself to chameleon-like adaptations when applying for
this or that professorial or directorial chair, and to wide-
embracing letterheads, it would reach a zenith in his seventies
in connection with plans for a 'whole College of colleagues' and
for an international *Cité Universitaire* in southern France.

Another trait, which intermittently worried friends and triggered
enemies, was his cavalier attitude towards certain tenets of
finance.   Although constantly preaching against the Mammon-
worship of an economy based on money-wealth, he could on occasion
utilise personal overdrafts, postponements and friendly loans or
advances in order to further what he considered a worthy project.
This was never done for personal gain or even the welfare of his
family: but always for the sake of some practical ideal like
improved housing for workers and students in Edinburgh, the re-
settling of refugees in Cyprus or the preservation of certain
World's Fair buildings in Paris for permanent international use.
Both family and friends had to live with this defect of his qualities, though not always without protest.

Coming to the many careers of Patrick Geddes, one will only
mention their nature and sequence here.   As Thomas Huxley's 'distinguished pupil' he should, logically, have continued pioneer
researches in borderline areas between plants and animals and in
cell theory and become a 'Scottish Darwin' as many contemporary
scientists predicted.   Instead, near-blindness and many weeks in
a dark-room while on a fossil-hunting expedition in Mexico,
together with his previous discovery of Auguste Comte through the
London Positivists, turned him from the microscope to contemplation
and the expression of thought by graphic 'thinking machines'.   At
the same time he moved 'upwards' into the latest-developing science of sociology (which for him included economics).   A logical
application of these new interests, given the youthful experience
of town and country, people and their work, was his 'valley-
section' approach to civic and town-planning problems.

Not winning the coveted Regius Chair of Botany at Edinburgh in
1888, he accepted a part-time professorship at University College,
Dundee, specially created for him.   This allowed him to spend
three-quarters of each year in Edinburgh, London, Paris; in
Cyprus, the USA, India, Palestine.   Between the 1890s and 1913
he devised and showed the itinerant 'Cities Exhibition' which made

his name as a planner, and ultimately brought him commissions to study and report on, in part or wholly, some fifty cities in Scotland, Ireland, India and Palestine.

At the same time as he served his apprenticeship with the 'Cities Exhibition' before and after 1900, he was giving University Extension and other public lectures on subjects ranging from 'The Origins of Science' for workmen in Scotland to 'Contemporary Social Evolution' and 'Universities, Past and Present' for audiences in London. Simultaneously he organised the Edinburgh Summer Meetings every August year after year, developed the Outlook Tower on Castle Hill as an instrument for Regional Survey and as the 'World's First Sociological Laboratory', and founded the first student halls of residence in Scotland.   Even earlier he and Anna had moved into historic but filthy James Court and begun their joint attack on the slums of Old Edinburgh.   There, in the 1880s, he first practised the 'Conservative Surgery' which, as a better alternative than wholesale clearance in many cases, would become famous in his Indian reports of 1914-22 and, after being forgotten, would be rediscovered by planners in the 1970s as 'rehabilitation'.

Still another activity dates from about the same time Geddes became a part-time professor at Dundee and a 'full-time generalist' in the British Isles.   Among the many roles he assumed, the most disturbing to fellow academics was the one revealed in his maiden public lecture in Dundee in 1888: that of 'Wandering Inspector-Critic of Universities'.   Not only did he have a knack for epithets like 'portly word-fog giants' to describe certain teachers and administrators; he also began a life-long campaign against the routine of 'cram-jaw-exam' which masqueraded as secondary and higher 'education'.   Indeed, with his self-governing halls of residence in Edinburgh and his pleas for continuous 'estimation' instead of solemn, final 'parrot-repetitions', he was about seventy years in advance of the student revolutionaries of today. Yet as a general 'disturber of the peace', to use his words, he awoke more ire from the establishments concerned than co-operation from hearers and readers.

The impact of Geddes has varied greatly from field to field, from very little today in biology to great actuality in city and regional planning.   Here much of his influence has been spread by pupils, colleagues and continuators like Sir Patrick Abercrombie, Sir William (later Lord) Holford, Sir Raymond Unwin and, perhaps most of all in many areas, by Lewis Mumford.   Another significant American was the regional planner, Benton MacKaye, who helped translate Geddesian 'geotechnics' into the philosophy and achievements of the Tennessee Valley Authority from the 1930s on.   Yet there are vast fields like human ecology, war-and-peace research, and peace-making in which Geddes's pioneer work has yet to become known and applied.   For instance, in 1884 when working out his own 'Principles of Economics', he sounded this ecological warning which still needs repeating and heeding in every part of the world: 'when any given environment or function, however apparently productive, is really fraught with disastrous influence to the

organism, its modification must be attempted, or, failing that, its
abandonment faced.' (3)

As for finding and applying 'moral equivalents for war' a phrase
which William James picked up from him - Patrick Geddes is also an
unexploited source of wise generalisation and practical suggestions.
From experience in Cyprus with Turks, Armenians and Greeks; in
Palestine with Jews, Arabs and Christians; and in Ireland with
Catholics, Protestants, James Larkin's army and rulers of Empire,
he distilled many a valid sociological and human dictum.   'Solve
the agricultural question and you solve the Eastern Question....'
By including the resettlement of refugees in his 'agricultural
question' of 1897, one can apply the next quotation directly to
current Israeli-Arab problems.
> Give men hope of better land, of enough food for their families,
> and you remove a main cause of bloodshed....   For wherever at
> this moment two Easterners are quarrelling in their poverty,
> four or six or ten might soon be cooperating in wealth and
> peace. (4)

In Dublin in 1914 he got the City Corporation to authorise a new
garden-village for Larkin's striking dockers, and the promise of
'New houses ... with no higher rent than for their present hovels'
was already solving this aspect of the 'Irish question'.   Geddes
then won over the Archbishop with plans for a cathedral, school
and art gallery to replace two churches which the Reformation had
taken away, while the Viceroy had already announced a competition
for an entire new city plan.   Here, indeed, was almost an achievement of 'constructive, dynamic Peace' which beyond any doubt would
have forestalled the Sinn Fein Rebellion, and prevented much of
today's hopeless impasse of long-standing religious and political
hatreds.   Yet all this was brutally thwarted by the outbreak of
the First World War.

Returning briefly to problems of individual human nature, one can
note that while Geddes steadily attracted many would-be disciples
and some able collaborators, both types soon left him: the former
because they could not understand him, the latter because of
Geddes's strange alternation of pleading, commandeering and
neglect which finally drove them away in frustration.   Actually,
he had only two doggedly faithful colleagues: (Sir) J. Arthur
Thomson in biology and Victor Branford in sociology, and his major
works in those fields were published jointly with them.

His relationship with a much younger colleague, whom he hoped would
replace his lost son and become the continuator par excellence, is
a sad tale of what appeared to the one as elderly wilfulness and to
the other as youthful stubbornness.   This is the quandary of the
dissident disciple, Lewis Mumford, which has been described at
length by him. (5)   Yet what Mumford took to be behaviour of on-
coming old age was standard routine for Geddes in proselytising
situations.   The American neophyte received very nearly the same
treatment as many others, including a Cornishman in Edinburgh
thirty years earlier.   This intriguing matter will be taken up in

its chronological place: suffice it to say here that Lewis Mumford
was unique in being able to combine his denial with a very selective
collaboration which first established his own independent career,
yet furthered many of Geddes's causes as well.

Another perplexing case is that of the psychologist and educator,
G. Stanley Hall, who came to Dundee looking for Geddes, the 'Professor of Psychology'. The two became good friends and visited
each other several times. Hall was so enthusiastic about the
Outlook Tower - 'the most interesting thing educationally' that he
had seen abroad - and its founder that he even dreamed in the early
1900s of being a Boswell to him.

> If I myself were a stenographer ... and could devote a year or
> two ... prodding him with all kinds of questions by day and
> writing it up at night, and reading what he has written Sundays,
> and put it together in good shape, I believe it would be the
> best contribution to the world I ever have or shall make. (6)

But how to explain that in G. Stanley Hall's autobiography there
is not a single mention of Patrick Geddes?

To the riddles of family- and colleague-relations must be added
those of religious and psycho-analytical nature. Both the evangelist, Henry Drummond, who graduated from Edinburgh University
around 1866, and Geddes who fled from it after one week in 1874,
were able quoters of Scripture. Both used 'faith, hope and love'
for their respective purposes: Drummond to convert and the scientist to confirm some interpretation of society. Each one also
saw evolution as the 'Ascent of Man', not 'Descent'. But even a
liberal theologian would have rejected Geddes as a 'believer' in
spite of his stating, on occasion, that he accepted every mythology, every philosophy and every religion. He designed in 1919
what might have been an inter-faith university for Jerusalem and
cited both the Old and New Testaments regarding his plans for rebuilding the 'Holy City'. In an educational pamphlet published
in India he declared: 'We are becoming more religious too, as we
learn through the great Teachers, how "in every nation he that
feareth God and doeth righteousness is accepted of Him"'. (7)   Yet
when a young relative of Drummond came to the Scots College in
Montpellier in 1926, Geddes outdid the Evil One in his efforts to
persuade this student to give up Christian theology.

As for depth psychology, he frequently expressed his distrust of
Freudian analyses and prescribed his own work-therapy ('ergo-
therapy') as better for the patient. On the other hand, he was
greatly interested in Alfred Adler and late in life became first
President of the New Europe Group in London, at the invitation of
Dimitrije Mitrinović. (8)   C.G. Jung's archetypes and four classes
of people ought to have appealed to Geddes as a re-interpreter of
mythology and disciple of Comte, but he never appears to have
commented on Jung's work.

That Patrick Geddes was a repressed poet and emotional, as well as
an avowed dramatist, was evidenced at intervals during his life.
When convalescing in 1922 in the Himalayan foothills at Simla he

suddenly found himself giving rhythmic expression to thoughts, feelings and fantasies. He told his close friend Victor Branford, in
blank verse, that this experience had cured him not only of his
'life-long writer's cramp' but also of some of his 'terrible Scottish
repression'. The spell lasted for weeks, but on returning to
planning jobs and to his new chair of Civics and Sociology at Bombay
University, the poetic urge vanished. In Scotland a year later,
after his daughter's singing had reminded him of Anna, he had a
brief impulse to learn to sing in a chorus, but that too vanished.

His interest in ballads and drama as a way of teaching history goes
back to his father's recitations in Gaelic and English, but it was
in 1912 that he first produced his 'Masques of Ancient and Modern
Learning' - to mark the Silver Jubilee of the self-governing Halls
of Residence in Edinburgh. In Bombay in early 1923, just before
leaving for his third lecture trip to the USA and for his first
'meeting in the flesh' with Lewis Mumford, he had the text of these
Masques reprinted as 'Dramatisations of History'. His preface to
this '5th Edition, Tenth Thousand' describes them as 'a more comprehensive presentment than has before been attempted upon any
stage, of main phases and salient events in the long and changeful
history of civilisation'. There also he made this challenge to
education and to the 'Making of the Future':
> We do not clearly think, much less clearly idealise, until we
> visualise: that is, until we dramatise. The War-world has
> long best known this, as its training in 'Kriegspiel' before
> the war has shown. So why not also be thinking out our aims
> and purposes as clearly, and learning also, as here for trial,
> to play the games of Peace? And even as something towards
> War's 'moral substitute'?

The story of Geddes's crowded years of thought and action, biting
criticisms and optimistic plans, warm affection and domineering
intellect will be told in its main lines, but with many illustrative details. Whatever the reader's and posterity's final judgment on the careers and enigmas of this Scottish life-scientist,
town planner, re-educator and peace-warrior, one ventures to predict that everyone will agree with the main quests of that rich
life. How to find ways of overcoming rural decay, urban disintegration and the world-wide threats of wardom? How to reconcile
individual freedom with social and civic responsibility in a
society based on friendly regional cooperation?

Though he seemingly lived and worked in many different worlds his
purpose was to show that they are all one. This one world of
nature and man, of labour and art, of science and religion is
guided by 'Love as Creation's final law', affirmed Patrick Geddes.
But it is up to today's men, women and children to make and keep
it 'Good, True and Beautiful'.

Chapter 1

CHILDHOOD AND YOUTH, 1854-74

ADVENTURE AT HOME

Spring had been in full possession of the old Scottish town of
Perth that day until afternoon brought release to the crowd of
boys in the Academy.   Into peaceful lanes and streets they
poured, shouting and scuffling for pure animal joy of freedom
regained: a ring of life and clamour which spread throughout
the historic City.   On the crest of this wave of youth was a
slender lad of ten who ran in the road because, as a comrade
later reported, 'he'd nae time to walk on the pavement.'   Pausing
briefly in a shop to pick up his father's newspaper, the boy
darted homeward across the Tay River bridge, bare knees flashing
under his grey kilt.

He glanced at the paper when the steepening slope of the Tay's far
bank slowed him down to a walk, but on this sunny day not even the
dispatches about the end of the war in America could hold his
attention for long.   To him the month of April 1865 meant
rejoicing mainly because another spring had arrived at last.   It
was the moment long awaited during the many winter weeks of rain
and dreariness.   It was the first warm day of spring!

A half mile up the winding hill road he turned into the gate of a
small cottage, standing in a large garden, just long enough to
drop his school-bag and newspaper, then dashed out again into the
sunshine.   A hundred yards more up the road, a scramble over its
bank to the edge of a field, and there he was at his 'aquarium'.
An adult would only have noticed a small spring draining into the
ditch below, but the boy saw it truly as a pool richly filled with
growing, moving life.

There, in his own later recollection:
  Back-spotted little 'water-spiders', as we called them, are
  ever gliding over its surface, dimpling its surface into tiniest
  ripples and changing lights; and strange little crustaceans
  swim below....   And along the ditch an exuberance of flowers,
  water forget-me-nots, water buttercups, a mimulus too, and

orpines on the near bank above.   Haunting those flowers, were
butterflies! - white and orange-tips, with coppers, and best of
all, blues!   In spring, too - Oh wonder! - frogs, egg-jellies,
then tadpoles!   Next budding legs, to froglings, then by and
by to big froggies, so beautiful! (1)

How fascinating to stay and watch, but today the hilltop above
beckoned even more strongly.   Passing his favourite quarry, he
swiftly climbed a stretch of wild moor and still uncut forest.
This ten-year-old observed the golden gorse, the beech, birch and
fir trees with the eye of an experienced naturalist, yet felt above
all the pure joy of a child to whom nature is both a commonplace
and a marvel.   Heart pounding, cheeks flushed under thick wind-
tousled hair, grey-blue eyes sparkling, he arrived at the climax
of his adventure, the 700-foot top of Kinnoull Hill.

At his feet the hill dropped in an almost sheer cliff several hundred feet down to the Tay River, which swung around in a great bend
before widening eastward into its Firth and finally joining the
North Sea.   Its near side was flanked by 'a long range of precipices accented here and there by a ruined tower or wall, a sight
which was to seem to me in later years more noble than any vista
along the Rhine'.   Across the river fertile farmlands stretched
to the south, and behind them ranged the mingled hills and valleys
of the old kingdom of Fife.   Upstream and at the bottom of the
hill, the Fair City of Perth lay spread out as in a relief map.
Steeples and factory chimneys, streets and buildings, all plainly
recognisable, even the now miniature Academy.

The boy loved to give his imagination full rein when thus looking
out over the world around him and to people it with all the characters he knew from legend and history.   First the Roman legions
marching up from the south and shouting, 'Ecce Tiberius!' 'Ecce
Campus Martius!', so much did the sight of the Tay with its broad
South Inch remind them of the Tiber and the field of Mars.   On
the corresponding North Inch, whose hundred acres now sprawled
between his school and the river, he saw taking place 'that
fiercest of all group duels' - thirty champions from Clan Chattan
fighting an equal number from Clan Quhele.   Then appeared the
other characters so vividly depicted by Scott: the Fair Maid of
Perth; the bandy-legged smith, Hal o' the Wynd; and the wild
young Highland chief who, when outlawed, hid in the very woods of
Kinnoull.

Perth was full of stirring figures, of memories of ancient conflicts between Highlander and Lowlander, between patriotic Scots
and the English.   Bruce's men had fought there, Cromwell's
soldiers had beseiged the city.   In contrast to its past, Perth
now seemed a sleepy provincial town content to dream of former
glories as capital of Scotland, but the world of nature beyond its
gates was still alive and exciting.   With his eye the boy followed
the Tay upstream as it wandered like a silver serpent under a
blue, cloud-sprinkled sky: past the tiny village of Scone where
Scottish kings were crowned in olden times, between the wooded hills

Mount Tabor Cottage, the boyhood home of Patrick Geddes on Kinnoull
Hill, Perth, Scotland

Patrick's mother, Janet Stevenson
(Stivenson) Geddes (1816-98)

Captain Alexander Geddes of
the Perthshire Rifles, father
of Patrick (1808-99)

Patrick in April 1864,
aged 10½

Patrick at the age of 15½

One of Patrick's favourite views from Kinnoull Hill, Perth, looking
eastward down the River Tay

of Birnam and Dunsinane, and on beyond till at last the river
became lost in the rising mass of Grampians, whose peaks made
the western horizon.

The sun was setting behind the purple Highlands when the lad
finally started on his way home, but even then he hunted ferns,
running from one to another not knowing which was the prettiest.
Though it was nearly dusk when he reached the cottage, he began
transplanting them in his little corner of the family garden.
For two years he had been building a fern-rockery with the finest
crystals the quarry yielded and decorating it with agates daringly
mined from the precipice of Kinnoull as he explored 'its face from
one precarious handgrip and foot-hold to another'. (2)

   'Patrick!' a woman's voice called from the kitchen window.
'Patrick!   It's away past time for supper.'
   'Yes, Mother.   I'll be coming.'
But the boy went on with his work.   There must be a nice border
of broad ferns outside the rock garden, with places of honour
inside for 'the dainty ones I well-nigh worshipped'.
Minutes later a man walked into the garden with a firm military
step and repeated the mother's words in a tone of authority.
   'Look Father!   See what lovely ferns I found on our Hill!'
When Mother came out she found both menfolk absorbed in planting
ferns.

FAMILY ... GARDEN ... LIBRARY ... KIRK

There were four persons around the supper table that evening.
The father, Alexander Geddes, originally a Gaelic-speaking Highlander from Speyside, was now serving as captain in the local
militia - the Perthshire Rifles - on his retirement from the
famous Black Watch regiment.   The Crimean War had led to his
recall to the colours and to this promotion.   He was a professional soldier whose thirty years of active service as a non-
commissioned officer had taken him over a considerable part of
the British Empire.   After rising to Quartermaster Sergeant he
had three times been offered a commission in the Black Watch, but
not having any private income he could not afford to accept it.

The mother, whose maiden name was Janet Stivenson, came from a
family of stern old Presbyterian Covenanters in Airdrie, a town
not far east of Glasgow.   The daughter, Jessie, born in Corfu
thirteen years before Patrick, was still living at home; unmarried
at twenty-four because her fiancé had died and she had never looked
elsewhere.   Instead, she devoted herself to helping Patrick
through a delicate early childhood; in fact it was she who once
nursed him back to life when the doctors despaired of saving
him. (3)   Finally there was the boy himself who would be eleven
years old next October.

Of his three older brothers, one had died in infancy aboard a
troopship en route to the Bermudas.   The others, Robert and John,

born in Dublin and Malta respectively, were his seniors by sixteen and eleven years.   Patrick was born at Ballater in West Aberdeen-shire on 2 October 1854;   the youngest child and the only one born in Scotland.   In 1857 his parents moved to Perth, then a quiet county town of some 25,000 inhabitants.   They settled in a modest hillside dwelling which Captain Geddes named 'Mount Tabor Cottage', after the sacred mountain of Northern Palestine.   There Patrick spent his next seventeen years.

John, however, left home in 1860 after an unhappy and rebellious time at the Academy, and went to seek his fortune in New Zealand. Brother Robert also left home three years later, first making a trip to New York and back, then emigrating from Scotland to become a banker in Mexico City.   Both of them nevertheless kept in friendly touch with the family over the years by writing and periodic visits.   Thanks to this family correspondence one has examples of the earliest letters written by Patrick.

The older boys had been brought up strictly, with almost military discipline, but the youngest, as he later told his own children, benefited 'by a modifying if not relaxing of parental supervision'. With brothers early gone from the home, it was natural that Patrick should become the main interest of the Captain's retired but active life, 'the Benjamin of his declining years'.   And so this son, at least, could afterwards look back on a 'rarely fortunate and happy childhood with the best of parents, passed in neither poverty nor riches'.

'Mount Tabor' was set in an old-fashioned and irregular-shaped garden 'hedged with beech and thorn instead of walled, and bordered by big wild cherry trees, glorious in spring blossom, and sometimes rich in small but delicious fruit.'   Here his earliest recollec-tions were:

> of trotting after Father with my little barrow and tools, or
> helping Mother with her flowers; and of watching things grow,
> of climbing the trees, of feeding the robins and pigeons out
> of my hand, and of many roamings....   I had my small barrow
> as my father the big one.   His 'The Tally-Ho', mine 'The
> Express' - and what races when they were empty, what loads
> when they were full! (4)

Though not a learned man, Captain Geddes was well informed on many subjects and keenly interested in everything in the worlds of nature and of man.   He found one of his greatest pleasures in rambling about the countryside, and he took Patrick with him as soon as the child could walk even a short distance.   Together they explored the hillside until the boy was old enough, at a mere seven or eight, to venture everywhere by himself.   Thus did Patrick acquire a wanderlust which a long life of travel and observation would never satiate.

For the inner world of mind and spirit it was likewise the old Captain who skilfully and unobtrusively served as guide.   He taught the boy to read and to write, and in fact gave him a general

schooling until Pat began attendance at Perth Academy at the age
of eight, the late start being the result of his early years of
poor health.   Even then the father supplemented formal instruction
by talks indoors and walks outside, and every evening after supper
he would read aloud to the family from the Bible or recite old
Scottish ballads.   It was these readings that first stirred
Patrick's imagination; he thrilled to the stories of Ezra and
Nehemiah, of the rebuilding of Solomon's temple, and to many other
Old Testament tales,   From the Book of Proverbs' many exhortations
he took particularly to heart, 'Wisdom is the principal thing,
therefore get wisdom and with all thy getting, get understanding'.

By his tenth Christmas he could write to his brother Jack that,
'I am seldom lower in any of my classes than second'.   That his
interests were also those of an ordinary boy was likewise revealed, though with surprisingly subtle humour:
> I hung up my stocking on Christmas Eve and Santa Claus
> generously filled it with potatoes, onions, wizened apples
> and 2 packages which made me suppose from his partiality to
> vegetables that they were Carrots, but to my agreeable surprise
> I found them to be Confections.

When he had learned to read well for himself, his father took him
one day to Perth and let him join the Mechanics Library, which had
a small but well-chosen selection of books.   To Patrick this
proved one of the greatest excitements and most enduring joys of
his whole boyhood and youth.   He was literally staggered by an
impression of limitless riches when he first saw the shelves upon
shelves of books.   Immediately he began to read at the astonishing
rate of nine or ten books a week, in addition to doing all his
schoolwork.   This pace he kept up for years until, in his own
expression, he had 'devoured the home library and soaked up the
public one'.   A boyhood friend, Harry Barker, has recalled that
Patrick read 'every novel in every library' and that 'at 4 a.m.
he was reading (not novels but philosophy) with a candle - till
time to get up, winter and summer'. (5)   The pattern of early
morning mental activity continued throughout life, though reading
would be replaced by the notation of his own thoughts.

Among the hundreds of books thus read were certain ones which
stood out as influences he would refer to throughout life, and
which he in turn would read to his own children.   'Pilgrim's
Progress' and 'Robinson Crusoe' were often named together, as
though these classics of spiritual and worldly adventure made a
logical educational pair.   Then came tales of King David,
Ulysses, Richard the Lion-Heart, Robert the Bruce, the Fairy Queen
and 'even the midnight witches'. (6)   The folklore of King
Arthur's Court likewise had a great fascination for him, that of
Merlin in particular.   Poets like Longfellow, Wordsworth and
Tennyson also strongly appealed to him with their varied combina-
tions of adventure, folktales, romance and nature descriptions.
Then, again bringing a more down-to-earth balance in the literary
fare, came the Leather-stocking novels of Cooper and Captain
Thomas Mayne Reid's series of standardised yet exciting stories.

Events in the contemporary world also made lasting impressions on
Patrick.   The Civil War in America and later, the Franco-Prussian
conflict, engaged him strongly.   He wrote over 60 years later:
   I remember, and vividly from childhood the American War, and
   the thrill of sympathy with the Negro people....   We sang
   their homely loves and sorrows ... we felt the horrors of
   slavery, and the sympathy and indignation, the vindication
   towards liberation, which these aroused.   And this all the
   more intensely in Scotland....   The old Kentucky and Virginia
   songs were sung in every gathering, by ladies and by men in
   turns - and from drawing-room to school, from ploughmen in the
   country to message-boy on street. (7)

During the siege of Paris in 1870 he wrote to brother Jack in New
Zealand, 'What a dreadful war this is....   Our sympathies are
with the French, at least mine are very warmly so.'   And at the
start of the First World War he told his oldest son how he had
even 'felt the thrill' to go to the front as a volunteer in 1870-1,
though he was only sixteen then.   Indeed Patrick would steadily
refer to childhood experiences, not only in general terms as
'deeply determinant' of his mature interests and deeds but pointing out specific incidents.

Sometimes it was to support a claim in his plan for elementary
education in home schools or to prove a point in his concept of
regional geography or to illustrate details in a town planning
scheme.   Again he would make a sweeping criticism of money-based
economic theory in terms of insights gained from his father's
teaching.   Yet, with few exceptions, there was little of nostalgic longing back to a 'Paradise Lost'.   He simply related
experiences from boyhood and youth in an objective manner for
whatever didactic value could be got out of them at the moment.
For example, in an article of combined exhortation and reminiscence written for a much later generation of Perth Academy boys,
he described his fern-rockeries as 'the real beginnings of all
my buildings and landscape gardenings'. (8)

Another time it was educational theory illustrated in terms of
the happy life at Mount Tabor Cottage.   To some extent he recalled the earliest incidents 'of that best of primary education -
of helping Mother' but much more clearly of 'early, even almost
infantile beginnings ... of secondary education - helping
Father'. (9)   One forenoon they planted what was to be the
winter's supply of potatoes, Father unobtrusively starting
Patrick in actual measurements and counting.   First an adult
foot, later a stick slightly longer, to determine the even
placing of drills;   then notches cut in another stick to mark
the 32 drills in one row.   The number of rows was noted first
by a potato for each;   then, after mutual discussion, by stones
so that the seed potatoes could be better used in the ground.
   But alas, when one went to school, there were no more such
   arithmetic lessons: only rules and tables, and examples to
   be worked in an exercise-book.   Paper drudgery with no
   interest, and thus no sense, meaning or significance to any

of us at all....   Returning from such book-cram to this real
and literal 'grounding' in arithmetic from my father, I dimly
recall that he soon also gave me from these notched sticks and
stones the idea of money and its real nature.   That is, a sign
and symbol of real wealth as real work: a notation for measuring these, and conservable, transferable, exchangeable, usefully superseding barter....   In this way it was impossible
to confuse these notches and tallies with the real potatoes and
rows, or with the future crop to which we had given our labour.

Ideal though it was in most ways, the Mount Tabor home was a
silent one in so far as music and song was concerned.   On Sundays
the grim Puritan tradition of silence and abstinence from all forms
of levity was rigorously observed.   Coming from militantly pious
forebears and having herself taught children in a Black Watch
regimental school, Mrs Janet Stivenson Geddes was inclined to
strict discipline.   Consequently Patrick's memories also included
incidents like this one.   Whether it was he and a comrade or he
and his sister Jessie who had momentarily relaxed on the Sabbath,
the result was that his mother called sternly to them from upstairs, 'Did we hear someone laugh?'

On a much earlier occasion, in Ireland, according to some brief
family data noted down by Patrick, the mother sharply rebuked a
boy in the Dublin barracks for whistling on Sunday.   However,
then Quartermaster Sergeant Geddes's brother John, who happened
to be visiting them, remarked very kindly to her, 'Read Matthew
7:1 - "Judge not, that ye be not judged".'   Her reaction was not
recorded.   Sergeant Geddes, on the other hand, had the reputation
of being persuasively gentle as well as a strict officer.   If
soldiers returned from leave drunk or quarrelling the mere sound
of his voice would often calm them down and save them from disci-
plinary action.   One of the habitual offenders, nicknamed
'Cursing Geordie', later gave him a valuable bonnet in gratitude
saying, 'You've had to confine me often, but never without a
cause.'

Alexander Geddes's parents died of the cholera when he was eight,
and afterwards he lived with an uncle and had some years of schooling in winter and herding in summer before joining the army at 17.
To Patrick he summed up his long life in ten words: 'Just a poor
boy; then enlisted; now here I am.'   When pressed for his
history, he merely replied, 'Get it in the Testimonials, from
friends, from the Regiment', but did add that he had received an
annuity of £15 since 1851.
    He was a most zealous Non-Commissioned Officer, and I have no
    hesitation in pronouncing him a strictly sober, trustworthy,
    conscientious, and moral man....   The conduct of his wife and
    family was likewise all that could have been desired.
                              Adjutant, 42nd Royal Highlanders
    The Commander-in-Chief's estimate of his irreproachable character
    has been such, that Her Majesty has been graciously pleased to
    grant the Annuity and Medal for faithful and meritorious
    services.
                    Commander, Reserve Battalion, 42nd Regiment (10)

The old soldier's friends and commanding officers were less taciturn.
Patrick records a family story about a captain in the Black Watch
Regiment once asking his mother, 'Not sorry you married into the
Army?   No?   Well you haven't got a rich man, but you've got a
good one.'   The father also told his son proudly that he had many
friends, adding 'I don't know of any enemy.   Never had an enemy in
my life.'

After moving to Perth in 1857 and being promoted, Captain Geddes
also became a leading elder in the Free Kirk.   There was naturally
much church-going on Sunday.   The whole family would walk down to
morning service in Perth taking with them a picnic lunch, which
they ate afterwards by way of sustaining themselves against an
afternoon service as lengthy as the early one.   These services
'which my parents and sister appreciated ... were to me tediousness
mostly unrelieved till the high tea on our return.' (11)

Besides the torture of sitting still for hours in an uncomfortable
pew at which any active boy would rebel, he was further depressed
by the church building, a bleak structure within and entirely un-
redeemed without by trees or by a garden of even a few flowers.
He could not reconcile this deliberate refusal of beauty with the
abundance of natural life on the hillside and in the home garden.
Even when his father with the other elders built a new church of
red stone in quite good Gothic style, he still found it uninspiring and hated the iron railing placed around it.   'Suffer, little
children,' it seemed to say to him.   'If you climb on us we'll
tear you!'

But when the day of services was at last over and the family
started homeward, Patrick's spirits quickly revived.   After high
tea, came:
>   the quiet joy of the day, and this throughout the year, from
>   earliest sign of spring to latest leaf of autumn.... For now
>   came an hour's ramble round the whole garden together, noting
>   the growth of everything, to leaf or flower or fruit, and even
>   with touch and scent and flavour also.

This garden stroll always came to a climax with the flower-beds
his mother tended: flowers she still loved and knew as well as
ever by touch even when long years of blindness came upon her.
>   Here was true Montessorian training, and at its rural best,
>   through senses to interests and sympathies;   and towards the
>   week's practicalities as well, from outdoor vegetable dishes
>   and stews, berry tarts, apple pudding and pies.   Life and
>   its growth, beauty and use, were thus all realized together.

The bonds between Patrick and his father seemed to have been much
closer than those with his mother, judging from the many thankful
references to the former's teaching.   Yet in one letter (12) -
written to 'My dear Father' not long before he died at 91 - there
is a whole-hearted tribute to both parents.   The old captain had
just given his gold watch to the favourite son who replied in
touching words only partly quoted here.
>   I cannot tell you how much pleasure it gives me almost every

time I look at it, as it calls up so many old and happy memories
of you and home, from the time when I used to creep into bed
between you and mother, and tremble at the big B.O. and the
fingers coming to gobble me [childhood mythology not otherwise
explained by Geddes] and then be amused and delighted with the
golden face and the tick-tick inside....   So your watch not
only tells me the present time, but calls up the old times
also; the watch pocket also with its embroidery by mother's
hands will always be a dear and sacred possession, and call up
her kind face also.

The most nostalgic reference to a childhood experience, however,
is one made almost unintentionally.   In a letter written from
India nearly sixty years after the event in question took place,
Patrick starts out to tell a geographer friend (13) some impressions of the great Ganges, but turns to its spiritual influence
as the 'Sacred River'.   This reminds him of the Tay of his
childhood which 'will always be for me among main impulses of
the life-stream as of the cosmos'.   Then, for the only time in
writing* as far as known documents show, he recounts this story
of deep childish faith and disillusionment.

[handwritten passage]

As a small child, soon I think after learning to say my
prayers, I saw what I afterwards learned (with disappointment!) to be but the Tay at Woody Island, with its strange

* However, some years later Geddes related this experience to
his son Arthur who, in turn, recorded these notes entitled,
'Autobiographical ... walk, 21 Nov 23':
  The Sunset!   He had just been taught to say his prayers - and
  about the same time he saw a sunset such as he had never seen.
  And the blaze of glory was to him the vision of God revealed!
  And he prayed with all his heart - not merely repeating the
  terms but with all his ardour.   For many nights this continued
  but at last faded - to his great disappointment.   Not till
  long after, perhaps a year or six months, did he find out the
  secret....   But (something of) the Experience remained within.

irregular cloud-shape aflame with the sunset, and so itself
a sunburst in the contrasted and darkening landscape around.
I had my first and still brightest vision of - what I took
to be - God.   And so prayed to, night after night at the
same time until the advance of the season moved the sunset
further northward and left me to discover its natural and
everyday character - with deep disappointment accordingly
at this lapse, as it seemed, into what I felt the too
prosaic world around.

SCHOOLDAYS ...'PERVERSION' AND 'CONVERSION' ... APPRENTICESHIPS

Despite its lack of music and song, except for the reading aloud
of poetry, and despite its Puritanical Sundays, Patrick's early
boyhood can be summed up as an unusually complete introduction
to the worlds of action and thought under the intelligent guidance
of that best teacher he ever had, his father.   This introduction
covered far more than garden or public library, extending as it
did beyond the horizons seen from Kinnoull Hill.   Father and son
once took a journey to Edinburgh for several days, and there
Patrick absorbed impressions of never-forgotten civic beauty
which again were 'deeply determinant' of his activities in later
life.

Another time they spent a fortnight tramping for 200 miles in the
Highlands of Dee and Spey, the father's home country.   Patrick
was always encouraged to adventure where he wished, among books
or along the precipices of the Tay.   In a field near his
aquarium he found his first fossil 'with sheer ecstasy never
forgotten nor surpassed';   and the ever-present attraction and
challenge of Kinnoull provided 'all the joys of treasure-finding,
with growing adventurousness of climbing too;   for year by year
the cliffs whispered more clearly - no fear, go anywhere and do
anything!' (14)

A century ago Perth Academy did not offer instruction which could
always engage the interest of a restless boy in his early teens.
The classics as then taught seemed too remote from Patrick's every-
day life which always had genuine, if sometimes unapproved, adventure to offer.   English he liked better, though his real enjoyment
of it was to read voraciously for himself in the evening.   The
study of Latin was tiresome, but he took to French with an enthusiasm which was to increase steadily the older he grew.   Indeed,
he played the role of Le Bourgeois Gentilhomme in Molière's
comedy at the age of twelve, and later won a prize in an inter-
scholastic competition in French.   German he found heavy and
dull like Latin, although the 'splendid German songs at the end
of Otto's 'Grammar' reconciled me to that'.

Mathematics was totally different, not merely because the class did outdoor mensuration of heights and distances, but even more because the teacher literally loved geometry and made it 'the greatest educational influence of all'.   This was old Rector Miller who used to stand at the blackboard enthralled by a proposition of Euclid he had just completed and murmur, 'What beauty!   What beauty!' He would solemnly tell his pupils:

Ge-o-metry, gentlemen, Ge-o-metry.   God governs the world by Ge-o-metry.   Hence Plato wrote over the portal of his Academe: 'Let no man ignorant of Geometry enter here!'   And when Pythagoras demonstrated this 47th Proposition, he offered a hecatomb of oxen to the Gods!   You sir, you're not attending!   You wouldn't have offered a hecatomb of mice!' (15)

At fifteen Pat Geddes was a recognised leader among the boys at the Academy.   School lessons always came easily, so he had plenty of time as well as inclination for games of all sorts, though cricket seemed slow and golf something 'intolerably old and grown-up'.   He delighted in football matches and in the great snow-fights which were traditional among the schools of Perth;   and in both types of encounter his quickness of eye and foot made him a valuable asset for the Academy.   In private combat, despite his short stature, Pat was no coward;   yet what he liked better than any kind of competitive game or fighting were the Saturday rambles which he took week after week with three or four comrades.   River boating and swimming occupied many a midsummer day, but with the opening of school and the coming of cool weather adventure could best be sought in the hills.

What he meant by 'adventure' as an adolescent, though, was not the same as his boyhood explorations on Kinnoull.   Now, typical Saturday outings for Pat - usually together with Harry and David Barker, James MacDonald and Hay Robertson - were the 10-15 or even 20-mile hikes upstream along the Tay to Birnam Hill and Dunsinane, or to any of a dozen other vantage points south, west and north.   But though they may have told their parents next day about the splendid views from this or that hilltop, they certainly neglected to mention visits to a farmer's field and to certain cottages on the outskirts of Perth on the way home.   The truth was that Pat was having 'an outbreak of impish practical joking' which he described over fifty years later in these words:

In this my demon made me a ringleader infectious to others. Not merely did we make appalling turnip-lantern ghosts, or rang bells and ran away;   we tied people's bells along a terrace to their door-handles on Saturday night, so that the more they pulled to open their doors to go to church, the more they were exasperated by feeling them held fast against them, and as if by some one ringing furiously with the other hand.

Kitchen chimneys were neatly closed with sods, houses were barricaded in;   a small disused cottage, belonging to a farmer who had resented our depredations on his turnip fields, was pulled down by us altogether.   In these and other ways we came obviously within the search of the police;   but we were cunning enough to vary localities and methods, and thus remain unsuspected. (16)

According to biographer Philip Mairet, (17) early correspondence between Patrick and his brothers shows that the latter thought he was too studious.   They cautioned him not to become a prig and a 'swot', and Mairet believes this may well have contributed to his spell of nigh juvenile delinquency.   Another, and perhaps even more plausible, factor might have been the years of enforced attendance at church.   In any case, the combination of lawful Saturday walks and secret evening mischief made Patrick so obviously worn out on his return and still so tired on Sunday morning that his parents often let him stay home to rest while they went to kirk!

From the vantage point of maturity Patrick Geddes used to look back on this period with a mixture of amusement and consternation, saying that if he had been less lucky or the police smarter he certainly would have been sent to the reformatory and there been 'educated as a professional criminal'.   But during the two or three months of Hallowe'ening inflicted on Perthshire, Patrick thought only of what great sport it was to match wits with farmers, townsfolk and police.   Then, happily for posterity, he was quite suddenly converted 'by the expulsive power of a new affection': to wit, from marauding 'to the new and frightful joys of experimental chemistry'.

> Hay Robertson and I made hydrogen, and what not, nearly every night for six weeks, until we were expelled from his room and home for burning the carpet, and next from mine for driving out the whole household, and blackening all the silver with that then most horrible of gases, hydrogen sulphide.   However, my wise and gentle father brought up the joiner next morning to build me a laboratory-shed against the house-gable, where I went on for a year or more, to heart's content. (18)

Temptations to renew exploits of devilry occasionally came even in the midst of his new hobby, but the youthful chemist resisted these impulses.   Meanwhile his father kept a watchful if distant eye over him suspecting perhaps that some of the recent events in the county might be connected with his own household.   He realised, too, that giving his son occupational outlets for adolescent energies at loose ends would be far more effective than any amount of scolding or repression.   When the chemical laboratory proved a success he had one side of it equipped as a carpenter's shop, with the result that woodworking soon became of even greater interest than chemistry.   As the summer of 1870 brought to a close the boy's studies at the Academy, the Captain carefully arranged a programme of activities to occupy each day.

Mornings were spent in the shop of a professional cabinet-maker, where Patrick quickly developed a skill to match his interest in building things - an experience which bore fruit throughout the rest of his life.   Afternoons were devoted mainly to the drawing class of a local art school, while evenings remained free for reading or experimenting in the home laboratory.   The purchase of a microscope with his French prize money turned him definitely into an 'amateur working naturalist', and the finding of fossils

started me in the direction of geology, which later, under James
Geikie's vivid influence, I nearly mistook for my profession.
Butterfly-hunting was a delight for a summer or two, but more
enduring was the quest for flowers and ferns, with the making of
a tiny botanic garden which fairly started me as a botanist.

Later in life Patrick would often condemn formal schooling and
preach the value of home instruction instead.   Yet in at least two
published articles (19) he also admitted that he not only was not
damaged by these eight years but even got a good foundation in many
subjects.   Considering how intellectually regimented and author-
itarian all schools in Great Britain were at that time, one may
even assert that he was extremely fortunate in being able to combine studies in 'modern' subjects like French and chemistry at
Perth Academy with living at Mount Tabor Cottage with 'the best
of parents'.

Patrick's industry as a pupil is further evidenced by an elaborate
notebook on geometry.   Completed in the summer term of 1870, his
last one in school, it was called a 'Fair Book' - for reasons unknown at the Academy today.   Many of its pages are still preserved
at the National Library of Scotland, including neatly lettered and
illustrated chapter pages.   One of these, 'Mensuration of Heights
and Distances', even bears drawings of Bell Rock Lighthouse and of
portions of two ruined castles.   A plausible explanation of this
unusually time-consuming homework has come from his daughter,
Norah, who once heard her father say that the old Captain had
considered Pat's handwriting to be in great need of improvement,
and she believed this was the remedy.

Whatever the reason for the highly decorated 'Fair Book', one of
Patrick's boyhood ambitions was to be an artist.   He was fascinated by the expert sketching and painting of his father's friend,
the Perth artist J.H. Armstown, and eagerly acted upon the
latter's suggestion that he study drawing in the local art school.
However, his teacher was a man trained at the National Art School
in London as a professional designer and whose ideal of art was
to copy perfectly.   Under such guidance Pat learned to design
symmetrically and to stipple expertly, and did so well that the
drawing master urged him to make designing his career.   One of
the boy's sketches was selected to be sent to the annual competition of the South Kensington Art Museum in London.

In due time the drawing came back with a prize, but this apparently successful achievement turned out to be the downfall of
Patrick's artistic ambitions.   Another boy in the class had submitted a sketch which was returned in the same bundle along with
his own.   Both of them had made sepia drawings from the same
cast and when they went to sort them out neither could tell for
the life of him which was whose without looking at the names on
the back!   In a flash of insight Patrick saw himself as a mere
copying machine, not a potential artist.   Thinking to overcome
this handicap he went up Kinnoull Hill to sketch from nature,
using as subject the striking line of crags along the Tay.   Alas,

it too proved a mechanical copy, and he went homeward in utter
discouragement, resolved to give up drawing altogether.   'Youth
often makes rapid decisions', Patrick would afterwards say, 'and
abides by them.'

During the year after completing school, his seventeenth, 'he
suffered from intermittent and unaccountable langours', (20)
according to his daughter Norah, and was allowed to go his own
way.   This meant geologising on Kinnoull as well as continued
observations in biology in the home shed-laboratory with 'his
precious microscope'.   At the same time he tried to make up his
mind as to what he should do in life.

His mother, like many a devout Scottish woman, had always cherished
the hope that her son would enter the ministry and even dreamed of
him in the pulpit of their own kirk.   But he, ever since his
earliest contact with its long sermons and the repellent ugliness
of its building, was quietly determined never to choose theology
as a profession.   His father, having witnessed the success of one
elder son in banking in Mexico and the other in a New Zealand
coffee and spice business, then tried to direct the youngest into
some similar path.   Though he knew at the start it was not his
field, Patrick agreed to give business a trial, spending a year
and a half as an apprentice in the local branch of the National
Bank of Scotland, and earning the following testimonial from the
manager:

PERTH 14 March 1873

Mr. Patrick Geddes has been in this office since Septr. 1871.
He now leaves in order to prosecute his studies, principally
the study of chemistry, for which he appears to have great
aptitude.   His conduct while here has been in every respect
unexceptionable; he is quick and expert at his work, & has
been most attentive to all his duties.   I never had a more
promising Apprentice & I am very sorry to lose him.   I wish
him every success, & trust he will prove an Ornament to the
Profession he may choose.

Sgn   D.H. Jolly
Branch Manager

FREE HOME STUDIES ... DISILLUSION IN EDINBURGH

His apprenticeships in cabinet-making, drawing and business duly
fulfilled, Patrick now claimed the freedom promised by his father
to go on with studies.   The commercial experience had made him
more than ever sure that his future lay somewhere in science,
though in which particular field he could not decide, since almost
everything from mathematics to biology attracted him.   Partly on
account of his uncertainty and partly because of spells of lassitude, he was not pressed to make up his mind or hurried towards
college.   He continued work in chemistry by going to an analyst
in Perth as well as carrying on systematic studies in geology,
mineralogy, botany, and physiology both by himself and under the
guidance of competent tutors.   Some of these, like the geologist

James Geikie, were in Perth; others in Dundee 25 miles away, a
distance which Patrick sometimes covered on foot!

In literature the Longfellow of his early schooldays gave way to
nature poets like Wordsworth, to Emerson and Tennyson, and to
moralists like Carlyle and Ruskin.   The latter was a great
favourite of Patrick's and more interesting personally than others
because he had spent part of his boyhood in Perth.   In fact,
Patrick would refer to Ruskin's description of the Tay as 'a perpetual treasure of flowing diamond to us children' and to his
'perpetual watching of all the ways of running water - a singular
awe developing itself in me, both of the pools of Tay, where the
water changed from brown to blue-black, and of the precipices of
Kinnoull...' almost as if these had been his own personal experiences.   Carlyle had also a high place among his favourites, and
such incidental facts as the author of 'Sartor Resartus' having
been born at Ecclefechan in Dumfriesshire and having walked the
one hundred miles from home to Edinburgh as a student must also
have intrigued Patrick.

Among the teenage readings often mentioned by the grown-up man
were the exploits of 'The Admirable Crichton': a sixteenth-
century scholar from St Andrews University whom Patrick greatly
admired for his skill both in learned disputation in Italy and
France, and in duelling.   Another favourite with a strong international flavour was 'The Scot Abroad', a book to which Geddes
referred periodically throughout his own career as an intellectual
adventurer in many countries.

Knowing Patrick's sympathies for France during her trials by
Prussians in 1870 and civil war in 1871, one can imagine him
following the frightful aftermath of the Paris Commune in newspaper accounts while working in the Perth bank.   The court-martial
of the famous geographers, the brothers Elie and Elisée Reclus,
would certainly have aroused him.   Escaping the massacre of
thousands of other Communards, both were sentenced to transportation to Devil's Island: Elie for acting as interim keeper of the
Bibliothèque Nationale, and Elisée, somewhat more logically, for
serving with the Communard aeronauts who flew balloons out of
beleaguered Paris.   Fortunately, a strong petition by men of
science all over the world, including England's Darwin and Alfred
Wallace, resulted in their punishment being changed to exile.   The
Reclus brothers were therefore alive and able, two decades later,
to accept the hospitality in Edinburgh of a former Bank of Scotland
apprentice.

Patrick carried on his informal scientific and humanistic education
almost until his twentieth birthday in October 1874.   It was a
period of intellectual fermentation entirely free from required
courses or pressure of examinations; it was the wise father's most
valuable legacy to his son.   Yet both agreed that it was high time
to fly out of the home nest.   The problem was where to go and what
to do.   Patrick was certain the four varied years since leaving
Perth Academy had not been wasted, and when comparing his lot with

those of friends cramming for degrees or caught in the routine of
office or shop, he felt extremely lucky.   On the other hand, the
conflicting claims and changing goals of his free studies had become
a real burden.

Still his father threw full responsibility on him for choosing a
career.   So at last, in the autumn of 1874, after consultation
with his tutor in botany, the science which was gradually demanding
more attention than the others, Patrick Geddes set out for Edinburgh to study botany at its famous old university.

Called 'Athens of the North' and 'third most beautiful city in the
world', Edinburgh was the Mecca of ambitious and talented youth
from all Scotland and even beyond her borders.   As on that first
visit to the capital with his father, Patrick again felt its magnificence and stirring history.   The silhouette of the Castle on
its rock against the Pentland Hills conjured up historic figures
like Robert the Bruce and Mary Queen of Scots, word magicians like
Robert Burns, Robert Louis Stevenson and Sir Walter Scott;   and
scientists like John Napier and Lord Lister.   What metropolis
could be more appropriate for his university career, and besides
all this lie only a short train journey distant from Perthshire
and his hillside home?

The new student found 'digs' in which he would live alone and ate
solitary meals as was scholastic custom during most of the nineteenth century.   He explored the Botanic Gardens where an added
attraction was a striking skyline view of the Old Town from Holyrood
Palace all the way up the Royal Mile to Castle Rock.   With great
expectations he frequented the lecture halls and laboratories
devoted to his chosen field of Botany.   Yet his encounter with
formal dissection and classification of living plants indoors,
and outside in the famous Garden as well, drove him from disappointment into despair.   The world of vital, harmonious nature
from his childhood and youth had disappeared.   Here was academic
disillusion too great to accept, while the alternative of returning home and admitting defeat seemed unthinkable.

In years to come, a maturely confident Patrick Geddes would survey
Edinburgh's 'Heritage of Good' and 'Burden of Evils', and courageously attack its civic and academic sins of omission and commission.   At this moment, however, he was still the youth,
uncitified and doubtless homesick, who was shocked and frustrated
by the lifeless urban approach to natural science.

One would like to imagine that at this crisis Patrick remembered
Carlyle and the pages of 'Sartor Resartus' wherein the latter
described *his* encounter with Edinburgh.   'ours was the worst of
all hitherto discovered Universities', followed by other such
comments on 'Mis-education' as practised there.   Yet after disillusionment, Carlyle had discovered that the university also
contained 'Books' and finally realised that 'we have brains to
read them;   here is a whole Earth and a whole Heaven, and we have
eyes to look on them.'

Whether young Geddes re-read Carlyle's lines at that time or not,
he did discover 'The Book' in Edinburgh: the one which solved his
hopeless dilemma.   With it he turned his back on Edinburgh and
returned hopefully to Mount Tabor Cottage one week after he had
left home.   The book was Thomas Huxley's 'Lay Sermons', and after
reading only the first few pages Patrick knew that its author was
the teacher for him.

Huxley!   The scientist who fearlessly championed the heresies of
Darwinism, who invaded even Scotland with public lectures on 'Man
and the Other Animals', and who delighted in hot disputes with
fundamentalist clergymen.   Huxley's very name was a synonym
among plain and God-fearing folk for 'infidel'!

Captain Geddes was of course greatly alarmed by this sudden turn
of the son's ambitions.   As an elder in the Free Kirk it would
be almost a calamity for his Patrick to go to that notorious un-
believer.   His poor mother too was deeply grieved.   Blindness
had been upon her scarcely a year, and now came the woe of her
youngest son wanting to study not for the ministry but with its
enemies.

Yet to the sorely-tried parents' great credit and to Patrick's
good fortune, they consented even to this plan.   No account of
the family council leading up to this decision has been recorded,
but a factor may have been his father's great relief over the
fact that his talented and long-hesitant son had at last found a
definite goal.   Whatever the inner facts and feelings were, here
is Patrick's tersely unemotional account of the conclusion,
written a half-century later: (21)   'they met the situation cordially and well: in faith too - which increased my respect alike
for them and it: so off to Huxley accordingly in 1874.'

Chapter 2

THE WANDERING STUDENT, 1874-80

WITH HUXLEY IN LONDON

Late 1874 marked the halfway point in both the 63-year reign of
Queen Victoria and the 16-year alternation as Prime Minister of
Conservative statesman Disraeli and his Liberal rival Gladstone.
London was already the sprawling capital of the British Isles and
of an empire with nearly 300 million subjects. Long a centre of
industry, finance and all the arts, it was now also a focal point
in the heated word-war between traditional theology and philosophy and the challenging natural scientists. Of the latter,
Thomas Henry Huxley was perhaps the most controversial.

An early champion of Darwin's 'Origin of Species' of 1859, Huxley
published his own classic 'Man's Place in Nature' in 1863 after
earlier medical studies and anthropological investigations around
the entire globe during his four years as assistant surgeon on
HMS 'Rattlesnake'. His active scientific career was interspersed
with agnostic public lectures for audiences of working men and
aggressive pen feuds with both leading clergymen and the politician Gladstone. (Witness Huxley's 'Science and Christian
Tradition' v. the 'Grand Old Man's' 'Impregnable Rock of Holy
Scripture ....')

Upon London's sophisticated scene appeared the home- and self-
taught country lad from Perthshire. Soon after his arrival
Patrick found himself face to face with Huxley, and he must have
described his anticipation and excitement in the letters he regularly sent home, but these apparently no longer exist. What
remains are his own terse reminiscences on the occasion of the
Huxley Centenary in 1925.

> I had, however, a disappointment; for at the first brief
> interview with the great man, he sentenced me to another pre-
> liminary year of chemistry, physics, and geology, before I
> should come to him. As I next got no credit from Dr.
> Frankland or others for my years of unofficial studies, but
> had to begin all over again, this year gave little more than
> revisal of what I knew already.... (1)

This categorical statement deserves a bit of attention.   The
revolt at Edinburgh can be explained as a vital reaction to a
lifeless presentation of botany, but here the student had no
quarrel for the time being with Huxley's teaching.   Furthermore,
the real cause of this disappointment was the stubborn aversion
to all forms of examinations and diplomas which Patrick had
acquired along with his free, 'unofficial studies' at home.
Mairet explains that on the lad's last day at Perth Academy, 'the
crowning moment of his success as a prize-winning scholar ... he
was suddenly overcome by a feeling that there was something
futile and unreal about prizes won by passing examinations'.
Whether this is the whole story or not, the fact is that Geddes
never took an academic degree in his life.   Yet as a youth of
twenty he expected the School of Mines to accept his previous
studies without the testimonials or certificates which he
apparently never asked geologist James Geikie or any other of
his Perthshire teachers to give him.

In any case, Patrick accepted Huxley's verdict and dutifully reviewed the physical sciences, even admitting afterwards that
'Ramsay's geology was a real stimulus'.   His ample free time he
spent enjoying 'the wide resources of London - museums, collections and libraries, galleries and theatres too, thus continuing
the self-education habit'.   (Although no family letters exist as
proof, Pat's first years in London must have been paid for by his
parents.   Not until his third year did he get a demonstratorship
to help defray expenses.)

Besides cultural pursuits he still had time, energy and sense of
humour enough to tease his fellow students and to play a capital
joke on the hallowed examination system.   A note in his diary
claimed that 'The only way of getting any mental activity out of
the School of Mines is to run down their occupation ... rude, but
good fun'.   He also, Mairet has related, ran down their curriculum, declaring that 'any fool could cram and pass exams'.   When
his comrades challenged him to prove this sweeping statement,
Patrick wagered that, given one week's preparation, he could get
through any of their written tests.

'He was as good as his word', writes Mairet whose source in turn
was Geddes's son Arthur.
> He passed the elementary stage in mining after reading the
> advanced textbook, and the advanced after re-reading it.
> This feat was accomplished partly by the aid of a remarkable
> memory for visual impressions: for he copied the diagrams in
> the textbook, reversed mirror-wise (to divert attention from
> the plagiarism), memorized them and then simply reproduced
> them.   The young satirist seemed to enjoy this result more as
> a demonstration that one could qualify as a sub-inspector of
> mines before ever having been down in a mine than as a proof
> of his own skill. (2)

Patrick's probationary year had at least two major consequences
for his intellectual development.   First, the wager and challenge

to the established exam system launched him, to use his own descriptive title, on a 'life-long career as inspector-critic of universities'.   The other result was to transfer his habits of exploration and observation from rural to urban areas.

This period, far from being only time wasted in reviewing elementary knowledge, was one of 'light discipline and large opportunity'
which in turn certainly was determinant of his coming work in both
town planning and sociology. (3)   Indeed, the very title of
Mairet's biography, 'Pioneer of Sociology', seeks its earliest
justification in Patrick's leisure-time wanderings about London.
Apart from daily journeys between his lodgings in Chelsea and the
School of Mines at Kensington, he must have covered all parts of
the metropolis either on foot or by omnibus.

Nothing could have resembled his native Perthshire less than congested London, but in the parks and by the Thames his country soul
could find relief from sooty railroad stations, dirty coal barges
and mean slum streets.   The walk home along the river at sundown
could be a memorable experience for Patrick.   He never failed to
be impressed by the great contrast between 'the open world of
nature in sky and stream, each a presence of the eternal, and our
hurrying, thronging human evanescence'.

Likewise, after passing the garish iron structure of Chelsea
Bridge, he delighted in the sight of the quaint old wooden bridge
of Battersea a mile distant.   Picturesque with the waving reflections in the water of its many piers, it made an unforgettable
sight on clear evenings: 'the red sun-glow burning through its
black ribs as through the phantom ship of the Ancient Mariner'. (4)

The period of elementary studies eventually passed, and
    The good time at length came: so I had two years of Huxley.
    His laboratory was open all day and every day throughout both
    winter and summer terms, though his lectures - always good
    measure over the hour (once nearly up to two hours, which
    left us exhausted!) - were in winter only.   Never, of course,
    had I heard such lectures; or indeed since.   Nothing could
    be clearer than his demonstrations of his well-chosen speci-
    mens, always sufficient for his exposition and argument, yet
    never in redundance; for his essential method lay in the
    educative value of the type-series and collection for the
    student, as compared with the redundant and bewildering wealth
    of the great museums.
       ... His lucid explanations went on with the gradual and
    creative up-building of first-rate blackboard drawings in
    colour; which he left for us to incorporate, after lecture,
    on the plain page of our note-books opposite the written page.
    His paper diagrams too were also of the best....   Among these
    too there sometimes appeared a touch of the dry humour which
    now and then twinkled in the lecture: thus I particularly
    remember our delight over a fine sheet of half-a-dozen heads
    of leading genera of Primates, in which the profiles of the
    big-nosed Tyndall, the bearded Darwin, the bright-maned Duke

of Argyll, as well as of himself, were unmistakably suggested
upon the simian level. (5)

Geddes would always look back to these years with unbounded gratitude to Huxley, both as a 'pioneering educator' and as a friendly
mentor.   His was 'the very first of laboratories, as also of
lectures truly and broadly biological'.   Together they gave his
pupils a 'not only elementary, but elemental, understanding of
the various viewpoints of science': anatomical, histological and
physiological.

> Taxonomy was not stressed, but clearly indicated; and the
> larger physiology of Nature - ecology - early opened to us in
> its colours and perspectives.   His introduction to embryology,
> as at once so protean yet so deeply orderly, was never to be
> forgotten; and his presentments of the palaeontological
> record - as for reptile and bird, and above all for his
> favourite battle-steeds, the horse-kind - transmitted to us
> his clear and concrete views of their gradual evolution....
>
> Through all this breadth of presentation the interest of
> morphology stood out clearest and central to all: witness
> his quiet but unmistakable intellectual pleasure in lucidly
> setting before us the unity, yet variety, of each related
> series of organic forms, as for his especially beloved cray-
> fish and lobster.   After that, who could not but understand
> Goethe's term 'Morphologie', and this not only as a culmination
> of his scientific work, but as perhaps the very greatest of
> his poems?

Patrick soon became 'a fairly good dissector' and 'grew fond of
setting myself tests of skill, like dissecting out more neatly
the growing point of Chara, the mouth-parts of Cyclops, and what
not.   So I was one day greatly honoured by having a specimen
kept for the museum....'   During his second year he became
'something of a real assistant', and one day Huxley told him it
was time to start on a research of his own.   'Choose any subject
you like, on which I can give you the material; and go ahead!' (6)

But the pupil still was at a loss, 'for if his teaching had any
fault, it was only too clear!   His exposition of an animal, a
part of a structure, was so perfect that it seemed to us finished,
and leaving nothing to be said by him, or asked by us.'   At length
the teacher himself had to think up a problem for the student;
namely to find out how the 'radula' or horny tongue-cover of
certain whelks and limpets works.

For a week Pat cut up several series of pickled shell-fish following out his professor's hypothesis that the tongue-cover was drawn
back and forth upon its cushion or by the attached 'odontophore'
muscles.   But he couldn't make it work that way and at last
timidly reported his difficulty.

'No, no!' said Huxley impatiently, 'Look at that, and that!
Now try again.'   With these words he disappeared.

Next day he returned, 'Well, have you got it clear?'   'Very
sorry', said I; 'but it seems to me that the thing works just

as a licking with the whole odontophore, and not a pulling to and fro of the radula.' 'Well, well, let me see.' So I showed him the set of dissections I had prepared. He looked through them keenly for a minute or two - which seemed to me long! Then suddenly he jumped up, gave me a great slap on the back, and said, ''Pon my word, you're right! You've got me! I was wrong! Capital! I must publish this for you!' So he made me draw three plates, and write my paper, which he then presented to the Zoological Society, for its Transactions, and as a correction of a bit of his own work by a pupil.

Huxley's frank admission of error made a lasting impression on Patrick. He was immeasurably encouraged and thereafter could always see far more problems for research than he could undertake. For a while he searched Huxley's books and papers for other little points of error, but failed to discover any: 'so the upshot was more respect and admiration for him than ever, and alike as anatomist and as man'.

CARLYLE AND RUSKIN ... COMTE AND SPENCER FEUDS WITH DARWIN AND HUXLEY

Patrick's work day was a long one. As a first-year biology student, he was told that 'to learn this subject you must apprentice yourself to all-time work at it, just as you would do for any craft or trade'. His second year, of combined research and demonstration, brought an even heavier schedule. Nevertheless, he still had time and energy for an astounding variety of extra-curricular activities.

His daily walk from Kensington, for example, provided both exercise and a fresh opportunity to observe the works and ways of urban folk. From the Embankment along the Thames he could review, beginning downstream, the 'squalid labyrinths of Westminster crowding up to its very towers', and the monotonous streets of Pimlico; then in Chelsea a mixture of new red houses and older 'and more irregular, simpler, quainter ones'. All of them were 'free from that dreary West End stuccoed respectability which is even more depressing than the gloom and grime of poorer London'. Among the red houses, at No. 5 Cheyne Row, lived his great literary idol, Thomas Carlyle; while upstream 'the view went on improving, even beyond Chelsea Church, with its memories of a gentler and yet greater social thinker - Sir Thomas More of the "Utopia"'. (7)

Reminiscing, Geddes would maintain that 'of the two contrasted poles of literature: that of clearest, keenest scientific writing on the one hand, that of deepest moral passion on the other, there stood out Huxley and Carlyle'. So when his father allowed him to give up 'previous plans of a Scottish University education for a wandering one', he settled down to study in Kensington, 'and to live in lodgings in Chelsea as near as possible to Carlyle - as it happened, a stone's throw from his door'. (8)

He soon discovered that this embankment was also Carlyle's
favourite walk.   'There was no mistaking the figure already
familiar from photograph and engraving, with its still vigourous
and steady stride, the shoulders only slightly bowed, the long
overcoat, the broad-brimmed hat, the hair and beard only grizzled,
not white.'

> Here, then, at length was the great teacher before me: my
> then hero as man of letters.   To give him more than ample
> space to pass, yet to take off one's hat reverently as becomes
> the student to his most venerated teacher was instinctive;
> one did not think of never having been introduced.   The sal-
> utation was courteously yet absent-mindedly returned, with
> eyes that only looked half into, half beyond my own;   so this
> liberty of salutation was never repeated.   And though
> meetings in the body frequently took place, I never dared to
> seek in any way the introduction for which I notwithstanding
> longed.

In hero-worship, Patrick re-read 'Sartor Resartus' and gazed upon
its author from both far and near;   yet never ventured to speak
to him.   Frequently the two would return to Chelsea at night on
the same omnibus, and Geddes would sit opposite Carlyle looking
into the deep meditative eyes without his ever noticing it.

> He was generally alone, as Old Age and Thought must ever be.
> Only two or three times have I seen him in company - once ...
> was near midnight with a companion not to be forgotten.   It
> was a scene startling then, curious to recall even now;   for
> here, in the moonless dark and but faintly shown by the poor
> street lamps, were to be seen - incredible, yet it seemed at
> first assuredly - two Carlyles!   Carlyle for one, sure enough,
> yet with another old gentleman almost his double: big over-
> coat, broad hat, grizzled beard and all!   Without superstition
> I felt startled by these two old wizards;   I looked with a
> perplexed awe not felt before or since.   Who it was I never
> knew;   doubtless some old friend who may have put on one of
> Carlyle's own characteristic overcoats to sally out with him
> for a final talk before going to bed.   But never have I seen
> two such figures, more strange, more satisfying also of one's
> dreams of ancient peripatetic sages. (9)

Whether consciously or unconsciously due to Carlyle's influence,
Geddes's own style of writing gradually took on certain unfortunate
traits.   His use of long superlative-laden, parenthetical sentences - partly salvaged by semicolons, dashes and exclamation
points - became so excessive in later years that many readers
simply gave up searching for the often brilliant ideas hidden
therein.   Even so, Patrick regarded Carlyle as 'One of the
greatest word-painters, who could either take in a man or a scene
with a flash, or reproduce a battle upon the spot, or from the
map with patient constructiveness ...', and his most enduring
memory is expressed in this word picture:

> I still see him ... his portrait as it were, most vividly
> framed, upon his beat between the two bridges.   He is walking
> upstream, and that stoutly: against the wind but towards the

sun, his back turned upon the iron bridge of modern utilitarianism, with its sham ornament and garish gilding, his eyes
towards the grey yet gleaming river, or upon the upper wooden
bridge: its old-world, simple, honest, rugged craftmanship
lending itself to effects of colour and shadow, now as strong,
now as unexpected and lurid, as those of his own style.

Patrick's admiration for John Ruskin was in great contrast.
Besides reading the exhortations to working men like 'Time and
Tide' - which 'cured me magnificently' (10) of a spell of depression - and 'Unto This Last', he actually corresponded with Ruskin.
Their first contact, according to evidence in the National Library,
was brought about by some hasty action taken against a member of
the Guild of St George by its founder.   Geddes obviously knew the
person* in question and wrote an intercession on his behalf.
Ruskin replied from Venice in January 1877, saying that he could
not do anything to help: 'I am not a saviour of sick men, but an
organizer of strong men.'

Geddes protested Ruskin's decision in terms strong and convincing
enough to cause the latter to answer that he was willing to give
the dismissed man further trial 'if you will undertake to manage
him under it ....'   A few days later came another note from Italy
saying 'I am very glad of your letter, and beg to enclose cheque
to be used as you see good for B-----'s help.   Many thanks for
your interest in the matter.'   In the same envelope which now
contains these three notes there is also an autographed portrait
of Ruskin, possibly sent to the young champion of justice at this
time.

A letter of December 1881 from Ruskin refers to the early incident
in these words:
    I quite forget the circumstances of the interference - and for
    whom it was.   But the only serious harm to the Guild is in my
    own laziness - or bad temper.   Believe me always, Gratefully
    & Faithfully ... etc ...   J. Ruskin.

A few years later the two were again to tangle by correspondence -
this time over the 'follies of Darwin and Huxley'.   That Ruskin
none the less remained Patrick's hero in one important field would
be documented not long after by a substantial booklet entitled
'John Ruskin, Economist'.

Patrick's awakening self-confidence was matched by a widening
interest in subjects peripheral to Huxley's teachings, and even
by an opposition to certain of the master's views.   On re-reading
the 'Lay Sermons', Patrick noted pages he had previously skipped
over: those dealing with Huxley's battle against the rapidly
growing cult of Positivism.   With eloquent ridicule the biologist

---

* John P. Reilly has identified this man as James Burden in
Chapter 1 of his PhD thesis, as well as giving much information
about the dispute.   (See Bibliography.)

attacked both Auguste Comte, its founder, and Dr Richard Congreve, the leader of the English Positivists; jibing at their worship of humanity and the Calendar of Great Men to be honoured if not prayed to.   Here Huxley made his famous remark that the Frenchman's philosophy, far from being the enlightened religion of the future, was only 'Catholicism minus Christianity'.   Yet to his great surprise Patrick found himself unconvinced by this onslaught against Comte. In all other matters he felt Huxley was right, but here, the more he read and re-read, the more his doubts increased.   Finally he decided to look into Positivism for himself and went on Sunday mornings to hear Dr Congreve's discourses at the mother church in Chapel Street.

> After one or two of these I timidly asked him some questions: a conversation arose, and I well remember his amused and gratified smile when he found that, although I had been so strongly impressed by Huxley's teachings as a biologist, his criticism in these other matters had sent me so directly in the opposite direction.   Good priest as he was, he could not but be delighted to find a brand thus plucking itself from the burning and henceforth I was welcome not only at Chapel Street but for long talks at his home. (11)

Congreve defended Positivism as 'Catholicism plus science' and held up Comte's philosophy of history as the most satisfactory interpretation of human progress ever made.   Yet when Geddes pressed him to justify the Positivist distrust of evolutionary theories, he proved impervious to the facts presented by biologists. He had 'that touch of pontificalism which emphasised the already sufficient authority of the Oxford don, and of the doctor of medicine as well; so there was no arguing with him'.   However, Congreve introduced Geddes to the week-night meetings of the Positivist Society, where there were always 'good and vivid' discussions of current questions' and where the young biologist met many well-known Londoners.   Geddes's friendship with S.H. Swinny, editor of the 'Positivist Review' and his acquaintance with Dr John H. Bridges, 'one of the keenest minds in the whole movement', were the two most lasting influences.

The latter's 'Discourses' (12) are an important primary source of ideas, maxims and philosophy which, consciously or unconsciously, will reappear in Geddes's life work.   There is for instance Dr Bridges's interpretation of Comte's motto, *Induire pour déduire, afin de construire,* as showing that 'between uncontrolled inquisitiveness on the one hand, and narrow utilitarianism on the other, there lies ... the building up of man's thoughts, feelings, and energies into a coherent whole', which would soon become the main goal of the Scottish neophyte.   John P. Reilly (13) strongly makes the point that Geddes found in Positivism the set of beliefs and even the explanation of prayer needed to fill the vacuum left by his rejections of parental piety.

Two further examples of this strong London influence from 1874 on are that Patrick, a decade later, converted his future fiancée to the 'Religion of Humanity'; and that he himself got an initiation

in Comtian social science.   In the 1870s also began his life-long
enthralment by Comte's classification of the sciences according to
which mathematics, physics, chemistry and biology were but 'preliminary sciences' and as such, incomplete and without human meaning until completed by the science of society.

Fifty years after he wrote in his Introduction to a biography (14)
of Dr Bridges that even though the Positivists 'could hardly be
but disappointed in my too rare and limited participation in their
work and teaching ...', he had not lost their 'essential interest
in the synthetic presentment of the sciences, and of sociology
above all'.   He also stated that 'I have constantly been applying
what I first learned from them.'

It was not just Comte over which Huxley and Geddes disagreed.
Once on returning from an inter-term vacation nominally devoted
to the study of chicken embryos, he enthusiastically told Huxley
that he had found time in addition to read Herbert Spencer's
'Principles of Biology'.
   'You'd have done far better to spend all your time on embryology!' came the snorting comment.

Whereupon Geddes immediately re-read Spencer to find out why
Huxley disapproved of him and soon got the answer in Spencer's
general view of nature: one far more humanistic than the Darwinism
of 'nature red in tooth and claw' which Huxley so energetically
propounded.   The 'Principles' claimed that while competition was
an undeniable part of animal and plant life, co-operation entered
into the evolutionary process even more importantly.   This interpretation of nature appealed strongly to Patrick, for his garden
and countryside experiences confirmed it.   The hours of reading
Spencer had not been wasted.

These minor clashes with Huxley brought to a focus certain doubts
that had been stirring in Patrick's mind for many months, doubts
as to the validity of the widely accepted 'survival of the fittest'
explanation of life.   Three years at the School of Mines had convinced him that his chosen master, despite a tremendous grasp of
comparative anatomy and the evolution of vertebrate structures,
was too much of a necrologist, too limited by skeletons.   Huxley
made excellent anatomists and dissectors out of his students but
he never once sent them outside the laboratory to study living
nature, even though Kensington Gardens lay right at the School's
door.

The great zoologist knew his limitations, for one time after
giving Patrick an especially brilliant explanation of the mechanics
of a crayfish skeleton he said, half to himself, 'You see, I should
have been an engineer!'

In dramatic contrast was this incident which occurred during
Patrick's final year in London and which stayed with him throughout
life as a 'vivid and memorable lesson in biology'.   He was in
Sanderson's laboratory one day filling in some spare moments by

examining samples of pond-water through a microscope. The first
slide revealed nothing much of interest - two or three common green
Euglenas swimming among a few motile bacilli - and he was about to
get a fresh sample when someone gently pushed him aside. A big
beard came over his shoulder, and there was Darwin! The famous
scientist, who had come in unnoticed, looked in the barren microscope field without saying a word. Then he broke out, 'positively
shouting for joy: "I say! They're moving, they're moving!
Sanderson! Sanderson! Come and see, they're MOVING! Look at
that!"' (15)

In spite of Huxley's mechanistic approach to life science Geddes
had him to thank for a good start in what promised to be a fruitful career as a naturalist. The summer following Patrick's correction of the error regarding the tongue-cover mechanism of whelks
and limpets, Huxley got him a job as demonstrator in the vacation
course supervised by Sir William Thiselton-Dyer, assistant director
of Kew Gardens. Next Huxley opened negotiations with two colleagues at Cambridge, Michael Foster and Francis Balfour, with the
intention of establishing his Scottish pupil at that venerable
English university. As Balfour's guest Geddes spent considerable
time at Cambridge looking over the situation, only to decide that
it, like Edinburgh, was not the place for him even as instructor.
On returning to London he thanked Huxley for providing this opportunity but told him that Continental centres of learning appealed
to him much more than either Oxford or Cambridge.
    'Hold on!' was Huxley's quick response. 'If you'll wait a
bit I'll put you up for the Sharpey Scholarship at University
College.' (16)

In due time this honour was awarded Geddes, and he spent his fourth
year in London performing the duties of senior demonstrator of
practical physiology under Professors E.A. Schäfer and J. Burdon
Sanderson. At the same time he carried on his own studies in a
field that greatly fascinated him: the lower forms of life in the
borderland of botany and zoology, where animals and plants seem
almost indistinguishable one from the other. In fact, his first
significant discovery in biology, soon to be made, would be to
prove that the basic plant substance chlorophyll actually existed
in some low forms of animal life! (cf. p. 54)

Yet with all his varied scientific interests and enduring assiduity,
there came a day (presumably during his first period in London)
when the ambitious Scot failed to appear at the laboratory. Two,
three days passed, and still no sign of him. Then, after a whole
month's absence, Geddes turned up and resumed work as though
nothing had happened. When his comrades asked what he had been
up to, he said, 'Oh, just looking at pictures in galleries.' They,
of course, were convinced that he had been on one long bender,
whereas the truth was that his month of 'folly' really had been
spent in visiting galleries, plus a few dinners and evenings at
the theatre. He had actually seen every art exhibition and
studied every famous painting in London, accompanied at first by
his boyhood friend, Harry Barker. Harry couldn't stand the pace,

however, and dropped out of the 'razzle-dazzle' after a week or
so. (17)   But no one believed Pat's story, so tradition at the
School of Mines held that Huxley's favourite pupil had indeed
'done London brown'.

The thousands of Geddes's personal and business letters, carefully
preserved by his daughter Norah and later turned over to the
National Library by her, bear witness to the tremendous correspondence carried on throughout his entire life, much of it written by
his own hand.   It is therefore all the more regrettable that this
student period is so lacking in documents.   His daughter states
that 'amongst the many letters he must have written home from
London, only one has been kept'. (18)   Dated October 1877 and
addressed to his sister Jessie, it contains Patrick's good advice
for patching up a quarrel between her and their sister-in-law
Maggie.

Biographer Mairet must, however, have seen other letters for he
writes:
> Correspondence with his sister Jessie at home shows that the
> parents' pride in his professional progress was still tinged
> with anxiety for his spiritual welfare; but his Sabbath occu-
> pations may have partly reassured them.   He took considerable
> interest in sermons - as well he might for London was never
> more rich in pulpit eloquence.   True, the preachers he liked
> best were theologically defective by Mount Tabor standards if
> not, like the Comtists, heterodox. (19)

In spite of Patrick's lapse from their communion, his father and
mother never considered him a lost soul.   Indeed, so strong was
their faith that it even justified in their eyes their son's
actions as being for the best.   Since he gave them constant
attention and affection as long as they lived, his break from
orthodoxy was accepted 'without any of that bitterness which con-
straint and revolt so readily engender between the elder and the
younger generations'.   Patrick always admired and respected his
father as 'the wisest guide, philosopher and friend among all
those more famous ones I learned from him to seek.'   He would
also say that nothing science taught him in later years was more
of a surprise than the so-called 'father and son difficulty', or
still worse, the tragic 'Oedipus complex' as revealed by modern
psychology.

ROSCOFF AND PARIS ... NATURE AND MAN REDISCOVERED

Although John Ruskin's 'Time and Tide' cured young Geddes so
magnificently of his spell of depression from over-work, it is
not recorded which of those haranguing and edifying letters to
English workmen were most medicinal.   It is certain, however,
that Ruskin's ideas on co-operation, wealth and political economy
were to bear a rich harvest.   For example, 'large fortunes cannot
honestly be made by the work of any one man's hands or head' will
return by 1884 as one of many pillars in Geddes's study of 'John

Ruskin, Economist'.   Similarly, the latter's admonitions to the
British public to demand that instead of millions being thrown
away on bad architectural ornaments like 'cast-iron cockades and
zigzag cornices', this money be used to procure 'land or lodging,
or books' for them, will crop up in spirit not only in 'Conditions
of Progress of the Capitalist and of the Labourer' in 1886 but in
a half-century of town planning.   Foreshadowing these developments
is Geddes's own diary comment that 'sociology is a better life for
me than physics....' (20)

As the winter of 1877-8 drew to a close, Patrick suffered what he
has described merely as a 'sharp illness', though in that one
letter extant to Jessie he had also explained that 'lack of wind
and laziness' had made him miss a church service.   This ties in
with the pattern of his adolescent lassitudes and of being ex-
hausted by taking notes during Huxley's two-hour lecture.   (Much
later in life Geddes would confess that he had always suffered
from writer's cramp.)   In any case, the patient went not to
Ruskin's books but to a doctor whose prescription was to use the
Easter vacation for a complete change from his indoor London life
of laboratory demonstrations, experiments, reading and museums.
Again it was Thomas Huxley who gave decisive help.   'Go to
Roscoff.'' he commanded on hearing of Patrick's ill-health, 'I'll
give you an introduction to my friend Lacaze-Duthiers.'

Located on the northwest coast of Brittany, the tiny port of
Roscoff had long been known among scientists for its marine biological station, founded by Professor Henri de Lacaze-Duthiers
of the Sorbonne, and in less learned circles for its excellent
sailors and fishermen.   As Scottish patriots had, in previous
centuries, sought refuge there from English rule at home, so now
Geddes made his escape from London.   This spring holiday was
'the first of two or three delightful mind-stirrings of convalescence which have been epochs of my personal life'.   After a
memorable month he came back to finish the term at University
College and to thank Huxley for health regained and for the
'inestimable service' of introducing him to life and learning
in France.

Patrick returned to Roscoff for the entire summer of 1878.   The
marine biological station there shared in the rugged hard-working
character of the little port.   Being a 'Roscovite' meant getting
up at dawn to board a small boat and head out into the choppy
waves of the Channel.   Marine fauna was to be found at its
richest and best along this north coast of Finistère but the students had to do their own finding.   At Roscoff there were no
laboratory boys to fetch and carry or to do the dirty work.

Geddes soon became expert in dredging from a boat and in combing
the seashore on foot, where, incidentally, the bathing was fine
in warm weather.   This immense change from sedentary student
life in London had very salutary effects on him.   It rescued him
from that isolation from reality which generally prevails in
institutions of higher learning, and put him into challenging

situations.   During boyhood he had by force of circumstance been
something of an only child, and though he was not spoiled in the
sense of being disagreeably selfish, he had become accustomed to
considering his own interests as of primary importance.   It did
him no harm to be socialised by the fishermen of Roscoff, who, as
he himself said, 'were at once his peers and his instructors'.

As for Lacaze-Duthiers, Patrick rapidly discovered in him an
inspiring field-naturalist, though not the equal of Huxley in
comparative anatomy.   Thanks to these two vacation periods with
'so splendidly life-intoxicated a naturalist' as Lacaze, one who
in this respect was 'the very peer of Darwin himself', (21)
Patrick was now back on the path along which his father had
started him.   Having advanced beyond both textbook and museum
collection, he was again able to observe and explore, 'in garden
and woodland, on hillside and seashore, the varied pageants of
life in actual performance on Nature's stage'.

The year 1878-9 marked yet another phase in student wanderings,
for after the summer in Brittany he followed the 'genial company
of Roscovites' back to Paris, there to continue work with Lacaze
in the Sorbonne and to study histology with Professors Wurtz and
Gautier in the Ecole de Médecine.   At Roscoff he entered into
some of the most valued friendships of his whole life.   In Paris
Geddes found his spiritual home.

France was then making quiet but tremendous efforts to redeem
herself after the recent débâcles of 1870-1 and to establish the
Third Republic on firmer bases than the first two.   The great
International Exposition of 1878 in Paris, which Patrick studied
as thoroughly as the museums in London, was clear proof that
though defeated by force of arms the French nation was again
supreme in the arts, and that she intended to resume her place
in the councils of Europe.   Everywhere and among all classes and
professions, from peasants to men of science, surged forth the
same spirit of strengthening and remaking France.   *Il faut
refaire la Patrie*!   This battle-cry to rebuild the mother
country, expressing as it did the purpose of millions of Frenchmen, made an indelible imprint on the 24-year-old Scot abroad.

He witnessed the beginnings of the promised emancipation of provincial centres of learning from long years of enslavement to the
bureaucratic and over-centralised governmental machinery set up
by Napoleon, a yoke which had definitely contributed to France's
defeat.   He felt the same spirit of renewal in the old Sorbonne
and in its students, and eagerly subscribed to one of their
manifestos which, reaching beyond university laboratories and
lecture-halls, claimed the whole culture of France as a necessary
supplement to the Sorbonne, the Ecole de Médecine, the Ecole de
Droit.   Thus the Bibliothèque Nationale in Paris was *their*
library, the artists of the Odéon and Comédie Française were
their instructors in French language and literature, the Louvre
and the Salons, the Conservatoire and the Opéra were *their* schools
of art and music.   In short, their university was the living city

in all the manifestations of its highest culture and thought;
while their city, their capital, was ideally the university in
action.

Patrick immersed himself in the keen Parisian atmosphere of scientific and social discussion which made a welcome contrast to
the staid mid-Victorian culture of London. His daughter Norah
says that 'Admiring French thought and adopting many French ways,
he practised assiduously to express himself with clarity and
even elegance in the written and spoken word.' (22) Geddes's
own description confirms his enthusiasm:

> The University and the City were each richer in impressions,
> experiences and impulses than all I had known before ... here
> the energy and helpfulness of Lacaze and the other teachers;
> there the superman-like intensity of Pasteur, beyond all men
> I have ever seen. The patriarchal Chevreul [at 90 he was
> still director of Gobelins and of the 'jardin des Plantes']
> I remember with peculiar distinctness and no little grati-
> tude.... And what vivid conversation everywhere! When I
> read Anatole France I hear his old master and mine - Pierre
> Lafitte - talking; and even the single lecture of Renan's I
> went to was enough to give an enduring idea of that subtly
> mingled mind. It was indeed a time of renewal. (23)

Stimulating as was intellectual life in France, Geddes found the
moral outlook of the French equally inspiring. On the surface
this morality seemed diametrically opposed both to the Free Kirk
conventions of his boyhood and to Victorian mixtures of holiness
and hypocrisy; yet he claimed that Paris was the ideal place
not merely to be more vitally educated but above all to be
moralized. 'Does this seem a paradox?' he asked. 'What
morality does one find there as compared with Edinburgh, Oxford,
Cambridge, London?' He gave this answer, which long years of
subsequent contact with France only reinforced:

> First and foremost the morality of truth. How so? *To see
> the thing as it is*, that is the perpetual quest, the essential
> atmosphere of French criticism; that is what it is ever seek-
> ing and ever teaching. What next beyond this? Morality of
> action: *to make the thing as it should be*!... What else
> does one learn in Paris? How its world-surpassing clearness
> of thought and excellence of workmanship have developed simply
> by following the one main road to these fundamental human
> moralities of truth and action: that of doing a day's work.
> For here is the hardest working of all great cities.

He experienced French mores at close hand during his year in
Paris and observed the various types around him: wastrels, *bons
vivants* and the ascetics of letters or science. He knew French
students who lived openly with mistresses or étudiantes and young
English gentlemen, notoriously holier-than-thou, who lived
chastely alone - between visits to prostitutes whom they des-
pised. To his French comrades, who made real love the condition
and justification of their affairs and trial marriages, such
hypocritical and frankly lustful behaviour on the part of Anglo-

Saxons was downright immoral, and he shared this opinion.   Judging from what Patrick records of those years, it would appear that he actually practised the ideal he ascribed to many of his French friends: *il faut passer son sexe par son cerveau*;   that is, to sublimate and express sex urges in terms of brain work.

To the writer's knowledge there are no written 'confessions' concerning Geddes's private life, though he did talk frankly on occasion with his children and certain colleagues.   Norah has thus noted his approval of French sexual morals versus Victorian but without any comment as to his possible practice of them.*   Arthur, on the other hand, firmly stated that his father assured him that he had never had sexual relations with any woman before his marriage. (24)

During 1878-9 Patrick wrote and published four scientific papers in French as well as lecturing in that language on certain occasions.   Apart from such biological investigations, he steadily broadened his spheres of interest both intentionally and by chance.   Wandering one afternoon along the Rue Jacob, he happened to see a poster in a doorway announcing some lectures by a M. Edmond Demolins on the new 'Science Sociale'.   Intrigued by the subject, he went in and heard the lecturer expound the work and social theories of Frédéric Le Play.   Though he had never heard of either person before, Geddes got then and there a new intellectual revelation.   Le Play, he learned, was a French mining engineer who had spent a lifetime in travel and first-hand study of social phenomena in worker-groups in all parts of Europe. His approach was concrete and comparative, on wages, family budgets, housing, stability of employment, and so on.   Sceptical of the abstract reasoning of classical philosophers and new 'sociologists', including Comte, Le Play had worked out an objective method for studying actual cross-sections of society. Expressed by his famous triad: *Lieu-Travail-Famille*, he saw in 'Place' the force of environment which everywhere determined what sort of work men might do, 'Work' the main conditioning factor of family life and organisation, and 'Family' as the basic social unit.

Suddenly Geddes realised that in Le Play's travels and observations there lay a method of study which could satisfy him as a scientist and inspire him, as one who now puzzled more and more over mankind's ways and institutions, to follow this literally down-to-earth lead.   After the lecture he presented himself to M. Demolins with eager questions about Le Play and the work of the 'Science Sociale' group.   When he left the Rue Jacob that evening, it was with a new idol to set up beside Thomas Huxley and Auguste Comte: Frédéric Le Play, both as scientific observer *and* as man of action.

* She has, however, written that 'It would have done him good if he had had a little temporary ménage in his Paris student days ...' in a letter to author 18 April 1945 (see also p. 393).

SELF-REVIEW IN MEXICO

In the autumn of 1879 Patrick Geddes carried out a plan which had
been ripening since his brother Robert had had some home leave from
Mexico City.   Already recognised in London and Paris as a brilliant
and promising young biologist, and with modest financial support
from the British Association for the Advancement of Science, Patrick
started out to gather geological, botanical and zoological specimens
in Mexican areas.   Yet what began as a perfect mingling of adventure and work for this many-sided, extrovert naturalist soon turned
into prolonged illness with a crisis of threatened blindness and
enforced meditation.

The inner story of this period of self-review has been authenti-
cally told in two pieces of the 'near poetry' into which he lapsed
sporadically in later life.   The first is from one of the many
'verse-letters' he poured out in India after an illness in the
summer of 1922.   Written in his own kind of tight yet flowing
blank verse, he crowded it with much factual and psychological
information along with dashes, parentheses and exclamation points.
Witness how the essence of his wander years 1874-9 is here condensed into almost the same number of lines:
>   ... Best of all in life is Convalescence!   This I tell
>   With Knowledge of what I'm saying, since once, again and now:
>   Vivid experience!   Thus, long ago - student in London - illness -
>   Then, six weeks at Roscoff!   There - after years concentrated
>   On Huxley's (Cuvier's) analyses, comparisons of form -
>   I woke anew, fuller than ever, to the living world.
>   Initiated now to Bio-drama-life of Sea!   Thence researches fresh;
>   Impelling years of work later, through life essential.

Specifically, this re-awakening led him to complete the academic
year 1878-9 in France and to spend a short time at the Zoological
Station in Naples, after which he went to the University of Aberdeen to help organise a similar station there during the summer
of 1879.   Then, having received a grant of £50 from the British
Association, he sailed from Liverpool on 10 September bound for
Mexico and a year of research.   By mid-October he was installed
in his brother Robert's home in Mexico City and hard at work in
the clear autumn air collecting stones for James Geikie, crayfish
for Huxley, and assorted reptiles and crustaceans for the British
Museum, as well as specimens of semi-tropical flora for himself.

Based on stories told him by Geddes's son Arthur, Mairet describes
the Mexican adventure as a 'toughening experience' and relates how
Patrick, one night soon after his arrival, had to help his brother
and staff guard the bank against an expected armed robbery.
Though this attack did not occur, he soon found that field work
was not only dangerous in this bandit-ridden country, but utterly
frustrating.   Many of the abandoned silver mines were rich in
prehistoric remains, yet the miners were unreasonably hostile.
>   Besides extinct species ... of elephant, he located mastodon,
>   glyptodon, and other precious paleontological relics, and he
>   was soon digging, sometimes with one or two hired Indians, at

Thomas Huxley's 'distinguished student' (Patrick Geddes) at the Royal School of Mines, London, around the age of 22

(right) Patrick with beard, Lowland Bonnet and walking stick in Aberdeen, August 1879, just before his Mexican expedition

Dear Marie! -- How goes it with you? Well, I hear; -- soon Better!
-Then Best! Best of all in life is Convalescence! This I tell,
- With knowledge of what I'm saying! since once, again, and now,
Vivid experience! -- Thus, long ago -- student in London -- illness-
Then, six weeks at Roscoff! There -- after years concen-
trated
On Huxley's (Cuvier's) analyses, comparisons of form -
I woke anew, more fully than ever, to the living world:
-Initiate now to Bio-drama of the Sea! Thence researches fresh;
Impelling years of work later, through life, essential.

Next breakdown, Mexico; both eyes endangered; bleedings
Fourteen or so; exhaustion! Ten weeks in total dark!
Naturalists, like doctors, know of heredity more than good
For them:- blind ancestors, from mother backward, haunted me.
What can a visual, not auditive, do, if blind?
-With returning strength, though darkness, came the gleam-
Graphics! -- Statistics! -- notations! -- symbolisms! -- ev'n mathe-
matics!

'Best of all in life is Convalescence!' Part of a verse-letter to 'Dear Marie (Bonnet)' written in the summer of 1922

sites within riding distance.   But to the natives, this energetic young Scot was a magician, and the miners suspected that
he was a rival prospecting for silver under false pretences:
they came by night and destroyed what he had carefully uncovered
by day.   It was impracticable to set a guard at night, one was
not too safe at any hour in a country where everyone carried a
revolver;   and Patrick refused to bear arms, being in no mind
to kill anybody.

He carried £5 about with him as a possible ransom if captured, and hoped to be able to administer a knock-out in the
French style he had studied if self-defence became unavoidable.
Sometimes he would work on late until his brother came galloping
through the dusk to bring him home, and as they rode back
Robert would draw Patrick's attention to the roadside crosses
erected over the graves of other young fools who had stayed
out and been killed under cover of darkness. (25)

But very soon Patrick's health began to suffer and, as he reported
to the British Association, 'indisposition soon passed into illness ... [which], aggravated by very severe, and as it afterwards
turned out, mistaken medical treatment, confined me to my room
for upwards of two months, and left me utterly enfeebled....' (26)
What he did not tell was that cumulative eye strain from years of
work at the microscope, brought to a crisis by the bright sunlight
of the Mexican plateau, made him a blind invalid sentenced to a
dark-room for an indefinite term.

His physical and mental crisis is poignantly described in the
reminiscent verse-letter:
   Next breakdown, Mexico; both eyes endangered; bleedings
   Fourteen or so: exhaustion, Ten weeks in total dark!
   Naturalists, like doctors, know of heredity more than good
   For them: blind ancestors from mother backward, haunted me.
   What can a visual, not auditive, do, if he be blind? (27)

Family history was indeed alarming, and Patrick could not help
reviewing it over and over again.   It was small consolation to
think how calmly Mother Geddes, now in her sixth year of blindness, accepted loss of sight or how much she still enjoyed the
Mount Tabor garden by touching or smelling her beloved flowers.
The son found himself stricken at twenty-five, at the very start
of mature life.   Friends might read him the latest monographs
and books - as his sister-in-law was now doing - but he would
always be barred from the two essential scientific steps of exploring nature and experimenting in laboratories.

In an unfinished poem called 'Preface' and written some time
around 1925 he again relives this
   ... time of darksome fears
   That stirred me to thoughtful man:

   For though I had had a student's life
   - Ay, ever since thoughtful child -
   I was fully alien in the tortured strife
   That blinded my mother mild.

Facsimile of the unfinished autobiographical poem 'Preface' of 1925, describing Patrick's temporary blindness in Mexico 'Five-and forty years ago ...'

As with winged eyes I had lived my life,
Gloating o'er all I saw:
Through nature and art, in beauty rife,
Observe! was my life's law!

But now it seemed ancestral doom
(That had fall'n so oft on age)
Hastened to turn my youth to gloom,
On first full-opening page!

From tropic rides and quests and finds
Prisoned in night-dark room!
Long weeks, then months, its boding binds
Hope between gloom and doom!

To help Patrick pass the long hours of solitary confinement,
Robert's wife Maggie used to read aloud for him sitting outside
his door.   But there were still hundreds of lonely hours to fill,
and he must certainly have resented as well as pondered over his
previous utter dependency on sight.   Why should scientists be
enslaved by the printed page?   Why did thought have to be so
bound up with black marks on paper that it could have no permanent
expression without them?   With some such protests he was standing
one day by his darkened window, feeling its small panes and criss-
cross pattern of frames.   Suddenly, a revelation:
   Yet youth is Hope, and searches far;
   Seeks Life, though maimed, ev'n blinded;
   Thus, touching darkened window's bar,
   Hope woke afresh - new-minded!

The fingers see! Oh wonders rare!
The window bars turn graphic!
Dark panes now each their vision bear!
Thus mind wins powers seraphic!

The visions and powers seraphic would be reflected in his thinking
and writing, in plans and projects for the rest of his life.   The
revelation was, in sum, that just as a chart's meridians and parallels help navigator and geographer to find their way in the physical world, so these window frames could serve to map out facts and
even ideas.

For example, his years as a wandering student might be represented
by three panes, for past, present and future, respectively.
Better still, by using nine panes, he could have debit, credit,
and balance columns as in a ledger (see Figure 2.1).   Thus his
two years with Huxley more than made up for the first year lost
at the School of Mines.   His meeting Lacaze-Duthiers at Roscoff
amply rewarded him for poor health in London, and so on.   Last
summer's work in Aberdeen belonged entirely on the credit side,
for both his chief, Professor Cossar-Ewart and his students
enthusiastically praised the way he had conducted laboratory
experiments and seaside excursions.

	Past	Present	Future
Credit			
Debit			
Balance			

Figure 2.1

Equally far on the debit side must go his failure to win appointment to the chair of zoology at Owens College, Manchester. It is
most likely that he had been rejected because of his youth and
lack of teaching experience. Yet the most obvious reason probably did not even occur to him; that of his not having an academic
degree. Not only had he scorned to take the BSc or MA which
every other young graduate in science had but he stubbornly
refused to admit its 'career-value'. True, only seven of his
scientific papers were thus far in print, but one of these, (28)
on the finding of vegetable chlorophyll and starch in planarian
worms, was known to biologists all over Europe. When the British
Association sent him in April 1879, for a short 'stage' at the
Zoological Station in Naples, he had won the admiration of a
group of European scientists by lecturing in French on his research
on chlorophyll in animal life.

As Director Hubrecht of the Dutch Museum of Natural History testified: 'Your talent of clear and lucid exposition of an intricate
scientific subject ... and in a language which was not your own,
certainly promises you a wonderful success as a teacher of
Science'. (29)   But as an antidote to excessive pride in his
accomplishments, Patrick could reflect on another experience in
Naples: that of watching an untrained laboratory boy discover
with the naked eye things which he himself had had to use a microscope to verify! (30)

With such thoughts painfully reminding him of his present afflic-
tion, Geddes moved on the second set of squares. Yet what was
there to record in the present except liabilities? He had perhaps
collected enough material during the first weeks in Mexico to
justify the British Association in having sent him on the expedition, but measured by his own expectations it was a failure.

Weakness from the repeated bleedings drove Patrick back to his
couch. Too bad the window frames weren't movable. But wait!
Fumbling on a table near by, he located a piece of paper, folded
it into squares whose creased outlines he could feel when unfolded
- and there was his *portable* device for classifying facts! With
this under his fingers he continued charting the accomplishments
and problems of his life. Whereas the present, up to a few
minutes ago, had held nothing but blindness and intellectual

frustration, his future now had one asset of discovery.   Meridians
and parallels could be used for many new kinds of mapping, even by
a sightless person, and by expressing them in a 'braille' of folded
paper the heartening result was that
      The fingers see! Oh wonders rare!

Though illness and darkness still imprisoned him as the New Year of
1880 began, Geddes was no longer completely at their mercy.   He
continued exploring the possibilities of thinking with pieces of
folded paper in his hands instead of pencil or pen.   It was
exciting to see how much of history, philosophy, and science might
be expressed and correlated by means of these 'thinking machines'
as he later called them.   Reflecting one day on Comte's hierarchy
of the sciences, he literally 'felt' that it begged his seeing
fingers to give it the staircase arrangement shown in Figure 2.2.

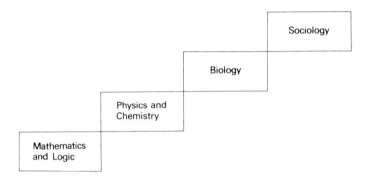

Figure 2.2

The blindfolded thinker visualised how clearly and concisely such
a diagonally ascending arrangement expressed the historic development and rank of the sciences.   His creased diagram showed how
the main fields of each pure science touch only at a corner point,
how those in the first three squares are preliminary to the crowning one of sociology, and much more.

In folding a sheet of paper to get these four ascending squares,
he found that he had twelve others in creased outline below, above,
and adjacent to, the main four (see Figure 2.3).   While feeling
these others with his finger-tips, he discovered that the lower
squares would serve admirably to show the applications and interrelations of the sciences.   The bottom row of squares thus revealed mathematics as basic to each of the succeeding sciences,
while the physical sciences were next shown as underlying biology
and sociology, with biology in turn as the preliminary science
most closely basic to that of society.   In his first enthusiasm
there seemed to be almost no end to the clarifications and interpretations which could spring out of such a charting of the
sciences.

Another day he turned to algebraic symbols as a change from the

			Sociology
		Biology	Public Health Medicine
	Physics and Chemistry	Biophysics Biochemistry	Industrial techniques
Mathematics (pure)	Mathematics (applied to Physics)	Biometrics	Statistics

Figure 2.3

lines and spaces of plane geometry, only to find himself combining
them all to make a new kind of thinking-machine.   Taking factors
A and B, and their two possible combinations as Ab or Ba, he soon
fitted them into four squares (Figure 2.4).

A	aB
bA	B

Figure 2.4

This led automatically to another graph expressing the possible
combinations of A, B, and C, this time six in number (Figure 2.5).

A	aB	aC
bA	B	bC
cA	cB	C

Figure 2.5

Still later he would come to substitute scientific factors and
concepts for algebraic symbols.   Biology's basic triad of environment, function and organism;   then Le Play's *Lieu-Travaille-
Famille* and the like in other sciences.   The use of 'thinking
machines' was to become one of Geddes's daily activities and a
trait which would both set him apart from all his contemporaries
and prove a stumbling block to many colleagues and potential
disciples.   He, however, considered the discovery of 'meridians
and parallels of thought' as significant as that of the slide-rule.
   Much mid these sharp-felt bars I see ...
   As 'Napier's bones' gave speed and power
   So here a further magic ...

After ten weeks the doctors allowed their patient to leave his darkened room.   Still very weak physically, Patrick found his eyes so painfully sensitive to light that the bandages could be removed only for short periods.   But he could see again!   At some time during his intellectual adventures the crisis of threatened blindness had been safely passed.   Convalescence was indeed 'the best of all in life', yet it went so slowly that even in the latter part of February he felt unable to resume his long-interrupted scientific work.   He did attempt a few botanical and fossil-hunting expeditions, one of them to the caves of Cacahuamilpa, but his condition soon forced him to yield to his brother's plea to return to Scotland and recuperate his health.

On 1 March 1880 he embarked for home at Vera Cruz, a voyage which then took a whole month.   Forbidden to read by his doctors, Patrick had to content himself with chess day in and day out, and with the new game of paper-folding.   His luggage consisted of crayfish for Huxley, fossils for the British Museum, deep-well boring-samples for James Geikie and graphic thinking-machines for himself. - Most important of all he brought back gradually restored sight and self-confidence re-won.

Those weeks of enforced leisure and meditation had given him a rare opportunity to assimilate the crowded experiences, readings, experiments, observations and writings of his past five years as a student wandering from London to Roscoff, Paris, Naples; from Aberdeen to Mexico.   The dark-room struggle had also stirred him 'to thoughtful man' and let his mind win 'powers seraphic'.

For the rest of his days he would tell and retell this story of physical and spiritual crisis in Mexico; emphasising it as 'the worst, yet best experience of my life'.

Chapter 3

WHICH IDENTITY, WHAT MESSAGE? 1880-6

THE ERRANT BOTANIST'S RETURN

> On returning to Scotland in the spring of 1880, I was appointed
> to organise and conduct the department of Practical Botany in
> this (Edinburgh) University.   For three years I also performed
> the duties of Lecturer on Natural History in the School of
> Medicine, and in this capacity delivered five courses of
> lectures, besides special courses on various departments of
> general biology.   Since 1882 I have devoted myself to botan-
> ical teaching alone. (1)

Patrick's account of his homecoming and earliest academic career
contains an enigma of phrasing which, though minor, points to a
trait that would become more and more obvious with time.   This
was a doubtless unconscious tendency to present his past accomplishments or current projects in the best possible light: as
they were inherently, or as they might become.   He thus writes in
the above application for a chair of botany that '... I also
performed the duties of Lecturer on Natural History.'   The somewhat confusing facts behind this choice of words are revealed by
documents in the National Library of Scotland and the University
of Edinburgh, as follows:
1   In April 1880 Geddes applied to the University Court for rec-
    ognition as an extra-mural lecturer in zoology, but before
    their decision was made Professor Alexander Dickson offered
    him an assistantship in Practical Botany.   In May the Court
    rejected his application 'on the grounds that there was no
    precedent for such double employment'. (2)
2   His friend William Stirling advised him not to 'attempt to
    give ambitious special courses ... few people care for Mor-
    phology or anything else.'   But according to Paddy Kitchen
    'Geddes ignored Stirling's advice and embarked on the
    lectures'. (3)
3   In June 1880 he withdrew his application for recognition, the
    University Court Minutes state but at the same time Geddes is,
    strangely enough, 'described as Lecturer on Natural History'.
    On the other hand, he is not included in official lists of
    Extra-Academical Lecturers. (4)

51

4   Four years later, July 1883, he again sought acceptance as an
    outside lecturer, but again 'this was denied "while you hold
    the University office of Assistant to a Professor," and he dis-
    continued his lectures'. (5)

The conclusion to be drawn in this case appears to be that while
Geddes did give various series of extra-mural lectures, he was
never officially recognised as a Lecturer.   Therefore, the phrase
'performed the duties of' avoided a direct misrepresentation of
the facts yet at the same time made it clear that he had actually
lectured on Natural History as well as serving as a practical
assistant in Botany.

Another minor mystery about Patrick's teaching début in Edinburgh
is the recurrent one in his life of periods of debility quickly
passing into those of robust, sustained activity.   Perthshire's
cool, damp and familiar climate must have agreed with him better
than Mexico's heat and intense sunlight, for within weeks of
leaving Vera Cruz he was in full swing again.

His rather prodigal return to Edinburgh was a fulfilment of his
own prophecy.   In 1878, in a humorous letter from Paris to Frank
Young, he had drawn a sketch of himself as a bartender in an Old
Town pub serving both students and workers.   'Never had I a truer
presage, for after a couple of years of roaming between Naples,
Aberdeen and Mexico, I came to Edinburgh and began my trade.   My
first barrels were of course biological.' (6)

A practical reason why he returned to that 'worst of all hitherto
discovered universities' which Carlyle had word-lashed in 1834,
and from which he, his ardent admirer, had fled after a week's
trial in 1874, was the new spirit prevailing in the department of
Practical Botany.   A quite sentimental reason was the deep
attraction which Edinburgh had held for him ever since that first
boyhood visit with his father.   To Patrick it was always 'our
City Beautiful, which had fascinated me in childhood', and which,
despite his early frustration as a student and the cold shoulder
it later turned on him, steadily 'brought me back to it for central home'. (7)   Unfortunately, the reverse of the medal has too
often been shabby neglect by city and university fathers, even up
to the 1970s.   But one is anticipating events by almost a century.

It is still 1880, and the 26-year-old naturalist is teaching both
botany and physiology with an enthusiasm hitherto unknown in that
venerable university.   The professor in charge at this time was
Alexander Dickson who had been appointed in 1879 to succeed the
late John Hutton Balfour, holder of the chair since 1845.   From
the start Patrick was given a free hand and encouraged to bring
living nature into the uninspiring laboratory.   After only two
years of assistantship, Professor Dickson could recommend him for
the vacant Chair of Natural History at St Andrews University in
these terms:

    A thoroughly trained and accomplished naturalist, of great
    intellectual capacity, and scientific insight and grasp, Mr

> GEDDES combines in a remarkable degree the qualifications of a
> successful teacher.   Easy, clear, and fluent in expression, he
> has the power at once of engaging the attention of his audience,
> and of enlisting their interest in the subjects treated of....
> Indeed, whatever success has attended the practical instruction
> in the Botanical Laboratory is, I may say, wholly due to his
> ability, energy, and remarkable organising power. (8)

The young teacher of 28 did not, however, receive the St Andrews
appointment and continued at Edinburgh for six more years.   During
his period as Demonstrator/Lecturer he had a remarkable influence
upon scores of students who themselves became successful and even
famous as teachers, physicians or men of science.   When Geddes
would apply in turn for the chair left vacant in 1888 by 'my late
master and friend, Professor Dickson', he could fill a booklet of
99 pages with the recommendations of renowned scientists from
Darwin to Alfred Wallace, of colleagues throughout Great Britain
and on the Continent, and with 'the unsolicited testimony of a
large body of senior students'.

The most enthusiastic was a young student of theology later to
become the famous zoologist and popular scientific writer, Sir J.
Arthur Thomson.

> When I entered your classes ... I at once felt your power as a
> true teacher.   It was not merely that you presented the facts
> in a fresh and always practical way ... but this above all,
> that you forced your students to think by your consistent pur-
> suit of a method which was not dogmatic, but critical. (9)

Patrick likewise displayed a skill and clarity worthy of his
master Huxley, while emulating his kindly generosity towards
pupils as well.   One of these has testified to

> that powerful influence which his character and conversation
> have over all his acquaintances.   It is a common remark among
> them that they never meet him without being the better of him,
> without being strengthened, encouraged, elevated, stimula-
> ted. (10)

Among all the favourable comments, though, was one which mentioned
a weakness that was to follow Geddes in varying degrees, throughout
life.   Frank Young, when a high school teacher in Dundee, revealed that 'Your voice, to begin with somewhat weak, has with
practice improved considerably'. (11)   With the years, other
audiences would experience dismay when only the blackboard and its
drawings or graphics could hear what the lecturer was saying.   A
great pity that Patrick was not given in time the same advice that
Huxley offered to one of his junior teachers: 'Lecture your
audience, do not lecture your blackboard'.   Huxley did, however,
write that Geddes

> was at one time a distinguished student of my class.   I have a
> very high opinion of his abilities....   He has published works
> of considerable interest and importance, and from the energy
> with which he throws himself into everything which he takes up,
> I should expect him to be, as I hear he is, an excellent
> teacher. (12)

Of the important works Huxley refers to, the first one, (13) based on research done at Roscoff, dealt with a primitive flatworm occurring in great numbers on the sandy beaches of Brittany and containing minute algae which gave it a green colour.   A pupil of Geddes gave this evaluation in 1954:

> These algae, as Geddes was the first to demonstrate, are capable of photo-synthesis, in sunlight building up into themselves nutritive carbohydrates from water and carbon dioxide produced as waste by the animal cells, and in so doing evolving oxygen useful to the animal.   Today this case of symbiosis is a biological commonplace; every young zoologist knows it; in 1879 Geddes's discovery was deemed worthy of publication by the Royal Society of London.   It is a good paper, clearly indicating its author as a man of ideas and ability. (14)

This discovery made Geddes known among European biologists, and some colleagues confidently expected him to become a 'Scottish Darwin'!   It is therefore rather a let-down to read further in the appraisal of his scientific contributions made on the occasion of the Geddes Centenary in 1954.

The discovery of chlorophyll in animals, says Peacock, was his 'only biological contribution of a strictly factual nature, all his subsequent work in biology being of another kind'.   He ascribes as a sufficient reason for this lack of detailed discoveries the fact that, after his near-blindness in Mexico, Geddes could never again apply himself to prolonged observations at the microscope.   This is verified by Mairet who has reported, from earlier access to diary notes now unavailable, that Patrick's eye trouble 'forbade more than the minimum of laboratory work, and punished it with severe headaches'. (15)

On the other hand, one may argue that even had his eyesight not been weakened, another basic factor would soon have hindered further specialised research: his manifold interests and his all-consuming desire to generalise, to synthesise.

Just as it took him four years of apprenticeships and private studies after finishing at Perth Academy to find out in what field he should concentrate, so would eight years pass in Edinburgh before his real career materialised.   Meanwhile he tried out several identities, all of which attracted him and any one of which he could have assumed with great success, as well as preached their messages with conviction.   One recalls the parting words of the bank manager in Perth who trusted that Patrick would 'prove an Ornament to the Profession he may choose'.   The only problem for the ex-bank apprentice was the choice!

INCURSION INTO SOCIOLOGY

During his first year as Lecturer on Zoology and Demonstrator of Botany, Geddes read two papers to the Royal Society of Edinburgh. The first (16) was precisely what was expected of him.   It treated

small details concerning a 'Species of Enteromorpha' and was, as
he himself afterwards described it, written in a manner dry-as-dust.
But the next paper was an insurgent milestone in the budding career
of this young man.   Not only did he invade the social sciences,
criticising their chaotic, 'pre-evolutionary' state and proposing
to organise all 'social knowledge', but he asserted that not until
the counsels of economics coincided with those of ethics, was any
intended course of action the right one.

Delivered in three instalments in March, April and May 1881, 'The
Classification of Statistics and its Results', (17) was both a
first anniversary tribute to his Mexican experience and a foretaste of what was to come.   To start with his own conclusion,
this paper was 'probably the first which has attempted to organise
the whole body of our recorded social knowledge into a form pre-
sentable to the cultivators of the preliminary sciences.'   What
he aimed at was, to quote an eight-point summary made a few years
later (18) nothing less than:
   1. To review the existing state of statistics;
   2. To define the nature of the subject, and its relation to
   history and the sciences;
   3. Broadly to group and co-ordinate the whole body of existing
   and possible statistics, in relation to the respective statistical sciences;   and
   4. In accordance with the preliminary sciences to frame a
   classification embracing all existing and possible sociological
   statistics.   Moreover,
   5. This was shown to involve, or rather actually to constitute,
   an aspect of the pressing problem of the systematisation of the
   literature of economics, of which
   6. The existing schools were briefly criticised;
   7. The relation of the conceptions of scientific economics to
   practical economics was outlined;
   8. As also their relation to ethics.

After invoking Comte's classification of sciences and Huxley's
contention that 'no natural boundary separates the subject matter
of Psychology and Sociology from that of Biology', Geddes launched
into his own arguments for re-examining the nature of statistics.
Finding that 'at least two hundred non-coincident definitions
have been given by statisticians', he criticised one of the latest
of their proposed systems as being 'closely analogous ... to that
earliest classification with which botanists commenced their
labours,that of the vegetable world into herbs, shrubs and trees'.
Then, more conciliatory, he added that 'Under these circumstances
the interference of the naturalist may be less impertinent than
might at first sight seem probable'.

While space is lacking to follow Geddes in all his steps of argument, here are the five 'sociological axioms' (19) which determine
his natural divisions of statistical matter:
   Axiom I.   A society obviously exists within certain limits of
              space and time;   therefore Group A, or *Territory*,
              includes all facts of political geography: the

quantity and quality of space occupied by the nation in question.

Axiom II.   A society consists of living organisms; therefore Group B, or *Organisms*, deals with the quantity, quality, and occupations of members of society: what they are and what they do.

Axiom III. Organisms modify surrounding nature, mainly by seizing part of its matter and energy; therefore Group C, or *Production*, co-ordinates the facts relating to sources of energy in the territory: to the exploitation, manufacture, and movement of products; and to premature loss of energy and matter.

Axiom IV.   Organisms use this matter and energy in the maintenance of their life; therefore Group D, or *Distribution*, would include the manner in which territory, products, services, or tokens for any of these are divided among or consumed by the society's members.*

Axiom V.   Organisms are modified by their environment, by their occupations and by each other: therefore Group E, or *Results*, would provide a place for all the observations of hygienist, physician, biologist, and psychologist, relative to the effects of environment and mode of life upon the organisms. (V is especially significant as *Geddes's prediction in 1881 of the need for a science of human ecology*.)

Reminiscent of his window-pane meditations is the broad framework of a 'Balance Sheet of Society' (Figure 3.1) wherein Tables A to E are based on Axioms I to V.   But as in Geddes's own chart, B and C are switched to bring the tables concerning Organisms and Classes of Occupations one after the other.   'The scheme', he argues, 'is scientific throughout - in accordance with the known truths of physical and biological science - as capable on the one hand of complete specialisation by the aid of minor tables, and on the other, of generalisation into a colossal balance-sheet'. (20)

Before leaving Geddes's statistical confrontation of his peers and seniors, one must cite two short but significant passages which augur other deviations from botany. Speaking of how 'little leavened' political economy is by the 'recent advances of our

* Actually, Geddes listed only four 'general truths' in his main argument (p. 304) but a few pages later (310) he wrote that 'since, in biological language, the organism is modified by its environment, it is now necessary to inquire as to the results of the given occupations....   The biologist has accumulated a considerable body of knowledge respecting these results among animals, but comparatively little is known of human society in this respect.' He also added a footnote to the effect that the effects of environment 'might, perhaps, more conveniently have been stated as a separate axiom'. Hence, at his suggestion, Axiom V is here listed.

knowledge of the laws of matter and of life', he delivered this open warning:

> To judge from their writings the economists would seem to be un-conscious of the very existence of such doctrines as those cf the conservation and dissipation of energy, of evolution, and the like, and of the evident fact that the students of the phys-ical and biological sciences can hardly much longer delay a combined invasion of their territory. (21)

Then he prophesied, 'As from our system of astronomical knowledge it is necessary to deduce the art of navigation, so from our system of sociological knowledge we must derive the art of conduct'. Finally, he invoked a 'higher order of considerations than the sociological ... the ethical' and postulates the 'coincidence of practical economics with practical ethics, of economy with morality'.

	CREDIT	CREDIT	DEBIT
A	**Territory** *Quantity*	**Territory** *Quality*	**Territory** *Decrease, Loss*
B	**Organisms** *Quantity* Occupations Class I: *Operations on Matter and Energy*	**Organisms** *Quality* Occupations Class II: *Services to Members of Society*	**Organisms** *Decrease* Occupations Class III: (negative) *Non-employed Criminals, Disabled, etc.*
C	**Production** *Sources of Energy* *Sources of Matter*	**Production** *Development of Ultimate Products*	**Production** *Loss* (In all stages and by all agencies)
D	*Distribution* of land, products, services, etc, among: Class I *Use* of these by: Class I	*Distribution,* etc. among Class II Class II	*Distribution,* etc. among Class III Class III
E	*Results* of environment, occupation, etc., upon members of Class I	*Results, etc.* upon: Class II	*Results, etc.* upon: Class III

Figure 3.1 The Balance Sheet of Society (after Geddes, but greatly condensed and simplified.   Table E is here added following Geddes's suggestion. Cf. note on page 56).

Though stating in his final section that 'Having thus reached the ethical platform we find a new series of ethical systems inviting study and criticism', he admitted that such comparisons 'however interesting, would lead into ground for unnecessary controversy'. Geddes concluded his lengthy 'interference of the naturalist' as follows:

> The object of the present paper ... will have been sufficiently gained if the unity and continuity of these (the preliminary sciences) with the social and moral sciences, has been made in some respects clearer than heretofore, and if the mode of treat-ment and arrangements of the facts of social science therein proposed be admitted as satisfactory and serviceable. (22)

ELLIS PRIZE ... NAPLES ... CELL THEORY ... TERCENTENARY CELEBRATIONS

The late summer and autumn of 1881 found Patrick in familiar haunts to the south.   First York, where on 6 September he read an abridg-ment of his original three-session paper on statistics to the British Association (23) and next London, where the three brothers had a reunion.   Robert had retired from banking in Mexico and John was on a combined holiday and business trip from New Zealand. He wrote to Jessie in mid-September at Mount Tabor:

> Father will be pleased to hear that my essay for the University prize will be finished in a few days more and will be a good one.   I did not know I had so many friends in London, but people never were so kind.   I cannot accept all the invita-tions I get, as two come for the same evening now and then, so I don't get so very much time with Jack after all.   Still we are becoming great friends....   Robert came up from Farnham the other day and stayed two nights with us.   We all went and got photographed together, so you will have a lovely trio! Mind you say I am the best looking....   I am glad Father and Mother were so pleased with that 'Times' notice.
>
> With dearest love to them and to yourself also,
>   Your affectionate brother, Pat.

It was probably late September when he made the journey via Paris to Italy and again occupied the British Association's table at the Zoological Station in Naples for six crowded weeks.   Research on sea-urchins, lecturing in French on his previous findings of chlorophyll in animals, putting the final touches on his essay for the Quinquennial Ellis Prize offered by the University of Edinburgh, and persuading two newly made friends there to trans-late his 'political economy' into Italian and Russian, respectively! On top of this he started a correspondence campaign (which proved unsuccessful, as had his try for the Owens College chair in 1879) for the vacant chair of natural history at Edinburgh which his father had telegraphed him about on 26 October.   Writing to his mother the same day, he warned them that the odds against him were considerable.

> I shall of course make as good a fight as I can, but shall take my probable ultimate defeat with the greatest composure, and I hope you will also do the same.   It won't be altogether lost

Mr Geddes exhibited living specimens of *Convoluta Schultzii,* his paper (*vide infra*) being postponed on account of the lateness of the hour.

Monday, 16th January 1882.

Sir WILLIAM THOMSON, Hon. Vice-President,
in the Chair.

The following Communications were read :—

1. On the Nature and Functions of the " Yellow Cells" of Radiolarians and Cœlenterates.   By Patrick Geddes.

It is now nearly forty years since the presence of chlorophyll in certain species of Planarians was recognised by Schultze.*   Later

Patrick's paper which won the Quinquennial Ellis Prize, is published in the 'Proceedings of the Royal Society of Edinburgh'

The Geddes Brothers (*from left*: John, Robert and Patrick) in London September 1881, 'Mind you say I'm the best looking ...'

time and money, as I'll get very thoroughly advertised as a
rising young naturalist, which may pay another time, and at any
rate enable me to preach my political economy more authorita-
tively.   It is very unfortunate for me that this vacancy has
occurred so soon.   I have such quantities of paper in the
press, and such quantities more in my head and notebooks
unfinished.

On his way to Naples, Geddes had stopped in Paris to renew old
contacts, and presumably as a result of this visit, two papers on
zoological research appeared in 1881 in the proceedings of the
Académie des Sciences. (24)   In his October letter he tells his
mother that he intends to send his paper on statistics 'to the
Institute of France in hope of getting a medal out of them'.   He
also is hopeful enough about winning the Ellis Prize to speculate
about its value: 'I presume about £60 or £70'.

At this point, one may again wonder how he justified competing
for medals and prizes while at the same time scoffing at university degrees.   An MA would have been a more valuable academic
investment, for either a 'rising young naturalist' or a preacher
of political economy, or both.   But Geddes had his own decided
opinions on this subject as well as many others: so decided that
in later years at least, there was as little chance of discussing
them openly with him as he had had of debating Positivism with
Dr Congreve, 'the Oxford don'.

In a short time Patrick's egocentric intellectualism would win him
the Quinquennial Ellis Prize, so let us return to Naples in
October 1881 and witness a pleasant break in work - as well as an
apparent touch of homesickness.   Already confident that his was
the prize-winning essay, (25) thanks partly to discoveries just
made, the researcher tells Mother that
　　I am going to take a holiday - hire a donkey for fifteenpence
　　for the day, and ride up to the top of Camadoli, a hill from
　　which you can see, not perhaps quite so far as Mount Tabor,
　　but at any rate a long way in that direction....   I am weary-
　　ing for news.   What of you all?   What of Robert and John?
　　The Weekly Herald - Jessie - is not so regular as of old.
　　　　Love to you all, Your affectionate son, Pat

The next year and a half was mainly devoted to research and publications in the field of cell theory along with a number of
articles for both the 'Britannica' and 'Chambers's'.   One of
these was among the 'quantities of paper in the press' referred
to, for early in December 1881 he was able to send a reprint of
'Insectivorous Plants' to the greatest living naturalist who
acknowledged it as follows:

9 December 1881

Dear Sir,
You were so kind as to send me a few days ago your article in the
'Encyclopaedia Britannica'.   I have now looked through it and it
seems to me wonderfully well done, and you have managed to give
in the space a surprising amount of information.

Permit me to add that I read with admiration your researches
on the presence of chlorophyll in the animal kingdom.
I remain, dear Sir, Yours faithfully,
Charles Darwin (26)

Geddes had written to Darwin the previous year asking permission
to copy some of the figures in the latter's book on 'Insectivorous Plants'. The request was generously granted in a brief note
dated 25 December 1880, Down, Beckingham, Kent. Its second paragraph reads: 'Pray forgive the manner of directing the envelope,
but no one in my house could read your signature'. Whereupon
Darwin cut it out and pasted it on the envelope, trusting that
someone in Edinburgh would be able to decipher it! Patrick must
have found this amusing, for he preserved both letter and envelope.

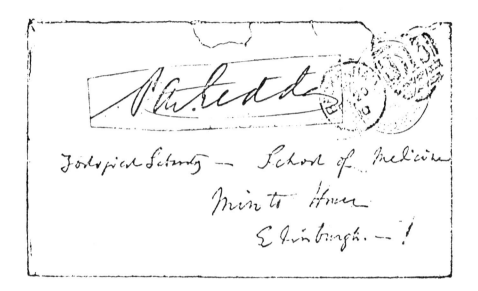

Concerning Geddes's work on cell theory, Professor Angelo Andres
at the School of Agriculture, Milan, wrote:
A few days ago I gave a public lecture on the cell theory, and
(modesty aside) I obtained a great triumph; but you deserved
all the praise, for I only repeated the very valuable ideas and
observations which you set forth in your little work 'A Re-
Statement of the Cell Theory', etc. (27)

But in contrast to these words stands the 1954 Centenary evaluation of A.D. Peacock. After citing the full title, 'A Re-Statement of the Cell Theory, With applications to the Morphology,
Classification and Physiology of Protists, Plants and Animals.
Together with an Hypothesis of Cell Structure and an Hypothesis
of Cell Contractility', Peacock states:
It has had no influence on the main current of biological
thought, the best monographs on cytology and protozoology

making no mention of it.   Yet in its day, bearing in mind that
these subjects then were undeveloped, it was a good paper.   Its
argument ... is worth consideration because it shows the essential Geddes.   Its very title, so comprehensive, is characteristic;   its content, compressed into 26 pages and a plate, com-
prises 14 topics, each alone worthy of an extended paper.
   The paper is bold and stimulating and though its hypotheses
are out-dated it is interesting today for three reasons at
least: it reflects biological thought of the time, also the
questing and speculative mind of Geddes, and contains the germs
of ideas which found full expression in Geddes's later work.
Here is an example ...
   ... on the Geddes view the organism 'is an active community,
of which some or many members, under the influence of any
favourable change of conditions, or the removal of any res-
traints, external or internal, immediately press into other
positions and functions, which however apparently new, are
either specialisations of the existing, or reversions to an
earlier type.'   The idea of the dynamic quality of living
things Geddes never ceased to stress. (28)

We conclude the cell debate with Professor Andres's words:
Allow me to say that those few pages are worth a whole book;
and they are the more valuable that in their succinct brevity
they effect a synthesis.   I wish you could find time to bring
together all your work on protoplasm and the cell: for it
would certainly be a new milestone in the progress of
science. (29)

The reason why Geddes did not consolidate this work was not just
his handicap at the microscope, for speculation and deduction
accounted for much more of his 'Re-Statement' than new observations in the laboratory.   Moreover, his major encyclopaedia
articles on 'Darwinian Theory', 'Cell', and 'Insectivorous
Plants' - to take three other examples from 1883 - reveal a
great amount of library research.   But the nature of what he set
himself to accomplish was changing, and the budding 'generalist'
was already beginning to overshadow the inquiring naturalist.
Witness this minor example just one year later.

The University of Edinburgh celebrated its 300th anniversary in
1884 with great pomp and circumstance.   Delegates from universities and learned societies all over the world attended the
ceremonies, and 120 eminent men of science and letters were
given honorary degrees.   In such an assemblage Geddes was only
one of scores of other ambitious workers in science.   Nevertheless, he left his mark upon the Tercentenary celebration in the
form of a biographical directory (30) of all the famous graduates
of the University, which he edited from information gathered by
sixteen of his colleagues and friends.

Yet, why should a serious young scientist have spent so much time
outside his own field?   Further proof of his lack of botanic
dedication was soon to come, and in a form that could only jeo-
pardize his ascent towards a professorial chair.

ASSAULT ON ORTHODOX ECONOMICS

In March, April, and July of the Tercentenary year of 1884 Geddes
reinforced his venture into statistics by appearing before the
Royal Society with the three instalments of 'An Analysis of the
Principles of Economics'. (31)   After a brief but challenging
summary of the 'Classification of Statistics', he stated his
plan as 'in short, once more to prepare for the construction of
a "system of economics" - not, however, by means of new definitions and old dialectic ... but in harmony with the organic whole
of the preliminary sciences'.
      For this, as in the preceding paper on statistics, two postu-
      lates are required - 1. the classification of the sciences,
      and 2. the main conceptions of each - the comparatively simple
      conceptions of physics preceding those of biology; those of
      biology being followed by those of psychology, and these again
      by sociology.
         ... to distinguish doctrine from practice, to separate
      principle from precept, and construct science apart from art -
      is the first aim of the present inquiry.   Precisely as biology
      underlies medicine, and astronomy navigation, so sound practi-
      cal economics can only be profitably attempted after sound
      scientific conceptions have been attained.

A logical consequence is that 'the economist must no longer
shrink from acquainting himself with the preliminary sciences'.
Yet he need not be alarmed about the labour involved, 'for no
specialist's knowledge is required'.   Just as simple equations
of algebra and the construction of rectangles and curves in geometry will suffice for mathematics, 'so a similarly rudimentary,
if real, knowledge of physics and physiology - of the doctrines
of the permanence of matter through transformation, of conservation and dissipation of energy, and of the functions of living
organisms - will here serve for a commencement.   Nor will more
be postulated in the present work.'

Let us follow a few of the lecturer's examples.   Passing over
pure mathematics, Geddes assumes we are first *physical economists*
and study economic phenomena from the material viewpoint only,
precisely as the physical geologist studies form and change in
the earth's crust.   Whatever we observe on this level - be it
change in the earth, in organisms, or in the interaction of organisms with their environment - is capable of expression in terms
of chemistry and mechanics.
      Social phenomena are to be viewed simply with regard to the
      matter and energy consumed or liberated, and physical economics
      is thus the study of certain forms of matter in motion.

Ruthlessly he eliminates the metaphors and the metaphysics of
economics.   Since human beings, or ants, when viewed from the
level of physics, are merely so many forms of mechanisms made out
of matter from the earth's crust and worked by the energy of the
sun, '"producers" are those automata devoted to the acquisition
of matter and energy from the environment; while all are

"consumers", and in this aspect in wonderfully similar degree'.
Likewise, 'capital' is but a part of the apparatus and energy
employed in production while 'money' is an apparatus of movement
for things which have been produced.

By treating the processes of production and consumption as one
vast mechanical process, by viewing society as a machine and
interpreting all its phenomena as integration or disintegration
of matter, with transformation or dissipation of energy, Geddes
arrives at an all-inclusive physical systematisation.   He proposes measuring production at every stage by the physicist's
metre, kilogram, and horse-power to determine how much matter and
energy are lost during these stages, and he calls for units of
energy like *man-power* and *man-day* to be used as additional measurements of industrial processes, thus anticipating by many
decades twentieth century technocracy.   As Lewis Mumford has
pointed out, Geddes was the first to make a sociological application of the modern concept of energy. (32)

Yet even on the basic level he emphasises that a great part of
so-called necessaries of life are not really needed, unlike fuel
or shelter.   These he calls the *super-necessaries*:   products
whose value lies in their stimulation of human sense organs.
The aesthetic element in production, he argues, is thus more
important than the fundamental one of sustaining life;   it stands
in the ratio of at least three to one.
>   And when we add up the aesthetic subfunctions of all 'neces-
>   sary' ultimate products, and add to this the vast quantity of
>   purely aesthetic products, we see how small the fundamental
>   element of production has become in relation to the superior,
>   and reach the paradoxical generalisation that production -
>   though fundamentally for maintenance - is mainly for art. (33)

After sketching the principles, Geddes turns to the practical
economic action that should be based on physical laws, such as
making improvements in the exploitation of raw material, and the
diminution of friction in transport.   The goal is to maximise
production, but not the production of transitory, ephemeral products which hold dangers even in physics and chemistry.   To increase the *wealth* of nations - not just the *population* - all
industry must be organised in terms of a new ideal: that of producing not more so-called necessities of life but more goods in
which the aesthetic element is supreme.
>   We have thus reached the new paradox that the sphere of prac-
>   tical physical economics is to discuss the ways and means of
>   increasing not so much bread, as Art.

As a living organism, man's protoplasm undergoes incessant waste
and so demands incessant repair.   'It is this fact which ...
[furnishes] the widest definition of productive labour' as performed by all the higher animals.   Namely,
>   obtaining the food needful for repairing the waste of their
>   tissues, from their environment by the performance of muscular
>   contractions co-ordinated by the nervous system.   [Biologi-

cally considered] ... the 'pain', the 'curse of labour' so
much insisted on, is at most merely an accompaniment, incidental either to excessive exertion or defective adaptation to
the task. (34)

Turning to the ways in which both animals and men perform particular functions in their respective kinds of productive labour, he
finds entirely similar results in 'the complicated co-operation of
the ant-hill or the city'.   Further, he asserts that 'the
"specialisation of functions" in *Formica* and the "division of
labour" in *Homo* are not merely "analogies between man and nature"
... but are absolutely identical.'   The effects of such specialised functions are also the same: polymorphic castes among ants
and occupational traits among men.

Biologists have long studied how function shapes organism, but
few economists, Geddes claims, have any knowledge of how occupation affects human beings for either good or ill.   All occupations
are merely considered 'productive' by them with no other factor
observed, far less taken into account.   Yet function not only
shapes the organism, but

other things equal, determines its quantity of health and
limits its length of life.   Ploughmen and weavers, joiners
or soldiers, then, are incipient castes as surely as Brahmin
and Pariah, worker and drone are formed ones;   and the dis-
advantages of the division of labour, so slowly forced into
prominence through the sufferings of the many and the moral
enthusiasm of an unscientific few, demand study and classification among the 'Variations of Animals and Plants under
Domestication'.

Another biological lesson for economists to learn is that of
degeneration in the organic world.   Degeneration occurs under
two distinct sets of conditions: from deprivation of food,
light, air, etc., on the one hand and from over-abundance of
food and too little activity on the other.   The first situation
causes undernourishment or extinction, and the second brings
about the far more insidious decay of life known as parasitism.

It is noteworthy that both these sets of conditions of organic
change exist abundantly in society, the former being known as
poverty, the latter as 'complete material well-being'.   The
influence of all this upon the degeneration of individuals and
upon the decline and fall of nations alike, need not be insisted upon.

Now comes a further biological definition of production: 'the
adaptation of the environment to human functions', and the further
statement that

every productive action thus tends either towards maintenance
and evolution, or the reverse.   This simple idea is not yet,
however, sufficiently active in our industrial age.   The
functions of production are undertaken by industrialists,
chiefs and proletaires alike, mainly with the notion of
obtaining 'wealth' in its very variable proportions of main-

tenance, power over others, personal immunity from function, &c.,
a conception of the nature and aim of production upon which our
surviving industrial anarchy mainly depends.

The action called for on this second level is to 'maximize the
maintenance and evolution of the community'.   Such action
    involves a criticism of life from a biological standpoint....
    The modifications of the organism must be determined and
    analysed into their various factors, viz, 1. the effects of
    organism on organism in heredity (education and competition);
    2. the influence of function on the organism towards degenera-
    tion on the one hand, and towards evolution on the other;
    3. the modification of the organism by its material environ-
    ment, such as food, dwelling, air, light, etc.

At this point Geddes brings a basic ecological message which,
though stated in 1884, is most pertinent to today's struggle
between urban man and the natural environment. (35)

*Proceedings of the Royal Society
of Edinburgh, Session 1883–84.*   971

in modification be observed and appreciated, but their modifiability
must be discussed and acted upon.   Thus, in the case, when any
given environment or function, however apparently " productive,"
is really fraught with disastrous influence to the organism, its modification must be attempted, or, failing that, its abandonment faced.

As a third step Geddes brings us to a view of economics based on
psychological principles.   After proclaiming the futility of
trying to base 'the psychology of economics upon the aspects of
value', he tackles the school of 'wants and desires'.

Its concepts cannot, he asserts, completely express the psychology
of action, 'since there is much ground for suspecting that complex
associations never formulated in consciousness play an important
part;   perhaps, too, that even lower states of cerebral activity
have their share in determining action'.   Having thus, though
unwittingly, described the basis of twentieth century advertising
and consumer-conditioning techniques, he points out psychological
principles parallel to biological ones. (36)   In the very simplest
forms of life there are two main forms of vital action: the nutritive and the reproductive.   The satisfaction of nutritive
wants is fundamentally egoistic but the reproductive desire contains the earliest germ of altruism.
    If this be admitted, as it must be, the exclusion of the
    altruistic element as a determinant of economic action is at
    once seen to be a mere artifice, alike impossible and absurd,
    if our psychology is to have any relation to living beings;
    while the deductively constructed fabric of orthodox economics

collapses without criticism, since one half of its foundation
('self-interest') alone was laid.

Starting, then, from this primal manifestation of egoistic
and altruistic desires, we may briefly follow the development
of these with the ever-increasing structural and social complexity of the organisms.... As the society reaches completer
polymorphism, altruism increases; progress towards the physical and biological ideal of productive synergy involves parallel progress to an ideal of sympathy or maximum altruism.

Even on the most sternly scientific grounds, Geddes affirms that
the basis of economics is not the 'iron law of competition'. On
the contrary, what may be deduced as the

highest generalisation of the phenomena ... is the exact converse of this - the golden rule of sympathy and synergy. And
it is a remarkable result that, without introducing into the
argument any so-called moral or sentimental considerations but
arguing soberly from the two fundamental functions and wants
of living beings - from nutrition and reproduction alone - the
noblest ideals of politics and morals arise before us. (37)

The action indicated on this third level follows logically upon
the principles just considered. If we accept the facts of biology and their subjective counterparts in psychology, then, says
Geddes, the psychological economist must approve of only those
wants and desires which are conducive to the maintenance and the
evolution of humanity. All others, just as was the case with
bad environment or unhealthful occupation, should be discouraged
or eliminated. Geddes concludes his 'Analysis' thus:

The problem of practical economics now demands that we produce
not that mere maximum of food and eaters which is the first
aspect of the physical ideal; not even that perfection of
quality and quantity of physical life which is the first
aspect of the biological; but the maximum evolution of mental
and moral nature which underlies the two former.

The problem, in fact, inverts itself, becoming not merely
how to fill bellies but how to place brains in the conditions
most favourable to their development and activity, and so the
problem of practical psychological economics passes into that
of education.

ENCYCLOPEDIAS, FRIENDSHIPS, SOCIAL CONSCIENCE

The brief exchange of letters with Darwin reveals that Geddes had
already begun writing encyclopedia articles by the end of 1880,
only a few months after Mexico. 'Insectivorous Plants' appeared
in the 1881 'Britannica', while vol. I of 'Chambers's' the same
year contained some minor articles (beginning with 'A': Agave,
Aloe, etc.). These were the first of many articles between then
and 1886. Major contributions from this early period include
Biology, Cell, Cell Theory and Darwinian Theory in 'Chambers's'
and Morphology, Parasitism, Protoplasm, Reproduction, and Sex in
'Britannica'. In 'Chambers's' the 1923 edition was the last to
carry either minor or major articles by Geddes.

The content of these many articles is now doubtless only of historical interest as far as biological facts are concerned.   On the
other hand, they contain much of interest to the biographer and to
students of Geddesian 'idea-history'.   'Darwinian Theory' for
'Chambers's' in 1883 is a good example of the interesting and
logical presentation of facts in a clear prose style, of which,
unfortunately, the naturalist will lose more and more as he gets
involved in sociology.   He warns that
> we must carefully guard aginst the confusion, still widely
> popular, of 'Evolution' with 'Darwinism'.   Evolution must
> clearly be retained to denote the entire drama of cosmic change;
> Darwinism, therefore, must as clearly be restricted to one par-
> ticular interpretation of the mechanism and plot of this cosmic
> drama, of many which have been thrown out by reflective spec-
> tators.

Geddes presents what still must be a valid account of the history
of this theory and an excellent summary of the arguments and the
vast amount of evidence presented in the 'Origin of Species'.
Equally balanced is his synopsis of how Darwin's views on evolution were received by followers and opponents.   He quotes Thomas
Huxley's assurance that not a single fact had been found that was
'irreconcilable with Darwinian theory', but has to point out that
this 'universal acceptance is not without its universally distributed exceptions'.   And among the 'complementary hypotheses' propounded he refers to his own article on 'Evolution'.

In fairness he also includes Darwin's assertion that 'the theory
of evolution by natural selection is no more inimical to religion
than is that of gravitation', and quotes in full his Envoy, which
ends:
> There is a grandeur in this view of life, with its several
> powers, having been originally breathed by the Creator into
> a few forms, or into one;   and that ... from so simple a
> beginning endless forms most beautiful and most wonderful
> have been, and are being, evolved.

'Upon every developing mind ... there presses at times the question
of the origin of things'.   Thus begins Geddes's 'Evolution' - a
lengthy but concise summing up of the various kinds of attempted
answers from theology and philosophy and modern science. (38)   He
traces the rise of dynamic and kinetic concepts in astronomy,
chemistry, geology and, above all, biology.   He gives a full
account of all the thinkers in many countries who, before and
after 'Goethe's epic of evolution', contributed to the break-
through of Darwin, and of those others who since have wished to
modify him (Spencer, Lancaster, Alfred Wallace and the Neo-
Lamarckians).

Then, after a synopsis of Darwinism as in the previous article,
Geddes turns to the moral implications of this theory.   Against
Huxley's well-known statement that 'From the point of view of
the naturalist the world is on about the same level as a gladiator's
show', he marshalls the evidence of material sacrifice for off-

spring in botany, zoology and in evolving 'sociality'.   Thereby, he argues, 'We escape from the conception that progress depends primarily upon the internecine struggle for existence' and come to the proposition that 'the greater steps of advance in the organic world compel us to interpret the general scheme of evolution as primarily a materialised ethical process underlying all appearance of a "gladiator's show"'.   Expressing that moral optimism which had such a great influence upon his early students and colleagues, Geddes boldly concludes:

> it is possible to interpret the ideals of ethical progress - through love and sociality, co-operation and sacrifice, not as mere utopias contradicted by experience, but as the highest expressions of the central evolutionary process of the natural world.

Many of the pupil friends Geddes made during these years of teaching in Edinburgh were to become famous men, and none more so than a Scottish clergyman's son named John Arthur Thomson who came to Edinburgh to study theology but who somehow turned up in the classes of practical botany and zoology in 1881.   This was the beginning of a lifetime of friendly contact and scientific collaboration between the two.   Of their lengthy correspondence between 1883 and 1931 the National Library has approximately 300 letters, which are fascinating sources of information on their thoughts and lives.   The early ones tell the virtually unknown story* of Thomson's struggle to decide between theology and biology besides revealing much about Geddes as a dynamic proponent of 'materialised ethical process' and as a helpful friend.

> It is impossible for me to tell all that you have done as my teacher since those first sessions.   To say that you continuously guided my theoretical and practical studies, that you taught me to use the tools of the scientific worker, that you gave me introductions to foreign professors and laboratories, that you supplied me with problems at which to work, would only be to mention a few external expressions of your generous educational enthusiasm.... (39)

One of these foreign professors was Ernst Haeckel, and by the end of 1882 Thomson was studying with him at the University of Jena. Letters in 1883 relate his difficulties in making a German translation of Geddes's 'Britannica' article on Morphology.   First of all, 'Haeckel cannot find the Morph MSS!', and after it turned up or was replaced several months later Thomson makes this blunt comment on its style: (40)

* Thomson's own son Landsborough did not know this until shown the letters in 1972 by this writer.

I am utterly – well I must be polite – rendered desperate by the sentences of your article 'Morph'. They are fearfully condensed & terse. I don't know when I shall get it done. Pray, don't send any more for a while. I have taken the opportunity of rereading your Cell Th. article, (which is better in style, I think).

At the same time Thomson was greatly troubled over his choice of career, for he writes early in 1883 to his Scottish master:
about the Challenger secretaryship I am very much obliged to you.   You really bother too much about me.   If everyone were as unselfish the aspect & relations of life would be somewhat different.

But I do not wish to apply.   I would gladly do so, if I intended to make a profession of Science, but I don't ... I am, as I said in my last letter, going back to the New College in November this year.

By March, however, he has decided to postpone theological studies for one year, during which he wishes 'to learn some Science'. 'I cannot rehearse all the reasons which have led me to decide to continue my theological course after a year.   I can only apolo-gise for my indecision and express my gratitude to you for your kindness.   Of course if you can *still* offer me any work to do I shall be delighted.'

Thomson's struggle with 'Morphology' cropped up again in a December letter.
Your article still discourages me, & for this reason.   I trans-late a piece ... I take it to a German student friend, and he tells me - *it is not sense*.   Then he takes it, twists it about and after a smelting and alloying process of considerable trouble - he says it will do....   Haeckel promises help too, but that must come afterwards.

Later in the same letter he again turns to personal matters.   For Geddes he is 'sorry you are not yet in your best health and vigour.   I wish I were at home to help you'.   Then he speaks of troubles of his own:
I am so unhappy when I resolve to give up the idea of being a minister that I cannot bear it.   I am not much fitted for being a pastor - after Ruskin.   I hope to be allowed to read your essay on Ruskin.   I cannot criticise him.   I do not know his works at all well enough yet.   But admire & respect him I can and do.

In Jena Thomson has just spent his second Christmas, and in a letter
just before New Year's Day of 1884 he returns to a familiar theme:
> I intended to do much of your article during the holidays now,
> but the fates are against it and me.   I cannot get the remaining
> sheets from Haeckel; he cannot find it anywhere! and I must
> therefore write to see if you cannot let me have them.

At the end of the letter is a financial accounting between author
and translator which at first reading seems slightly confused.
> ... you promised me £5 as part payment of some work I did not
> do ... I lent you £3/10 in Berlin & you sent me £5.   The
> deficit is obviously £3/10.   If you can lend me that amount I
> should be much obliged, or if £5 still more obliged.... *But*
> if it should be an inconvenience to you, pray do not do it ...
> especially since I think it is more probable that I shall go
> back to Theology the less you bother with me the better ... I
> hope at least you will send the article soon.

Thomson's struggles were ultimately successful, though anonymous,
and the translated work is recorded in Geddes's 'Letter' of 1888.
Another result of his early collaboration with Geddes was a summer
tutoring job in 1884 'for which opportunity I have you to thank'.
He must also have joined Geddes at some of the evening get-
togethers on social problems at the home of James Oliphant which
occupied not a little of Geddes's time between 1883 and 1886.
(Mairet writes of 'enthusiastic discussions between Geddes the
biological economist and Oliphant the philosopher, often protrac-
ted far into the night'. (41)   In any case, there were such
meetings the previous year and there were also at least two
attentive female listeners if not participants: Mrs Oliphant,
née Edith Morton, and her older sister, Anna, who was on a visit
from Liverpool.   From the brief note that follows, one may
gather that Patrick was not unaware of Anna's presence.

50 Palmerston Place,
Edinburgh
March 1883

Dear Mr. Geddes,
I am VERY sorry to find that we shall not be able to go and
see you tomorrow afternoon.
     I wanted to thank you very much for all the pleasure you
have given me during my visit, but I must content myself, I
suppose, with writing my goodbye and thanks.

Believe me, Sincerely yours,

Anna Morton (42)

As prophesied, the scholars' and workmen's pub which Patrick opened
in Edinburgh had many kinds of brew on tap, including that of
social responsibility.   Not only did he mix potent portions of
biology and ethics into his principles of economy but he proclaimed Ruskin one of his heroes and, furthermore, took an active
part in social work.   In the reminiscence explaining how the
fascination of Edinburgh, 'our City Beautiful', had always brought
him back to it from his wanderings, he again refers to his early
education as having presented nature and humanistic studies as a
unity.

My roamings from childhood round Perth, among interesting city
well framed in natural beauty, had prepared me for this further
union here - so that my studies of life natural and social
became more and more clearly unified.   The long skyline of
Edinburgh towering over the framework of the Botanic Garden,
and framed within its trees, was thus a joy for every working
day;   while to find the like conditions for study windows I
searched through Edinburgh old and new and happily found those
in what I still think the best outlook of our great boulevard
of Princes Street: in Barry's big 'Veneration Palace'....
For here the Rock looms high over the gardens, the Castle
buildings group together to their best and the Old Town ridge
is piled up high, and runs clear against crags and the seat
[Arthur's Seat]. (43)

Even more than other European cities of the late-nineteenth century, Edinburgh was a mingling of monumental architecture and
sordid slums.   Dirty, overcrowded tenements in the old quarters,
and wide boulevards and fine villas in some of the newer sections,
with a vast middle ground of areas of flats in row upon row of
redundant mediocrity.   Edinburgh also surpassed at least some of
the other cities in the aloofness which the various classes had
for generations maintained one against the other, and by the
neglect with which its responsible authorities treated the tenement dwellers.   Geddes was well aware of the reality behind the
magnificent façades of public buildings and back of the Princes
Street Gardens.   He and James Oliphant, aided by other public-
spirited intellectuals and professional men, began agitating for
action, and proposed an organisation to co-ordinate the spirit of
social consciousness which, after long stirring in London under
the leadership of Arnold Toynbee and Octavia Hill, was beginning
to be felt in Scotland.

For an eloquent account of this new interest of Geddes's we turn
again to Mairet.   After describing how the historic city - the
Royal Mile from Holyrood Palace up High Street to the Castle - had
'declined into a collection of famous monuments surviving in an
insanitary slumland of high tenements, filled floor upon floor
with impoverished humanity', and asserting that 'their rent-pay-
ments helped to maintain the comfortable citizenry on the other
side of Princes Street', he writes:
    The new demonstrator of zoology was hardly installed in office
    before he began exploring this maze of squalor and misery with
    the curiosity of a social scientist, rapidly kindling into the
    humanitarian zeal of the reformer.   The more he saw, the more
    scandalous he found the contrast between the two halves of the
    city, and the more he had to say about it to anyone within
    hearing.   This old town, he exclaimed, was a whole serpent-
    brood of evils, a gorgon's head held up in the sight of the
    new townsmen, turning their hearts to stone....   There was no
    answer to his argument that the state of the old town was an
    inexcusable scandal....   The University took no interest in
    the problem whatever, except in the abundance of clinical cases
    it provided for the School of Medicine. (44)

The first result of Geddes's public and private agitation was the
founding of the Edinburgh Social Union in January 1885. Its aim
was rather cautiously stated as 'to bring together all those who
feel that the misery of the poor arises in a large measure from
the want of sympathy and fellowship between different classes, and
that all charitable effort which seeks to remedy this evil should
apply those methods which economic science suggests as tending most
permanently to the mental and moral development of the community.'(45)   Still far from revolutionary, the members of the
Union 'believe that the immediate question to face is how to make
the best of present conditions, how to raise the standard of comfort without waiting for the operation of legislative changes.'
They proposed to 'begin their crusade against intemperance and
other such evils by providing opportunities for higher tastes and
pleasures.'

Despite the vague and highly moral purposes, practical action was
taken.   Several properties were acquired and managed and rents
were collected weekly by 'ladies and gentlemen, who undertake this
task as a means of gaining influence among the tenants, and helping them with their counsel and sympathy'.   Any surplus of rent,
beyond 5 per cent interest on capital placed in the property and
'working expenses', was to be expended on the property or saved
for future improvements.

By its sixth year of existence the Union had bought fourteen
properties, organised groups 'For the Study and Practice of Industrial Arts' as well as 'Recreative Evening Classes'.   Among its
500 or so members could be counted 15 reverends, several professors, a score of architects, artists and decorators; about 250
'Misses' listed only as 'Miss Bell, Miss Black' and so on down
the alphabet; and finally three titled 'Ladies'.   Among the
better-known academic names are those of Professor James Mavor and
J. Arthur Thomson.

The Social Union is the first example of a pattern of behaviour
which was to recur periodically in Geddes's life of action.   He
would have the idea, the plan of a campaign, and would take an
important part in the early stages of implementation.   Then
having got things going, he stepped out or aside, leaving others
to carry on.   For him it was not an abandonment of a project he
believed in, but rather that he had had another new idea and
found another field of activity.   As he used to explain it, referring to one of the least reprehensible of his adolescent
pranks, he was 'the boy who rang doorbells and then ran away'.

Before launching himself into new deeds, however, Geddes did devote
much time to the Union.   He went to London as its delegate,
studying the housing reforms of Octavia Hill and even lecturing
at a conference on industrial remuneration on how to improve the
standards of living of the poor.

Yet all this intellectual and social work did not seem to agree
with his health.   On certain 'cryptic memoranda, made on scraps

of paper' he recorded his own rather gloomy thoughts about himself
and his work at this period.   He vowed to reform his habits of
living to 'maximize energetic cerebration' and upbraided himself
for having taken too little exercise and no holiday.   On top of
which, 'old Annie his housekeeper was not much of a cook and his
digestion suffered accordingly'. (46)

Even his protégé Arthur Thomson, who later became a member of this
Edinburgh group, gently rebuked him for the pace he was setting.
    I am afraid you are making a martyr of yourself for the sake of
    the Social Union.   You are too intense.   I could not live in
    bustle of organising such a thing.   I wonder how you can get
    on with so much to think about. (47)

ANNA MORTON ... 'JOHN RUSKIN, ECONOMIST'

Had it depended on outward circumstances alone, Patrick Geddes
could have led a happier and more healthful life at this time.
He had many friends in and near Edinburgh, but either his 'terrible Scottish repression' that he would confess to in late years,
or his self-centred program of 'maximized cerebration', or both,
kept him aloof from likely young women.   Information about the
female acquaintances of his first thirty years is very sparse.
To this writer's knowledge only two names have turned up from
student days in London, and none at all from France.   The former
are those of Annie Besant (well-known champion of women's rights
and, later, of Theosophy - seven years his senior), and the
daughter of Charles Bradlaugh, the then notorious atheist.
Patrick tutored them both in natural science after they had been
refused admittance to college in London.   But on settling in
Edinburgh he had the opportunity of meeting the women who attended
his public lectures as well as female relatives of his colleagues.
One of the latter was Anna Morton, a sister-in-law of James
Oliphant.   A long friendship developed between Patrick and Anna
starting with her visit to Edinburgh in 1883, but caution and shy-
ness dominated his feelings.

Anna was the daughter of Frazer Morton, an Ulster Scot and well-
to-do merchant who had settled in Liverpool.   Though he came from
a strict Presbyterian family, he had secretly learned to play the
violin and so not only permitted, but encouraged music in his own
home.   Anna was thus sent to Dresden to study singing and piano
for a year when she was eighteen.   She also came in contact with
the reform work of Octavia Hill in London and even planned at one
time to follow in her footsteps.   When her younger sister Edith
married James Oliphant, Anna went to visit them in Edinburgh.
How inspired she was by the 'social conscience' discussions she
heard at their house, and how intrigued by Patrick is suggested
by the facts that she founded her own girls' club in Liverpool
after that first visit, and that she returned frequently to Edinburgh in the ensuing three years (despite her mother's occasional
protests).

Meanwhile the seemingly confirmed bachelor suffered from indigestion
and self-deprecation, eating housekeeper Annie's poor meals and continuing his over-strenuous and intensely intellectual life.   He
published another challenging pamphlet - this time on 'John Ruskin,
Economist' (48) - and gave extra-mural lectures on subjects like
'The Production and Use of Wealth in Relation to Social Progress'.
These provocations, compounded by his getting the Social Union to
meddle with long-established slum patterns, aroused much enthusiasm
among his students and young colleagues but great annoyance in
other quarters.   Both city and university fathers developed cases
of angry self-justification and guilty conscience.   For much as
they resented this meddling, they saw that public opinion was slowly
awakening in favour of the meddlers.   So began the long, pitched
battle between the attacking radical botanist and the Edinburgh
establishment.   That his early successes aroused in the latter
a growing desire, conscious or unconscious, for sabotage and even
revenge, comes as no surprise.

Before examining Geddes's pages on Ruskin, the art critic who
challenged the values and deeds of nineteenth-century industrialism, we may quote from their correspondence of 1884-5, presumably
about articles which Geddes wanted to discuss with him.   The
latter, writing from his home in Coniston in August after one of
Huxley's lectures, stated in no uncertain terms that 'I am every
day more sick of the names and more indignant at the follies, of
Darwin and Huxley'.   In October, in another note to 'P. Geddes,
Esquire, 81 A Princes Street, Edinburgh', he wrote: 'Sorry to
have missed you at Coniston, & let me hope for some other opportunity.'   The following spring Geddes sent him a paper, perhaps
the 'Britannica' article on 'Darwinian Theory'.   Whatever it was,
it elicited this temperamental reply on 20 March 1885.
> Your instalment unluckily did not come till I had lost your
> letter with references - and I was so furious at what you
> said of Darwin - who, whether he himself be right or not, is
> simply the nucleus of all the fools in Europe - that I threw
> the whole thing with a curse into the wastebasket.
> Will you please send me another copy and I'll look at the
> points referred to in your note of 6th March now found.
>   Ever gratefully yrs,
>   JR

Being 'a quiet student of science and economics, one of those
scholars of Huxley and Darwin, of Spencer and Comte, of whom Mr.
Ruskin has so often spoken other than smooth things', Geddes feels
sure that his 'John Ruskin, Economist' will explain the misunder-
stood economic message of this 'veteran art teacher, critic and
man of letters'.   Even common-sense people, Geddes admits, see
in this 'would-be delivering knight' only the latest version of
'Don Quixote', 'and so either join merrily in the hooting, or pass
by in sorrow, as their own moral temper happens to incline'.

Indeed, what can be learned 'from a man who speaks contemptuously
of all the highest practical achievements of the nineteenth
century'?   For Ruskin its science is 'either of mere mechanism or

evolutionary nonsense ... its modern commerce is little better than complex thieving ... our vast and prosperous industrial cities are so many working models of hell.'   Before answering this question, Geddes digresses at length into the classification of the sciences as needful for his purposes, and into the attempted excommunication of its economic section by the British Association in 1876, with repercussions two years later.   In 1878 the section's new president, Professor J.K. Ingram, delivered 'a destructive criticism of the past and present of British economics - a criticism exceeding anything of that kind ever attempted by Mr. Ruskin.'   And Geddes eloquently carries on from this point, reviewing with obvious relish 'what the defects of our orthodox economists, as now exposed and admitted, really are....' (49)

Their 'extensive literature' presents formidable barriers of both style and content.   What endurance is necessary, he exclaims, as the critical natural scientist goes 'wearily wading through shallow seas of verbiage, or toiling patiently through deserts of details, useless and numberless as the sand; now silently evading some dismal swamp of error, often crushing a whole stony volume for a few grains of genuine gold.'

In all concepts from Adam Smith's 'enlightened self-interest' to Stanley Jevons's 'utility' and John Stuart Mill's 'wealth', he finds only 'the whole spirit of mediaeval metaphysics' and figments of 'antique scholasticism'.   As for 'the legal and literary economists, like those of the school of Ricardo', they imagine 'that by adroitly spinning and weaving definitions and syllogisms in their logic mills, they manufacture a body of "natural laws"....' Next, Geddes appraises Freedom of Contract as a myth unrelated 'to any known modern sociology' but useful in reminding economists of their indebtedness to the 'Contrat Social' and to 'its illustrious author, that ingenious metaphysician ... M. Jean Jacques Rousseau'.   In short, such scientific conceptions as they may have are 'curiously archaic and erroneous ones', while 'their intellectual apparatus consists largely of broken down heirlooms, which the attempt to work is what anthropologists call a "survival in culture"'.

Just as in 'An Analysis of the Principles of Economics', Geddes refers to the joint attack on the economists' citadel which Comte started a half century before and which Spencer, Huxley, Haeckel and cohorts have continued.   But now he imagines the final battle and wonders, when faced with 'these hungry and all-devouring hordes of scientific invaders ... whom neither the flapping of theologians' robes nor the wagging of lawyers' wigs can frighten from beginning to meddle with even their special business', what will become of the defenceless 'metaphysicians who have so long had economics in their keeping'?

Answering his own question, the botanist predicts the 'providential interference' of an as yet unknown aspect of Natural Selection.   'This goddess, more powerful and more beneficent than Supply-and-Demand', first tells them they are doomed to extinction.

Yet take courage, I will prolong your days many years: here is
the secret.

Acquire as fast as you can a deceptive external resemblance
to the invaders.   Do not name your sacred dogmas as of old but
conceal the old matter under their newer manner;   its aridity
and difficulty will at once keep off the public and impress
them with profound reverence, while its superficial resemblance
to science will long satisfy even the scientists, who have
plenty to do yet awhile among their telescopes and balances,
their fossils and their flowers.

This do and live!   You and your children shall go in and
out under their very noses in safety;   nay, you shall have
'scientific' societies of your own, even a whole department of
the British Association all to yourselves.   And though here
and there some impassioned socialist or quick-eyed art critic
may detect your true nature, nobody will believe them;   it
will be ... I know not how long before you are finally extir-
pated.

Fear not, therefore, this all-devouring march of science.
Become memetic organisms in its ranks and all shall long be
well. (50)

After matching Ruskin in sharp irony, Geddes makes two good points.
He defines 'freedom of contract' as letting the worker 'be free to
contract between work there in "Bastilles for Labour built by
Capital" and starvation anywhere else'.   He further asserts that
'criticism of the aesthetic consumption' is the 'most needful of
all conceivable contributions to production' and that

Art-criticism, in short, is a special province of the practical economics of production and consumption - belongs to it as
food-analysis does.

Geddes reiterates his own sweeping ecological warning that wherever
and whenever a function or an environment is found to have a bad
influence on the organism, 'its modification must be attempted,
and, failing that, its abandonment faced'.   Further, he prophecies that if man is

to remain healthy and become civilised ... [he] must take
especial heed of his environment;   not only at his peril
keeping the natural factors of air, water and light at their
purest, but caring only for 'production of wealth' at all, in
so far as it shapes the artificial factors, the material surroundings of domestic and civic life, into forms more completely serviceable for the Ascent of Man. (51)

Returning to Ruskin's disputed merits, Geddes claims that the
former's evaluation of which kinds of work are best accomplished
by hand or by machine, and of

the effect of machinery in gathering and multiplying population
and its effects upon the minds and bodies of such population,
equals or exceeds at once in clear biological insight and in
social wisdom anything else in the entire literature of practical economics....   [Moreover, Ruskin's] clear enunciation
of the essential unity of economics and morals in opposition to

the discord assumed as a deductive artifice, will remain
especially and permanently classic.

Later, having appraised Ruskin as a vital teacher, he is inspired
to give his own scathing definition of
> the miserable mixture of pseudo-literary and pseudo-commercial
> cram ... miscalled 'education': that jumbled compromise into
> which academic fossil and commercial Philistine everywhere
> settle down for the supposed maintenance of their supposed
> interests, and the actual stupefaction of their children's
> lives.

With eloquent optimism Geddes sums up the reforms in progress to
improve the health of worker, to ennoble function, to purify the
environment.   There have been Crusades, the French Revolution,
and 'once again throughout Europe a new enthusiasm is arising,
deeper and wider than of old'.
> The sorely needed knowledge, both of the natural and the
> social order, is approaching maturity; the long-delayed
> renaissance of art has begun, and the prolonged discord of
> these is changing into harmony: so, with these for guidance,
> men shall no longer grind on in slavery to a false image of
> their lowest selves, miscalled Self-interest, but at length,
> as freemen, live in the Sympathy and labour in the Synergy of
> the Race.
>   And for this, the last Crusade, herald, knight, and preacher
> are not wanting; and yet in our land and day there has been
> no clearer herald, nobler preacher, nor truer knight than
> John Ruskin, Economist.

Still another year passed in the bachelor routine of teaching and
lecturing, discussions and dyspepsia, intellectual friendship
with Anna Morton, and correspondence with friends.   Extra-mural
lectures took him occasionally to boyhood haunts in Perth, to
Dundee where Frank Young was teaching in the high school, and to
Balruddery where another boyhood friend, J. Martin White, would
soon take over both his father's fortune and his position in
public life.   Martin was planning a trip to Greece for early
1886 and invited Patrick to accompany him as companion-tutor.
Mairet writes that:
> He yielded to this highly attractive proposition but betrayed
> a marked confusion of motives.   Anna was in Edinburgh when
> the date drew near, and the prospect of parting brought him
> to sudden self-realization.   At his urgent invitation she
> came to the Botanic Gardens the following morning, on a Sunday
> when the place was closed to the public but not to him. (52)

In this setting of still winter-bare trees which made his favourite
view of the Old Town's skyline even more clear, Patrick overcame
the years of hesitation and proposed marriage.   Anna's joyful
acceptance was followed by a unique engagement scene.   Patrick
produced a rough opal matrix, the size of a large orange, which
he had found in Mexico and broke it neatly in two with a geologist's hammer.   He then gave Anna one of the halves as his pledge
of betrothal, keeping the other himself.

Clues to dates are found in the engagement letters which Anna
wrote from her home while Patrick, as she would later teasingly
remind him, toured Grecian isles and cities on his solitary
'wedding trip'.   One of them mentions Sunday 7 February as the
day on which 'we came here together': that is, to Egremont,
Liverpool, where her parents lived.   Within the next day or two
they went to Perth where Anna stayed with his parents while
Patrick returned briefly to Edinburgh.   Her very first letter to
'My own dear love', dated Thursday 11 February 1886, discloses
that they had parted that same day, she taking the boat to Liverpool (presumably from Glasgow) and he leaving by train for London
the next day.   Anna confesses how much she had been thinking
about him, in spite of herself, ever since they first met.

  I suppose I was always so afraid of letting you see too much
  of what I felt when I thought you were only kind to me as you
  were kind to so many others; and I went sometimes to the
  opposite extreme & made you think I did not care at all; and
  then you did not make as distinct signs as you thought even
  you did, - but you are never to reproach yourself, darling,
  darling, for there is compensation, ay, and far more than compensation for it all.   Again and again I think it is too
  good to be true....

  Don't be disappointed if some of my letters are colder.
  I won't really feel colder, but perhaps I shall not be able
  to say things as I can tonight.   I'm not even going to read
  this over, I want to think I have said it to you already.
  Sometimes in these next two months I know I shall feel that I
  cannot bear any longer to have you away.   Even in the few
  days I was at Perth, I felt sometimes as if I MUST run away
  and get to you, as if I could not stay there a minute longer
  without you.   But then I shall try to think of all the things
  I have to do & of what you want me to think about!

What more fitting conclusion to this chapter than to let Patrick's
finally-found companion continue her first real message to him?

  I wonder if you DID feel the parting today more than I did!
  I don't think so - but it doesn't matter.   When I got on the
  boat & was walking up & down on the upper deck to be away from
  the people, I could not help thinking I had left something
  behind - forgotten it.   I felt so strangely *incomplete* (it
  wasn't my glove).   And I was inclined to go up town again to
  look for it, but bethought myself in time that it was no use,
  & that I would have to wait awhile....

Anna closed her first day of waiting with these words quoted for
Patrick: '"Good night, sweet friend; thy love ne'er alter till
thy sweet life end".   (Do you know what that is?   I'll read it
to you some day perhaps).'

Chapter 4

MARRIAGE, AND THE CIVIC CRUSADE, 1886-8

SOLITARY 'WEDDING TRIP' TO GREECE

The eight of Anna's engagement letters which have been preserved
are a unique source of both factual and psychological information
on her life and that of Patrick.   Above all they are love letters,
and one feels it is an intrusion to read the intimate thoughts
which were only meant for her beloved.   Still, there are so many
authentic revelations of their ideas as well as feelings that one
must make discreet use of this material.   For instance, on the
nature of their religious belief in contrast to that of her
parents.

On the first Sunday evening after Patrick's departure she tells
of having gone to church 'where I had some pleasant thoughts
during the sermon.   I was never so happy in our church before.'
The clergyman 'said some good things in his sermon (when I
happened to be listening!) but he condemned the "religion of
humanity" more than once, and when we came home Mother said she
thought the sermon must have been meant for me, for wasn't that
the religion we professed?   I said Dr Muir didn't know what he
was talking about, for he hadn't tried the religion of humanity,
whereas I had tried both that & Christianity....' (1)

> I am more & more pleased to find how broad Mother is on ques-
> tions of religious belief, and that she sees when I put it to
> her how much we have in common on the subject.   She is never
> in the least troubled about the safety of our souls ... and
> she thinks our *religion* must be good since she is satisfied
> that *we* are good.   The only thing I regret is that she is not
> young enough to make our beliefs hers - of course Father's
> state of mind would prevent her trying to do that, for he is
> much more orthodox.

Materialist topics are very few, but here is part of Anna's report
of an afternoon walk that Sunday spent in discussing her future
husband's finances with her brother Frazer.

> Being a business man, he would have liked more exact figures
> about what we are to live upon before he would declare that he

understood it fully.... However, he did not see any need for
further discussion ... since we have quite settled to be married
in April; nor does he think it at all necessary to tell Mother
any more particulars of how your affairs stand than I did in my
letter. So it's all right, and you needn't mind saying anything more to anybody, & you needn't think anything more about
it until you come back either. *I* am not at all uneasy, and no
one else need be - nor *is* anyone else. Now, you said business
was always to be dismissed as soon as possible, & I have only
taken up one page with it!

After telling how little opportunity she has even to talk to her
brother on week-days, Anna exclaims: 'Wouldn't it be *dreadful* if
you were a business man? I should never see *half* enough of you.
Why, it's as good as living twice as long - better even - to have
you in your present position - at least I *hope* we shall find it
so.' She then relates how

Mother and I got into a warm discussion about the amount of
liberty that should be allowed to girls and how much attention
should be paid to the proprieties; and your *prim, conventional*
friend gave utterances to some exceedingly outrageous opinions
on the subject ... I instanced ... some of my escapades with
yourself in past times as examples of what would be termed most
improper conduct by Mother if other girls had been guilty of
them, and maintained that I would encourage other girls in the
same course if I thought they had sufficient self-respect.

No details were given, but in a later letter Anna writes how
lonely she is having tea all by herself, unlike 'in Princes Street
where you were across from me'. (2) Having tea in a bachelor's
flat in the 1880s was very likely an 'escapade', even though old
Annie the housekeeper was surely their chaperone.

The gifted musician then confides a deeply personal experience
to her eye-minded and tone-illiterate fiancé.

Do you know that my unmusical old 'lecturer' is going to be
my music teacher after all? I played a little last night, &
never had so much delight from my piano before! Don't be
jealous of my poor music. You wouldn't be, Pat dear, if you
could know how your love speaks in every note, murmuring or
chanting or singing in triumphant ecstasy. In ten minutes
I found out more new meanings in my favourite Chopin Scherzo
than I have done in many hours before - it's a whole love
story, I find: and if I only had the requisite execution I
could play it magnificently now.

She is very sorry that 'I cannot speak much to you in that
language (of music) yet, but there is scarcely room for *any*
regrets about you, except that you are away from me.... Sometimes I have a horrible fear that you will never come back, and
that it is too much happiness for me to expect - as if the gods
would need to be appeased in *some* way - you know the story of
Polycrates and the ring? - but that doesn't last very long.' (3)

Portrait of Patrick Geddes
on the occasion of his
engagement to Anna Morton in
early 1886

CO-OPERATION

VERSUS

SOCIALISM.

BY

PATRICK GEDDES.

REPRINTED FROM THE CO-OPERATIVE WHOLESALE SOCIETIES' "ANNUAL"
FOR 1888.

ed. cf p.15

MANCHESTER:
CO-OPERATIVE PRINTING SOCIETY LIMITED, 92, CORPORATION STREET.
MDCCCLXXXVIII.

Title page of one of
Geddes's many incursions
into non-botanical fields
and issues: 'Co-operation
vs Socialism'

How many letters Anna wrote in all is not known, but quite probably
twice as many as these eight extant: 11, 14, 28 February, 14, 28,
29 March; and 3 and 6 April.   On 14 March, for example, she
received two from Patrick in Athens who complained that he had had
none there.   Anna hastened to say that she had sent four letters
to Athens but did not mention their dates.   In any case, four have
been preserved from the last ten days or so of their separation so
her average was at least two letters per week.   Yet what of
Patrick's replies to Anna as he roamed through Mediterranean
scenes?

Thus far there is no trace of these, either at the National Library
of Scotland or in the possession of his heirs.   Tantalising
clues, however, are found in Anna's responses to what he has
written.   His health is mentioned several times: 'I'm only sorry
you still have attacks of dyspepsia - that is not good news.   Are
you are as careful as you can be, mein Lieber, of yourself?   I
know it goes rather against the grain for you to take care.'
'... how naughty of you to have dyspepsia.   I believe you do too
much, & fast too long don't you?   And then you relieve your conscience by a gentle lecture to me?   *I'll* promise to take care if
you will.'   On her side she had to tell him of staying home from
church on account of neuralgia, and on another Sunday she confesses:
    'The cares of this world' (preparations, etc.) *have* tired me
    rather, and besides I often can't sleep as much as I'm accus-
    tomed to do ... but I think we shall be alright when you come
    back, shan't we?
        I wonder if you look as well as Mr. White said you did.
    I suppose you are a little disappointed about your dyspepsia
    not going altogether?   Well we'll have to take very good care
    of you, the 'goodwife' and I.   And if you're not punctual
    every day for meals!! - I'll go out I think!

The nearest approach to a mild quarrel appears in hers of Sunday
28 March:
    For the first time (in yr letter posted at Athens last Sun.)
    you have grumbled a *little* not only *to* me but *at* me - about a
    letter.   Well, I daresay you're quite right.   I don't remem-
    ber what was (or wasn't) in the letter you speak of, but I
    know some of them weren't satisfactory - and then you know it
    is a little hard upon *me* that you should get so few of my
    letters, for when you get one with not much in it it seems
    worse than it would if you had got them all.   And I wrote 4
    to Athens & two to Cple [Constantinople], and so far you seem
    to have got only one at each place.

By the next page she is her adoring self again and writes that
even though her letters have sometimes been 'more of a pain than
a pleasure' to him because of their being lost in the mails, 'yours
have been everything to me!'   '... I hope your fine weather has
continued....   The time will soon pass now - and this day three
weeks (i.e. 18 April) what a Sunday we shall have!   I think we
won't go to church!'   'You've guessed quite wrong about the cook-
ing!', Anna continues in the same letter,

I haven't been learning that at all.   I thought the 'good-
wife' could do everything, but we'll see about the macaroni
& some other things; it isn't very difficult.   I was looking
over those silly papers of mine y'day that I wrote for you 3
years ago in Edinbr & on one of them on the margin is written
a remark about the model housekeeper who devotes herself to
stimulating the gluttony of the men of her household, but as
this cookery is for a different end I suppose that severe old
lecturer doesn't disapprove of it!!   Do you know I'm quite
maliciously glad to be able to tell you that it is one of *your*
friends who has bought us the first electro plate for a wedding
present.

Anna's days are filled with a variety of activities.   Practising
her music, going to 'Prof. MacCunn's last lecture on Socialism'
with her brother, shopping in Liverpool, writing to prospective
wedding guests, including his parents and brothers, and of course
to Pat himself.   In one letter Anna 'was very angry because a
tiresome boy cousin came in and stayed the whole evening, and I
had to talk to him.'
   I don't feel at all good or nice to-night - except when I think
   of you - and I must go to bed now.   But first I want to tell
   you that it does me good to have you say such beautiful things
   as you have done in this last letter about our life together,
   and I answer 'yea and amen' to them with all my heart.   You
   said when you asked me to marry you that you thought I would
   be 'a help & not a hindrance', and when you talk to me like
   that I feel as if I could really be a help.

Another time, however, she tries to look at her enthralment more
objectively.
   Sometimes I think, how much better I would have worked and
   read & thought & done everything, if I had known I was doing it
   for you.   And then again I think, perhaps it was as well you
   did not make me belong to you sooner, or else I should have had
   no individuality of my own at all, but would have been an
   absurd shadow of you; for I feel sometimes as if I could not
   help thinking just what you choose to think, and then I resolve to have a will of my own!! but I don't know really whether
   I have or not!   And a line of Browning's runs through my mind
   constantly: 'There is no good of life, but love - but love.'
      Often when I used to read poetry & lose myself in the *ideal*
   world it used to be so hard to have to come back to the real
   one, but now the ideal & the real are one; there is no break.

Only two short letters were written in April: to Rome and Cannes,
the 3rd and 6th.   She tells him that his sister Jessie will arrive
on the 12th and will be a bridesmaid.   The groomsman seems to be a
bit uncertain: Martin White or another of Pat's friends*, but one

---

*   On 28 March Anna had received a letter with '1½ sheets taken up
with names of friends, & only ¼ for me....   We shall talk over the
list when you come.'

who can't yet give a definite answer.   She reminds him in both
letters to send her the size of his wedding ring
>they don't keep a stock of such things for husbands, only for
>wives ... if you haven't an old ring cut a hole in a piece of
>card to fit your finger neatly....   I want you to have yours
>on the 17th too.

In one letter Anna tells Patrick how sure she is that he is the
right companion for her, asserting
>for me it is always always perfect bliss to lean upon you.
>It is easy, very easy to do without the hope of immortality
>when one has this full perfect life.   What does one want with
>another cold calm existence after the raptures of this?   In
>my former life - before you came into it - I used to think
>sometimes when I looked forward to always living alone that I
>would be glad of another chance for a fuller & better life.

Commenting on how many of her friends have remarked how happy she
has looked since her engagement, and on a relative who told her
she had changed for the better, she says
>It would be strange if I had not changed, I think!   'Except
>a man be born again, he cannot enter into the kingdom of God.'
>This is being 'born again' - of *love* & *joy*, instead of 'water
>& the spirit'.   Whatever that may mean, I don't quite under-
>stand.
>   Some of your friends and mine would be rather shocked at
>our interpretations of bible quotations.   Good night, my
>darling.   Anna.

FIRST BRIDGES IN OLD EDINBURGH

A few days after Patrick's safe return to England the nuptials
took place at Egremont on Saturday, 17 April 1886, as was
announced in the many formal invitations.

Anna's joy can only be imagined, for the informative love letters
naturally ceased, and what Patrick may have reported to his parents
who apparently could not be present, is likewise not available.
All that has been recorded from family tradition is simply: 'his
wedding with Anna was celebrated in a blaze of spring flowers at
the Mortons' house.' (4)   What the good clergyman thought about
their not using his church is also only to be guessed at.

Mute evidence of the ceremony, the wedding rings themselves still
exist (now worn by a grand-daughter of Geddes and her husband):
plain gold bands inscribed inside 'A.M.' and 'P.G.', respectively,
followed by '17th April 1886'.   There is also an August letter
from J. Arthur Thomson in which he wishes the married couple a
happy vacation and gives 'much personal news' to Geddes.
>I am really stronger intellectually with each year lately, and
>if you have patience may still be of use to you....   I meant
>to speak to you and to Mrs Geddes about a recent experience of
>mine, but conditions were not just favourable, so I shall do so

by letter.   More than a brother are you to me, and I am proud
to think of Mrs Geddes as a sister.   Hence I tell you of my
experience.

Long, long ago I was regenerated at the hands of faith, and
all things became really new, nor have I lost all my early enthusiasm brought me.   I was really born again in faith.

A time came however, with the dawning of clearer light when
... by your help, I was slowly led, not without pain, to a
wider synthesis and a surer knowledge.   I was born again of
hope ... all things became a second time new in the light of a
scientific synthesis.   For this I thank you.

A third time, however, I have been born again.   I have
listened to a third regenerating voice.   All things are again
new, though my new enthusiasm can coexist with the old.   I
have been born again of love....

I was betrothed on the first of this month....   I feel sure
both Mrs. Geddes & you will rejoice with me.

> Glückliche Ferien
> Yours Ever very truly
> J. Arthur Thomson (5)

It is thanks to reminiscences that we have any information at all
about the early years of marriage.   Thomson has recalled his
earliest impression of Anna nearly fifty years afterwards: 'My
first picture is of a midsummer morning when a lot of us climbed
the Pentlands.   I think it was soon after her marriage, and she
looked like a young goddess - very nimble & joyous & radiant.' (6)

In his seventies when sentences had become more cumbersome than
Carlyle's, Geddes himself recalls bachelor days in his Princes
Street lodgings facing the Garden.

There too came the Love of my life, and with her that fresh
impulse to action, which rouses student to man and woman to
comrade, as next to mother.   Social conscience was then stirring throughout the cities, and we had both felt it strongly -
and so strengthened each other: so after a single winter of
bonnie home, so small within, so spacious without, we crossed
to the high James Court tenement of the Old Town opposite, with
opposite northern view accordingly, and thus enabling us to
endure, by facing and tackling of dirt and overcrowding and
disorder of even more infernal slumdom than now exists in
Edinburgh; and to begin such changes as might be, thus became
problems as scientific, as technical, as had been those of
living nature and its science for myself, or of music for my
companion. (7)

Just as Patrick had condensed his student life into a few lines of
verse so does he here compress into one long sentence the years of
his and Anna's joint campaign which was to shape their married
life and ultimately lead to his main career in town planning:

Beginning within our limited range, with flower-boxes for dull
windows and colour-washing for yet duller walls (than which
there is no better, no simpler and brighter beginnings for city
improvements) we soon got to fuller cleanings and repairings,

next even to renewals, and at length to building as through Lawnmarket, Castle Hill to Ramsay Garden, of course with thanks to
growing cooperation alike from students and citizens, increasingly becoming good neighbours.

Repercussions of the courageous action of this unconventional
couple spread both near and wide.   Members of the young Edinburgh
Social Union were doubtless their first visitors, since the
Geddes's settling in James Court was a logical extension and
application of the principles of that group.   Yet, the earliest
recorded appreciation of this deed comes from a Russian prince and
exiled anarchist, Peter Kropotkin.   Writing from London to
another distinguished exile, the French geographer Elisée Reclus,
he penned these words in April 1886 (the date apparently indicating
that the newlyweds had planned to move from Princes Street even
sooner than they did):
> a young teacher in Edinburgh who, four years ago, was making
> plans of statistical sociology beyond all bounds, has now just
> got married, leaving his house and taking a very poor flat
> among the workers.   Everywhere, in one form or another, one
> finds similar things.   It is a complete reawakening.   What
> direction will it take?

Before applying Kropotkin's question to Geddes's own work, we may
record that it was in this slum dwelling that Anna's and Patrick's
first-born arrived in October 1887: daughter Norah.   When in
turn reminiscing in her seventies, she would verify that the Old
Town, unlike the old centres of cities in the Low Countries, was
in a shameful state of disrepair and unwholesomeness.   In fact,
the chief use of Old Edinburgh was 'to provide clinical material
for the School of Medicine.   There the hardships and deprivations
of poverty were aggravated by the squalor and dirt following on
the indifference of land-lords and town councillors.'   Norah
recollects:
> Their neighbours were one-roomed families with whom they
> shared a common stair, and they experienced through window and
> ceiling many uncongenial sounds and sights....   Not all our
> neighbours were quarrelsome, drunk and disorderly by any means;
> but were on the contrary douce, hard working and well conduc-
> ted.   In any case, my infant memory has retained no pictures
> of unseemly behaviour. (8)

Gedd s threw himself into slum cleaning with the same zeal he
showed in reorganising a botanical laboratory or redefining the
principles of economics.   He took part in manual jobs himself,
sometimes in rather curious attire.   'Clad in night shirt as
overall', says Norah!   From other bits of family legend we have
the following picture of the newlyweds in Edinburgh.
> Patrick quickly endeared himself to working people young or
> old by his warmth and humour, his enthusiasm and ready co-
> operation;   and by talking with them, as he always did, in
> good Scots.   Anna was not, in the same way, one of them, but
> her sure, dignified manner commended her to the women 'as one
> lady to another'.   One by one, some denizens of the courts

began to give their own time to the jobs that Geddes persuaded
them to tackle with him, clearing, whitewashing, or gardening;
nor could they work beside him, listening to his flow of ideas
about the job in hand and the further possibilities, without
catching something of his sanguine spirit.   For the first time
they began to feel that something could be done to change their
surroundings.   'What a pity more people don't back us up,' he
said to one of them.   'Man,' was the reply, 'if they did we'd
go right down the old street all the way to Holyrood!' (9)

Courageous and optimistic as the Geddes family's example was, and
enthusiastic as many neighbours were, years had to pass before
their civic crusade really began to overcome municipal inertia
and 'landlords' lethargy'.   Moreover, a full century and more
may have elapsed before the Royal Mile between Holyrood and the
Castle Rock has really been improved as those pioneers of the
1880s intended.

One may well wonder, confronted with Patrick's terse memoir and
family traditions about the daily struggle against slum conditions, how the young couple got on with each other and what
happened to Anna's musical expectations for Patrick.   In late
March 1886 she wrote to him in Naples that 'I've not forgotten
to think about music for you especially'.   She had bought a book
with 'some nice old things in it' which even two of her non-
musical friends appreciated.   'I mean their musical taste has
not been much cultivated.   And besides, I've done something else
in the way of music for you which I can explain better when you
come back.'

While it is not known how he reacted to her plans, Anna did have
a piano* at James Court from the start, and their three children
would grow up able both to sing and play musical instruments.   On
the other hand, the record clearly shows that the father remained
a visual and that 'Observe!' was still his 'Life's law'.   What
the newlyweds really shared was Patrick's ideas and plans.   He
set the stage and pace, and Anna followed him as an essential yet
tactfully critical helpmate.   His acquaintance with the facts
of domestic life was nevertheless astonishingly limited.

In a letter about her parents' early married life, Norah states
that her father had no other knowledge of marital relationships
than from the fiction he had read.   He told her once that he was
quite surprised 'when he found young women did not faint away as
described in novels'.   Norah's conclusion:
   His trouble was coming to marriage with entire inexperience of
   the nature of women, or interest in or comprehension of their
   characteristic make up.   He was the romantic and idealistic

* Dr John Reilly has found evidence that Prince Kropotkin, when
visiting Geddes in 1886 at James Court, went 'straight to the piano
and sang a revolutionary song': 'Early Social Thought of Patrick
Geddes', Ch. V.

lover who then quite needlessly suffered some sort of disillusionment for lack of experience and comprehension.   I have
gathered the first year of married life was as a result *not*
happy.   That over, they made a real success of life
together. (10)

The fullest account of their early crusade in Old Edinburgh has
been given by James Mavor* in his two-volume autobiography, 'My
Windows on the Street of the World'.   After comparing Geddes to
William Morris to whom 'he was in many ways nearer in his points
of view ... than either he or Morris realised', Mavor describes
James Court as 'filled with a population belonging to the lower
ranks of skilled labour - shoemakers or rather cobblers, black-
smiths, etc.;   there was even a sweep who occupied a portion of an
ancient palace that formed part of the court'.

> The people, I believe, looked upon the advent among them of the
> Geddes family with amusement, not altogether unmingled with sus-
> picion.   Some of the younger people more or less enjoyed the
> receptions the Geddeses gave, and the infinite patience and
> loyalty to her husband's ideals of Mrs. Geddes must have had a
> good influence upon them.   In course of time the court began
> to assume a new aspect....   The Geddeses had furnished their
> house with good examples of Scots furniture of the eighteenth
> century.   They brought some of the beauty and the joy of life
> into a spot where unredeemed squalor had reigned....
>   Geddes was really on the same track as Morris.   With
> scarcely inferior practical sagacity, though with greatly in-
> ferior material means, Geddes had done something to bring back
> the surroundings of the period before the factory system had
> divorced the fine arts from production....   Geddes's theory
> was, however, different from that of Morris.   He did not
> believe in razing society to the ground in order to rebuild a
> new society in its place.   His biological training was of
> value in revealing to him, through the hard experience of
> direct social experiment, that, important as surroundings
> might be, the inherent factor was not less important, and that
> the degradation of surroundings was an index of the degrada-
> tion of the people who inhabited them. (11)

A much-needed supplement to the descriptions of male observers are
the intimate facts given in Norah's memoirs and letters.   For
instance, although the work of Geddes in slum rehabilitation and
in starting the first student residences in Edinburgh finally won
the official recognition of being noted in a history of the University, no public mention has been made of Anna's share of the
burden.   But here are Norah's comments:

> Biologist though he was, P.G. did not make enough allowance
> for the strain of pregnancy, & my mother worked too hard
> during the first and third, certainly.   Lister House University

---

* Scottish contemporary and friend of Geddes;   editor, later Professor of Economics at St Mungo's College, Glasgow, and at the
University of Toronto.

Hall was opened sometime in 1887 (for the winter session I suppose).   Everthing near the end was done in a hurry & Mrs. G. had too much responsibility.   At one point when alone, she sat down on one of the beds & cried with strain, weakness & fatigue.... (12)

   Our mother had a good deal to put up with in daily life owing to habits fostered by our father's early life as a wandering student and his childhood's solitary meals;   owing to his dyspeptic condition in early manhood, and due to the vagaries of his unpredictable temperament.   Their social background had been different too, and some of his ways jarred on her fastidiousness. (13)

Such facts were not known outside the immediate family, and apparently were confided only to the loyally taciturn daughter. Indeed, after writing the first letter about problems of adjustment she added in its margin: 'Better not dwell on 1st year of marriage as being difficult: it was not known or referred to.' On the other hand, Norah emphasised that her mother was 'able to provide what he had ... need of: judgment, discernment, steadiness and staying power'. (14)   J. Arthur Thomson, in recalling his early impressions of Anna, was certainly aware of some of these problems she faced.   He once wrote to the children:

   I have never seen anyone excel her in courage, not even your
   father.   For often as he burned his boats, he was less aware
   of the details involved;   and then there is a reward to the
   initiator.   Sometimes, if not often, the result of some
   decision meant years of frugality and self-denial.   She
   seems to me in this way one of the most heroic people I have
   known. (15)

HISTORY OF BIOLOGY ... VERDICTS ON CAPITAL, LABOUR AND ART

The chronological list of Geddes's publications just before and during his first two years of marriage reveals the same mingling of biology and social-economics that began in 1881.   Thus, 1885 credits him with a revision of W.J. Behrens 'Textbook of General Botany';   and 1886 with three major papers read before the Royal Society of Edinburgh.   The meeting of 7 June heard the reading of 'History and Theory of Spermogenesis' by Geddes and Thomson - the first joint work of teacher and pupil.   This date is of interest in the light of Thomson's first recollection of Anna. He relates that, after meeting the 'young goddess' in the midsummer of 1886, 'She told me that I was coming to mean much to your father ... and that she hoped that whatever happened, she would never come between us.   As far as I know that was true for all the years.' (16)

At the Royal Society's next monthly meeting on 5 July 1886 Geddes presented two of his own papers: 'A Synthetic Outline of the History of Biology' and 'Theory of Growth, Reproduction and Heredity'.   The first one contains a diagrammatic summary of the parallel development of morphology and physiology, i.e. the study

of form and function, which foreshadows his future use of thinking
machines. Having placed ten classic originators of the basic
lines of research into appropriate squares under 'Morphology' and
'Physiology', he leaves spaces underneath into which the work of
all successors can be arranged in synthetic outline (see Figure
4.1).

MORPHOLOGY.					GENERAL SURVEY.	PHYSIOLOGY.				
Protoplasm.	Cells.	Tissues.	Organs.	Forms.		Habits and Temperament.	Functions of Organs.	Functions of Tissues.	Functions of Cells.	Functions of Protoplasm.
Dujardin.	Schwann.	Bichât.	Cuvier.	Linné.	Encyclop ↓ Buffon.	Haller.	Müller.	Bichât.	Virchow.	Bernard.

Figure 4.1

Then comes a further adaptation of his Mexican 'window-pane'
justaposition of facts and ideas.
 If we suppose the diagram rolled into a cylinder, the meeting
 of the two edges will readily illustrate how, in the study of
 protoplasm, morphology and physiology come into ultimate contact. Again, if the diagram be folded along the middle per-
 pendicular lines, a gradual unfolding from the centre outwards
 will, as column after column is exposed, illustrate the historic evolution of the sciences. (17)

Geddes starts his next paper, 'Theory of Growth, etc.', by referring to the one on biology and pointing out the urgency of now
reversing 'the usual order of investigation'. That is, instead
of merely adding accumulations of facts to the above categories,
the biologist should now boldly
 set about interpreting these in terms of their fundamental
 secret, that of constructive and destructive metabolism -
 anabolism and katabolism. Selecting a set of problems at
 once peculiarly comprehensive and peculiarly difficult, which
 the author has in recent essays discussed inductively, it is
 the object of the present paper to apply the modern conception
 of protoplasmic anabolism and katabolism to the phenomena of
 growth, reproduction, sex, and heredity.

Some 40 years after its reading in the Royal Society, Sir J. Arthur

Thomson would describe the synthetic outline of biology in superlatives. 'Unsurpassable ... a forgotten parergon [sic], without
the light of which some big histories of biological science are
dull and dead. (18)

Returning to 1886 and Geddes's mingled contributions to science,
we find that despite one foot firmly planted in biology, he
steadily ventured further and further afield. Not many weeks
after the wedding, for example, he took part in a series of
popular lectures devoted to the question: 'Is the Present System
of Distribution Satisfactory?'

James Oliphant, his wife's brother-in-law, had been entrusted
with the thousand-pound surplus left from an industrial remuneration conference held in London in 1885, which sum Geddes was to
spend studying the problem. Accordingly he arranged for leading
speakers from the conference to expound their views on the subject
before audiences in Glasgow, Dundee, and Edinburgh. A labour
organiser put forth the cause of trade unions; a manager of a
large cooperative society demonstrated how his system would
improve distribution; William Morris championed the socialist
cause. A recognised economist from London gave his explanation
of the 'Irregularity of Employment'; Alfred Russel Wallace analysed the causes of and remedies for depression; and Patrick
Geddes, FRSE (Fellow of the Royal Society of Edinburgh) appeared
on the scene to explain the 'Conditions of Progress of the Capitalist and of the Labourer'. (19)

Admitting that he was coming before his audiences 'as a student -
an observer, not an actor in the great world of industry', he
asked for 'something of that consideration which men show to a
foreigner, whose ways of speech may seem quaint ... and whose
criticisms are so apt to give offence'. 'Yet with all these
drawbacks ... the foreigner has often ... something to say which
may be worth while listening to.'
     So, while the heads of my discourse are evidently Capitalist,
     Labourer, and Progress, I must warn you that I have no inten-
     tion of flattering any of the three. A little plain-speaking
     may be agreeable by contrast on this eve of a general elec-
     tion.... Even though you should both resent the criticism
     and reject the theory of this paper, it may at any rate interest
     you as giving a rough sample of the way in which social matters
     are being talked over by scientific men.... The world of
     thought cannot be permanently divorced from the world of
     action; nay, our present anarchy in the one is but the too
     faithful reflection of that which prevails in the other.

Geddes admits the difficulty of giving 'anything like a just and
fair idea of labourer and capitalist alike'. Comparing the descriptions of one another made by the opposing camps, he finds that
'The characters seem those of an unreal world, like the stock
Irishman or the wicked uncle of the play'. The capitalist is 'a
benign lord, incapable of wrong' and the labourer 'a foolish, un-
appreciative and rebellious subject'. Alternatively the orthodox

socialist sees the former as 'a vampire battening on wealth he does
not create' and the latter 'one of the blameless, long-suffering
elect'.

But the lecturer proposes letting Bastiat and Marx, Giffen and
Henry George cancel each other so that one can look at labour and
capital 'in a quiet natural-history sort of way'. What do we find
in real life? 'Truly, all sorts and conditions of man, a host of
irreconcilably different types and varieties of labourers and
capitalists, struggling for existence among each other.' Contrasting with the admittedly prevalent exploitation of labour in
nineteenth-century England was the shining example of the Leven
Shipyard in Dumbarton, the owners of which let their workers regu-
late wages even in years of depression. But on the other hand
Geddes pointed out that at the recent industrial remuneration conference in London 'there was no graver charge of systematic
oppression of any class of labourers than that alleged against the
highly paid and successful ship-platers with respect to the
labourers who assist them'.

Venturing into the future, he prophesies:
    I don't imagine the average English capitalist of the present
    generation will be looked back to with any very great regret or
    enthusiasm; but - don't let us suppose the average workman
    will be either. This is not an heroic age.... And admitting
    that the modern capitalist is largely a hard man, and ... that
    he thinks much of the rights of wealth, and little of its
    duties - would it not be even worse if we replaced such capit-
    alists by labourers, chosen by lot or suffrage, or as you
    will, tomorrow?

To illustrate his scepticism concerning the great things promised
by new masters, he tells of a little town in Italian Switzerland
which had been taken possession of by three of the Swiss federal
states. Instead of granting the new territory 'liberty, equality, fraternity', the Swiss built
    three enormous castles ... put in garrisons, and sold the abso-
    lute government of their brethren, taxation and all, to the
    highest bidder.... And this went on until the Powers put an
    end to it in 1815....
        That's human nature - capitalists' nature, labourers'
    nature, your nature, my nature, every man's nature - when temp-
    tation is strong enough.

The lecturer's scepticism also includes the apparently simple
proposition that 'the average share of the labourer can only be
increased by diminishing the percentage appropriated by the capitalist'. Here Geddes uncovers two 'vast' and 'misleading' assump-
tions. First, that there will be no increase in the labouring
population (which then would diminish the percentage taken from
ownership), and second, that 'the social machine is assumed perfect'. Workmen and employers everywhere go over their machinery
to improve it.
    But the social machine ... does anyone think of repairing it?...

Wholesale, without understanding it, yes - that's politics;
but in detail by detail, city by city, no - that would only be
practical economics, and you aren't interested in that.

Everyone assumes that we are always making progress, industrially
and politically.   Thus, 'A man may think as he pleases, may vote
as he pleases, and (as long as he is in the majority) may say what
he pleases; but who ventures to speak irreverently or despondently
of progress, save perhaps Mr Ruskin in his wildest vein?'   Appeal-
ing again to biology, Geddes points out that
    the essential scientific fact about the evolution of any species
    - man or beast, plant or animal, it matters not - is improved
    average *quality*.   Increase of quantity is not evolution....
    Your apparent progress in quantity tends indeed to be the
    opposite of real progress in quality: your supposed evolution
    is - degeneration, in fact.

After this verdict, Geddes examines over-population, urging the
economist to get beyond the early theories of Malthus and Darwin
and grasp Spencer's law.   Namely, 'the rate of reproduction of
all living things becomes lowered as the development is raised,
and conversely.'   Once this modern theory is understood practical
action
    at once assumes a new and higher aspect - a third line of
    action becomes clear.   Neither preventive check nor struggle
    for existence are the main thing.   The remedy lies in higher
    and higher individuation - i.e. if we would repress excessive
    multiplication, we must develop the average individual standard
    throughout society.

Geddes asserts that poverty is connected with so-called progress.
    The secret of the connection ... lies primarily in the depart-
    ment of production, not that of distribution, let the reformers
    of the latter say what they will; and the practical economist,
    who would increase the well-being rather than the mere number
    of the population, must attempt a vast proportional increase in
    the industries which elevate life over those which merely main-
    tain it, and must make his ideal of production for a long time
    lie in raising quality of production over mere quantity of
    it....
        The stupendous increase of material resources, upon which
    our age has so congratulated itself, and the portentous increase
    of a poor population over which it commences to be alarmed are
    associated as cause and effect.

He warns economists that without steadily directing more and more
of our industry from the production of these forms of wealth
which merely support life to those which evolve it ... 'degenera-
must go on'.   Without this 'an infinite increase of coal and
cotton, of cattle and corn, is but a curse to us; and - paradoxical though it seems - taken alone, they tend only to the increased
production of increased poverty.'
    in short, the development of new resources pushes back the
    limit of misery, only ultimately to increase it.   For were man

bathed in an ocean of nectar and ambrosia, he would not only come
to multiply as fast as the tapeworm but degenerate as far. The
progress which we hear so much about from Canada and the United
States lies in always growing more cheap corn and cotton - to
feed and clothe more cheap labourers - to grow more corn - to
feed more labourers - to grow more corn still ... till finally
we have an indefinite population certainly, but nothing to eat.
'However,' Geddes ironically observes, 'the goal of that sort of
progress - statisticians' progress - is reached; its ideal is
realised.'

The lecture proper ends on the philosophical note of applying the
new concepts of biology and sociology to human progress.
    Reproduction has outrun individuation; the mere growth of our
    cities has outrun their real development. Remedial treatment
    then demands a raising of the whole character and aims of our
    civilisation ... of reorganising cities, of reforming indus-
    tries, of transforming the ideal of progress from an individual
    Race for Wealth into a social Crusade of Culture.
A vast problem, admits the lecturer, yet
    the resources are at hand, nay, the process is fairly begun:
    art and education ... are commencing to reassert their ancient
    leadership of civilised industry. Only thus can we ever hope
    to realise the aim of practical economics which is not illusory
    progress visible only in census returns and bank ledgers, but
    is the progressive development of the highest human and social
    life - not the Increase of Wealth, but the Ascent of Man.

Notwithstanding this eloquent close, Geddes remains on the platform with 'a postscript to anticipate your criticisms'. To those
who thought the lecture too scientific: 'Well, I can't help that:
since the world is complex, we must just take the trouble to
understand it.' To those who found him too indefinite, he
explains:
    More wages for the ship's crew is all very well; I sincerely
    desire it. But ... let us make sure that we are sailing for
    the right port and that our cargo is of real treasure; then
    it will be time enough to talk of larger shares.
    My business to-night has been to show that capitalists and
    labourers - like barons and retainers of old - are very much
    alike at the bottom; that for both of them too life is decid-
    edly a poor affair ... life is equally blank at present. The
    capitalist in his big ugly house is no happier than the labourer
    in his little ugly one; if the one has more of fatigue the
    other has more of worry.

For those wanting to learn about social ideals, Geddes suggests
    all kinds of social literature.... Read such criticism of
    modern life and industry as we owe to Carlyle, Ruskin, and
    Morris; read, if you have nothing else, the Book of Ecclesias-
    tes. Above all, read history, of ancient Greek cities, better
    of medieval ones, best of all of ancient Flemish ... [which] were
    organised on a higher plane of civilisation than we moderns
    almost dare to dream ... and how their inhabitants, though

without our industrial powers or our scientific knowledge, had
yet, on the whole, unquestionably a better life of it than we
have yet reached with all.

Finally, Geddes throws out two more 'ways of making ideals
definite':

I might speak of saving - of the real saving which lies first of
all in getting the permanent surroundings of a good and healthy
and civilised life, of saving in house and furniture and in
mutual insurance.... I might point out, too, that the excellent ideal of shortened working hours is only to be got in this
indirect way of leading production and consumption into more and
more permanent channels, for our day's work is ultimately
fixed, not by the capitalist, but by the consumer; each day we
have just to replace what the community consumes.

  Or if you have any capital, the first duty it owes to labour
is that of wise investment.... Don't for instance invest in
more foreign loans, nor even in more corn or cattle raising in
America. We have plenty of all these; but invest it in your
own town, among the people who made it for you, and in permanent realities. Not in more smoke and nuisance, more percus-
sion and corrosion, nor in more factories, and more back streets
full of workers in them - we have plenty of these, too - but in
nobler dwellings, in giving the higher industries their long-
delayed turn, and so producing a larger individual return for
labour than is to be got by our too exclusive tending of
machines. That is the kind of investment which pays, the
kind of risk for which there is ample compensation.

After this lecturing event, Geddes steadily took part in an increasing number of activities that were outside the field of Botany. A
printed syllabus shows that he gave a course of twelve lectures on
the 'Outlines of Modern Botany' at Dunfermline in the summer of
1887, sponsored by the Extension Service of the University of St
Andrews. (20) But two other printed course syllabuses also exist
bearing quite unbotanical titles. One, likewise sponsored by St
Andrews, announces twelve lectures on 'Social Science and Social
Life: an Introduction to Practical Economics'; the second, with
no sponsor named, publicises twelve lectures on 'The Use and Production of Wealth in Relation to Social Progress'. No dates
appear in either outline, but many phrases in the one on wealth
are reminiscent of the 1886 lecture on capitalist and labourer.

The 'Wealth' syllabus is of particular interest for its evidence
of the revolutionary procedures in teaching which he already then
used, and for his invitation for student participation which
appears on the last page. 'At close of each Lecture, those
interested are invited to remain for discussion or inquiry....
A small reading and working party, or "Seminar" (without fee)
will also be formed if possible.' In addition, the very syllabus
itself with its outline of what was to be covered lecture by
lecture, and its list of suggested readings, was a radical break
with academic tradition. The University Extension Movement had
of course started earlier in England, but Geddes immediately

grasped the possibilities of the new extra-mural way of teaching.
In fact, he had learned its possibilities over a decade ago from
the example of Thomas Huxley's lectures to working men.

Strangely enough, the first recognition of Geddes's considerable
part in this field of education came from Scotland. Unlike both
the city and university of Edinburgh, St Andrew's University had
no hesitation in recognising and praising useful pioneer achievement. An official report from St Andrew's stated, in 1888, that
    in any account of the steps taken to organise the University
    Extension Movement in Scotland special mention must be made of
    Mr. Patrick Geddes, to whose zeal and energy the formation of
    a large committee of university professors and others is en-
    tirely due. He has advocated the scheme and laboured at it
    with unwearied patience and disinterested ardour.

'Its aims were to bring to the smaller provincial centres the
best the Universities had to offer', Norah writes about her
father's contribution.
    At the same time he expressed more than a fervent hope that
    the methods of teaching current in the Scottish Universities
    would not be repeated; that is of lectures feverishly trans-
    cribed into notes and crammed thereafter for examination
    purposes. He wanted the printed syllabus distributed to
    each student, to do away with the need for note-taking: he
    hoped the University Extension students would prove that
    serious studies could be pursued without the yoke of examina-
    tions or the goad of competition being applied. (21)

As though all this work in promoting and delivering such popular
lectures was not enough, Geddes launched into another time-consuming pursuit in 1887 and 1888. Varied though his thoughts and
deeds had already become, one is nevertheless taken aback by the
new activity: an invasion of art criticism!

One pamphlet of 32 pages and another of 58, both entitled 'Every
Man His Own Art Critic' and published, respectively, for the
Manchester Exhibition of 1887 and Glasgow's of 1888, bear witness
to the ever-widening forays of Geddes. The first 'Every Man'
expounds his triple approach to criticism by seeking to appreciate a picture in terms of the painter's vision, arrangement,
and thought. It also contains this ironic comment on successful
artists of the day:
    Your Royal Academicians are no more academic than they are
    royal; Respectable Artificer is all those coveted letters,
    R.A., really mean (when indeed so much). (22)

The 1888 pamphlet, however, is more interesting. In it he
reproves the public for its habit of first looking in the list
of exhibits 'To see what it is called', instead of looking at
the picture first, 'till they are ready to mark on their catalogue what it is'. This popular weakness, he asserts with
typical irony, has 'been the making of the literary painter'.
    Only concoct a title with a pun in it, or turn up a happy

quotation from Longfellow, a good pathetic sermonising ... and
an engraving of your picture shall adorn the British drawing-
room, you are safe to become an R.A., you stand a fair chance
of being knighted. If a German, the choice of subject is more
limited - a broad practical joke ... princely spike-helmets and
imperial jack-boots - best of all a 'battle piece' with plenty
of copper-coloured fiends in French uniforms running away - any
of these will do for the new Berlin National Gallery. If, on
the other hand, it is to cut a figure in the Salon you want,
you cannot do better than to go in for the ghastly or the
indecent. (23)

Here Geddes refers approvingly to a recent article by his old
Positivist friend, Frederic Harrison, who says the great masters
painted what was 'simple, familiar, noble, traditional and beautiful, while he laments bitterly, and with much justice, over the
subjects which modern painters have adopted instead'. Yet
Geddes realises that 'The painter also feels himself a man among
men, to whom nothing human is foreign, nothing henceforth common
or unclean. The painter will not be behind his scientific
brother in his resolute inquiry into all things visible.' He
understands why some seek inspiration in 'our foremost expert in
putrefaction and the utmost horrors of contagious disease, M.
Pasteur ... and the specialist in moral putrefaction and conta-
gion, M. Zola'.

> The wonder is that even more painters should not choose kin-
> dred themes of material and spiritual loathsomeness. Still
> we are getting the good out of this uncompromising realism.
> Much that is highest in modern science, literature, and art
> is called forth and strengthened by its very contrast with
> this. Synthesis, and poetry, and moral enthusiasm, are
> arising fast in reaction to a generation of too much analy-
> sis, of too prosaic literalism, of widespread moral decay;
> for there is in human as in natural history a strange alter-
> nation of generations. Moreover, through all these stir-
> rings and soundings of hitherto evaded depths of rottenness
> we are rapidly determining the conditions of healthy life on
> all sides, material, moral, and aesthetic; and may now more
> surely devise our measures of overcoming all this evil with
> good, in rational confidence of not only survival in the con-
> test but victory. We may thus adopt Mr Harrison's criticisms
> as alike useful and timely, but in hopeful not pessimistic
> mood.

'It is a great period,' concludes Geddes, 'though not a final
one, this phase of realism: it may be necessary thus to prove
all things, before we can fully hold fast the good.'

His booklet is a mixture of science of colours, art of seeing,
criticism of individual paintings in the Exhibition, and liberal
doses of biology and philosophy. Though at first glance it
seems quite off the track of even his wide interests and messages,
it bears not only clear traces of his past, but also foreshadows
his future. Quoting Harrison turns back the years to Positivist

sermons in London, and to his month's art-gallery truancy from
Huxley's laboratory.   It also recalls his reading of 'Time and
Tide', with traces of Ruskin's 'art-rantings'.

The art criticism of Geddes is of most interest for what it
reveals about him.   For example, his reaction to a picture of a
midsummer sleeping beauty is that of a 'speculative naturalist'
who sees it as a 'supreme visible rendering of ... that waxing
potential energy of life in repose'.
> And thus the fairy tale *is* science;   yet science, despite her
> new strange language, is better than the tale, for the fairy
> fancy has sprung into universal reality: no spot on earth
> but is the Enchanted Palace where one-half of being waits its
> awakening with the other's kiss.

Again, looking at a symbolic picture of 'Pan and Psyche', the
critic lyrically recalls that 'although "great Pan is dead", his
avatar (Darwin) was but lately with us to link anew the life of
man and beast and grass'.
> shall we listen, as he did, to the complex piping of the old
> woodland Pan with an ear which strives to know its many notes
> and changeful melodies?   Or shall our souls ever be lifted
> from the hurrying stream of vicissitude into the presence of
> the All?

After the biologist's, Geddes applies 'the thinker's perception'
to art and claims to have 'a new canon of criticism' to use not
only at exhibitions but 'also everywhere without'.   And so he
interprets modern life and art in terms of two factors: 'Hellen-
ism and Hebraism'.
> In the one mood we shall ... live again in the delightfulness
> of the Hellenic world, the joyous freedom of the Renaissance....
> Yet in the second mood again, when we let the world of facts
> fully confront us, and face the ideals of life and death to
> which these sooner or later tend, we feel once more the iron
> grasp of Hebraism.
>   It is only after grasping the Hellenic and Hebraic atti-
> tudes ... that we can fully interpret a single picture, a
> single edifice, a single man.

Geddes tells of the brief reconciliations of these two ideals but
mostly of their unending conflict which finally has fallen 'to
its present level in the "hardly human abjection" of our modern
city'.   Yet, he ironically reports, a peaceful compromise has
been reached:
> The claims to the life and enjoyment of the senses, success-
> fully starved by the Puritan on every higher plane, have now
> victoriously reasserted their irrepressible vitality upon the
> lowest animal one;   hence the prosperous labour only for
> domestic comfort in the sense of upholstery and long dinners,
> while the unprosperous again labour primarily for drink,
> probably with a deeper if briefer satisfaction.

Like 'Capitalist & Labourer', 'Every Man' ends on a socially
optimistic note.   The poet's inspiration has been passed on to

the 'ideal painter' and to his 'brethren of all humbler industries' who likewise 'will work no longer for sale only, but for perfection, for truer mutual service'.

> Possibilities of new action are thus nearing us: every man may be more than merely his own art critic, but something of his own artist also....   Already he disputes abundantly of how to bring in a better order of things, in politics and social life, in industry or education.

REGIUS CHAIR CANDIDACY

The first weeks of 1888 must have been unusually crowded ones, even for such an active scholar-teacher-lecturer-civic reformer as Patrick Geddes. His 'master and friend', Professor Alexander Dickson, died at the end of December 1887 leaving vacant the Regius Chair of Botany at Edinburgh.

Sorrow notwithstanding, Geddes realised that he must lose no time in making as good a case for himself as possible, for applications were due in February. For the fourth time during his assistant-ship at Edinburgh, he prepared the formal document required for petitioning a professorial chair. But this time it was the ideal chair in the ideal place for him, and he went all out to win it. In late January and early February letters of recommendation and encouragement, both solicited and unsolicited, poured in to him from Europe and the British Isles, from former teachers and pupils as well as colleagues. His testimonials were arranged in two series: the first from 7 educationists, 10 physicians, phys-iologists and pathologists, 5 well-known former pupils, 23 university extension students at Dunfermline; and a collective letter signed by 56 colleagues. The second series numbered 35 biologists and botanists, ranging from Charles Darwin to Alfred Russell Wallace. In between was a bibliography of the appli-cant's scientific work grouped under such headings as 'General Botany', 'Algae and Fungi', 'Chlorophyll (Vegetable and Animal)', 'Protoplasm and Cell', etc., a total of 3 books and 42 papers. Two, however, were labelled 'under preparation' - 'A Re-statement of the Theory of Organic Evolution' (appeared in Chambers's 'Encyclopedia' as 'Evolution' later that year), and a textbook (published in 1893 as 'Chapters in Modern Botany').

Conspicuously yet understandably absent were all titles on stat-istics, economics, capital and labour, cooperation vs socialism, and John Ruskin.

Dated 14 February 1888 and addressed to the curators of the University of Edinburgh, 'The Letter of 1888' made an impressive printed booklet of 100 pages. (24)   It opened most formally:

> MY LORDS AND GENTLEMEN,
> I beg respectfully to present myself as an applicant for the Chair of Botany in the University of Edinburgh, and to submit the following statement of my qualification for the appoint-ment.

Divided into two parts describing, respectively, his practical
qualifications and his research, it is a clear and condensed
summary of his major career thus far: biology.   In fact, a
reader judging from its contents alone would get a convincing
impression that here was a keen natural scientist devoted to
his field and with a brilliant future before him.   Note how, in
the applicant's pen, all the hesitations and experiments of
youth, all his wanderings and uncertainties of purpose, have
been marshalled to appear as one steady preparation for this
Chair.

> I. Studies and Experience in Teaching. - Having early decided
> upon a course of independent study, I spent the four years
> usually allotted to undergraduate life chiefly in private
> scientific studies, chemical, botanical, and geological.   In
> 1874 I went to the Royal School of Mines, and after some
> further preliminary work, entered the laboratory of Professor
> Huxley, where for two years my time was divided between lab-
> oratory work, research, and teaching.   In 1877 the Council
> of University College, London, conferred upon me the Sharpey
> Physiological Scholarship ...

Of special interest is his summary of eight-and-a-half years of
teaching at the university.

> I have acquired considerable experience in examining, through
> conducting the regular class examinations in Botany, and as
> an examiner in Biology in the Victoria University for three
> years.   As University Local Examiner in Botany, my attention
> has been constantly directed to the teaching of Botany in
> schools, and to its value as an instrument of general as well
> as elementary scientific education.   I have hence endeavoured
> to advance the teaching of the subject, and to give it reality
> and concreteness, especially by the organisation of small
> typical botanic gardens, whose rapid adoption by public and
> private schools and other institutions gives encouraging
> evidence of their utility to the actual work of education.
> In more general ways, I have also tried to increase the use-
> fulness of the University beyond its own immediate bounds,
> particularly in work connected with the rising University
> Extension movement, as well as with other recent developments
> of academic life.

What was cautiously referred to in that last phrase was the
development of halls of residence for Edinburgh students.   The
omission of their names was doubtless a conciliatory gesture in
line with certain bibliographical omissions in later pages.   On
the other hand, Geddes allowed himself 'to call attention to the
increase of the number of students working in the botanical laboratory - from 10 per cent of those attending the lectures in
1880 ... to 28 per cent in 1887.'   While he did not enter into
details of his teaching methods, he claimed that his long experience in biological laboratories of many kinds 'has given me some
measure of success, not only in presenting the essential facts of
Botany in fresh lights, and in redeeming these from the traditional reproach of dryness, but in bringing the subject more fully

into line with other departments of scientific and medical education.'

To confirm this he presents first, 'the statements of former pupils,
now themselves teachers and investigators'; second, the testimony
of 'representative educationists' as to his practical teaching and
dealing with large audiences; and finally, recommendations from
'physicians, physiologists, and pathologists,' bearing largely on
the 'kind of botanical instruction of most professional usefulness ...' and 'expressing distinct approval of the general biological standpoint of my teaching, as distinguished from the traditional systematic and anatomical one.' For, says Geddes, the
claims of botany to continue to be preliminary to the study of
medicine 'can no longer be based upon the collection or dissection
of plants ... but now alike depend upon the reading of the laws
of organic life from these their simplest manifestations'.

'II. Original Work. - ' follows with 'a list of my publications
with testimonials bearing on these' from 35 biologists and
botanists. Here he takes care to explain that while his scientific papers deal with almost all departments of biology, they
purposely range 'in each case from special researches on concrete
points up to a summary or rearrangement of the general principles
of the subject'. Further, he emphasises the risk of misunderstanding attached to such apparently scattered work.

> That our present extreme subdivision of intellectual labour
> necessitates a corresponding attempt at concentrating and or-
> ganising our knowledge, is universally admitted. Neverthe-
> less, while work within any one of the established fields of
> specialism gains immediate recognition and reward, the more
> arduous labour of re-surveying a definite number of these,
> and of reuniting them under a more systematic culture, has
> not only usually to await approval until its results can be
> clearly set forth towards the close of life, but is even apt
> to be mistaken for the uncertain wanderings of the beginner
> who has as yet found no definite task.

The candidate points out that his studies of phenomena common to
the vegetable and animal worlds have trained him for writing 'a
series of comprehensive "Encyclopaedia" articles, which constitute the framework of an ultimate treatise on the Principles of
Biology'. (A treatise which would take him forty years to complete.) Most of these articles 'contain a considerable amount
of new matter, and possess more unity than at first appears'.

> Thus the articles dealing with Morphology and Cell introduce
> a re-statement of the Cell theory, which receives a rational
> basis by co-ordination with our knowledge of Protoplasm.
> This, then, throws light upon the processes of Reproduction
> and Growth, and for the first time affords an interpretation
> of the phenomena of Sex in plants and animals.

After this detailed review and defence of his career as both
teacher and original researcher, Geddes swiftly and neatly ties
up his arguments:

At this point, therefore, I may fairly claim to have ended my
apprenticeship, and to be ready to return to the collection and
interpretation of the details of Botany with renewed interest,
and to the teaching of its principles with increased energy....
I have, in conclusion, to lay before you the testimony of professed biologists and botanists....

I have the honour to be,
MY LORDS AND GENTLEMEN,
Your obedient Servant,
PATRICK GEDDES.

Botanical Laboratory
of the University of Edinburgh,
Royal Botanic Garden,
14th February 1888.

As a source of contemporary information on Geddes, the 'Letter of
1888' creates a problem because of its very wealth of material.
Thirty-five leading men of science on the continent and in Great
Britain each write something significant about their candidate,
but as a solution to the difficulty of choice I quote all of
Darwin's second letter* and select fragments from those of five
other well-known sponsors.

Down, 27th March 1882.

Dear Sir, -
I have read several of your biological papers with very great
interest, and I have formed, if you will permit me to say so, a
high opinion of your abilities.   I can entertain no doubt that
you will continue to do excellent service in advancing our knowledge in several branches of science.   Therefore I believe that
you are well fitted to occupy any chair of natural history, for
I am convinced that example is fully as important as precept
for students.

I remain, dear Sir, yours faithfully,
Charles Darwin.

The first excerpt is from Thomas Henry Huxley who, already in
April 1882, wrote a recommendation which has been partly quoted
earlier.   The whole first paragraph reads:
Mr Patrick Geddes was at one time a distinguished student of
my class.   I have a very high opinion of his abilities; and
I am well aware that his knowledge is unusually varied and
extensive.

Professor Henri de Lacaze-Duthiers (Institut de France,
26 January 1888)
Your activity in research ... your knowledge of histology and
physiology make me augur for you a brilliant future....
Your candidature has my best wishes.   Become Professor,

* This letter was written originally for Geddes's unsuccessful
application in 1882 for the Chair of Natural History in Edinburgh.
Darwin's first letter, also re-used in 1888, has been quoted in
full in chapter 3, pp. 60-1.

and come to Roscoff and Banyuls with a legion of young naturalists.   You know what a reception you will get there, and what
a harvest you will reap....

Alfred R. Wallace (Codalming, Surrey, 2 February 1888)
I have much pleasure in stating my opinion that Mr PATRICK
GEDDES is exceptionally well fitted for the post of Professor
of Botany at your University.
   He is well known as an original thinker and worker in some
of the most interesting and difficult branches of biological
study....

Professor August Weismann (University of Freiburg, Naples,
3 February 1888)
... Mr GEDDES ranks among those of the living English investigators who have most deeply thought out the general biological
problems which equally concern both the vegetable and the
animal kingdom.

Professor Emile Yung (University of Geneva, 26 January 1888)
... To a power of minute analysis he adds that of synthesis,
a quality which is too rare not to entitle Mr GEDDES to be
called an excellent Professor....   He knows science by having
contributed to its advances; his travels in France, Italy,
and Germany, have put him in relation with men of science, who
esteem him highly, and reckon still more upon him for the
future.

Both Anna and Patrick must have felt a sense of achievement and
relief when the bulky 'Letter' was finally proof-read, printed,
stapled as a paper-bound booklet, and delivered to the Curators.
While there is no record of any discussion the two may have had,
there did exist a sheet of paper* on which he had, presumably
several years earlier, noted his plans for the future, his thesis
of defiance to the academic world:
   The writer has set before himself two intellectual problems:
   1. to weld somewhat more compactly, in theory and mode of
   teaching, the biological sciences; 2. to organize upon these
   a system of economics.   If he succeeds in half of either -
   much less the whole of both - doctors' gowns will be had for
   nothing and letters after his name can be had cheap; for
   from him the University will have to take its degree so far
   as these subjects are concerned.   If he succeeds not, flat
   hats and red hoods will not console him; titles of Bachelor,
   Doctor, Pundit, Siccopedant, Dry-as-Dust and Heavystern will
   do him no good.

Though none of these revolutionary thoughts were expressed in his
application, they were not hidden from friends,   Witness Mavor to
the effect that Geddes 'was not a normal academic product ... he

* Part of a MS. seen at the Outlook Tower in 1935 and typed by
the author.

did not trouble about taking a degree, but pursued his own course in his own way.' (25)

With the completion of the 'Letter', let us see Patrick and Anna at home at this time.   George Eyre-Todd relates:
> The flat was furnished with beautiful old chairs, tables, bureaus (sic) and the like, retrieved from second-hand shops where they were looked on mostly as derelicts; and their appearance in the Geddes domicile went a long way to set agoing the craze for the antique which is a noted and wholesome feature of the present day.   On those uneven old floors, stained and polished, on which the furniture was apt to sit uneasily, one met many of the coming men of the time.   Indeed, James Court was the preferred rendezvous of that circle of university and town folk whose interests ran to social and economic questions and who were known throughout the city as the 'Geddes group.' (26)

A typical gathering is described in Mavor's autobiography in the chapter on Peter Kropotkin.   The princely anarchist was visiting Edinburgh in 1886 after his release from the French prison of Clairvaux, 'and one evening', writes Mavor, 'we met at Patrick Geddes's in James Court.   There was a large party.   In a group of biologists there was a youth with yellow hair and blue eyes, taller by almost a head than anyone else in the room.   He was a student in the Marine Biological Station at Granton.   His name was Fridtjof Nansen.'

Three of the social economists present: Thomas Kirkup, 'a thoroughly convinced Marxist,' Prince Kropotkin and Mavor
> formed a little group by ourselves....   Although Kropotkin's positive views were not such as I could accept without great qualification, his hostility to Marx was at least as great as my own....   Kirkup was an exceedingly shy man, and it was hard to draw him into an argument.   Kropotkin and I alternately hammered Marx, and Kirkup spoke up for him, and we had an excellent discussion ... and from that evening we became firm friends. (27)

The two years which elapsed between Patrick and Anna's engagement in February 1886 and his all-out campaign for the Chair of Botany in February 1888 were particularly significant ones in a long life filled with seminal thoughts, bold deeds and crucial decisions.   Not only did he take the tardy step of getting engaged and married but courageously launched himself and his helpmate as pioneers in the rehabilitation of the Old Town of Edinburgh and in the reform of the equally neglected conditions of student life.   Intellectually, these years also marked his appearance in newspaper columns, in pamphlets and on public lecture platforms as a force to be reckoned with in adult education, social economics and industrial relations.

Yet in all this expansion of interests Geddes merely followed what to him was the self-evident development of a naturalist who

steadily widens his area of observation of organisms functioning
in their environments.   Such a widening brought him quite logically to consider the highest organism, man, as he lived and
worked in his rural and urban surroundings.   With Patrick in the
Regius Chair and with both him and Anna as friendly neighbourhood
leaders and catalytic hosts to key citizens at their James Court
gatherings, what might they not achieve together towards the renewal of his 'City Beautiful'?

Chapter 5

PART-TIME PROFESSOR, FULL-TIME GENERALIST, 1888-97

DUNDEE

It was June 1889. Patrick Geddes, now a full-fledged Professor of Botany, walked from home to his lecture room enjoying summer as manifest in leaf and flower in this northern latitude. His path, however, did not lead from the Regius Keeper's mansion through the spacious beauty of the Royal Botanic Gardens of Edinburgh. It followed instead dull streets lined with the dirty-grey buildings of Dundee, then probably the most dismal town of Scotland spoiling the most beautiful natural setting imaginable: that of the north shore of the Firth of Tay.

Exactly what happened to Patrick's weighty application for the Edinburgh chair will perhaps never be known. All efforts made in later years by his son Arthur to find documents relating to the case were in vain, though one surviving Curator did admit that there was no formal discussion. Pressed as to whether he had studied the application enough to see that Darwin had written not one, but two letters of recommendation, he confessed that he did not know this. (1) Having been asked to investigate the records of filling the Chair of Botany, the Keeper of Manuscripts of Edinburgh University Library has replied: (2)

I can find no notice of the vacancy in any official record, nor of the names of the candidates. Professor Dickson's death is the subject of a minute of condolence in the Senatus Minutes for 14th Jan. 1888, and Professor Isaac Bayley Balfour presented his commission as Professor of Botany at the Senatus meeting of 24th March 1888.

The Senate Minutes contain no reference to the Candidacy of Patrick Geddes ... and there are no curators of chairs, or curators' minutes.

One can imagine how great the disappointment of Anna and Patrick was at this rebuff to his career in biology and at this implicit disavowal of their civic labours. That he fought actively to retain his connections with Edinburgh is also revealed in the Keeper's letters.

> Patrick Geddes ... applied for the post of Examiner in Botany
> (in succession to Prof. Balfour) on 19 March 1888.... The
> successful candidate was Prof. H. Marshall Ward.   On 7th July
> 1888 Geddes applied for recognition as an Extra-Academical
> lecturer on botany (in the Medical School).   His application,
> with details of his course at University College, Dundee is
> preserved.   His application was granted by the Court of
> Edinburgh University, 1 August 1888.

Concurrently with this rearguard action, Geddes's friend J. Martin
White was extremely active on his behalf.   The result is given in
White's own words as quoted by an editor of the 'Scots Magazine':
'Mr. Patrick Geddes was then lecturing on botany.   He was an
eminent man, whom all would be glad to have made a professor.
My family and I decided to endow a chair of botany as a memorial to my father and as a summer course, and Professor Geddes
occupied it.'   The endowment was £6,000, and Geddes ... was
paid half the salary of a full-time professor. (3)

The practical arrangements of the Martin White Chair of Botany
were that he should teach only during the summer term, approximately mid-April to mid-June, while an assistant took care of
students during the winter term.   Consequently, Geddes could
earn his academic cake in Dundee, so to speak, and eat it for
three-quarters of the year anywhere else he wished.

A recent history of Edinburgh's Royal Botanic Garden written by
Professor H.R. Fletcher, present incumbent of the Regius Chair of
Botany, states that the vacancy in 1888: 'was strongly canvassed
by Patrick Geddes'. (4)   Nevertheless, the successful candidate
was Isaac Bayley Balfour, whose father had been Professor Dickson's predecessor and who, in 1888, was holding the chair of
botany at Oxford.   During the second Balfour's thirty-four
years of incumbency, this history reports, the Gardens were
developed and expanded and made into one of Europe's finest.
Dr Fletcher has told the writer that Balfour, in his opinion, was
the best possible man for the Garden and that Geddes probably was
able to do mankind an even greater service by not getting the
Chair.

In the absence of any official record of the meetings of the Curators, one may easily lean to the view that the appointment was a
foregone conclusion.   What is certain is that Bayley Balfour
lived in Edinburgh 'within a stone's throw of the Garden', and
that he was there almost daily as he grew up, 'in contact with
the staff from the Curator downwards, subconsciously or perhaps
quite deliberately, receiving a practical training in garden
craft.'   He later studied botany in the University, and 'in
1871 ... was one of his father's assistants, a duty he undertook
every year thereafter until 1878'. (5)   He graduated with a BSc
in 1873 and won a DSc in botany in 1875; so there can be no doubt
but that he was well qualified for the chair.   Certainly his two
academic degrees weighed more than Geddes's none at all.   Furthermore, Balfour had not diverted his attention from botany to

things like political economy or the cleaning of Edinburgh's
slums.

The question of what Geddes would or could have done as Regius
Professor in Edinburgh, though interesting, is largely a hypo-
thetical one.   He definitely would not have occupied the Keeper's
Mansion (a large manor house now used as The Gallery of Modern
Art), for financial and social reasons.   But would academic
pressure have made a full-time botanist of him even though it
might not have softened his attacks on negligent landlords and
slothful officials?   Some clues to his likely behaviour may be
found in the story of his thirty-year tenure of the part-time
chair at Dundee.

In his maiden lecture in 1888 entitled 'The Rise and Aims of
Botany', delivered to both students and the Dundee public, Geddes
was immediately controversial:

> From the petrifying predominance of letter over spirit, no
> science has indeed been wholly exempt.   Yet happily, for
> the past century at least, no department of knowledge save
> botany has ever fallen into such intellectual torpor, lain in
> it so long, nay, even now escaped from it so incompletely....
>   The best botanist was he who had described most plants and
> had accumulated the richest herbarium; but the art of des-
> cribing plants, once clearly learned, became a mechanical
> routine, a mere Latin clerkship....   In their new-won aca-
> demic seats the systematic botanists speedily absorbed all
> the vices of the old-world pedantry around them ... the
> simple descriptive language of Linnaeus was elaborated into
> a barbarous terminology which he would have been the first
> to denounce, and the concrete teaching of the facts of botany
> became more and more pushed aside ... hence it is that the
> majority of beginners soon instinctively abandon the whole
> subject as 'dry', while the minority tend to become ... in-
> tellectually lost and smothered amid accumulations of mere
> unused hay.

Geddes soon proved to be a highly unconventional teacher of
botany, and many were the tales told about his classroom performances at University College, Dundee (UCD).   For instance, even
when both end of term and the visit of the external examiner were
approaching, Geddes continued unperturbed with his mainly Socratic methods.   One day instead of reviewing possible examination
questions, he lectured on wheat stalks.   First he showed photographs and sketches of the Firth of Forth railroad bridge in
various stages of construction, and expounded the various engineering problems involved.   Then at the end of the period, tradition says, he folded up his illustrations, remarking that 'there
are many similarities between this bridge and stalks of wheat.
See if you can discover for yourselves what they are'.

On another occasion, he gave the class a written test which
started thus: 'Ask any question you like on botany and answer
it.' (6)   As stories like these, plain and embroidered, seeped

back into Edinburgh there were doubtless prayers of thanksgiving
on many a set of academic and municipal lips.   Suppose this man
had got a professorship in their city!

It was no victory for Geddes to take a chair in a small, struggling institution, though UCD's academic standing rose greatly
after its affiliation with St Andrew's University in 1897.   No
greater contrast in equipment could have been found anywhere in
European universities than that between Edinburgh and Dundee.
At the Royal Botanic Garden there were many gardeners and ample
funds for any project undertaken.   At Dundee he found no gardens,
but a wide expanse of lawn and gravel walks in front of the row
of dwelling houses which had been joined by a corridor and
turned into University College.

'So much the better!' was his comment. (7)   'Here I can plan
things exactly as I want them.   I may have the smallest botany
department, but I intend to make the most effective gardens for
teaching in the British Isles.'   Whereupon he pressed the UCD
administration for enough money to hire one gardener, and set to
work to make good his promise.

Lecturing and writing were accompanied by much physical labour.
With his lone gardener Geddes dug up some of the lawns and walks
to make room for a Type Botanic Garden like the one he developed
so successfully in Edinburgh.   Of the many hundred thousands of
plant species found in the world, they chose those which best
illustrated the different types of flora and the main steps of
vegetable evolution.   In variously shaped beds, large and small,
stretching both in front of and behind the college buildings,
were laid out the natural orders, sometimes to show affinities
and again to show contrasts.   The relationship between lilies
and rushes, irises and common grasses, arums and palms, and so
on, was thus made far clearer than it could be on the pages of a
textbook.   At the same time the whole garden was designed to
reveal what Geddes saw as the vast antithesis of the green
world: on one side plants like weeds or lettuce growing 'in an
ecstasy of leaf' and on the other side those like lilies or
irises growing 'in an ecstasy of flower.'

By 1893 the gardens had developed into a thing of beauty as well
as a summary and index of world flora.   He excelled in 'garden-
writing', in using the lines and colours of nature both to
express facts of biology and to create scenes pleasing to the eye,
a composition which he enjoyed far more than arranging words on
paper.   On the other hand, the scientific aspects of botany were
not neglected.

It was in the garden and laboratory of this smallest department
of botany in the United Kingdom that several notable botanists
were trained.   It was here that the project originated for surveying the plant life of Great Britain.   Some of the best
botanical maps ever made were done by pupils such as Robert Smith
and Marcel Hardy, and their work in turn greatly stimulated the

whole movement of studying floral distribution.   Moreover, the
external examination results of his students showed, when looked
into at the request of the unconventional professor himself, an
average above those of other departments. (8)

Further justification of his Socratic approach would come much
later when former pupils were established in their own careers.
'I have never met anyone who impressed me so much', said a young
woman, looking back on her botanical studies in after years,

> and before that I couldn't have imagined that any such person
> really did exist.   Coming directly as I did from an orthodox
> nineteenth-century academy, Professor Geddes was at the same
> time a mystery and a revelation to me.   His clothes were not
> of the latest fahionable cut and he never was perfectly
> groomed, but this was passed unnoticed by most of us.   His
> hair was thick and dark and he had bushy eyebrows over very
> wonderful lively eyes.   His whole appearance and gait and
> demeanor were those of a man full of vitality and a secret
> fund of joy and certainty.
>
> It was impossible to take notes on his lectures; he spoke
> rather fast and was most of the time talking away over the
> heads of his students.   As often as not he went far away
> from the subject with which he started but he had a great
> sense of humour no matter where he wandered.
>
> I liked him best when we were in the country on excursions,
> for he was then like a schoolboy.   He was untiring, regard-
> less of weather, and content with little in the way of food
> even on the longest jaunts.   And although he did not give us
> much in the way of preparation for a degree examination -
> that was left to his assistant - he did far more by taking
> us into the open out-of-door, exposing us to undreamt-of
> beauties and making us ask the 'how?' and 'why?' of nature. (9)

Similarly G.R. Tudhope, President of the Association of University Teachers in 1954, declared at the Centenary that 'It was my
great privilege to know this man and to be one of his pupils'.
He recalled how the new students of his year looked forward to
experiencing the 'thinking-shop', as Geddes's class was nicknamed at Dundee.   But the day and time of the first lecture in
botany conflicted with a total eclipse of the sun, and everyone
was torn between watching it and the duty of attending the
opening lecture.

> Like good Scots students all obeyed the call of duty.   A
> first impression of the Professor was of a slightly-built,
> but wiry figure with an impressive head, bright and alert eyes
> and a rather untidy beard. 'What a splendid morning', he
> said, 'on which to commence the study of botany.   There is
> an eclipse of the sun in ten minutes' time and I have provided
> smoked glasses for the whole class so that we may go out into
> the garden to see it!'   Out on the College lawn we saw that
> eclipse as I think few can have seen it.   While the Professor
> talked to us quietly we saw how the whole of nature shared in
> the eclipse.   We felt the growing chill as the sun became
> obscured, the colours of the grass and flowers changed, the

daisies closed, the bird-song ceased as the darkness of night
spread over us. Quickly once more night gave place to the
dawn, and with Geddes we realized that the eclipse was not an
isolated event in the heavens. (10)

Readily admitting that Geddes neither admired the educational
system of Scotland nor approved of the teaching methods of its
universities, Mr Tudhope stated that
> A university, in his (Geddes's) view, should be the spiritual,
> the intellectual and the artistic centre of its region....
> Geddes was essentially a teacher by the spoken word. Formal
> lectures did not greatly appeal to him, but in talking to
> small groups of students he was inspiring. His class walked
> the gardens with him while he talked; and not only did he
> teach in the garden, but he taught by the garden for the
> flower beds were planted as scientific groups showing the
> relationship between one plant and another and the evolution
> of the groups. Nevertheless it was his genius that the
> garden of the College which he had planned was visually beauti-
> ful with a complete and lovely unity. As he himself said:
> 'I am something of a painter in greens'. The College garden
> was not to be the only one planned by Geddes in the City of
> Dundee, for he was invited to plan a Convent Garden and with
> his remarkable gift of discernment and original mental pattern
> he there presented the Life of Christ in flowers.

'THE BOOK ON SEX' ... 'A DRYAD HIDES IN EVERY TREE'

The early years at University College coincided with Geddes's and
J. Arthur Thomson's first major publication in biology, 'The
Evolution of Sex' (1889) and with the former's monograph,
'Chapters in Modern Botany' (1893). (11) Of the joint work,
Norah relates an amusing story which her father told her.
> At U.C.D. in the garden one day he heard his old friend and
> colleague, Professor Steggall (Mathematics), murmuring:
> 'I always stood up for you, old chap.'
> 'What do you say?'
> 'Oh, nothing.'
> 'Yes, but tell me.'
> 'I only said I always stood up for you.'
> 'But why & when?'
> 'Oh, you know, the book on Sex. But I always told them you'd
> given up that sort of thing long ago.'
> My father was quite non-plussed and told the story as an
> example of lack of comprehension on the part of those who
> might have been expected to know better. (12)

That 'book on Sex' was an epoch-making contribution to a subject
which the nineteenth century scarcely ever dared to mention aloud,
much less discuss in print. It first appeared in London at the
end of 1889 as one volume of a scientific series edited by Have-
lock Ellis and was also distributed in the USA by a New York publisher. In July 1890, the Humboldt Library of Science brought

out a special American edition.   By 1892 the French biologist,
Henri de Varigny, had translated and published the work in Paris
as 'L'Evolution du Sexe', while in Great Britain it went through
three printings and two different editions.

Naturally the reviewers were out in full force to hail or condemn
the book.   Typical of the general recognition of its scientific
worth was the review in 'The Nation' (New York), while representative of the school of alarm was 'Nature' (London).

'It is very much to be regretted', wrote the latter's critic (10
April 1890) 'that the authors have included a discussion of certain social and ethical problems absolutely unconnected with the
title of their book.'   Though admitting they had brought to
their task 'a wealth of knowledge, a lucid and attractive method
of treatment, and a rich vein of picturesque language' and that
it was an excellent controversial book for biologists to grapple
with, 'Nature' felt obliged to warn off the general public.

Like the article, 'Sex', which Geddes contributed to volume XXI
of the 'Britannica' in 1886, 'The Evolution of Sex' dealt mainly
with such questions as the physiology and determination of sex
in plants and animals, treating the subject in a detached, scientific manner.

'This little book', states the preface, 'has the difficult task
of inviting the criticism of the biological student, although
primarily addressing itself to the general reader or beginner.'
The authors explain that they had come to take 'an altered and
unconventional view' of many problems in biology and further
that they frankly faced the responsibility of popularising discussion of a subject 'from which there are so many superficial
reasons to shrink, and which knowledge and ignorance so commonly
conspire to veil'.

Three of the book's four divisions are taken up with description
of processes of reproduction in representative forms of life,
with summaries of experiments performed and of theories propounded up to the year 1889.   But the final section, and the one of
greatest interest today, put forth Geddes's remarkable theory of
the why and wherefore of maleness and femaleness, a theory which,
curiously enough, received experimental confirmation some forty
years later in the laboratories of American scientists.

During the London years Huxley had told him not to waste time
reading Spencer, so he read Spencer and seized upon the latter's
emphasis on anabolism and katabolism, the processes of building
up and tearing down, as fundamental to all forms of life.   From
this starting point Geddes read and observed, reasoned and
guessed, till he convinced himself of a number of things in con-
tradiction to currently held ideas.

First of all, as in Geddes's article on 'Evolution', (13) the
joint authors restate the theory of organic evolution, rejecting

Patrick Geddes and colleagues
Professor J.E.A. Steggall
(*standing, left*) and Professor D'Arcy W. Thompson
(*seated*) at University
College, Dundee

The Geddeses at Martin
White's home in Balruddery,
c. 1895: *From left:* Norah, 'a
nice enough little girl, but
badly dressed' (according to
her 'Reminiscences'), P.G.,
Anna, and *at extreme right*,
the host

Chapters

in

Modern Botany

By PATRICK GEDDES
PROFESSOR OF BOTANY, UNIVERSITY COLLEGE, DUNDEE

LONDON
JOHN MURRAY, ALBEMARLE STREET
1893

THE

EVOLUTION OF SEX.

BY

PROFESSOR PATRICK GEDDES

AND

J. ARTHUR THOMSON.

With 104 Illustrations.

LONDON:
WALTER SCOTT,
24 WARWICK LANE, PATERNOSTER ROW.
1889.

Title pages for 'Chapters in Modern Botany' and 'Evolution of Sex'

the Darwinian conception of indefinite variation brought about
through the haphazard working of natural selection and resulting
in an unlimited number of forms of life.   Despite this apparently
infinite variety, they see plant and animal life as governed by
certain definite laws of growth which limit variation to definite
forms and make evolution an orderly, even predictable process.
These two main determining forces are the now alternating, now
mingling ones of nutrition and reproduction: the desire to preserve self and the desire to perpetuate the species.   Similarly
the differences between male and female are interpreted as a
related manifestation of the same fundamental rhythm of life.
The male is by nature preponderantly katabolic, living very
actively but at a loss of energy and protoplasm; the female is
inherently anabolic, living with a surplus of energy which gives
her the capacity to bear offspring.

On the question of the origin of sex, Geddes and Thomson claim
that one reason why it had not been solved was the way naturalists beat about the bush just as did clergymen or doctors when
this subject was to be treated.

> Modesty defeats itself in pruriency and good taste runs to the
> extreme of putting a premium upon ignorance.   Now this re-
> flects itself in biology.   Reproduction and sex have been
> fenced off as facts by themselves; they have been disassocia-
> ted from the general physiology of the individual and the
> species.   Hence the origin of sex has been involved in
> special mystery and difficulty, because it has not been recog-
> nised that the variation which first gave rise to the difference
> between male and female, must have been a variation only
> accenting in degree what might be traced universally. (14)

Geddes had earlier traced back to the simplest one-celled plants
and animals what he claimed was the key to both the nature and
the origin of sex: the universal antithesis or alternating
rhythm of anabolism and katabolism.   Among these self-dividing
amoeboid cells there sooner or later developed certain ones that
were better nourished than others; the hungry, active cell
became a flagellate sperm while the quiescent, well-fed one
became an ovum.   From this simple beginning he examined the
higher organisms, pointing out wherein they show evidence of this
same variation between anabolism and katabolism, between the conservation and dissipation of energy.   The forms, functions, and
organs of the sexes are the outcome and expression of the basic
fluctuation in metabolism.

As one follows up this antithesis through all levels of life, the
active males are found to be more variable and thus the main
leaders in evolutionary progress, while the more passive females
tend to preserve the constancy and integrity of the species.   In
mankind

> the feminine passivity is expressed in greater patience, more
> open-mindedness, greater appreciation of subtle details and
> consequently what we call more rapid intuition.   The masculine
> activity lends a greater power of maximum effort, of scientific

insight or cerebral experiment with impressions, and is associated with an unobservant or impatient disregard of minute
details, but with a stronger grasp of generalities. Man
thinks more, woman feels more. He discovers more but remem-
bers less; she is more receptive and less forgetful. (15)

Towards the end of their book Geddes and Thomson take up 'certain
social and ethical problems,' as 'Nature's' reviewer has already
warned. Insisting on the essential differences between man and
woman ('What was decided among the prehistoric Protozoa cannot be
annulled by Act of Parliament'), they demand that the education,
the ethics, and even the economics of the sexes be based on biological fact, not on ignorance and tradition. The problem of
over-population comes in for its share of attention with first a
review of Malthus's, Darwin's, and Spencer's theories and next a
discussion of Neo-Malthusianism.

By daring to mention, and even describe, contraceptive practices
then current, the authors were among the first to strike early
blows for freedom of discussion in a field hitherto forbidden.*
Also shocking to Victorians was their crass assertion that a
prejudice against birth-control even more culpable than that
resulting from moral cowardice, is the one
    consciously or unconsciously derived from the profitableness
    to the capitalist classes of unlimited competition of cheap
    unskilled labour. For never did the proletariat more literally
    deserve its name (from the Latin *proletarii*: the lowest
    rearers of offspring) than since the advent of the factory
    period, their rapid and degenerative increase indeed primarily
    representing 'the progress of investments'. (16)

Yet Geddes's unshakeable faith in life ran all through his
writings before and after and in 'The Evolution of Sex'. He did
not share that unobservant optimism which finds in animal life
only 'one hymn of love' and admitted that much of struggle,
cruelty, and selfishness exists among creatures as well as men.
But he saw altruism coexistent with egoism in even the lowest
organisms, and proclaimed the importance of cooperation as a
factor in evolution even before Kropotkin's 'Mutual Aid'. 'The
ideal of evolution is indeed an Eden; and although competition
can never be wholly eliminated ... it is much for our pure
natural history to recognize that "creation's final law" is not
struggle but love.'

A contemporary has written:
    in the 1890's, multitudes of young men in Scotland and in
    England owed their souls to the teachings of Patrick Geddes....
    Even a noble soul like Huxley could see in life essentially a
    'gladiator's show'. Geddes, pupil of Huxley, challenged the
    verdict in his books, in his lectures, in the flood of viva-
    cious speech which leaped from him like a fountain. I recall

* Annie Besant's 'The Gospel of Atheism' was published in 1877.

the thrill which went through an audience as he traced the
basal feature of all life to be the sacrifice of the mother
for her offspring and closed by saying, with his usual finger-
ing of the abundant locks and the phrase over the shoulder:
"So life is not really a gladiator's show; it is rather - a
vast mothers' meeting!"' (17)

This theme is even expressed graphically in 'The Evolution of
Sex'.   Plate 9(a) shows the 'two divergent lines of emotional
and practical activity,' as they spread out upwards from 'Protoplasmic identity' towards 'Ideal unity'. (18)

These find a basal unity in the primitively close association
between hunger and love, between nutritive and reproductive
needs.   Each plane of ascent, marks a widening and ennobling
of the activities; but each has its corresponding bathos,
when either side unduly preponderates over the other.   The
actual path of progress is represented by action and reaction
between the two complementary functions, the mingling becoming
more and more intricate.   Sexual attraction ceases to be
wholly selfish; hunger may be overcome by love; love of
mates is enhanced by love for offspring; love for offspring
broadens out into love of kind.   Finally, the ideal before
us is a more harmonious blending of the two streams.

'Chapters in Modern Botany' did not appear until 1893, five years
after its mention as in preparation in the 'Letter of 1888'.   The
only textbook Geddes ever wrote, it is still worth reading for
its skilful motivation of the reader to observe things for himself, and for its freshness of style.

He describes, for example, how the fall of the leaf is prepared
for in plants by a partition of soft juicy cells growing across
the base of the leaf-stalk where it is normally firm and tough.
These cells multiply and expand

into a springy cushion, which either foists the leaf off, or
makes the attachment so delicate that a gust of wind serves
to snap the narrow bridge binding the living and the dead.
That the scar should thus have been prepared before the operation is one of the prettiest points of the economy of woodland nature.... (19)

Virtually dead the leaves now are, empty houses from which
the tenanting molecules of living matter have vanished, leaving little more than the ashes in the hearth.   But these
ashes - how glorious! for in yellow and orange, in red and
purple, the leaves shine forth, glowing in the low beams of
the autumn sun.

'It is the misfortune of biology that Darwin was not a teacher',
Geddes writes in his preface and frankly admits how hard it is
to organise a morphological training that is 'truly Darwinian in
spirit from the beginning'.   One which lets both teacher and
pupil start out

neither with conning an inventory of plant-mummies, nor with
the tissue-unwrapping of samples of these; but with childlike

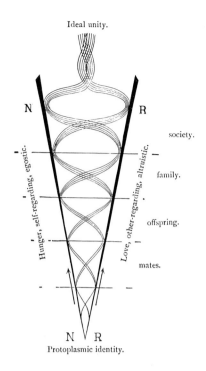

Ideal unity.

N   R

society.

Hunger, self-regarding, egotic.

Love, other-regarding, altruistic.

family.

offspring.

mates.

N   R
Protoplasmic identity.

P.G.'s diagram of the Evolution of Sex from 'Protoplasmic
identity' towards 'Ideal
unity'

University Hall Extension
Castle Hill for Prof. Patrick Geddes
S. Henbest Capper M.A. Architect

Ramsay Garden or University Hall Extension, facing the Esplanade of
Edinburgh Castle. The entire third floor (above the ground) was
the Geddeses' flat

watching, scene after scene, of the actual drama of nature, in which life interacts with life, and fate with all.

'Were it worthy,' he says of his little book, 'it should be dedicated to the memory of Darwin'.   From early encyclopedia articles on to his and Thomson's final opus, 'Life: Outlines of General Biology', Geddes praises Darwin as a lover and understander of nature.   In 'Life' he relates a favourite anecdote* of Darwin having invited a group of young scientists to his country home and spending a whole evening 'questioning each, and drawing him out on his subject; for no man was more open and eager to learn'.   Then, leaning back in his chair, Darwin said:

'I am always feeling my ignorance, but never have I had it more strongly brought home to me than to-night.   You have surprised me! - and again and again!   What you (pointing in turn to each) know about cryptogams, and you tell me about phanerogams, and you about bacteriology, and you about embryology, and you about fishes, and so on, is most interesting!   It's something astonishing!   You do indeed make me feel my ignorance, and what I have missed!'   Pause: then jumping up from his chair, and with thump on table: 'But - damn you! - there's not a Naturalist in the whole lot of you!' (20)

That Geddes himself took this lesson to heart is repeatedly proved throughout the 'Chapters'.   He warns that all textbooks including his own are poor, or downright harmful, substitutes for living nature.   'At the drama of evolution mankind are but the awakening spectators.'

We cannot have, it is true, too full a list of the kinds or 'species' of the innumerable and strangely varied *dramatis personae*; we cannot look too closely into their corpses as they fall, else we shall fail to understand much....

But not the smallest living scene - not even this bee upon its flower - is to be understood from our museums and herbaria: for this exhaustive division of labour, with its entomological and botanical specialists, in winning extension of exact and detailed special knowledge, had lost sight of developing that vague general knowledge with which childhood begins.   Watching the bees among the flowers is an old and happy occupation, not only for children but their elders.... (21)

'Am I to read no text-books then?' the dismayed student constantly asks.   The writer for one answers, with deeper and better justified conviction every year: Read? certainly not; Consult? yes, constantly, by help of the index, for every point and difficulty as it arises, for all information as it is desired.   Thus you will gradually get all the facts and results and methods which it contains, while thus, and probably thus only, can you avoid that elaborately formalist analysis of the subject from which every science has such difficulty to

* Told to Geddes by his friend George Murray (later Keeper of Cryptograms, Edinburgh Natural History Museum) on the latter's return to London from Darwin's home at Down, c. 1879.

escape.   Botany is a drama of nature, and this summer is your
opportunity of seeing it....

If the many teachers, colleagues and former pupils who supported
Geddes were indignant when 'My Lords and Gentlemen' ignored them,
a greater disappointment was in store.   The years passed, but
their man did not become either a 'Scottish Darwin' or even as
well-known academically as his own faithful, hard-working student.
To borrow someone's happy phrase: 'Pat Geddes's greatest contribution to biology was J. Arthur Thomson'.   Scientists who knew
both men intimately have said that in general Geddes had the
ideas, the challenging theories, while Thomson had superior talent
as lecturer and writer.

Many years later Thomson generously explained the gap between
their public achievements in this way:
> If he (Geddes) had even published the interpretations of floral
> and indeed organic structure which he scatters generously among
> pupils and friends, his reputation and value would have been
> much greater.   Had he followed up these interpretations by re-
> search, he might have been the greatest of botanists....   As
> one who understands plants, he is probably ... *facile princeps
> botanicorum*;   but the pity is that many botanists know him only
> as a sociologist! (22)

Even so, Geddes equalled both masters and colleagues as a teacher
of living nature, and he himself possessed the imaginative intui-
tion and the almost mystical reverence for nature which he so
admired in Darwin.   Whatever value will be retained by Darwin's
special theories of evolution, he writes in the botany textbook,
'the world will always owe him thanks;   for his books have a
deeper use and significance'.   They bring back that close contact with nature which primeval man had in the forest, where
formerly 'a Dryad hides in every tree, while Pan roams through
the glade'.

RAMSAY GARDEN ... UNIVERSITY EXTENSION AND REFORM

What did Geddes do the nine months of each year when not teaching
botany?   How could he ever support himself and family on his partial salary from UCD?   The basic fact is that he kept his headquarters in Edinburgh and simply carried further all the projects
he had either started on or dreamed of during the years 1880-7.
One of these was 'University Hall Extension' consisting of Ramsay
Garden, a five-storey co-operative block of flats at the top of
the Royal Mile, adjacent to the Castle Esplanade;   and of Ramsay
Lodge, a new residential unit with rooms for forty-five men
students.   The latter was inaugurated in April 1894, the former
in the autumn of 1893 at which time Geddes moved his family from
James Court to the spacious twelve-room flat that took up the
entire third floor of Ramsay Garden.

In order to finance the block he had invested in it £1,500 which

Anna had inherited from her father and persuaded a group of people
to buy the other flats in advance, each paying his share as construction progressed.   One overly cautious lady, however, refused
to pay until she saw her quarters actually completed, and this
annoyed Geddes so much that he bought what was to have been her
flat himself.   He could then make her pay rent as a penalty for
lack of confidence, but only by tying up capital he did not have.
Later, he would confess to Norah that this was the beginning of
the money troubles which periodically beset him and his family.
Indeed, the building of Ramsay Garden inadvertently caused Anna
much emotional stress even before the financial worries came
along.

For most of the period mid-December 1892 to mid-January 1893 Geddes
lived alone at James Court in Edinburgh while Anna, with Norah 5
and Alasdair 1½, shared a flat in London with her sister Bex,
recently widowed.   He was so wrapped up in the construction and
plans for decoration, along with other business including feuds
with legalistic theologians of New College which owned much adjacent land, that he kept postponing his return to London.   In a
series of poignant quotations from frequent letters to Patrick,
Paddy Kitchen (pp. 126-8) shows how upset Anna was at times even
though she realised how important it was for him to stay on in
Edinburgh.   A brief sampling:

> 22 Dec. ... No word from you again this morning....   Is there
> any chance I wonder of your being home for X'mas? ... I feel
> so in the dark about you.
> 27 Dec. ... This is very sad news, but there's no use mourning
> about it; & further I much prefer knowing when I am to expect
> you, than being put off from day to day.
> 4/1/93 ... Of course I'll be back on Sat. to receive you,
> [Anna was visiting Patrick's brother Robert and his wife
> Maggie at Ryde, Isle of Wight], whenever you come, in the in-
> fernal hole you are good enough to call home!   I appreciate
> the compliment.

On the other hand, reading through all twenty of her December-
January letters, one finds some mitigating information.   Patrick
also wrote almost every day but his letters did not arrive many
mornings until after Anna had gone to the British Museum to look
up this and that book at his behest.   An earlier comment she
made on the 'infernal hole' was that 'in this small house *I* in
particular never seem to find a quiet corner'.   Though she continues to ask about his date of return, there is mainly cheerful
news in her letters, and always an affectionate salutation - sometimes even two!

> 29 Dec. ... I couldn't go to the Brit. M. this morning, because
> it was so foggy, & they can't get at the books I want when it's
> foggy....   Thanks for the photo of the house [Ramsay Garden],
> it looks very nice indeed.
> 5.1.93 ... Yr letter from Perth reached me here [Ryde] this
> morning.   Thanks, dear, for writing.   Very glad of news of
> grandparents [Patrick's father and mother].
> 9.1.93. ... I am sure a *great many things* will be very beauti-
> ful in the new house.

Not until Friday 13 January did Anna get a telegram confirming
'My fears that you were going to stop away till the very last
moment', i.e. Saturday or Sunday night.   But she promised to
clear all engagements
    so as to have all the time with you that I possibly can.   I'm
    wondering how you'll ever get time to tell me all about things
    in Edinburgh!   I've got all yr letters to question you upon!
    ... Auf Wiedersehen - for this is my last letter - really.
    'I'm well nigh dizzy wi' the thocht'.

Beginning on Monday 16 January 1893, 'Patrick Geddes, F.R.S.E.,
White's Professor of Botany at University College, Dundee (University of St. Andrew's)', as he was described in the Syllabus
put out by the London Society for the Extension of University
Teaching, gave a course of ten weekly lectures on 'The Theory of
Organic Evolution'.   And about ten months later he and his
patient, loving wife could move into 'the seven-towered castle'
he had built for her at the top of the Royal Mile.

The upper floors of Ramsay Garden had incomparable views from all
windows.   The bay at one end of the large double drawing-room
looked due north across city and Firth to the old Kingdom of
Fife, with a foreground vista of Princes Street Gardens.   At the
east foot of the house was the old cottage of Allan Ramsay the
poet, now incorporated into the new Ramsay Lodge.   From the
south and southwest windows another wide panorama was visible:
the Esplanade and Castle right at hand and, far across the city,
the Pentland Hills, where Robert Louis Stevenson had been living
and writing just a few years before.   'No king or queen,' commented one visitor, 'ever had finer outlooks from palace windows.'

Norah, who lived in Ramsay Garden as a child and again when
married, has described its interior in detail.
    My parents' bedroom was spacious and beautiful.   Along one
    wall and over the fireplace were frescoes by Charles Mackie.
    The long wall showed a series of country scenes arranged in
    sequence according to season and time of day....   Their
    double bed was sumptuously carved to illustrate the theme of
    'My heart, my heart is like a singing bird', Christina
    Rossetti's love song.   Two dissimilar doves carved in the
    round faced each other from the ends, and a peacock in relief
    adorned the head of the bed.   Some mornings we climbed over
    the end and got in beside my parents.
        August was a time of great doings: much entertaining on
    the part of my parents of guests, foreign and British.   The
    house was planned for receptions, with less emphasis on dinner
    parties, for the dining room was relatively small.   But there
    were two large drawing-rooms divided only by double curtains.
    They had frescoes on all the walls.   Four panels, one on each
    side of the curtain, were by Charles Mackie, illustrating the
    seasons....   The other panels were all seasonal too, painted
    by Mary Hill Burton, daughter of the historiographer Royal.
    A scene of daffodils, of apple blossom, of hedgerow, tall cow
    parsnip and on the other side the autumnal undergrowth in the
    Highlands with rose hip and tawny bracken in abundance. (23)

Her father's many projects in the 1890s impressed her greatly.
'I could not but be aware of all this activity and felt it to be
very important.   My father's study with three secretaries and
its business room bore witness to this and I imagined him and his
work making history.'

His early involvement with University Extension teaching has already been briefly mentioned in Chapter 4, and the much expanded
syllabus of some of his own extra-mural lectures is recorded in
'Chapters in Modern Botany'.   He heartily approved of extending
university teaching to students and adults unable to attend the
regular centres, and one of his main reasons for working in the
movement was to reform the universities themselves.   He told the
people of Dunfermline in 1887:

> Were the proposed Extension to consist of university instruc-
> tion as it now exists, I for one would not be asking the manu-
> facturers and merchants of Scotland and the provincial towns
> to provide themselves with it.   Undeniably something very
> different is required. (24)

A complete reversal of academic policy was needed, he wrote in
the 'Scottish Review' for January 1888, so that teaching would
dominate mere routine *examining*.   As a case in point he emphasised the positive effects of extra-mural teaching on the
established centres of learning.   First, the 'strikingly fresh
and original lecture syllabuses, and the vivid and enthusiastic
teaching and learning which lecturer and pupils mutually elicit.'
Next came the

> education of the teachers themselves, each of whom has to be
> far more fully on his mettle to keep his country audience
> well in hand, than in his class-room at the University;   for
> too many students of the latter seem like sullen and dispiri-
> ted prisoners receiving punishment before trial, after one
> has had experience of the naive and stimulating freshness of
> the other.   And a yet more important side of the teacher's
> own education is in progress - the moral one - he learns
> that study can be well done for love, and without competition;
> his every day's work goes towards righting the vicious modern
> subordination of teaching to examining. (25)

In his own case, the printed syllabus proved a special boon to
students.   Discursive by nature, all-inclusive in interests and
sometimes too quiet in delivery, he needed the restraining influence of a formal outline to bring him somewhere near his goal
at the close of the lecture.   When words got lost in the beard,
or were addressed to the blackboard while he drew some diagram
thereon, it was no small comfort for listeners to be able to
refer to the already prepared notes.   Yet, all things considered,
he was able to put ideas across to his listeners, and often to
stir them to action.

Take the night of 16 October 1891.   A public meeting was being
held in Aberdeen to discuss the aims and the means of promoting
technical education.   Midway in the proceedings the chairman

announced that the audience 'had the advantage of the presence
that evening of one of the most able workers in the cause of technical education in Scotland: Professor Patrick Geddes of University College, Dundee'. (26)   This introduction was quite accurate,
for along with all his other activities he had found time to
pioneer in this movement as well, just as Huxley had done in
England.   When the welcoming applause subsided, Geddes began by
telling the Aberdonians what serious damage and loss occurred in
every industry because of imperfectly educated workers.

> We have marvellous smiths and metal workers, better than any
> others that have ever existed. We have the best ship-
> builders in the world and the greatest miners (applause), for
> it is in these very industries that technical education is
> best developed. But we are certainly not as good architects,
> not as good artistic producers in any line; there is a very
> noticeable inferiority between the beautiful and dignified
> buildings of an ancient city and the dreadfully coarse forms
> and dreadfully dull and uninteresting styles of the present
> speculative jerry-builder.

> There is an art which is almost entirely forgotten in this
> country, which is practically unknown - the art of forestry
> (applause). The knowledge of that art would develop our re-
> sources tremendously, yet there is no forestry known. Still
> we plant trees and we do it, I am bound to say, in the most
> ignorant and chaotic manner of any nation on the face of the
> earth. In the same way, we have very famous Scotch garden-
> ers, but, for all that, the practice of horticulture is not
> so far advanced as it might be. Everybody knows that fruit
> and vegetables, compared with other countries, are very scarce
> and dear.

He then called for a new college of agriculture:

> Every one of the Universities already possesses three-fourths
> of all that is required for an agricultural college; it would
> be sheer economy to adopt this system.... We are proud in
> some respects of our democratic Universities, but they are
> largely middle class, they are largely the school guilds of
> lawyer, doctor, preacher and teacher. We want to make them
> besides that schools of industry; schools of farmer, crafts-
> man, painter and architect. We want to avoid that separation
> which has taken place in Germany with disastrous results, that
> separation of the school of industry from the school of sci-
> ence which produces *pedants in the University and Philistines
> in the workshop.*

> There are many who shudder from the thought of an education
> commercialized by industry but I shall ask the working man
> and his representative in Town Council or County Council to
> hold fast, and to teach the doctrine that what we are coming
> to is really *industry ennobled by education.*

Although such an integrated college of agriculture was not established, Geddes, aided by his friends Martin White and Frank Young,
did succeed by the end of that same October in organising 'The
Scottish Society for the Promotion of Technical and Secondary
Education'. This body later accomplished much of what he called
for.

He furthermore played the role of 'Wandering Inspector of Universities', as he later described it, having assumed its self-imposed
duties even before going to Dundee.   Not a year passed without
some criticism of academic evils, some suggestion for their reform,
being woven into an article, a lecture, or a book.   For instance,
in 1890 Geddes brought the University College summer term to an
end by delivering the traditional public 'closing address'.   For
his subject he chose 'Scottish University Needs and Aims'.

> The occasions on which a Professor has any opportunity of
> speaking to a wider public than that of his class-room are so
> rare that I must be pardoned if, instead of endeavouring to
> make the sort of after-dinner speech which might best suit the
> present festal occasion, I deliver myself of some more serious
> thoughts which have long been in my mind....
>
>   I am first going to say some unpleasant truths, such as
> people too rarely hear.   But let me urge in extenuation that
> I am not a candidate for political honours from the other side
> of the Tweed, that I should repeat the usual cheap flatteries
> about our being the best educated and the most advanced people
> in the world....   On the contrary, I claim to be no less
> enthusiastic a Scotsman than any here, and to have that pat-
> riotism, too, which a man never feels so fully as when he has
> lived some thousands of miles from home, but which does not
> shrink from honestly comparing the strong and weak sides of
> one's own people with those of others. (27)

After noting that 'historical studies do not as yet even exist in
Scotland', he proceeded to interpret her history himself.   On
the one hand: world-famous scholars, writers and men of action;
on the other, both popular and cultural movements always two generations or so behind those of other lands.   The Scottish Reformation was one example, while in politics he saw 'the noblest of
our ancestors in each century, dying manfully for a dead cause,
that of the ideas of the century before'.   'In short, our history may be summed up in this one sentence - that while the
Scotsman has often led the age, Scotland has no less often lagged
behind in it.'

At this point Geddes reminded his academic audience of the very
current event of 'the present University reform, which we are all
discussing', and put it into his interpretive nutshell.   It is

> just a ripple of that wave of academic progress which began in
> Germany in 1809; and which out of a jumble of small, sleepy
> hide-bound, so-called Universities, essentially mere secondary
> schools, made the vast thought centres from which the world
> has ever since been learning.   This new renaissance has fol-
> lowed the same laws as the old one.   It took, indeed, forty
> years to reach England, and here is coming into sight after
> fourscore.   Is it indeed fully in sight?

The Scottish Universities Commission, appointed by Parliament in
1889, was spending two years looking into conditions north of the
Tweed.   Aside from financial support and the changes 'of mere
curriculum and staff, which the Commissioners are doing their

best to give us', said Geddes, there are other needs to satisfy
and aims to reach.   For example, 'some rational adaptation of
that College life which gives the English University man his
superior geniality and breadth, his greater readiness to enter
upon the best work of the world'.   He then referred to 'our
rising University Hall in Edinburgh' as an experiment proving the
value of student residences in the Scottish milieu.   Further,
he wanted each University not only to have such Halls for under-
graduate students, but also 'to send its best graduates, helped
by scholarships if need be, for a year or two of foreign work and
travel'.

Geddes had spent several months the previous winter visiting universities in France, Germany, Belgium and Switzerland and stated:
> The student ... needs a better greeting than the railway
> porter's when he arrives at his foreign destination.   Friends
> and a home, studies and expenses;   all must be provided for in
> advance.   Nor is such an organisation hard to arrange, for it
> almost exists already.   At Montpellier or Lyons, for instance,
> at Geneva, Jena, or Freiburg, I can positively promise a stu-
> dent far more than is yet arranged for him, outside University
> Hall at anyrate, in any Scottish University....
>
> He will be received when he arrives, introduced to some of
> the best among his fellow students and to the cultured society
> of the town;   he will be looked after in sickness, his studies
> will be arranged for and directed, his work and regularity
> faithfully certified to his University.   Such a reception ...
> is often a veritable escape from the Slough of Despond to the
> Interpreter's House;   nay, it may be from the dungeon of Giant
> Despair and even graver perils to within sight of the Delect-
> able Mountains. (28)

In this connection the speaker disclosed that while in Paris he
had got the idea of reviving the 'ancient Scots College' and had
organised a French committee of distinguished scientists and
scholars which included Pasteur and Ernest Renan.   A St Andrews
committee, of which he was secretary, was likewise involved in
the plan to purchase the old Scots building in Paris dating from
1325 and use it as a hostel for Scottish students attending the
Sorbonne, as in the Middle Ages.

Of all the witnesses appearing before the Scottish Universities
Commission, none could have been more challenging and disturbing
than Professor Geddes from UCD.   On his first appearance in
October 1890 he gave its members a complete history, illustrated
by charts, of higher education from Grecian times to the present.
Another document was his 'common denominator diagram' which outlined, for purposes of comparison, all the rival proposals for
improving the universities.   Presumably, he also distributed
copies of his Dundee closing address on 'Needs and Aims' which
had been printed in the 'Scots Magazine' of the previous August.
His next appearance was in mid-July 1891, not many weeks after
Anna had given birth to their first son, Alasdair.

What he had in the way of new testimony is clearly indicated by a
one-page, seven-point 'Abstract of Evidence' which begins: (29)
'From results of an additional winter's travel (1890-1) through
foreign Universities ... witness is prepared to confirm and continue his evidence laid before the Commissioners in October 1890,
if desired.'   Point V had to do with the 'Report of University
Hall' for 1890-1 with emphasis on the fact that the residents lost
none of that independence which rightly is an old and cherished
tradition in Scotland.   Instead of having University Hall admin-
istered by wardens or masters, the students themselves assume full
control of the internal management of the houses.

> They decide who may be a resident, what the rules of conduct
> shall be and how enforced; they take turns in supervising the
> domestic staff which prepares meals and cares for the rooms;
> and finally, after dividing the actual cost of rent and pro-
> visions among their number, they live more comfortably and
> more cheaply than is possible anywhere else in Edinburgh.

If asked for figures, Geddes could reply that from the modest
beginning in 1887 with seven students in one flat, the Hall four
years later comprised the whole tenement at No. 2, Mound Place as
well as a former mansion in Riddle's Court with a combined total
of forty residents.   Not an imposing number but still quite an
achievement, for despite lack of support from civic and academic
sources his plans for tripling this figure were already under way.
Yet the greatest significance of University Hall was that it
brought together for the first time in Scotland, undergraduates
and graduates from different fields of study and research.   That
young men of science and law, of medicine, theology and liberal
arts were able to converse at meals and in the common room, and
cooperate in self-government was, in Geddes's view, a start
towards bringing synthesis into fragmentary specialisms.   Furthermore, by themselves living in the midst of acute slum problems
and of attempts at civic renewal these students got some awareness of what existed outside the shelter of academic careers.

Despite the length and variety of his testimony thus far the professor of botany had still, under Point VII, to report on his
Summer Meetings and on:

> Experimental results of this as regards - 1. Furtherance of
> University Extension Scheme.   2. Continued higher training of
> teachers.   3. Advantages of unified curriculum, i.e., assoc-
> iation of Humanities and Natural Science.... (and) 4. Higher
> Education of Women.

THE EDINBURGH SUMMER MEETINGS

The relief felt in certain quarters of Edinburgh when Geddes got
the chair at Dundee in 1888 proved to be very short-lived.   Given
his insatiable interests and fertile brain plus eight or nine
months of leisure each year, it was not surprising that rever-
berations of 'P.G.' were soon felt from Glasgow to St Andrews,
from Aberdeen to Edinburgh, and even beyond.   The initials P.G. -

standing either for Patrick Geddes or Professor Geddes - became known to Members of Parliament, Lord Provosts and working men as well as students of botany; the two letters were the trade mark of ideas and deeds which spread, first over Scotland in the 1890s and later to Europe, America and India.

With an equal amount of free time, energy and cerebration at their disposal, academics would have written shelvesful of contributions to some field; while personally ambitious men would have climbed high on social, political or financial ladders.   P.G., however, restricted himself intellectually to the biological and social sciences and to the history, needs and aims of universities.   In action he was content, until 1897, with mainly local projects of an academic and civic nature.

Every August from 1887 to 1899 Geddes, with a dozen or so collaborators in many fields, organised a unique series of vacation courses for teachers, graduate students, artists, musicians, men of letters and anyone else who was interested in the reconciliation of specialisms with synthesis of knowledge.   The prospectuses from these years give a tantalisingly meagre summary of all that was planned in the way of lectures, seminars, excursions, and special events in art and music.   Yet between their printed lines, one can still read the fascinating tale of growth from two small courses of 'seaside Zoology and garden Botany', offered to a handful of students in 1887, to a full-fledged summer school of art, letters, and science which by 1893, numbered 120 participants from a half-dozen countries and nearly a score of lecturers.

Geddes attributed the idea of organising these Summer Meetings to the well-known series of vacation lectures held at Chautauqua, New York since 1874, but he developed his courses along quite different lines.   For one thing he chose as their location, not an isolated spot on some enchanting Scottish loch but the workaday city of Edinburgh with its life of mingled sordidness and beauty.   The motto of the Summer Meetings was 'Vivendo Discimus' (By Living We Learn) and, asked P.G., what better way is there of learning something new than by taking part in actual life as people live it?   Secondly, he held constantly before both teachers and students the single goal of reuniting the separate studies of art, of literature, and of science into a related cultural whole which should serve as an example to the universities still mainly engaged in breaking knowledge up into particles unconnected with each other or with life.   His project can be called the first real summer school in Europe to combine art, philosophy of education, and science.

Each August for a dozen years the Lawnmarket quarter of Edinburgh became the focus towards which men of fresh ideas converged from the British Isles, Europe, and America.   Among them at different times were well-known men like Emile Yung, Swiss botanist;   Ernst Haeckel, the great German evolutionist;   and Henri de Varigny, French biologist.   From France also came Paul Desjardins,

publicist and philosopher; Abbé Félix Klein, widely-known educator; Edmond Demolins, the continuator of Le Play; Elisée Reclus,
renowned geographer, and his brother Elie, the anthropologist.
From Scotland, England, and Ireland came an equal number of prominent teachers, scientists, and men of letters, while America contributed William James of Harvard, Charles Zueblin of Chicago, and
many others.   Several of Geddes's Scottish colleagues in the
vacation courses later crossed the Atlantic to occupy important
university chairs.   James Mavor was to become professor of economics at Toronto.   Richard Green Moulton, of 'Modern Reader's
Bible' fame, was to be professor of English literature at Chicago;
and R.M. Wenley, professor of philosophy at Michigan.

The following composite schedule of a day at the ninth Summer
Meeting shows what activities the one hundred-odd participants
had at their disposal during four weeks in August 1895:
    8.00 a.m. Breakfast was served at the various houses of Uni-
versity Hall, which now included two new residential units:
Ramsay Lodge, opened in April 1894, holding forty-five men, and
Blackie House, a rehabilitated Lawnmarket tenement.   Riddle's
Court and Mound Place housed the women members of the school.
    9.00 a.m. Professor Geddes delivered one of the key lectures
which opened each day's programme under the blanket title of
'Life and Thought'.   This day he re-affirmed:
    Education is not merely by and for the sake of thought, it is
    in a still higher degree by and for the sake of action.   Just
    as the man of science must think and experiment alternately,
    so too must artist, author and scholar alternate creation or
    study with participation in the life around them.   For it is
    only by thinking things out as one lives them, and living
    things out as one thinks them, that a man or a society can
    really be said to think or even live at all.
        At this point the highest principle of our Summer Meetings
    comes into view, that of seeking to fit the student for some
    of the higher activities of life by letting him actually share
    them.   He is invited to become not a mere passive auditor,
    a receptacle for such tidbits of knowledge as may be tossed to
    him, but an active collaborator in all that we are carrying on
    here....
        If we have any dogma it is to teach a utilitarianism which
    treats life and culture as a whole and which may sometimes
    find the Beautiful more useful than the Useful.   For the
    rest we hold, if I may repeat, that thought does not exist by
    and for itself, as is too much the view of the old order of
    education.   It arises from life and widens in proportion to
    its range of action, of observation and of social intercourse.
    In a word, we learn by living! (30)
    10.00 a.m. A choice of civics or architecture was offered, the
latter course given by Professor Henbest Capper, soon to go to
McGill University in Montreal.   During the second fortnight the
civics course was replaced by one in history led by Victor Branford, MA, a man destined to play a large part in P.G.'s life in
the 1900s.   Another new colleague was William Sharp, a man of
letters involved with Geddes in an ambitious but short-lived
publishing project.

Victor Branford had graduated from Edinburgh University in 1886
with a distinguished record in mathematics, and for several years
served as a coach in natural sciences.   He was also a member 'of
the most variously distinguished group the University Halls of
Residence have as yet on record: since including Arthur Thomson,
later of Aberdeen;   Andrew Herbertson, later of Oxford;   W.S.
Bruce the Arctic and Antarctic explorer;   John Duncan, now R.S.A.;
and R. and W. Smith, ecologists'. (31)   Branford had also
studied history, and 1895 was at least his third year of summer
lecturing in addition to leading a daily seminar of which the
main activity was making a 'Chronological Atlas'.   The Art section of the summer school supplemented his work by preparing 'a
series of designs illustrative of history' and of the 'Historical Personages of Scotland' led by artists W.G. Burn-Murdoch and
John Duncan.

11.00 a.m. Again a choice of subjects: geography or linguis-
tics during the first fortnight;   French literature or anthropology the second.   Under the successive guidance of Geddes, Elisée
Reclus, and P.G.'s brilliant young assistant from Dundee, A.J.
Herbertson, the geography course portrayed the origin and growth
of cities in a manner as fascinating and imaginative as though
the subject matter had been a plot in fiction.   A great travel-
ler and the first to write a Universal Geography, Elisée Reclus
was also a colourful figure in politics.   It will be recalled
that young Patrick was a bank apprentice when both Elisée and his
brother Elie were exiled from France for their participation in
the Paris Commune of 1870.   Elie was also at the Summer Meeting
and lectured on anthropology.

Another distinguished Frenchman who shared this morning hour was
Abbé Félix Klein of the Catholic University in Paris, and he too
lectured in French.   Abbé Klein has written the following
account of his part in the 1895 gathering: (32)

> Having once attended the Edinburgh Summer Meeting as a stu-
> dent and without any special introduction to Geddes, I became
> associated with him so quickly that he invited me to return
> the following year as professor of French literature and let
> me share in his family life and in his friendships.   While
> treating thus cordially a Roman Catholic priest he at the
> same time carried on similar relations with Elisée Reclus, the
> great geographer and anarchistic sociologist, finding a way
> to link under his auspices two such different minds.   He com-
> pleted our small intimate group with that remarkable person-
> ality, Edmond Demolins, the founder of the *Ecole des Roches*
> and one of the renewers of education in France.*

12.00 noon. Students could now attend either J. Arthur Thomson's
courses in biology or another series of foreign language lectures.
The latter dealt with contemporary conditions in France, Germany,
and England and were given by Louis Hamon, Professor Delius of

---

* Demolins also wrote a best-seller extolling Anglo-Saxon
schools: 'A quoi tient la supériorité des Anglo-Saxons?' Paris,
Didot, 1897.

Bonn University, and Edmond Demolins.   The end of the midday
period was marked by the firing of the one o'clock time-gun at
Edinburgh Castle, which reverberated so suddenly and so loudly
that poor Monsieur Demolins involuntarily leapt out of his chair
daily at exactly one o'clock.

The time-gun also signalled lunch at University Hall.   When
plates had been emptied observant eaters noticed that they bore
the Geddesian motto, 'Vivendo Discimus', baked into the pottery
along with a University Hall coat-of-arms adapted from that of
Edinburgh University.   The cutlery bore the same motto.

   2.15 p.m. The afternoon lecture period was given over sometimes to pedagogical discussions and again to chemistry or geology, followed by various seminar and studio projects.   (The
Sloyd workshop directed by a native Swede had, however, been in
progress since the close of P.G.'s morning lecture.)   One group
made costumes for a historical show to be put on during the last
week in August, a pageant re-enacting some early legends of
Scottish history.   Norah relates:

   My father arranged excursions to make the past live again, and
   one I recall vividly.   The party had been landed by row boat
   on the island of Inchcolm and were busy making fires for a
   picnic tea when they heard voices across the water and, looking up, saw tall armed men standing and chanting in an open
   boat which approached the island in menacing fashion.
      Skirmishes resulted, for the peaceful 'natives' tried to
   resist the Nordic invaders.   I tried throwing things at them
   but presently was being convoyed as a prisoner between two hel-
   meted stalwarts while perched on the shoulder of the young man
   who had charge of me: to my intense humiliation and annoyance,
   for I must have been seven or so. (33)

In 1895 Professor Wenley, of Glasgow and Michigan Universities,
states:

   No matter what Professor Geddes's services may have been in
   the early days of the Scottish Extension Movement, there can
   be little doubt that his greatest achievement - next to his
   University Hall triumph - is his inception and entirely successful conduct, during the past eight years, of a Summer
   School of Art and Science....   Mr. Geddes's success is the
   more remarkable that it had been attained entirely without
   official assistance either from the University of Edinburgh
   or from any of the sister seats of learning. (34)

On the other hand, the Edinburgh Town Council proved more co-
operative, at least at first, and voted £200 in aid of P.G.'s
summer school for the 1892 session.   (Even so, he had to make
up a deficit that year of over £80 out of his own pocket.)   In
1893 and 1894 the grant was increased to £300.   In the latter
year a number of councillors attended the series of archeological
tableaux vivants produced by the art studio, but the sight of
primitive man discovering the use of fire or an ancient hunter
making the first musical instrument out of his twanging bow
caused a majority of them to disapprove of such 'bairns' shows'.

The result of this experiment in 'teaching history by dramatiza-
tion' was that the city council made no more grants-in-aid to the
Summer Meetings.

3.15 to 6.30 p.m. For those not taking Sloyd or expressing
themselves in some form of art, the main part of the afternoon was
devoted to scientific field trips.   On Wednesdays Geddes usually
arranged a special sociological excursion either in Edinburgh or
to some town near by.

8.00 p.m. Turn by turn there were dances, formal concerts
arranged by Mrs Kennedy-Fraser, the collector of folk songs from
the Hebrides, informal musicales planned by Mrs Geddes, or
popular lectures.   This evening P.G. himself took the chair to
discourse upon 'Edinburgh, Its Region and its Outlook'.   Here
was indeed the genius of these summer gatherings: the same in-
defatigable, enthusiastic and wrily humourous man who had opened
the day's events almost twelve hours ago.

10.00 or 11.00 p.m. (on one memorable occasion).   The forty-
five inmates of Ramsay Lodge were in various stages of disattire
and in various mental states as they reviewed the day's round
of lectures and work-projects.   Suddenly there came sounds as of
an alarm from the entrance hall.   Pyjama-clad men rushed to
their doors.   Was it fire or robbery?   It was P.G.   'Halloo!
Wake up!' he cried, 'It's a marvellous moonlight evening.   Come
along, we're going to climb up Arthur's Seat!'   When the same
scene had been enacted in Riddle's Court and at St Giles House,
a volunteer band of young men and women followed him on foot
down High Street and Cannongate beside Holyrood Palace, and
ascended the steep slope of that ancient volcanic cone which, as
tradition has it, was once the seat of mighty King Arthur.

Eight hundred feet below them lay Auld Reekie with myriad lights
and steeples now visible through, now shut off by, a blanket of
mist.   Beyond stretched the waters of North Sea and Forth, the
Pentland Hills, and even distant Fife, all bathed in strong
moonlight.   Geddes was silent and completely lost in the beauty
of the night for many minutes.   Then he began to talk of olden
times in this region, of early Celts, their legends and their
beliefs, and of his own dream of reviving past glories of Edina,
the old city, until it seemed one was listening indeed to an
ancient bard relating the history and foretelling the future of
his beloved land.   P.G. was at his best that night on the hilltop, and, as one of his friends said, he made those around him
think of the lines in the Kubla Khan:

  For he on honey-dew hath fed
  And drunk the milk of Paradise. (35)

JEKYLL-HYDE'S RETURN ... 'THE INTERPRETER'S HOUSE'

The original Dr Jekyll and Mr Hyde was a man wearing sombre
clothes and a mask who, on dark nights of the 1780s, was wont to
prowl in and out of the closes bordering the Royal Mile long
after honest folk had gone to bed.   During daylight hours he
was one of Edinburgh's most respectable citizens, being a well-

to-do craftsman and influential member of the council of city
fathers.   Yet under cover of darkness, he sneaked out of his
Castlehill mansion as a daring and highly successful burglar.
Deacon Brodie carried on this dangerously mixed life of respectability and lawlessness for many years until at last, denounced
by a confederate, he ended his Jekyll-Hyde existence on the
gallows.

Exactly 100 years later another striking figure was haunting High
Street and the Lawnmarket, but this time it was by day as well as
by night.   He knew each close and alley inside and out, and
could find his way through nocturnal fog as well almost as in
broad daylight.   But since this nineteenth-century prowler
carried no dark-lantern and wore no mask, every passer-by might
quickly recognise him as 'The Professor'.   That a part-time
holder of a provincial chair should be given this title in an
Edinburgh filled with eminent professors, tells much about the
impact of Patrick Geddes.

Residents of University Hall's various components inevitably experienced P.G. at first hand as well, and the glowing testimony
of J. Arthur Thomson and Victor Branford might lead one to assume
that all who met the pre-1900 Geddes must have been greatly inspired by him.   However, a medical student named Riccardo
Stephens not only found P.G. a mixed blessing but apparently
sought to even up matters by making him an incidental target in
an occult-ridden novel which satirised academic Edinburgh of the
early 1890s. (36)   Disguised in name, position and physical
appearance except for hair, 'The Professor' Stephens presented
was a two-faced schemer dominated by a proselyting Mr Hyde.
This was a fictitious professor of psychology called Grosvenor
or '"Shock-headed Peter", as he was familiarly dubbed by the
students.'

> Red-haired and red-bearded, his head was a perfect burning
> bush, and his temper was as fiery as his hair.   Nevertheless,
> he was a most astute diplomatist ... surprisingly frank at one
> time, but at other times working for his object in an un-
> scrupulous and roundabout way....   He was sanguine to silli-
> ness, yet far-sighted and intuitive to an astonishing degree.
> He would promise heaven and earth to anyone at any time, if
> he thought it necessary for his schemes, which were many....
>
> I have known him to turn aside quite unnecessarily to do a
> stranger a kindness.   I have never known him to spare a
> friend who seemed to stand between him and success.   One was
> taken up and dropped frankly, according to one's momentary
> usefulness or uselessness.   When the appropriate moment re-
> turned one must be ready to reappear, or the Professor was
> hurt beyond measure at what he was pleased to term disloyalty.
> He never spared others, and, to do him justice, was equally
> hard on himself.

The novel's hero, having just completed his medical studies, was
approached by Grosvenor after the capping ceremony about helping
him in a scheme 'which later on I will explain to you more fully'.

But the next time they met the psychologist had quite forgot this plan, and on a third encounter began to sketch out 'a fresh scheme'.

> Even now, mistrusting him as I always did, I could not but be moved by the breadth of view and bigness of conception - only to be jarred presently by some little word suggestive of fickleness and sharp practice....
>
> We walked through one street after another while he poured out his ideas for my sympathy. For it was characteristic of the man that he longed for a sympathetic hearer....   Often he talked a kind of shorthand of shadowly outlines, suggestions, and dashes, and at these times I found that one left him impressed by one knew not what, and with faint recollections of great possibilities hinted at, but no more.

The Summer Meetings came in for their share of ridicule as being the result of Grosvenor's paradoxical 'importuning of lecturers, eminent and otherwise, to take their holidays in Edinburgh, and spend them in lecturing, with or without pecuniary profit to themselves'.   Various characters in the novel attended the summer classes, themselves obviously more or less caricatures of academic and social figures in contemporary Edinburgh.   One was a Miss Verney who 'had enrolled herself in his [Grosvenor's] little army of female enthusiasts', and their joint presence had a stimulating effect.

> He grew positively boisterous, his sentences longer and more involved than ever, his diagrams more ingeniously far-fetched and incomprehensible. He held long discussions with Miss Verney, from which he came radiant and hopeful of everything. He talked of modern teaching methods as if they were entirely superseded. To hear him, one would think that he held the key to all knowledge, and shortly intended to unlock all the secrets of the universe.

To balance this picture of Geddes one will quote from his letter to 'Dear Dr Stephens' of 26 October 1895, the year before the novel appeared.*   The young doctor had collected fees from 'patients belonging to Riddle's Court', whereas, according to P.G.'s interpretation of 'those amicable discussions out of which our agreement arose', Stephens was supposed to act as medical officer for all 'residents and servants in University Hall'.   Financial difficulties were at the bottom of their dispute, for Geddes refers to a recent interview in which 'I again clearly explained the disasters which delayed my attempt to take over your whole debt.'   He also 'expressed regret and offered amends for the occasion on which I failed to write you by the day promised ... with regard to *the loan*'.   P.G. is sorry that

---

* The 'Scotsman' and 'The Glasgow Herald' reviewed the book with very faint praise and as a '... third-rate romance', respectively, on 9 and 12 March 1896. Unfortunately, neither reviewer made any reference to the Grosvenor-Geddes satire, so one has only P.G.'s reproaches and Stephen's ridicule as source material.

Stephen's disappointment has led him to take 'the course of failing me in the daily work itself' and closes with these words:

> As a sharer in my financial misfortunes - (ay, and as neces-
> sarily one of the very causes of that incessant anxiety and
> overwork which made me forget to write you the day I promised)
> it would ... have relieved your irritation instead of allowing
> it to accumulate and gnaw had you continued to work with me
> as I can say I have done, as I am still doing for you.   And
> so I state unhesitatingly my view that it is now your turn to
> express regret to me, your turn to offer amends - and which I
> would gladly accept - a return to that cordial co-operation in
> the interests of the whole Hall in which you were of old so
> energetic and so valued a Colleague.
>
> Yours faithfully,
>
> Pat. Geddes

We now turn back from what appears to be semi-fictional revenge
to more constructive realities around the year 1892.   What with
student residences successfully running and slum-cleaning projects well under way, P.G.'s comings and goings involved a tall
stone building on Castlehill, then the last one on the right
before reaching the Castle Esplanade.   Traditionally supposed to
have been the town mansion of the 'Laird of Cockpen', this structure was known in the 1880s as 'Short's Observatory' from the
viewing instrument which Mr Short, the optician, had in the
highest turret.   Again, it is thanks to James Mavor that we
know of what seems to have been P.G.'s first inspiration, if not
first actual visit to this vantage point.

> I happened to be with Geddes when the idea came into his mind.
> One day in a moment of leisure we paid our coppers and ascen-
> ded the tower to look at the passing show as it appeared in
> this huge periscope. (37)

Finding that the Observatory was available on lease, Geddes
immediately took possession of it and named it 'appropriately
Outlook Tower.   It was indeed symbolical of a new outlook upon
life'.

What he intended to do with this latest acquisition was widely
conjectured.   It was not suitable as a hall of residence, it
enclosed no courtyard in need of cleaning, nor could its rooms
accommodate all activities of the Summer Meetings.   In later
years P.G. liked to explain that, from the very start, it was to
be an Outlook from which to survey city and countryside, an
Index-Museum providing synthesised clues, not mere alphabetical
ones, to other institutions and movements all over the world.
At the same time it should serve as an institute for action with
solutions for the problems of educators, captains of industry,
social workers and civic leaders.   In sum, it was the nerve-
centre and the keystone of all his projects in Edinburgh.

In 1895, nevertheless, P.G. was not so eloquently certain about
what the Outlook Tower would become.   In a letter to a collaborator which accompanied 'oldest jottings of notes for this
Tower of about four years ago ... and the big bundle that has been

accumulating through the summer', he expressed his intentions in
vague language.   He asked the student to keep these documents
because they tended

> to furnish a kind of teaching series for the essential thing
> I have got to teach ... the gradual building of Castles in the
> Air into Castles of Stone, of floating fancies into schemes of
> culture ... out of these once boyish sentiments and fancies
> and Castles in the Air I build you and your comrades this small
> towerlet of that great Northern citadel of Culture I have so
> often dreamt of but must leave others to build. (38)

Yet by 1899 P.G.'s fancies had taken such concrete form as to inspire an American visitor to hail it as 'The World's First Sociological Laboratory'. (39)   We shall shortly reconstruct one of
Geddes's guided, commentated tours of the Outlook Tower, after
quoting a few more words of praise by those who saw it in its
nascent heyday.   G. Stanley Hall, President of Clark University,
used superlatives.

> It is a magnificent new idea into which a vast amount of care-
> ful intellectual work has been invested.   It is so unique and
> original that the conventional mind would hardly be likely to
> appreciate it, but every intelligent man and woman deeply
> interested in science and education will see in the Tower a
> new departure full of untold possibilities.

The occasion for Hall's tribute was the public lecture delivered
in June 1905 by a churchman friend of Geddes, the Reverend John
Kelman, Jr, on 'The Interpreter's House on the Castle Hill'.
Afterwards, letters from scores of prominent men in Europe and
America were 'intimated and partly read' and a committee of
leading Edinburgh citizens was formed to secure financially the
Tower's completion and future.   The speaker began by expressing

> the immense debt of gratitude which I personally owe to him
> for illuminative and far-reaching thoughts;   and the immense
> debt which Edinburgh owes to him, not for thoughts only, but
> for the institutions which have been the outcome of some of
> them, and for the reserves of suggestion which still wait
> their embodiment. (40)

The fact that the Reverend Kelman did not comment on the title
chosen must show how generally understood in Edinburgh was the
transfer of The Interpreter's role from 'Pilgrim's Progress' to
P.G.   When printed in pamphlet form, the lecture bore the sub-
title, 'The Ideals embodied in the Outlook Tower, Edinburgh' and
served as the first guidebook for visitors.   In 1906, thanks to
Anna Geddes and certain members of the committee mentioned above,
a more systematic guide with illustrations was published: 'A
First Visit to the Outlook Tower'.

Let us now imagine The Professor charging up the Royal Mile with
several puffing persons in tow who probably have just been shown
all the student residences.   We move on up Castle Hill to the
Outlook Tower.   There we are herded up five flights of stairs on
to a flat roof, then driven into an eight-sided turret and up a

The Outlook Tower seen from the top of High Street

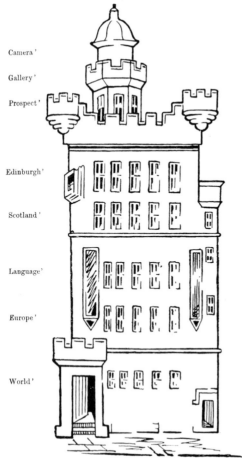

Camera'

Gallery'

Prospect'

Edinburgh'

Scotland'

Language'

Europe'

World'

THE OUTLOOK TOWER

Diagrammatic elevation of the Outlook Tower showing the purpose or contents of each storey. (*In margin:* Camera Obscura, Gallery, Prospect or Outlooks, Edinburgh, Scotland, Language or English-speaking countries, Europe, World)

steep, narrow wooden staircase with ropes for handrails.   About
half-way up we file out on to a narrow gallery which encircles the
turret some eighty feet above the ground.

'Now you can see what I mean by the "Outlook Tower"', says the
modern Interpreter sweeping his arm out towards a panorama as extensive as it is magnificent.   Edinburgh and its surrounding
region lie spread out before us to every point of the compass.
As we walk around the panorama balcony, Geddes keeps up a steady
commentary on places of historical or geographical interest,
mingled with items of philosophy.
    Perhaps you wondered why I hurried you up here from the street?
    Simply because the exertion of climbing makes one's blood cir-
    culate more rapidly, thus clearing fog out of the brain and
    preparing one physiologically for the mental thrill of these
    outlooks.

Here spoke the boy who used to rush out of school and up past the
family cottage to his discoveries on Kinnoull Hill:
    I have rambled through many cities but have found no better
    site for such a Tower than here in Edinburgh.   Not even from
    the heights of London or of Paris, nor from the historic pin-
    nacles of Athens or Constantinople, is there so complete a
    view of the natural and social world to be had as there is
    from this Castle Hill.
        Our greatest need today is to conceive life as a whole, to
    see its many sides in their proper relations, but we must
    have a practical as well as a philosophic interest in such an
    integrated view of life.   Hence the first contribution of
    this Tower towards understanding life is purely visual, for
    from here everyone can make a start towards *seeing completely*
    that portion of the world he can survey.   He can also grasp
    what a natural region actually is and how a great city is
    linked to such a region.

Back in the narrow stairway we climb still higher to reach the
hollow dome of the turret.   It is dimly lit by one small window,
which Geddes promptly closes, thus plunging us into pitch darkness.   'This is the Camera Obscura, or dark room, where for
practical purposes you are inside the bellows of a huge photographic apparatus.'   We form a circle around what seems to be a
white table-top suspended by cords from the dome.   The Professor
manipulates a lever, and there flashes on the round white surface
a moving picture of Edinburgh Castle.   People are walking along
the Esplanade, trees are blowing in the wind, but even more
striking are the sharp contrasts in colour;   the usually drab
rock of the cliff now appears vividly tinted.

The whole panorama at which we were just looking from the gallery
passes in review on the table-top, but magically different as
highly coloured miniatures of country and city scenes.   The most
ordinary tenement house is revealed as a composition of lights
and shadows with its tiled roof and chimney-pots done in beautiful
shades of red and orange.

It's very simple, a mirror at the top of the dome picks up
images in whatever direction I turn it with this lever and
reflects them through a lens which in turn focuses the picture
on this white surface as on a film in a camera.   The colours?
Your eyes are first made more sensitive to light by the darkness of the room.   Then the mirror picks up only the light-
rays reflected directly from the objects without the cross-
reflections which confuse our vision in broad daylight.   The
result is that here you see everything in its true colours
with fresh eyes.

With Ruskin, Geddes tells us that not many people ever learn to
see and laments:

How few in Edinburgh know the magic beauty of colours!   How
the grey, dark Castle, sable on its field argent, as the old
heralds picturesquely saw, in early sunrise has its ugly roofs
aglow with sapphire: or how the old High Street, in the morning a sunlit thoroughfare, is in the evening a dark blue river
of agelong sin and sorrow, a visible Valley of the Shadow of
Death, between high, impenetrable walls, over which floats a
misty fretted crown of thorns. (41)

Turning to material and social problems, Geddes asks how anyone
can understand this world, not to mention improve it, if he does
not have effective visual contact with external reality?   The
complementary panoramas from gallery and through the Camera can
re-awaken and re-educate unseeing eyes.   The first provides
that all-inclusive view of the world which both practical man
and philosopher need, while the other calls forth the artist who
finds beauty everywhere.

We now go back down the steep stairs and out on to the Prospect
Roof where the other specific viewpoints of the Tower are symbolised.   One of Edinburgh's chilly east winds has just sprung
up.   P.G. notices our shivers and is prompted by the wind to
describe us all as meteorologists.   He shows us the simple
apparatus consisting of thermometer, wind-gauge, and barometer
which serves to illustrate the methods and outlook of the
meteorological observatory.

Pointing to the eastern horizon, he asks what mighty forces have
created the Salisbury Crags or the volcanic cones of Arthur's
Seat?   Or, behind us, the rock of Edinburgh Castle?   'As soon
as you pose such questions you look at the world through the
eyes of a geologist.'   Geddes then rushes us through a dozen
other outlooks.   As botanists we are interested in the verdure
and flowers of the Princes Street Gardens, the apparent barren-
ness of the Pentland Hills, and the tiny herbarium which, shel-
tered in a nook of the roof, contains vegetation typical of the
region.   As historians we have relics of kings and queens, re-
formers and heroes, authors and statesmen spread out before us,
and traces of Viking, Roman and prehistoric times.   Adding the
viewpoints of chemist, engineer, economist and more, we observe
the region through many other pairs of eyes.   The sum total of

all outlooks of scholar and scientist is what the city-planner
calls 'regional survey', and Geddes points out that it is also
good civics.

Every region, he says, has its heritage of good and its burden of
evil.   Every inhabitant should strive to know what his region
contains, not only its wealth of natural resources, scenic
beauty, and heritage of culture but the opposite picture as well:
the evils of ugliness, poverty, crime, and injustice.   The
citizen must first study all these things with the utmost realism,
then seek to preserve the good and abate the evil with the utmost
idealism.

We then turn to the octagonal room and discover that it contains
apparatus which can extend the visitor's observations to the
widest extent of human comprehension.   There are devices to show
the earth's path through the seasons, and its relation to the
sun and the polar star.   There are models of a celestial sphere
and a larger cosmosphere to relate the earth to this universe and
to others.   There is an ingenious 'Episcope' which allows one
to visualize the world in the perspective it would have from this
Tower, with continents and oceans seemingly turned inside out and
backwards.   Scandinavia becomes a large imposing mass, Australia
is shrivelled up to a tiny spot, and other lands far and near are
similarly distorted.

At this point our heads are reeling from the rapidity with which
we have journeyed from prehistory to the future and from Edinburgh
to the limits of the universe and back again.   As P.G. motions
us towards a corner of the room we protest that we cannot cope
with anything more just now.   'Come, come!' he insists.   'Here
is the needed complement to all those outlooks on the external
world.'   Behind a curtained doorway is a tiny bare-walled cell
containing nothing but a single chair: the beginning of an Inlook Tower.   This is to symbolise the solitary meditation with
which every observer must complete his studies of the outside
world.

After a few minutes' relaxation we are ready to tackle the five
storeys of the building proper which constitute what The Professor
calls 'an Index-Museum to the world'.   Starting with the top
floor devoted to Edinburgh and region, we pass down through the
others, which treat of Scotland, the British Empire, and the
world in general, in this order.   A relief map of the Firth of
Forth region is modelled on the floor of the Edinburgh room,
while on its walls are sketches, prints and photographs illustrating the city past and present.   Other documents show the
mineral, industrial, cultural, etc., resources of the area.
There are maps and drawings portraying what the future of Edinburgh might be, how its defects can be remedied, and how its
heritage of culture and art may best be preserved and improved.
As Geddes puts it, 'after regional survey should come regional
service'.

The Europe room's most striking exhibit is a vast, coloured chart covering three walls to portray European history from the fourth to the nineteenth century.   The widening and narrowing of bands of purple for Roman Empire, yellow for invading Goths, green for Moslems, etc., present an unforgettable picture of the ebb and flow of these powers through the centuries.   The chart demonstrates that by such graphic representation of facts and ideas the alert visitor can emancipate himself from the tyranny of detail which, in history especially, is such a deadening influence.

At the stair landings between certain floors we are struck by some curious diagrams on stained glass windows.   Geddes explains that they, too, are 'Index' exhibits, but not in the sense of a mere alphabetical list of disconnected items.   As an example Geddes points to a diagram in coloured glass showing a landscape from mountain peaks to the sea with a text underneath naming the fundamental occupations that correspond to the natural divisions of this valley section.   Wherever you may be, he asks, between Alps and Mediterranean, between Highlands and North Sea, do you not have a definite, natural relation to all other places of that valley section?   Does not your viewpoint change according to whether you are miner, fisherman, or city-dweller?   The Tower, on the contrary, commands the whole region and instead of merely cramming facts into an unrelated A-to-Z catalogue, interprets them in terms of the three basic elements of sociology: Place, Work, and Folk.

Having arrived at his favourite science, P.G. discourses on Comte's classification of the sciences, Le Play's practical field studies and his own discovery of 'thinking machines' in Mexico.   Like a musician running over scales for the thousandth time, he explains the workings of algebraic logic in giving the possible combinations of A, B, C, as he folds and sketches on a piece of paper.   Two diagrams quickly take shape, first the nine juxtapositions of A, B and C (as illustrated in ch. 2);   then one using Le Play's Place, Work, Folk instead of algebraic symbols

PLACE	place-WORK	place-FOLK
work-PLACE	WORK	work-FOLK
folk-PLACE	folk-WORK	FOLK

Figure 5.1

(see Appendix, Figure A3).   At this point a lengthy lecture would
have ensued in reality, but we imaginary visitors move on quickly
to the next coloured window.   Depicting an Egyptian obelisk, it
is covered with Geddesian hieroglyphics and bears the Latin inscription, *Lapis Philosophorum* (see Plate 11).

My 'Philosophers' Stone', says Geddes, is another example of how
we may free ourselves from the limitations of the printed word.
By the juxtaposition of such idea-symbols on paper (or as in this
case on a window), one can see not only the most obvious relations
between them but actually discover new ones.   Watch how this
modern Lapus coordinates the arts and sciences into their logical
objective and subjective groups as well as according to their
historical development.   He interprets the symbols chosen to represent these divisions and their figurative relation to each
other, pointing out how the butterfly, representing psychology,
gets its sustenance from the flower, which is the art of education.   The function of education, he says, is to provide proper
nourishment for the developing soul.   Mathematics (at the bottom
of the stone) and logic (at the top) together make up the general
method of all the sciences.   The arrows pointing up and down
suggest two opposite ideals of action: the one which would use
knowledge and power primarily for the sake of increasing material
wealth, and the other which holds that material things should be
subservient to the ideal and the spiritual.

Moving on to the last window, we find in *the Arbor   Saeculorum*,
a Geddesian version of the Tree of Life drawn from both historians
and philosophers.   It portrays the temporal and spiritual aspects
of human history with the streams of power and culture caught and
defined at each succeeding age by means of the signs or objects
which characterised them.

> The tree has its roots amid the fires of life, and is perpet-
> ually renewed from them.   But the spirals of smoke which curl
> among its branches blind the thinkers and workers of each suc-
> cessive age to the thought and work of their precursors.   Two
> sphinxes guard the tree and gaze upward in eternal questioning,
> their lion-bodies recalling man's origin in the animal world,
> their human faces the ascent of man.   The branches symbolize
> the past and passing developments of society, while the bud at
> the tree-top suggests the hope of the opening future.   Issuing
> from the smoke-wreaths at the top you can also see the phoenix
> of man's ever-renewed body and the butterfly or Psyche of the
> deathless soul of humanity. (42)

The Tree at length explained, we are returned to the ground floor
where study of the whole world is suggested by a great globe and
books on geography and travel.   Geddes sends us on our way with
a final discourse:

> The Tower is incomplete in many ways, but each visitor may
> help to complete it as well as deepen his understanding of the
> world if he will return as a collaborator.   Read the mottoes
> inscribed in the entrance hall: 'Here may ye see infinite
> riches in a little room' and its complement: 'The eye sees

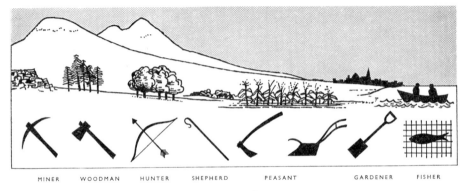

MINER   WOODMAN   HUNTER   SHEPHERD   PEASANT   GARDENER   FISHER

The Valley Section with basic occupations

Lapis Philosophorum or Philosopher's
Stone according to Geddes

Arbor Saeculorum or Geddesian
Tree of Life

only what it brings with it the power of seeing.'   With every
visit to the Tower and every application of its methods, one
may feel, at every stage of this widening survey and of his
growing powers of observation and understanding that 'In
Nature's infinite book of mystery I can a little read'.

That P.G. and his Tower were as nearly synonymous as a human
being and a material creation can be is well vouched for by Mr
Edward McGegan, curator of the Tower for many years.

> It was, in a very real sense, both one of Geddes's greatest
> inspirers and his most constant collaborator.   The point
> cannot be emphasized too firmly that Patrick Geddes whether
> in his personality or as a thinker or as a man of action -
> cannot properly be understood without a clear and sympathe-
> tic perception of what he meant the Tower to be, and of what
> the Tower itself constantly gave to him. (43)

He often said that it should be an Inlook Tower as well, and
that the Meditation Cell in the octagonal room on the Prospect
Roof was the beginning of this.   Any other plans he had exist
only in brief references in manuscripts and letters.   For
instance, in January 1896 Geddes wrote these lines on an otherwise blank page* entitled 'Plans for an Inlook Tower':

> No religions are true, for we have outlived them all.
> All religions are true, and we must relive them all!
> Cowards and fugitives hiding themselves in church while the
> Devil completes his organised conquest of their city.

P.G., UNLIMITED!

If the 1880s had seen a young demonstrator of botany develop into
a thinker whose searching criticisms and whose constructive
thought reached out far beyond his own field, the 1890s witnessed
his further evolution into a combined philosopher and man of
action.   Patrick Geddes became a leavening force in the life of
Edinburgh, of Scotland, and even of London.   By dint of forceful personality, an inexhaustible supply of ideas, and tremendous
physical endurance, he stood forth as a one-man university, a
one-man 'public service' company whose equal the Victorian Age
did not produce.   In short, he became 'P.G., Unlimited!'

The difficulty is to portray, by means of words on paper, qualities which in his case above all need the living man himself to
reveal them.   Patrick Geddes was a teacher in the Socratic tradition.   He preferred conversation to print as a medium of
sharing his thought with others.   Lewis Mumford characterised
him perfectly when he said that his books 'are but notes written

---

* Found and copied by the author in 1935 when, greatly helped by
Mr McGegan, he was gathering material for his PhD thesis on P.G.
At that time there were, he noted, 'Many sketches, thinking
machines and notes on this subject'.

as it were on the margin of his thinking'. One had to be in personal contact with P.G. in order to sense his magnitude, and even then, he was so complex and so universal that few could grasp the full measure of his mind and his activity.

Certain contemporaries have, however, recorded valuable clues as to the looming stature of this Scot already in the closing years of the nineteenth century. Israel Zangwill's report of a visit to Edinburgh in 1895 in 'Without Prejudice' is most evocative:

> It was a stormy morning when the mercurial Professor of Botany, recking naught of the rain that saturated his brown cloak, itself reluctantly donned, led me hither and thither, through the highways and byways of old Edinburgh. Everywhere a litter of building operations, and we trod gingerly many a decadent staircase. Sometimes a double row of houses had already been knocked away, revealing a Close within a Close, eyeless house behind blind alley, and even so the diameter of the court was still but a few yards.... Those sunless courts, entered by needles' eyes of apertures, congested with hellish, heaven-scaling barracks, reeking with refuse and evil odours, inhabited promiscuously by poverty and prostitution, worse than the worst slums of London itself - how could they have been left so long to pollute the fairest and wellnigh the wealthiest city in the kingdom?
>
> 'Do you wonder Edinburgh is renowned for its medical schools?' asked the Professor grimly, as he darted in and out among those foul alleys, explaining how he was demolishing this and reconstructing that - at once a Destroying Angel and a Redeemer.... His own destruction was conservative in character; it was his aim to preserve the ancient note in the architecture, and to make a clean old Edinburgh of a dirty....
>
> But whence come the sinews of war? Evidently no professor's privy purse would suffice. I gathered that the apostle of the sanitary picturesque had inspired sundry local capitalists with his own patriotic enthusiasm. What a miracle, this trust in a man overbrimming with ideas, the brilliant biological theorizer of 'The Evolution of Sex', the patron of fantastic artists like John Duncan! Obviously, it is his architectural faculty that has saved him. There stand the houses he has built - visible, tangible, delectable; concrete proof that he is no mere visionary.

The climax of P.G.'s building activity was Ramsay Garden, the co-operative block of flats, already mentioned,as facing the Castle Esplanade just above the Outlook Tower (see Figure
At the time he called it 'the seven-towered castle built for his beloved', yet in partial reality it was also one of the last straws which came close to driving him into bankruptcy and Anna to a nervous breakdown. For in making the sceptical shareholder pay rent, he came to 'punish' his own family more than her. Norah has written that before Arthur was born at the end of October 1895 her mother 'had too many worries which interfered

with her digestion and the nourishment of the foetus.   P.G. was
in the midst of his Celtic publishing, a ruinous venture.' (44)

Very fortunately for them, Patrick and Anna had many good friends
in Edinburgh who were also hard-headed Scots and who undertook to
save them from the 'defects of P.G.'s qualities'.   In May 1896,
with the help of such friends, was organised the 'Town and Gown
Association, Limited', a stock-holding company of which the primary purpose was to take over from Geddes most of the enterprises
he had started and put them on a strictly business basis.   Bearing in mind that this part-time professor earned only £200 a year
and that his wife had inherited just enough money to purchase
their Ramsay Garden flat, one can really be astounded by this
rough listing of the possessions he turned over to the T. & G.
Association:

1 The properties bought or held by Geddes during the ten
  years, 1887-96: Riddle's Court, St. Giles House, Ramsay Garden Lodge, and Blackie House, all four being
  parts of University Hall with a total of 120 residents;
  some eighty-five flats or apartments built or recondi-
  tioned in slum areas for working men; a number of
  shops along the Royal Mile, and a few building sites,
  the whole of which were valued at   £42,000
2 New properties just acquired,   £6,000
3 Furniture and furnishings,   £2,500
4 Reimbursement for sums advanced by Geddes for educational undertakings at University Hall and for repairing buildings,   £2,700

Yet at heart P.G. was loath to give up both burdens and managerial
rights.   Something in him wanted always to be planning, acquiring, directing.   Having a wealth of ideas was not enough, they
must be put into practice as well.

Thus, out of the grand total of £53,200 worth of buildings and
equipment P.G. actually received only a tiny percentage.   Not
only had much of the capital been furnished by friends and by
banks, but he accepted shares of stock in main payment of his
personal interest in the properties.   Furthermore he stipulated
that no dividend should be paid on the bulk of his shares until
the common stock should have received a $4\frac{1}{2}$ per cent premium for
five years.   When it became evident that the Town and Gown
Association could not pay a dividend one year, Geddes gave the
value of his Ramsay Garden flat to the company so that a make-
believe profit might be distributed.   Yet while he made nothing
on this T. & G. deal, it did remove the great burden of admini-
stering the numerous properties for which he was legally
responsible.

As its name implied and as stated by its Latin motto, *Floreat Res
Publica, Vivat Academia* (borrowed by P.G. from the student song
Gaudeamus Igitur), the Association was also intended to carry on
his projects for civil and academic betterment and serve as a
common meeting ground for those too commonly isolated groups of

men of affairs and men of learning.   In pamphlets and lectures
Geddes had long attacked 'Philistines in industry and pedants in
the university', and now he offered a practical opportunity for
townsmen and gownsmen to get together and fight their respective
accumulations of evils.

Probably the formation of the T. & G. Association proved more of
a relief to Anna than to Patrick, who looked on it more as a
means of furthering his ideas than as salvation from financial
difficulties.   While 1896 brought more good things than the
wife and mother had dared hope for a few months earlier, the
husband and father continued plunging into more projects.   The
tenth anniversary of the Summer Meeting was coming up in August,
the Outlook Tower was in the midst of its creation; and there
was the bold new enterprise, 'Patrick Geddes & Colleagues'.

For many years he had been interested in publishing.   His early
booklets such as the 'Analysis of the Principles of Economics'
and 'Every Man His Own Art Critic' were printed at his own expense.   Sooner or later he was bound to have a fling as a publisher and so his meeting with the Scottish writer William
Sharp in the autumn of 1894 had proved merely the opportune
spark.

Sharp and he organised a publishing firm of which Sharp was
manager and for which Geddes evidently furnished most of the
funds.   'P.G. & Colleagues' aimed to be a medium for the expression and dissemination of all that was stirring in the self-
styled 'Scots Renascence' of the middle 1890s.   Accordingly
he planned lists of books in these fields that an experienced
editor would have viewed with alarm, especially since the basic
principle of the new house was 'to the authors belong all
profits'.   Established publishing firms condemned his venture
as contrary to the tenets of successful business, while even
close friends held the private opinion that it was a foolhardy
undertaking and did not deserve to succeed.

In defence of Geddes it is now recognised that, regardless of
financial success or failure, his is the credit for having
launched the literary career of one of the most conspicuous
Scottish writers of the closing nineteenth century, Fiona
Macleod.   P.G. & Colleagues first published 'The Washer of the
Ford' and 'The Sin-Eater' (collections of Celtic-flavoured
stories) which were reissued by a London publisher (Heinemann)
when the original editions had been sold out.   Fiona Macleod
was a gifted and mysterious young woman about whom there circulated no end of rumour and speculation, for no one seemed to
know who she was or where she lived.   No one, that is, except
Fiona herself and Mr and Mrs Geddes.   The secret they kept for
many years involved a famous case of dual literary personality.
Fiona Macleod, who wrote with such feminine insight and gracious-
ness, was in reality William Sharp.   According to his mood he
wrote under either name, and as manager of P.G. & Colleagues he
was in a strategic position to edit his books and at the same

time guard the identity of their author.   Manager Sharp, unfortunately, was not able to provide the other books of the company
with the success of his own, and great was the blame heaped on
his head for getting P.G. into business difficulties that never
should have concerned him.

In the agreement between the Town and Gown Association and Geddes
it was specifically stated that his publishing venture was to
remain 'a matter of individual responsibility until its standing
and productivity have become sufficiently established'.   How far
away that state of affairs was would be documented, among other
incidents, in 1902 when Sharp's successor as manager brought
suit to recover £100 allegedly owed him by P.G. & Colleagues.
(The case will be returned to early in ch. 7.)

Besides publishing, other economic worries were the Old Edinburgh
School of Art, led by John Duncan and partly financed by Geddes,
and the big country house at Lasswade in the Esk Valley a few
miles south of Edinburgh.   He had envisioned it as an ideal
rural retreat for artists and academics on week-ends and during
summer holidays, but it, too, hung on his hands as a nearly total
loss, and he was obliged to let the Ramsay Garden flat and move
to Lasswade in order even partly to balance the household budget.

However painful the burdens of his financial incursions into the
realms of art, The Professor fulfilled all the requirements of a
patron, playing the role of a modest Medici in the Athens of the
North.   He directed the decorational activities of the Edinburgh
Social Union and was instrumental in getting local artists to
paint colour panels for the Royal Infirmary and murals for the
Sick Children's Hospital and the schools of St Mary's Cathedral.
The Edinburgh School of Art carried on an up-and-down existence
from 1892 to 1900 when John Duncan went to teach at the Parker
School in Chicago.   But before this, P.G. had his protégé
execute a number of panels and murals depicting Celtic figures
of legend and history (45) for the dining and common rooms of
Ramsay Lodge and St Giles House.   (The Ramsay Garden panels by
Charles Mackie and Mary Hill Burton have been described in ch. 5.)
Not forgetting the Outlook Tower, P.G. engaged another Scottish
artist, James Cadenhead, to paint friezes in the Edinburgh Room
portraying the main aspects of the city.

In 1724 Allan Ramsay had published 'A collection of Scots Poems
Wrote by the Ingenious before 1600', called 'The Ever Green', in
which he pleaded for 'a return to nature' and the old native
poetric tradition.   The residents of the new Ramsay Lodge and
Ramsay Garden, 170 years later, printed a Christmas book entitled
'The New Evergreen' in memory of Ramsay, whose house and whose
tradition they inherited.   This little book then suggested to
P.G. & Colleagues the possibility of establishing a semi-annual
review also called 'The Evergreen', as a medium of expression
for University Hall, the Outlook Tower, and Scotland in general.
Hence appeared the four numbers, 'Spring', 'Autumn', 'Summer',
and 'Winter' during 1895 and 1896.

In 'The Evergreen', which P.G. and William Sharp edited, may be
seen work in black and white by both Duncan and Cadenhead and by
a dozen other artistically inclined young men and women of the
Geddes entourage.   The literary contents of 'The Evergreen' were,
however, superior to the artistic.   The first number, 'Spring',
created something of a stir among critics.   A few Londoners
thought it was just 'a counter-blast at the established reviews',
and a young journalist by the name of H.G. Wells remarked of it:
'It's bad from cover to cover and even the covers are bad.'*
But other reviewers found it 'fresh in thought and beautiful in
form'.   Israel Zangwill said that to understand 'The Evergreen'
one had to know not just Edinburgh, but The Professor too: 'For
Patrick Geddes is the key to the Northern position in life and
letters.'

P.G.'s purpose was partly to carry on the spirit of Allan Ramsay.
'The Return to Nature', he stated in a prefatory note in 'Autumn',
    is a rallying call which each age must answer in its own way.
    The ending century has written its answer large in Science
    and Industry, in Literature and Art;   yet many solutions are
    still lacking.   Many of us are no longer satisfied with
    analysis and observation, with criticism and pessimism;   many
    begin to ask for Synthesis, for Action, for Life, for Joy.

He aimed at thawing out the 'frozen ice-pack of culture' in
Edinburgh and at bringing some feeling for art to 'that inferno
of industry', Glasgow.   Another part of his purpose consisted
in renewing local feeling and local colour in Scotland, not in
terms of a narrow 'patriotism' but to the end that she might again
become, like Norway, one of the 'European Powers of Culture' and
share in 'that wider culture-movement which knows neither nationality nor race'.

Geddes's own contributions to 'The Evergreen' represent some of
the best writing of his lifetime.   In 'The Scots Renascence',
for instance, written for 'Spring', ideas and words are happily
matched despite some long sentences.   He describes the signs of
a better future for Edinburgh and its people:
    Now the old courts and closes from Holyrood to Castle Hill
    are slowly but steadily changing, and amid what was and is
    the most dense and dire confusion of material and human wreck
    and misery in Europe, we have every here and there some spark
    of art, some strenuous beginning of civic sanitation, some
    group of healthy homes of workman and student, of rich and
    poor, some slight but daily strengthening reunion of Democracy
    with Culture;   and this in no parliamentary and abstract
    sense, but in the civic and concrete one....   Through the
    old town, so oft aflame, the phoenix which had long 'lain
    among the pots' is once more fluttering....

* This trite witticism was duly quoted by 'The Evergreen's'
editors in a publicity leaflet - along with other and more favourable comments!

THE

EVERGREEN

A NORTHERN SEASONAL

1895

Spring

PUBLISHED

IN THE LAWNMARKET OF EDINBURGH

BY PATRICK GEDDES AND COLLEAGUES

AND IN LONDON: BY T. FISHER UNWIN

One day noble traditions long forgot will rouse a mightier
literature, nobler localities still unvisited bring forth more
enduring labours for their crown.   Though Charlie may no come
back again, though the too knightly king, so long expected
back from Flodden, lie for ever 'mid the Flowers of the Forest,
though Mary's fair face still rouse dispute as of old, the
Wizard's magic book still waits unmouldering in his tomb.
The prophetic Rhymer listens from Elfland, Arthur sits in the
Eildon Hills, Merlin but sleeps in his thorn.   For while a
man can win power over nature, there is magic;   while he can
stoutly confront life and death, there is romance.   Our
recent and current writers have but touched a fringe of their
possibilities.   The songs of militant nationality may lose
their power, the psalmody of Zion no more stir the sons as it
was wont to do the fathers, yet gentler voices may reappear,
older runes win a reading.

Perhaps Edinburgh may some day regret the neglect of her greatest
practical visionary and far-ranging generalist, and seek to fulfil
the spirit of his Summer Meetings, his Interpreter's House and his
Scottish Renascence.

Chapter 6

FROM NEAR-EAST PEACEMAKER TO INTERNATIONAL EDUCATOR, 1897-1901

CYPRUS: *'IL FAUT CULTIVER SON JARDIN'*

At the turn of the century Anna and Patrick Geddes were taking part in the affairs of a world extending far beyond the horizons of his Edinburgh Tower. From its ground floor, where the globe made by Elisée Reclus symbolised earth-wide relationships, they stepped out into the Royal Mile to begin travels as far east as Asia Minor and as far west as St Louis, Missouri. P.G.'s international projects sometimes bore immediate fruit, sometimes not, but they were always tangible expressions of his interpretive thought and forceful enthusiasm.

An early result of his internationalism was the publication by P.G. & Colleagues of a booklet devoted to the Dreyfus Affair, then shaking France from Parisian boulevard to tiniest village. Written by a young Frenchman supposedly named Georges Guyou, the booklet went into three editions, for it was revised as new developments in Paris threw more light on what in the late 1890s seemed a hopeless confusion of accusations, counter-charges, spying, forgeries, suicides, and interference with witnesses.

'Guyou' himself served as an excellent example of how varied were P.G.'s contacts in Europe. In reality he was Paul Reclus, son of Elie and nephew of Elisée. Geddes had become friends with the latter even before they settled in Brussels in 1894, inviting them to lecture at the Edinburgh Summer Meeting. He also generously took Paul in his charge for many years, under the name of Guyou, which permitted him to travel more freely in France, and found him employment in the Summer Meetings, in the publishing house, and also as a skilled translator of scientific articles. Naturally, then, Paul carried on the tradition of friendship and collaboration between the families Reclus and Geddes after the deaths of his father and uncle.

That Geddes was an ardent Scot is conspicuous in his writings for 'The Evergreen'. That he was an equally loyal and intellectual son of France stands out in many a deed and thought since his first trip

to Brittany in 1878.   Yet with the approach of the twentieth century he placed himself no less convincingly in a third category,
of world citizenship, without abandoning either France or Scotland.
He set a pioneer example by his down-to-earth philosophy and practice of that vague abstraction called internationalism.   What P.G.
proposed and did was so unspectacular and so full of common sense
that it ought to have been rediscovered and reapplied by the statesmen of every generation from his on up to now.   He expressed it all
by the famous phrase of Voltaire's Candide: *Il faut cultiver son
jardin*.

'We must cultivate our gardens.'   Is this the language of international diplomacy?   Does this resolve war and peace?   By way of
explanation consider a concrete example, one particular instance of
violence and misery out of the thousands in recorded history.   It
was at the beginning of the year 1897 in the island of Cyprus that
Geddes appeared in the new and very active role of economic missionary to the Near East.

This small island, situated in the extreme north-east corner of the
Mediterranean, had shared the vicissitudes of 3,000 years of ancient
and modern history.   Phoenicians, Greeks, Egyptians, Romans, Cru-
saders, Venetians, Turks had each taken their turn at plundering or
ruling Cyprus, until in 1878 John Bull got the island as his share
of booty distributed at the Berlin conference of that year.   For
the next ten years Britain thus had one more interest in the
'Eastern Question', as the problems of all countries in the eastern
Mediterranean region were collectively termed at home.   The British government was considered at this same time to have assumed
responsibility for the protection of the Armenian minority in
Turkish territory, but the unrestrained massacres of 1895 and 1896
showed that Downing Street was unwilling or unable to champion the
unfortunate Armenians.

In August 1886, 6,000 of them were slaughtered in Constantinople,
and thousands of others tried to escape from Turkish terrorism.
Well-meaning individuals and societies in Great Britain deplored
these happenings and charitably tried to send food and clothing
out to the suffering refugees.   But Geddes saw that a far more
effective solution was imperative.   In January 1897 he and his
wife sailed from Marseilles, determined to study the 'Eastern
Question' at first hand.   They landed at the port of Larnaca in
Cyprus and immediately made a tour of the island.   Anna was happy
to share in this undertaking, even though it meant leaving the
three children in care of friends at home (and 15-month-old Arthur
had just had the measles!).   But these were slight inconveniences
indeed, compared to the hardships of the refugees she hoped to help
in some way.

For three months P.G. and Anna lived and travelled on the island.
What struck them on every hand was the need for agricultural improvements, since among Christian and Mohammedan peasants alike
'almost every conceivable mistake is made, every sin of omission
and commission' (1):   olive trees either unpruned or over-pruned;

the land under cultivation merely scratched with primitive wooden
ploughs; and so on.   Behind all this individual ignorance the
centuries-old curse of deforestation lay heavily upon every part
of Cyprus.   Where in ancient times great forests had flourished,
there were now only fever-swamps, dry river beds, barren hill
slopes, and skeleton hills.   This was Nature's answer to human
short-sightedness, not only in Cyprus but in the whole Mediterranean region from Spain to Syria, where drought, poor soil, and
poverty were the general rule.   Given such adverse economic conditions in Cyprus, plus the annual tribute of about £100,000 which
Britain collected for the Turkish government, how possibly could
the Armenian refugees be cared for?   Every steamer from the main-
land brought a score or two of destitute human beings in need of
food, clothing, and shelter.   Yet Geddes insisted that Cyprus was
exactly the haven to receive the Armenians.

He said that John Bull had here the opportunity of getting beyond
the old 'Spanish imperialism', which ruins both mother country and
colonies, by making the island an experimental station for colonial
education and development.   Instead of alms and soup-kitchens,
P.G. urged, give the Cypriots technical colleges, geologists, and
silk-experts.   Instead of sending out more police* and bureaucrats
from London, try shipping fresh seed, grafting-knives, and agricultural implements.   By so doing, the British might justify their
occupation of Cyprus and at the same time give the world an example
of reclaimed natural resources and salvaged human lives that could
restore hope throughout the whole Near East.

'The Eastern Question is ultimately an Agricultural Question',
asserted Geddes, but politicians, diplomats and administrators are
all agriculturally inept.   The futility of their efforts heretofore 'is but the common urban incapacity to govern agricultural
populations, to deal with rustic questions'. (2)

Geddes made plain in actual deed as well as in words what should
and could be accomplished.   Near the port of Larnaca he established several Armenian families on small farms rented for a period
of years, providing them with the necessary seed and implements and

* Describing the vicious circle of usury, debt, embitterment,
hunger, drinking and crime among the still oppressed Cypriots, P.G.
figuratively sees the Lord Chief Justice writing 'a report (innocent of any glimpse of social facts or theories), saying that ...
an increase of the Police Force already doubled since the British
occupation is the one thing needful'.   He gets local reinforcements which means that 'the best of growing youths are taken off
the fields to this army and new taxes are levied to pay for larger
barracks and larger prisons.   So these surviving peasants go to
the usurer again to borrow once more - are then doubly poorer.
New money = new crime = new report ... = new police and so on, in
downward spiral.   This is what they call the progress resulting
from British Rule.'   (From letter of 10 February 1897 to Mary and
Mrs John Hill Burton, quoted by Paddy Kitchen, p. 163.)

a small cash loan without interest.   At Nicosia, capital of Cyprus,
he organised a school of sericulture where both native Cypriots and
refugees could learn modern methods of raising silk worms and winding thread.   From the Armenian Monastery of St Maghar he took over
rent-free a hundred acres of land on which to settle a whole village
of refugees, complete with new houses (built by themselves under
direction of an Armenian architect) and with adequate farming implements.   Then, near the capital, P.G. bought a 1,500-acre farm
as a private investment, repaired its ruined irrigation works, and
planned for extensive fruit-growing and mulberry culture which
would give steady employment to many workers.

During their three-month sojourn in Cyprus, Geddes and Anna invested some £2,000 in 'productive relief'.   Instead of dissipating
the funds in outright and short-lived charity, they placed them in
projects that enabled refugees to earn their own living and to repay
the sums advanced to them.   Most of the capital was supplied by
British committees on Armenian relief and by hard-headed Edinburgh
business men whom The Professor persuaded into better human invest-
ments than more slums or more factory chimneys.

> All industry is no doubt good in its way ... but ... we have
> first to reconstitute the self-supporting agricultural village,
> in Cyprus, in Armenia, everywhere through the ruined East,
> before we seek to reproduce a miniature manufacturing and ex-
> porting town. (3)

In letters to a main supporter in London, Geddes reviews an astonishing amount of travel in many parts of the island and of almost
daily practical accomplishments.   Sometimes it was placing a
family on a piece of land, sometimes buying a whole farm.

> I am committing myself, in the first place *personally* as not
> only a proprietor in Cyprus with one fairly large estate to
> develop and soon probably another - (thereafter it may be
> another and another!) but also 2. *educationally* with Agricul-
> tural School (for Cyprus and for *our* young Colonists too!) (4)

P.G.'s brief but active period as 'economic missionary' clearly
revealed his brilliance in analysing all factors of a given human
situation, and his ability to find swift and sensible ways of reme-
dying both material and spiritual ills.   He fully realised the
vast amount of sustained work required to improve even the smallest
segment of society and conscientiously performed as much of this
follow-up labour as his multiple activities would permit.   But
the final success of his projects depended of course on how inspired others were and whether they had the necessary vision and
courage to carry them out, and this required him to combine leadership with teaching.

Armed with some knowledge of the geology of Cyprus, Geddes went out
in the arid mountain valleys and several times performed, to the
astonishment of Cypriots and to his own secret pleasure, the
ancient miracle of Moses's rod: he smote the rock behind which
mountain springs had sealed themselves up with heavy lime deposits
and the imprisoned waters gushed forth as of old.   But instead of

cloaking the 'miracle' in mystery, the Scot explained to his companions the elementary geological principles involved, so that they
might continue to increase the island's water supply.   He went on
to interpret the whole of Mediterranean history and most of its
current problems in terms of interaction between man and that basic
necessity, water.   While any geologist could easily duplicate the
beginning of his experiment, few sociologists or politicians have
followed Geddes to the conclusion of his reasoning.

He imagined our Aryan forefathers as 'driven from the ancient, well-
watered paradise garden by the flaming sword of drought, the piti-
less arrows of the desert sun'.   With the passing centuries shepherd turned into marauding nomad, sailor into pirate, and peasant
into bandit as the once fertile land, through climatic change,
deforestation, and erosion, became a desert.   At the bottom of
racial and religious conflicts Geddes therefore saw the primeval
struggle between flock and field, shepherd and hunter, peasant and
townsman: struggles engendered primarily by want and hunger, not
by human cruelty.   'Give men hope of better land, of enough food
for their families, and you remove a main cause of bloodshed.'
   And so we go home to Nicosia to buy and tend that first-seen
   palm oasis, to reopen its ruined wells, to mend its broken cisterns;   for here for Arab or Turk is the old-world earthly paradise....   Thus we may read and - if it may be - write in silent
   yet living and spreading symbol what is so hard to say in these
   days of futile word and bloody deed: that the future of the
   East lies not in the struggle, not in the victorious or beaten
   isolation of its contrasted races, but in their co-operation as
   complementary races;   not in the conflict but in the synthesis
   of its fragmentary philosophies.   It lies in such union of
   labour and thought as may again literally lead from the ruined
   well its life-giving waters, and melt from these frozen religions their imprisoned waters of life.   For wherever at this
   moment two Easterners are quarrelling in their poverty, four or
   six or ten might soon be cooperating in wealth and peace. (5)

The interpreter of international affairs continued:
   War we understand in terms and images concrete enough, from the
   fate of nations down to individual deed and suffering, life and
   death.   But of Peace ... how many have more than a mere abstract idea - a mere whiff of rhetoric, a mere colourless negative - of Not-War...?
      Who has not heard of Kriegspiel ... [but] How many have
   heard or thought of Friedenspiel?   Do we not need to understand
   peace in the concrete, to follow it from individual lives and
   labours up to its natural and human resultants?   The inquiry is
   a long one, as long and broad as history, yet we shall have
   begun if we grasp again its concrete symbol: the living olive
   branch of old.

Geddes pointed out that twenty or thirty years of constructive
peace must elapse before an olive tree can mature and bear fruit.
Consequently, one could
   begin to see how, for the future as for the past, the long-tended

olives stand with the house of peace, and how amid the deep-
rooted palms there is literally flowing ... the water which
bears the essential concrete possibility of restoring at once
material and social order, and with these the moral order also,
of renewing the sound social mind in sound economic embodiment.

Coming back to practical problems, he re-emphasised that permanent
agricultural and industrial openings must be provided
for those whom we now go on relieving, and at the same time
demoralising.... Many a lost leader is by this time, thanks
to our uneconomic philanthropy, settling down to become a begging
letter writer, since we do not set him to work. Cyprus then may
become one of the best of rallying centres ... provided the
available leaders are utilised on the one hand, and the capital
to start them with, be forthcoming on the other. (6)

He concluded a report to the International Conference on Armenian
Aid (London, May 1897) by saying 'we are now prepared to employ any
capital which may be intrusted to us, or to help so far as possible
any who wish independent investment, on lines in harmony with the
objects of this Conference'. Indeed, after Anna's and his
return to Scotland that spring he organised a joint-stock company,
'The Eastern and Colonial Association Ltd.' which, with a proposed
capital of £50,000, was to administer and expand the combined
humanitarian and economic enterprises they had started in Cyprus.

At least two versions of its 'magnificent prospectus', as Mairet
termed it, are extant. The first, of twenty-two pages, was signed
by Geddes himself, dated 12 October 1897, and lists him as chairman
of five directors. It contains maps, a description of the island's
geography and resources, its communications and agricultural possibilities, and the confidential predictions of a merchant, a civil
engineer and an agriculturalist. The second version, of 10 June
1898, contains only fifteen pages in that much descriptive material
had been omitted, and the predictions replaced by an account of
what the Association had already done in the field: invested about
£10,000 in farms, mills, wells, irrigation channels, livestock,
aqueducts, a wine factory and a silk school; '30,000 wild olive
and carob bean trees have already been grafted ... the ploughs and
reaping machines have arrived and are being worked satisfactorily.'
The same five Directors are listed but with a civil engineer as
chairman instead of the professor of botany. An office was
established in London with a full-time secretary while a resident
accountant was sent to Cyprus. All in all, the picture was very
rosy in the summer of 1898, but unforeseen circumstances were soon
to upset this most promising project. Mairet writes: (7)
Besides the constant difficulty in keeping sufficient contact
between the promoters and the operatives of a relatively small
but complex concern at such a distance, there was the disastrous loss of the ... manager.... But a decisive reason for
the failure of the Association was that it was formed specifically to solve an Armenian problem in Cyprus, and that problem
melted away of itself.... Geddes's effort was thus deprived
of its basis. The capital, of which something over £2000 was

lost, had been lent on terms that would enable the refugees to
repay without interest, so the subscribers expected no dividends
and they must have been partly prepared even to lose their principal.   Geddes lost some money of his own too.   But whatever
its ultimate fate, the work had been abundantly worth while.
And later foresters* and agriculturalists of the Colonial Service
have recognized its value.

The basic principles of eastern peacemaking and resettlement of
refugees which P.G. sketched out in deed and word are as timely
today as they were almost 80 years ago.   Any real improvement of
life for either refugees or regular inhabitants, he said, would
not come by merely signing treaties and increasing commercial
activity.   It would come through restoration of the earth and its
resources by applied science and by the renewal of society in its
renewed environment.   These, indeed, are the games and tasks of
Friedenspiel.

> Peace is not fundamentally a question of high concert, confer-
> ence or arbitration, good though all these may be;   it is fun-
> damentally a question of industry and this mainly of the main
> industry, agriculture....   For social health as for individual
> health must not the essential matter be hygiene?
>   Il faut cultiver son jardin.   That is the hygiene of
> peace. (8)

HOME LIFE AND SCHOOLING ... 'WE HAVE LIVED AND LOVED'

The mission to the Near East took place in the middle of the
family's three-year residence at the otherwise unused 'country
resort' at Crauford, Lasswade.   What with financial losses from
both P.G. & Colleagues in Edinburgh and The Eastern & Colonial
Association of London and Cyprus, this was certainly one of those
periods of 'frugality and self-denial' which J. Arthur Thomson has
referred to.   But Norah's recollections of the time do not reflect
any of the parents' troubles. (9)

> The large garden was much overgrown when they first moved in, and
> My father set about with a saw carving out views.   There was
> a pear tree that I was very fond of climbing, on which he had
> designs.   To reconcile me to its being cut down he gave me a
> little frame that he had for looking at views, in the hope that
> I would see the need for removing that tree.   I saw his point
> but refused to concede it, so that he was never aware that I
> saw what I saw.

On Norah's tenth birthday in October 1897 her father
  made a great autumn festival of it, decorating the house with

* One of these, Alistair Foggie, wrote to Arthur Geddes, 10 April
1940, with information about the manager's house at 'Lakkos tou
Franggou' which P.G. had presumably occupied for a time and which
still has mulberry trees in the lands near-by.

autumn branches and enthroning me in the middle, but he also had
the unfortunate idea of saying he was making me a birthday
present of a thousand bulbs and I knew it was because he wanted
a thousand bulbs.... Then came the tedium of planting them, so
that I simulated a pain in my inside and can still recall standing in melancholy fashion at the window of my bedroom watching
my brother and his father planting away and wondering which fate
was worse.

Norah, and Alasdair, four years younger, were given a long border
of the garden as their own, but
it was too big an undertaking and all our gardening efforts were
spent in maintainance and we never had any time to sow according
to our own fancy. In the autumn we had a great deal of tidying
up of leaves and I remember one fine autumn afternoon on being
called in to tea, Alastair who was very sensitive to beauty,
said 'Beauty is better than hunger', which was a phrase much
quoted in the family. Another example of his sensitivity was
that he could not bear my mother singing the ballad of 'Jean
Renaud', so that on one occasion he was lost during the singing
and was found in a cupboard shut away from the sound, and in
passionate tears.

Their early schooling consisted of lessons from the mother and, at
the time, Norah had to keep a diary as homework. 'I used to
wander round the house asking the maids to tell me what I had done
the day before.' She also longed to be free from lessons and
would have played truant 'if only I had punishment to face instead
of the anticipated reproach'.

Norah particularly recalled a donkey her father had acquired for
the children (without knowing much about its care) and a pig their
mother bought from an old Irishman which
every now and then opened the bolt of its stye and got loose in
the garden. I still remember the cat clambering up a tree out
of harm's way, the housemaid making a bolt for the safety of
the house and the cook pursuing it with an open sack round the
gooseberry bushes!

In view of the family's straitened circumstances, the presence of
both a housemaid and cook at Lasswade seems a bit contradictory,
yet these must have been part of the bare necessities of life even
during times of 'frugality and self denial'. However, a real
economic puzzle is raised by Norah: 'When we first went to Crau-
furd [Lasswade] there was just one house in the garden ... but
this did not satisfy my father; he must have another house. He
built it.' She relates that an American couple were tenants but
says nothing about its financing.

While Norah does not give many details of home lessons, she notes
what the parents read to the children, which in turn reflects
something of what Patrick heard from his father: 'The Old and New
Testaments, Paradise Lost, the Volsunga Saga, Pilgrim's Progress,
Tales of a Grandfather, Border Ballads, Tanglewood Tales ...' In

At Lasswade c. 1898.
Back row from left:
'Auntie Jeannie'
Bothwell Currie, Anna
Geddes and P.G.;
middle row: the cook,
the maid and Arthur;
seated: Norah, the
nurse and Alasdair

Mount Tabor Cottage
in 1898: P.G., Anna,
Alasdair, the nurse,
Norah and ? (perhaps
'Auntie Jeannie')

addition they heard a great many French short stories read by
friends and, after 1900, by governesses.   She also emphasises the
seriousness of their upbringing:

> My father had wanted us to know the nature of a day's work and
> to be able to do it.   We always had cold baths.   For some
> reason we had chapped hands which glycerine made very painful.
> It was not a soft upbringing; we learnt to endure cold, hunger
> and fatigue.

There is a side of P.G.'s nature which the daughter does not mention: it is his occasional, but deep, expression of feelings in
writing.   His old and blind mother died suddenly in early February 1898 while he was away from Edinburgh lecturing.   Even Anna,
who was home at Ramsay Garden, could not get to Perth before she
passed away and could only write to Patrick:

> They can't have expected the end so soon, or they would have
> wired me in reply to mine sent this morning offering to go
> today.   I have done what I think you would have done, dear,
> had you been here.   I am so sorry to have to write you this
> sad news in the midst of your work.   I shall wire you re
> funeral arrangements to Cambridge tomorrow. (10)

It was old Captain Geddes who suffered most, for life lost its
meaning without his beloved Janet.   One day he collapsed into the
arms of the nurse and was bedridden thereafter.   In April he sent
his treasured gold watch to the favourite son, who then wrote the
touching words already quoted (p. 17) about the happy childhood
memories called up by this gift.   Patrick continues:

> Now that I have the responsibilities of a father in my turn,
> dear dad, it is a great thing for me to have your example to
> look back and fall upon.   As I have told you before, I have
> been a pupil of many great naturalists, each of whom knew far
> more than you ever dreamt of, but I have to thank you for my
> love of nature and of gardens.   Here I am making a beautiful
> old place, I trust, more beautiful: if all goes well and I'm
> spared, it will be one of the very nicest little gardens in the
> County (aye, or in the island) but the one thing I wish for it
> is your presence, to walk round it with me and let me show you
> what I have been doing with my little spade and barrow, since I
> used to trot round with the little 'Express' after the big
> 'Tally Ho'.

Patrick wishes that his father 'could start your grandchildren as
you started me; but I must try and do it for you, and as you used
to do'.   Then he says that on Sunday they will all go round the
garden

> together as you used to take us, and we shall think of mother
> and you and of dear Jessie too: and we shall call the new
> apple-trees after the children, and ourselves, so that each one
> shall have his or her tree as in the dear old Garden at Mount
> Tabor.   And the big, beautiful old pear tree (winter pears,
> like that on your wall just outside the window, but tall and
> grand like a forest tree almost) shall be 'Grandfather's tree',
> and the old apple in the same way shall be 'Grannie's';   and

already it wears over its roots a great crown of white blossom -
a wreath of memory, yet also of joy.
    And last of all, dear father, the watch speaks of the future
also.   I am passing through middle age towards age itself;   and
believe me, I feel the responsibility;   it helps me to look
beyond this hour and day, into the years, and even to see things
from the widest standpoint, of eternity.

                            Believe me always, Your loving son
                                                    Pat. (11)

Two other revelations of his innermost nature belong to these years.
First, a letter (12 December 1898) to Anna at Crawford from Patrick
who was in Invernesshire attending the funeral of a beloved old
friend of theirs, the widow of the late John Hill Burton, Historio-
grapher Royal of Scotland.   He described his journey by gig and
the 'solemn splendour of winter pageantry' en route as the right
background for coming to the 'house of sorrow'.

    Then here, warmly welcomed, dried, warmed by the kind greetings
    no less than by the material fire;   then to the room with the
    dear, dead face, like a bust in tinted marble, strong and sweet
    as of old.   In daylight, the whole house as it should be and as
    she would have wished it.   One thinks more than one can set
    down: it is a great thing to have so much to remember: friend-
    ships are so rare in the world and this was more;   there was no
    exaggeration in our all feeling her as 'mother' and 'granny' -
    but the simple fact.   Here again, *wir haben gelebt und geliebet
    - wir leben und lieben und erinnern noch...* [We have lived and
    loved - We live and love and still remember.]

The second occasion was in May 1899 at Mount Tabor Cottage where
Patrick had gone to say farewell to his own father.   The story is
from the youngest son Arthur:

    The old soldier of ninety-one felt little left to live for since
    the death of his wife, Janet: rather, the hope of going where
    she had gone was something to die for.   Yet, as he began to
    descend the valley of death, there loomed out of the shadows a
    dreadful doubt, shaking this consolation, of which their faith
    had assured them.   This was more than he could face alone: in
    his last moments he appealed to the best-loved but agnostic son,
    for some re-assurance that he had not hoped in vain.   This was
    one of the most poignant moments in Patrick's life;   it remained
    vividly in his memory, and years after his own bereavement it
    was with evident emotion that he told the story to his son;   'Oh,
    will I see her, Pat?'   And I lied to him for the first time.
    'Yes, oh, surely yes'.   Then he passed away. (12)

The question of P.G.'s beliefs is a complicated one, in that he
pendulates between rejection of 'Christian Myths' and acceptance
of them and all others.   Among the pertinent documents is a long
narrative letter to 'Dear children over sea' [i.e. his brother
John's children in Auckland, N.Z.] written at Christmas time 1898.
He tells them how instead of throwing out the 'great Tree' as usual
the day after Christmas, he had proposed relighting it that
evening.   After explaining to his own children the pagan calendar

and the Scandinavian evergreen, he gave a demonstration of the
solar system with Alasdair carrying a tilted and turning globe
around the drawing room where a centre lamp served as the sun.
'But enough of Yule', said Geddes and suggested they read for themselves 'the actual story of Christmas in the Gospels (1st Matthew
and Luke)'.   Then, having relit the tree, they watched it as it
seemingly 'mounted into the sky, its buds kindled into stars, its
candles into suns, its gleaming globes their planets.'   When the
candles had burned out they saw

> the stable which had passed almost unheeded the other evening
> ... the Mother and Child, Joseph tending the weary ass, the
> kingly shepherds: at once ... the whole embodiment of a wealth
> of medieval art, till in the dark there seemed to be with us a
> hundred painters, some working on their knees like Fra Angelico
> of old....

> At one moment we see the glories of the world-tree, but the
> next we are glad to shelter under the homely roof and see here
> the birth of human, as there the cosmic religion of nature.
> Around us the infinite and omnipresent, the unchangeable yet
> protean energy of the Universe; within, the Divine humanity,
> the hope of the human world.

Though he 'will not try to restate the Christian doctrine', P.G.
does express some of the meanings he has found as a student of
nature, 'briefly in my own way'.

> First then there is ... the most wonderful fact of the whole
> Universe, more marvellous than suns and systems - the perpetual
> renewal of human life, so that for each moment of the year a
> new child is somewhere born.   In another of its many meanings
> this Child is the symbol of humanity in its perpetual renewal.

Each new child 'is no ordinary babe, no average, but a unique individual' as every mother feels.   Each one is a possible genius
if its development is not hindered.

> But in all this vast range of human possibility, what is great-
> est?   Practical energy - scientific intellect - poetic emo-
> tion?   All these are good, yet are but the elements of a higher
> unity, like the three colours which make up white light.   We
> must unite action and knowledge and sympathy, are we to reach
> wisdom.   We must widen wisdom till she live not for herself
> alone but for others, nay even when need comes die for others,
> then and only then our world evolution is complete, - the Child
> Wonderful is born - to live and to die for men.

SUBURBAN PROJECT ... RECLUS'S GREAT GLOBE ... FIRST VISIT TO THE
USA

The years 1897-9 were not merely devoted to 'Eastern and Colonial'
business, Geddes also kept on with housing projects at home even
after the Town & Gown Association took over his first crop of
burdens.   Evidence that he had, by 1897, started constructing a
group of cottage-villas at Coltbridge, a west suburb of Edinburgh,
is found in a letter from John Ross, an associate in his friend

Victor Branford's firm of Chartered Accountants.   Ross informs
Geddes that the agents want an immediate settlement of their account
due: £198.12.6.   He then makes these frank comments after having
gone over, at P.G.'s request, the whole set of transactions:

> Whilst there is no benefit to be gained by crying over spilt
> milk, I want to point out to you that you seem to me to have to
> a great extent crippled and handicapped the whole original idea
> of your scheme by what you must pardon me for calling your very
> great laxity with regard to the arrangements and agreements into
> which you entered. (13)

A profit was made on the first part of the constructions, Ross
continues.

> But alas, what did you do, - I cannot imagine why, it seems so
> wholly unnecessary and unusual - but take into partnership not
> only the man from whom you borrowed the money at a good rate of
> interest, but also your law-agent from whom so far as I can see
> you did not borrow any money to speak of, but of course paying
> interest as is usual there too....
>
>   Well, you will probably think me considerably more plain than
> pleasant in my remarks, but I am sorry to see the apparently
> inevitable ruin of the scheme.   The only way out of it seems to
> me is, now that you have done so well for your friend who lent
> the money and for your law-agent, that you should ask them to
> join you in completing the whole plan.   Of course my prognos-
> tications as to the result of erecting the back tenements may
> be all wrong.   *You* certainly, if anyone, can work out a plan
> to pay, but after the attempts I have made I have not much hope.

(The Coltbridge cottages were built, after all, but further comments
belong a decade hence, see chapter 7.)

The suburban project is of added interest in the light of a contemporary letter (14) from Geddes to a member of Edinburgh's New
College (School of Theology), which was the Outlook Tower's nearest
landowning neighbour.   After pointing out that its writer has completed a fifteen-year series of improvements which have 'touched
or included some thirty seven of the Old Edinburgh courts and
closes, and involved a turn-over of upwards of £120,000 ... without loss of principal or interest to any person concerned other
than myself', the letter announces that he is removing his business from Edinburgh to quarters (i.e. Coltbridge) where it meets
'if not with less apathy at least with less opposition'.   The
epistle next frankly reminds the theologian of all the misdeeds
his School has committed against Geddes's work for civic and
hygienic improvement.

> Of all the harsh, i.e. not only ungenerous but to my mind unjust
> dealing of which I have been sufferer or spectator of during
> twenty years of business your Body stands out absolutely and
> unquestionably first....
>
>   I need not recall in detail the innumerable large and small
> difficulties which we have had ... from the material vandalism
> which wantonly destroyed my gift of decorative paintings, to
> the material injustice of your many times renewed rejections of
> arbitration on each and every point on which I have protested
> against your exactions.

Some conciliatory lines follow in which P.G. first admits, 'I am
clearly conscious too that I cannot always have been right', and
then asks his adversary to consider whether the strictly legalistic methods of New College are in its own best interests of 'good-
neighbourhood', civic responsibilities, and public example.   He
concludes, skilfully combining a blast against barristers with a
sermonette:

> Our Edinburgh legal idea of business [is one] which eliminates
> all considerations of feeling, individual or public, which
> attains the ideal of utmost coldness to all, thus coinciding
> with the lowest circle of the Inferno - that of Ice.   For your
> own sake & that of others, why stay there.*
>
> Yours faithfully,

By autumn, 1898, the incorrigible P.G. Unlimited was in the midst
of a campaign to get financial backing for Elisée Reclus's proposed 'Great Globe of the World'.   Geddes attended the British
Association meeting at Bristol that September with a view to making
useful contacts.   Though he told Anna that 'Having been away so
long from the Brit. Assn., I have lost or lacked my old acquaintances very much, and I know too few faces', he soon had a 'Committee arranged for the Globe'.   A colleague from the Summer
Meetings, T.R. Marr, joined him in Bristol, and there they had
long talks with Reclus and a Monsieur A. Picard who was to be the
Director General of the great International Exhibition to be held
in Paris in 1900.

That coming event touched off in P.G.'s mind still another plan:
to organise an 'International Association for the Advancement of
Science, Arts and Education' which would sponsor a vastly expanded
'Summer Meeting' at the Exposition Internationale.   The plan,
writes Mairet,

> was to get together an international committee of patronage for
> this school, strong enough to organize it efficiently as a re-
> cognized department of the exhibition.   The school was to
> attract an intellectual élite from Europe, Britain, and America;
> it would then function, under his direction, as the guide and
> interpreter to the bewildering wealth displayed in the pavil-
> ions.   Visitors who attached themselves to the school would
> not only have a better tour of the exhibits;   they would be en-
> abled to see them in their historical, sociological, and cul-
> tural relations.   The great terrestrial sphere of Reclus had
> an obvious part to play in this enterprise, both as its central
> exhibit and as a superb instrument of demonstration.   Unfortu-
> nately, it might cost as much as £200,000 to build. (15)

Geddes envisaged the committee mentioned above as also being involved with 'the promotion of The Globe Tower Syndicate' and, in
a circular letter drafted in January 1899, asks what the existing
agencies are whose support could be enlisted: geographical,

---

* This last line was added in P.G.'s hand on the carbon copy now
at the National Library of Scotland, without a question mark.

ethical, photographic, cyclists and other kinds of societies?   What
about political clubs, trade unions and working class organisations,
teachers and current events clubs?   He sketches the evolution of
clubs from 'active discussion over coffee' to 'restaurant, bar,
smoking-room and loafing-shelter', and comments that 'clubs have all
more or less undergone this degeneration':

> You cannot tell from anything you see at a club whether it is
> Liberal or Conservative, whether for literature or for science.
> Private letters and meetings, chops and bitter, coffee and
> 'baccy, whiskey and billiards make up the essential and general
> elements....   I am not proposing to alter this state of things
> very greatly.   There must be always a restaurant and meeting
> place, a resting place, in the big city; but I do not see why
> they should not have among all the many specialities e.g. a
> globe....   Nor do I see why there should not be somewhere a
> central Information Club, which is practically what the Outlook
> Tower had always proposed to be, but one which would have the
> inestimable advantage of uniting all sorts of specialists and
> conditions of men. (16)

P.G. then states that 'I had a good preliminary talk with Nansen
and if I had the time would go to Christiania to see him'.
Instead, however, he undertook his first, and shortest, trip to the
USA from February to mid-April 1899.   Westbound, he sailed on the
RMS 'Campania' which, he writes to 'Dear Children Three' just
before leaving Liverpool, 'is as yet the finest ship afloat they
say'.   After several lines of recalling home scenes of both them
and their pets and of imagining how they will all meet him at the
garden gate, he refers to his new mission. (17)

> So beyond working and playing comes remembering, in some ways
> the happiest of all.   Then too there is planning - I have to
> build my Tower and the Globe too if I can - at least in some-
> body's mind who will take it up and carry it on....   Now I
> must stop and write some business letters, but I thank you for
> your flowers, which I'll unpack in my cabin, to keep me company
> if I'm sick.   But I'll be as jolly as I can, and be with you
> all oftener than you perhaps think.   And I'm sure you'll often
> be with me, and certainly every bed-time, won't you?
>
> Your affectionate
Daddy.

Arriving in New York around 20 February, P.G. dictated a six-page
letter home describing his impressions and activities from Monday
to Friday 20-25.   He found New York

> startling beyond anything I had expected ... fearfully and
> wonderfully made - sublime and ridiculous in one.   Ridiculous
> of course those many storeyed sky-scrapers - dwarfing the city
> and the landscape till in one aspect for all the world the im-
> pression from the boat is little better than of a wharf piled
> with packing cases, standing on end, their hard sky lines re-
> lieved into irregular ugliness by an occasional inverted piano-
> leg or cheap paraffin lamp stand.

Yet on coming nearer

> you cannot but recall the piled up picturesqueness of Old Edin-

burgh, of Stamboul itself, and if one could but see this at
dusk, it would have a quality by no means altogether inferior
to either.   (One might do something with an Outlook Tower upon
one of these pedestals...)

The flying cars, the ubiquitous overhead railways making the
streets sordid skeleton tunnels, are extraordinarily efficient.
There is no comparison between New York and London in this respect; the former is the place to move about in - but the
latter for a quiet life! However, I didn't come here for a
quiet life, so won't complain.

Disembarking, Geddes strolled from the wharves through the town to
the University Settlement in Rivington Street where he was expected by the 'head-worker' (Mr Reynolds) and given accommodation.
On the way he noted 'high-piled mountains' of snow from a recent
storm, 'covered with dirt, banana-skins and ashes worse than in
Old Edinburgh'.   However, 'the wonderfully clean and smokeless
air, the ample sea breezes etc., make it free from the smell and
stuffiness of London'.   Living at the Settlement pleased him and
he gladly made it his headquarters.

It is very interesting again to feel a student, and to go out
to one's meals as in Paris.   I only wish you could join as
that winter.   It is good to renew sympathy with one's fellows
in their poverty once more; we have been too long away from
the Lawnmarket and tend to forget; at least I do.

He mentioned that 'files of unemployed line the roadways every
morning to get organised for snow clearing', and confessed: 'If
I had only had old breeks and boots to match this old jacket, I'd
have knocked my hat in a little more, and imposed on Reynolds,
and gone off with one of his squads to scrape snow yesterday
morning!'   P.G. was also restrained 'by that reluctance to face
a day's work common to tramps of all classes!' and for fear 'of
the healthy public opinion of the gang' when he would have had to
throw down his shovel before they did.   Consequently, 'I did not
get beyond my café'.

A quite different experience for him was supper at Dr Adler's
Ethical Culture School where he met Carl Schurz, 'a magnificent
Prussian exile of 1848'.   Other contacts included lunch with
'J.K. Macdonald of "Progressive Review" and Fabian Society' but
'I never got anything from a Fabian somehow - No understanding in
common - of course I've not had many opportunities.'   He visited
the Adlers' home, went with Dr Tolman to the Brooklyn Merchants'
Association meeting and listened to addresses containing 'Anglo-
Saxon gush and Russian bogey etc. in as full and chauvinistic
misrepresentation as any London paper'.

The same letter contains one of the eye-minded observer's very
rare references to his own hearing.   He asked Anna to send him
a weekly paper regularly to keep up on European news.

I can't stand these yelling head lines.   (Never before have
I heard such audible yelling of the damned as around here.   A
music hall vocalist on the 'Campania' 'idealised' these effects

with more than foghorn power! which pierced me hidden away at
the farthest end of the ship with ears stuffed and jammed in
agony.   I am not exaggerating.   I did not know of such possibilities of pain.   Then the applause - apparently unanimous
from England and America alike!)

Turning again to intellectual matters, Geddes reported 'Invitations from Patton to Philadelphia and from Century Club, Chicago.
Of course accepting both, Patton's new book evidently quite extraordinary.'   Telling of a visit to Adler's Ethical Culture School
on Washington's birthday (22 February), he noted cryptically:
'Adler as Confessor and Counsellor....   Cross-examined me on my
own notions of relations of thought and work.   Promised to
advise me *re* Outlook Tower, Architects, etc.'   There are also
two references to lecturing which, in view of P.G.'s apparent
unawareness of his own peculiarities, are most significant.
   Tuesday. Stayed at home to unpack, prepare lecture etc., rested
   before I dined with Chubb (a teacher at Ethical School) (who
   introduced me in a few kindly words ...);   lectured pretty well
   for me and *passably*, Chubb thinks, for that audience;   though
   he recommends *lessons* and hearing *types* - we'll see what can be
   done.   Beer with Chubb afterwards!
   Wednesday ... Brooklyn.   Attended Lecture on Florence.
   Ideal in all respects as an example of what I have to learn -
   the business of lecturing ... I must go to some more.
   Friday ... lots of thinking - here dictated a long essay to
   typist (who came this morning)! ... Dined at Ladies' Settlement where I am to board henceforward instead of prowling the
   streets!   While appreciating both the material and social
   advantages of this scheme, I'll leave them till next letter.
                                   And remain,
                                   Always yours,

What that letter contained can only be conjectured, for the next
one extant is dated nearly a month later, from Boston. (18)
   Darling Winsome,
   This is just a wee line for yourself.   (I wrote today already
   by ordinary mail; and while I am waiting for a cab for a
   return journey to New York for Brooklyn lecture I am thinking
   of you, and so take pen.)
   What shall I say?   That absence does make fonder: that it
   constantly makes me realise how great and rare our happiness
   is; how delightful and beautiful our home; how noble our
   city and country - for oh, woe's me! this vast wealth and
   energy as yet produces little save a pandemonium city;   its
   very luxuries, of hot blasts and ice, of whirling electric
   cars, of decoration and the Press, of feasts and flare, making
   up an impression which is generally more painful than pleasant
   - and which forces the impression that America is the martyr
   of her own progress....   Yet there are better things here, in
   part beginnings, too, of neotechnic future.   And it is coming,
   too, a great ferment of changes....
   People are moving fast in thought, and are more ready for
   what I have to say than at home; their own thought too, is

often more congenial and complimentary than I find at home,
and, as I said today, I have found no such mine of ideas as
at Worcester.

But, Oh, dear lassie, how I long with it all for you, and
to have you in my arms again - and all, and all - and *all*.
And the dear little ones too.   I wish often I could see them
at play and asleep and round the table.

I am glad to be coming home in time for my session, etc.,
though not, I fear, for much of Crauford.   Still, I hope for
Sunday - but one must not hope too much, for steamers are apt
to be late.

Always your loving
P.

The final epistle from his first American journey was written on
the RMS 'Lucania' in mid-April, when approaching Queenstown.   As
he says, it is mainly a love-letter, and one recalls Anna's engagement words of early 1886: 'You *do* write a nice love-letter
when you write one at all'. (19)

Dear Lassie,

We have had a very good voyage: I have scarcely been sick at
all, and though today for the first time the ship is rolling
vastly, I am now fairly accustomed to the sea and expect to
hold out.   Everyone had enjoyed the voyage - as much as
voyages can be enjoyed.   One should be grateful for the rest,
the freedom from all cares and anxieties, all calls to duty
or even pleasure; the silence and the fresh air, each so
healthful in its way; the feeding-up too is not to be forgotten.   I am very well indeed, and quite rested now.

I hope to arrive by the first afternoon train from Liver-
pool, or failing that, by the second on Saturday....   But
I'll wire you from Queenstown, and if need be again from
Liverpool

That mainly established, the reason of my letter is to say
how penitent I feel for not writing more fully and posting
more carefully - though I really took more thought and care
than you can have supposed (Ship very wobbly!).   It was,
however, a very full and busy time.

But I'll be a better husband now that I come back, you'll
see: and recover myself by every penitence and obedience and
submission and devotion; and obedience and penance and worship and adoration that the heart of man can offer and the
heart of woman desire!   Yes, dear, our constant affection is
only strengthened by parting for a season, and now it glows
all the brighter as we approach re-union.   Need I say how I
have counted the time, and now the days and nights and hours!
... I am very well, as I said above; and shall be quite ready
for the summer's work.   One result too will please you - I
feel more ready to write now also.

But this is a love letter, dearest, and I feel as young as
ever to write that, as I am sure you do to read it.

Yours
P.

PATRICK'S SECOND, ANNA'S FIRST AMERICAN JOURNEY

The last year of the nineteenth century was a busy one for the
Geddes family in that Patrick now had a world-sized project to
occupy his non-teaching months.   The quick trip to America and
the response there to his Outlook-Tower approach to both sociology
and education made him wish for a return tour, with Anna as necessary partner.   How this could be financed on his meagre salary
was not a problem to stop him.   In practice, his favourite maxim
that 'It is ideas that count, not money' did come true at critical
times in his various careers.   The summer of 1899 was one of
these times.

After his father's death in April P.G. had to visit Perth on
several occasions in connection with inheritance matters.   Mount
Tabor Cottage had been willed to the three sons, but, according
to Mairet, it 'was eventually made over to Anna, who had done
most for the old couple in their declining years'.   Meanwhile,
Patrick
    was brought into closer contact with Sir Robert Pullar, of the
    world-famous Perth dye-works, who was an old friend of Captain
    Geddes and a strong believer in Patrick's mission to the world.
    Now, of course, he heard all about P.G.'s plans for holding an
    international school at Paris, and of his recruitment of a
    committee of intellectual leaders from Europe, Britain, and
    America to promote and support it.   Near the end of this
    summer Sir Robert gave P.G. a cheque for £3000, to be used at
    his own discretion in furtherance of the whole design. (20)

Consequently, after September spent in further recruiting of supporters at both the British and French Associations for the
Advancement of Science (held simultaneously just across the
Channel from each other at Dover and Boulogne), Geddes was able
to marshall an imposing list of presidents, vice presidents,
secretaries and lecturers representing France and Great Britain,
and later Germany and Russia.   All that was lacking were similar
names for the American Group of the coming Paris International
Assembly of the International Association for the Advancement of
Science, Arts and Education (IAASAE).   It was logical then that
among the first-class passengers aboard the RMS 'Germanic',
leaving Liverpool on 20 December 1899, were Mr and Mrs Patrick
Geddes.

Writing that day to her children, Anna gives news of their present
undertaking:
    I have just been copying a very grand letter from the President
    of the Paris University, M. Gréard, to the American Universities
    accrediting Daddy as his representative ... to work for the
    International Assoc'n & explain about it & the Paris Assembly
    to the American professors.   We are very pleased too because
    the Director of the Exposition had allowed us to have beautiful
    lecture rooms in the Hôtel Palais des Invalides & also in the
    Palais des Congrès....   So all that is very good news, for it
    means ... that we are sure of the 'bienveillance active de
    l'Exposition'.

This first letter was followed by at least ten others to the children which together provide a running account of the Geddes team in action.   There were follow-up meetings with contacts made the previous year and with new prospects, visits to museums and the classic sights of New York, Philadelphia, Washington, Boston and Chicago, and of course the lectures given by P.G. and the steady round of luncheon, dinner and evening invitations, most of which called for additional talks by him.   Anna also kept an engagement book, and merely to read the entries therein is to marvel at their stamina.

Judging by certain newspaper accounts of his movements, P.G. gave the reporters a hard time of it when they endeavoured to get 'a good story' from him.   The New York 'Daily Tribune' bravely started out on 30 December with an account of the 'well-known Scottish sociologist, biologist, and geographer', who had come to America in the interests 'of an important movement already afoot in England and France', but lost sight of him thereafter.   Other papers chronicled from time to time the doings of Professor Patrick Geddes, assigning him, with utter impartiality, now to the University of London, now to Glasgow or Edinburgh, then to St Andrews, and at least once to his correct post at UCD.

In Philadelphia, apart from historical sightseeing, he spent much time in the Commercial Museum studying its organisation and talking with its director.   In Washington he conferred with the United States Commissioner of Education, presenting him with letters of introduction from French and British scientists and educators.   The Commissioner in turn gave P.G. a free hand, in so far as the Bureau of Education was concerned, to carry on his mission in the USA.

One day Geddes accosted the information clerk at his hotel, a bright-appearing young man:
    Do you know if Professor Graham Bell is in town?
    Who?
    Graham Bell, the inventor of the telephone!
    Never heard of him.
    Not heard of your great inventor?   Why look at your telephone!
    Oh, come now, retorted the clerk, We've always had telephones! (21)

P.G. located Bell nevertheless, and although no details were given of the meeting its outcome was successful, for the latter's name duly appeared on the American list.   So it went in every city or university centre along the eastern coast; from college, museum, or business firm Geddes drew out some leading spirit, persuaded him to lend his name if not his time to the cause.   However, it was in New York that he made an essential 'convert': Robert Erskine Ely, a young man whom he had met in New York the previous winter through James Mavor.   Ely was then in charge of Harvard's unofficial extension work in the Prospect Union, and afterward the well-known director of the League for Political Education and moving spirit in the famous Town Hall of New York.

To him P.G. told the story of organising 500 members of the British Group under the Right Honourable James Bryce, M.P., and Sir
Archibald Geikie as Vice Presidents and himself as Secretary.   A
similar French group had been formed with Rector Gréard as President and, among others, the historian Lavisse and the mathematician Henri Poincaré as Vice Presidents.   The General President of
both groups was Léon Bourgeois, former Minister of Education.   In
fact, all that was now lacking were similar officers for the American Group, plus a capable salaried secretary to do the work.
Fired by P.G.'s enthusiasm, Ely accepted the job and its challenge,
working over home territory at first and going afterwards to Paris
for the summer's bout of lectures.

This accomplished, Geddes the recruiter moved on to new territory
and tasks: Yale, Princeton, Johns Hopkins, Columbia.   At Harvard, President Eliot (like Seth Low of Columbia) could enjoy the
unique experience of talks with, and from, Patrick Geddes.
Besides the President, a dozen professors were singled out in
Cambridge and in Boston for verbal encounters and, during the
whole month of January, The Hub and surrounding territory as far
west as Amherst and Worcester felt repercussions of the Scottish
visitor.

In the midst of this New England activity he dashed back alone to
Philadelphia, Baltimore and Washington for three days.   Just
before leaving he had lectured at a Ladies Settlement about civic
improvements in Edinburgh.   Afterwards, Anna reported, a lady
said that if only your 'Daddy could go through the world speaking
as he had done that night she was sure everything would come
right, for he not only saw how to make things better, but made
other people want to work at improving them.' (22)   On 5 January
1900, under 'Amusements', the Boston 'Transcript' carried a
short one-column advertisement of 'Four Lectures by PROFESSOR
PATRICK GEDDES of Edinburgh'.   Competing for attention with
Tissot's '500 Paintings Illustrating the LIFE OF CHRIST' and
David Belasco's version of 'ZAZA', it named the Twentieth Century
Club as sponsor and Tremont Temple as the place on 'Saturday
mornings at 11 o'clock'.   The titles appeared in small print:
'Jan. 6 - Evolution of Sex; Jan. 13 - Sex in Evolution; Jan. 20 -
The Sexes in Education; Jan. 27 - The Sexes in Social Life'.   (A
minor yet typical detail is that P.G. let himself be presented,
not by his professorship at Dundee but as 'of Edinburgh'.   This
flair for optimum professional publicity also characterised his
many letterheads.)

Six hundred Bostonians turned out for the first lecture, but the
numbers dwindled on succeeding Saturdays partly through disappointed curiosity and partly because not all of the lecturer's sentences cleared the bushy beard or got beyond the blackboard.   As
far as the 'Transcript' was concerned, every word must have been
inaudible or unquotable, for one may search through pages of
print given over to the Boer War, Russo-Japanese incidents, the
Filipino Insurrection, and reviews of 'The Girl from Maxim's'
without finding any mention of the Tremont Temple lectures.   The

Boston 'Herald', however, succeeded in reporting the first one, in which P.G. merely reviewed the history of the scientific study of sex and then expounded his own theory of maleness and femaleness. Then it, too, apparently called off its reporters.

The amount of space devoted to the Scottish lecturer in the public press is no indication of the personal success he had or of the influence which spread through other channels. The diary kept by Anna Geddes of the American journey reveals in crowded, terse entries how great was their private and social ascendancy. In Boston they were showered with invitations to lunch, dine, take tea, go riding, attend concerts. P.G. was given enough occasions for talks and discussion to occupy even his supply of energy and ideas.

On 20 January, for example, having returned from New York just in time, he delivered his third Saturday morning lecture, 'The Sexes in Education', after which he stayed in Lorimer Hall for about an hour answering questions and giving additional examples of how those two basic evolutionary forces, Nutrition and Reproduction, express themselves in human history and even in literature. At one o'clock he and Mrs Geddes went to the Beacon Hill quarters of the Twentieth Century Club for lunch and discussion of its President, Mr Edwin D. Mead's International Peace Foundation. On the stroke of two, the president called to order nearly a hundred of Boston's public-minded business and professional men who met each Saturday to lunch and to hear well-known speakers. Thereupon Geddes told the story of his IAASAE, emphasising that for probably the first time in history a world's fair would be something more than 'vast shop-windows and refreshment bars of super-magnificence'; for the international school would make the 1900 Paris Exposition a cultural event as well.

Three p.m. was the accepted deadline for the Twentieth Century luncheon talks, but P.G. swept on a good while before he could be turned off. At four he was in full tilt again, a college club in Cambridge having invited him to talk informally on whatever topic or topics he wished. Shortly before six o'clock Professor Cummings of Harvard rescued the club members by taking the speaker away to dinner. At eight Geddes once more stood on a platform, this time to lecture on 'Nature and the Study of Society' under the auspices of the Boston Normal School. His theme was the necessity of knowing something of the natural world before attempting to study either individual or social behaviour, and his presentation included charts of Comte's classification of sciences and the Place-Work-Folk thinking machine. He tackled his favourite bogey of excessive specialisation and slew it for the Boston teachers with weapons from his Outlook Tower arsenal. The Tower he next built for them, storey by storey, and wound up by suggesting that there were many tall buildings in the Hub which would make excellent 'index-museums' of its region.

Anna had her own programme after the Saturday morning lecture, ending up in the evening at Cambridge, 'a little town or village

3 miles from Boston', where a new host took charge and where P.G.
turned up that night.   She wrote the children a diary letter
'which I shall explain when I come back'.
>   Sun.:   Beautiful sunny day.   Nice walk in morning;   lunch with
>   Mr & Mrs Horace Scudder (of Atlantic Monthly) ... 3 o'clock to
>   a Mr D. Ross, art critic & lecturer....   Then on to a meeting
>   at Mrs Ole Bull's, widow of the violinist....   Supper at Mrs
>   O. B.'s, interesting people & beautiful house;   enjoyed playing
>   in her fine music room....   Back here to letters & arrange-
>   ments - then Daddy off for N.Y. by midnight (sleeping) car. (23)

After two days in New York and one at Yale Patrick rejoined Anna,
both then going to Clark University in Worcester, Massachusetts
as guests of President and Mrs G. Stanley Hall.   Patrick and G.
Stanley had a marvellous time together, and Clark students of that
time carried away memories of the dynamic Scot which would still
be vivid forty years later.

'Here we are on our travels again', Anna wrote to Norah and Alasdair on 2 February 1900, 'having left Boston & our dear kind hos-
tess finally this morning.'   Their destination was Chicago, with
several stopovers en route, the first being Albany.   P.G. had
been there early in January to see the US Commissioner for Education and Social Economy at the Paris Exposition who was soon
leaving for France.   He also met Mr Melville Dewey, 'one of the
greatest librarians in the world, who advised Carnegie about the
Edinburgh Public Library....   Daddy liked Mr Dewey so much that
he thinks we must go back to Albany together ... to see him & also
to see Governor Theodore Roosevelt.'   Hence Anna could note on
2 February, 'Today we reach Albany at 2.40 (6 hours' journey),
interview Governor Roosevelt & see a Mr Melville Dewey.   Then on
to Buffalo, where ... Daddy lectures'.

On his way from Boston he had lectured not only at Buffalo, but
Toronto (where Professor Mavor arranged a welcome for him), and
Ann Arbor, Michigan as well.   At Ann Arbor it was his old Summer
Meeting colleague, Professor Wenley, who rounded him up an aud-
ience (and who saw that he received the customary honorarium, for
P.G. did not have to talk merely for the joy of it.   He earned
from $25 to $75 every time he stood before a university audience).
When he reached Chicago two other friends, Professors Richard
Green Moulton and Charles Zueblin, jointly provided host and guide
service.

The Geddeses lived at Hull House for a time, there beginning a
long friendship with Jane Addams, 'the Abbess of Chicago', as
Patrick called her.   His sojourn was afterwards commemorated by
a photograph hanging in the gallery of distinguished visitors in
the 'Octagon Room' of the settlement.   He spent much time at
Colonel Parker's new school and in exchanging pedagogical ideas
with John Dewey.   He also became well acquainted with the University of Chicago, taking especial pleasure in the company of
its 'bad boy economist', Thorstein Veblen.

Geddes and Veblen developed a high regard one for the other.   Both were academic rebels and more concerned with ideas than in observing the proprieties that surrounded each field of learning; both had a gift for finding or coining *le mot juste* and took delight in using it when found.   Veblen's 'Theory of the Leisure Class' had recently appeared in its first edition with the phrases like 'conspicuous consumption' and 'vicarious leisure', which were destined to become classic in American speech.   Meanwhile, quite appropriately, a Geddes paper of 1884 with delightful comments on 'reincarnated metaphysicians' posing as economists and 'portly word-fog-giants' holding down professorial chairs was being reprinted in New York by the 'International Monthly' (March 1900) under the slightly revised title of 'John Ruskin, as Economist'.

According to those who heard him in 1900, P.G. made both a striking and favourable impression in Chicago, even more consistently than in the East.   Wherever he spoke, whether at the University of Chicago, at Northwestern, at Hull House, or in private homes, the same enthusiasm greeted his words, the same stimulus fired his audience.   Mrs Charles Zueblin has told of hearing John Dewey exclaim, after listening to P.G., that it was the greatest, most idea-provoking lecture he had ever heard.   George Hooker, pioneer worker in Hull House and pioneer civic planner in Chicago, looked on Geddes ever afterwards as the 'second most admired person' he had known, and took every occasion to study his rebuilding work in Old Edinburgh.   Miss Flora Cooke, principal of the Parker School for over thirty years, reported that Geddes held his listeners from start to lengthy finish, fascinating and astounding them with his wide range of ideas and the inexhaustible fund of knowledge he drew on afterwards to answer the questions that everyone put to him.   After forty years, she said, the memory of his talks was still vivid. (24)

The printed syllabus of P.G.'s lecture at the University of Chicago on 'The Real France' on 15 February noted his introduction as: 'Varying current estimates, sympathetic, pessimistic, of France, her history, character and influence'.   The full text, however, contained remarks such as 'The Real France is an unknown country; it is a land about which circulate tales as wild and as inaccurate as about Darkest Africa', followed by a Geddesian defence of Latin Quarter morality as being superior to Anglo-Saxon hypocrisy.   To those who were thinking of the Dreyfus Affair and saying 'Thank God, we are not like these Frenchmen!' he insisted that the very fact this scandal could be made public was proof of French superiority.

>Americans have Dreyfus Affairs; we British have ours; but they never come into the light!   They are smothered in hypocritical silence, they are squelched in order to save the face of the Army or University or whatever happens to be the power threatened by ugly disclosures.   It is only the French who dare to hang out their dirty linen, before the eyes of the world if need be.

Anna has written the following account, in a letter home, of a similar talk held for a women's club near Boston.

He lectured on 'The Real France', because we find that over here
as well as at home, people do not know much about the best side
of French civilisation, and they are apt to think our Anglo-
Saxon civilisation better in every way.... Daddy worked out
his lecture on his historical diagram, pointing out that the
French had been the leaders in all the great movements in the
Middle Ages with their chivalry & their great cathedrals &
castles - at the Renaissance, at the Revolution, & in later
times too. You will often hear him talk about this when we
are in Paris; or if not I'll tell you if you ask me. These
ladies were delighted with the lecture, & some of them ... said
they had never heard anything that interested them so much. (25)

Learning that St Louis was planning to have an exposition in 1903,
Geddes spent two days reconnoitring the city with a view to turning loose his International Association there. Back in Chicago,
he gave a few more lectures, including one at the home of Mrs
Emmons Blaine, patroness of progressive education and social
leader, and then he and Anna departed near the end of February for
Pittsburgh and points east. In March they set up headquarters
once more in New York, staying for about three weeks.

During his three months in the USA P.G. collected about $1,200 in
lecture fees, which was not at all bad for those days and for a
little-known botany professor. His expenses, of course, exceeded
that sum, for they included salaries to co-Secretary Ely and an
assistant as well as travelling costs. But he took with him a
great surplus of ideas, impressions, and anecdotes, gathering much
from John Dewey and Colonel Parker. Strangely enough, his first
direct contact with the Hindu way of life came via the New World,
for it was in Chicago that he met the Swami Vivekananda, apostle
of the Vedanta. The eastern discipline of body and mind made
such an impression on both Anna and Patrick that they later handed
on to their young children the simple Raja Yoga exercises for
'control of the inner nature'.

The meeting of the Swami and Geddes had not only interesting consequences, but preliminaries too. In the spring of 1898 a Miss
Josephine MacLeod of New York met, near Calcutta, the English
woman Margaret Noble who had become the Swami's disciple. The
latter said to the American, 'If you ever hear of a man called
Patrick Geddes, follow him up. He is the type of man to make
disciples'. (26) How Miss Noble knew about P.G. is not clear,
but in any case two years later, when Miss MacLeod was visiting
in California, she chanced to read in the papers that a certain
Professor Geddes was lecturing in New York. Thereupon she wrote
to her sister, wife of wealthy New York grocer Francis H. Leggett,
with the result that both Mr and Mrs Geddes were taken into the
Leggett mansion as guests in March on their return from Chicago.
Miss MacLeod journeyed east in turn and met face to face the
Scottish professor she had heard about in India. It was the
beginning of a long friendship between her and both P.G. and Anna.

However, such proximity to a potential Maecenus was irresistible.

At the breakfast table P.G. brought up Elisée Reclus's project for
a great globe at the Paris Exposition representing the whole world
on a scale of 1:500,000.   In glowing terms he told Mr Leggett what
a valuable contribution to science such a globe would make, how
spectacular an appeal to visitors from all walks of life.

   How much would it cost?

   I think one million dollars would build it.

   What practical use would it have?   How would it help my or anyone else's business? (27)

For once here was a question with which P.G.'s eloquence could not
cope, and Mr Leggett returned to his breakfast.

By the spring of 1900 the Geddes-Ely drive had resulted in a general
committee of some 400 members presided over by US Commissioner of
Education Harris and President Woodward of the American Association,
and with executive offices in New York, Philadelphia, Boston, and
Chicago.   On the membership list appeared names distinguished in
science, industry, politics, letters, and high society: Andrew
Carnegie, Alexander Bell, Woodrow Wilson, Grover Cleveland, D.C.
Heath, Nicholas Murray Butler, G. Stanley Hall, John Dewey, Jane
Addams, the Reverend Edward Everett Hale, Mrs Julia Ward Howe,
William Dean Howells, Louis Tiffany, Mrs Emmons Blaine of Chicago;
and Mrs Schuyler Van Rensselaer and Mrs Francis H. Leggett of New
York.   Of course, no such list can be taken quite at its face
value.   For every active member, there were doubtless two who knew
little of what the Scottish professor was trying to accomplish,
though both kinds lent their names to the cause.

Beyond all such practical results there was the intangible yet widespread influence of Geddes's 'winged words' and fertile ideas.
Anna has reported a typical instance to the children.   After his
second Boston lecture on the 'Evolution of Sex' (Anna called it
'his biology lecture') a lady came to him and

   said she had enjoyed it so much, that it was the music of life.
   I think she must have meant that Daddy helped her to understand
   the beauty & harmony of all life, of flowers & birds & beasts &
   men & women & children.   I tell you these things about Daddy
   because I know you like to hear them & because I hope it will
   help you to grow up worthy of him. (28)

On 21 March the Geddes team ended its American journey and embarked
for Liverpool and home.   Immediately on arriving in Scotland they
carried out a commission for Colonel Parker and Mrs Blaine, by en-
gaging John Duncan as teacher of art for the Parker School in
Chicago.

WORLD'S FAIR IN PARIS ... INTERNATIONAL SUMMER MEETINGS

In May 1900, visitors began to converge upon Paris from all parts
of the world to find the 'Exposition Universelle' in various stages
of completion.   P.G. and staff, on the other hand, were ready and
waiting with a super summer-school equipped to instruct and to
shepherd people in English, French, German and Russian.   In strat-

egically located offices and lecture-rooms he, Mavor, Ely and a
score of lecturers prepared to cope with the incoming crowds of
knowledge-seekers.   But by June they realised there was no danger
of being overwhelmed: most people hadn't come all the way to this
great World's Fair to improve their minds.   They came for its
sights and the amusements of 'gay Paree', and if they were thirsty
after even an hour or two of tramping around the exposition grounds,
it was not for knowledge.

A minority of curious visitors, however, did find their way to the
'International Assembly', either by word of mouth from the hundreds of British and American Group members or by coming upon the
excellent 'Guide to Paris, The Exhibition and The Assembly'.   Published in London, New York and Edinburgh (from the Outlook Tower,
Castlehill) and bearing many traces of P.G., this pocket-sized
booklet contained a good introduction to Paris as well as the
summer meetings.   It is still an interesting historical and sociological document, providing a brief, yet comprehensive, account of
the city and its region from pre-Roman times up to the greatest of
world fairs.   The latter's 18 main groups with their 131 classes
are described in a nutshell, while the 9 geographical areas are
both described and shown on 3 two-colour maps specially made for
the guidebook by the Edinburgh Geographical Institute.

Indeed, the result contains valuable contemporary evidence of
aspects of Paris in 1900.   The conflict of French and Anglo-Saxon
customs is presented in these words:
> Besides the offensively conspicuous necessaries for men found
> everywhere along the Paris streets, there are at intervals
> *chalets de nécessité*, with a woman guardian who furnishes toilet
> conveniences to both sexes.   For the sake of comfort, and even
> of health, it is almost necessary that Anglo-Saxon timidity or
> prudishness should be overcome in this connection.   The victory
> may be aided by a clear knowledge of the fact that those who
> live habitually in Paris will not even be aware of the mental
> struggle which takes place in the newcomer.

Twenty pages or so of the guide are devoted to the Assembly itself.
Advantages provided by membership are for specialists 'the means of
meeting with fellow-workers in France and from other countries',
and for the 'intelligent public ... a method of seeing and appreciating the important features of the Exhibition with economy of
time, effort and money, by means of daily lectures and systematic
visits with skilled guidance'.   The cost varied from 25 Fr. (including the guidebook, printed programmes and five entrance tickets)
for 'any one week between June 1st and October 31st' to 250 Fr. for
'Life Membership in the International Association, with participation in the Paris Assembly throughout its duration, and in all
future Assemblies'.   The booklet's final pages recorded the
officers of all national groups together with their many hundreds
of members, and two early pages announced the publications of
Patrick Geddes & Colleagues of Edinburgh.

For those who sampled it, this summer meeting in Paris provided a varied and attractive bill of fare.   After visits to points of interest in the city and its environs, Saturday trips to Chartres, Fontainebleau, Reims, and weekly social gatherings, furnished the needed relief from daily tours of the Exposition and from detailed studies of exhibits.   Such widely representative personalities as Jane Addams, J. Arthur Thomson, Lester Ward, and Senator Henri La Fontaine of Belgium (who would be awarded the Nobel Peace Prize in 1913), the Swami Vivekananda of India and Jean de Bloch of Warsaw, gave lectures in English along with some twenty-five others from Britain and the USA.   Among the twenty-five should be mentioned James Mavor and John Duncan, the American secretary, Robert Ely, and two young Scots, Edward McGegan and T.R. Marr.   The latter two had already had sporadic periods as junior colleagues in various Edinburgh activities, and many more Geddesian experiences were in store for them.

P.G.'s main helper, as always, was Anna.   She was the ex-officio member of all committees, the pillar of all his varied projects. She kept track of his appointments, an especially difficult task that summer in Paris, and supplied the tact and social grace necessary to make day-by-day life possible for those in contact with him.   Her duties also included reminding Patrick to pay this bill or be on time for that engagement, diverting him from an attack on Mr X's ideas when Mr X was a dinner guest, and a hundred other things.   As wife, general manager, and diplomat, Anna was indispensable.   Everyone agreed that what P.G. achieved on both material and intellectual planes was in great part due to her.   To quote a young French woman who at this time was governess in their home, 'The best thing Monsieur Geddes possesses, it is neither his ideas nor his kindness; it is his wife'. (29)

In addition to such 'normal' burdens Anna underwent a severe crisis early in their sojourn in Paris.   Norah relates how 'one day there was a sense of impending doom: my father said to me "You and Alastair (he was barely 9 then and I was 12) must take a fiacre, engage it by the hour, and go to these addresses.   You must find a nurse for your mother and bring her back with you and go on trying until you do"'.   They succeeded, but 'Another day, with heavy hearts, we were taken to spend the day ... with friends so as to be out of the way, because our mother had a miscarriage and her life was in danger'. (30)

Norah, Alasdair and Arthur, as children of P.G., had much fun along with the responsibilities and the steady pressure of serious example imposed, often unwittingly, by their moralistic and hard-working parents.   They were well taken care of by friends (Miss Bothwell Currie and Miss Mary Hill Burton) in the absence of their parents; spending, for example, the winter of 1899-1900 'in a large old house, called Comrie Castle in Fife' where they had an extraordinary number of Christmas presents (but few formal school lessons) and where they ran wild in woods and garden.   In April the whole family settled in Paris, for P.G. was too busy in 1900 to go to Dundee, living first in a *pension de famille* opposite the Luxembourg Gardens on the Boulevard St Michel and then taking a flat on

the other side of the Seine, near the Champs Elysees and the Exposition.   Geddes took Norah and Alasdair on their first visit to
the great fair, and it seemed so marvellous to the children that
they later returned for half days at a time, frequently alone, but
on condition that they never separated.   After nine months in Paris
all three had an excellent speaking knowledge of French for their
age, even 5-year-old Arthur.   Thus early in life were P.G.'s children started in the 'wandering Scot' tradition which he at the same
age had known only through reading.

They also 'were privileged to help' with the great amount of cleri-
cal work involved in running the Assembly, chiefly by delivering
urgent letters and invitations.   Norah recalls,
   This we did with pleasure, but unfortunately Mother was not very
   discerning about social distinctions in a foreign country.   We
   often went dressed in overalls of grey-blue check material worn
   only by the school children of the People ('Enfants du peuple').
   The result was that when we asked the concierges for directions
   ... they directed us up the back stair.   But we had our dignity
   and the dignity of our mission to maintain so we insisted on
   going up the stair proper or else outwitted the concierge - a
   dragon in human form.   I remember one day we were proud because
   in the same afternoon we had a letter for Monsieur le Comte un
   Tel, Monsieur le Duc de Quelquepart and as climax one for Monsieur le Prince Bonaparte! (31)

If the youngsters had a good time at the Exposition, the father had
a superlative one; Paris was always his spiritual home, and the
added attraction of the World's Fair, its exhibits, scientific congresses, and visiting celebrities, made this sojourn the most
eventful one of all.   He used the Exposition of 1900 as a vast
laboratory in which to demonstrate his sociological ideas and his
system for unifying all knowledge.

Even more than the Edinburgh Summer Meetings, this international
school provided a full challenge to his intellectual and linguistic
prowess.   A French participant in one of the former has paid an
eloquent tribute to Geddes's command of French in conversation and
lecturing:
   He seems so much at home among us that involuntarily I try to
   identify him with one of our provinces: I find in him the grace
   of Angevine and the poetry of Bretagne....   He speaks, and the
   hurried elliptical phrases quickly arrange themselves in rhythm
   with the thought which bears them.   His language is a very pure
   French: elegant, savorous, enlivened by a trace of Anglicism.
   A slight hesitation, which barely betrays the foreigner, enhances
   the complexity of his thought much more than it impedes its
   nuances. (32)

In a high gallery of the Trocadéro, which dominated a great part of
the city, P.G. set up a miniature Outlook Tower and index-museum,
and from there he started each general tour of the Fair.   Whether
to parties of workmen or professors he always drove home the point
that only by such devices could they hope to understand the 350

acres of exhibits either in general or in detail.   The Tower with
its vantage-point for physical orientation and with its specific
outlooks (of scientist, artist, citizen, etc.), with its classification of sciences, for giving intellectual bearings, said Geddes,
provides the means of triumphing over what inherently is incompre-
hensible chaos.   Once in possession of a method of interpreting
history and of linking together the scattered details of human
science, industry, and art, the visitor might then grasp the significance, in part and as a whole, of the 'Exposition Universelle'.

Inimitable cicerone, Geddes led his charges through a world summary,
a laboratory of contemporary social evolution.   The favourite
object lesson he drew from the Exposition and its 120 international
congresses was that here was the raw material of lasting world
peace.

How to occupy our community constructively, is not that the
problem upon which the ideals of the Exposition and those of the
older culture must more and more unite?   From this change of
treatment of the peace question, no longer abstract and ethical,
legal or critical, but that of concrete geography and history,
the corresponding practical policy appears - the material re-
organisation (agricultural, hygienic, educational, economic,
etc.), of region by region, city by city, on the comprehensive
scale hitherto mainly considered for their disorganisation by
war.

An active policy of constructive peace, unattainable by mere
vague aspiration, by passive negation of war, or even by legal
adjustment, is yet gradually organisable, map by map.   Let
those who desire peace think of this....   For as soldiers play
their game of war upon the map, so it must be with the game of
peace.   To have done with Kriegspiel, we need a no less definite Friedenspiel. (33)

Mairet has also emphasised this aspect of Geddes's work in Paris,
rightly pointing out that the 'interludes of passionate preaching
or prophecy in P.G.'s lecturing had a quality of realism too often
lacking in the discourse of social moralists'.

Writers and preachers innumerable have extolled the labours of
peace as worthier of men's devotion and invention than those of
war, but their efforts to infuse the joy of battle into the reclamation of the common life have generally been frustrated by
inability to give precise and immediate content to this general
idea.   But Geddes would demonstrate urgent tasks of peace,
often in detail, before one's eyes: one felt as though the war
on ignorance, squalor, and militarism had been declared - almost as though Geddes were already directing the operations. (34)

Month after month Geddes served as both an informational intellectual landmark and as a unifying force in a Paris teeming with tran-
sient scientists, public figures, and ordinary visitors.   For him
it was a golden opportunity to renew ties with friends of student
days or from the Summer Meetings.

Then came a host of new contacts: Henri Bergson;   Charles Gide,

famous French economist; Paul Otlet, creator of the Mundaneum
(world centre for the organisation of knowledge in Brussels) with
whom Geddes collaborated from then on; and finally a considerable
number of Americans, some of whom, like Jane Addams and Lester Ward,
he had already encounted in the USA and others whom he met in the
Leggett's Paris home where he and Mrs Geddes were frequent guests.

When Mrs Leggett and her sister, Miss Josephine MacLeod, left New
York in the spring of 1900 to settle in the French capital, they
were accompanied by Margaret Noble, the Swami Vivekananda's disciple.   But Sister Nivedita, to use her Hindu name, very shortly
had enough of the luxury and round of entertainments in the
Leggett home and so she fled this worldliness to live in a bare
garret above the flat occupied by P.G. and Anna.   She spent much
of the summer trying hard, even desperately, to assimilate P.G.'s
philosophy and to learn his method of observing and interpreting
life.   She followed him on visits to the Exposition and the city,
listening to his every word, taking notes, and rewriting these
notes afterwards in her garret.   For a time they attempted to
collaborate on a book that would express her idealism and his
science.

Yet despite her devoted efforts and his generosity with time, ideas
and interpretations, the attempt did not succeed.   Well might he
be an intellectual common denominator for minds working in natural
science, the arts and even in industry, but neither his synthesis
of factual knowledge nor his 'evolutionary ethics' could satisfy
her quest for spiritual values.   [Miss MacLeod's explanation was
that he was too elusive, that his mind darted here, there, and
everywhere like a flame always just out of reach. (35)]   Still
baffled after months of apprenticeship, she gave up the search for
an absolute clue to Geddes, nearly ill for a time with disappointment.   Nevertheless, Sister Nivedita did get a great deal from
him, as she acknowledged in her book, 'The Web of Indian Life',
published in 1904.   It was dedicated to Patrick Geddes 'who, by
teaching me to understand a little of Europe, indirectly gave me
a method by which to read my Indian experiences'.

The Swami Vivekananda and the Scottish scientist met again during
this summer in Paris, a meeting which further deepened the latter's
interest in India.   Ten years later P.G. wrote the preface to a
French edition of the Swami's philosophy of Raja Yoga, (36) and
four years after that he embarked on a mission to India that was
to occupy nearly a decade of his life.   What Geddes once wrote
about Sister Nivedita's appeal to children seems to have been true
of his own experience with Vivekananda:
    She would sit with them upon the floor in the firelight and tell
    them her 'Cradle Tales of Hinduism', with a power and charm even
    excelling her written version of them, and thus touch this or
    that ardent young soul to dream of following her to the utmost
    East.

On 18 October 1900, the quadrilingual International School brought
its work to an official close with a great reception held in the

USA Pavilion.   Under the chairmanship of Léon Bourgeois and in the
presence of the American Ambassador, the officers of the French,
German, Russian, and British-American groups submitted to one
another reports of their various activities.   The French had enrolled the largest number of students, but the total work of all
groups made some impressive statistics.   One hundred lecturers,
8 secretaries, and 10 miscellaneous employees had participated in
the four-month session; 300 formal lectures were delivered on
main features of the Exposition, and 800 talks on special subjects
of exhibits to some tens of thousands of visitors; more than 450
expertly guided visits were arranged to various parts of the Fair,
not counting numerous excursions about Paris and the surrounding
region.   As the general secretary of the International Association
reported to the assembled officers and members:
> There is many a university which does not offer as much in one
> semester.   And I believe that never has an exposition provoked
> a similar movement of study and teaching by six nations and in
> four languages: a fact which is not the least novelty of the
> movement.   There, Gentlemen, is your work in a nutshell.

But Geddes, this year a complete truant from UCD, was not content
even with this extra-curricular record.   He arose to present plans
for next year's work at the Glasgow Exposition and for the St Louis
Exposition of 1903.   When these had been approved by the Association and after appropriate speeches by various French, German,
Russian, and American personalities, the 1900 session of the International School was declared officially ended.

RUE DES NATIONS: SEEDS OF UNESCO

After the festivities and the departure of all visitors came the
anticlimax of dismantling the great show.   Machinery, paintings,
scientific apparatus and a thousand other kinds of exhibits were
made ready for repatriation, while gangs of wreckers prepared to
demolish exposition palaces and national pavilions.   'What a pity
to destroy all those buildings!'   With such a comment the passer-
by went on about his business, for ultimate destruction was the
accepted fate of every local or world's fair.   But to P.G. came
an audacious idea, and instantaneously he followed its commands.
A typical example is the long letter he wrote to the Norwegian
polar explorer on 12 November 1900.
> Dear Dr. Nansen,
> You will be surprised to hear from me: but if you will first
> look at the accompanying roll - the Panorama of the *Rue des
> Nations* which has been by far the finest feature of this great
> Exhibition - & note the ... suggestions of our *Avant-Projet*
> below you will see more clearly that there is something to
> interest you - alike as an internationalist & as a good Nor-
> wegian - as a lover of science & of art - & as feeling I am sure
> that we have constantly to freshen our education by a fuller
> contact with life - & to bring together progressive culture &
> the most general and popular education.
> But I won't teach you what you have thought out as fully as I:

PARIS INTERNATIONAL ASSEMBLY
(ÉCOLE INTERNATIONALE DE L'EXPOSITION)

General Secretary: M. LIARD   *General President:* M. LÉON BOURGEOIS   *Asst. General Secy.:* M. ÉMILE BOURGEOIS

BRITISH GROUP

Vice-Presidents: { RT. HON. JAMES BRYCE, M.P.
{ SIR ARCHIBALD GEIKIE, F.R.S.

AMERICAN GROUP

Vice-Presidents: { WILLIAM T. HARRIS, LL.D.
{ PROF. R. S. WOODWARD, PH. D.

OFFICES IN PARIS
Within the Exposition

Secretary: PROF. PATRICK GEDDES
Assistant Secretary: MR. T. R. MARR
Treasurers: ROSS, BRANFORD & CO.

PALAIS DES CONGRÈS, SOUS-SOL
(Place de l'Alma)
PALAIS DE L'ENSEIGNEMENT, CLASSE I
(Champ de Mars)
Outside the Exposition
7 AVENUE DE L'OPÉRA, (RESTANTS')

Secretaries: { MR. ROBERT ERSKINE ELY
{ PROF. PATRICK GEDDES
Treasurers: { MR. R. C. OGDEN, NEW YORK
{ MR. FRANCIS H. LEGGETT, PARIS

19 Rue Marignan

PARIS   12/11/   1900

Dear Dr. Nansen

*You will be surprised to hear from me: but if you will first look at the accompanying roll — the **Panorama** of the "Rue des Nations" which has been by far the finest feature of this great Exhibition, & note the red with suggestions of our*

Geddes appeals to the
Norwegian explorer,
Fridtjof Nansen, for
help in preserving
the *Rue des Nations*
in Paris after the
World's Fair of 1900

Anna Geddes with
Norah and Alasdair at
back, Arthur seated,
Glasgow, Summer 1901

only let me ask you to put this panorama up upon your wall - and meditate upon the various possibilities it suggests - then give us the benefit of them - of your name also & support upon our committee - especially of course for the groups which most interest you.

This done as an abstract matter, of pure science, let us talk of the business of it.   You know my constructive interests (Old Edin'g buildings as well as Globe, Tower, etc) & so can easily see that I could not readily work six months opposite this pano- rama & then let it be pulled down.   So after our International Assembly our fresh business is as *Comité pour la Conservation et l'Utilisation de la Rue des Nations*.

Our practical problem is to get the national commissions to give their buildings to the City of Paris for such uses - and this the majority of them are willing to do - often with detailed difficulties in each case, but none with which we do not hope successfully to grapple.

Another problem discussed in this letter was how to get home auth- orities not only to make up any deficits already incurred by their pavilions but also to provide more money.   P.G. then suggests to Nansen, as he already had to Norway's representative at the Exposi- tion (Mr Wilhelm Christophersen, Consul General, and later Norweg- ian Minister of Foreign Affairs), that he ask the national parlia- ment for the gift of the building as 'useful to Paris & to the world at large, and also suitable and creditable to the nation'. 'Give us a grant to make up our deficit,' he should urge, 'and so you can have this permanent national monument on the most conspic- uous spot in the centre of Paris.'   Concluding, P.G. hopes that Nansen can use his

so deservedly great influence in directing Norse public opinion towards this gift.   If it has been worth each nation's while to spend so much money and effort on this Exposition - which I quite believe - it is also worth while to let their house remain - is that not so?

> Yours ever faithfully
> Patrick Geddes
> Sec. of Committee for
> Conservation & Utilisation
> of Rue des Nations -

Léon Bourgeois was chairman of the committee, and many other key persons of the Assembly supported the new project as well as re- cently recruited politicians and diplomats.   But it was the in- defatigable secretary who bore the brunt of this campaign to achieve what now can be described as a UNESCO nearly 50 years ahead of its time.   Of the twenty-two pavilions along the 'Street of the Nations' official architects pronounced twelve as well enough built and suitable for preservation.   Whereupon Geddes submitted a detailed plan for the disposition of each pavilion and for its future maintenance as well.   The British building, because of superior lighting, was to shelter the Pasteur Museum and the lab- oratories of scientific societies.   Germany's would provide meeting places for other learned societies and congresses, and

Norway's would contain exhibits of fishery, navigation, and Arctic exploration.   The Finnish pavilion was to house geographical collections.   And so it went, Greece providing for archaeology, Hungary for history, Monaco for oceanography, Sweden for industries, Belgium for civic collections, the USA for a museum of comparative education; and Austria for a palace of music, and a truly Geddesian Museum of Peace.

As all-purpose secretary, P.G.'s duty was to interview and explain, to lobby and persuade, wherever or however he thought best.   As inherently a man of action, his daily joy for several months was to do battle for the *Rue des Nations*.   He sought out representatives of a dozen foreign governments, struggled with the red-tape of the Third Republic, hounded exposition officials, Parisian city fathers, and dignitaries of all kinds.   At first his success was amazing: Germany immediately offered its building as an outright gift; Finland followed suit, as did most of the other nations involved.   Publicity in the Paris newspapers resulted in substantial gifts of money, and by December even the contractors, whose wrecking crews were impatiently standing by, had come to terms.   Collections to fill the salvaged pavilions were pledged in abundance. The Prince of Monaco promised duplicates of specimens in his own museum, Fridtjof Nansen undertook to organise the museum of geography, and similar offers were made for each and every one of the institutes of the original plan.

The argument P.G. used on Nansen about reviving cultural Delphi as well as the 'Olympian Games' must have had a wide appeal.   He referred to the plans and elevations showing the 'magnificent result of the excavations of Delphi' as a precedent in Paris.

> See there the great theatre, literally the Salle des Fêtes of the Exposition; and if central temple and great statue be still wanting here, note at least on either side of the way thither the striking and varied range of buildings, one from each of the many little states and commonwealths which made up the Hellenic civilisation of the time, and to which each sent what seemed best of its contemporary art and of its historic treasures.
>
> Now here again at this Exposition, after two thousand years, the nations who make up the civilisation of the time have again sunk their jealousies and ennobled their rivalries in the same way; each has built again its treasure-house, given its own individual expression of its own ideals, yet in harmony with all.   It is no evil omen, then, no unhappy augury, this re-opening of the Sacred Way at Delphi, these even transient buildings of the Rue des Nations. (37)

In his zeal Geddes may occasionally have trodden upon a bureaucratic toe or upon a point of diplomatic procedure, but the implacable enemy was time.   Foreign commissioners and French contractors alike were eager to wind up their business.   The latter wanted their wrecking-contracts either adhered to or else well and quickly paid for if broken.   The municipal council of Paris went into a long recess, while a legal tangle over the ownership of the *Rue des Nations* arose which would have delighted any lawyer, had there been time to unravel it.   Rights over the river-front of this street belonged to the Ministry of Public Works, jurisdiction over the thoroughfare was vested in the city of Paris, while ownership of an intermediate strip of land was claimed by the railway company whose tunnel ran underneath.   But the deadlines for saving the *Rue des Nations* expired with the old year, and in the first days of January 1901 the valiant committee had to acknowledge its defeat and disband.

P.G., however, refused to give up the fight; he fell back and began another offensive.   Though the picturesque line of national pavilions was doomed, the valuable collections still were available and needed only to be housed.   Towards finding such museum space a new committee was constituted, which in turn presented a request to the municipal council that the ground floor of the *Petit Palais*, a permanent building of the exposition, be given over to these collections.   What finally happened to this proposition is not clear: politics and waning of public interest were partial factors, and Geddes had to return to Scotland to his other undertakings, notably the forthcoming Glasgow Exposition.   Thus the second project ultimately met the fate of the first.

It was splendid, everyone agreed, this vision of the *Rue des Nations* as an enduring monument to the finest achievements of the nineteenth century.   Its institutes and the international co-operation they were to have fostered would have constituted a veritable League of Nations on cultural and scientific planes if not immediately on that of international politics.   This bold project contained in germ much that was to be implemented from two to five decades later by the International Labour Office in Geneva, the International Institute for Intellectual Co-operation in Paris and above all by UNESCO, the United Nations Educational, Scientific and Cultural Organisation.

In retrospect the stirring attempt to save the *Rue des Nations* has to be looked upon as one of P.G.'s 'Magnificent Failures', the first of several great battles in which his defeat, inherent in the circumstances, proved almost as glorious as victory.   Yet these same battles are still being fought, the same ideals and principles are still there to inspire new champions.

The years 1897 to 1901 were filled with conflict and bloodshed: Armenian massacres, the Spanish-American War, the Boer War, the Filipino Insurrection.   Everywhere raged the rivalry of predatory empires.   This was the world which Rabindranath Tagore described in his poem, 'The Sunset of the Century', written on 31 December 1900.

> The last sun of the century sets amidst the blood-red clouds of the West and the whirlwind of hatred.
>
> The naked passion of self-love of Nations, in its drunken delirium of greed, is dancing to the clash of steel and the howling verses of vengeance.

Patrick Geddes also experienced this world of violence and destruction, but he interpreted its evils in basic terms of occupational strife.   He saw hunter and shepherd against peasant, and
he saw agricultural degeneration.   Upon these age-old evils were
piled all the economic maladjustments of the nineteenth century,
all the rapaciousness of palaeotechnic civilisation and of con-
quistador-imperialism.   Yet, instead of merely talking about 'the
brotherhood of man' and the 'blessings of peace', he demonstrated
in both rural Cyprus and metropolitan Paris, that men can only be
brothers and keep the peace if they have work to engage their
energies, food to nourish their families and visions of a better
future to challenge their minds.   An adventurous, constructive
peace is the only one that can compete with war and its glory:
action.   Therefore, said Geddes, real peace must be an unending
fight against disease and slums, ignorance and economic injustice,
against deforestation and waste of natural resources: such a
peace means, both concretely and figuratively, that everyone must
care for his garden.

To paraphrase his wise comment on Cyprus in 1897:
  Wherever at this moment two Easterners (or Africans, Americans,
  Asians, Europeans) are quarrelling in their poverty, or dis-
  puting resources wastefully plundered from nature, four or six
  or ten might soon be co-operating (reclaiming rural areas,
  humanizing cities) in wealth and in peace.

Panorama of the *Rue des Nations* at the Paris World's Fair, which P.G. nearly succeeded in having preserved as a 'UNESCO' of 1900!

Chapter 7

LIFE PROJECTS DISCOVERED: TOWN PLANNING AND SOCIOLOGY, 1901-14

GLASGOW FAIR 1901 ... 'THE TEMPLE' ... GLOBES & TOWER ... MUSEUM DIRECTORSHIP

The failure of P.G.'s 'UNESCO' project in the *Rue des Nations* in no way discouraged him.   Rather, it whetted both his appetite for more such spare-time activities and his zeal in pursuing them. First came the Glasgow International Exposition of 1901 where, in accordance with the Paris resolution, a bilingual summer school was held throughout the summer.   Next was the framing of a simi- lar resolution aimed at continuing the work of the International Association at the Exposition planned for St Louis in 1903.   Then followed a Geddesian exhortation to the Glasgow Corporation to preserve as permanent museums some of the most valuable pavilions of the Fair.

This time the aftermath was neither successful nor glorious.   The municipal and exposition authorities did not follow up P.G.'s nine- teen-page report on, and preservation plea for, 'Museums and Insti- tutes Possible....'   Moreover, and unlike Paris, there arose a dispute between him and the local committee of the International Association over certain financial matters.   In two letters to his friend Mavor in the summer of 1902 P.G. refers to the matter as 'that unlucky and disastrous dispute' and 'this weary question', respectively. (1)   He had sent his whole dossier to a capable lawyer, asking for an impartial statement of 'the rights & wrongs of both sides'.   After three months the legal report came: 'prac- tically ... a confirmation of all my contentions & a conviction of their arithmetical blunders, & of worse.'   But still the case was not re-opened, and P.G. entreats Mavor's 'good offices towards a fair trial' since he 'can ill afford to drop the money, but still less to bear what a minute & detailed inquiry proves to be error & injustice'.

On 20 October 1902 Geddes wrote to the Lord Provost of Glasgow, re- calling 'the interview last July which you kindly granted me' and the latter's promise 'personally to read that report ... obtained from Mr. James Macdonald S.S.C. Edinburgh, and which, with all

relevant documents, I left in your hands'.   He is sorry to seem
'in any way to press your Lordship', but explains that he is
heavily burdened by 'having had to advance almost the whole outlays
of the Association ... by overdrafts upon my personal A/cs.'.   He
further appeals for arbitration to determine what is due him 'after
hearing both parties, and checking their mutual allegations of
arithmetical and other error'.   Meanwhile, says P.G., the Local
Executive Committee has offered a settlement of 'nearly £200 less
than that portion of our actual outlays which we claim ...' and
intends to compel 'me by their stress of personal poverty to accept
this in full, or abandon the whole amount'.   His only hope of re-
dress lies with the Lord Provost: 'without your Lordship's speedy
intervention, this mode of coercion must soon become effective....
I entreat you not to compel my Association and myself to leave
Glasgow with our usefulness permanently injured, and with an abid-
ing sense of unredressed wrong.'

The outcome of this 'disastrous dispute' is not known,* nor is that
of another controversy which came to a legal climax in 1902 in the
'Sheriff Court ... at Edinburgh'.   The latter story is here condensed from a draft of 'Defences' prepared by Geddes's counsel,
with additions in the 'Defender's' own hand. (2)   When the publishing firm of P.G. & Colleagues got into difficulties in 1896 one
of the contributors to its review, 'The Evergreen', a wholesale
stationer named William Cuthbertson (now referred to as 'Pursuer'),
offered to supervise its business transactions.   Described then by
Geddes as 'loyally enthusiastic', Cuthbertson acted for a time as
'manager-partner' to 'prove his confident prediction of a great
advance' in selling the firm's publications.   Their agreement 'was
reduced to writing' in a letter of late November 1896 of which 'no
copy was preserved by the Defender' but which stated that 'Pursuer's
renumeration was to be amicably arranged later on'.

Such unbusinesslike terms could not fail to lead to misunderstanding.   When the 'anticipated success in selling did not come off'
the part-time manager not only 'ceased interesting himself in the
work' but later on 'took great umbrage' at an alleged under-payment
for stationery supplied to the Eastern and Colonial Association,
Ltd.   In consequence, 'The Pursuer ... rudely called on Defender
to pay a sum of £100 as being the remuneration to which he was entitled'.   In 1899, however, another 'amicable arrangement' was

---

* The National Library has no letters from Mavor in 1902, while an
inquiry made to the City Archivist, Corporation of Glasgow elicited
the reply (11 May 1972): '... I am unable to locate any correspondence on this matter now surviving in the City's Archives.   No
special file on the International Assembly survives and the letter-
books of the Lord Provost 1902-6 are missing from the series ...'
However the Minutes of the Town Council meeting of 12 January 1905
acknowledged receipt of a cheque to the Glasgow Corporation for the
amount of the International Association's surplus after its affairs
were wound up: nearly 200 times what Geddes had claimed, £39,000!
(Archivist's letter of 10 February 1976.)

made whereby Cuthbertson accepted £100 capital in the concern and
was to that extent a partner'.   But in 1901 Pursuer again demanded
payment of the £100, this time with interest.   'The Defender having
replied somewhat warmly there followed a series of abusive violent
letters from Pursuer to Defender' as well as the bringing of legal
action against Geddes in 1902.*

The fragments of evidence recorded by P.G. in the Glasgow and Edinburgh disputes well illustrate his behaviour in the financial
tangles which now and then cropped up in his long life of practical
affairs.   Sometimes there was arithmetical or other error on the
part of others, but again the misunderstanding would reflect a recurrent pattern of unshakable confidence in his own recollection of
enthusiastic oral agreements and in his interpretations of essential
points.   Added to this was an impatience with petty routine which
he once vented to James Mavor in these words: 'I can't and won't
keep accounts!' (3)

Wisely, he did not make such confessions to other than close
friends, for his enemies would have rejoiced and claimed confirmation of their many criticisms, and wavering supporters found reason
to back out.   Indeed, while Geddes was at his busiest at the Paris
Exposition in August 1900, an initially friendly investor** in the
Town & Gown Association attacked him for neglecting its interests
in Edinburgh.   The man's wife even sent Mrs Geddes a copy of his
protest to the T & G's directors, with a note which ended, 'Believe
me dear Anna, Your affectionate friend'.   Other attacks followed
during P.G.'s struggle with the aftermath of the Glasgow Exhibition, climaxed by a list of the T & G's manifold schemes wherein
ideal claims and aims were confronted with poor practical results.
Anna loyally defended these projects against her friend's allegations, and Patrick composed a lengthy rebuttal justifying the
intent of his admittedly unfulfilled plans.   Unconvinced, the
hard-headed investor made this not unfriendly exhortation:
    Suspend - if possible give up altogether - your attempts to
    realize your dreams.   The world is not ripe for them nor are
    the means at your disposal adequate.

Geddes had long been accustomed to such advice, but it was as impossible for him to heed it as it was for others not to give it.

* Asked about a possible verdict the Scottish Record Office in
Edinburgh replied (22 April 1974) that their last entry in this case
showed 'that the closed record was entered on 21 November 1902'.
They had no date 'for bringing proof or for extracting of decree'
and stated: 'The inference from this is that the case did not in
fact proceed to decree, having been settled out of court at some
date later than 21 November'.

** The Edinburgh bookbinder and printer, Thomas James Cobden-
Sanderson.   See Kitchen, pp. 190-1 and 201-3 for details of his
and others' complaints about P.G.'s 'very much too sanguine' forecasts.

Among the Geddes documents in the National Library are four sheets
of intriguing handwritten notes from early 1902.   The first two are
marked 'To V.V.B.' and dated 19 January; the others 'Private: ie
Esoteric pro tem' but undated.   All four, plus certain letters referred to but not extant, were written to Victor Veratius Branford
who by now was almost as close a colleague of P.G. in sociology as
J. Arthur Thomson in biology.   These notes concern a possible extension of the Outlook Tower beyond geography and civics into the
'actual *autogenetic* process ... education in best sense'.   How far-
reaching these esoteric interests of Geddes were is best revealed
by him.   He had been largely occupied 'in Ethical Meditation, &
indeed in trying to discern the equivalents in our modern life &
phrase for the essentials of the religious life of past periods'.

Schuré's *Les Grds* [Grands] *Initiés* wd [would] interest you - but
returning to my best youthful source of insprn, I find none
better than Emerson.   But all are suggestive & profitable.
Thus the spl [spiritual] exercises of St. Ignatius! (wh. [which]
a Cath. neighbour perhaps hopeful of my soul's health has brought
me) has thrown light - some of course upon that militant imper-
ialist of his times - but also into oneself ...

The Tower of Thought and Action needs a corresponding basement
& not merely that of Arts & Sci's in Gen'l as hitherto but a *sub-
basement or catacomb proper* in which the Life of Feeling sim.
[ilarly] be recog. [nised].   Is there any escape from this
argument? & if not to what does it lead?   Do not imagine that I
have in any way lapsed into a Quietist or delirious mood.   This
is only a clearer devt of what has been more or less implicit &
incipient all along.

Ethicalised social activity, industry etc, all good & well,
but how reach the devt. of *personality*: How, in short, effect
what in theol. phrase is called the Conversion of sinners!   How
hold Revival Meetings, & organise a Salvation Army?   This, as I
indicated before, is the large problem of my past winter - largely concerned it has been with 'makin' my soul' as the vivid
Irishism goes!   In nobler (or at least less vulgarised) phrase,
we have the Temple, but what of the Mysteries?   What of the Initiation?

Get hold of a book - (it is worth buying ...) Schuré's 'Les
Grands Initiés' - (Pythagore, Orpheus, Plato, J.C. etc.) and you
will see better what I mean and how I am quite sane over all
this....

If this be a clearer statement of the personal ev. [evolution]
process than the usual ones, & one 'reconciling science and religion' as that much-invoked phrase goes, the process of ed'l
work becomes clearer & the Ethicosm becomes functional - alive - .
The bearing of all this on School & University I have of course
always so far *seen*, but never yet *vitalised* or succeeded in
putting in action save a little at the best moments of the summer
meetings.   I think I see more clearly & feel more strongly - and
so I go back to my plans with a more cathedral-building spirit, &
tenacity.   And to you I say - either we have or have not a means
here, not only of carrying out our dreams of kg, [knowledge] education - action - but of carrying these farther & deeper for ourselves & others than we have dared to dream before - So I ask you
again - come soon - and help - and I am confident of your
answer -

Victor Branford replied two days later from a village in Buckingham-shire: 'To be allowed the privilege of the glimpse into the working of your mind, disclosed in your letter, is a great thing for which the offer of formal thanks seems almost an impertinence.' He says that this letter reminded him of P.G.'s paper of 1885, 'A Synthetic Outline of the History of Biology', and eulogises:

> Even if I had not known you personally I think that this paper would have struck me as being one of the most interesting docu-ments in the history of science.   For in this paper one sees the rare sight of a science visibly passing from the stage of being predominantly inductive to that of being predominantly deduc-tive....   We have an instance of what might be called the birth of a new master science not less sharply defined in outline ... than the birth of modern mechanics with Newton.

Branford philosophises about Geddes's twin towers of Outlook and In-look saying 'that as the former interpreted the world as predomi-nantly will and idea, ... so the latter interpreted the world as predominantly will and emotion'.   He makes no mention, however, of the plea to 'come soon - and help'.   (Or did even this most faith-ful 'disciple' at times prefer correspondence to daily contact?) The only assistance offered is some advice regarding health.

> I am distressed to hear of your inability to get that troublesome writer cramp cured.   I feel sure you would be amply repaid for the trouble of using a type-writer by the astonishing diminution of physical strain in writing....   [Branford says he does the greater part of his own writing on a small Blickensderfer.]   In a very short time one learns to write on this quicker than with the hand and with vastly less fatigue.

He concludes by mentioning 'Galeron's models' and wonders whether 'your article on these has appeared'.   This refers to the gran-diose joint-proposal of geographer J.G. Bartholomew and Patrick Geddes for the creation of a National Institute of Geography for Great Britain.

As a repository of maps and books on special subjects, it was to supplement, if not incorporate, the long-established Royal Geo-graphical Society.   As a co-ordinator of all the sciences and activities related to geography, it would be a super-Outlook Tower. The ground-plan and elevation published in the 'Scottish Geographi-cal Magazine' (March 1902) show how skilfully Geddes brought toget-her in the proposed institute his favourite world- and universe-surveying ideas.   One side of this large building was to house the huge celestial globe, brain-child of Paul Louis Albert Galeron, a French architect.   At the centre behind the main edifice the plan called for a tower 250 ft high and 60 ft square at the base, the Tower of Regional Survey.   Two amphitheatres completed the insti-tute: one to serve as a lecture and congress hall, the other as an exhibition gallery for landscape panoramas.

With this half-practical, half-philosophical bait, Geddes went angling for some 'patriotic and wealthy patron' who would finance the project.   The Right Honourable James Bryce, MP, DCL, FRS,

expressed approval of the scheme and declared that the Outlook
Tower part of it would 'bring facts into new relations and stimulate reflection'.   Sir Archibald Geikie, the geologist, waxed
enthusiastic about the service such an institute could render by
providing legislators, 'who are not always as well informed as we
could wish', with accurate information, not only on this or that
point of the far-flung empire, but on their own electoral districts
as well.

Sir Clements Markham, president of the Royal Geographical Society,
wrote Geddes that he had always been interested in the latter's
ideas and in his efforts to give them practical shape, and suggested that the Royal Geographical Society already provided a nucleus
around which the more complete national institute might be built.
In fact, Sir Clements asserted that the subject would have the
serious consideration of the Council of the Society 'in a year or
two, when Mr Bartholomew, yourself, and other leading geographers
will no doubt be invited to meet and thus form a more representative deliberative council'.   However, the fishing apparently was
very poor in the British Isles of that day, for despite approbation in high places nothing came of the proposed Institute.   An
inquiry in 1972 to the Royal Geographic Society brought this reply
from the Archivist:

> Our council minute books contain no reference to it, nor to any
> communications from Sir Patrick Geddes or J.G. Bartholomew on
> the subject....   [Sir Clements Markham's] correspondence with
> the other officers of the Society contains no reference to the
> proposed National Institute of Geography. (4)

A few months later Geddes moved on to the summer school at Cambridge University in 1902, where he gave a course of lectures on
Nature Study.   (This was a subject, incidentally, on which he was
becoming a widely recognised authority.   Through his and J. Arthur
Thomson's efforts, it had been officially adopted as a part of the
curriculum of Scottish schools in 1899 and of English schools in
1900.)   That same summer a conference was held in London at
Regent's Park on how to teach the new subject, so naturally Geddes
was on hand, reading two papers.   Geography and nature study
appear to have taken up practically the whole year, for in December he turned up in Dunfermline, Scotland, to give an inaugural
address before the Naturalists' Society of that town.   But by
March of 1903 his energies were applied in still another direction.

The Edinburgh Museum of Science and Art was at that time without a
director, and this was a temptation too great for P.G., Unlimited
to resist.   He made application for the job, sending in a bulky
dossier containing: a copy of the 100-page 'Letter of Application'
which fifteen years before had confronted My Lords and Gentlemen of
Edinburgh University;   a set of programmes from the Edinburgh
Summer Meetings;   documents relating to Geddesian activities at
the Paris Exposition;   a copy of the Glasgow exhortation on preserving museums;   and a lengthy personal letter of application
which, reviewing his activities from 'museum work' under Thomas
Huxley to the recent fair in Glasgow, made it appear that he had

been preparing solely for the Edinburgh directorship for the past
fifty years.   Here is his own interpretation of the varied experiences and the multiple aims of his life thus far:

> As regards technical and artistic education, I have not been
> without direct experience.   In the field or upon the sea the
> naturalist is accustomed to take part in the simple nature occu-
> pations; in the garden and the laboratory he becomes in some
> measure initiated into more developed crafts.   Since a biolo-
> gist's outlook tends to rise into the human and social one, I
> have sought to improve the material environment, the hygiene
> of the city, the housing of its workers and its students.   And
> in employing architects and artists, in planning or repairing
> buildings, in scheming decorations, even in searching out the
> antique furniture of students' houses, one purchases experience
> of a kind for which a museum may have obvious use.
>
> As regards fine art, besides frequent teaching in museums and
> galleries, I have been mainly responsible for nearly ten years,
> and not upon the administrative side alone, for a good deal of
> public and private decoration, book-illustration and craft
> design of different sorts, which latterly developed as an 'Old
> Edinburgh School of Art'.

Then followed an account of the Outlook Tower and its index-museum
as bearing on the problems of large museums and as having provided
Geddes with much valuable experience.

> While thus not lacking the training and the detailed discipline
> of a museum curator, I may fairly claim to have had a real pre-
> paration for the duties of a directorship.   That this prepara-
> tion, though wide, has not therefore been superficial, may be
> ascertained by reference to any or all of the correspondingly
> various experts whose names I am permitted to submit below....
>   In summary, then, I base my candidature upon three points:
> 1.   a long and critical acquaintance with Museums and Exhibi-
>   tions ...;
> 2.   a special and experimental intimacy with the problems of
>   classification ...;
> 3.   the experience of an educationist, whose essential problem
>   has always been the awakening or freshening of interest in
>   student and teacher.   For it is not enough to amass col-
>   lections, nor even intelligently to display them; the most
>   pressing problem of all is that of the museum-visitors:
>   teachers, pupils, and public alike.   It is to renew the
>   healthy spring of wonder - in our day too much depressed -
>   and to guide it onwards, as admiration towards art, as cur-
>   iosity towards science.   In a word, I should hope not only
>   to administer and develop the Museum as a centre of educa-
>   tional supply, but to increase and improve the educational
>   demand.

Yet neither titled patronage (he had sought the support of the Earl
of Rosebery) nor the weighty application succeeded in getting him
the Edinburgh directorship, and the months of April, May, and June
1903 found Geddes as usual at Dundee.   August saw a revival of
the Summer Meetings in Edinburgh, the first to be held since 1899
and the fourteenth and next-to-last of those inimitable Geddesian
gatherings.

The theme for 1903 was 'Edinburgh and Its Region', one chosen to
appeal impartially to 'Naturalist and Humanist, Teacher and
Tourist', and to give them all a taste of 'regional survey'.
> As befits a Survey the course of study is first of all practi-
> cal, and will be conducted as far as possible in the open air.
> But an adequate Programme of Interpretative Lectures, Demonstra-
> tions, and Recitals, of Museum visits, of Laboratory and Studio
> work, has also been arranged. Active and sedentary studies may
> thus be combined in proportion varying with individual needs and
> strength, and as far as possible kept outdoors in sun, indoors
> in storm.

CITY DEVELOPMENT IN DUNFERMLINE ... CIVIC AWAKENING IN LONDON

Although eight months of 1903 had already passed, well filled with
thoughts, deeds and plans, there was still time that year for Patrick Geddes to establish his main, double calling in life. The
two proving-grounds were vastly and appropriately different from
each other: a small town in mid-Scotland; and overgrown, metropolitan London. What he there sought to accomplish would shape
thinking and action for the rest of his life.

In August 1903 Andrew Carnegie set up a trust fund of £500,000 for
Dunfermline, the little Scottish town in which he was born, and in
addition gave the adjacent 70 acre Pittencrieff estate to the municipality. Some years before, Carnegie had presented his birthplace with the first in the great chain of free public libraries he
was to scatter over the world, but this time his gift was an experiment in civic renewal. To the twenty representative citizens selected by him as trustees, he confided the task of bringing into
'the monotonous lives of the toiling masses of Dunfermline more of
sweetness and light'. 'Remember,' he charged in his deed of
trust, 'you are pioneers, and do not be afraid of making mistakes.
Not what other cities have is your standard. It is the something
beyond this which they lack.'

Without delay the trustees engaged two men to study and report
separately on the best means of making the Pittencrieff estate into
a public park and providing it with recreational and cultural facilities. One was T.H. Mawson, a professional town-planner, and
the other a teacher of botany named Geddes. The two competitors
lost no time in getting under way; Mawson with the competence of
a trained architect, P.G. with his typical enthusiasm and far-
sightedness.

For about three months the latter haunted the streets of Dunfermline, tramping up and down every square rod of the future park,
studying from every angle the historic ruined abbey and palace
which lay between park and town. On clear days he was accompanied
by a local photographer, Mr James Norval, who served as a kind of
Boswell, recording with camera whatever P.G. looked at: vistas
over the estate from all approaches, detailed landscapes, views of
public buildings, alleys, dump-heaps, broken sewers, and so on by

the score.   With this photographic survey of his subject and a
trunkful of notes and sketches, he departed for London there to
write the major part of: 'City Development: A Study of Parks,
Gardens and Culture-Institutes', as his report to the Carnegie
Dunfermline Trust was entitled.

He arrived early enough in November to help Victor Branford complete some arrangements they had started in June involving representatives of 'various departments of social investigation - economic, anthropological, historical, psychological, ethical, etc. -
of philosophy, of education, and of practical social interests'.
A general meeting of these men was held later in November at which
the Sociological Society of London 'was duly constituted'.   The
Right Hon. James Bryce was elected first President, J. Martin
White Treasurer, Victor Branford Hon. Secretary, and among its
thirty Councillors were names such as Sir John Cockburn, former
Premier of South Australia, Mr H.G. Wells, and as thinly disguised
instigator ex-officio, 'Professor Geddes: President, Edinburgh
School of Sociology'.

Branford, now a financier as well as accountant, was the supporting
force behind the new Society, and it would be an open secret for
years that he used both private money and influence so that his
Scottish teacher and colleague might have a London forum for his
ideas.

A detailed account of the founding was published by R.J. Halliday,
in the 'Sociological Review', November 1968, which throws interesting light on both preliminaries and aftermath.   It was only
after an attempt to create a Scottish Institute of Sociology at the
Outlook Tower had failed that Branford and P.G. turned for support
to London.   The result, writes Mr Halliday, was a national Sociological Society formed as 'a coalition between three distinct movements; the civics, racial [i.e. eugenist] and social work schools'.
(The 'hiving off' of the eugenists in 1907 into their own Society
would weaken the parent group but also enlarge the role played by
the civics or Geddesian school.)

The Sociological Society with its monthly meetings and its quarterly 'Review' (later a monthly publication) served to bring P.G. to
the attention of academic and literary circles in London; it provided him with audiences for the exposition of his pet subjects:
sociology based on Place-Work-Folk and regional survey as pre-
requisite to planning.   But neither President nor Treasurer nor
Secretary could ensure that its members would always understand
what Geddes was driving at and follow his suggestions for action.
When Francis Galton appeared before the society at the opening
meeting on 18 April 1904 to expound the new subject of 'Eu-genics'
; the science of Good Birth - he was received with intelligent
interest.   Yet when Geddes came along in mid-July 1904 with a
complementary paper on 'Civics as Applied Sociology', in which he
held that eugenics was inseparable from *politogenics* or *Eu-polito-
genics* (interpreted by him to mean the science of Good Cities) not
everyone followed his reasoning.   With valley-section sketch,

historical charts, and unfamiliar words like 'Hebraomorphic thought'
and 'Eu-topia' (meaning 'good place' instead of 'Utopia' which
derives from the Greek 'Ou-topia', or 'no place') he proved too
much for some of the intellectuals of London.

On the other hand, two famous workers in practical civics had no
trouble in following him.   Charles Booth stated from the Chair
that it was 'one of the most complete and charming papers on a
great and interesting subject' he had ever heard and hoped that
the ensuing discussion would 'emphasise and, if that is possible,
add to the wealth of ideas that this paper contains'. (5)   Ebenezer Howard, the first to make comment, said: 'I have read and re-
read - in the proof forwarded to me - Professor Geddes's wonderfully
luminous and picturesque paper with much interest'.   Taking up the
speaker's account of the geographical and historical development of
a city, Howard prophesied that solutions would be found for the
'twin problems of rural depopulation and of the over-crowded, overgrown city'.   He could already read the signs
> of a coming change so great and so momentous that the twentieth
> century will be known as the period of the great exodus, the
> return to the land, the period when by a great and conscious
> effort a new fabric of civilisation shall be reared.

Howard suggested, a propos P.G.'s diagram portraying city development, that 'for one of Prof. Geddes's interrogation marks might be
substituted "Decentralisation of Industry" - as a great, but yet
incipient movement, represented by Port Sunlight, Bournville,
Garden City.'

Precisely what influence Geddes and Howard had upon each other is
a study that falls outside the limits of this biography, but the
former wrote in 1922 that Howard 'was good enough to tell me once
he had been encouraged by my beginnings long ago in Old Edinburgh!. (6)   Geddes had earlier paid tribute to Howard in 'Cities
in Evolution' (1915) for 'The note of social idealism, and in
practical yet most disinterested form' which he struck
> in his famous Eutopia ... of 'Garden Cities'.   In this notable
> book is set forth the town of the Industrial Age now opening -
> that neotechnic order, characterised by electricity, hygiene,
> and art, by efficient and beautiful town planning and assoc-
> iated rural development, and by a corresponding rise of social
> co-operation and effective good-will.

A leading London Comtist, Dr J.H. Bridges, commented favourably
upon the new regional survey approach to the basic study of cities
and civic problems.
> Everyone who heard the lecturer must have been fascinated by
> his picture of a river system which he takes for his unit of
> study; the high mountain tracts, the pastoral hill-sides, the
> hamlets and villages in the valleys, the market town where the
> valleys meet, the convergence of larger valleys into a county
> town, finally, the great city where the river meets the sea.
> The special note of Prof. Geddes' method is that he does not
> limit himself to the greater cities, but also, and perhaps by

preference deals with the smaller, and with their physical environment; and, above all, that he attempts not merely to
observe closely and thoroughly, but to generalise as the result
of his observation.

Israel Zangwill wrote ('To-day', 10 August 1904) that Geddes must
'be congratulated on a stimulating paper, and upon his discovery
of Eutopia.   For Eutopia ... is merely your own place perfected.
And the duty of working towards its perfection lies directly upon
you.   "Civics - as applied sociology" comes to show you the way.'
'The Times' (20 July 1904) not only printed an abstract of his
paper but stated in a leading article that it
     contained ideas of practical value to be recommended to the
     study of ambitious municipalities....   Professor Geddes truly
     said ... the beginnings of a concrete art of city-making are
     visible at various points.   But our city rulers are often
     among the blindest to these considerations.

The months between the founding of the Sociological Society and his
lecture on the heels of Galton were again more than normally full
ones for P.G.   He helped Branford with recruiting of both members
and lecturers.   He gave winter lectures on nature study at the
Horniman Museum, on cities at the London School of Economics, and
in the late spring on botany at UCD.   Such leisure moments as he
may have had must have been fairly well occupied also, for when he
returned to London in the middle of July he was able to lay on the
Sociological Society's table a printed and generously illustrated
advance copy of 'City Development'.   The regular edition was not
in public circulation until the autumn, but when it appeared nearly
every periodical and large newspaper in Great Britain carried laud-
atory reviews, although approbation was mingled with doubts as to
its acceptance by the Trust.

This quarto-size volume, whose 230 pages are filled almost as much
by photographs, artists' sketches, and architects' drawings as by
printed text, is a rare example of what can result when a modern,
town-planning Leonardo is given, or takes, a free hand.   Historian, archaeologist, naturalist, gardener, architect, builder,
decorator, museum-maker, educator, and sociologist, P.G. mastered
the past and present of Dunfermline and moulded its possible
future with the deftness of a sculptor working in clay.   Yet with
all this sweeping back into history and the cutting across all
segments of contemporary life, he never rambled without definite
purpose.   Whatever he touched on had a definite connection with
Pittencrieff Park and its accompanying culture-institutes.

'As the wandering student of old, though seeking ever to learn as
well as teach, was wont boldly to nail up his theses against all
comers, so do I here.'   With this challenge in his preface, the
author of 'City Development' stressed the need of a threefold study,
not merely of Dunfermline, but of every town in the world that
sought to improve itself.   First, a book of the past, an interpretive guide-book of history and geography.   Second, a book of
the present; a social survey of people, their condition and

occupation, their real wages, family budget and cultural interests.
Third, a book of the city's hope which,

> taking full note of places and things as they stand, of people
> as they are, of work, family and institutions, of ideas and
> ideals; yet patiently plans out, then boldly suggests, new and
> practicable developments; and these not only for the immediate
> future but for the remoter and higher issues which a city's long
> life ... involves.

It was the sequel to guide and survey, the book of the future, which
Geddes wrote for Dunfermline in 1904.

> Civics as an art, a policy, has thus to do, not with U-topia but
> with Eu-topia; not with imagining an impossible no-place where
> all is well, but with making the most and best of each and every
> place, and especially of the city in which we live.   Here,
> then, is such a Eutopia for Dunfermline.

There were two distinct yet intermingling aspects of the Eutopia
P.G. proposed to build with Carnegie's money: Nature, as revealed
in lake and garden, museum and conservatory; and the Humanities
as expressed in history-palace and art-institute, outdoor theatre
and concert hall, in revitalised library and 'Thinking House'.
From the wealth of details as well as far-seeing generalisations
crowded into his report, some typical examples of each can be given.
A device Geddes used repeatedly was to present a photograph of some
existing evil - the mill-stream heaped with rubbish, an ugly street,
a bare corner of park - and then beside it show, by means of re-
touching the same photograph, how each burden could be turned into
an asset.   He removed rubbish, landscaped the stream, planted
trees along the street, put flower-beds or an artificial pond in
the park corner, and so on.   Whether in building or gardening
he insisted on utilising classic and romantic, exotic and native
styles, but each in its appropriate place.   His guiding principle
was that of 'neither too radically destroying the past in the
supposed interest of the present, nor too conservatively allowing
the past to limit this, but incorporating the best results of the
past with the best we can do in the present.'

Geddes planned everything usually found in public parks, including
gardens, playgrounds, tennis courts, gymnasium, wading pools, duck-
ponds, oriental tea-house, an orangery, and a miniature zoo.   In
particular a rock garden in which both plants and visitors should
have ample room.

> Children will always run up and down the rocks of a rock garden,
> and it should therefore be constructed from the first with paths
> and steps sufficiently broad to admit of their doing this with-
> out injury to the plants or themselves.   Hence my roomy and
> winding rock paths, nearly one-third of a mile, with occasional
> pools and masses of shrubbery, are arranged so as to give con-
> tinual variety and fresh points of view and interest. (7)

This was only a starting point.   The garden would also serve to
illustrate the evolution of plant life and the geological structure
of the world.   In the botanical gardens of Edinburgh and Dundee he

CITY DEVELOPMENT

A STUDY OF

PARKS, GARDENS, AND CULTURE-INSTITUTES

A REPORT
TO THE CARNEGIE DUNFERMLINE TRUST

BY

PATRICK GEDDES

PROFESSOR OF BOTANY, UNIV. COLL., DUNDEE (ST ANDREWS UNIVERSITY)
PRESIDENT OF THE EDINBURGH SCHOOL OF SOCIOLOGY

WITH PLAN, PERSPECTIVE, AND 136 ILLUSTRATIONS

GEDDES AND COMPANY, OUTLOOK TOWER, EDINBURGH
AND 5 OLD QUEEN STREET, WESTMINSTER

THE SAINT GEORGE PRESS, BOURNVILLE, BIRMINGHAM

1904

Title page of Geddes's first great classic of town planning, a study made in 1903 for the trustees of Andrew Carnegie's gift to his birthplace, Dunfermline

had already experimented with scientific 'garden-writing', but to
combine a rock garden with reproductions of actual geological formations, complete with fossils and even models of animals of different periods, was a new and fascinating problem even for him;
one full of 'splendid possibilities'.

Like his pleasure gardens, P.G.'s suggested buildings reached
beyond their immediate functions into economic and sociological
problems.   Though limited by his commission to treatment of Pittencrieff Park and its 'culture-institutes', he still expanded his
ideas until they touched the whole town.   For example, when discussing the stream running through the new park, he emphasised
the uselessness of attempting any improvements there until the
whole problem of pollution and sewage disposal had been attacked,
not only in Dunfermline but upstream throughout the entire county
and beyond to its source.   Similarly, since park entrances and
boundaries would greatly affect the nature and value of adjacent
properties, Geddes urged the Trust to acquire all it could of
those in order to pioneer actively in housing reform.   The Trust
should become a model landlord: first providing tenants with
better habitations for the same rent than they could find elsewhere, better 'in actual floor and cube space, in sanitation and
decoration, in garden and outlook';   and second, a landlord leading tenants on to new and better houses as their earning power
increased.

P.G. exhorted the Trust's architects to utilise in all its properties, whether purchased or built, the known facts of hygiene and
up-to-date building ideas from other lands.   Sunlight and fresh
air should have easy access to the house by means of windows that
would open, and by balconies and gardens.   That traditional
British relic of barbaric days, the back kitchen and scullery,
should be redesigned on American lines.   Geddes wrote that 'after
spending more time in America than many more prolific writers',
he was firmly convinced that those American superiorities which
'surprise and disconcert old Europe very largely turn, indirectly
and directly, upon the superior culture and status of women'.
This superiority, for him, was derived from the well-designed
kitchen, and
     from that diminution in domestic drudgery which distinguishes
     the American from the European home.   When this begins to be
     realised, masculine chivalry will take the form of improving
     the kitchen and its appurtenances, alike for Cinderella's sake
     and for her mistress's.

The conclusion he put before the Scottish trustees was: 'To adopt
every improvement, then, that housewife and architect can devise
is thus a matter of increasing importance in domestic comfort,
well-being and leisure, in civic prosperity and culture, in
national and racial struggle'.   In other words, the kitchen is,
or ought to be, one of the foundations of a better equalised
society.

P.G.'s Outlook Tower colleague Edward McGegan, has related how com-

prehensive this report was, how amazingly it touched every aspect of
civic life, and states that 'Such a combination of rapidity and
thoroughness could come only from the possession of a highly-devel-
oped sixth sense of practice and discipline'. In addition to keen
observation, to have expressed what he saw and thought on paper in a
compelling and at times poetic manner was no mean literary achievement for Geddes. 'I was privileged to accompany him on some of his
surveys of Dunfermline', says McGegan, 'to discuss his plans with
him, and to be by his side while he wrote much of his Report; and I
remember vividly how hard he struggled to keep within the terms of
his reference.' (8) The result of this struggle, 'City Development', is Patrick Geddes at his best. It still can give an authentic glimpse of the botanist at work as a city-planning philosopher
and as an evangelist of civic rejuvenation.

Returning to the park, we discover next the plans for open-air museums of types of native dwellings like those in Norway and for reconstructions of primitive dwellings in appropriate sites, from prehistoric cave and underground house of Pict to Roman wall and Scottish 'crannog' or lake dwelling. A genuine Geddesian touch to this
latter project was that groups of boys, not workmen hired by the
Trust, were to dig the caves and build the huts: as one step towards the replacement of futile 'education by Exercises' by the
vital 'education of Experiences'. Not far from the primitive village lay a crafts village consisting of old mills and smithy restored to active use as an example of crafts such as flour-grinding,
bread-making, spinning and weaving, and metal work of all kinds.

In a great Nature-Palace Geddes had, as might be guessed, provided
for Galeron's celestial globe and Reclus's terrestrial globe in reduced format along with the usual exhibits representing all the
natural sciences. There was also a set of three-dimensional panoramas, like those in the Swedish pavilion at the Paris Exposition,
which would represent typical scenes of the earth from Lapland to
Greece, from Alaska to Florida, from the Nile to Capetown, and
similarly for every continent.
    Thus, as the series became comprehensive the visitor would not
    only know more of the world than any one mortal has ever seen,
    but realise it also, and see beyond his too narrow limit of
    daily street the larger world of Nature and Humanity.

Then, in rapid succession, came plans for a history-palace, an art
institute, an outdoor theatre, and a large concert hall. The history building was planned in segments, each one to portray a period
in Scotland's past, all culminating in a large round tower for the
twentieth century which naturally would also serve as an Outlook
Tower for Dunfermline. In the art institute Geddes was more concerned with the 'art of seeing' and the raising of public taste in
art than with building up a large collection of pictures. He pleaded for revolt against the dead hand of traditional instruction with
its 'freehand and model drawing, perspective and shading from the
cast' which mainly results in producing a crop of 'innumerable inferior draughtsmen' and not artists. His revolt was to be made
durable by teaching observation and 'healthy and joyous seeing' out
of doors.

The child in sunshine sees the violet shadows upon the dusty road just as the impressionist paints them: it is only the mis-educated grown-up, who has been trained from old pictures, or perhaps still more from printed descriptions of them, who persuades himself that the same shadow is brown.   To escape from common literary epithets and to be encouraged to observe how often earth is purple, grass gold, and the sea all possible colours, is a training which most of the older generation have missed and which the younger are not yet by any means sufficiently receiving.

Concert hall and theatre had also their missions of educating young and old, of indirectly though effectively elevating the level of popular culture.   'We are not laying out and prettifying this or that garden for a nine days' wonder, not setting up this or that museum as a new sarcophagus.'   Everything Geddes planned had an ideal purpose and in this case his ideal harmonised perfectly with that of Andrew Carnegie.   'Not what other cities have is your standard.   It is the something beyond this which they lack.'

Two paragraphs from the Report fittingly summarise both the method and spirit of its author:

Starting, then, with the fundamental problem of purifying our stream and cultivating our garden, we naturally and necessarily progressed towards the idea, first of bettered dwellings of the body, and then to that of higher palaces of the spirit.   The whole scheme - material and intellectual, domestic and civic, scientific and artistic - is thus thoroughly one; whereas without such fundamental basis of natural and industrial reality much of our present-day idealism but flutters in the void; while our would-be practical world, as yet too much without this evolutionary idealism, is continually sinking into material failure of stagnation, moral discouragement of decay.

Let us, then, unite both elements and, in the immortal phrase of Socrates, at once 'labour and make music.'   For even modest practical effort, a high note must be struck from the very outset.   'Except the Ideal build the house, they labour in vain that build it.' (9)

As one could expect from the sheer number of 'Parks, Gardens and Culture-Institutes' it proposed, P.G.'s lavishly illustrated report completely frightened the Dunfermline Trustees.   As Mairet says, these responsible citizens 'seem to have shown less understanding of its merits than alarm at the cost of its preparation'.   Their first act was to refuse to pay for its publication; whereupon Geddes had the volume printed at his own expense.*   But the real

---

* Ultimately the Trust did pay Geddes almost all of his account for fees and outlays, including the printing of two hundred copies for them and one hundred for him - 'In the end both parties emerged with dignity from this rather squalid disagreement.   Geddes was subsequently allowed the use of the plates and blocks, presumably so that he could run off more copies for distribution to his numerous correspondents' (letter to author, 16 July 1976, from Fred Mann, Secretary of the Carnegie Dunfermline Trust).

shock was the estimate of what his transformation of Dunfermline
would cost: one million pounds, or exactly double the amount of
Carnegie's donation.   To the trustees this was madness.
> Not at all! [countered Geddes] you have an annual income of at
> least twenty thousand pounds from the trust fund.   Invest this
> income in the gradual realization of these projects and in
> fifty years you will have spent the needed million, yet the
> capital will remain untouched!

Unconvinced, the trustees turned to the plans and estimates prepared
by T.H. Mawson.   Second great shock, for his also demanded a million pounds!   And so the two rival planners found themselves brothers in adversity.

The rejection was a deplorable decision, says Mairet who points out
that
> one circumstance that worked against P.G. may have been perso-
> nal.   Most unfortunately, the key man among the trustees had a
> legalistic mind peculiarly unresponsive to Geddes's aims, and
> happened to be passing through a personal crisis.   At one time
> or another there seem to have been some warm exchanges of opin-
> ion between them in the course of which P.G. made remarks that
> he would have expressed very differently had he known of this
> personal tragedy.   The trustee who had been an uncomprehending
> critic changed into an active enemy of Geddes and all his works.
> This does not excuse the trustees as a body for responding so
> unadventurously to Mr Carnegie's gift and exhortation;   they
> seem simply to have banked the capital and spent the interest on
> maintaining the park and some other worthy cultural objects. (10)

Twenty-five years later the Dunfermline 'Press' commented: 'Whether
the Trustees were justified or not in the attitude they adopted
towards Professor Geddes's work, the Trustees of today might find
inspiration in "City Development". (11)   We believe that some of
the present day members have never seen the book, to their own loss
and indirectly to the loss of the community.'* Whatever the rights
and wrongs of the case, one fact remained unchallenged, the paper
said.   'Only a genius could have produced, in the short time at
his disposal, such an amazing wealth of constructive proposals.'

Geddes foresaw the opposition he would meet and urged both citizens
and trustees to re-read Carnegie's deed of trust and accompanying
letter before branding his report as too ambitious.
> For since the keynotes there given forth are not those of our
> everyday practical life, but express ideals of exceptionally bold
> initiative, struck out at moments of highest insight and enthus-
> iasm, the practical policy of the Trust and the proposals of the
> present report must aim at, must be attuned to, the corresponding

---

* The present status of two of his practical proposals is: 'The
streams of Dunfermline have to a limited degree been cleaned up, but
catchment area controls are non-existant ... the [green-belt] linking of parks and recreational areas has only *partially* been executed
and comparatively recently' (Mr W.G. Stephenson, Retired Burgh
Engineer, to author 20 April 1977).

height.   It is not simply in his everyday business mood that
the reader must judge of them, but in his highest moments of
hope and resolve....
        The members of this Trust ... are, or should be, for the time
    the world's foremost council of sociological pioneers....   Thus
    viewed, the creation of this Trust may be considered as a move
    of the highest importance in that civic evolution of the world
    which claims hearing amid the political clamour of the times....
    Here then, once more in Scotland, as in stirring times of old,
    we see opening before us 'actions of a very high nature, leading
    to untrodden paths.' (12)

As an interlude between spring teaching of botany in Dundee in 1904
and autumn preaching of sociology in London, Geddes wrote still
another letter of application.   This time he sought to become
Principal of the Durham College of Science and in September laid
before its Council a skilful accounting of all his activities which
for years had constituted a preparation for such a headship.   He
vowed:
    Should you entrust me with the high responsibilities of this
    appointment, I should regard the busy and many-sided life they
    would involve, not so much as terminating my present lines of
    study and constructive work, but as an opportunity of adapting
    their experience to a larger field ... I am, My Lords and
    Gentlemen.

                            Most respectfully yours,
                            Patrick Geddes.

An interesting detail is that P.G. no longer claimed, as in his
1888 Letter, to be 'Your obedient Servant'.   To his application
he appended the names of fifty referees, among whom were two Americans: John Dewey, educator, and Earl Barnes, sociologist.

But, as in the case of the Edinburgh museum directorship, the responsible authorities shrank from the risk of appointing such a
generalist 'jack of all subjects'.   Or did they carefully reason
out that P.G. would be of greater use to humanity in his part-time
circumstances?   Whatever the basis for decision, he was left free
to continue all the varied, but financially uncertain, activities
with which he filled his months and years.   Thus, for the next
decade, he shuttled steadily between England and Scotland with
stop-overs in many places for varying periods of time.   His purpose
was now frankly two-fold: to expound the sociological synthesis of
Comte - Le Play - Geddes; and to work as a practical planner and
renewer of cities.   P.G.'s double identity had at last found clear
expression.

There are many accounts of Geddes by contemporaries in this period.
S.K. Ratcliffe, a British journalist and lecturer who was honorary
secretary of the Society for a time, once tried to help P.G. with
publicity for one of his civic schemes but without much success.
'And any one', he said, 'who ever tried collaborating with Patrick
Geddes, especially in a writing job, will understand why.'   Regarding P.G.'s relations with other members of the society, Mr Ratcliffe
has commented:

Shaw, Wells, Graham Wallas, etc., had, I think, a kind of affectionate respect for Geddes, but his attitude and methods were so
far apart from theirs that they usually ignored him.   From their
quite different standpoints, they would object - among other
things - to his formulae and his habit of always applying them;
to his trick of going over them almost every time in making an
exposition of any problem; to his folded papers and diagrams,
and so on.   And they had also an impatience with any thinker or
teacher who quoted Comte respectfully. (13)

Yet from his point of view P.G. objected even more strongly to the
conventional prose-limited methods of his objectors in handling
ideas and to their 'urban-limited' methods of action.   In the early
days of the Sociological Society he even devoted parts of his lectures to analysing what, intellectually, was wrong with certain
well-known writers.   Once he put H.G. Wells, so to speak, through
the sociological apparatus of the Outlook Tower, weighed him in the
balances of regional survey and of synthesis, and found him wanting.   Despite superb imagination, excellent brain and good style;
Geddes had to conclude that his colleague in sociology remained
fundamentally what his London upbringing and his public schooling
first made him: an 'intellectual Cockney'.   That is, one whose
thought and action are limited by the prejudices, the isolation from
real life and the false self-sufficiency of the city-dweller.   Despite vast culture-resources and an intellectual élite, P.G. used to
say, London stunts the mind and warps it to a viewpoint of fancied
superiority over the provinces.

A friend of Mairet's who attended this lecture has related how a
latecomer who sat in a back seat turned out to be Wells himself:
    Suddenly P.G.'s eye, wandering to his listeners at the back of
    the hall, caught sight of H.G.W.   My friend said it was very
    curious how this completely destroyed Geddes's style.   He was
    really rather overcome with confusion.   Wells just grinned, and
    presently when P.G. had changed the subject he got up and tip-
    toed out. (14)

Another story from these London days tells of Geddes and G.B. Shaw
occupying the same lecture platform.   This time the former did not
analyse his fellow but went on at great length expounding his
thinking-machine and regional survey approach to social science.
At such length, in fact, that the usually calm and well poised Shaw
for the first and last time in his life, as he himself later confessed, lost control of himself.   Like Job he found existence
frankly unbearable, at least on the same platform as P.G.; like
Job, Shaw felt consumed by a 'fire not blown', and when his turn to
speak came at last, he was a mortal quite beside himself who un-
burdened his soul in a most heated and un-Shavian manner. (15)

What Wells and Shaw had to say in turn about the sharp-tongued, discursive Scot has apparently not been recorded.   The former's heirs
have given all documents to the H.G. Wells Collection at the University of Illinois, which kindly lent the one letter it had from
Geddes in 1929 but with no trace of a reply.   (It starts 'Dear

Wells, Many years since we met! - as at Sociolog'l Society etc...'
and continues with an offer to collaborate, which will be returned
to in a later chapter.)   While the playwright mentioned neither
Geddes nor this incident in his autobiography, Augustin Hamon did
compare the two Celts in his standard work on Bernard Shaw. (16)
The English translation of 1915 reads:

> Shaw possesses the rare quality of having an original view on
> everything that comes up for discussion, new, if not in sub-
> stance, at least in form, and from this it results that even the
> substance often seems new.   So individual a manner of looking
> at everything, the manifestation of a rich imagination, is a
> quality I have encountered in one other man only, a Scotsman,
> Professor Patrick Geddes.

In the original French version of 1913 ('Le Molière du XXe Siècle:
Bernard Shaw', p. 69), however, Hamon's comment was somewhat longer.
A nearly literal translation of the last sentence follows:

> Such an entirely personal fashion of looking at everything - the
> manifestation of an extremely rich imagination - I have encoun-
> tered thus far only in one other man, almost a compatriot of
> Shaw since he is a Scot, the scientist Professor Patrick Geddes:
> and yet in my already long life I have kept company with quite a
> few eminent personalities.

Of greater significance than being accepted or not by his more literary contemporaries are the town-planning results of 'P.G.'s Progress' in the first decade of the 1900s.   Though his ideas, initiatives and arguments could sometimes weary or offend, they most certainly could not be ignored.

CROSBY HALL ... TOWN-PLANNING ACT ... CITIES EXHIBITION

The earliest traces of building activity on the part of Geddes date,
as related in Chapter 3, from his involvement in the Edinburgh
Social Union in the mid-1880s.   Although he was neither a gambler
nor an alcoholic, something of the same inner compulsion and habit-
forming indulgence was also symptomatic of his intercourse with
real estate.   In 1898, just two years after the Town and Gown
Association, Ltd had taken over most of his property problems, we
found him in new difficulties at Coltbridge.   In May 1903 a Feuing
Plan case, presumably that of Coltbridge, came up in the Guild
Court in Edinburgh but action was postponed.   'I meantime hold
over, uncashed, your cheque', writes his lawyer in a note addressed
to P.G. at Dundee. (17)

A printer's proof of the Coltbridge prospectus still exists describing 'a group of Cottage Villas' with 'modern improvements,
electric lighting, etc.' the intention of which was 'to bring
within the range of very moderate incomes, advantages not always
enjoyed by even the richer class'.   There are corrections in P.G.'s
handwriting changing promised dates of occupancy from Martinmas
(11 November) 1902 to Whitsunday 1905.   The cause of this delay is
hinted at in a letter of 2 May 1905 to a trustee of the T & G

Association who is accused of 'holding back'.   Geddes says 'I have
long ago taken this initiative at Coltbridge and am now about to
develop it' and blames the others for keeping back this and other
projects and 'so losing more, probably, than I'd have done by
action, long ago!'

To unravel the details of P.G.'s life-long financial problems, if
this were possible, would very likely point to one main deficit
factor.   Namely, a recurrent and irrepressible urge to invest in
or construct dwellings and institutions, with the resulting hardships for Anna which J.A. Thomson has described.   Another interesting document bearing on finances dates from 1906 but refers only to
their state, not the causes.

Marked 'Private and Confidential', it is an appeal by nineteen of
his friends for subscriptions for a 'GEDDES LECTURESHIP FUND'.
Starting with the Rev. Canon Barnett of Toynbee Hall, the list included J. Arthur Thomson, now Regius Professor of Natural History
at Aberdeen, and P.G.'s most faithful financial backer, J. Martin
White, J.P.

It was hoped to raise a minimum of £1,400 in order to 'provide £200
a year for not less than five years, to enable Professor Geddes to
continue the educational, sociological and geographical courses, he
has for more than a quarter of a century been giving in Edinburgh
either wholly gratuitously or for merely nominal fees'.   Reference
is made to the article 'Sociology' in the 'Encyclopaedia of Education' 'where the Outlook Tower is noted as one of the signal
achievements of the sociological movement in this country'.   Also
mentioned were the facts that 'the "Nature Study" movement sprang
mainly from this origin' and that eminent geographers have praised
its 'initiating impulse', 'particularly Elisée Reclus, who made
more than one visit to Scotland for the purpose of inspecting and
studying the Tower'.
> The long-continued and persistent efforts of Professor Geddes to
> make the Outlook Tower a living expression both of the methods
> and of the results of his teaching, have entailed serious perso-
> nal sacrifices, which it is thought ought not continue.

Attached to the document (18) was a slip saying: 'It is particularly desired that the present proposal should not be made known to
Professor Geddes himself, and that information of the project be
withheld from him until the total sum is raised.'   Whether the
goal of £1,400 was ever reached seems doubtful, since a letter from
John Ross informing P.G. of the project only says that nearly £500
is at hand.   However, Ross proposes that he devote one fixed term
for two years to the exposition of his 'Synthetic Philosophy' and
hopes he may long be spared in health to continue this important
work. (19)

A new milestone in the career of civic planner Geddes came two
years later: the saving of Crosby Hall.   This historic old residence of Richard III and of Sir Thomas More, author of 'Utopia',
was demolished in the spring of 1908 by the bank which had acquired

the property after a public subscription campaign had failed to
save it.   However, the Earl of Sandwich, inspired by his friend
P.G., had been able to persuade the bank to have the stones and
timbers carefully numbered and turned over to the London County
Council for safe-keeping.   (This was done 'under the watchful eye
of Mr Walter Godfrey', a young architect and council member of the
Chelsea Society who, later, also supervised the re-erection of the
Hall.) (Ref. pamphlet, 'Crosby Hall, 1966, pp. 15-16.)   The Earl
had previously supported the Geddesian campaign for residential
halls for students in London, then in its tenth year, and both
agreed that Crosby Hall should be resurrected as part of this campaign.   But how to get possession of the precious debris?

On arriving in London after his term at Dundee, P.G. discovered
that while the County Council also had authority to dispose of the
materials, there were two influential and wealthy competitors in
the field.   The more formidable of them was a department store
magnate who wished to incorporate the famous mansion in his new
building just begun in Oxford Street.   Geddes lost no time in
taking up the challenge and, aided by the Earl of Sandwich, began
to hound officials and members of the London County Council.   A
dialogue resulted, and P.G. made his proposition.
      What can you pay for these remains?
      Nothing!   We have no funds at all: just an important idea.
      What, then, is your proposal?
      Give us these materials and we will do our best to raise enough
      money to reerect Crosby Hall on the one site in all London
      which is most clearly indicated for this purpose.
      And where is that?
      In Chelsea: the site of the country residence of Sir Thomas
      More, now partially vacant land.   Last December we organized
      a hall of residence in a group of flats known as More's Garden,
      adjacent to the vacant lot.   This residence has been officially
      recognized by the University of London; so what more natural
      than to add Crosby Hall to this nucleus, and to let More's city
      mansion serve now as a dining hall and common-room comparable
      in architecture and in history to those of Oxford and Cambridge?

The remarkable part of the tale is that the London public officials
were won over, and they actually gave Crosby Hall to P.G. on his
own terms: 'A fact', to quote the Earl, 'which bears testimony to
the persuasive power of Patrick Geddes.' (20)   But they still had
to raise the many thousands of pounds needed for transportation of
the large quantity of stone and timber to Chelsea and for skilled
labour to re-assemble the hall.   Throughout the summer of 1908
P.G. campaigned on behalf of Crosby Hall, writing, lecturing, and
talking about Sir Thomas More's friendship with Erasmus and his
introduction of enlightened humanism into England, and about the
necessity of renewing such links with the past as a means of preparing the future.
      This will be no mere act of architectural piety, still less of
      mere 'restoration,' but one of renewal; it is a purposeful
      symbol, a renewed initiative, Utopian and local, civic and aca-
      demic in one....   In sum, it is a new link between Chelsea
      Past and Chelsea Possible.

Although the journalist S.K. Ratcliffe found it most frustrating to
try to help P.G. with the project, he wrote this homage:

> Patrick Geddes seemed to be in touch with every creative person
> and enterprise.... He was in his prime, and no one could paint
> what then he was: a flame of energy, darting hither and thither
> with projects.... He was an inexhaustible fount of ideas,
> designs and suggestions. His schemes might seem remote or fan-
> tastic ... but you were wise never to treat any project of his
> as unreal. You could always depend upon its having a founda-
> tion of value, and as a rule you would find that Geddes had seen
> into it and beyond, and had a notion of its actual working that
> left the practical man standing. (21)

P.G. clearly visualised how Crosby Hall would look on the Chelsea
site with a view across the Embankment and the Thames and how
greatly it would enhance the embryonic University Hall already
there. His only task was to convince others of the worth of his
vision. Old friends like J. Martin White did what they could to
help, but obviously some fresh and wealthier benefactor had to be
found. So Geddes ferreted out the identity of an anonymous donor
who had pledged the largest single sum towards the original public
subscription. It was a Mrs Wharrie, and when the Earl of Sandwich
learned this, he excitedly told Geddes that he knew her brother
very well, and that he was an influential man of affairs. Both
men hastened to call at his home in Buckinghamshire and through him
soon reached the sister. The Earl reported afterwards that

> All went well from that moment, and not only was a large sum of
> money given us by Mrs Wharrie, but further donations from that
> generous benefactress made it possible, with the assistance of
> other donations, to rebuild Crosby Hall where it stands today,
> to purchase a portion of land behind it and to take over a five
> hundred years' lease from the County Council for the whole
> site. (22)

He also related the incident which took place when the two men
finished their call in Buckinghamshire. The brother, then past
middle age, responded 'so much to Patrick Geddes's attractive personality that as we were leaving the house he came up to me, almost
with tears in his eyes, and expressed the regret he felt not to
have known Geddes in his younger days, as if he had done so, he
would certainly have become his disciple!'

The testimony of these men reveals P.G. at his best in persuasive
action, yet that he also had the defects of his qualities has been
brought out by friends as well as enemies. His energetic public
altruism often had to be paid for by his family, not only in material hardships but in impaired home life.

To read Anna's letters of the decade just before and after 1900,
when Patrick was away on winter lecture tours or pursuing practical
matters, is to understand what constant support she gave him in his
work for others and with what devotion she forgave the neglect this
often brought upon her and the children. Yet concern for his
tasks was mingled with disappointment as in December 1892 when it
appeared that he could not join them for Christmas:

Only do let us try to have one day if possible without a heavy
burden of business before the freshness of your homecoming has
worn off....   I don't want you to feel that I am murmuring at
this prolonged absence.   I understand and sympathise too much
with the quantity and the importance of your work to be in that
mood.   [See also ch. 5, p. 122.]

On another occasion, this time in summer, she fears he will return
tired out for a new burst of excitement over the Town & Gown
Association, & not get rested for the Summer Meeting.   I know
you won't like me to be croaking like this; but I have never
known you come home from London other than so worn out (without
knowing it) that you had heavy arrears of rest to make up.

Anna had apparently written some sort of ultimatum the night before,
and though it had 'nothing whatever to do with what I write now ...
I send it all the same!'

This morning I feel I shall be quite content to go on if you
will only just not be too tired and weary.   I know you work for
the best, dear, but you have to take more care of yourself than
you used to do, you know. (23)

In December 1905 Geddes started on a two months' Riviera trip of
combined lecturing and planning gardens for wealthy British winter
exiles.   Anna stayed in Edinburgh with the children and to carry
on his endless struggle with Outlook Tower deficits.   Despite much
space devoted to problems of business and of trying to reconcile
his manuscript instalments for a guide to the Tower with the wishes
of its finance committee, she writes cheerfully.   Indeed, part of
a mid-December letter recalls the tone of those of twenty years ago
to her fiancé.   J. Arthur Thomson had given a lecture at the Tower
which was

very charming in style, the interest always sustained, full of
little humorous & poetic touches, and not requiring any great
effort to follow....   You will have to look to your laurels,
for J.A.T. is without doubt a very attractive lecturer to follow
you! [Geddes had lectured there just before leaving for the
south.]

But I hope, dearest, you are now rested enough to be giving
your best lectures, and enjoying sunshine & change + your variety
of hosts - & hostesses - new witches?...

I do hope I shall have a letter this morning ... 1/6 of our
two months of separation is over.   We shall miss you most in
the holidays. (24)

From 1908 to 1914 the town planner's star rose more steadily than
that of his sociology, but this did not matter to P.G., for whom
both interests were inseparable.   The interrelations of Place,
Work and Folk in the ecologically interdependent parts of a valley
section were the basis of all his practical work, which in turn
served to illustrate the generalisations of his social science.
Yet he was not the slave of his formulas or thinking-machines when
out in the field.   Of this the Dunfermline report bears full witness, as would later his reports on Indian cities.   Even those
who found his diagrams and sociological charts difficult, fantas-
tic, or reprehensible could not find any such faults in the prac-

tical proposals resulting from his regional and civic surveys.
Geddes planner and Geddes sociologist made an excellent working
team which pioneered in its new field with great success.

The Town and Country Planning Act passed by Parliament in 1909
was the first of a series of important laws concerned with the improvement of rural and urban areas.   Another significant event
took place in October 1910, the town planning exhibition and conference in London which was attended by an international group of
over 1,200 architects, municipal engineers, town councillors and
the like.   It was the first such meeting in Great Britain and one
of which the influence went on steadily spreading in time and space
as the years passed.

Characteristically, both the occurrence and the results of these
events can in large measure be traced to Patrick Geddes.   To begin
with, it was he who, through his omni-present yet behind-the-scenes
influence, helped to start the legislative ball rolling.   John
Burns, M.P. and member of the Cabinet, was the man who drew up the
1909 Act and who succeeded in getting it approved by Parliament,
but he did so under Geddesian stimulus.   Similarly, at the exhibition held in 1910 at the Royal Academy, work influenced by P.G.
filled an entire gallery!

Assisted by an able young Scottish architect, Frank C. Mears, Geddes
had prepared a comprehensive exhibit of the geology, history, economic life, architecture, housing and social conditions of Edinburgh.   It was, in short, a planner's survey of a great city and
its region.   In surrounding galleries were exhibits sent from
British Colonies, the USA, and the major European countries.
Photographs, sketches, and perspectives which surpassed in quantity,
and in the quality of their frames, those in P.G.'s survey.   Yet
even London newspapers recognised that in his gallery lay the keynote of the whole international exhibition.   The 'Standard', for
example, told its readers to head straight for the Edinburgh room
if they would understand what town-planning was all about. (25)
   This collection of models, maps, plans, drawings, and photographs is of quite extraordinary interest and value.   It, so
   to speak, explains the whole exhibition, and prevents its becoming for the unprofessional visitor a collection of unrelated
   facts and illustrations.

As for the professional town-planners and municipal architects, one
of their number, Patrick Abercrombie, the widely-known planner of
Dublin and Sheffield, ascribes to P.G.'s appearance at the 1910
exhibition the modern trend of city planning throughout the world.
He said:
   There was a time when it seemed only necessary to shake up into
   a bottle the German town-extension plan, the Parisian boulevard, the English garden village, the American civic centre and
   park system, in order to produce a mechanical mixture which
   might be applied indiscriminately and beneficially to every town
   and village in this country, in the hope that thus it would be
   'town planned' according to the most up-to-date notions.

Pleasing dream!   First shattered by Geddes, emerging from his
Outlook Tower in the frozen north, to produce that nightmare of
complexity, the Edinburgh Room at the great Town Planning Exhibition of 1910.
It was a torture chamber to all those simple souls that had
been ravished by the glorious perspectives or heartened by the
healthy villages shown in the other and ampler galleries.
Within this den sat Geddes, a most unsettling person, talking,
talking ... about anything and everything.   The visitors could
criticize his show - the merest hotch-potch - picture postcards
- newspaper cuttings - crude old woodcuts - strange diagrams -
archaeological reconstructions;   these things, they said, were
unworthy of the Royal Academy - many of them not even framed -
shocking want of respect!   But if they chanced within the range
of Geddes's talk, henceforth nothing could medicine them to that
sweet sleep which yesterday they owned.   There was something
more in town planning than met the eye! (26)

Fortunately we have a reprint of his 'Civic Survey of Edinburgh'
which catalogues and describes some of the exhibits.   In a 'Preliminary Note' he emphasises that the 'Survey' is important
as affording evidence of the necessity, practicability, and
fruitfulness of a clear understanding for each town and city
(a) of its geographical situation, (b) of its development (and
corresponding decline) at each important phase of its history
from earliest to most recent times.   Natural environment is
thus never to be neglected without long-enduring penalties.
Neither can historic phases be considered as past and done with;
their heritage of good, their burden of evil, are each traceable
in our complex present City: and each as a momentum, towards
betterment, or towards deterioration respectively. (27)

Specific points are driven home in P.G.'s captions, sometimes with
biting irony.   Taking a fifteenth-century plan which showed the
city walls fencing in the high ridge leading up to the Castle, he
comments:
To this is directly traceable the long overcrowding and under-
housing of Edinburgh, with high rents and land values: a marked
influence also in Scotland, and on industrial age therefrom.
(Note analogous evil influence now radiating through USA, etc,
from narrow site of New York City.) ... [of Old Edinburgh there
are] ... Photographs recording the appalling (still tolerated)
squalor of the Old Town buildings, and correspondingly of its
slum life.   This mainly accepted as a permanent supply of
material for charity, medicine, anatomy, and religious endeavour.   [More modern sections are labelled] 'The long unlovely
street' - Photos recording miles of tenement rows with further
decadence of rival styles.   This essential continuance of the
historic overcrowding of Edinburgh has been and still is encouraged and maintained by its educational trust acting as ground
landlords, in the supposed interest of the development of the
child life of Edinburgh!

Arriving at the main argument, Geddes takes his listeners or readers

swiftly through the geography and geology of this region, repeating
the admonition 'that natural environment is never to be neglected
without long-enduring penalties'.   The same injunction applies to
history, as evidenced by the inherited evil of overcrowding.   Originally due to the need for safety, the walled-in space with its
inadequate water supply, density and uncleanliness became traditional, even when unnecessary.   Here he points to a sketch made by
F.C. Mears showing the Royal Mile in medieval times.   The most
striking thing about it is that today's narrow slum-bordered High
Street was then 100 ft broad: 'in its day, as the letters of
French or Venetian ambassadors show, the stateliest street in
Europe''.

Then, using as evidence the relief model made by Paul Reclus, along
with maps and photos, P.G. challenges the
> town-planner boldly to confront and scrutinise the railway
> system of his own town and of every other town.   Let him
> criticise this ... from his more extensive and more clear-headed
> grasp of the topography and the economics of the town and
> region, which the railway directors and their engineers have as
> yet so astonishingly little time to inquire into.   He will thus
> discover that the 'utilitarian' here, as so often elsewhere, has
> been the 'futilitarian'.

He urges the planner, for further proof, to look at mazes of railway lines and termini in London, Paris, and even in 'the newest
capitals, like Berlin and Chicago'.
> All this will surely be sufficient to warrant the present attack
> upon most railway planning, whether in Edinburgh or beyond, as
> the most fortuitous bungle in the long history of cities, and as
> far exceeding in its present disorder and waste of space, time,
> and energy (to say nothing of natural beauty or human life),
> anything that has been or can be alleged against the decay of
> the Mediaeval, the Renaissance or the eighteenth-century cities
> and city plans, defective though we have seen each and all of
> these to have been in its turn, and disastrous in its decay.   I
> labour this point, not as vituperation, but to bring out the
> essential origins and tasks of our present town-planning move-
> ment;   it is the necessary rebound of a new generation against
> the ideas, and the lack of ideas, of our elders of the railway
> and industrial age, and the practical endeavour now to mitigate
> the material confusion and the social deterioration in which
> their lapse of well-nigh all sense of civic responsibility and
> well-being has plunged us. (28)

No wonder that Patrick Abercrombie called the Edinburgh Room a
'torture chamber' for those wanting only fine vistas and healthy
villages.   Geddes marshalled example upon example, exhibit upon
exhibit, as he hammered home his criticisms of planners' and politicians' blunders.   Always using Edinburgh as an object lesson,
he would generalise:
> Architecture and town planning in such a city, we thus plainly
> see, are not the mere products of the quiet drawing-office some
> here would have them;   they are the expressions of the local

history, the civic and national changes of mood and contrasts of mind.   Here, indeed, I submit is an answer to those town planners who design a shell, and then pack their snail of a would-be progressive city into it, not discerning that the only real and well-fitting shell is that which the creature at its growing periods throws out from its own life.   This is no doctrine of *laissez faire*;   it is simply the recognition that each generation, and in this, each essential type and group of it, must express its own life, and thus make its contribution to its city in its own characteristic way.

After many pages (equalling hours of talk to visitors) Geddes reaches an eloquent summary:

Our Civic Survey thus has ranged through wide limits: from the fullest civic idealism on the one hand, to the most direct and ruthless realism on the other.   For there is no real incompatibility between the power of seeing the thing as it is - the Town as Place, as Work, as Folk - and the power of seeing things as they may be - the City of Etho-Polity, Culture and Art....

Yet as each phase of development of our survey has come and gone, so in turn may this presentment of it.   All surveys, we have seen, need perpetual renewal;   and our final exhibit is thus a plain office-model of the Outlook Tower - reduced to its simplest expression - that in which it may be adapted by anyone to the problems and the tasks presented by his own immediate environment, his own region and neighbourhood, quarter and city....   *In conclusion then, here is my thesis and challenge: City surveys are urgent, practicable, and useful, so useful that they must before long become for civic statesmanship and local administration what charts now are to Admiralty and to pilot.* (29)

Within two weeks of the close of the 1910 Town Planning Exhibition in London, Geddes publicly proposed to enlarge his Edinburgh 'show' into an exhibition

not merely of town-planning, but of cities and civics generally - in a word, a cities exhibition proper....   This should first arouse the visitor's interest by varied and panoramic glimpses into great historic cities, the strange magnificence of Ninevah and Jerusalem, the beauty of Athens, the grandeur of Rome.   It should show the Mediaeval City within its walls, and with its town house and cathedral;   the Renaissance City within its palaces and their magnificence, and then the Industrial City in its alternate gloom and glare.   Upon this the various developments and purposes of modern town planning would follow. (30)

In February 1911, this idea bore fruit, and the 'Cities and Town Planning Exhibition' was officially opened by the Rt Hon. John Burns, MP, at Crosby Hall, Chelsea.   Aided by fellow planners Adams, Lanchester and Unwin and by Frank C. Mears, Geddes had in this short time gathered together the first 'Cities Exhibition' of its kind anywhere.   It represented cities from ancient times to modern, but this was no mere gallery of curiosities to be stared at and quickly passed by.   Every single picture or plan, every panel of carefully related pictures, was a vehicle for the ideas of P.G., who through them proved that he was a 'master of town-planning' in all its aspects.

The walls of Crosby Hall offered one course in 'rational geography' (the valley-section interpretation of the origin and significance of cities everywhere) and another in 'rational history' (the study of cities in terms of alternating temporal and spiritual forces, from early Egypt to twentieth-century Europe and America).   They gave examples of types of urban development and interpretation of city life, the origin of its evils, the means for abating them.   In addition, Crosby Hall presented Geddes, the interpreter.   S.K. Ratcliffe paid him an unqualified tribute:

> His collection of historical, architectural, and imaginative material was a remarkable expression of his mind and method, and I would assert that no interpreter of our age, in the wide province of social evolution and institutions, was in the same class with Geddes as, accompanied by a group of students, he made his progress along the road of civilisation as it was illuminated by the maps, plans, and diagrams on the walls and stands. (31)

During the spring and summer of 1911 the Cities and Town Planning Exhibition became itinerant, being displayed in Edinburgh, Dublin and Belfast.   In Edinburgh it, and P.G., scored a real triumph: the city which had refused him as Regius Professor of Botany now welcomed him officially and popularly as a town-planner.   His exhibition was held in the Royal Scottish Academy galleries under the auspices of the city corporation.   It was opened with addresses by Lord Pentland, His Majesty's Secretary of State for Scotland, and by the Right Honorable the Lord Provost of Edinburgh.   In three weeks a total of 17,000 persons visited the exhibition: workmen, school teachers and their classes, business men, politicians; everyone came to see Geddes's 'show'.   A similar official and public response occurred in Ireland when the collection was shown in Dublin and Belfast.   The Earl of Aberdeen, Viceroy of Ireland, and his wife the Countess of Aberdeen, took special interest in both the exhibition and its organiser, and from then on they enlisted P.G.'s help in their ambitious schemes for the improvement of Irish cities.   In fact, three years later, he was to have the chance of a lifetime, the replanning of Dublin.

KNIGHTHOOD DECLINED ... HOME SCHOOL ... JUNIOR COLLEAGUES

Following close upon the successes of the exhibition in 1911 came potential Royal recognition of P.G.'s new identity.   His name was scheduled to appear in the New Year's Honours of 1912 for civic and educational services to his country.   This Knighthood would be official evidence of his conquest of the high places of the land and of his acceptance by those in power, whom he had more or less harassed for the past thirty years.   Lord Pentland was eager to recommend Geddes's name to King George V.   All that remained was for P.G. himself to agree to accept the honour.

A major struggle ensued in the sociologist-town planner's mind.

Portrait of Patrick
Geddes ('P.G., Un-
limited') by Ehona
Mycale MacGilli-
vray, Ramsay
Garden, 1912

Cities and Town Planning Exhibition

EDINBURGH

13th MARCH to 1st APRIL, 1911

Explanatory Guide Book

— AND —

Outline Catalogue

BY

P. GEDDES and F. C. MEARS

Title page of cata-
logue of the Cor-
poration of Edin-
burgh Cities and
Town Planning Ex-
hibition in the
Galleries of the
Royal Scottish
Academy

To win such public acknowledgment for his labours, to bear the title
'Sir', the very sound of which would silence philistines into res-
pectful attention, to be quoted by the press: 'Sir Patrick says';
these were certainly legitimate rewards.   But on the other hand
P.G.'s basic training was that of a 'quiet student of science', a
gardener, a man of action, whose own deeds and ideas were after all
far more important to him than any official title that might be be-
stowed upon him.   Had he not always fulminated against the shallow-
ness of degrees and titles, roasting with irony the 'quadruple
doctors', the 'Heavy-sterns', and the 'portly word-fog-giants' of
universities and of governments?

Carlyle's reply to Disraeli's offer of a baronetcy in 1874 perhaps
also came to mind: that titles of honour were out of keeping with
the tenor of his existence and 'would be an encumbrance, not a furtherance to me'.   In any case, Geddes finally told Lord Pentland
that 'for democratic reasons' he must refuse the Knighthood which
was his for the asking.   For the next twenty years, he was to remain simply Patrick Geddes, and when A.G. Gardiner included a sketch
of him in 'Pillars of Society' in 1913 it was on the strength of
personality and ideas which needed no title to commend them to
readers.   Gardiner wrote:

> To meet Patrick Geddes for the first time is an intellectual red-
> letter day.   It is like stepping over a stile into a new country
> - like passing, let us say, out of the tunnel at the top of Glen-
> gariff Pass and seeing all the wonders of Kerry spread out before
> you.   Perhaps you discover him at some Town Planning Exhibition.
> You have gone in without emotion, and have wandered round the
> rooms hung with great maps and diagrams and charts.   You find
> them very important and very dull.   You are glad that you have
> come; but on the whole you will be more glad to go.   Then good
> fortune brings you Professor Geddes and the whole place is illu-
> minated.   The maps cease to be maps and become romantic visions.
> His talk envelops you like an atmosphere; your mind becomes all
> windows - windows into the past and windows into the future.
> The old city leaps to life again; the map echoes with the tramp
> of armed men; it becomes a pageant of history, a sudden inter-
> pretation of the present.   But it becomes more; it becomes a
> promise of the future, a vision of the City Beautiful, with
> squalor banished, with learning and life no longer divorced, but
> going hand in hand to the complete triumph over the misery and
> confusion of things.

It would be 1915 before the many lectures, articles and private exhortations of P.G. as planner would appear in book form, but then
'Cities in Evolution' could begin to take its place as a Geddesian
classic even more influential than 'City Development'.   (In fact,
its increasing influence and popularity would reach a high point
in the 1970s with three new editions and a translation into Italian; see Bibliography.)   Its message and its practical examples,
however, all stem from observations and generalisations first made
almost a century ago in Edinburgh, London and Paris; then verified
in Dunfermline and in the Cities Exhibition.

While Patrick Geddes was in London in late 1903 lecturing on civics
and writing his report on Dunfermline, his three children were, as
they had been for years, getting some very unconventional schooling.
Norah aged 16, Alasdair 12 and Arthur 8, were in various stages of
work and study guided by what was called the 'Home School'.   Its
philosophy, curriculum and methods were as unlike those of state or
private schools as P.G.'s other undertakings were different from
their established counterparts.   The gist of his educational
theory can be glimpsed in the following anecdote related by Geddes
himself.

> Yesterday in town I met an old friend, who tells me his son is
> soon leaving school with classical honours, to win scholarships
> and glory in like manner at Oxbridge....
> And how is your boy, and what is he doing since he is not at
> school? I am asked in turn.
> He does some lessons at home; and he is learning to be a pretty
> fair gardener.
> Ah! And will that be enough for him by and by?
> Oh, no! Not quite! When I left home he was making a box.
> Ah! said my friend again, and dropped the conversation, evident-
> ly thinking nothing could be made of my surly and paradoxical
> impracticability. (32)

Yet there was a logical basis for P.G.'s theory and practice.   He
explained that, to his mind,

> there are two main pieces of work in a boy's education; and one
> of these is to garden, and the other is to make boxes.   When
> our boys can do these, and not till then, they have got their
> essential education for their work in the world....   Each does
> best what he enjoys, and he enjoys best what he has done long,
> what he did as a child....   To get the true hand, the true
> eye, one must get them early.   The great masters of the Renais-
> sance, the smaller artists of today, how do they differ?   Very
> largely in that the master began his apprenticeship as a boy of
> twelve or fourteen at most, while the hand and brain centers
> were still fully adaptable; while we make our contemporaries
> wait to begin their artistic education until late adolescence or
> even manhood, that is until it is physiologically too late to
> make high skill an organic and subconscious functioning of brain
> and hand.

Like every great teacher, P.G. looked on the complex process of
learning as a part of every-day living.   His motto and philosophy
of education was *Vivendo Discimus*; and if we 'learn by living' the
most important thing is to live.   Ideally and all-inclusively,
what he prescribed was: Discover the world around you from earliest childhood, the physical world, until you know what it is
from mountains to the sea and until you know what it contains of
human occupations and culture, from miners to fishermen, from upland
village to coastal city; study history, art, and literature, first
in the lives and work of the people who now inhabit your 'valley-
section', and afterwards in records of the past, observe at first-
hand in the open air, then read in the library; and take part in
the varied life from mountains to the sea, don't merely watch people
work.   *Be* a **forester**, a shepherd, a fisher, a farmer for a season.

This was the sort of training old Captain Geddes had instinctively given his son, and it was what the son consciously and systematically wanted to give his children in their turn.   He and Anna, assisted by an aunt skilful in dealing with youngsters, set up a home school for Norah, Alasdair, Arthur, and a fourth child, the daughter of the aunt.   Victor Branford has given this first-hand account:

> The children opened the school day by singing in chorus a chant of the Roman Breviary.   It was a memorable experience for a visitor in the Geddes household to hear the sonorous Latin hymn rolling from the fresh, true voices of the youngsters as they stood round their mother at the piano.   Morning school thus begun was followed by two or three hours of book-learning not widely different from the customary.   The afternoon course consisted of work in the garden, alternating with music or dancing lessons, out-of-door sketching expeditions, play-acting, masquerading and concert-giving by the children; with seniors, guests, and neighbours for audience.   Each of the children according to age and capacity rendered some practical assistance in the tasks of the working gardener - who was Professor Geddes himself. (33)

The gardener was also the teacher of literature who introduced his pupils at an early age to the poetry of four languages, starting with Scottish ballads which he recited;   then English, French and German ones.   From such forms they turned to other types of poetry and prose, each to his own taste.   Geddes often read aloud to them just as his father had read to him.   Anna directed the children in the more formal aspects of language studies and also gave them a grounding in instrumental music and singing.   Alasdair took up the 'cello, Arthur the violin, and Norah the piano, and as they became old enough to perform, gave regular family recitals. Patrick grew up in a silent home, but his children never had that handicap, thanks to their mother.

Norah has already been quoted as not always sharing her father's enthusiasm for home schooling (pp. 160-1), and Arthur would come to look back on much of his part in it as very unsatisfactory.   On one side he felt the constant expectations of nigh-perfectionist parents, while on the other he resented not having good outside tutors and blamed the family's poor economy for his having been 'let down' educationally.   The matter of family relations belongs to later pages, and with it comments on the obverse of the home school medallion.   But here we shall let P.G. expound more of his personal philosophy of education.

He emphasised the responsibility of parents not to abandon their children completely to 'bookish misinstruction'.   'Much of our so-called education is literally definable as the *production of artificial defectives*.'   Again he would say that 'the wildest of all hallucinations is that widely current one which imagines individual growth to be a matter of examinations passed and marks received'.   He insisted that for the home to reassume its part in education would be good for both youngsters and elders - always

assuming, though not always saying so, that relationships would be
like those between him and his parents in Mount Tabor Cottage.

> The healthy curiosity of an intelligent child can always puzzle
> all the Doctors of the Temple; so the only possible discredit
> to any adult from failing to satisfy the juvenile inspector
> arises if the questioning intelligence be crushed down with a
> brutal 'Never mind, don't ask questions!' or even disappointed
> with an honest 'don't know' if it be in the tone of 'don't care'.

He believed fully that on the shoulders of parents, possibly helped
by some exceptional teacher, rests the burden of

> leading children out into freedom, or giving them that franchise
> of the world of culture which the routine education of the three
> R's, despite all machinery of standards, addition of special
> subjects and what not, hopes and promises to give but neces-
> sarily fails.

Rather than the three R's, Geddes promoted the three H's of Heart,
Hand and Head.   These terms and their sequence simply meant that
priority must be given first to the child's emotional development,
thereafter to physical growth, and only finally to strictly intellectual training.   For him the basis of all elementary education
was to be found in childish interests in the natural world and in
the wonderment it evoked.

> The child's desire of seeing and hearing, touching and handling,
> of smelling and tasting are all true and healthy hungers, and it
> can hardly be too strongly insisted that good teaching begins,
> neither with knowledge nor discipline, but through delight.   As
> for art and music, so for nature and other studies; better do
> no teaching at all than without 'the feeling for the subject.'

To counterbalance such idealistic generalisations one can recall
Norah on the 'cold, hunger and fatigue' which was part of a day's
work in their Home School.   Her father also spoke and wrote very
plainly on occasion:

> Any preparation I have had for doing and saying something in
> education is based not primarily on academic but on *solid ground*;
> that is, on a long silent experience of going up and down the
> hill of my diagram [the valley-section], learning literal gar-
> dening, literal fishing, literal tree-planting, literal building
> and the like: seeking, in short, the Wisdom of the Crafts.

To a friend's suggestion that her son come to the Crawford residence to work along with Norah and Alasdair, Geddes replied:

> Your son must come here to work regularly or not at all, and
> with written excuse from you for necessary absence.   He must
> learn to work three hours, albeit to perspiration and soreness,
> and by way of promotion - and getting half-way to being a fair
> average man - he may look forward to being able by and by to
> work four hours, and this with more perspiration, if with less
> soreness.   Hardest of all he must work - and that best - when
> my back is turned, when I am away for an hour or two, or all day,
> or as will happen this winter, for two months.   I leave my Dun-
> dee gardener for nine and a half months at a time; that's the

sort of man he is!   I wish I could say as much for all the
people I have to work with, but they were not caught young
enough, and have not the drill I should like to give your son
and Alasdair.   It is easy for them to try this; but it will
be harder to stick to it when the first freshness is off, and
the results have not begun to be seen or felt, and new pleasures
call, and public opinion presses.   But apprenticeship must be
apprenticeship. (34)

Yet the ideal and the general always beckoned.   After outlining 'a
busy enough week's' programme of morning studies, afternoon chores
and evening reading, music or dance, P.G. philosophises:

What is wanting for the Sunday?   Complete freedom from ordinary
lessons and labour being of course assumed, may we not touch the
much discussed subject of moral and religious education by help
of the most vividly didactic elements of the whole Hebrew literature, the Proverbs and the Parables?   For what are the Proverbs?   What but the homely yet poetic wisdom of the rustic and
urban labour, of the every-day domestic economy of the people,
yet also of their result in national economy and statesmanship,
in personal and national destiny.   What are the Parables if not
primarily subtler and more spiritualised interpretations of the
same homely experience, drawn from the same every-day familiarity with simple and educative toil?
... do we not see in most of these Parables the very essence ...
of rustic wisdom; and in that of the house foundations, the reflective experience of the urban craftsman as well?   That the
carpenter of Nazareth had shared both rustic and urban labour as
a boy is surely plain....
    The principles we have been pleading for thus hardly agree
with the practice either of State schools or Church ones.   Yet
... Epictetus and Antoninus, slave and emperor alike, knew that
freedom lay in the mind itself; and what more have we been
trying to prove than that the 'Kingdom of Heaven' is within you?
What more to plead for than to 'suffer the little children'?
For the ideal to which the child is dragged or driven is not
ideal at all, but only its wooden image at best. (35)

As Norah and Alasdair reached their 'teens, a practical aspect of
the Geddesian pedagogy began to show itself.   For years the emphasis had been on their experiences and understanding of the worlds
without and within, although the element of pleasing Mother and
Father was always present.   But with their approaching maturity
the father counted more and more openly on them as potential colleagues and continuators.   Indeed, a case can be made that P.G.
very early had selfish or self-perpetuating motives in his concern
about the children's education, utterly unlike his own father.

For all his emphasis on Heart and Hand before Head, Geddes insisted
on jotting down ideas and making diagrams at an early age.   Along
with the thousands of his own sheets which have been preserved are
a number of cards and scraps of paper with notes by Alasdair and
Arthur which also found their way into the family archives.   'Would
Daddy want me to do this - or that?'   'Would he be pleased should I

do such and such?', is the gist of many juvenile documents.   These
are now in the possession of the daughter-in-law who has commented
that P.G. certainly could be called a perfectionist parent.   He
urged them from early years to take notes, put down the pros and
cons of a project or a thought.   But judging from their notations
and early letters, she feels that they took up his suggestions more
with an anxious effort to please him, rather than from spontaneous
desire so to reason and weigh the various aspects of a problem. (36)

From Geddes's point of view, however, this activity was gratifying
evidence of their mental development and ability to face and answer
questions of daily life.   He regarded their home studies and occupational 'apprenticeships' as the best of all possible schoolings.
Alasdair, in particular, was to him proof beyond any shadow of
doubt as the superiority of home school methods.

It was Alasdair who stayed home to garden and make boxes, and who
was a steady truant from conventional schools except for two short
periods 'to give him a taste of what he was escaping'.   Occupa-
tionally, his was also an almost complete 'valley section' education.   He herded sheep for a season, was cook on a herring-boat
for a summer, he worked as a mason, and learned practical agriculture on the experimental farm of Joseph Fels in Essex, 'that socialised millionaire' from America.   (It is said that Mr Fels became
so attracted by Alasdair's pleasing personality and many abilities
that he wanted to adopt the Scots lad as his son and heir to the
soap fortune.)   At fifteen Alasdair served as laboratory boy at
the Millport Zoological Station on the west coast of Scotland, and
at sixteen he passed the official tests which qualified him as
steersman of the coastal life-saving boats.   On land he progressed
from childhood donkey-riding to breaking in horses for army use.
But the most adventurous of all Alasdair's youthful experiences was
joining an arctic exploration led by Dr W.S. Bruce.   Throughout
the summer of 1909, at the age of eighteen, he served as assistant
to Dr Bruce in the mapping of an island near Spitzbergen, where
today the names of Mount Geddes and Alasdair Horn commemorate his
work.

Taking part in basic occupations was, however, only one side of
P.G.'s ideal, and he never failed to stress the need for living in
the world of thought as well.   The best-written case he ever made
for this duality in education is a fascinating tract-like booklet,
'The World Without and the World Within: Sunday Talks with my
Children' (London, George Allen, 1905, 38 pp.), which a footnote
explains as 'Sunday "Thinking Lessons" to my children, jotted down
by their mother, and now but little altered for Press'.   Published
in 1905, some of its contents date from 1898 when the father 'was
going a journey ... to the very middle of the world and back' and
when Arthur was the 'baby brother' of three.   The core of the
lessons is that just as children live turn by turn in an Out-world
of play-work and roaming and in an In-world of remembering and make
believe, so should this daily rhythm be continued and developed
throughout life.   P.G. expressed this in a simple thinking machine
based on the planning of the family garden at Crauford.   The whole
circle of their activities was expressed in its four quarters.

Out-world	1	4	Facts	Acts
In-world	2	3	Memories	Plans

First, the outer world we see; second, the inner world we remember. But we are not content merely with seeing nor with remembering: we went deeper into the In-world. We made a new step
in this when we began actively thinking and planning; and then
in carrying out our plan we came back into the Out-world once
more. So with this coming Spring the new garden-scene you have
prepared will begin for you. You see the need then of being
able to live and be active in the In-world as well as the Out-
world; not merely to dream there, but to be awake and all alive,
if you ever mean to do anything. From the hard World of Facts
to the no less real World of Acts, you can only travel by this
In-world way.

Two passages in these 'Sunday Talks with My Children' are significant in their application to Geddes himself. The first is really
his credo, his lodestar:
To be at home in the Out-world and in the In-world, and to be
active as well as passive in each by turns; that is what we have
seen you can aim at in your education. Not only to enjoy more,
see more, remember more; but to do more, plan more, carry out
more.

The second shows the origin of what later would become the thirty-
six-squared 'Chart of Life'. He tells of another father going on
a journey from which he might not return who wondered what he could
leave of value to his children instead of money.
So he bethought himself of an ancient, yet inexhaustible, talisman, indeed, an ever-strengthening one, which had been his own
best possession, too late though he had found it, too little use
though he had made of it. But now his children could carry and
use this all through their lives; the magic wand, say rather the
key, the sign which should open each of the four worlds - the Out
and the In, the Active and the Passive in each - Life in its many
aspects or possibilities. That talisman is simple. It is
before you; it is one of the many meanings also of the Celtic
Spiral, of the world-old Cross.

Yet with all his accomplishments and varied experiences, Alasdair
was not an exceptional person either in physique or in mind. 'He
had', explained his father, 'simply a good all-round character, and
a fair, but not exceptional mental ability.' Even the son once

described himself as just 'an ordinary person and not specially
gifted in any direction.'   The key to his success was, to quote
the father again, that he was

> clearly possessed of - and by - the idea of being at home upon
> the Valley Section from snows to sea - and thus from ski-running,
> and glacier crossing to ship or life-boat....   Nothing for him
> was painfully acquired or 'got up' as separate 'subjects'; but
> all by turns were felt as fresh modes and moods of life worth
> trying and mastering, and thus genially entered into.   So in
> social intercourse he was easy and natural with all sorts and
> conditions of men, from forecastle to quarterdeck, from labora-
> tory boys to students and professors, from scientific men to
> artist and poet, from labourer's fireside to court-functions;
> and thence back again. (37)

While Geddes makes no specific reference to sex-education in connection with his own children, he does take up the subject in the
biological works written with J. Arthur Thomson.   Thus they urged
that sex-education should arise almost imperceptibly from nature-
study: from observation of flowers, from experience of pets such as
rabbits and doves, cat and kittens, dog and puppies - and even from
visits to the farmyard.

> While there may be a legitimate silence or postponement of
> answer, there must be no shirking or beating about the bush once
> an answer has been embarked upon.   Nothing must be said which
> will have to be unlearned afterwards, for no one can do a child
> much greater harm than telling it something which it will after-
> wards discover to be untrue....   While there should not be any
> suggestion of any shadow of shamefulness over the subject, it
> must be treated with reverence and as a great mystery - as it
> certainly is. (38)

Of everything the two biologists have written on sex, their interpretation of the text, 'Consider the lilies ... how they grow', is
perhaps the most arresting and original.   It first appeared in
print in the Summer volume (pp. 75-6) of 'The Evergreen', in 1896,
but undoubtedly dates from much earlier lectures of Geddes. (39)
In speaking of how the timid are alarmed, and the pure repelled,
whenever sex questions are discussed, he insists that here as everywhere the road lies forward, not back.

> We must grapple with each question, whoever be shocked; not
> shirk it, gloss it, retreat from it, in our feeble virtue.   Con-
> sider then the lily: face its elemental biologic-moral fact.
> 'Pure as a lily' is not really a phrase of hackneyed sham-morals;
> for it does not mean weak, bloodless, sexless, like your moral
> philosopher's books, your curate's sermons.   The lily's Purity
> lies in that it has something to be pure; its Glory is in being
> the most frank and open manifestation of sex in all the organic
> world.   Its magnificent array is to show forth, not conceal:
> these wear their lucent argent for the passion-fragrant night,
> and these roll back their swart-stained robes of scarlet orange
> to the sun-rich day; naked and not ashamed, glowing, breathing,
> warm - each flower showers forth its opulence of golden dust,
> stretches forth to welcome it in return.   This, when we consi-
> der, is How they Grow.

While music was naturally left in Anna's hands, there is one interesting exception to this rule.   In June 1904 when Alasdair was
thirteen, P.G. wrote him a partly autobiographical letter which
began: 'For your birthday present I propose to revive an old interest of your own - that in possessing a set of pipes'.   He realised that Alasdair had 'practically had to give up piano for
'cello; why therefore another instrument, and that a comparatively
rude one?' Over nearly two-and-a-half typed pages the father gives
a well-written and self-revealing explanation.   The first reason is
remarkable in that it is a rare confession of the Home School's in-
adequacy on one score.   He thinks Alasdair's '(and perhaps by and
by Arthur's) education will be better for this', and that
> it should help to make up for the disadvantage of your home edu-
> cation, with its lessened social opportunities and its less of
> sharing in games.   As myself the largely home-educated son of a
> quiet and student-like father, I feel I have too much shrunk from
> society of all kinds, and also that I am not so able to lead and
> inspire others as I wish you to be.

What follows is P.G.'s romantic description of the bagpipes as an
element of Scottish character and even history.   The piper possesses 'in a very high degree good personal and social qualities...'
> Practically unarmed and unresisting, the piper takes the post of
> danger, and blows on, wounded or no, sometimes rallying defeat
> into victory.   And though I hope you will never need to use the
> pipes in war, peace has need of all the military virtues it can
> preserve or redevelop.   Simple though it is, this is of all in-
> struments the one that most fully goes into life, that not only
> storms in the battle, but with its high strenuous voice enlivens
> the steady monotonous everyday trudge which is so much of the
> ordinary duty of life.   It throbs and leaps in the dance, it
> laughs and rejoices at the wedding, it wails at the funeral...

Another reason for learning to pipe is that 'In a summer or two you
will lead some of our excursions, and almost from the first you will
be able to start the march and help the fun.'   Here the hopeful
parent lists eight possible activities from field-naturalist to
photographer, in the performance of which 'you may find this
strange old piercing song stir yourself and others, as you send its
joy or sadness singing over the bens and moors, and through the
glens...'
> You have always worn the costume of our Highland forbears, as I
> did as a boy, my father as a man, but we have both lost their
> language.   Learn then this wider language, that by which the
> Celt at once appeals to every Scottish ear - indeed to many
> others....   Go on then and learn to play the old Celtic laments,
> the marches too, the pibrochs: blow loud and clear till men
> think of the long-lost Arthur returning in his might;   croon too
> with the doves of peace, and chant like Columba and his breth-
> ren....   Take up the pipes then, and carry on into your gentle
> home and college life, and the strenuous working years beyond,
> more and more of the intensity and the splendour of war and of
> religion.   As you know, of the pipes there is many a tale of
> old magic: do you begin another, of renewed Romance.   For in

the study and laboratory of the Evolutionist, in the work and
play of the Artist, there is again beginning the Holy War.

In 1907 Norah was 20, Alasdair 16, Arthur 12, and their father 53.
Almost ten years before Patrick had written to his old father about
'passing through middle age towards age itself', yet there was no
sign of any lessening of vitality or in number of projects being
launched.   Nevertheless, P.G. was now openly concerned about finding new colleagues and successors.   He had Thomson in natural science, Branford in civics-sociology, John Duncan in art, A.J. Herbertson in geography, but none in planning.   The following letter
to Norah, who was having her turn at studies in Montpellier, reveals
both his far-ranging interests as a planner and his concern about
the future.   The letter-head itself is symptomatic of something in
his make-up that steadily sought expression and proof of achievement, in print at least.   He must have new work-companions, colleagues, comrades-in-arms, for his wish-needs were insatiable.
Here is an early plea for junior colleagues.

PATRICK GEDDES AND COLLEAGUES

LANDSCAPE ARCHITECTS, PARK AND GARDEN
DESIGNERS, MUSEUM PLANNERS, ETC
OUTLOOK TOWER, EDINBURGH
AND 5 OLD QUEEN ST, WESTMINSTER

CITY PLANS AND IMPROVEMENTS
PARKS AND GARDENS
GARDEN VILLAGES
TYPE MUSEUMS
EDUCATIONAL APPLIANCES
SCHOOL GARDENS

To her daughter in Montpellier

OUTLOOK TOWER

EDINBURGH

5 Jan.   *1907*

Dear Lassie

Dear Lassie,
Since you ask for a serious letter from each of us, saying what
we'd like you to think of and prepare for, here is mine; or at
least an instalment of it.   The very paper will show that I mean
business - and of the largest kind.   Lately I have been in correspondence with various people in Canada ... (regarding Grand
Trunk Pacific Railway and their new western terminus at Prince
Rupert.) ....   I might be of use towards laying out this and
other cities.
     Again, I have, by Bailie Dobie's invitation, written him in-
dicating some of the things I should like to try to organise for
Exhibitions - Edinburgh, 1908 - civics, education, etc.
     This means a lot of work as well as thought.   I have set
about learning to draw! and after a few trials on different evenings, generally after work, I feel something coming back....   I
have been stirring up Alasdair and he is going to try too....
He will tell you himself of this first lesson yesterday in the
field with me.
     Of course neither of these two jobs may come off, but this
will at least show you that I mean business, and that on more
ambitious lines than ever; so the more and the sooner you and
Alasdair are ready to be colleagues the better!   It is a great
pleasure to think of you both being associated with me in these
endeavours, and I'll be able to work with far more enthusiasm if

I can think of myself as beginning a business which will not end
with my years - now necessarily few, at best - of active life.
It is in West and North-west Canada that the next great development of a new country is beginning, comparable to that of the
Middle and West of the U.S.A. in the last generation, and seems
to me to offer very interesting careers to you all. It is more
attractive than finding here and there a rich man's garden in the
country, or even on the Riviera...

Your affectionate
Daddy

This letter also contains suggestions for Norah's and Alasdair's
further studies so that they would be better prepared to help.
However, the Grand Trunk job did not materialise, apparently because
P.G. did not make time to go to London to meet one of the key Cana-
dians involved. As Philip Mairet phrased it, 'Geddes's problems of
time were growing insoluble'. (40)   He was carrying on a 'volumi-
nous and exacting correspondence' with friends who wrote him about
their planning problems. Victor Branford had made a trip to
Mexico, being involved in projects there and in South America.
Marcel Hardy, a Belgian whom P.G. had helped to settle in Scotland
and who became one of the latter's assistants at Dundee, was having
problems managing a plantation in Paraguay. Even the American
millionaire, Joseph Fels, wanted advice by mail in connection with
a proposed Zionist settlement in Central America.

This conflict between too many interests and too little time had
disastrous results for the 'civics school' whose interests the
Sociological Society was originally meant to further. Martin White
generously endowed a Chair of Sociology at the University of London,
and as at Dundee, his intention was that Geddes should get the
chair. However, several candidates were invited to try out, and
according to Arthur Geddes's recollections, P.G. 'gave a very bad
lecture beforehand'. He 'rushed up by train and he hadn't thought
it out. It was a scrambled talk such as P.G. sometimes gave instead of a lecture, so he didn't get the chair'. (41)

An 'ethical' sociologist, T.H. Hobhouse, was not only selected instead for the London chair but also became editor of the 'Sociological Review'. His concept of sociology was as 'a science for
social work' and it involved an 'unequivocal rejection of civics
sociology'. Branford complained to Martin White that Hobhouse had
admitted his lack of 'knowledge of both Eugenics and Civics' and
that in spite of this, 'As an editor he refuses to be guided'. An
immediate consequence was that the eugenists 'hived off' in 1907 to
form their own organisation; the town-planners likewise, in 1911.
The total result, as summed up by Halliday sixty years later, was
that

Geddes's failure to secure the Martin White Professorship in
London and Hobhouse's editorial policy for the 'Sociological
Review' effectively prevented the civics school from exercising
a sustained influence on academic sociology. (42)

CAUTIOUS COLLEAGUES ... 'SINS OF EDINBURGH'

Still more onerous than Geddes's lack of time, Mairet has pointed
out, 'and often emotionally distracting, were his affairs in Edinburgh'.

> The Outlook Tower had been saved from financial failure during
> one of his absences by Anna: it was still the home base for all
> his sociological operations and as such he regarded it to the end
> of his days; but its maintenance gave rise to recurrent prob-
> lems.   Often, too, he was drawn into the politics of the Town
> and Gown Association which had taken over most of his earlier
> Edinburgh responsibilities, and these colleagues did not admini-
> ster their properties as adventurously as he thought they
> should. (43)

In fact, P.G. did not hesitate on occasion to express his frank
opinion of some of these men.   In a letter of 2 May 1905, for
example, he takes Thomas B. Whitson (chairman of the Town and Gown
Association) bluntly to task.   After first describing the faults of
a proposed new board member, Geddes writes that, even so, he and his
ilk

> have a redeeming quality ... namely this - though caring far too
> much for themselves, they *really want to get something done*, and,
> consequently, despite their inferiorities, they do: (and our
> wars, slums, speculating, and chaos generally are no doubt large-
> ly the result!)   Per contra, it is the fatal limitation of you,
> the business and professional gentlemen of Edinburgh, that -
> simply and comprehensively - you DON'T want to get things done:
> you are there to criticise, to 'be cautious', to 'prevent loss',
> to 'protect your clients' and so on, and thus, in short, to be
> the council of war that never fights - and the surest, because
> the steadiest, pilots to destruction.   For while you damp down
> fires and let off steam lest we should go ahead into 'danger',
> the vessel is meantime drifting on to worse rocks.   Hence the
> above chaos is *your* fault, not the bounders.

Such blasts are temporarily softened with conciliatory words characteristically followed by more hard hitting:

> No one can more loyally recognise his true and good friends, I
> trust, than I do in you and M.   But....   You fellows would
> build express engines out of the best Westinghouse brakes *only*,
> and you think of the vital steam simply and solely as a *dangerous
> explosive* to be *kept in total inaction* - not to be sanely regula-
> ted at its intensest power, and even then by steam, not ice.
>   That is the use that has been made of me all these years by
> Town and Gown; and accordingly, just now you are offering huge
> commissions to get rid of property, because you would not spend
> a tithe of this in T. & G.'s working for London University and
> the like.

He refers to the Coltbridge Garden City project adding that even if
he were wrong in this case he still believes that 'if there were
fifty more cases they would be settled in the same way'.   Then
comes a mingling of broadside against the real enemy, Edinburgh, and
of more conciliation.

My criticism of Edinburgh is the general one of frozen legality - of the paralysed respectability, which in turn develops the British hypocrisy, that culminates in the Churches and the Parties, but now runs off into 'philanthropy' also, and 'supports' Garden City or Garden Suburb - while asking ME (!) to find the capital.

Now I am writing not to hurt your feelings, goodness knows, but to help you more keenly and sharply to feel what honest men like you and your friends are partially feeling - that it is time to wake out of that fool's paradise of a west end, with its routine W.S.-ing and C.A.-ing [Writer-to-the-Signet-ing & Chartered-Accountant-ing] and amateur speculating, instead of the constructive modesty of the young Germans or Americans who will soon be our masters.

For the due development of this House of Thought and Action through the City and beyond, it is well that I should at the outset say my say strongly. If it offends, better now than later: if it leads to vigorous reply and ultimate co-operation, all is well.

Ever yours sincerely (and affectionately)
Patrick Geddes

P.S. Communicate what you think fit - or all if you like - to our mutual friend; but don't let him think he won't do: at worst, he has *some* interest, and who else has so much?

An incident which the younger son, Arthur, later recalled is appropriate to P.G.'s public relations even though it has no connection with Town and Gown colleagues. When he was thirteen or fourteen he asked this question:

'Mother, why is it that Daddy has so many enemies?' And with infinite sadness she said, 'Well you see, if a man does something that should be done, and tries to do it - perhaps succeeds in doing it - then others will say to those who should have done it: "Why didn't you do it?" And that makes them enemies'. I think that is a profound remark which is typical of my mother's insight. (44)

An additional explanation must be that P.G. had a flair for discovering and spelling out in black and white the errors and stupidities of others, academics and officials in particular. In 1910, for example, he wrote to Victor Branford at greater length about the 'sins of Edinburgh' than he had to Mr Whitson. (45) After praising the breweries' endowment of a chair of bacteriology at Heriot-Watt College and the good co-operation of manufacturing pharmacists with the School of Medicine, he prepared for the coming thunder: 'But not always are science and industry kept together thus'.

A generation ago we expatriated Prof. Melville Bell, and his Visible Speech. True, he was only a professor of elocution, and in this city of the letter that killeth it was only natural to give but the humblest status to the exponent of the living word. Now however this invention of visible speech is better known as his son's Telephone, and also as Edison's Phonograph. (So by the way Dundee threw away its local inventor's initiatives of electric lighting and of wireless telegraphy.) Returning to Edinburgh: so we lost the Students' Microscope (designed here) to Germany; and so on in other cases.

Another indictment lay in Cambridge's celebration of Darwin whereas
Edinburgh, 'the University of three generations of Darwins', took no
notice of the great Charles 'in his lifetime, though there was time
and again occasion for honouring him, and when he would have appreciated it.   So here the next generation of Darwins have never set
foot - and no wonder!'

> Just as it refused Carlyle ... so I can remember their refusing
> Robert Louis Stevenson....   We want 'safe' men here you know,
> and so we generally get them.   Since Blackie, Masson, etc., no
> more such fiery spirits have been admitted ... and though it is
> fair to note that good men still manage to slip through the in-
> spection, they are pretty free from the stigmata of genius which
> characterised the older generation.

As a final, extreme example of pen-lashing we quote from P.G.'s
letter to H.B. Cunninghame Graham of 31 August 1909 in which 'I have
been letting myself go (indeed as I have rarely done to anyone)'.
He invites Graham to come back to Edinburgh for a week-end 'and look
with me at this sad old city'.

> You see her pinioned by her judges and preyed on by their wig-
> lice, that countless vermin of lawyerlings, swollen and small.
> You see her left in squalor by her shopkeepers, her bawbee-
> worshipping bailie-bodies and pushioned by her doctors; you hear
> her dulled by the blithers of her politicians and deived by the
> skreigh of the newsboy-caddies who squabble at their heels, and
> you know how she has been paralysed by the piffle of her profes-
> sors, more than half-docted or driven into alternate hidebound or
> hysteric nightmares by every chilly dogmatism, every flaring
> hell-blast imagined by three centuries and more of diabologiac
> Divines.

PAGEANTS OF HISTORY

University Hall, Edinburgh, completed its twenty-fifth year of successful existence in 1912.   From the original seven residents its
yearly membership had increased to 150, lodged in four houses, and
the University itself had finally been moved to establish two student residences.   Of the many suggestions made for celebrating the
semi-jubilee of the first autonomous student residence in Great
Britain, the most imaginative and appropriate was that of its
founder.

During the third week of March 1912, Edinburgh's large Synod Hall
was eight times filled to capacity by paying spectators who thronged
to witness 'The Masque of Learning', a pageant of the history of
civilisation, devised and interpreted by Patrick Geddes.   It was
performed by 'about 650 active participants, as players, orchestra
and choir ... and repeated for 2500 school-children of Edinburgh.
Thousands failed to obtain admission: hence further performances'. (46)   Such was P.G.'s triumph as pageant producer in the
city whose town council seventeen years before had withdrawn support of his summer school because of the historical 'bairns' show'
at Inchcolm Island.

This achievement was repeated in London the following spring in the
Great Hall of the Imperial Institute where the enthusiasm aroused
by the first five performances in March 1913 caused five more to be
given early in April.   Whereas the Edinburgh performers were organised around University Hall and the Outlook Tower, the London masquers appropriately had their headquarters in rebuilt Crosby Hall.
P.G.'s publishing house revived itself for both occasions to the
extent of issuing a booklet containing his directions for and reflections on these scenes of dramatised history.   Revised three
times within a year, its pages varied from 80 to 186 and the number
of scenes from 24 to 44, plus eight new masques suggested!   Unlike
certain titles in P.G. & Colleagues' Celtic Library, 'The Masque of
Learning and Its Many Meanings' sold out all four editions totalling
at least 9,000 copies.

How well Geddes's wide interests and vast number of acquaintances
served him in this, the original 'Outline of History' is apparent
in the Scenario of the first edition which names the organisers of
each scene and the dozens of scholars, artists, musicians, curators,
theatrical staff, missionaries, overseas students, robemakers and
others who gave advice and material help.   Besides his multifarious
tasks as deviser and director of the Masques in Edinburgh and London
he corresponded with persons who wrote to him about this project.
A notable example is his contact with Dr Ananda Coomaraswamy of
Ceylon who later became the first keeper of Indian Art in the Boston
Museum of Fine Arts.

In a letter of 30 March 1912 Dr Coomaraswamy thanked P.G. 'for your
delightful booklet', made several suggestions for improving the
section on Hindu culture and sent 'good wishes for your many works'.
One comment was used in the following edition, while Geddes in turn
filled up such blank space as was left in the letter with suggestions for future cooperation and sent it back to Coomaraswamy marked
'Please return to P.G.'.   His reaction to the mention of Aryina,
Krishna and Asoka was 'Would not [each of these] need a whole stage
for itself?'   'Such scenes however are examples of how admirably
rich & vivid, simple & inspiring, might be the "Masque of India"!
When and where are we to do it?'   His contact with this scholar
also bespeaks the steadily increasing interest which Geddes was
showing in the life and civilisation of the Orient.

Moving on to London in the spring of 1913, the dramatist became even
more hectically involved than the year before.   An English eye-
witness, Amelia Defries, tells how P.G. staged the greatly enlarged
'Masque of Medieval and Modern Learning' at the same time as he
served as a planning consultant for Edinburgh's new Zoo.   Furthermore, his botanical duties in Dundee would soon recommence: on top
of which he was also working on plans for a town-planning exhibition
in Ghent that summer.   No wonder there seemed to be mainly chaos
in the crypt of Crosby Hall where the hundreds of London participants came to go over their parts.   The witness, who was also a
group leader, relates:

Rehearsals proceeded in an unorganized way which made some of us
wonder whether there would ever be a performance at all.   But in

and out of the various groups of performers the thin, agile figure of the author might at times be seen moving about, like a
shepherd's dog among sheep. Occasionally he came to my group
and acted the part of each person, with complete absorption and
with the dramatic force and finish of a fine professional actor,
as indeed I at first took him to be. In these rare visits, he
inspired us with an almost ferocious vigour; and he gave us an
insight into the different characters in the Masque which went
far beyond our ordinary ideas of history. (47)

Anna Geddes, 'a little lady with grey hair and a pale, smiling face,
and the tranquillity of a Quakeress, was hovering around the performers and weaving order out of chaos; with invisible wires she
pulled us together into a whole'. Yet at times when the author-
producer was urgently needed, the players were told he was back in
Edinburgh, which 'seemed to us a little mad!' However,
there was method in the madness of the wizard who turned to touch
us, each one, with his magic wand when necessary; but who left
us alone to plough through our difficulties and find out for ourselves, instead of drilling us in the ordinary way. Towards the
end he was back again, quietly giving confidence here and touching up a performance there, now in a passion of earnestness and
now smiling or talking softly and rapidly into his beard, until
the Masque began to *live*.

In addition to marking the University Hall anniversary, the 'Masque
of Learning' was a convincing defence of his thesis
that there is no subject of study into which dramatisation, historical and other, cannot brighteningly be introduced; as
obviously into all the humanities, and even into each and all
of the sciences. Nothing is too abstract, from philosophy to
mathematics and logic; nothing too prosaic or arid, even to
economics in its controversies, bibliography in its labours....
We do not clearly think, much less clearly idealise, until we
visualise and energise: that is, until we dramatise.

The Prologue shows the oral teaching of Geddes at its clearest and
best:
THE SCHOOL BAG

Scene - The street, outside the Portal of the University. BOY
enters, swinging his school-bag: he pauses and looks in dubious-
ly, thinking of the matriculation examination for which he is
preparing.
A friendly PROFESSOR accosts him, and asks what he is doing at
school. The BOY shows his crowded bag.
The PROFESSOR takes out the books one by one and musingly explains them - to himself, as well as to the boy:

This overgrown arithmetic book is the very spirit of the commercial and financial age: this old examination paper bears the
stamp of its bureaucracy: and this cram-book to prepare for it
is the encyclopaedia in miniature.

All this reading in living languages, English, French, and German, has come on from the golden moment of the Renaissance; and the grammars and lexicon are from its silver age.   Here is an essay, dated yesterday; yet with unmistakable traces of the medieval thesis and disputation.

Virgil and Homer; the heritage of Rome, of Greece.   The Bible; it renews the voices of the patriarchal world.

What's this?   New story-book?   Not really new, nor yet trivial or contraband: It is continuing the tradition began 'once upon a time': for the tale-teller comes from the remote unwritten past of folklore.

A fresh apple; a new ball!   These are the oldest of all. For this is the raw food, and that the ready missile of Primeval Man.

BOY - If all this be in my school-bag, what must there be in the University, and its big Library?

PROFESSOR - The same, only more fully.   A book is not merely a fossil or a treasure from some phase of the past.   Its right reading - not the words from without, but the thought from within - is a spell by which you may recall this past, re-enter it when you will.   This test of this power of reading is the old matriculation examination, and the coming one too.   It must be made by the aspirant, and not merely of him.   Will you try it?

BOY - Yes.   How?

PROFESSOR - The spell is simple: the reason why so many fail is by using only one or the other half of it.   You must throw your ball, and with all your might; and eat the apple of knowledge also: only by help of both can you or any youth get so far as that earliest development of conscious man.   To take either alone is a fall, an evil: it is a real enchantment, an arrest - for some by the brute's strength, for others at the parrot's memory.

But with this elementary education, with apple and ball, of mind and body together, one's higher education goes on with the world's.   Term by term the spell continues to work; the pageant goes on opening, phase by phase; each lives again, by the magic of its rightly read book....

(Boy throws the ball, proceeds to devour the apple, and thus matriculates as Student: the Pageant opens accordingly.) (48)

While specialists may question the choice of certain great moments and men, no one can fail to share P.G.'s enthusiasm as he recreates essential steps of the 'long, eventful, ever-arrested, ever-renewing Ascent of Man'.   For as J. Arthur Thomson put it, Geddes had a remarkable visualising power, 'picturing the pageant of history as if he had been an eye-witness, discussing the aeonic process of organic evolution as a drama in which he had personally shared'. (49)

There unfolds before the boy the pageant of countless generations
of life and labour, of ideas and ideals. Beginning with pre-his-
toric man mastering fire and inventing musical instruments from a
twanging bow-string, the scene moves to the dawn of recorded history: Babylonian priests begin to measure time; Egyptians stretch
ropes to measure land; astronomy and geometry come into existence.
Moses appears with the Tables of the Law; Confucius and Lao-tze
meet; Hindu mathematicians and poets form a procession; and so on
for the highlights of Oriental culture. Then follows the heritage
of Greece personified by gods, goddesses, and Muses; by Homer,
Hippocrates, Socrates, Plato, and Aristotle. Each of the latter
three is accompanied by a friend and pupil, 'for philosophy, like
music, lives in its discourse and dies down into silence and
nothingness with mere retrospect and criticism'. Next comes Rome,
its law and engineering, its poetry and prose; its fight against,
then adoption of Christianity; and much more. The masque of
ancient learning draws to a close with Celtic culture as typified
by Ossian, St Patrick, Arthur, and St Columba.

The second half of the pageant commences with the fall of Rome and
brings the boy to his own twentieth century. The scenes from
Mediaeval, Renaissance, Reformation, and recent times are too complex even to enumerate: Faustus, Lorenzo, and Leonardo da Vinci;
Sir Thomas More presenting Erasmus and Holbein to Henry VIII, Queen
Mary and John Knox, the immortals of the Mermaid tavern, Milton
visiting Galileo; such is but a sampling of the great moments of
these centuries. As a climax to man's achievements up to the
present comes Beethoven and the playing of his music by the orchestra. In P.G.'s next lines one feels the influence, if not the
actual words, of Anna.

> In him a vision of the world, a passion of life, vast as Shakes-
> peare's, a power of evocation like Homer's, find utterance in
> creations no less glorious than theirs; and in the high perfec-
> tion of an art which at the time of their inspiration was still
> but in its infancy.
>   History is thus no mere death-mask, impressive symbol of the
> past though that may be. - Its commemoration is no mere wreath-
> ing with laurels, right and necessary though that also be. It
> is the hearing of the voices of the past; and more - the con-
> tinuance of their music. More still, its variations also, to
> meet the fresh situations and new themes of the present and
> future.

The final scene, portraying City and University as they are and as
they will be, is a sharply focused illustration of Geddes's philosophy. A typical academic procession enters one side of the stage.
Gaudily berobed professors of all Faculties accompanying Alma Mater,
who is the modern Eve, Sibyl, and 'Mother Church' in one. From the
opposite side arrives a civic procession: Mater Civitas, the Mother
City, followed by chief magistrate, councillors, the trades, crafts,
and occupations. But the two groups remain aloof; it being the
era of philistine towns and pedantic colleges. Meanwhile the en-
cyclopaedists dissect Alma Mater's apple of knowledge into so many
tiny pieces that the philosophers themselves are unable to puzzle

Patrick Geddes as the 'Medieval Scholar' at the Court of Lorenzo the
Magnificent in the Masque of Learning performed in 1913 in London

it together again.   'The educationalist sweetly promises its fragments to the people, while the pedant and the bureaucrat substitute
its husks.   The people perish for lack of knowledge, and most of
all where there is no vision.'

At length comes the new era of cooperation between University and
City.   Graduates of each Faculty offer their services to Mater
Civitas, who sets them to work among her people.   In return she
gives the University new colleges of technology, fine arts, and
music, but this union of Town and Gown is best symbolised in their
joint ministrations of medicine and public hygiene.   When the pro-
cessions leave the stage, they go out, not separately as they came
in, but together, with students and workmen, professors and merchants intermingling as together they form the 'latest and greatest
of Faculties, that of Citizenship'.

GRAND PRIX AT GHENT ... SUCCESS AND DÉBÂCLE IN DUBLIN

Ghent, the capital of the Flemish population of Belgium, became a
centre of international importance throughout the summer of 1913 by
reason of its great 'Exposition Internationale'.   It also was,
thanks to P.G., the 'capital of civic sociology' and the meeting
place of the first 'World Congress of Cities'.   Visitors in general
were struck by the emphasis on things urban: the Communal Square
with its four civic palaces representing Ghent, Antwerp, Liège, and
Brussels; the grandiose exhibits of German city improvements in the
German Pavilion; and the itinerant Cities Exhibition of Professor
Geddes, housed beside the Palace of Brussels.   While the architects, engineers, politicians, and other professionals attending the
'Congrès International des Villes' took this emphasis for granted,
no observant person could have failed to notice the great contrast
in exhibits.

The Ghent Congress had largely come into being through the efforts
of two of Geddes's Belgian friends: Paul Otlet, creator of the
Mundaneum in Brussels, and Senator Henri La Fontaine, who would
receive the Nobel Peace Prize later that year.   Various points of
view in the embryonic field of urbanism found expression there, some
in almost clashing opposition to one another.   The German exhibits
were all beautifully framed and labelled, arranged with typical
Prussian method in spacious galleries, as befitted an exhibition
subsidised by the Prussian state to show its achievements in urban
reconstruction.   The Cities Exhibition, on the other hand, was
Geddes's own show and for financial backing had only the voluntary
subscriptions of such Britons as were interested in his ideas.

Like the Edinburgh Room at the Royal Gallery, his exhibits lacked
such niceties as gilt frames and printed labels; and whether because of lack of funds or not there was no printed catalogue as
for the showings in Great Britain.   However, a reprint of an
article in the 'Town Planning Review' of July 1913 partially served
the purpose, containing a one-page plan of the Ghent Exhibition and
fifteen pages of guidance and persuasion.   Alasdair, then twenty-

two, came from Montpellier, where he, too, had been studying botany, in good time to arrange the exhibits as the full-fledged junior colleague he already was.   But two days before the official opening in late July there was still no sign of P.G.   True, he had made a quick trip to Ghent in May to give Alasdair general instructions and a cryptic lay-out to follow, then rushed back to his Dundee duties with side-trips to Edinburgh for the new Zoo project with which Norah, now a landscape designer in her own right, was helping him.

Amelia Defries has written an amusing account of how everyone was hunting for the elusive professor who was still in Scotland.   Paul Otlet, 'a white-bearded, exquisitely groomed and top-hatted Belgian gentleman, with a decoration in his buttonhole', came to Alasdair in great perturbation: 'Mais, où est-il, ce bon Geddes, hein?'
    Alasdair shrugged his shoulders, spread out his hands like a
    Frenchman, and said simply and smilingly, as if it were a joke:
    'Il n'est pas encore arrivé'....   Agitated visitors from dif-
    ferent countries, as well as Belgians, were wandering about look-
    ing for an interpreter.   Alasdair, busy among his finishing
    touches, was able to enlighten some, but my general impression
    was of frock-coated gentlemen, top-hats in hand, decorations in
    button-holes, rather excitedly exclaiming: 'Mais M. Geddes, où
    est-il donc?'

The day before the opening ceremony Miss Defries arrived at the Exhibition especially early, only to find there a group of workmen who had already been busy for some hours.   In the midst of them was Geddes, himself, in shirt-sleeves and working at white heat.   On the floor were scattered many of the pictures and diagrams that Alasdair and his helpers had so painstakingly hung during the previous weeks.
    For the first and last time I saw Alasdair in a rage.   But no
    word was said; he was obeying orders like a conscript and it was
    towards the middle of the day, when helping him to get a great
    map of Paris into place, that I asked him if we had really made
    so many mistakes as to hang all those things wrongly.
    'No,' he said quietly, with tight lips and almost on the verge
    of tears.   'No.   Daddy had an inspiration in the train last
    night.   He saw all at once a way to make things clearer.'

The price of P.G.'s inspiration was a terrific day's work for all concerned to make the necessary changes in arrangement before the formal opening.   The incident is a good example of intellectual tyranny, Geddesian style.   His life was dominated by ideas, incessant and self-propagating, which governed his waking hours and which at night brewed themselves subconsciously until the approach of daylight should turn them loose.

'Ideas at any cost' describes a great part of his life and explains his relations with his fellows.   To him thoughts were inseparable from action, and it was woe betide friends and foes alike when the sparks of cerebration, particularly last-minute ones, began to fly. He did not spare himself in effort or fatigue; neither did he spare those who helped him willingly or those whom he practically forced to aid him.

All, however, was not lost at Ghent.   Since there was no detailed
catalogue to be revised, this saved finances from strain and the
personnel from further anguish.   Happily, the tardy arrival of P.G.
brought more than consternation.   His wife came with him, the calm
grey-haired lady who could bring order out of chaos.

Immediately on arriving at the Exhibition galleries Anna Geddes set
about doing what the menfolk had overlooked, such as tidying up the
library room which was to serve as a meeting place for the Congress
of Cities next day.   But even more valuable than restoring order
was her power of intercession, her ability to tone down Pat's cerebral high-voltage when some bewildered soul was in danger of elec-
trocution.
    Mrs Geddes found time, while sorting books and jotting down notes,
    to inquire as to my health and living arrangements; and a few
    days later she had me in much better rooms, working shorter hours
    and living more normally than during the last three months. (50)

Interest in the exhibits at Ghent was heightened by the open competition among the various exhibitors, for a jury was to award a
prize to the collection best portraying civic development and
planning.   Geddes and the Germans were obviously the two main competitors.   P.G.'s compatriots naturally desired his success, for
patriotic reasons if for no other, but even experienced architects
and planners doubted the appeal his method would have for the
judges.

'The Germans may have the frames and labels', he retorted, 'but we
have the ideas!'   The thoughtful visitor who read the reprint of
'Two Steps in Civics' had quick proof of this.   As in all P.G.'s
exhibitions since 1910, his aim was to stir up the 'practical man'
to 'see more of his City's roots in the past, of his responsibilities in the future'.   He also wanted to arouse 'the best minds of
each city to distinguish, in the past, its "Heritage" (respect for
which makes the Conservative at his moral best) from its "Burden"
(revolt from which makes the Radical and the Revolutionary at his
moral best)'.   To both of them he urged the common-sense practice,
as in medicine, of 'diagnosis before treatment', instead of, 'as so
much hitherto', adopting 'the best advertised panacea of treatment,
before any diagnosis worth the name'.   The rival quackeries of
'party politicians have too long been delaying the survey and diagnosis of the civic sociologist'.

Despite their lack of professional presentation, P.G.'s exhibits got
through to alert visitors such as the American planner, N.P. Lewis,
who found this 'show of ideas' the most important feature of the
Ghent Exposition.   Twenty years later an editor of a town-planning
journal in England wrote: 'We cannot forget the thrill of that
personally conducted tour around Geddes's town-planning exhibition
at Ghent in 1913.'   Yet the most spontaneous tribute
    came from an old gentleman of distinguished appearance.... He
    had come out of the 'Cell' (which suggested the need of medita-
    tion as well as practical surveys) and, taking off his soft hat,
    bowed low several times!   Looking at the other exhibits, after

studying them awhile, he repeated his bows, backing at times as
if from a royal presence.   When at length he caught sight of me,
he asked in French: 'Who is responsible for this?' - waving his
hands expressively.
'It is an exhibition of the ideas of Professor Geddes.'
'Ah!' He looked around for half-an-hour more, and then came
back to me and bowed.   'I take off my hat', he said, 'to the
genius whose thoughts are here.   I take off my hat to him.'   He
bowed again, saying: 'Tomorrow I return', and next day came
back.   He was Emile Claus, the father of Belgian Impression-
ism! (51)

That Alasdair was following convincingly in his father's best footsteps is testified to by an incident that summer.   The British
educator, Sir William Mather, had been shown the galleries by the
son who explained the history and future universities as unfolded
by the Exhibition.   Sir William, 'before leaving, put his hand on
the youth's shoulder, saying, "You will reform the Universities!"
"That is one of my dreams", was the firm yet modest reply.' (52)

By his conventional university colleagues P.G. may still have been
looked on as a 'jack of all subjects' and a menace to the isolation
of specialised fields of learning, but to the larger world of geographers, architects, municipal engineers, councillors, and urban-
ists he was already a trail-blazer, a master of the many complex
elements that make up the science and art of city-planning.

In recognition of his pioneer work in the civic survey and of the
notable superiority of his Cities Exhibition, the international
jury of the Ghent Exposition of 1913 awarded the *Grand Prix* to
Patrick Geddes.   Thus did the regimented methods of Prussian
planning, in this preliminary round, go down in defeat before the
unbounded ideas of a Scottish naturalist.

In the early summer of 1914 Dublin was the 'geotechnic capital' of
the British Isles.   This phrase of Victor Branford's meant that
the Irish city was then the converging point of forces there working more fully towards civic and regional improvement than anywhere
else.   Ever since 1911, when P.G. and his travelling Cities Exhibition had first stirred up public interest in 'geotechnics', Dublin
had been seriously taking stock of its burden of evils and considering how to reduce them.   The Viceroy of Ireland, Lord Aberdeen,
was an active leader in this movement.   He in fact had invited
Geddes to put on his 'idea-exhibit' in 1911 which resulted in the
forming of the National Housing and Town Planning Association and
its undertaking of a civic survey of Dublin.   By April 1914 plans
for a broad campaign of slum improvement and for replanning the
whole city were actively under way.

But to most outward appearances Dublin at this time was mainly
a hotbed of strikes and revolt like many an Irish city.   Since
August 1913 a bitter fight had been raging between organised employers and organised labour, with attendant riots and bloodshed,
strikes and lock-outs.   While the British Parliament debated the

generation-old question of Home Rule for Ireland, that country experienced even greater unrest than it had been accustomed to through
centuries of rule by John Bull's bureaucrats.   Protestant Ulster
wanted independence from the rest of Ireland as well as from Britain, and in Belfast an army of 90,000 had been recruited to defend
this stand.   In Dublin two armies sprang up: one to buttress
Catholic interests and the other, Larkin's Citizen Army, to combat
capitalistic tyranny without regard to creed or politics.

From the slums of Dublin, where over a fifth of the population lived
in miserable one-room flats, James Larkin had arisen as a formidable
champion of the poor.   He incited workers to strike, defied police
orders against holding mass meetings, and when arrested and brought
to trial for sedition, defended himself in a way that won the sympathies of working men everywhere in the British Isles.   Sentenced
to imprisonment, Larkin became such a popular hero and received so
much support against his judges that he was shortly released.   'The
government has made outlaws of the working-class of Dublin', he
thundered.   'But if we are treated as outlaws we shall act as outlaws!'   And he continued war on the stubborn employers who refused
to recognise his union or to accept mediation offered by a disinterested committee.   From the strike of transport workers in the
autumn of 1913 he carried the conflict into other trades.   With
business half paralysed by 1914, Dublin was a city of poverty, fear
and hatred as well as a 'geotechnic capital'.

Into this city came Geddes bringing ideas and action.   On a preliminary visit in March he suggested to Lord and Lady Aberdeen, whose
guest he was, that a civic exhibition be held there, representing
all Ireland and that plans for improving Dublin be drawn up and displayed.   The Viceroy opened a competition with a prize of £500 for
the best replanning scheme for the city, of which the judges were
to be P.G., John Nolen (American landscape architect and city-
planner), and the official architect of the Dublin municipality.
Having thus rung a first door bell, Geddes returned to Scotland in
April with a stop-over in Cardiff, to lecture on the history of
zoological gardens and on his planning of the Edinburgh Zoo.   Back
at the Outlook Tower he took a hand in the Easter vacation course
which had been arranged by his regional-survey colleague, Mabel
Barker, daughter of his boyhood comrade Harry.   Out of this course
grew the Regional Survey Association, later to bear fruit in schools
in all parts of Great Britain.

Shortly before reassuming his spring duties at Dundee, P.G. sent
a cablegram to agents in the USA accepting a lecture-tour offer for
1914-15 which could well lead to some city-planning practice while
there and a Cities Exhibition tour for the following season.   But
the next day a letter arrived from Lord Pentland, then Governor of
Madras, with an official invitation to bring the civic exhibition
with him and 'enlighten municipal administrators and others in
India upon the subject of modern town-planning'.   Since this was
exactly his kind of work, he postponed his America tour for a year
and accepted Lord Pentland's offer, for the following October.

In July 1914 the botanist went back to Dublin as man of action, as geotechnician; not to ring the bell and run away this time, but to face problems which had defeated generations of Irish citizens and would-be British rulers.   With him he brought his special weapons: the *Grand Prix* Cities Exhibition, now nearly trebled in size;   and a picked squad of helpers.   Among these were Victor Branford, Professor H.J. Fleure, geographer and anthropologist, Mabel Barker, and Alasdair and Norah Geddes.   Alasdair was again his father's right-hand man in transporting, setting up, and demonstrating the civic exhibition, while Norah, as garden-designer, took part in the campaign to provide Dublin with adequate school and public gardens.

In the Linen Hall, a vast unused building which had been repaired and added to for the purpose, father and son set up their graphic history of urban civilisation, their object lessons in the growth, flowering, and decay of cities.   Supplementing this master exhibition were local exhibits from every town in Ireland, the material gathered thus far in the survey of Dublin, and the Child Welfare Exhibit lent by its American creators.   The work of Sir Horace Plunkett in renewing agriculture and farm life in Ireland was also depicted in the Linen Hall.   This, said Geddes, meant that the rustic and urban movements which had so long run separate (and mainly unsuccessful) courses were now to be coordinated into one: that of a *regional* revival of life and labour in which country and town would regain their lost unity and with it their health and prosperity.

The Linen Hall exhibits plus the action of Geddes and team made a marked impression at all levels in Dublin.   The mere repairing of this deserted building and cleaning up its grounds stimulated the whole neighbourhood into similar tidying and repairing.   Then the mid-July opening of the restored hall with a procession of eighty mayors of Irish towns all in their robes, the Lord Mayor and Corporation of Dublin, and government officials from London showed that politicians themselves realised something new was stirring in Ireland.   Even slum children saw that better things were coming to them: playgrounds and gardens for their enjoyment;   while a little theatre and ballroom in the Linen Hall provided what was doubtless the first entertainment in their lives.

Yet the rival political factions remained unchanged, and the labour war continued with the same bitterness.   Larkin made a dramatic plea to send children from the intolerable one-room slum dwellings of Dublin over to England, where more fortunate working families would care for them until the housing situation was improved. This suggestion met first with approval then, as religious bigotry arose, with complete failure.   Certain Catholic clergy refused to let the children of the faithful escape from hell on earth for fear that during their sojourn in English Protestant homes they might win hell in the hereafter.   'Anti-Christ has come to town', a bishop said.   'It is Larkin!' (53)   Inevitably, then, the fight between labourers and employers became more savage.   As the exhibition was being prepared Larkin organised longshoremen and dockers into a strikers' corps that needed only a spark to drive them into bloody revolt.

At this point Geddes took a hand.   As an important figure at the
Linen Hall and as guest of Viceroy Aberdeen, he had access to anything and anyone in Dublin he desired, and accordingly, spent much
time exploring the city, talking with citizens and officials.   One
day he announced to his host that he wanted to call on James Larkin.
Lord Aberdeen raised no objections, though warning P.G. that the
strike leader had the reputation of being a dangerous man.   To
which Geddes replied there was nothing to fear since he already knew
Larkin from his visit to Edinburgh in 1913.   After addressing a
mass meeting there, the labour champion had accepted P.G.'s invitation to the Outlook Tower where, says Mairet,

> his personality made a great impression upon P.G. and his col-
> leagues.   This intense rebel, with his searching, fiery eyes,
> haunted by the memories of generations of suffering, won their
> respect by his courtesy and his readiness to listen and to learn.
> Larkin, for his part, was impressed by the intellectual energy
> and quick understanding of this full-bearded Scot, who almost
> completely outflanked his proletarian suspicions, more by what he
> evidently was than by what he said. (54)

If ever an adequate film or TV programme is to be made of P.G. Unlimited, it must recapture some of this 'biotechnic' drama which
took place in Edinburgh and Dublin, not least his encounters with
Larkin.   Authentic background information has also been provided by
Mabel Barker who tells of meeting 'Jim Larkin' in Edinburgh, at
lunch at Ramsay Garden, 'so he was already a friend' before the
summer of 1914.   She relates further that she then had a camp outside Dublin '& cycled in daily being P.G.'s organising secretary
for the School of Civics.   Larkin came out to visit it & some of
us went in to tea with him.   He was rather charming!' (55) Geddes
himself has provided this account of their meeting, saying that

> he had tackled the formidable James Larkin ... and had found him
> most reasonable, and not a little conciliated by the hope of a
> garden village for miserably housed (indeed practically homeless)
> dockers.   [P.G. then confirmed] ... how the Corporation had
> offered their estate just at the City's edge, and only a mile
> from the docks, on which he had planned 'the biggest of workers'
> garden villages as yet, and albeit necessarily the simplest and
> poorest, a garden village still'. (56)

His next move was to approach the Catholic hierarchy of Dublin
offering plans for a cathedral, a school and an art gallery.   The
cathedral was to be a monument to the new Ireland of Home Rule as
well as a sacred edifice replacing the two churches which the Reformation had taken away from the Catholics.   The Archbishop was
quickly won over by these plans (although originated by a Protestant), and bought the site indicated for the buildings.

Thus P.G. went from success to success until he was assured of support from dockers, clergy, the municipality and even the upper layer
of intellectuals.   Many of the latter were converted to the geotechnic cause in the 'School of Civics' organised in connection with
his Cities Exhibition at the Linen Hall.   In the space of three
weeks his imported 'regional-survey squad', together with local

teachers and scientists, provided a large body of students with what must have been the most comprehensive survey of a city and its region ever achieved in such a limited time.

The dinners at the Vice-regal Mansion arranged by Lady Aberdeen contributed in no small way to P.G.'s influence in Dublin.   Many a hard-headed employer, whom several Linen Halls full of exhibits would have left untouched, came to dine and remained to be converted to the economic doctrine of 'mutual aid', when the botanist showed them how mere 'survival of the fittest' was not workable even among the lowest forms of life.   Other captains of industry whose wives had social ambitions were probably more easily won over by an invitation from Lady Aberdeen than they would have been by argumentation.

One evening in the fourth week of exhibitions and the second of the School of Civics the dinner conversation turned from local problems to the facts of war in the Balkans, and general mobilisation. Still no one wanted to believe that Great Britain would become entangled in a continental conflict.   'War between England and Germany is inevitable!' exclaimed Victor Branford.   'Some of us have seen it coming ever since 1900.'   'There IS war already', said P.G.   'It's only a question of time until we are in it too.' Someone remarked that if so, there would be neither money nor man-power for any civic projects at home.   'You must pursue them, war or no war!' insisted Geddes.
> The health, the unity, the existence of Dublin and of Ireland is
> at stake here, not on distant battlefields.   No foreign war is
> going to remove your responsibility of fighting poverty and
> filth and economic injustice here at home.   You may have to
> carry on two wars, but I urge not only that the collections in
> the Linen Hall be preserved permanently but that the replanning
> scheme which wins the Viceroy's prize be carried out coura-
> geously - and beginning this very summer.

The discussion was still going on after dinner when Lord Aberdeen was called from the room.   He returned several minutes later, pale and intense, to tell his guests that the British Government had declared war on Germany.   It was the evening of 4 August 1914.

P.G. and collaborators carried on the exhibitions and summer school as planned, except for the addition of training courses for Red Cross nurses.   Yet by the end of August the renovated Linen Hall was no longer a centre of regional survey or a headquarters for city replanning.   It was first turned into a barracks and later into a hospital.   One by one the projects which dould have made Dublin the 'geotechnic capital' of the British Empire were abandoned: the dockers' garden village, the new cathedral, and more. Even the selection of the winning plan for the new Dublin could not be made, since John Nolen, the American judge, cancelled his sailing on the outbreak of war.

Geddes and his elder son rediscussed their Indian plans, as the ruthless destruction of Belgian and French cities aroused the father

to righteous anger and Alasdair to youthful fighting fury.   Both
knew those cities and their people, but Alasdair was not free to
enlist in the British army.   The Cities Exhibition had been contracted for showings in the Madras Presidency since April, his
father was engaged as planning consultant and he was pledged to
accompany him as assistant.   No substitute possessing the requisite training and experience could be found, and so on 18 September Alasdair and P.G. sailed for India.   At about the same time
the exhibition, its maps, photographs, and documents carefully
packed in bulky cases, left Liverpool on board the freighter 'Clan
Grant'.

The debacle in Dublin just when success was at hand, was a bitter
disappointment to Geddes who already foresaw the consequences.
The lack of vision and courage of leaders on both sides of the
Irish Sea would prove a social and political boomerang: the never-
ending nemesis of Sinn Fein Rebellion;   continued religious strife
and increasing Home Rule tribulations from 1916 on.

Meanwhile Patrick Geddes, having served his apprenticeship as
planner from Dunfermline 1903 to London 1910 and worked afterwards
as master of civic arts in Ghent and Dublin, was himself following
the call of Sister Nivedita 'to the utmost East'.

Chapter 8

FIRST YEARS IN INDIA, 1914-19

REFLECTIVE VOYAGE

Early on 2 October 1914 the Peninsula & Orient Line's S.S. 'Nore'
was sailing out of the Gulf of Suez into the Red Sea. On deck
P.G. watched 'the fine sunrise of the cloudless type we hardly ever
see in the north' and the changing light effects on both sides of
the Gulf. It was his sixtieth birthday.

Alasdair was also on board, having decided to make this trip to
India even though he still felt the urge to get into action against
the Germans as soon as possible. But first he would heed the
philosophic and personal pleas in his father's letter of early
August: 'What is our duty? Your duty? To go to the front as a
volunteer? I have of course felt that thrill once and again since
1870-1 itself, but also saw better.'
> The war is not a crusade of new ideals but a Gadarene rout of
> dying ideas and ideals, the legions of Devils of the past enter-
> ing into the people and driving them to ruin. Here are the
> Devils of Machiavelli and the theorists and warriors of the Bal-
> ance of Power, the old religious hatreds reawakening, the old
> tyrannies and revolts. Here are the mechanical and the romantic
> ideas of the paleotects, the jingoisms of the imperialists and
> their bureaucracies, the protests of the Socialists, the great
> doings of the financiers and the anarchic discontent they es-
> pecially create. Their ideas have now to fight each other out
> ... while we have to work at and for better ideals and begin-
> nings - the savings of a better future.

The parent had argued further that just as a staff officer is more
valuable than a line one,
> so you and I have to keep back from the front and attend to more
> difficult and important duties far in the rear of the immediate
> war.... So if ever you have trusted me, do so once more! I
> need your help - and you will find that we are of more use, alike
> to the homeland and to the France we love, than if we went to the
> front.... For we have our place in the scouting and pioneering
> of the better order which has now to struggle for existence. (1)

Now, just over half way to the scene of their kind of battle and
reconstruction, P.G. was looking forward confidently to what the
future might hold and found in the sunrise both contrasts and
prophecies.   To the east were the Arabian mountains, but on the
western, Egyptian side he saw mainly 'barren and uninhabited isles,
rising to hill heights, but hardly hill shapes, mere models of de-
nudation by wind and rain'.

> Nowhere else is such a perfect contrast to be seen, so far as my
> geography goes, as between this unresisting process of collapse
> into the sea on the one side, and the sublime resistance of these
> Arabian mountains on the other; with their nobly individualised
> sierra- and peak-alternation, keen against the sky.   It was
> indeed interesting to recall this as the Sinaitic peninsula –
> with its great associations of the individuality, and Union, of
> God and Man.

Watching this eastern horizon, which ranged from the highest peaks
of Mount Sinai southward down through table-land and lower hills to
sea level at Cape Muhammad, Geddes saw it become from south to north
'a vast graphic sharp-drawn upon the sky – the course of life!'

> Emergent from the sea and first, but near its unconscious level,
> the child's course – then the boy's – the youth's; then serra-
> tions of increasing sharpness seemed to work out the years of
> education.   Then a narrow valley pause, and a long slope uphill
> again: where our son seemed to be climbing, at the outset of
> his professional life, and towards that first individuation of
> the latest twenties when the long apprenticeship ends & journey-
> manship with its touch of personal style is fully reached.   Then
> a long sierra which seemed to stand for the thirties – another
> valley, and a higher sierra for the forties, passing on into
> fifties....
>
> ... as one counted on in these broad spacings, came a little
> valley-notch, which seemed to mark my present stand at this
> birthday of Age – and beyond it for the sixties – three or four
> fresh rises and into the main peak of the range.   Then declining
> heights for a time, and a pleateau valley – from which again rose
> a succession of peaks – and for the seventies, it seemed plainly,
> first two, the most definite of all, mostly finely individua-
> lised, then a long slope more to the final peak, from which the
> gently descending table-land flowed and faded softly above the
> earth mists into the upper sky.

To Patrick Geddes at sixty this was 'A comforting vision of life,
and a fresh notation from that of the Olympus' – coming when and as
it did, on this particular birthday morning, not without its fore-
bodings, it seemed a response of personal hope in life as well as
Universal faith in its possibilities for normal man – a touch of
'geomancy' as it were.

The entire voyage was a transition and a preparation.   'At this
change from Europe to the East, and at this climacteric of life ...
one feels ... how it is time to be less dependent on knowledge and
preparation and work, needful though all these are, and more free,
more reliant upon the direct response of one's life and nature to
each occasion – difficulty – opportunity.'

Having devoted the first stage of his journey to tasks from the
past, P.G. could report to Anna on entering the Suez Canal:
> Bulk of correspondence done with - Branford's letter of demand
> for a paper for Sociological Society on 'War Problems' answered
> with 5,000 words or so, and best of all that weary book [The
> classic 'Cities in Evolution', published 1915] at last fully
> sent off. So one has time for a day or two to 'feel one's soul
> one's own again'.

He describes at length the new variations on the theme of Place-
Work-Folk which passed in review on both sides of the canal. (2)
The Arab coaling gangs at Suez impress him with their 'rapid intensity of toil' and 'their strange chanties and handclapping'. It is
'A great example and symbol of the forces and possibilities of
Labour - when again it feels the drama of affairs as these fellows
do that of swiftly coaling the hurrying ships; and when again it
feels free to sing.' He looks across the partly fertile plain and
has 'a vivid feeling' of 'what splendid work to extend these oases'.
But after a spate of visualising how local and foreign skills might
unite in such reclamation, he has to admit that the peoples of both
East and West are 'degenerates ... forgetful of their nobler times,
when once and again they revived the spirituality of the world'.
So P.G.'s new oases 'were but the mere quantitative expression we
have so much of in the Industrial world', and 'one's whole geotechnic Utopia crumbled down'.
> Then I remembered we were beside the Peninsula of Sinai, and be-
> tween this and the mountains of old Egypt; homes of idealism
> each in its way - but the spiritual and ethopolitic vision of
> the one far exceeding and transcending the geotechnic mastery of
> the other.
> The Renewal of the Desert thus needs again the religion of the
> Desert and the confraternities of the Desert; spiritual brother-
> hood in some form such as flourished of old.... With this idea
> one saw again Moses descending from the mountain-vision, and
> stirring his people from sordidness and slavishness to a new
> idealism, bracing them to a new simplicity. And so on through
> their history, constantly falling back, yet ever renewing toget-
> her ideal and ethopolity, ritual and labour, temple and song.
> Till at last sounded out anew the ancient voices of prophesy; -
> Prepare ye the way - Prepare ye the way of the Lord! Make
> straight in the desert the pathway of our God.
> And then the oases returned, extended, multiplied, grew and
> flourished, into beauty and sacred art, because of again en-
> nobled life.

Sailing farther into the Red Sea, Geddes finds the near tropical
temperatures conducive to 'leisure and passiveness - to reading at
most, not to writing certainly'. 'One can read of India now with
more detachment from Europe. Yet beyond this, and even our work
there - I begin already to see - beyond all this detachment - a re-
education, in India, for life in Europe again on our return.' P.G.
outlines the problem awaiting them of combating 'the latency of war,
and the growing and accumulating of its tendencies as well as of its
direct preparations' in periods of so-called peace.

The Militants with their prayer 'Our Wardom Come' have answered
it - while the incomparably more numerous so-called (and self-
believed) religious, with their daily prayer for peace and of
'Thy Kingdom Come' have failed to realise it. Why? Because
they failed to realise it - subjectively, and so can't get it
objectively; whereas the warmen have been thinking and working
out the details and these both great and small; great for King-
doms, for empires, for the world - and so the small; frontiers
and routes, provinces and districts, cities and towns, villages,
hamlets. And so with the strategic points for all, from bridge-
head or road turn to hilltop and region, seaport and seas....

To think ourselves into 'Peacedom' in like manner, with
Friedenspiel accordingly, for *Kriegspiel*; that is not Utopian,
but Eutopian - we have but to think with a will '(*furieusement*)
(*solidairement*) à penser'. But this is the University Militant
- the Tower really outlooking. Well, why not?

He continues to prepare for his meeting with India both by 'socio-
logising' and reading:
as with help of such as a good book on Deccan Agriculture I read
yesterday. In these old Indian villages there is more of Peacedom than under great cities of Wardom. So, despite all its
cumulative martyrdoms and individual evils ... the Indian village
stands out as a main human unit to be understood for *general*
purposes....

Furthermore, instead of over-idealising this and that village,
a region small or great, but admitting its undeniably recurrent
evils - its peacedom too much tainted from within, as well as
ever shattered from without - let us ask where and how has any
great vision of peace been formulated - and where applied.

The answer, says Geddes, 'is scattered everywhere in the history of
Civilisation'; and he has already found an important clue in
India's past.
One concrete idea begins to come up, like a distant isle on the
horizon, that of all times and places where the Kingdom has Come,
and Peacedom had its day, one of the greatest, most significant,
most truly classic - perhaps *biblical* in significance and value
(and even portent and suggestive guidance?) is that of Asoka. (3)
But it is too soon to begin writing of this; it is an idea to
examine; a civilisation to learn about and try to figure in
one's mind.

After noting the temperature as ninety degrees in the shade with
even more predicted for the next two days, 'till we get away from
Aden', the thirteen-page birthday letter closes:
... Peacedom is no continuing State or City, the great thing is
that we should see that it has at times existed - that here and
there for a season, its Kingdom has actually come.
                                        Enough this time
                                            P.G.

THE 'EMDEN'S' EXPLOIT ... IDEAS STILL VICTORIOUS

The 23 October was a notorious day for P.G. and Alasdair. They had
disembarked at Bombay on the west coast of India in mid-October,
continuing by train with Madras as their final destination after
many weeks of study-travel. Their first stop was at Poona as
guests of Lord and Lady Willington who were friends of Geddes's
friends the Pentlands. The Poona hosts were 'quite in love with
India, and Indians, and thus much more to Alasdair's and my mind
than all other people we have met, nice to us though all have been'.
Patrick tells Anna of visiting 'a series of Hindu temples' and having a busy day of preliminary talks with town councillors and officials, and that they would 'begin study of Poona tomorrow'. Then
a laconic understatement: 'Got back well pleased with ourselves, to
find news of 'Emden's' exploit. Are we downhearted? NO!'

Yet what had happened was complete catastrophe. The 'Clan Grant',
having headed for Madras directly without calling at any west-side
ports, was near the southern tip of India with the end of the voyage
practically in sight, when the German raider 'Emden' suddenly
appeared. No one expected enemy warships in the Indian Ocean, and
there was no help at hand from British or Australian navy. The
'Clan Grant' went to the bottom and with her the famous Cities
Exhibition.

A week later Geddes wrote to Lord and Lady Aberdeen in Dublin,
making this stoic comment:
> The best I can say is that having raged so much over Louvain and
> other cities, I have not lost sleep over the loss of even the
> best of plans & pictures of them! Still, it is hard - espec-
> ially when one is feeling what the sixties must bring with them -
> to lose years of work!
> Of course we are not sitting down under it: quite the con-
> trary, we are busy taking measures to reorganise as speedily as
> may be. Unfortunately, since penury (as well as pride in Brit-
> annia's ruling of the waves) prevented *war* insurance in addition
> to the ordinary policy, we get nothing towards renewal or recoup-
> ment; & I must I suppose take all upon my own shoulders, as
> before in establishing it, like previous ventures. (4)

On studying the records* available of P.G.'s first year in India,
one is astounded by the mere itinerary.   He and Alasdair travelled
between two and three thousand miles in the two months or so between
disembarking at Bombay and arrival at Madras in mid-December.
Their route went first north to Ahmadabad, Ajmer, Jaipur and Agra to
New Delhi, then across India to 'Lucknow & Cawnpur, Allahabad &
Benares' and to Calcutta on the north-eastern coast;   and finally
southward to Madras.

At Ahmadabad came a gratifying surprise in the form of a cable from
London, probably 4 November.   'Emergency Committee Lanchester
chairman endeavouring collect and forward within fortnight small
representative Exhibition replace loss.   Have you any instructions?' (5)

After cabling his 'heartiest thanks' and requesting survey material
from the Outlook Tower, Geddes wrote to John Ross and H.V. Lanchester on 5 November with these opening words: 'The wire you sent has
made us very pleased & proud.   When a man is in trouble, it is a
great consolation when his friends thus stand by him, and unasked!'

He then told them to 'take three weeks longer' for the collecting
because of his and Alasdair's 'round of study of Cities and Town
Planning conditions' which would not bring them to Madras before
Christmas.   They had already reported tentatively on Bombay, 'a
fearful tangle and slum in parts, though of magnificent situation &
fine features, & now being Haussmannised'** and on Poona, 'a good old
city in danger of having its features spoiled'.   '... we are getting
a better understanding of the origin & growth of cities, their diseases & decay than we ever reached at home.'

As for Ahmadabad, father and son were already engaged in trying to
save 'the fine ramparts of this old city' from demolition (for roads
not needed) by the 'Public Waste Dept', the local name for 'Public
Works Dept'!   Hence this prediction and call for specific help:
  So we shall have fights!   And I hope Lanchester will fortify me
  for the coming fray by loan of tracings or reprints to replace
  the fine originals I have lost, as of Lashkar, etc, with its
  conservative surgery instead of the futile vivesection (extrava-
  gant too beyond description) into which Govts. are in danger of
  being tempted here.

* A number of letters to Anna and to colleagues in Great Britain,
but only fragments of one report out of thirteen made on towns in
the Madras Presidency.   Significant quotations from five other reports survive in the little book, 'Patrick Geddes in India', London,
1947, 193 pp.   Fortunately, however, thanks to Dr Helen Meller's
researches in India in 1972, xerox copies of all thirteen of the
Madras Reports will ultimately be deposited in the National Library
along with several others from later years.   See Bibliography.

** Georges Haussmann, French Prefect (1853-70) responsible for cutting the wide boulevards of Paris through former residential quarters.

The rest of the letter had to do with how to raise money for the new Cities Exhibition.   P.G.'s own finances were in their usual state of old deficit and new expenditure.   The original Exhibition still owed him money and he had not yet received any planner's fees.   Yet he offered £200 from himself and £50 from Alasdair to head a subscription list, not as 'cash available for purchases, but a step towards solvency'.   Then from his 'separate honorarium ... with which the Exh. has nothing to do, if necessary I shall try to advance what cash I can, badly though that is needed to reduce overdraft etc. at home, & even keep pot boiling there as well'.

City after city was visited, including the pride of Sir Edwin Lutyens and of The Empire, New Delhi, which Geddes would refer to scathingly ever after.   In a letter to Frank Mears, for example, he fires this brief salvo: 'Delhi is wholly unspiritual - & with lowest standards yet reached by (in)-humanity for housing of humbler workers & of temporary ones - for which I am giving them the plainest speaking.' (6)

In early December they came to Benares, 'this wonderful old city of religion'.   They spent an afternoon in rambling through lanes which ran from temples and shrines down to the Ganges and the bathing 'ghats'

which are of all kinds and degrees from the simplest and rudest of old stairs to the palaces of state, and these again standing stately as of old, or overwhelmed and collapsed, shattered and half-buried, by the tremendous violence of the great stream in its floods!   Contrast of cosmic indifference and human religions can go no further!

Yet the religions too are right;   and in the main they hold back the cosmic stream, and make it the human one it is.   Yet how simply! - that nature is sacred, that sex is sacred, that creatures are sacred, life sacred, and that even out of destruction comes new life; - these seem to be the main teachings; while the burning of the dead and the sweeping of the ashes of the pyre into the river which we have just been watching, are fitting and frank expressions of the great fact of death.

It is a great relief, after the totally materialistic character of our civilization, and of most of that of Mohammedan and Hindu life also, in the cities we have come through, to find ourselves in a world where ideals, and meditations on them, are recognised as the main business of life;   and where architecture and art are frankly in the service of religion - and this religion one with both hygiene in its bases and poetry in its origins! (7)

Two days later, on the train to Calcutta, he wrote still more about the wonderful river-front of Benares.   It was

a medley of architecture and life, of colour and verdure, of palace and ruin, of temples and shrines, of life - death - the like of which is nowhere else to be seen!   Then in the midst of all this, great mud deposits and worse - vast spaces and gashes of river-destruction, where the hill-side and its buildings have collapsed into the stream....

> What a climax - Alasdair and I have been thinking - to our
> town-planning and city-revivance ideas it would be to repair
> this!   Who knows?   We talked it over with one of the most
> attractive and productive as well as responsive Indians we have
> met, himself active in the Central Hindu College, the New Uni-
> versity and so on - and he thinks it might take on well.   How-
> ever, that problem must be left to simmer.   Alasdair is staying
> on a couple of days longer;   for this is one of the great exper-
> iences and uplifts of his life. (8)

Geddes appreciated the action his colleagues were taking on behalf
of the Cities Exhibition but he could not just sit still and wait
for the results.   He confessed that he must do his best for this
cause 'by extorting work (not I hope to be all unpaid!) from
friends'.   Whereupon he asked Mears to help reconstruct a chart of
the development of Edinburgh and to make purchases of 'Plans, Maps,
Engravings etc, illustrative material generally!' in London and
Paris.   'Very, very urgent!   *All expenses and fees can & will be
met.*'   (These parenthetical and emphasised words indicate P.G.'s
awareness of his reputation among friends as a 'deficit-financier of
worthy causes', and illustrate how persuasively he pleaded for
them.)

In Calcutta he met municipal and university officials as well as
Lord Carmichael, the Governor, lectured on his educational theories
at the University, and made arrangements for the showing of his
future exhibition.   He was, however, mildly apprehensive about the
hospitality arranged, being in 'the delicate situation of staying
with the Chairman of the Improvement Trust - like a sanitary smoke-
inspector staying with the manufacturer he has to look after!'
From there he journeyed in December to Vizagapatam and Guntur, northern cities of the Madras Presidency and among the first on which
he published reports. (9)   In fact, some page proofs of his comments on these two cities still exist (thanks to Lewis Mumford who
salvaged and gave them to the writer) to show how P.G. mingled
practical concrete details with ideal aims, and made life temporarily a burden for typesetters and printers!   Plate 19 showing the
first paragraph of page 63 on Guntur, is an extreme but by no means
a solitary example.   Even a final proof could become a rough draft
when it fell into the hands of Geddes!

After reaching Madras around 20 December and greeting his employer
Lord Pentland, P.G. shortly turned up in the southern city of Bel-
lary.   His schedule was admittedly a tight one: 'Five cities to
report on (averaging 50,000) in less than a fortnight - a strenuous,
but immensely interesting and I hope useful job.'   'There is no
doubt we are at the making of a new science, a finer geography, a
more concrete and vital history - a more real interpretation of
human life, and this in all its aspects, from economic to psychological and ethical!'

> However, difficulties were waiting in these minor but unique towns:
> unique in past, present and possible.   But oh, woe's me! with
> how little wisdom the world is governed - and this, whether by

Guntur.

My visit to Guntur was too closely concentrated upon two pressing practical problems — one the improvement of a suburban extension scheme delayed, & the other the treatment of a Bazar neighbourhood congestion, — to admit of any general study or even view, of the City as a whole. Each of these problems, moreover, may here be illustrated & more fully from other cities. Still, on the principle of these lectures, that of repeated illustrations of main principles, a brief instance may here be made. But first a word of City Sanitation in general — there are

In a general way, and so far as my necessarily limited observation goes, I cannot but warmly concur in the sanitary recommendations embodied in the "Inspection Notes" of my friend and travelling companion Dr. Matthew, Deputy Sanitary Commissioner. The improvement of the water-supply is there rightly given the foremost place. His constructive recommendations given as to provisional improvements of the Black Tank supply, as to wells, etc, seem to me urgent and economical. Similarly as regards conservancy, latrines, dustbins and so on. There can be no doubt that these simple and inexpensive improvements would yield a rich return in the health and well-being of the town. It is the misfortune of cities that there has not as yet been organised, a system of Civic Book-keeping; which would show the profitableness of thus diminishing waste of matter as dirt, and the deterioration of life, and its social efficiency and productiveness which dirt involves; but the general principle of such social finance is surely becoming clear. This is gradually becoming plain to the more intelligent minority of every town; and I could even point to cities in which the majority have grasped this, and with little delay after their Councils

MADURA. *

But of these monuments I have already spoken (Chap.); and as my impressions of Madura have gradually disengaged themselves from an active inspection in detail, hence at the outset of this summary I may best conveniently follow the same order.

Our first visit was to Ponnagaram, a site of 13½ acres lately acquired for the benefit of people evicted by clearances, more particularly the fishermen of the Minkara block demolished last year. The ground has been taken from paddy cultivation and raised several feet and has thus been doubly expensive; while the lay-out has the frequent defect of an excessive road and lane system, with corresponding narrowing of plots, though they are still too large for poor purchasers, who are not coming forward. A more economical replanning of this whole area was of course suggested; and this has since been attended to, more on garden village lines, with the engineer, in the recent practical class at Madras.

In the foreground is a new school building, on standard plan; to this I see make no objection, as regards the building itself. But the play-ground is very limited; and there is no school garden at all. The explanation is given me that "this is an elementary school, and the Government does not insist upon a garden." But I would here respectfully refer the Government, and the municipal authorities, to the experience of France and Germany, of America and Russia alike; and though last in this matter to an increasing degree that of the British Isles also. In every case where the garden is sympathetically kept—i.e., with and for the children, and as far as possible by them—the educational result is found to compare favourably with that from any other improvement—material or æsthetic, hygienic or intellectual, economic or moral—which can be named as having taken place in education in our times: nor is this to be wondered at, since a school garden offers peculiarly all these six elements of life and education, vitally united into one.

I plead then for a practical test of this large claim here. The ground can still be allotted.

Looking over the space allotted to this new suburb, one is struck by the enormous prominence of new latrines defaced its foreground. These have been arranged at the back of the existing slum of cotton operatives in the immediate neighbourhood, but evidently without any reflection as to their foreground effect, in diminishing the attractiveness of the proposed new suburb to its purchasers of a more prosperous class. Here as elsewhere, people work at each point on a partial plan, without bringing these together, or comparing them with the town's plan.

Approaching this slum region we find the latrines are not yet in use; but beside them a dismal expanse of mudholes, with wandering and wallowing swine; a loathsomeness unsurpassed in my large experience of filthy and neglected quarters. I am told that a notice has been served on the proprietor, and this six months ago—but I venture to deprecate such delay; first in serving it, and now in enforcing it. Entering the village we find it bad enough, though hardly deserving so neglected an approach such surroundings. The huts are the most crowded and the smallest I have seen: worse even than in

Two examples of 'final page proofs' after being read by Patrick Geddes: from his respective reports for Guntur and Madura in the Madras Presidency, 1915

ourselves or by the Hindu! ... I am undergoing a steady increase
of disillusionment - if that be possible, did you say?   Yes, I
did not realise what a curse the best intentioned sanitation can
become, for instance, before I came here....

   I have a new fight before me, as with the Housing at Delhi.
Here it is to be with the Sanitary Authority of the Madras Government, with its death-dealing Haussmannising and its squalid
(Belfast 1858) industrial by-laws, which it thinks, enacts and
enforces as up-to-date planning; and, for the least infraction
of these mean, straight lines it scolds, abuses and delays this
poor municipality, and at length not only bullies, but threatens
it with extinction altogether!   From the callous, contemptuous
city bureaucrat at Delhi, I have now to tackle here the well-
intentioned fanatic of sanitation - perhaps an even tougher
proposition. (10)

Christmas Day was spent in Madras where Lord Pentland gave them
'Thoughtfully chosen Xmas presents - to each of us the right book
etc.'   Geddes found this part of India greatly to his liking

   People here more open-minded than at Delhi, of course: they know
   that they have not yet succeeded with their cities; whereas in
   the north the new toy naturally excites hopes! ... the head of
   the Local and Municipal Department, Mr Francis, is to meet me at
   Madura next week for two days clinical study before he returns to
   his desk, and the head of the municipality here is to travel with
   me for ten days out of the fortnight....   Fancy the head of the
   Home Office coming on tour a couple of days! that of the County
   Council ten! - and you'll see how these people are getting
   stirred up.   And what is more encouraging, it is partly by the
   situation, and not merely by Lord Pentland - nor by me; though
   I hope to advance the process somewhat!

      Very busy however, our real work fully on; and our great
   holiday quite over until the [return] voyage.

                         Love to each and all from Your affectionate
                            P.

The first shipment of exhibits from Great Britain arrived very
appropriately at this season, and P.G. afterwards declared that 'No
youngster ever put his hand into a Christmas stocking with such excitement as I did into those cases from home'.   The opening of the
new Cities Exhibition was set for mid-January, with Alasdair again
in charge of mounting it while the father continued his lone reporting on the southern provincial towns of Conjeeveram, Coimbatore,
Madura and Tanjore.   Again the letters home were filled with eloquent descriptions and appreciation of Indian temples which he, a
European, saw for the first time.

   What unexpected, what astounding magnificence of architecture!
   What a stupendous magnitude, intricacy, exuberance, variety of
   designs and of execution! ... two cathedrals would go inside its
   [Madura's] walls and far more ... its extraordinary cloisters
   surpassing in magnitude and in richness of effect, in wonder of
   lighting all else in the world....   Imagine within these cathedrals, each with its vast nave and choir, the essential temple
   itself in dim and deeply impressive shadow into which one can

only peer - and again, sometimes, a labyrinth one cannot enter of stately colonnades and statued chapels, leading up to the distant and indistinguishable shrine - the 'Sanctum Sanctorum' as Indians call it to us....

Imagine again outside all this, yet led into by these cloisters, the Hall of a Thousand Columns (really 960 or so may actually survive!), with its changing perspectives, its curiously varied similarity, its crowded intricacy....   Outside all these, the magnificent Tank - a great bathing reservoir with beautifully stepped walls and cloister walk again, painted with mythologic splendour - the old fading out in quietest yet living tones, the new coming on, in fanfaronade of vermilion, blue and gold!   Then garden-courts, old and neglected, and with minor temples falling into decay, but now and then the faint lamp and fading mangold flower of some last loyalty.

Yet from such courts, what wonderful views!   The plan, I should have said at the outset, is one of indefinite growth, yet with regularity, which solves the problem of such planning, and this for temples and cities alike, in a way and to a degree both undreamed by other styles of architecture - and with a simplicity and unity, yet a variability and freedom as well, which put to shame all else in the world!

To conclude the long letter on temples Geddes climbs the east 'Gopuram' or gate tower and looks out over Madura.*

Fifteen towers from S. to N., nine at least across! all rising around the central holy place - a low dome, ablaze with beaten gold!   And all this crescendo!   The last is stupendous beyond description, with monolithic gate-pillars each forty feet high; a design new and original, that of the great builder-King Tiramala....   And a man, since he built over his whole land, and for the gods as well as for his own gigantic palace-hall! This, like all his works ... stands unfinished - too vast and too costly to be realised, they say - but not at all! *Sursum corda* - lift up your heart.   Build in each age more greatly than ever; that is the ideal of this style - the spirit of hope, of impulsion, of growth, the temple of the Elan Vital, the spirit of Evolution, of whom these Hindu gods, whom fools call idols, are as yet in many ways (I do not say all ways) the most vital and vivid expressions yet reached by man.

Here, too, is the four-squared city of the Apocalypse - yet the city of man! city of the Ideal, yet also of man in his growth.

From the high outlook of the East Gopuram with its vast landscape ... I saw how to complete the unfinished cycle of Tiramala

---

* Geddes strongly reproves an established critic of Indian architecture, James Fergusson, for calling Madura a 'disappointing diminuendo'.   '... his criticism for which there is no other word than stupid - because Europomorphic - is copied into every text-book and guide-book and so has concealed the real wonder of Dravidian architecture from the world.'   P.G.'s censure is expanded in 'The Temple Cities ...', 'Modern Review', March 1919.

- perhaps even how to initiate a new one from the mean modern
chaos growing up around.   But that takes me back to work, and
the party and motor are already waiting to take me out for a
busy day.

Yours,
P.G. (11)

On 17 January 1915, in the Senate Hall of Madras University, the
opening took place of the Cities and Town Planning Exhibition.
After Lord Pentland's formal introduction, P.G. and Alasdair promptly put the assemblage through a graphic history of the rise, fall
and possible renewal of western cities, illustrated by some three
thousand maps, prints, and photographs spread out on a quarter-mile
of wall and screen.   But most important of all there were also
exhibits to show how 'diagnosis before treatment' and 'conservative
surgery' were even more applicable in the East.

Using ideas and examples that would soon appear in his Madras reports, Geddes preached his practical message of 'Regional Survey for
Regional Service', skilfully adapting it to Indian traditions and
values.   He likewise demonstrated that his philosophy of civic
renewal had universal validity and popular appeal.

> Town-planning is not mere place-planning, nor even work-plan-
> ning.   If it is to be successful it must be folk-planning.
> This means that its task is not to coerce people into new places
> against their associations, wishes, and interest - as we find
> bad schemes trying to do.   Instead its task is to find the
> right places for each sort of people, places where they will
> really flourish.   To give people in fact the same care that we
> give when transplanting flowers. (12)

To Western-trained architects and engineers such words might at
first smack of romantic dilettantism or - if they knew of Geddes's
first career, of 'Dryad-in-tree' sentimental botany.   But turning
a page or two in any of his Indian reports, they would discover a
penetrating analysis of methods and costs of renewal and development.   For example, P.G. assesses their favourite means of attempting to relieve congestion, as found at Tanjore:

> In this town, as usual, it is proposed to drive a new grid-iron
> of forty feet streets through a congested and insanitary area.
> Again as usual, this dreary and conventional plan is quite un-
> sparing to the old homes and to the neighbourhood life of the
> area.   It leaves fewer housing sites and these mostly narrower
> than before, and the large population thus expelled would, again
> as usual, be driven into creating worse congestion in other quar-
> ters, to the advantage only of the rack-renting interests.   This
> interest often consciously, but sometimes, I am willing to
> believe, quite unconsciously, is at the bottom of this preten-
> tious but spurious method of 'relieving congestion', which has
> been practised in European and in Indian cities alike.   Nor, so
> far as my knowledge goes, has the offer of suburban sites met
> this difficulty ever or anywhere.   Even if, as rarely happens,
> the new site offered is both suitable and acceptable to the
> people expelled, they are practically excluded by the present

cost of building in favour of the more prosperous classes.
Hence the result of these would-be improvements is to increase
the serious depression of the poor and make this ever more difficult to relieve.

By way of contrast P.G. demonstrates how his method of conservative
surgery would achieve the desired goals in ways more effective, more
friendly to the inhabitants, and far more cheaply.

First it shows that the new streets prove not to be really required since, by simply enlarging the existing lanes, ample communications already exist; secondly that, with the addition of
some vacant lots and the removal of a few of the most dilapidated and insanitary houses, these lanes can be greatly improved
and every house brought within reach of fresh air as well as of
material sanitation - a point on which the more pretentious
method constantly fails, as is evident on every plan. The estimated cost of the engineer's gridiron is, in this town, some
30,000 rupees, merely for the portion selected as a start;
whereas, by Conservative Surgery, the total expense for this
typical area (including necessary outlays on roads and drains) is
officially estimated at only 5000 rupees - one sixth of the preceding amount. The same method could, of course, be continued
over the whole town and the 30,000 rupees, originally voted as
the first instalment for gridiron clearance, would go a very long
way towards accomplishing a reasonable plan for the whole area.

These sketches of a part of Tanjore Fort illustrate the vast difference between Plate 20a, the official plan for driving three
broad streets through the area, and Plate 20b: P.G.'s careful
utilisation of all actual and possible open spaces without disturbing the bulk of good existing dwellings.

The contrast between these methods is so extreme, says Geddes, that
he constantly wonders how 'the customary system of slicing through
new sanitary lanes ... at once so costly and so inefficient, can
have become so general both in India and in Europe'.

Yet, when we realise that not only does this system cost from
six to tenfold that of the commonsense methods of Conservative
Surgery, but that it is less efficient in the locality and causes
an intensification of congestion elsewhere - in fact that the old
difficulties persist - surely the awakening of public interest
must be at hand.

He also realises that his conservative method has its difficulties.
It presupposes a careful 'diagnostic survey' like the one shown in
Plate 20c of Tanjore Fort which is the connecting link between
Plates 20a and b.

It requires long and patient study. The work cannot be done in
the office with ruler and parallels, for the plan must be sketched out on the spot, after wearying hours of perambulation -
commonly amid sights and odours which neither Brahmin nor Briton
has generally schooled himself to endure, despite the moral and
physical courage of which each is legitimately proud. This type
of work also requires maps of a higher degree of detail and

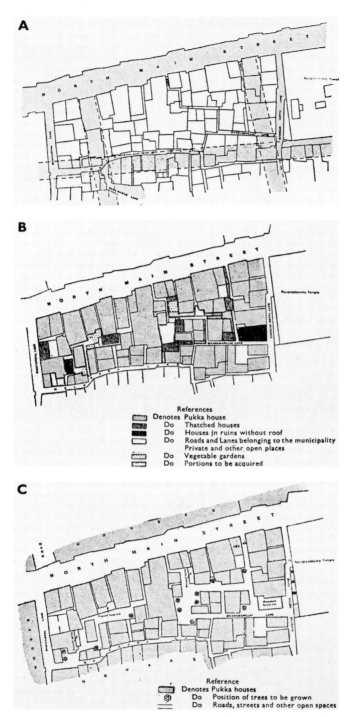

Three plans for a portion of Tanjore Fort (1915) from 'Patrick
Geddes in India', pp. 42-3
  a The Municipal Council's proposals for the relief of congestion
  b A 'diagnostic survey'
  c The congested area as it would appear after the application
     of 'conservative surgery'

accuracy than those hitherto required by law for municipal or
governmental use - indeed, in this town, it was found necessary
to establish a practical class for engineers and surveyors for
this purpose.

Even when a detailed and corrected map has been produced (instead of a rude tracing from the revenue atlas, necessarily
largely out of date) the task is still difficult.   Even after a
good deal of experience of the game, one constantly finds oneself
in check;   now and then so definitely and persistently as to feel
tempted, like the impatient chess-player, to sweep a fist through
the pieces which stand in the way.   This destructive impatience
is, indeed, an old vice of beginners in a position of authority;
and their chance of learning the real game is, of course, spoiled
by such an abuse of it.

After the Exhibition and P.G.'s formal lectures were over he worked
steadily on reports for other towns of the Madras Presidency until
time for return to Scotland.   A little item in a letter to Anna of
9 February takes one back to student and tutoring days in London,
for he meets his former biology pupil Annie Besant, now President of
the Theosophical Society and a persistent fighter for Indian independence.

Yesterday, Sunday, Mrs Besant and two of her friends took us a
motor-run to the old temple-city of Conjeveram - one of the seven
holy cities of India, and the most unspoiled and undegenerated I
have seen anywhere....   Nowhere have I seen so spacious and
well-built an old garden city - for this it almost is, and doubtless still more was: so this was an extraordinary object-lesson
in that conservatism which I represent here, and confirmed all I
had been preaching.

Another example of 'conservative surgery' is found in the report on
Madura where P.G. arrived to find that:

One of the poor quarters of this same town is at present threatened with 'relief of congestion', and we are shown a rough plan
in which the usual gridiron of new thoroughfares is hacked
through its old-world village life.   We are told that this
sweeping and costly plan is not the original one, but is regarded
as a moderate and even economical substitute for the first one of
total demolition, that was happily too expensive to obtain the
sanction or support of the Government.   It is not suggested that
the new thoroughfares to be made through this area are required
in any way for city communication;   the streets outside the area
are amply sufficient for this purpose.   This local scheme is
only one of 'sanitation'.

He then studied the quarter on foot, and the first doomed house he
came upon was 'substantial, decent, and even pleasing as one could
wish to see'.

Why then should it be demolished?   The explanation is 'straigh-
tening the new lane beside it'.   This new lane is not intended
to be appreciably broader than the present one and the only
merit claimed for the destruction is that it will bring the new
lane about sixteen degrees nearer to the draughtsman's straight

line than at present.   In short, the 'sanitary' improvements
begin by destroying an excellent home and squandering its value
(at least 3000 rupees) for the sole purpose of inclining the
present lane from a position slightly oblique to the edge of the
drawing board to one strictly parallel to it.

Geddes could find no common-sense reason for such planning but explained it with biting irony as an example of what evolutionists
call the 'principle of functional substitution'.

Were this a question of a new conservancy lane or a new latrine I
could understand it.   These are the sacred shrines of the sanitation engineers who originate these clearances.   But draughtsmen care no more for sanitation than do other members of the
public.   When copying the plans of a sanitarian their prime
interest is in its neat straight lines.   Thus a crude sanitation plan gives place to a still more elementary aesthetic, and
we here do obeisance to the straight lines of the drawing board
and the set square.

Whereupon he and his Indian assistants leave the first house intact,
only removing rubbish behind it.   With over 3,000 rupees thus saved
they can acquire two vacant sites overlooked in the old plan and
offer these to owners of two bad houses that must be condemned.

This is but the opening of the game, but it commends itself to
the commonsense of my companions.   We work on together in this
way hour after hour, and gradually a new plan evolves.   A plan
with as much new vacant space as was contained in the former
plan, but without any of the sweeping destruction, and conse-
quent displacement of people and overcrowding of other quarters,
that it threatened.

As a final illustration of the advantages of Geddesian conservation
versus wholesale clearance, look at two plans from a section of
Balrampur: first Plate 21a 'the existing labyrinth which is crowded
and dilapidated, dirty and depressed'.   Next, Plate 21b shows
P.G.'s plan which 'has resulted from an intensive study of the area,
house by house as well as lane by lane.   It will be seen that the
lanes have now become reasonably spacious and orderly, though not
formally so, and that open and easy communications exist in every
direction.'

In case one thinks this is the result of extensive, costly demolitions, says P.G., 'examination on the site will show that this is
not so'.

Here, as so often, the right starting points have been provided
by the existing open spaces, each with its well and temple.

These spaces have been slightly extended by clearing the sites
of all fallen buildings and planting trees to protect the enlarged spaces against future encroachment.   The open spaces can
then be linked by further small clearances, mainly at the expense
of ruined and dilapidated buildings.

As this study of the locality proceeds, one is encouraged by
the results, alike for sanitation and for beauty.   As these depressed and dilapidated old quarters re-open to one another it

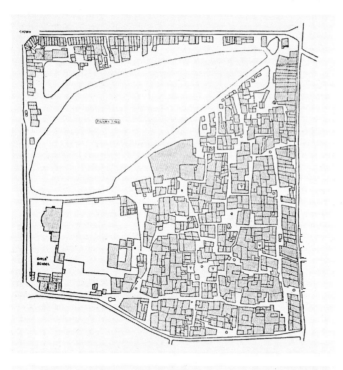

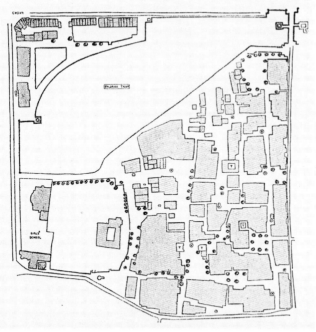

P.G.'s 'conservative surgery' or, in modern terminology, 'rehabilitation', as he proposed it for part of Balrampur, 1917
(above) The quarter south of the Palace and of Pajawa Tank from
the Municipal Plan
(below) The same quarter as improved

can be seen that the old village life, with its admirable combination of private simplicity and sacred magnificence, is only
awaiting renewal.

Geddes knew from daily encounters that most city engineers looked
upon the past as something to be rid of, and upon any attempt to
preserve 'old village life' as impractical romanticism.   Yet he
continued to fight for the best of past traditions and constructions
as essential factors in solving present urban problems.   The vaun-
ted 'industrial order' of the nineteenth century, he told them, had
merely succeeded in ruining the environment and deteriorating the
worker.   Even the practical plans of engineers and sanitarians resulted only in 'standardised semi-slums ... which are but the slums
of tomorrow'.   He steadily hammered the point that it was
   the recovery and renewal of old-world village life, which is the
   vital secret of the working quarter, both for east and for west
   alike.   Yet there must be no mere sentimental renewals of village customs now obsolete, or of artistic embellishments now out-
   worn.   Such only discourage the renewal of the village at its
   best....
   The problem is how to accomplish this return to the health of
   village life, with its beauty of surroundings and its contact
   with nature, upon a new spiral turning beyond the old one which,
   at the same time, frankly and fully incorporates the best advantages of town-life.

Before leaving Geddes's first season of planning in India, we cite
his observation on our contemporary problem of traffic which is all
the more significant in that motor cars were at a very early stage
of development in 1915.   He pleads for the wise Indian tradition of
narrow lanes which 'admit of shade and quietness without, and leave
an ampler space for the houses within', and predicts that even
though the engineer
   too often snorts or hoots at all such narrow lanes ... as people
   recover from this contemporary intoxication of motorists and see
   it as but a malady of youth communicated from the machine to its
   driver and master, others will learn to distinguish once more, as
   planners already do, between main routes of communication and
   homely village lanes.   At that time we shall be able to make
   each in its right place and not continue to spoil both by imposing upon each some of the limitations of the other, as is now
   almost universally the case. (13)

ALASDAIR ENLISTS ... 'THE WAR: ITS SOCIAL TASKS AND PROBLEMS'

It was Alasdair's intention, after the winter season of demonstrating his father's exhibits, to spend the summer in the Himalayas
studying mountain flora as had been planned since his graduation in
June 1914.   The Vans Dunlop scholarship he had won would have amply
met expenses of the expedition, and afterwards he could have prepared his doctor's thesis for the University of Edinburgh.   The war
obstructed these plans, however, and radically changed the course of
Alasdair's life.   Even though there was yet no conscription in

Britain, he conscientiously had no choice but to fight against the
Prussian militarism that threatened to overrun and destroy all
Europe.   While still working for the Cities Exhibition he found
time to utilise his horsemanship by training Australian remounts
for the British army, and at the close of the exhibition he gave up
the Himalayan project to leave India with his father in the spring
of 1915.

P.G. went immediately to Dundee and his teaching duties, arriving
after the term had begun.   Though he roamed the world or replanned
its far corners during nine and a half months, he still was UCD's
visiting Professor of Botany.   Alasdair, however, remained in
France long enough to discover that if the Allies were to win it
would require every combined resource of France and Britain.   'It
was his habit to do nothing in unreflecting haste', Victor Branford
related after the young man had visited him in London.

> With care and thoroughness he set about inquiries and investiga-
> tions as to how and where he could render most effective ser-
> vice.   And these preliminaries he carried out with that modesty
> of gesture, that simplicity of demeanour - saved only from
> naiveté by a certain graciousness - that good-humoured considera-
> tion of all points of view, which were amongst his most engaging
> qualities. (14)

Alasdair's first move was to qualify as driver of motor vehicles,
his next to go through the course of training at the Roehampton
School of Aeronautics and thereby receive a commission in the Royal
Naval Air Service.   He was then sent to the front, where his sup-
eriors, discovering in him remarkable powers of observation, shortly
transferred him to the Army Balloon Corps.   Thus began, at the age
of twenty-four, a military career for Alasdair which astonished and
puzzled those who did not comprehend the 'valley-section' education
he had received.   As observer in captive-balloons he soon won the
reputation of an 'ace', so successfully did he ferret out the location of enemy batteries.   On the ground he served as field instructor for other observers and as a link between the French and British
air services.   He adapted a number of French inventions and improvements to the equipment of his corps, and after only a few
months of service won his captaincy.   By the end of 1916 he was
Major Geddes, the youngest in that branch of the army, and in addition to being considered by his fellows as the best observer on the
western front, he received the Military Cross in official recognition of that fact.

It was Alasdair's grasp of geography and systematic explorations
between mountains and sea which served him so well.   He was educated for active peace, for geotechnics, but his training proved
equally effective in war.   P.G. had always scoffed at the uselessness of English public-school (that is, private-school) education
which prepared neither for genuine peace nor for genuine war.   It
was ridiculously inefficient as the Boer War so clearly showed, despite the 'boasted playing fields of Eton, where Waterloo was not
won'.   'My young geographers and geotects', said Geddes, 'were not
kept between a barrack called a "schoolhouse" and its desert exer-

cise-yard called a "playground"; but were prepared to go anywhere and do anything.' If, after Alasdair had received the ten different offers of civil employment in June 1914, sceptics still doubted the value of this kind of education they could now consider his army career, one which any professional soldier might envy.

Meantime the father, too, was fighting battles. At sixty he lacked neither physical vigour nor mental alertness for the campaign he carried on during the war years and afterwards. This was nothing less than to interpret the causes of the European holocaust, to sketch out a lasting reconstruction, and to re-educate citizens and governments. During the years 1913-23 Patrick Geddes was active on fronts extending from Ghent and Dublin to Madras, London and Paris to Bombay, Jerusalem and New York. He appeared as public lecturer, as professor of divers subjects, and as town-planner; yet always his purpose was to point the way of escape towards Eutopia.

The sum total of P.G.'s activities can be expressed in his lofty terms as 'to engage the militant energies of the race in adventures of constructive peace'. Taken separately, however, each activity was a hard-headed, yet idealistic effort to understand and solve problems which were baffling men in the aftermath of 1914 and which still are today. Take, for example, the Summer Meeting organised in London in July 1915 devoted to 'The War: its Social Tasks and Problems'.

Though a year had not passed since the outbreak of hostilities and though the outcome was still uncertain, Geddes, ably seconded by Dr Gilbert Slater, principal of Ruskin College, Oxford, stirred up great interest both in the study of war as a sociological phenomenon and in practical measures to lessen its evil results. King's College in the Strand provided lecture halls and library facilities, while a staff of over forty professors, statesmen, Members of Parliament, and relief workers contributed their teaching and lecturing services. For three weeks, every day except Sunday and from 10.30 a.m. to 10.30 p.m., these experts reviewed the geographic, historical, and economic factors leading up to August 1914, surveyed the situation in all countries and forecast the shape of post-war conditions.

Serbian, Polish, Russian, Belgian, and Dutch scholars contributed their first-hand analyses to the more general view of the war made by British lecturers. Emile Vandervelde, Belgian Minister of State, conducted a conference on the reconstruction in Belgium and northern France already under way or proposed, and Herbert Hoover led a discussion on current relief work. Other distinguished participants in this London meeting included town-planners H.V. Lanchester and Raymond Unwin, sociologist L.T. Hobhouse, geographer and MP H.J. Mackinder, publicist S.K. Ratcliffe, and geographer H.J. Fleure.

As in the Edinburgh gatherings before 1900 Patrick Geddes was himself the foundation and the continuity of the whole course. Each morning he started the day's programme with one of his all-inclusive lectures on 'The Sociology of War and Peace', and nearly every afternoon Dr Slater followed up with the 'Economic Aspects of the War'.   In the first week P.G. tackled geography as a determinant and deterrent of human conflict.   An article appearing in the 'Sociological Review' for January 1915, will serve to reveal much of what he discussed in July, for its title and that of at least one lecture are identical: 'Wardom and Peacedom'.   What he expressed on this subject is of exceptional interest and relevance, whether in connection with contemporary struggles against Prussianism or against later kinds of military dictatorship.

It will not be denied that we in our lifetime have practically known only wars and rumours and preparations of wars; that, when not in patent war, we have lived in latent war.

But do not let us go on with the absurd misnomer of giving to this period of latency, to this governmental and industrial task of tending the germination of dragon's teeth, the great name of Peace.   Absurd! ... Must we not condense our unmistakable wars, our thin-veiled, war-preparing pseudo-peace, under some one single common category - say, of 'Wardom'?   For war kinetic, that is, open strife, and our commonly so-called 'peace' - that is, war static and potential - are but rhythmic phases of what we should call Wardom.   Whether as imperialists or financiers - in whatever muddle or combinations, crossings or blendings matters little, and however we may talk of 'peace' matters perhaps even less - it is in Wardom that we live, move and have our being.

What have been the main and characteristic wars of history, particularly of recent history?   Can any order be observed in their recurrence; and if so, of what kind or kinds?   In what regions have wars especially prevailed and where have they been rarest? (15)

Geddes suggested the mapping of war centres upon world maps of different periods much as a seismologist maps volcanic centres and earthquake areas.   That branch of geology works confidently 'in each field of catastrophic and seemingly fortuitous activity until an orderly vulcanology and seismology are attained'.   Why, therefore, should not the science of war or 'strategology' be similarly worked out as a branch of sociology?

This physical map of warfare should be compared with one showing the distribution of occupational types throughout the world: i.e. areas preponderantly inhabited by hunters, shepherds, nomads, peasants, fishermen, and the like.   To him the basic law of Place conditioning Work and both together shaping Folk explained why some areas were especially belligerent.   It revealed the hunter as the archetype warrior and war-maker, the peasant as by nature and occupation a man of peace.   After this distribution of folk-types in space, P.G. proposed charting their vicissitudes in time and then juxtaposing the three maps to see what this might yield.   'Why, for instance, have the hunter and warrior Assyrian vanished, while their contemporaries, the peaceful Chinese peasants, still inhabit the earth in ever-increasing multitude?'

As for history proper, Geddes called for more charts, which would
mark 'no longer merely the successions of princes and their few most
decisive battles but, with a more vivid notation, the long waves of
surging eddies of international and national wars'.   That is,
charts which would generalise wars in terms of Comte's categories of
'people', 'chiefs', 'intellectuals', and 'emotionals', and further
according to the spiritual and temporal forces involved.   Possessed
of these graphics the 'socio-seismologists' or students of war
might, after checking all possible correlations, be able to deduce
theories of the cause and course of warfare in history.

Written history is inadequate, he claimed.   It is unable to reveal
some of the most vital facts of social development.   'History is no
more a book science than are the sciences of nature!'   Just as
botany stagnates when catalogues and texts usurp the place of living
plants and experience of them, so does history become sterile when
not based on active observation of social phenomena.   From the
changing plan of each city, from survivals of all kinds, one may reconstruct both its main branching and fruiting and its detail of
individual twigs and leaves.   The dead branches left by time are
there;   likewise the broken limbs and scars caused by war.   A city,
in sum, is a natural and social palimpsest where one may read, in
half-effaced, overlapping, yet unmistakable symbols, the true
records of history.

During the second week at King's College Geddes displayed the 'Arbor
Saeculorum' as an example of how temporal and spiritual history may
be condensed and contrasted in symbols, and how deductions can be
made from graphics that are impossible to make from ordinary history
books.   From this and other thinking machines he threw off 'ideas,
projects and theories, as some plants eject their spores', to re-
quote the phrase of J. Arthur Thomson. (16)

He interpreted the World War then raging as the logical outcome of
nineteenth-century Darwinism.   British and German minds alike were
dazzled by that 'impressive nature-myth' of tooth-and-claw competition which Darwin and his followers mainly saw in organic evolution.
In reality, P.G. asserted, the whole trend of natural science and
politics for half a century was based on half-truths and guided by
colossal errors of interpretation.   Darwin had read nature largely
in terms of industrial conflict, of economic survival of the fittest
and in turn, the industrialists and economists found in Darwin's
projection of their system upon nature the justification for continuing in their ways.   German scientists and Prussian imperialists
then went all out in adapting this British-industrial conception of
evolution to their *Kultur* and their goal of world-dominion.   And
since 1914, concluded Geddes, the Prussian statecraft of brute force
has openly been hurling this Darwinism of 'might is right' back at
the Allies.

Such, in brief summary, is P.G.'s wardom.   What now of peacedom?
We shall be told, of course, that no such state as peace proper -
free from war and war-makings alike - exists, ever has existed,
or ever will exist;   but a statement so grandly independent of

biology, of anthropology and history, of psychology and ethics,
is not for sociologists.

Peacedom offers in reality a truer view of life and evolution, both
organic and social, than does wardom, said P.G., though admitting
that this is a hard saying to those who, like himself, were brought
up from youth upon Darwin and Huxley.   Yet to counterbalance their
tooth-and-claw interpretation is Kropotkin's 'Mutual Aid', 'likewise
a classic rendering of nature's order, method and purpose', and the
scientific observations of zoologist J. Arthur Thomson and botanist
Patrick Geddes which led them to hold the ideal of evolution to be
'no gladiator's show, but an Eden' and to see 'no longer struggle,
but love as "creation's final law"'.   He who disbelieves in the
possibility of peacedom, challenged Geddes, has first of all to
overturn these optimistic post-Darwinian theories of nature and
society.

Realising that the path towards peacedom is infinitely difficult for
mankind to follow, he nevertheless sketched out, in the third and
last week of summer lectures, his conception of the Eden which some
day would cover the earth, and how it might be created.   He admitted that

> Active war is in many ways definitely superior to and more desir-
> able than the so-called 'peace' of wardom.   Warfare is neotech-
> nic in its efficiency, its training, its cooperation, its utili-
> zation of science and machinery;   whereas negative peace is
> muddling, inefficient, distinctly paleotechnic in nearly all its
> aspects.   Times of war bring forth greater qualities of heroism
> and sacrifice than does the 'peace' of money-counting and indus-
> trial expansion.   On the other hand, war is by nature destruc-
> tive of cities, of culture, of human life.   But is not the
> 'peace' of wardom almost as unmindful of life?   Does it not all
> too often stunt the body in its slums and warp the mind by its
> mis-education? (17)

Geddes's remedy is easy enough on paper.   Take the positive qualities, the neotechnic efficiency of warfare and put them to work for
peacedom.   In other words, as William James had expressed P.G.'s
original idea a decade earlier, find 'moral equivalents for war'.
Of the constructive substitutes for war, Geddes had an inexhaustible list: survey cities and their regions, then begin their long-
needed replanning and rebuilding;   clean up slum areas;   reforest
denuded lands;   renew village and urban life.   'But surely you do
not propose such things in the midst of war?'   To this he replied
that with artists, architects, and builders victims of unemployment
because of the war, it was the best possible moment to busy them
with public works.   Renewing Britain's cities and raising their
industries from the sweatshop level would be an economic endeavour
far more enduring than any attempt 'to collar Germany's trade'.

ANNA AND PATRICK IN INDIA ... PARIS 1916:   'THE CITY RECONSTRUCTED'

Alasdair's younger brother, Arthur, chose to enlist in reconstruction work rather than in the destruction at the front.   Following
the London Summer Meeting he joined the forces of the Society of
Friends who were achieving incredible success in the relief and re-
housing of refugees right in the midst of fighting and havoc in
France.   Sister Norah went on her honeymoon in July 1915, having
become the wife of Frank C. Mears, her father's architect colleague.
In September P.G. made his second trip to India, with Anna as his
colleague and companion instead of Alasdair.   Together they continued his rounds of lecturing, surveying, and fighting bureaucrats.
January 1916 found them in Dacca from where P.G. wrote a long letter
to Alasdair about his work.

> I have had a good time over Dacca, & I am proposing to Gov't and
> municipality to clean up & regenerate with a part of their absur-
> dly extravagant sewerage scheme - 40 lacs & more!...   Then too,
> after all my slating of the engineers, I have been asked to plan
> new Ry [Railway] towns for Kanchrapara, the E. Bengal Ry town.
> 6-700 workmen = 30,000-40,000, people, at least - ... (18)

He tells of their meeting the physicist and plant physiologist, Professor J.C. Bose, in Calcutta, and of plans for a Hindu University
of Benares which he hopes to be asked to work on.   He even sketches
out a general scheme for Alasdair to reflect upon.

> My idea of buildings is of long series of one-storey court-yards
> each a quad for its dept. with shade (& ventiliation through, by
> open verandahs communicating).   All simply built within their
> *temple* scheme, as at Srirangan...
>   What of Cosmo, drama etc. or as scheme for Univ. Depts?   And
> what form would it take?   Each leading out to the various depts
> - & there branching again into their minor infinities - minor
> quads accordingly.
>   To build in mud & bamboo in first place, yet with a main
> feature opposite entrance Verandah, in more dignified character,
> some day to be replaced by something statelier in appropriately
> carven wood or stone;   or in brick sometimes.
>   History of each Dept. to be expressed.
> Bibliography   "   "   "   "   "
> Personalities "   "   "   "   "
> Problems stated diagramatically & so on.
>   If any suggestions occur to you, send them: it is a good
> problem to play with, in the intervals of your war-work!
>   Again how can the living of students be improved (& with caste
> etc in view).

Some of those promoting the Benares plan, he informs Alasdair, want
him to give an address on 'University Ideals' at the laying of a
foundation stone, which is to take place even though the project has
not been worked out.   Others oppose his participation, fearing that
Geddes 'is an idealist'.   He, however, is counting on a new friend
to turn the tide and remarks: 'It would be interesting if our hopes
of Benares were thus to take form'.

The Cities Exhibition had been shown in Calcutta as soon as Anna and
Patrick arrived there in the autumn of 1915.   From there it went to
Nagpur at Christmas, but was not invited to Delhi - as P.G. had
clearly foreseen.   The Geddeses spent much time in Calcutta and
became good friends of Professor and Mrs J.C. Bose, whose guests
they were.   P.G. was fascinated by Bose's studies of plant sensitivity and his technique of taking moving pictures of their growth and
would in a few years publish the first biography of this Indian
'Pioneer of Science'. (19)

In January 1916 Geddes also wrote to his colleague and son-in-law,
Frank Mears, giving accounts of his planning jobs in and around
Dacca, similar to those sent to Alasdair.   As in most of his
letters from India, shocked mention is made of the 'wasteful' and
'absurd' plans which have been adopted by various cities.   'You
have to come here', he tells Mears, 'to realise the wild and wasteful ways of engineers, though I thought our railway plan at Edinburgh had opened my eyes.   I have learnt lots more!'

En route to Dundee in April for the term of 1916, Geddes took Anna
with him as far as Paris.   There he left her with selected materials brought along from the Cities Exhibition and some directions
for arranging these into a section of the 'Exposition de la Ville
Reconstituée' to be held there that summer.   While he returned to
botany, Anna struggled with exhibits on the spot and with distant
and uncertain lecturers by correspondence.   Chief among the latter
was her own husband to whom she explained that, in view of the extensive plans of the French exhibitors,

> it would be wasted & misplaced effort for us to commit ourselves
> to dragging in many other lecturers, or you & Prof. Fleure to
> give many.   You know, my dear, you *always* undertake too much:
> & also reckon too much on other people's interest & help.   You
> interest people always in the most wonderful way yourself;   and
> it is well worth your while talking to the best of these men;
> but lectures to which you expect an outside public to come are a
> different matter, & my strong advice is not to put too many into
> your programme....   No, come over as soon as you can, without
> being too tired, after the D'dee session ends, & exercise your
> own magic influence. (20)

The opening was scheduled for 11 June, and poor Anna, arranging exhibits, wrote on the 10th that she 'was supposed to cover the 180
sq. meters in the one day!'   The day after the opening she wrote
again, this time with a mild complaint.   'I don't see how I am to
prepare any programme with so little to go upon as you give me - No
fixed dates, save that you arrive sometime before 9 July....   No
word either from or of Mr Fleure.'

If P.G. did not give prompt notice of his Paris plans, it was mainly
because of other activities, of which a mid-June letter to Alasdair
bears witness.   Written from Dundee, it notes the City Architect's
Office, Dublin as his address 'for week or so, then c/o Marie Bonnet
[in Paris] about or after July 1'.   He tells that Lord Aberdeen has
been persuaded 'to let the adjudication of Dublin plans go on - & I

leave accordingly on Friday 16th without waiting for exams'.   He
and the Dublin City Architect are to 'report in draft to Nolen, who
will settle any differences of opinion we may express'.

> It is a difficult job, as I understand there are very good men
> in, some of whom you will doubtless know, when the names can be
> announced. (Eight in all.)   Then as soon as may be to Paris,
> for July, with Fleure.   That is a new friend who steadily im-
> proves on acquaintance - a wide and deep-thinking geographer &
> humanist.   You should see something of him when you get back to
> geography in constructive lines....   I hope your mother will be
> none the worse of all her work.   I fancy we have felt the sep-
> aration!   (I think it has turned me a little greyer!).

The same longing is expressed to Anna by an impatient Patrick who is
still in Dublin near the end of June.
> Dearest -
> Our last Sunday of separation, if all's well!
>   I have got along all right here....   The work has been in-
> teresting, & instructive too - suggestive as well; an excellent
> & needed step, as pupil of the competition, as well as judge!...
> But Lord, what fools these politicians be - those of each &
> every colour apparently equally blind to any & every form of con-
> crete life or labour, efficiency or happiness!   Citizen or
> scholar, Lord Mayor or Bishop - all without vision of anything
> we planners see.

The delayed lecturers finally showed up, and the Geddesian part of
the 'Exposition de la Cité Reconstituée' could be carried out according to the four-page programme which Anna had succeeded in getting
printed.   Afterwards P.G. used to refer to the main exhibition as
an example of French realism and courage, for they were studying
aims and means of rebuilding devastated cities not only in the
midst of the war but literally within earshot of German guns.   He
also once mentioned to Arthur that the Paris Ecole d'Urbanisme had
arisen after this exposition, while Anna, even during her preparations, could report that the organisers 'will make as much capital
out of us as possible & try to arrange next Ex'n on our model....'

In Paris Anna and Patrick renewed some contacts from 1900 and other
visits: among them M. Schrader of the International Peace Organisation, André Gide, the economist, and of course old friends like
Marie Bonnet.   But P.G.'s sojourn was relatively short, and after
meeting Alasdair on leave in Paris, he and Anna went to Scotland for
a family reunion.   But first they stopped over in Oxford where,
according to Mairet, he
> addressed a brilliant gathering at University College upon *Uni-
> versities and their Re-planning,* ... and explained in some detail
> his design for the new University of Benares.   This was the one
> occasion upon which Geddes made a real impression at Oxford: the
> chairman, Sir Michael Sadler (who was then Vice-Chancellor of
> Leeds) said at the end of Geddes's lecture, 'What we have heard
> today is pure gold; the concentrated wisdom of a life of toil,
> of travel, of thought and of high courage....   I hope that

England will recognise in him one who speaks with genius on university organisation'.   P.G.'s gratifying reception at Oxford was also a happy and heartening reunion with many old friends of his and Anna's before they went back to India. (21)

DARJEELING SUMMER MEETING ... DOUBLE TRAGEDY

After their active summer on intellectual reconstruction fronts in France and Great Britain, Patrick and Anna again made the long journey to the East.   His third season in India, however, was to consist of disappointments, illness and finally bereavement in its most tragic form.   Almost as soon as they reached Benares he discovered that a change had been made in the council of Benares University, with anti-'Geddesian idealism' forces in the majority, and all his dreams and concrete plans for making a temple of higher education in the Sacred City vanished.

But Geddes worked on at other projects, never giving up hope of convincing some of the officials some of the time that they should and could save their cities from blundering, costly errors in planning. In January 1917 he writes to Alasdair from Lahore:
Good hunting here: great work for all of us, each province like a European country, & with cities no less interesting & often far more beautiful.   Wonderful is Lahore - no wonder *Kim* is Kipling's best! with his impressions of youth!
How they have been spoiling it - oh, if I had only been here a few months sooner!   I continue to like the Indians I meet; & am often disappointed with my countrymen's wooden inability to get on with them!*

Another letter from Lahore to his son shows P.G. in energetic, optimistic form.
Don't you wake up with this or that idea the inner Daimon has worked out for you while you were sleeping?   To me he has always brought my best, & the ideas & resolves worked out in daylight - & now more & more.   For this work (of survey and planning) with its ever-widening opportunities, keeps one young & growing. Each new city is an experience as fresh as was the first going to College, & with far less of disappointments, for I get more & more of my way now....
I am often sorry to think that you had so much of the drudgery of the two Exns [Exhibitions], & missed my touring to Madura etc: as also that of last winter, & now this.   I have learned my job too ever so much better, & there is work for us all in this - and with good pay, honourably earned, as a trifling decimal of 1% on the waste & ruinous bungling one replaces.

* An inability which Sir Edwin Lutjens, for one, has explained in these self-revealing words: 'The natives do not improve much on acquaintance.... They are very different and even my ultra-wide sympathy with them cannot admit them on the same plane as myself' (quoted from A.D. King, 'Colonial Urban Development', London, 1976, p. 238).

> Today I have finished a big garden-suburb of 200 houses by
> simply filling up the agricultural & waste land of a big quarter
> with all sorts of interesting corners & compounds, temples & even
> mosques. (23)

Instead of the expected hundreds of demolitions, Geddes needs to
make only four with this latest application of conservative surgery.
Again he saves thousands of pounds and gains the advantages of the
'hatred of people saved us, & their good will assured'.   The letter
continues with typical diatribe:

> What a gorgeous old city is Lahore! - far finer in buildings than
> *anything* we saw together.... But it makes one sad & sorry to
> see what European and Anglicised Indians do to spoil it.   In
> some ways bombardment would be preferable - to the electric light
> installation for instance, which is the most extraordinary be-
> devilment of poles, wires, girders etc. etc. ... (Wait till you
> see the photos, if you think I exaggerate.)

On the optimistic front he reports that the Public Works Director,
'an old pupil and warm admirer & friend of Lanchester's, has become
a warm ally' and 'is keen for me to tidy up the whole Punjab towns,
& is going to Govt on that line!'   In fact, Geddes is considering
making his headquarters at Lahore instead of Lucknow.   However, in
February he not only writes from Lucknow but has to tell Alasdair
that 'the P.W.D. (against whom I become more and more seditious!)
has dished Exhibn at Lahore, & (of course) Sir Malcolm Hailey etc
wouldn't want it at Delhi, so it will sleep this winter.   Constructive work is of course far more interesting, so I'm quite consoled'.

The letters to Alasdair also tell of his mother's illness, a dysentery and fever.   In January P.G. urges him 'to send us short
letters often'.   '... now that mother has had this illness (though
convalescent & even described as well) she'll need to be protected
from anxiety: so do write as often as you possibly can find time
for.'   In mid-February: 'Mother is about all right again - though
she'll have to be careful.   I'm always quite well.'

The next letter from 1917 is one of mid-April to Branford but there
is no word of Anna's health.   What occupies Geddes at this time is
again his 'Daimon'.

> I am having in three months - Feb. March, April especially - a
> very distinct phase of intensified lucidity & vision: sometimes
> so distinct in mornings at awaking as to realise how the 'Daimon'
> or 'the Low's voice' appeared so distinctly an extra-self phn.
> [phenomenon] or prophet; (although as a visual, but not vision-
> ary, since not auditive, I remain completely without impulse &
> temptation to objectivation of hallucination, of course).

He interprets this as a result of his being at 'the grand climactive
(62)' and continues:

> I find this in various ways to be a life-climate
> with *intensified* will, even passioned
> with serener *contemplation* and passionless calm also.
> & with corresponding *intensification* of all essential life-
>   interests (active & speculative.)
> yet   "   *detachment* from them also.

with correspondingly increasing power then, both in action and in *thought,* in *civics* and in *education*, (so that my Reports & Plans improve...)

P.G. urges that Branford and he should come out into the open and not hide behind the Sociological Society, Town Planning Exhibitions, the Outlook Tower and so on.

It is no doubt a good instinct in the cloisterer to pull down their cowls; for thus they shut off interruptions to think: but in all preaching, teaching or leading, the cowl is thrown back, frankly & altogether! though not thrown away (no fear of you or me doing that!) (Pan has got his cowl back, and is preaching with a will, is he not!)

The day before this letter, Geddes started a long one to his friend Fleure in which he speaks of the development his Valley Section concept is undergoing in India, namely 'to that of the *Sacred River*'.

For the Ganges (its sister streams in some measure also) has been educating me, sometimes consciously, & also gradually & sub-consciously, to realise this, & something of what it has meant for civilisation - what it continues to mean - what it may mean also for the future. (24)

The Ganges reminds him of his own childhood river, the Tay, 'which will always be for me my main impulse of the life-stream and of the cosmos'. This leads in turn to his early experience of sunsets reflected in the river and his 'first - and still brightest - vision of - what I took to be - God'. Reminiscing about the fine views from the Kinnoull Hill cliffs, he sees that 'it must have been in the climbings & ramblings over this fine valley landscape ... that I got the feeling of the valley section which has been a main vision of geography in later years'. These views of town and countryside also aroused his interest

in the plans & detailed aspects of cities, & also in their generalised aspects & their ideal significance - & these as in direct continuity one with another, & not belonging, like the religion & politics around me, to different worlds, both always uninteresting, & even repellant, since as I later came to see - unreal.

P.G. comes back to the Ganges and its 'mighty convergents' which sweep down from 'Himalayas to delta & ocean ... & which make the journey from Calcutta to Dacca so impressive', and finds this too vast in comparison with European distances and valley sections.

Yet the extraordinary magnitude with its extensiveness is more of a world-vision, & so completes our otherwise too micro-cosmal & local ones.

You see too the importance of this greatness of scale in the spl. [special] metropolitance of Benares - which it is well worth coming to India to feel, as you can't do until you have spent long mornings & afternoons & evenings upon the river with its marvellous arch'l [architectural] medley, & its strange intensity & variety of religious & ritual life.

Geddes turns from geography to current planning blunders he has come
across and to their political consequences. He tells of a riot in
Cawnpore of 1914 'caused by discontent with a Town-planning improvement which took a (supposed insignificant and unconsecrated) corner
from a Mosque'. The crowd was fired upon
> and so trouble spread through India - with grave bitterness be-
> tween Moslem & Hindu, (for the former said their buildings had
> been injured to save touching a Temple near by, & so, sample con-
> sequence arising from this feud, this winter there are *no* Hindus
> in the Lucknow Town Council!

The letter next reports a current rumour that the 'amateur town
planner' who suggested the 'intended improvement which put the fat
in the fire' was identical with the official 'who read the Riot Act
... & gave the order to fire'. 'I have still to verify these alleged particulars ... but be they verified or no, the serious thing
is that people ... should believe them!'
> Returning now to the Draft Report, here is a grim light upon it -
> of confirmation of evil presages. I believe there is enough
> mischief in this proposed city scheme alone to light a discontent
> enough to lose the Indian Empire.

Anna, meanwhile, had recovered sufficiently from dysentery to be
removed from the Lucknow hospital to a place outside the city. In
fact, she even began organising the Summer Meeting to be held at
Darjeeling in the cool foothills of the Himalayas, and everything
seemed to be working out well for their first summer in India. The
increased activity of German submarines had made it impossible for
them to return to Scotland for P.G.'s teaching duties. But then,
only a week after the letters to Branford and Fleure quoted above,
came the fateful cable reporting the death of Major Alasdair Geddes.
Caught by enemy shellfire near their observation post, he and two
fellow officers took shelter in a small shell-hole. To give them
better protection Alasdair made a dash to another hole only to be
hit and killed instantly.

For over four harrowing weeks Patrick read to Anna the letters which
still kept coming from Alasdair, forced to playing an actor's role
to cover up the tragedy as long as possible. The doctors had
warned him that she would not survive the shock, if told. When
time for the Darjeeling course came nearer, he took Anna as far as
Calcutta to the house of an Indian doctor friend whom they knew from
the latter's study time in Edinburgh. But still the letters
arrived.

In the midst of this trial of nerves and emotions P.G. wrote to J.C.
Bose who had suggested some practical changes in the programme for
the sake of participants. Geddes agrees, but adds in parenthesis:
'Were this meeting really for them!!!' He continues with a remarkably frank statement of their own motives as scientists and
thinkers. If they were a 'concert company' dependent on the public, then they would have to 'fit its ways'.
> But *we* are at bottom - you & I & all the others who really matter
> - a little *conference* of musicians, considering our art on one

Geddes in India: (top) Madras
1915; (centre) in 1915/16 and in
1917/18 after the tragic deaths
of Alasdair and Anna
(left) Alasdair Geddes, older
son of Anna and Patrick

> hand, singing & playing to & for each other; & purposely indif-
> ferent to our public - to their quantity at any rate, their mass
> approval - as good painters & good men of science, & good monks
> & good religious - & good soldiers & practical men too - always
> are!... Our main *theses and problems to be solved*, & our own
> *inward speculative urge* is the main thing, & thereafter the app-
> lications to general thought, & to education & life accordingly.
>   Now this meeting is my laboratory! - my Outlook Tower, which
> I carry on my back like a snail, yet also climb on it, like a
> watchman, & a muezzin!

Geddes expects at least two promising students will be attending:
R. Mukerjee, for whose 'Foundations of Indian Economics' he wrote a
preface in 1916, and Principal Sherhadi of Benares University.   But
these are exceptions, just as 'Arthur Thomson, or Herbertson, or
Branford' were in years past.

> Again even your & my idle, half-interested, sight-seeing public
> expect you & me to be working, though they may rarely drop in, &
> then only half awake.   But you go on like the strenuous smith,
> experimenting at his forge, like the subtle weaver at his pat-
> tern, with its forms & colours changing as he dreams: - well, so
> do I!
>   You feel the coming of age, the uncertainty of health, the
> lack of successors, you feel too the numerous problems to be
> solved, & the daily urge of speculative search; the rarer ecs-
> tasy of solution, incomplete though this ever be, & only a
> stepping-stone to new ones!   Well, so do I ... & this in my
> way - & workshop of education. (25)

Yet daily reality called him back from this world of thought to
Anna's illness and the reading of letters from their dead son.
Alasdair still told about cheerful things that happened even in the
midst of his serious duties.   He had almost run out of ways to
keep his men occupied when poor visibility kept them from going
aloft in balloons.   Then a sudden 'craze', as he used to call ideas
as a boy, struck him.   He went foraging around the countryside till
he found a plough and two horses, and taught his men to plough
fields.   'There's an example of geotechnics for you!' commented the
father proudly.

Another time it was an exciting experience which ended well.   The
young major was on observation duty one morning with his own
brother-in-law, Captain Mears, curiously enough, when a German aero-
plane suddenly appeared.   It had shaken off Allied pursuit planes
and now proceeded to riddle their balloon with incendiary bullets.
Both observers bailed out, however, and parachuted from the height
of a mile to a safe landing behind the British lines.

About this same time the French government awarded the Cross of the
Legion of Honour to two British airmen: the ace who, as fighter,
had shot down most enemy planes and the observer, Major A. Geddes,
who had located for destruction the most enemy batteries.   But what
Anna could not be told was that this decoration arrived only in time
to be laid on her son's grave.   Mairet describes Geddes's tragic
quandary as husband and father:

When the time came for him to go on to Darjeeling, and her condition had not improved, P.G. was in an agonizing dilemma.   To
cancel the engagement would add to her distress, and perhaps discourage her by making her suspect that the doctors took a graver
view of her illness than they did.   Yet how could he leave her?
In the end he was persuaded to go, heavy with anxiety, after
arranging to return to Calcutta for the week-end. (26)

So well had Anna done her work as executive secretary, in spite of
illness, that lecturers such as the physicist J.C. Bose and the poet
Rabindranath Tagore were recruited, programmes printed, and so on,
in time for the scheduled opening on 21 May 1917.   P.G. carried on
an arduous existence of lecturing, leading botanical and geographical excursions, and illustrating the field techniques of regional
survey.   At the same time he wrote daily letters to Anna.   On
learning that she had developed enteric fever, apparently contracted
in the Lucknow hospital, he planned to visit her the first week-end
in June.   But the doctors discouraged the trip at this time for
fear the news of Alasdair's death might have to be told, since his
letters had ceased arriving.   A week later a wire summoned Geddes
to Calcutta in all haste.   The journey took twenty-two hours, and
in the meantime Anna succumbed to the fever despite all efforts to
prolong her life.

The Indians who were sent to meet Geddes at the morning train had
not the heart to tell him the truth; so he reached the door of the
doctor's house thinking he had only to run upstairs to see his wife.
The shock was frightful.   He spent the next hours in a daze beside
the bier covered with lotus flowers, and that evening Anna was
cremated.

Nevertheless, he wrote three letters to his children that day, for
Norah has copied parts of '3rd letter, Calcutta, 9 June 2 p.m.'   He
tells how a delayed letter from Alasdair had arrived only the week
before and how happy Anna was 'thinking of him and you all'.
We exchanged letters daily these weeks past - and as lovers ever.
But what a hardship to have been separated!   Yet each of us had
been accustomed to that division of labour too, & I was carrying
out what she largely had willed and essentially had organised -
and good work it has been.   Our summer meetings have always been
of use & happiness to many & she was keenly interested in this
even to yesterday when she cross-examined Joyh after his return.
She had no idea she was dying - only needing to sleep - that is a
comfort after so much pain that her last day was of peace.
    You will I am sure feel the fitness of the Indian burial &
cremation, since she gave up home & health, and life as it has
proved to help me here with Indian civics & education and this so
fully & definitely as ever of old at home in our young days.
And it is among the Indians far more than among our countrymen
that we have found our friends & fellow workers.
    I think I shall go back to Darjeeling for a time, though not
to lecture again.   Nature is the best anodyne & I can be as free
to stay alone with this new sorrow as I was with the first.   And
when I am fit for science or plan - as at times I shall be, just

as since the previous blow - I have the conditions too.   So do
not be anxious about me.   And now again to my vigil - of tears.

Writing to a friend some weeks later, Geddes related these details.
She was beautiful, like a bride among her flowers under her
veil, though alas when we raised it she was worn to a shadow!
I spent the day beside her - and then in evening the old Indian
students she had mothered, as they said, when in Edinburgh ...
came at short notice, all in Indian costume and barefoot and
carried her, six by six, on an open floral bier all the three
miles to the Crematorium, I following.... Then on the steps all
sang Rabindranath Tagore's 'Farewell' - a strangely penetrating
funeral hymn, and they sprinkled incense over her and flowers;
the doors opened and closed - and so now have but her ashes to
bring home. (27)

Such was the final scene, far from her homeland, of Anna's life of
unselfishness and devotion.   A life which for thirty years had been
the inspiration and mainstay of her beloved Patrick.

Letter-writing must have been both a burden and a relief to Geddes.
In May he appeals to 'Dear Son Frank, to whom I must now turn - with
all separateness of temperaments forgotten, & with real trust', to
write all his impressions of Alasdair's last years.   In June he
wrote again to the son-in-law about material for the memorial booklet on Alasdair 'which would be a pleasure to his friends & valued
by his family - and its unborn members not least in some ways'.
I have not yet recovered sufficient balance to make any [plans],
nor are circumstances at present pressing me into any definite
course.   This is a good place for convalescence from the alternate shocks & strains of the past seven weeks, and my brain is
clearing.   My health too as good as can be expected, though
vigour has ebbed appreciably, save at times of excitement, such
as these friendly & active-minded human surroundings also happily
give.

P.G. returned to Darjeeling and the Bose's summer home as a refuge
after the loss of Anna, and remained there until early August,
judging by letters to Arthur.   Since an exchange of answers between
India and Scotland took up to two months, this time-lag caused additional poignancy and strain, as when Norah wrote on 5 June:
Parents dear, Daddy's sad brave letter came at last, telling he
had heard the worst.   It was a renewal of the sorrow for me & a
relief as well.   To hear that Mother wasn't well enough to know,
filled me with some anxiety & the miserable feeling of a fresh
blow still to come.   So Daddy bore it all alone too.
How I long to hear that Mother got strong again & safely up
to Darjeeling & that she was not immersed in business worries.
They are no anodyne: only a cruel smothering of the soul.   Only
congenial work, or work that in some way is from within out, can
be an anodyne....   Otherwise leisure is better....
Poor Arthur is often lonely I think....   Just after Daddy's
letter of 30 April came one from him describing a waking vision
he had had of Mother.   It was a sad one rather, and after
Daddy's news, added vaguely to my anxiety.

Addressing Arthur on 4 August, the father first complained of receiving two weeks' mail on the same day.   '(Pray post when you
write, each week;   though of course the delay may not be yours.)'
Then came appreciation of the letters.

> Each has given me pleasure & though it is sad to have you still
> writing to the dear mother who cannot read them, I still think
> it best not to have cabled - & hope you agree?   (Say frankly if
> I was wrong.)
>
>   Yes, I am glad to have your reflections & recollections re
> Alasdair.   Write too as you feel about Mother, & from time to
> time, & as fully as you can.   Each helps me.

From that unhappy summer on, all of Geddes's letters to Arthur were
more filled than ever with well-meaning advice about his education
and future career.   The father expected Arthur to take over all of
the projects and collaboration that Alasdair would have engaged in
after the war, and Arthur wanted to do so at first.   Later pages
will have to tell something of what happened to his intentions and
P.G.'s increasing demands.   Suffice it to mention here that at the
top of another August letter with six full pages of fatherly suggestions, Arthur wrote the significant comment: 'This time, again,
Education - exclusively!'

ANODYNES OF 'NATURE AND HARD WORK' ... ENCOUNTER WITH GANDHI

What took place in the next year and a half Geddes himself has summarised in these lines to John Ross written from the Bose Research
Institute in Calcutta in January 1919.

> I found such anodyne as might be between Nature at Darjeeling &
> hard work in a year's planning at Indore - the best job I've yet
> done.   Then again at Darj'g in autumn, and now here as a natu-
> ralist again, lecturing on my life theories & trying towards
> pulling my long-dreamed opus together - a welcome interlude from
> planning - though not a paying one!

The results of his hard work were published in 1918 as a two-volume
town planning report on Indore.   In this milestone-study of civic
problems in India Geddes's insistence on 'diagnosis before treatment', on carefully examining a city's past and present before
trying to shape its future growth, frequently upset town councillors
anxious to get quick results.   His practice of 'conservative surgery' often revealed the past or proposed actions of some supposedly
practical engineer as incompetent and wasteful.   Whether it was a
question of imposing a needlessly wide Parisian boulevard or a
costly English system of public water-closets upon poor native
quarters, P.G. would ridicule the plan with an effective combination
of seriousness and sarcasm, and then make a better and cheaper one.
In place of western WCs, which would have cost more 'per seat' than
the dwellings of the Indians who were to use them, he proposed army-
style latrines which could be rotated over the parks or open spaces.
These, he demonstrated, would make possible great savings in initial
outlay and would contribute, as in China, to the fertility of the
land.

When it was a matter of reducing overcrowding, Geddes would take
engineers, sanitarians, and city fathers on a tour of the area involved.   Their intended wholesale destruction of houses, he pointed out, would mean simply the 'Removal of Congestion' from one
quarter to another.   Far better to weed out only the worst hovels
and repair the more substantial dwellings.

> Simply follow an existing lane a little way, and then pull down
> a few houses, enough to make a little square; plant a tree, and
> let the people make a little shrine if they like; women will
> sit and children will play there.   Then go on a little further
> and make another space.   Your way of 'driving streets through'
> means the destruction of four hundred houses or more; my way
> means destroying about fourteen.   Try it and see if it is not
> good. (28)

An interesting supplement to the Indore Report is found in correspondence with Norah and Arthur from October 1917 on to January 1919.
From the beginning Geddes was confident about his planning and its
results, and in one letter he previewed for Arthur one of his many
ideas for Indore:

> This is on junction of two small rivers, giving varied landscape
> effects through city.   At present these are made little of, but
> I hope to bring the whole 20 miles of banks nearly into public
> view & yet without double riverside ways.   Great squalor & much
> delapidation here as everywhere, but more willingness & readiness
> for big schemes than I have met elsewhere.   This will be best of
> my city schemes as yet, & the likeliest to be carried out.   The
> best also for training for reconstruction. (29)

The remark about reconstruction reflects his hope to find employment
in the rebuilding of French cities, mentioned in the same letter.
He did not plan to return to Scotland 'before I must, for Dundee
(- if I really go there - i.e. if not wanted for Town Planning on
continent)'.   Then the questions and exhortations: 'Are you learning French with any accuracy?   Reading?   Tell me of such studies &
thinkings as you have, even more fully than last time....   Tell
more too of Place, Work & People.   You never write of Town Study
since your first attempts, which were good.'

A few days later the father writes: 'life almost wholly divided
between work and sleep' and describes more of his Indore planning.

> Fancy making not only all manner of beauty-developments of this
> city's landscapes on one side, but a Cottonopolis - mills & rail-
> way sidings, workers quarters etc on the other - & besides fight-
> ing a scheme of drainage - charging 15 X £6666 - for making water
> run up hill, providing 48-seated latrines, & other follies with-
> out number, as the manner of such paleotechnic devilries is - &
> planning a new one, to cost a tithe of amount by turning all into
> gardens through & around city.

At the same time he is making a Masque for Diwali, 'the New Year
Festival of Hindu calendar - Nov. 20 or thereby'.

> Subject - the *Chasing Out of the Black Death*.   For Plague is
> master of the town - killing out hundreds - & chasing out

thousands - perhaps soon tens of thousands!   (You need not fear
for me.   We Europeans don't take it - booted & gaitered & well-
fed.   But the frontal attack methods, instead of flight methods,
may answer - we'll see!   If so, it will have been worth making,
& for more than Indore.)
    So you see there is War everywhere!   Reconstruction too.

Just after Christmas 1917 Geddes wrote to 'Dear Norah - Arthur too'
to say how glad he was that the souvenirs of Alasdair (among them
his war medals) had arrived after much delay.
    I am glad to have these things to keep with Mother's ring, &
    lock of hair, & photo.   It is good to look at the bright ribbon
    stainless (& the button dingy!).   I still feel their loss more
    than the old happiness - but the proportion begins to change, &
    I consequently shrink less from thinking of the past.   To you
    young ones I hope the change is easier.
        But I am full in the St Martin's summer of my working life &
    never worked so steadily or better;   & now at times with some-
    thing of the flame I felt in writing the best of the Dunfermline
    book.   You will like I hope my chapters & plans of gardens, &
    though I may well fear they will not all be executed, something
    may.

P.G. is not too happy with the draughtsmen at his disposition, presumably in the local planning office.   'Awful duffers', whom he
never goes near himself, but the fault is not basically theirs:
    The compound of 'English education' of *copy-exam- & jaw* on top of
    the decayed Brahmin ditto, *squares* the evil product.   What a
    fate for a race naturally as bright as any!
        The new doctor of the big School here kindly asked me to Xmas
    dinner.   He has unusual lights....   But there was a (Univ.)
    college Principal, an ass - complacently superior to all we could
    talk of, from Upanishads to Bergson or Bose: for had he not been
    at Dunderhand School & then Deadminds College, Oxbridge, & fin-
    ally at Dead Souls Theol. School & then sent out here!   How our
    poor Commonwealth or this vast Empire is to survive, or be
    cleaned of, these barnacles, & be navigable at all, is more than
    I can fance!   Yet they too are fundamentally good fellows,
    spoiled!

The letter returns 'to our own affairs', asking what Arthur is drawing, 'And don't you, Norah, sometimes sketch gardens?'
    And couldn't you make beauty for kailyards?   I have often
    dreamed of trying, but never did it.   Though in its way every
    handy garden is beautiful, this might be ordered & intensified.
    What finer than rhubarb & green & blue cabbage, than an apple-
    tree, than curly kale & carrots?
Geddes asks for news of Edinburgh people whom he has not heard about
for some time.
    I could not overtake the correspondence which came to me after
    our sorrows.   I thought of printing an acknowledgment card - but
    that is a poor affair!   I'll write some day, & do now & then to
    one here & there, as the mood & time come together - but that is
    rarely!

I don't like to lament, and sadden you; but once for all may
I say to relieve myself, how different is the home-coming now -
this home-coming that is no home-coming, but desolate.... And
there are only happy memories save when I think of my own omissions - commissions I daresay too.   But what a contrast from
our happy little bungalow at Nagpur, for instance, this is! (30)
                                     Your loving Daddy.

According to family information he had at least once a vision of
Anna which came to him so clearly as to make him fear hallucinations.   His remedy, as he also wrote to Norah, was to tackle the
job at Indore day and evening, never sparing himself.
    So, with hard work - motoring, with constant descents and plan-
    nings on foot - active talking, explaining, arguing, and winning
    decisions; and then at the planning table at every available
    moment, I am ready for sleep, which always comes.   Truly, work
    is the best anodyne!

The loss of Anna was far more than a personal one for Geddes.   Not
only could she arrange summer meetings but helped carry them through
with tactful skill, as in Paris at the 1916 Exhibition 'at which
Mother did so much, dear brave wise soul & clear brain!'   Furthermore, she kept him out of many a rash venture or, if he had already
got entangled, saved what could be saved.   But after 1917 the impulsive man of unlimited interests had no one to counsel and res-
train him.   Norah, especially, and even Arthur tried on occasion,
but only Anna could have succeeded.

Two instances of possible financial loss date from Geddes's time in
Indore, both of them typical of the impetuous appraisal of persons
and projects which would occur during his widower's years ahead.
First, the impulsive guarantee of passage from the Bahamas to England for a young painter.   Arthur was simply informed afterwards
that, on hearing that the painter had been 'rejected by military,
fool-regulations' on account of his small stature, P.G. had written
to him guaranteeing second class passage home, and employment in
the Friends' Reconstruction Corps
    (for which if necessary I shall repay them outlays, just as I
    have done for you), also his painting materials - if he will 'do
    his bit' by painting in & for the reconstruction....   I have
    told him to cable me if he accepts ... promising that you will
    make the necessary arrangements! (31)

The second hasty involvement, a half-year later, was in a project
to market a new kind of Indian wall-tile in Europe.   This time
Arthur was informed about one of P.G.'s assistants who
    has made a first class world-invention, of which I have built
    first house - for Boy Scouts - here, & am having a cottage built
    by Garden City connection near London, preparatory to general
    attack on Housing-cheapening everywhere.   Indian mud walls cased
    in tiles adjusted to stand & hold! & so nearly as cheap as former
    - a fraction of cost of brick walls, & looking as pukka (neat &
    finished) as stone.
        His patent will be given free from royalties to reconstruction

areas & cheap everywhere.   So you may tell your Reconstruction
friends.... This method will utilise also ashes, shale-heaps
etc. which become quarries for future, instead of permanent
horrors. (32)

Of the numerous brief encounters which Patrick Geddes had with great
men of thought or action, the one occurring at Indore in late March
and early April 1918 is perhaps the most tantalising in its lack of
documentation.   The person involved was Mahatma Gandhi, and the
surviving evidence at the National Library consists of two letters
from P.G. and one from Gandhi.   We examine P.G.'s second one
first. (33)

For eight typed pages of folio size Geddes analyses the Hindi Conference just held in Indore and, addressing Gandhi as its President
offers the 'frank and friendly criticism, which you of all men will
least deny is within the rights of membership'.   He asks why the
Indians have merely copied 'the customary and orderly ritual of
every British Congress' when there are other examples in the West:
the Eisteddfod of Wales (where P.G. heard Lloyd George *sing* as well
as speak);   the Highland Gatherings with 'splendid old Herculean
feats', dance and pipe-music;   the revival of Provençal life and
culture by Frédéric Mistral, 'their Robert Burns and Tagore in one',
who re-opened the Graeco-Roman theatre of their region and who, with
his Nobel Prize money, built the *Musée Provençal*, 'no mere glass-
case museum!'

The letter concludes with a plea to rival and even surpass 'all
these examples, and so make the needed step beyond your present enlarged edition of the English Public Meeting', and is signed 'Yours
faithfully, P. Geddes'.   But an arrow below the name points on to
a P.S. of two pages, which begins 'Now, since you think me a little
mad about Town Planning ... let me add a word on that'.

P.G. says that Gandhi's Pendal (an open-air platform with canopy) is
a good example of seeking 'the needed material *environment* for
effective action - the fulcrum for your lever, before you can move
the world'.   But he suggests that what is needed 'is no mere tran-
sient Pendal, and with its poor acoustics', but the open air theatre
and amphitheatre, 'the supreme material achievement of the Hellenic
culture'.

The intertwined initials P.G. closed the P.S., only to have another
arrow indicating an eighth page with 'Another P.S.'   This one took
up Gandhi's plea 'for the Union of the Hindi with the Urdu vocabulary' and reminded him of how modern English owes its best qualities
to the long mingling of Saxon and French.

In less than a week came Gandhi's reply:
Dear Prof Geddes.
I am truly thankful for your very kind letter.
    You could not be more pained than I am over our base imitation
of the West - I want a great deal from you but nothing undiscri-
minatingly.   I take part in the spectacles such as the one at

Indore in order that I may reach & touch the hearts of the people
& wean them from materialism as much as possible...

I tried last year to do away with the pendal for the congress
and suggested a meeting on the maidan early in the morning.
That is the Indian style & it is the best - I wonder if the
Amphi-theatre is an improvement.   My ideal is speaking to the
crowd from under a tree, never mind if the voice does not reach
the thousands, nay millions.   They come not to hear but to see.
And they see far more than we imagine....

But what is the use of my writing.   Both of us are preoccu-
pied.   The wretched fever of the West has taken possession of
us.   We have no leisure for things eternal.   The utmost that
can be said of us is that we do hanker after the eternal though
our activity may belie our profession.

I shall treasure your letter.   May I make public use of it?

And do please tell me how I may build cheap & durable houses
- from the foundation to the roof.

Yours sincerely
M K Gandhi (34)

Although it may never have reached Gandhi, P.G.'s first letter is
the more interesting. (35)   At the top is noted by hand: '(Written
after our Town-Planning talk & outing 30.3.18, but now sent with
Report)'.   Then follows, also by hand, a swift summary of Geddesian
thought and activities, documented by Part II of the Indore Report
and these four papers:

Universities in Europe & India - written to my old friend &
pupil, Nivedita, in 1903; & Universities, Historic & Possible,
1915, an Oxford lecture expanding the opening of the former
paper, & summarising my main study through life - that of universities - (from which I have come to cities).   With this I'll
try to send copy of my Evidence to the Calcutta Univ. Commission
1918.   So here will be four papers in all: a large demand for
reading on a busy man like you!   But though I chaff the barristers, I credit them with a rapid power of reading & assimilating
& criticising: so I hope I may be sure you'll run through all
four.

Geddes also hopes Gandhi will give him an opportunity to expound his
'unwritten fifth attempt' - the Regional Approach though this is
'but "one" among the needful ones'.   Another approach is that of
drama as in his Masques of Ancient & Modern Learning, 'performed in
Edinburgh & London University: (carrying the war into the enemy's
country, as you see)'.   Like himself, P.G. assumes that Gandhi is
fundamentally interested in the reflective, abstract, meditative
approach to education, though forced into action also by the surrounding bungle and failure.   We agree, do we not, that this
degradation of Learning into cram, (as of Art into Copy, and of
Religion and Social Science into what schoolboys call 'jaw') is
not of intentionally evil intention, despite all its evil result.
And so we are thrown back upon our meditation, and into our
studies, to discover, if we can, the pathology of this perpetual
withering of the spirit into the letter, of the life into the
form.   We are compelled to solve this, or fail in turn, if &
when our turn comes, as it is coming!

[Handwritten letter facsimile:]

Dear Mr Gandhi

    Herewith Part II of my Report — that entering
a question of "University of Central India" for Indore.

    But before this, I send you a couple of more
general papers — "Universities in Europe + in India — written
by my old friend + pupil - Nivedita - in 1903. + Universities, Actual
+ Possible ~ 1915. an Oxford Lecture only expanding the opening of
the former paper, + summarising my main study through life -
that of Universities - (from which I have come to this).

At some length P.G. runs through the many ways by which he has
attempted his solution: all the sciences, travel, arts and crafts,
books, and more.   He has had experience as 'Librarian & Biblio-
grapher', he served on the 'Britannica staff as a young man, thence
became sub-editor of Chambers'.   He made approaches through religion, mythology, ethics and 'in restless questioning of the philosophies'.   He has been 'hostel-builder & warden', he has been
active
> in college building, University planning & so on.   Again in art
> - as architect, as playwright, manager & actor; & so on - in
> short, through a life of incessant experimental quest, still in
> progress, (of which all this town planning is but a part &
> phase).

Geddes hopes Gandhi will not be alarmed or bored by this letter and
explains that his view 'is like that of the Ancient Mariner....   "I
know the man that must hear me - to him my tale I teach!"'   Whereupon he goes on narrating.
> ... *in a measure, I have got my solution* ... so far clearing up
> though not yet written....   [He will attempt to express it]   as
> a further reorganisation of the evolutionary sciences - in short,
> a re-reading of Life;   as the common factor of all the above....
> Here then I have got a move beyond Bergson, William James etc
> etc - as they beyond my old masters - Darwin & Huxley, Haeckel,
> Weissman & Co.

Like the Mariner, P.G. comes at long last to his point:
> Hence, just as I found in Bose the man of science with & for whom
> I can best work here in India, so it appears to me that *you* are
> the man of action to whom I can best turn on that side.   Am I
> right?   (Or wrong?   If so, to whom?   I fail to see him!)

And as this summer I have enlisted with Bose, for Calcutta Institute, & for repetition of Darjeeling Summer Meeting of last year, this time at Dunga Paja in October, *so I now offer to come to you, at any practical place or time* (consistent with my town-planning & other engagements, & not *too* hot, for in those conditions I am unfitted.)

But you are busy, you have your engagements & you naturally dread a fresh demand upon your precious & crowded time.   Still mine too is precious, & I have not made this offer to any other, save Bose, before.

In any issue, at any rate, believe me, Cordially yours,

Pat. Geddes

[handwritten reproduction of the first paragraph]

Whether this letter was ever sent, and if so, what Gandhi replied to it, are questions not yet answerable.   In any case, the fact remains that there regrettably was no meeting of minds or synergy of action between the compulsive Scot and the Indian folk leader.

At the end of July 1918 Geddes wrote to Arthur that he had finished nine full months of service at Indore, plus one of partly doing what he pleased.   'I have at length got the Maharaja interested: so I trust all may go on;   (though one never knows!).'   In early November he could also report having had a real holiday at Darjeeling with 'no duties of any kind', not even letter writing until now.

I've been riding ... botanising, dreaming, theorising, versify-
ing.(!) by turns, taking in the landscape....   It's a great
thing to have such a holiday - & for the first time, without dis-
loyalty to the past - to feel happy & young again.   It has been
a St. Martin's summer for my life - & I won't forget it: even if
I can't keep it up.

Books are coming together more clearly from their innumerable
fragments & speculations: so much so that I feel tempted to
write all winter!

The task of putting his manifold and steadily developing ideas into book form was something that P.G. was always verbally struggling with, but only rarely was writing actually begun.   This ration-alised procrastination became more and more a part of his daily routine, with periodic mentions of progress.   Thomson and Branford had to plead and nag to get any written results at all from him. His Darjeeling holiday was thus partly interrupted by a 'bit of solid drudgery', finishing up a 34 page booklet, 'Westminster: an interpretative survey', with Victor Branford in the 'Papers for the Present' series.   Another interruption occurred when, riding home one evening, my pony stumbled in the dark, & came down, sending me on in advance by overhead route!   A few slight cuts, scratches rather - but a bruised shoulder, for which Dr Circar has kept me 6 days in bed....   But I have still 14 days here - so I'll be fit as ever for the winter's work.   I am first to lecture for Bose Institute - on Biology - & then, I'm not sure where.

In early March 1919, however, he was still in Calcutta busy with plans for the Barra Bazaar while waiting for his passage to England. As usual he found that previous planners had bungled:
I am trying to save a waste of several £ millions (3 or 4: indeed even more) in this area of 90 acres!
 . I am scoring here by a new warehouse scheme.   (I who know 0 about them really, but see how past planners here have known *less*!)....   Town Planning is fundamentally *human consideration* ... whereas the Engineers etc are without this, & so bungle even a warehouse! (36)

P.G. really did return to authorship despite these planning jobs and the fall from his pony, for he tells Arthur in the same letter that he is 'Busy also writing Bose's life - as a study in Biography, Science, & Synthesis - of India too.   Learning to write my book at last!   Begin getting notes & ideas for yours!'.

A UNIVERSITY FOR CENTRAL INDIA ... DIWALI PAGEANT AT INDORE

While Geddes is working 'all the oracles I can to get a passage' on 15 March to Europe, one may look at two of his best, and inherently still valid, legacies to India.   These are a plan for a university with both interrelated sciences and humanities and genuine contacts with town and region, and a successful case of citizen participation in civic renewal.

The plan was first published in Volume II of his famous Indore Report, the one piece of writing which he was able to finish in record time.   Reprinted separately as 'The Proposed University for Central India', it commenced with his nutshell-history of learning as a dwindling heritage of good from past ages and an increasing burden of old and new academic evils.   For higher education, he said, is a subject 'which cannot be omitted from any Town-planning forecast;   least of all by the present writer'.

Even before 1918 there was considerable talk of founding a university at Indore, so P.G. did not have to sow his ideas in an entirely unprepared field.   The ideas themselves, however, were such as to throw contemporary educators into consternation.   For example, his basic contention was that
No true University has ever been 'founded', either by statesmen or by millionaires: they have all historically arisen from a preliminary growth and demand of culture in their cities;   and they can be at best but watered and guarded by external wealth and power.

Accordingly he did not ask the Maharajah or wealthy citizens to put
up funds for a brand-new university in Indore. The city already
had a normal school, a school of medicine and several scientific
institutes, but while encouraging each of these to expand, Geddes
warned against any premature organisation into the prevalent form of
western universities and against being 'cramped into the stereotyp-
ing mould of the examination-machine'. He suggested the creation
of more such independent units of the coming university: museums of
agriculture, of history and art; a central library with both fixed
and itinerant branches; a civic theatre, and, as instrument to co-
ordinate and inspire all these institutes and museums, an Outlook
Tower. The need for each and every one of the various university
departments is, he said, already felt by the people of Indore;
donors and founders are only waiting for the signal, and yet there
is lacking the right man to head the university as chancellor.

> In my life of University wanderings I have met many bearers of
> this high title.... Often retired veterans of other experience
> more or less adaptable; sometimes a kindly patriarch; sometimes
> a mere dignitary of conventional stuffing, at one time sitting on
> the safety-valve of youth and at another letting its energies run
> to waste in play, when not to stagnation in routine. Sometimes
> a great head-janitor, perfected in his low-level efficiency.
> Often too, in America especially, a super-mendicant, returning
> chequeladen to the college-treasurer from his rounds; yet too
> often also an anxious business man, perplexed to make both ends
> meet. (37)

Obviously Indore must find a different type of university principal,
one able to unite Indian traditions at their highest with western
science at its best, one who has the energy and ability 'which can
at once revive the oldest or most weary teachers, encourage and help
on the youngest, and inspire the students above all; and, beyond
and through all these, the citizens, until they feel the University
as their own, as part of themselves, and henceforward of civic
interest and pride'. But until such a combination of skilful
general and spiritual leader can be discovered, continued Geddes,
and until Indore has some conception of what the genuine University
Militant will be, far better to have no university at all than to
set up just one more institution fixed and bound by 'administrative
and examinational fetters'.

The University Militant! This phrase, launched in 1911 by an American writer, (38) was adopted by P.G. to designate his own conception of higher education at its best. It fitted admirably into his
special history of learning as the goal which lay beyond all the
established 'Germanic' and 'Napoleonic' universities of the world.
Though writing the Indore Report in 1917-18 in the midst of slaugh-
ter and destruction in Europe, Geddes gave a remarkably fair appraisal of German civilisation. In the first part of the nineteenth
century, when 'freedom of learning and freedom of teaching' really
existed, German professors and students made theirs the most necessary of all great languages because their work in science, philo-
logy, and all subjects of the Encyclopaedia, was the most systematic
and authoritative in the world. But on the other hand,

Of the deteriorative influences upon Berlin University from the
Prussian state and from the German Empire since 1871, I have had
vivid evidence since my first contact nearly forty years ago,
with the old spirit of German studies in—little Jena, and with
its contrast in the Imperial megalomania of great Berlin.   And
in subsequent visits and studies in Germany, I have seen and felt
the increasing spread of these Prussicating influences throughout
Universities and Cities formerly free from them....

I have dealt with the past of German learning and with its
world-services while sober, rather than since its intoxication.
But what is now most important for us to note, is that such
potent intoxicants are not a Prussian monopoly; but that they
are more or less in active distillation wherever the State over-
dominates education; and hence active in London and in Oxford
too not a little, let alone in India.   Education, like religion, can only be truly vital in the measure of its freedom from
external authority; since truth, like goodness, cannot be imposed from without, but can only grow with mind and soul
within. (39)

Coming back to Indian problems, P.G. warned that the greatest immediate need was the widespread improvement of agriculture.   Two of
the most significant advances in India of this century may well
prove to be the new plough perfected at Ewing College and the improved seed-strains of Pusa wheat.   Certainly India will get nowhere if all that her 'educators' can offer are examinations imported from Britain plus the starvation diet of textbooks which,
whether Indian or foreign, are too often 'the dry dung-cakes of the
cram-trade publishers'.

The new 'University for Central India' was to have a group of buildings which, erected at the junction of Indore City's two rivers,
would constitute the most unusual civic centre in the world.   Although he credited the Maharajah with suggesting such a group, only
P.G. could have crowded the whole of human history, science, and
literature into the projected library, museum, and theatre.   The
secret of this feat, on plan, was that the Outlook Tower, which
dominated the civic centre architecturally, also dominated intellectually.   It co-ordinated all the book-collections and museum-
exhibits, and served at the same time as an interpretative index to
the city and its region, just as the original Outlook Tower did in
Edinburgh.

Beyond all functions of being a focal point for regional survey and
service, of guiding and harmonising the industrial and cultural
forces of the city, Geddes commended the proposed tower to Indore's
citizens as an instrument of vital education.   Let no one disparage
or underestimate the eagerness and wonderment of a child who for the
first time views the world from a high outlook tower, who glimpses
its hitherto hidden beauty through the magic glass of the Camera
Obscura.   For the 'great originality' of any of the famous investigators - Darwin or Huxley, Haeckel or Pasteur, Stanley Hall, William
James, or Bergson - is essentially that of the eager child on the
tower.   'This, if anything, I experimentally know', said P.G.,

'having had it out directly, with each of these men and more, and
from Darwin himself to many another nature-loving child.'
     The Town-Plan, which should be painted upon the roof-platform of
     the main Tower beneath us, is thus but the condensed and pallid
     abstract of the living city below; the reality, in all its full-
     ness of details, all their synthesis into beauty, thus lies all
     around us.
          Around, in this concrete wealth of varied impressions unified
     as landscape, lies the world of Nature and of Human Life, to
     which Education, if not an Initiation, is worse than no education
     at all.   Life and Nature in the city, Nature and Life in the
     surrounding plain, in the horizon of hills, and in the changing
     sky, with its birds and clouds, and measureless blue, and the
     great sun which rolls over this, from sunrise-glories to sunset-
     gold and dark.

Reviewing the status of his main thoughts and deeds in India, Geddes
confessed in 1925 that 'only once have I really laid hold of the
imagination of a whole community - of the population of an entire
city and its surrounding villages'.   His methods and his results
on that occasion, in Indore at the beginning of his planning work
there, deserve an accounting in some detail. (40)

He had been shocked to find it one of the most plague- and malaria-
ridden cities in India, with a life-expectancy of only 18.6 years,
and tried to find some effective means of improving these conditions.   But as he tramped through crowded lanes and along the
dirty river-fronts, marking on a map the most serious menaces to
public health, the Indorians displayed signs of open hostility.
The sight of Europeans prowling about with maps always made the
Indians fearful of what demolition might soon strike their homes or
neighbourhood, but the presence of the bearded Scotsman with his
face marked by recent sorrows and overwork spread near-terror among
the townspeople.   Finally, P.G. asked his Indian assistant why
everyone pointed at him, and it was reluctantly explained that they
thought he was 'the old Sahib that brings the plague!'.

Geddes went that very afternoon to the Home-minister of the ruling
prince of Indore and, after explaining the problem, boldly requested
to be made Maharajah for a day!   Consent was speedily given, and
thus armed with princely authority and with the enthusiastic help of
Indore's mayor ('an able Brahmin doctor'), the Scottish Maharajah
launched a campaign that revealed him as an able general of reconstruction.   They spread news throughout theccity that a new kind of
pageant and festival would be given on next Diwali day, this being
an important holiday representing several great occasions: a day of
harvest; the New Year's day of one sacred calendar; a day commemorating the slaying of a fearsome giant by Rama, and
     most appropriate of all, for my purpose, Diwali is the signal for
     that strange and terrible domestic cataclysm, that annual insur-
     rection of the women from which all men can but flee, and which
     is as well known in West as East - here as 'spring-houseclean-
     ing.'

After widely announcing that the new festive procession would not
follow either the traditional Hindu or the Moslem route through the
city, but take instead the one along which the most houses had been
cleaned and repaired, P.G. and the mayor enlisted the aid of each
priest and 'mollah' by having the roads and pavements outside all
temples and mosques cleaned and mended, and trees planted around
them.   Free removal of rubbish was advertised far and wide and in
the six weeks of preparation for this special Diwali, over 6,000
loads were carted away from homes and courtyards, 'with much incon-
venience to the rats formerly housed therein'.   These plague-
spreading pests were trapped by the thousands in the city and along
the river banks.   Meanwhile a wave of housecleaning, painting, and
repairing swept through every quarter of Indore, for each one wanted
to win the honour of having the procession pass along its streets.
    Then on the great day came forth our Pageant, with streets
    athrong with villagers from far and near.   First the procession
    of the State - music, cavalry, camelry and elephantry, as well
    as infantry and artillery: and after these a chosen series of
    beautiful led horses, richly caparisoned, from the Maharaja's
    vast stables;   and one more marvellous still, in golden trap-
    pings of which none had seen the like.

Agriculture and the harvest were portrayed by chariots carrying the
Sun-god, the Rain, and so on.   Elephants laden with cotton-bags and
carrying merchants in silver howdahs on their backs signified the
importance of cotton to Indore.   The climax of this section of the
parade was Lakshmi, the goddess of prosperity, on the dazzling white
elephant of her legend.   Here P.G. had encountered some difficulty,
for the nearest white elephants belonged to the King of Siam, and
even his were only light pink.   But an idea inveitably struck
Geddes:

With a little persuasion we were able to give this mount two
coats of whitewash, from trunk to tail.   What snowy brilliance
in the sunshine - a paragon of a white elephant, such as neither
king nor goddess had ever ridden before!

After the gaiety of harvest, came a dismal change of scene and tone.
There appeared:
melancholy, wailing, and discordant instruments;   weird figures,
as tigers, as demons, as diseases - the latter breaking jointed,
bacilli-like twigs and casting them at the crowd.   Types too of
poverty and misery as well as wretched disease-sufferers;   and
among and after these came sinister swordsmen, barbarous raiders,
threatening with dagger or with lance: in short the ugly aspects
of war.   Next followed models of slum-dwellings, well-carcica-
tured with their crumbling walls and staggering roofs, broken
windows and general air of misery and dirt.   Then the Giant of
Rama's legend, but here presented as the giant of Dirt - a formidable figure some twelve feet high....   Then following him, the
Rat of Plague, also made by clever and skilfull craftsmen: a
good six feet long, this rodent, and quivering all over with the
rat-fleas which carry plague, fleas here similarly magnified by
use of locusts dipped in ink and mounted on quivering wires.
Nor did we forget huge model mosquitoes for malaria.
    Again a brief break after all these instructive horrors.
Then cheerful music, heading the long line of four hundred
sweepers of the town, two abreast all in spotless white raiment,
with new brooms, flower-garlanded.   Their carts were all fresh-
painted, red and blue, and their big beautiful white oxen were
not only well-groomed and bright-harnessed for the occasion but
had black polished hoofs, blue bead necklaces and golden flower
garlands, with their great horns gilded and vermillioned by
turns.   Every sweeper too was wearing a new turban, and of the
town's color - as were all the employees and higher officers of
Indore, as well as the mayor and myself;   this had been arranged
with his warm approval as symbol of the democracy of civic
service.

As the sweepers began their march, Geddes warmly greeted the leader,
a stately patriarch with a magnificent white beard, and took a mari-
gold for his button-hole from the old man's broom-garland.
    Thereupon a burst of cheers went down the line.
    Well done; a good idea! cried the mayor to me.
    Why?   What? said I.
    Said he, Custom would not let me do that, as a Brahmin, to an
Untouchable; but as a European you were free to.   You could not
have done better: you have treated them as men, as equals, and
thus encouraged them more than I can tell you!   (And so indeed
it afterwards proved.)

Behind the sweepers marched a civic procession worthy of the free
cities of Europe at their apogee: caste labourers, firemen, and
police; officials, mayor, and Maharajah Geddes; and after them,
enthroned on a stately car, a new goddess evoked for the occasion:
Indore City.   Her banner bore on one side the city's name in illu-

minated letters and on the other the city-plan in large outline, with heavy red lines showing the proposed changes to be made. Following this goddess were big models of the public library, museum, theatre, and other buildings P.G. had projected; and a whole group of floats contained models of the private homes that were to replace slum dwellings.   Next came floats representing all the crafts, on which masons, potters and others busily acted out their parts.   Then

> the future gardens: great drays laden with fruit-laden banana plants, papayas and more: and with flowers as well, and sacks of fruit, to toss to the children.   We even sacrificed the Maharaja's biggest and best orange-tree, which went swaying through the streets, and dropping its golden burden.   And to wind up all, a dray giving away innumerable tiny pots with seedlings of the Tulsi plant, (*Ocymum sanctum* of Linnaeus) the 'sacred basil' of European poets, which is the central symbol of the well-kept Hindu home.

> Thus we perambulated pretty well the whole city for the long afternoon; and then wound up at dark at the public park, where the Giant of Dirt and the Rat of Plague were burned in a great bonfire; and their disappearance announced by fire-works.

The results of this dramatised lesson in civics were quickly apparent.   A new spirit of house-pride and self-confidence spread among the Indians whom generations of disease had defeated and discouraged; even the sweepers performed their humble tasks with renewed zeal.   Practically all of the thousand plots laid out in garden suburbs were taken up in a short time.   But most important of all, the plague came to an end, partly through cleaning up the city and partly because its season was over.   Geddes was the leading figure in Indore, and people followed him in the streets, pointed at him, talked excitedly.   Now they called him 'the old Sahib that's charmed away the plague!'

As the first halfoof Patrick Geddes's career in India comes to a close with his return to Scotland in 1919, what better commentary on the vicissitudes of these years than his own definition of magic and romance:

> While a man can win power over nature, there is magic; while he can stoutly confront life and death, there is romance.

Chapter 9

THE MAKING OF THE FUTURE, 1919-24

PLANS AND SELF-REVIEW ... FAREWELL TO BOTANY AT DUNDEE

In the last week of April 1919 P.G. wrote to an old friend of his
and Anna's from the P. & O.'s 'Armande', bound via Gibraltar to
Plymouth, that he would arrive a fortnight late for his final term
at UCD.   It had been very difficult to get a passage 'among the
thousands of candidates for hundreds of berths', but he would soon
be back in Scotland after a continuous absence this time of two-and-
a-half years.   His plans?

> After May-June in Dundee, I'll come south for a few days ... and
> then I hope to cross to the Reconstruction Front somewhere - as
> my Indian experience & economics might be of use.   I'd like too
> to have a run through the Irish Towns & see whether the Sein
> Feiners have any constructiveness in them - & it's just possible
> I may have to lecture for a few days at Aberystwyth.   So far my
> programme, as far as I at present see it.
>
> Then back to India in autumn - partly by choice, for I have
> put in so much time & fight there that I'd like to assure it -- &
> am also offered a Chair of Sociology in Bombay (though that is
> still private).   Partly too by necessity.   No pot-boiling pos-
> sible in Edinburgh nor indeed anywhere at home, since my sort of
> writings bring in 0, or - [minus], as with 'Future' ['Making of
> the Future'] books like their predecessors, even the last ['Evo-
> lution of Cities'].   So don't think me running away from home
> duties: I really can't help myself.   I'm resolved to make some-
> thing of my Tower - but even for that I have to earn. (1)

Some months before leaving India he had written an extraordinary
letter to Victor Branford, in the form of a self-review covering
most of their joint careers. (2)   But unlike P.G.'s confident letter
of self-introduction to Gandhi, this one was a long Jeremiade of
what had gone wrong, yet also an honest attempt to analyse why.
For, he said, 'while we *have* ploughed and sown for ideas ... we have
alike had less time, and still less inclination, *for making these
successful*'.

> (Thus I *think*, but without publishing - e.g. 0 in botany these 30
> years!   So it is not to be complained of that my colleagues
> think me sterile).

But one does sometimes publish, yet with little effect, e.g.
'Evolution of Sex', (Thomson's and my best known book).   This
has been practically boycotted by the physiologists, zoologists
and botanists - why?   Simply because I dropped out of the San-
derson-Schafer connection in which I started;   and dropped out
too of my initial circle of Cambridge friends also, F.M. Balfour, etc. etc. ... so with my Evolution theory: when disapproved, as it could not but be, by the Darwin-Huxley-Wallace,
Haeckel group (to which I at one time seemed a *very* hopeful man)
I simply left the matter alone, and neither submitted to them,
nor fought them.

Geddes continues probing into other ideas and deeds with the same
mixture of stern criticism and extenuating pardon.   In his relations with the universities where he taught he was doomed to be mis-
understood.   'Holding the views I do, it was impossible to take
active part in Senates, Council, etc. etc.   But I have necessarily
seemed to them ... as a wilful and unpractical (even unpracticable)
outsider.'

In Halls at Edinburgh and Chelsea, etc. we were up before the
dawn....   The Summer Meetings did so far appeal to live people,
but these more from France.

The Tower too, has not been understood - even in Edinburgh,
hardly ever by its supporters.

Again my Dfne [Dunfermline] plan was not carried out.   Why?
Simply - and here I come to point - just as I was asked to do
this through friendship with Beveridge and acquaintance with
Ross, I fell out with Ross's view: and was friendly with White-
house, of whom Ross was jealous.

Or again, I lost Prince Rupert [Canadian Project]:   I did not
go to London to see the responsible man.

A great asset, however, was the important part played in his work by
women.   His relative success in Dublin he ascribed to 'friendship
with the Aberdeen's, while his coming to India was 'made positive by
Lady Aberdeen (and her daughter)'.   His friendship with Bose came
about through Sister Nivedita and Miss Macleod, beginning in Paris
in 1900.   'Such success as the Summer Meetings and the Tower had
was due to the women - (my wife, and others).'

Returning to the 'Evolution of Sex', P.G. repeats that it failed to
reach the scientists because he 'dropped out of their society ...
(deserted "the Pack", as it were)'.

But we also neglected the advanced people - from Shaw, etc. etc.
who might otherwise, if vividly talked to about it, have written
plays, novels, etc. not to speak of reviews, on these lines, instead of simply thinking it technical - (or reactionary, as many
advanced women did).

After generalising about the futility of politics without women actively involved, and about the 'anarchy of past and present social
formations' being due to the 'separation of the sexes, without their
normal cooperation', he again lists his own projects from the Edinburgh Social Union of 1885 on.   'Despite heavy losses, and present

millstones round my neck, these have all been more or less instruc-
tive as experiments, and some useful.... And in so far as successful, you know how much they owed to my wife.' Two concluding
thoughts in the letter are, among others:

> But the essential is that we learn from our mistakes, or rather
> limitations, and see how to apply what time and strength remains
> to us more effectively.
>   It is as with a shop: we have stocked it with goods: but
> where are the customers?

Just before sailing from Bombay Geddes wrote again to Branford, but
this time it was to plan the walltile project for which he 'at last
got my agreement fixed up ... with tile sample & drawings.... I am
still quite clearly convinced of its efficiency & I submit we should
proceed at once'. Whereupon P.G. proposes names for a group of
directors, lists a dozen cities where local companies should be set
up, since 'it does not pay to transport tiles, except by canal', and
reminds himself to 'write article, reproduce plans, etc.' (3)

Geddes promised to have a brief visit with Branford as soon as he
reached England, 'Don't attempt to meet me, but be free & at home,
relying on my coming straight to your house for the night (& following day too if possible).' But being late for Dundee duties, he
soon had to go north, and what happened to the tile plan is unclear.
On the other hand, there is a record of his farewell lecture:
delivered thirty-one years after his first public lecture at UCD.

In 1888 his subject was 'The Rise and Aims of Botany'; in 1919,
'Biology and its Social Bearings: How a Botanist Looks at the
World', and each title reflects the Geddes of two different centuries. In the 1880s he was still enough of a brilliantly theorising biologist to be considered by many as the successor of Darwin
and Huxley, whereas in 1919 he was frankly a city-planner and an
interpreter of the condition of mankind.

To P.G.'s farewell lecture came numbers of students and citizens,
but his colleagues the professors were conspicuously absent. They
apparently still looked on him as an irresponsible truant who, to
the injury of abandoning the specialised fold, added the insult of
periodic returns to exhort the faithful to self-improvement. Un-
mindful of the absentees, Geddes spoke in his rambling way about all
things, using botany as a springboard from which to plunge into
economics and sociology, politics and town-planning. He drew diagrams on the blackboard, recounted his experiences in India, talked
now to the audience and now to his beard; but everything was made
to emphasise the need for individual re-education, for regional and
national re-construction, for the re-conciliation of culture and
industry, for the re-union of ethics and politics.

He preached the old sermon on biology as the basis of the social
sciences and their applied arts, as well as the interpreter of life.
> This is a green world, with animals comparatively few and small,
> and all dependent upon the leaves. By leaves we live. Some
> people have strange ideas that they live by money. They think

energy is generated by the circulation of coins. Whereas the
world is mainly a vast leaf-colony, growing on and forming a
leafy soil, not a mere mineral mass: and we live not by the
jingling of our coins, but by the fullness of our harvests.

P.G. belaboured the medical schools for neglecting botany and insisted that not only had botanists first showed that germs 'are
vitally necessary to the soil and to all life, since they remove
decay', but also were well in advance of 'the modern departments of
Public Health'.
    How so? Doctors are far too easily satisfied when their
    patients are out of pain, and call them cured when they are able
    to get out of bed and move about again. But this freedom from
    pain and release from inactivity is not yet Health. Most people
    - indeed, most of whole nations - are more or less neurasthenic
    today.
        Modern medicine thus needs to be renewed and reorganized
    afresh from current biology, just as from our germ biology in the
    recent past. For we are coming to a conception of high stan-
    dards of life, to conceptions of health physical and mental, com-
    parable to that of the rose and the lily, the peacock and the
    song-bird, and thence to ideals expressed of old by the Greeks,
    and in their Gods and Muses.

Turning to an old theme of his, the need for city children to have
unlimited access to flowers and fruit without gardeners calling in
the police, he said:
    In France ... and other sensible places, too, they grow so many
    cherry trees that they neither fear thieves nor birds.... There
    is no limit to the possibilities of such gardening, even here.
    That would be real wealth, real economics, vital industry.
        Thus you see how gardening comes to town, 'making the field
    gain on the street, and not merely the street on the field', as
    Ruskin put it. True town-planning begins with thus simply
    amending the surrounding of the people; and it may soon get
    inside their homes, as I have found these many years in Edinburgh
    and in other cities too. It grows on from small gardens and
    semi-public ones like this, and thence to parks and boulevards,
    and so to better houses for all upon their course or beyond it.

Having brought in city planning, Geddes told the dramatic story of
his work in Dublin during the summer of 1914 and how 'with the war,
men's hearts failed them, and all these civic schemes were dropped
by all concerned.' At this point he thundered out:
    With a hundred thousand pounds well spent in carrying out the
    beginnings of all this - aye even half of it - there would have
    been no Sein Fein Revolution of 1916. I do not merely suggest
    this: I know it! And from both sides, from all concerned. (4)

Before reaching a conclusion Geddes covered many other favourite
subjects: 'tooth and claw' Darwinism which the Germans have 'fired
back at us these four years and more'; the growing lily as 'the
fullest splendour and frankness of sex in nature, naked and not
ashamed'; the history of universities; the need of Re-education by

means of nature study, regional survey, and through the Towers of
Outlook, Initiation and Inlook.   Finally, he drew a diagram on the
blackboard to emphasise once again that 'we must cease to think
merely in terms of separated departments and faculties, and must
correlate these in the living mind; in the social life as well.'
It showed how each interrelated science is associated with its related arts and crafts, from simple occupations to complex ones and
how 'Beyond the attractive yet dangerous apples of the separate
sciences, the Tree of Life thus comes into view.'

As P.G. finished on this theme of intellectual and spiritual synthesis, the lecture hall rang with cheers.   Truant or not, discursive or not, he was alive, and students responded to his stimulus
even if they could not always follow his swift mental pace.   As the
audience filed out an old lady said, 'He has been talking to the
next generation.   It is too much for us.'

Geddes left the hall in turn, his teaching days in Scotland ended.
At sixty-five he was Emeritus Professor of Botany, a widower and
twice a grandfather.   Friends urged him to devote his retirement
to collecting and giving literary expression to the myriad thoughts
of a lifetime.   But P.G. Unlimited had no intention of retiring,
and though his letters proclaimed that he was 'more ready to write'
or that 'thought is now clearing up', he still kept on delaying.
'When an idea is dead it is embalmed in a textbook' he would say,
or: 'When one crystallizes his thought into print he ceases to
think'.

A fragment of a letter to Rachel Annand Taylor, poetess and biographer of Leonardo da Vinci, reveals both his feelings and activities on finishing at Dundee.   (A former botany pupil, she had long
admired his gardens, even dedicating poems to them and him.)

University College,
Dundee.

It is ill being here without you: still more to have to realise
that that chapter of my life as botanist & professor is over &
that I can expect no new appreciator/collaborator of flowers &
gardens & their meaning....   Still I am in some measure comfor-
ted by the collaboration of young Berrington [an artist who had
helped with the Cities Exhibition] for a few days, preparing the
diagram-perspectives of Olympus, for my talk to the Hellenic Club
at Aberdeen.

   We squabble over details & work out more & more gorgeous fancies, as they at least seem at the time, & of which I hope some
may survive to show you – & perhaps, at best possible, inspire
you to that once & again half-promised expression in your own
medium. (5)

The next spell of work was in July 1919, a series of lectures in
London at Le Play House, an offshoot of the Sociological Society
devoted to such practical aspects of Geddesian philosophy as regional and civic surveys.   His subject was the 'Devolution and Federation of Cities'.   As for other activities, it was announced that
summer that Patrick Geddes had accepted appointment as Professor of
Civics and Sociology at the University of Bombay and also that he
had been commissioned by the Zionist Federation to design their
University of Jerusalem.   In addition, he was to prepare plans for
the creation of the brand-new coastal town of Tel Aviv and for the
improvement of historic Jerusalem itself.

'IDEAS AT WAR' ... 'THE COMING POLITY' ... 'OUR SOCIAL INHERITANCE'

Before following P.G. on the second part of his career in the East
we must briefly examine the trilogy dedicated to reconstruction and
winning the peace.   In 1917 came a manifesto launching a series of
pamphlets and books under the general title and slogan of 'The
Making of the Future', using these hopeful words:
   Since the Industrial Revolution, there has gone on an organized
   sacrifice of men to things, a large-scale subordination of life
   to machinery.
      Things have been in the saddle and ridden mankind.   The cult
   of force in statecraft has been brought to logical perfection in
   Prussian 'frightfulness'.   The cult of 'profiteering' in business has had a similar goal in the striving for monopoly by ruthless elimination of rivals.   Prussianism and profiteering are
   thus twin evils.   Historically they have risen together.   Is it
   not possible they are destined to fall together before the rising
   tide of a new vitalism?

Assisted by his colleague Victor Branford and the historian Gilbert
Slater, P.G. plunged into the contemporary war world, bringing forth
both analyses of its ills and solutions for its difficulties.   Between 1917 and 1925, more than a score of pamphlets and books

appeared in 'The Making of the Future' series or as 'Papers for the Present', all of them expositions of Geddesian ideas or methods. The three main books were 'The Coming Polity' (1917), 'Ideas at War' (1917) and 'Our Social Inheritance' (1919).   The first volume bore a dedication to Woodrow Wilson, 'The Student-Citizen who, in the Presidential Chair of a great and generous Nation, embodies the Platonic Ideal of the Philosopher-Statesman'.

There are many explanations of P.G.'s lack of influence on the would-be peacemakers and rebuilders of 1918 and thereafter.   Probably not one Member of Parliament in a hundred, nor one citizen in ten thousand ever even saw the three challenging volumes, let alone read them.   Of those who did, few grasped their significance, for however keen Geddes and Branford were as thinkers, their pens did not do justice to their thoughts.*   Branford was inordinately fond of capitalising all abstract nouns, and P.G. frequently lapsed into the parenthesis-burdened sentences which already had begun to mar his writings.   Yet underneath these surface barriers of style was a wealth of historical interpretations and of suggestions for action.

If either of them had only possessed the literary ability of J. Arthur Thomson and his skill in reaching a wide public, these books could have been as widely known as the latter's 'Outlines of Science'.   Even so, they saw and described clearly the extraordinary efforts made by entire peoples to save themselves from armed invaders;   and the effective team-work of financiers, industrialists, workers, and soldiers which culminated in the military defeat of Germany.   They proclaimed that the hour had come for the great transition 'from a machine and money economy towards one of life and personality and citizenship', from the old era of open war and latent war (called 'peace') to the new age of genuine, constructive, and militant peace.   Beyond the war and peace that mankind had known for centuries, Geddes and Branford pointed towards what they called the 'Third Alternative':   the building of 'Eu-topia'.   With complete faith in the good intentions of the Allied nations chastened by four years of war, they believed that they had only to point point out the real causes of world conflict and to sketch the kind of material and spiritual reconstruction that people surely must be ready for this time.

* The 'Times Literary Supplement' greeted the series on 26 July 1917 with two columns of one-third approval of their intentions but two-thirds sarcastic comment on their style, their generalisations, and their use of 'symbolic trees'.   'O for one hour of Swift or Newton!   O for one hour of almost anybody who has learnt to write a Latin prose!'   But the reviewer concludes that they have honestly tried 'to lay sound stones of the Perfect City of the Future'.   The 'Manchester Guardian', likewise, in its partly favourable review of 22 November 1919, claimed they wrote 'in an unfortunate dialect, somewhat after the manner of Carlyle'.

P.G.'s view of the aims of war and peace can be gathered in paraphrase under five main headings which also represent five principal
steps towards the 'Third Alternative':

1   To crush utterly the Prussian military machine and free the
    world, including the German people, from its menace for all
    time.
2   To liberate the Allied peoples not only from the threat of
    Berlin but from their own war-capitals as well; from the
    bureaucratic and financial octopuses of Paris and London,
    Rome, New York and Washington.
3   To rebuild both the war-torn areas of Belgium and France *and*
    the industry-devastated slums of Liverpool, Chicago, and a
    hundred other cities behind the lines. In short, to rehab-
    ilitate both vanquished and victorious nations in terms of
    Eu-topia with its regional independence and return of govern-
    mental powers to individual citizens.
4   To free schools and universities everywhere from their evil
    burden of lifelessness, of Germanic over-specialisms and re-
    pressive systems of 'cram & examine'. Upon the new 'Univer-
    sity Militant' would fall the chief responsibility for guid-
    ing world-reconstruction and for putting 'moral equivalents
    for war' into every-day practice.
5   To create a workable League of Nations: that is, one guided
    and implemented by a Federation of Cities and a 'Concert of
    Universities'.

Geddes first encountered Prussian militarism as a young student just
a few years after its conquest of France in 1870. Through subsequent visits to Germany he saw the dominant results of this *Kultur*
appearing in the form of pedants in the universities, philistines in
industry, and tyrants in government and army. In 1913, as we have
seen, P.G.'s concept of nurture of life as a main basis of city
planning clashed head-on with the militarists' emphasis on strategic
road systems and broad avenues in cities. Yet it was Geddes who
carried off the *Grand Prix* in Ghent.

The other encounter took place in Berlin itself. P.G. went to
visit some colleagues at the university whom he had not seen in a
long time. With intense pride the German professors showed him the
glories of their university: the new equipment in laboratories, the
libraries and lecture-halls; and finally a museum of German history. That evening they gave a big dinner in honour of the visiting Scot and afterwards called upon him for a speech. The guest
arose to thank the assembled professors for their kindness and to
praise what he had seen. Then, with characteristic and fearless
irony, Geddes concluded: 'But most of all I want to thank you because you have taken me into your Holy of Holies, and there in the
inner-most shrine of your University, you have shown me - the
Emperor's Jack-Boots'. At this a grey-haired professor jumped up
and shouted with the greatest indignation, 'Yes, we do worship
those Boots! We would die for those Boots!'

'War is the national industry of Prussia.' This often quoted
phrase of the French statesman Mirabeau inspired P.G. to give a

running sociological explanation of militarism.   First in the
'Sociological Review' of January 1915, then in lectures at the
London summer school on 'Problems of the War' in 1915, and most
fully in the 1917 volume, 'Ideas at War'.

Briefly, he interpreted the main cities of Europe as so many war-
capitals, so many octopuses of bureaucracy and finance, stretching
their tentacles into every province and district to suck corn and
meat, taxes and dividends, men and ideas, into the central administrative maw.   He declared that within Petrograd, Rome, Vienna,
Berlin, London and Paris,

> the legions of functionaries maintained by imperial taxation have
> gone on growing from year to year, and this at incredible rate,
> until in Paris the established term for the functionary is not
> simply 'mandarin' but 'budgetivore'....   Each imperial city at
> once exhausts and depresses the intellectual and spiritual life
> of the smaller centres.   It crushes them by the arrogance of its
> superior prestige; it kills their local literature and journa-
> lism; it attracts to itself and puts its own stamp on their
> rising men; it replaces them with its own products; and with
> its sneers at the *vie de province*, at the *Krähwinkel* and at the
> *parish pump*; it belittles in the minds of the provincials them-
> selves their own most vital interests.

'War is the supreme among centralizing processes', said Geddes,
pointing out that this applied even more to home provinces than to
foreign territories.   For 'when peace returns, "improved administration" steadily goes to work to consolidate the provincial conquest'.   But of all octupus-capitals, how could Berlin, 'upon its
poor sandy plain, its rye and potato field of Prussia', grow as
fast as Chicago?   How could it, like the rich American capital of
meat and railways, spread out interminably 'like a mould in its
jam-paradise'?

> Obviously by two methods and two methods only: by consuming its
> provinces on the one hand, and by conquering more provinces with
> them on the other.   Here, in fact, briefly and harshly stated,
> is the true inwardness of the history too long and generally
> called Prussian, but now better seen and termed 'Prussic'.   As
> the Iliad is summed now as the 'Epic of Troy', so that tremendous
> sage-cycle which includes the deeds of Frederick, the wars of
> obscurantism against the French Revolution, the wars of Bis-
> marck, and now that of Kaiser Wilhelm, will all increasingly be
> remembered as those of 'the Hunger of Berlin'.
>
> In the old decentralized Germany, of many region-states and of
> *free* as well as provincial cities, each a capital in itself and
> often significant in the European world as well as in the German-
> ic one, there was little word, much less foreboding, of this
> great and terrible Berlin.   But with the Rome-like evolution of
> modern capitals, Berlin has come to the very front and success-
> fully exploited anew for her own purposes the medieval Germanic
> myth of the 'Holy Roman Empire'....   Here, then, is the model
> and ideal Empire City, that most purely Assyroid of any since the
> days of Assyria herself.   What more natural, more inevitable,
> than that she should now stake her very existence, with that of

her conquered Germany, in an alternative and adventure which her
own phrase of 'World Dominion or Downfall' so precisely and
frankly states and boldly faces?   Never more fully in history
has appeared the mighty image of Empire, with its head of gold,
its frame of iron and its feet of clay.   And certainly never
more resolutely was its shattering resolved upon.

'Ideas at War' is the most complete published record of Geddes's
thinking about war and peace.   Consisting mainly of his 1915 lectures in London as edited and supplemented by Dr Gilbert Slater, it
was finally put in print by Victor Branford two years later in the
absence of both author and editor.   Despite its heterogeneous composition and its high content of generalisations, 'Ideas at War'
should some day win recognition for its interpretation of contemporary civilisation and its explanation of the real 'war guilt' on
both sides.   'The difference', said P.G., 'is that Prussia ... has
done thoroughly the evil that all others have done but half-heart-
edly.'

After proposing exhaustive studies of war-phenomena in space, time,
and society, and summarising human history in his Tree-of-Life diagram, Geddes, leaning on Comte, reinterprets the era preceding 1914
as consisting of three distinct, yet interwoven ages: the Mechanical;   the Imperial;   and the Financial.   (These are abbreviated in
letters and diagrams as MIF.)

The Mechanical Age came into being as machines supplemented or dis-
placed man-power and multiplied the social injustices already existing.   It did not invent slums and the sweatshop, it merely
standardised these evils and increased them a thousand-fold.   The
economic gospel of this age was that 'the highest duty of man is to
buy in the cheapest and sell in the dearest market'.   Aided by
'Liberalism' in thought and politics, the Mechancial Age achieved a
system of free public instruction in the three R's - falsely referred to as 'elementary education' - so that the quality and
quantity of clerks and bureaucrats might be improved.   Incidentally, the emphasis on arithmetic as a key to success diverted the
attention of workers from *real* wages to *money* wages;   hence their
demands were for 'more money', not for better housing or cleaner
air to breathe.

The Imperial Age continued the Mechanical by extending the latter's
methods and goals to all corners of the earth.   Hand-in-hand with
this imperialism, the Financial Age developed, for wherever pounds,
francs and dollars went, the flag soon followed, and vice-versa.
The mainsprings of the Financial Age were the legislation of limited
liability companies in England, the creation of monopolistic trusts
in the USA, and the perfection of profiteering-techniques in both
countries.

Today the most widely known Geddesian interpretation of social history is the one, made at least as early as 1898, which divides human
progress into the opposite yet mingled phases of *paleotechnics* and
neotechnics.   This concept first occurred to him in the heyday of

the Edinburgh Summer Meetings and of his lectures on 'Social Evolution'.   Reflecting upon the two phases of the stone age of man,
paleolithic and neolithic, he realised that the industrial age presented a similar division of old and new technical methods.   The
earlier *paleo*technic period was that based on coal and steam and
typified by waste of resources, smoke- and soot-covered cities,
blighted landscapes, and stunted human lives.

> A time of making money anyhow and having wars anyhow, with only
> utilitarian economists and liberal lawyers, or else imperial
> bureaucrats and bards, as our rival priesthoods: the whole
> system being crowned at its summit by the ruling financier.

The *neo*technic period, however, which was just beginning to subor-
dinate the older one, is marked by the use of electricity as motive
power, the combining of beauty with utility in technological products, and the planning of cities wherein men may really live.
Neotechnics thus leads to geotechnics, the remaking of the earth
into an environment favourable to human life.

But it was not until 1915 that 'Cities in Evolution', P.G.'s one
widely circulated book on town planning, brought this twenty-year-
old idea before a more general public.   Almost another twenty years
passed before Lewis Mumford, in his 'Technics and Civilization'
(1934), applied Geddes's idea to the last thousand years of industrial development, adding a third term, *eo*technic (the dawn age of
machinery), to complete the cycle of technology.   By 1940, the
triad of eo-, paleo-, and neo-technics became sufficiently established to be used in the New York 'Times' as a filler-article.

> It was neither for pittance of pay, nor routine of drill ... that
> the youth of Europe marched out from home, from school and col-
> lege, from workshop, counter and office, in Garibaldi's immortal
> phrase, 'to face hardships, privations, wounds and death'.   Why,
> then should we assume the cessation of the heroic appeal on the
> resumption of peace?   Surely youth returning from the fight will
> see to it that life will be tuned and led on its reconstructive
> march by a different music from that of the turning of wheels,
> the scratching of pens, the chinking of coins and rustling of
> papers of our passing chaos.

Thus did Patrick Geddes describe in 'The Coming Polity' what he believed would be the major force in bringing Europe out of the old
impasses of alternate war and peace and setting her on the path
towards the third alternative of local, regional, and international
co-operation.   Although this book was written jointly with Victor
Branford, the final section is unmistakably from Geddes's pen with
whole passages borrowed from his Indore Report.   The tone is
optimistic; nevertheless, he clearly saw disillusionment in all
countries with the achievements of the nineteenth century.   He felt
the symptoms of open rebellion in Berlin and Petrograd, in Paris and
London, and he sensed the disenchantment of men everywhere 'with the
imperial world, with its promise of peace and pride of power, its
victories and glories; and with the financial world, with its in-
calculable and crushing debts'.

Yet he feared that very little of constructive nature would come out
of this mass discontent. First, because so many people in all
countries could 'still see nothing beyond the industrial progress,
the military power, or the financial enterprise, which have thus led
down to pandemonium', and consequently expected and desired an
after-war destiny more violent and mercenary than that preceding
1914. Next, because those critics who did rebound from this chaos
were mainly wasting 'life and usefulness in mere criticism: here
radical, there socialist, and elsewhere anarchist in character'.
'Compound these three insurgent types of social critic', went on
P.G., 'salt them with millennial idealisms, add a mingling of traditional politics and conventional creeds, compound this concoction,
fling it into a seething cauldron of poverty, discontent, and disillusionment, and you have the disorders of Revolution, actual in
many countries, latent in all.'

The final chapters of 'The Coming Polity' partly repeat arguments
from 'Ideas at War' but emphasise problems and procedures of reconstruction. Sometimes in hopeful generalities, again in passages of
striking practicality leavened with idealism.

> We have to re-open the coal mines, renew the machinery, and mul-
> tiply the products like our predecessors of the industrial and
> liberal age; but now not merely for sale and personal profit,
> but for clothing the naked. More important still, we have again
> to till and plant the ground; but now not merely or mainly for
> market, but to feed the hungry. Again we have to build houses,
> but now no longer merely as properties, as comfort-villas or
> luxury-palaces - still less as speculations in rise of land
> values or on profits of jerry-building; but to house the home-
> less. We have to rebuild the schools; but not to pass exami-
> nations in, or provide returns for metropolitan clerks to pigeon-
> hole; but to teach the children. (6)

By teaching the children P.G. meant introducing them to 'their still
undestroyed and indestructible heritage of the spirit', and at the
same time training them to help in every home, village, and city
with the rebuilding of their shattered material heritage.

> We have to do all this, as on the battlefield, with its stren-
> uousness; and as behind the battlefield, using for the tasks of
> peace the very maps they use for war in the Staff-Office; but
> with even fuller Civic and Regional Survey of every material
> feature and element of the situation; yet with increasing incor-
> poration of the other elements as well, mental, moral, and
> social.

At the end of the First World War the politicians talked eloquently
about remaking Great Britain 'a land fit for heroes'. Yet, as H.G.
Wells pointed out, by 1920 both the British Ministry of Reconstruction 'and its foreign equivalents were exposed as a soothing sham.
The common man felt he had been cheated. There was to be no reconstruction, but only a restoration of the old order - in the harsher
form necessitated by the poverty of the new time'.

Geddes had warned against such a betrayal of Europe's hopes even

earlier.   In the 1919 edition of 'The Coming Polity' he had
written:

> We hear of Reconstruction Committees by the score, even by the
> hundred, and all of them strenuously at work on necessary prob-
> lems.   But of the one supremely needed committee there is so
> far no mention.   The missing committee is one that would vita-
> lize, energize, spiritualize all the others.   How?   By using
> the psychology of war to quicken the psychology of peace.   It
> would get to work upon plans for a 'great push' in making beauti-
> ful, healthy and efficient the ugly towns, wasteful cities and
> dreary villages which are the legacy of our paleotechnic peace.
> And this planning our missing committee would do in the spirit of
> an army preparing for battle and with like command of national
> resources.
>
> Here would come into play the civic verities guiding into
> action the military virtues and the rustic energies.   For in
> execution the vital committee, passing from synthesis to synergy,
> would become the General Staff Office serving analogous groups of
> regional initiative by the clearing of activities.   Why, for
> instance, in level of aim and achievement, should a Ministry of
> Peace fall behind the Ministry of War that organized so effec-
> tively the supply of ammunition as to justify its boast, 'no gun
> unemployed'.   The energy of twelve thousand tons of shot and
> shell directed daily to destroying an enemy camped on allied
> soil, if redirected to the making of the future, would leave no
> willing worker unemployed. (7)

When men of affairs and politicians tried to tell P.G. that they
didn't have enough money even to rebuild cities the way they were
before the war, let alone make utopias, he retorted:

> We do not reconstruct with money but with *life*.   A nation re-
> stores itself with the life and labour of the future, not with
> savings of the past.   We shall be impoverished, but when we no
> longer divide wealth between animal comforts and munitions, we
> shall find our resources ample for greater achievements than in
> our days of fat utilitarian prosperity we ever dared dream.

'Our Social Inheritance' is two-thirds Branford and one-third
Geddes, yet it is the latter's Part III, 'Re-Education, National and
International', which is the most challenging.   The tone, however,
is early set by Branford's phrasing of this bit of Geddesian social
history:

> The ancient Hebrews ... enriched our civilization with the ideal
> of righteousness yet also set examples of pharisaism of which the
> world seldom fails to take exemplary advantage....   The Romans
> showed how justice should be conceived and how it may be attain-
> ed; they also invented forms of social parasitism, hardly im-
> proved upon till our own times....   The Industrial Era has fur-
> nished undreamed wealth and boundless power, and at the same time
> abject poverty and the futilities of despair.

Typical of P.G. is this later passage on the League of Nations:

> Have our national statesmen, our representatives, our prime mini-
> sters done so well by us that we can hope great things from a

mere extension of principles underlying them into the sphere of
international control of states?   How can they accomplish as
super-statesmen what they have failed to accomplish at home?
[The League is a] temporal project perilous in its incomplete-
ness unless it be balanced and supplemented by a correlative but
wholly independent spiritual power ... a concert of universities
is a necessary counterpoise to the League of Nations.   Without
counsel and education from sources at once informed and untainted
the public interests embodied in the League will suffer all the
old political temptations and some new ones.   If left to face
unsupported every gust of national passion, what will happen to
the League?
     But warmth of impulse and loftiness of aim are also needed and
in fullest measure.   An alliance of the University with the
Church is therefore imperative;   for assuredly no full-orbed
society of nations is possible without that ancient mother, of
whom Alma Mater is herself the daughter.

Speaking of the equally difficult task of renewing human societies
and groupings that have been shattered, Geddes writes:
     Though family losses are so far irreparable, Life does not end
     with retrospect;   and the needs of the rising generation are
     thereby the more clamant upon us as survivors;   and the consola-
     tion best worth having comes with the call and the response of
     the children.   Towards this human and social renewal our mobil-
     ization has to be more thorough still: all of goodwill are
     ready, and even those too embittered or too apathetic have to be
     aroused to it anew.

He not only had his full share of the day-after-day loneliness and
sorrow that followed the war, but he sensed the emotional burdens
of whole populations, and called upon religious as well as scientific groups to help with the needed 'human and social renewal'.   He
expected that Industry and Art would now work together in 'true
neotechnic and eutechnic fashion', and that Public Health and Education would jointly be concerned with 'life in its full activity
of body and brain'.   That is, a 'psychorganic life':   'soul and
spirit directing, energizing and conserving body and thus reinvig-
orating them in turn.'

The book ends on an optimistic note as Geddes invokes past examples
of reconstruction and imagines the potential achievements of revi-
talized institutions like the University Militant.   In ancient
Greece there were
     nobler examples than our current civilization can yet offer.
     Recall, then, Athens after the Persians had done their worst,
     leaving on its shattered Acropolis no single sign of life among
     the ruins;   for even of Pallas Athena's sacred olive-tree there
     remained only the charred stump.   Yet from its base there sprang
     one small green shoot: pointing to this as sign of hope, one
     brave spirit inspired the rest;   and it was in this high rebound
     from despair that the Parthenon was built, and the nearest to the
     golden age in human records was begun.

For the future Geddes envisioned, as in the Indore Report, a new
higher education which would revitalize Allied universities and
'even penetrate Germany herself'.   It would coordinate her separated specialisms, out-think her State-philosophy and bring her
>   back to reason, and even to human loyalty, from her fanaticism
>   of an imaginary Teutonic race and its aggressive superiority -
>   thus returning to her good for present evil, and good for pre-
>   vious good.

JERUSALEM AND THE ZIONIST UNIVERSITY

In July 1919 P.G. lectured in London on the 'Devolution and Federation of Cities', a typical Geddesian dichotomy.   On one hand he
urged reversal of the usual process of city development from small
beginnings to the ever larger metropolis, while showing on the
other that a world federation of free cities was also a *sine qua non*
of a successful League of Nations.

Also in London, and of far more immediate significance, were the
negotiations between him and the Zionist Organisation concerning the
proposed Hebrew University in Jerusalem.   The outcome was full of
promise for both parties.   He was to work out a complete plan with
the architectural assistance of Frank Mears while the Zionists
sought the necessary international financial support.   Mairet's
biography provides these facts:
>   It was his friend Dr M.D. Eder, a distinguished Freudian physi-
>   cian and a social thinker, whose wife was one of the keenest of
>   the English Zionists, who was chiefly instrumental in persuading
>   the Zionists to employ Geddes as a planner.   On 21 August a con-
>   tract to engage Geddes in this work for a short preliminary term,
>   at a salary of £400 a month, was signed by Dr Chaim Weizmann, and
>   Geddes proceeded immediately to Haifa via Marseilles.   In Pales-
>   tine he would have something less than three months to survey the
>   situation and prepare his first report, before going on to India
>   in November. (8)

Dr Eder has given this eye-witness account of how their planner set
about his task:
>   The first weeks Geddes prowled round Jerusalem at all hours of
>   the day and night.   To my wife and myself, who accompanied him
>   whenever possible - and often, because he insisted, when it was
>   impossible! - he would say no word of the planning of the Uni-
>   versity or of the town.   As he went to this hillock or that,
>   examined a sukh, peered into a house, reverently touched a tree,
>   Geddes had no set plan in his mind but he followed some inner
>   vision.   Ideas, too formless yet to find expression, were brood-
>   ing in his mind.   It was the period of fecundation - not a note
>   was yet put upon paper, not a line drawn.   On any other subject
>   he conversed freely and gaily; when I say 'on any other sub-
>   ject', those who knew Geddes will rightly interpret as 'on *every*
>   other subject.' (9)

Within a short time, however, he had produced results that were

incredible to those who did not know how intensely he worked and how
he could draw upon, without seeming effort, the vast amount of experience he now had in both 'diagnosis' and 'treatment'.   A few
months after his arrival, reported Dr Eder,

> The main lines of the Jerusalem University had been made;   a plan
> for Jerusalem had been mapped out;   suggestions, carried out in
> plans,made for Tel Aviv, for settlements on Mt Carmel, accompan-
> ied by helpful suggestions for the educational side of the Uni-
> versity.

As early as 1913, while working on his Cities Exhibition in Ghent,
P.G. revealed his strong interest in Jerusalem in a letter to a
Jewish friend.

> The great example, the classic instance of city renewal is that
> of the rebuilding of Jerusalem, and my particular civic interests
> owe more to my boyish familiarity with the building of Solomon's
> temple and with the books of Ezra and Nehemiah, than to anything
> else in literature.   Jews probably know more or less how the
> Old Testament has dominated Scottish education and religion for
> centuries;   these were above all the stories which fascinated me
> as a youngster, and though I lapsed from the church of my fathers
> well-nigh forty years ago, I still feel these as the great
> example for the Town Planning Exhibition. (10)

So it was that, thanks to old Captain Geddes and his daily Bible
readings, the son found himself a half-century later spiritually
qualified to plan improvements for the city of David.   Written
results included his preliminary stencilled report to the military
governor in November 1919, entitled 'Jerusalem Actual and Possible'
(36 pp.);   and, for the Zionists in December, another stencilled
report on 'The Proposed Hebrew University of Jerusalem' (46 pp.).
The first plan was the customary exhortation of conservative surgery, of cleansing and brightening from within instead of the
wholesale demolition urged in official quarters.   As in India he
demonstrated the utter uselessness of many of the new and costly
streets proposed by the engineers.   'If a penny will do the task
properly, why spend a shilling?'   Tackling the political situation,
he boldly asserted: 'The fears of unending strife between Jew,
Arab, and Christian over Palestine do not exist for me.   There is
never any permanent need for people to kill each other'. (11)

Again,as in Cyprus a generation before, Geddes pointed to reforesta-
tion, improvement of water supply, and general revival of agriculture as the keys both to material prosperity in the Holy Land and
to the solution of its internal conflicts.   In Cyprus he had found
out how easily 'Turk and Armenian, Greek and Jew could, would and
did work together - wherever the constructive task was clear and
regular employment forthcoming', and he claimed that what worked in
Cyprus would also work in Palestine. (12)

Now a veteran planner, his method, as Dr Eder related and as he himself stated in the report, was first of all

> that of thorough and repeated perambulation day after day, and
> practically without use of any plans at all, until considerable

familiarity with the whole city, old and new, has been obtained.
...   In this way one gradually comes to see the qualities, the
defects and the possibilities of the areas under consideration.

What he considered included not only housing in new suburbs and
'conservative surgery' in the old city, a chain of parks, the restoration of pools generally (and those of Hezekiah and Bethesda in
particular), the need for accurate contour-mapping and so on, but
also religious, cultural and educational aspects of life.

His very first proposal was to make a small park on a little hill
near the railway station so that visitors could get a magnificent
general view of 'the noble City Wall leading on to the ancient
Castle and Gate'.   'Most visitors come to *see* Jerusalem, and these
desire to feel as deeply as possible what Jerusalem has meant to the
world, or at least to their own faith.'   He suggested placing there
a simple but dignified stone platform with a shelter behind....
On this the visitor, of whatever faith, in devotional mood, may
make his prayer on arrival, and again it may be on leaving.
This park, then, is of 'Hail and Farewell' (*Ave atque Vale*) for
pilgrims, but also of attraction to citizens.

Matching the insight of this introductory project was Geddes's
understanding of and respect for the spiritual significance which
Jerusalem has for Jews, Christians and Moslems alike.   His desire
to reconcile and evoke cooperation was as great as his urge to renew
or rebuild.   Whether it was a question of Christian monasteries,
Moslem mosques, or the Jewish Wailing Wall, he diagnosed and proposed treatment on a basis of equality and mutual respect among all
civic groups.   To exemplify such constructive working together of
all faiths, he pointed repeatedly to the Pro-Jerusalem Society
which had been started by the Military Governor, Colonel Storrs.

Of special interest is the plan P.G. outlined in his Jerusalem
Report for improving conditions at the Wailing Wall.   By acquiring
and completing some unfinished buildings near the 'Mograbin village', one might exchange these
for the very few and small Mograbi houses which are alone necessary for the improvement of the Wailing Wall, leaving the rest of
this village undisturbed, until it can be dealt with independent-
ly - and by the Municipality, not the Jewish community.
For with the removal of a single row of houses, and with the
acquirement of the small garden at the north end, the length of
the Wailing Wall will be about doubled, and the space in front of
it sufficiently increased, while a row of Cypress trees can be
planted along the west side, and the whole enclosed by wall and
gates.
A fresh access, independent of the present steep and awkward
lane, may readily be obtained, not through the Cadi's Court as
has been suggested, but immediately to the west of this, either
by removing the latrine immediately west of the Court Hall, or
west of this again.
A good staircase can easily be constructed from the street
level here and down through the present little garden, and an

access also provided from the lane to south.   The accompanying
sketch shows how simply, yet sufficiently this Wall may be improved.

Geddes also made important suggestions for replanting trees and remaking terraces on the eroded sides of the Mount of Olives and other
historic heights as well as for creating garden suburbs.   The
latter, he insisted, were not matters 'of drawing board, compasses
and ruler but of geography, history and present requirements';   for
only thus 'gradually arises a Garden Village' with a character of
its own.   Concerning Moslem parks, he pointed out his success in
India in making 'Zonana Parks', shielded by trees for privacy, which
were 'increasingly appreciated by Moslem ladies and children'.   He
anticipated that, though the past and present of Jerusalem have been
almost exclusively of religious   interest', its future would also
'be that of a City of Education'.

To this end he suggested the creation of a 'National and Civic Museum' that would be both scientific and popular in the same way as
his Cities Exhibitions.   He proposed showing selected historical
milestones, as in his own 'Repertory of the Masques of Ancient
Learning', and making relief models of Jerusalem 'from its earliest
Jebusite days, to its glories under David, its greatness under
Solomon'.   He appealed for help from all geographical, historical
and archeological authorities, including 'the American and British
schools of Archaeology'.   Confident that the new University would
also 'do its utmost to aid, to support and to advance such a comprehensive scheme', he concluded the Preliminary Report, somewhat
as he finished its short introduction, by referring to his and
Mears's intentions:

> On our return in spring we shall adjust details together, invite
> the criticisms and suggestions of the various authorities on the
> topography, archaeology and history of Jerusalem, and then sub-
> mit plan amended and completed to the best of our ability, and
> with fuller report accordingly.

P.G.'s report to the Zionists was short in text but typically vast
in its range over the past, present and future of higher learning.
Accompanied by perspectives and a ground plan drawn by Frank C.
Mears, it was the most definite contribution yet made by the 'wandering inspector of universities'.   It comprised both a philosopher's guide and an architect's design for the University Militant.

After the expected historical introduction and the analysis of current trends in education, Geddes took up the concrete problem of
buildings and grounds.   Seeking a location where future city
growth could not block the university's material development, as
has happened to most western ones, he found it on Mount Scopus, a
hill just outside Jerusalem to the east.

> No other site in the world is at once so magnificently panoramic
> and historic as this!   Rightly named as the 'hill of seeing',
> Mount Scopus overlooks on the south the Mount of Olives, on the
> west the outspread ancient and modern city;   and eastwards it
> commands the ranges of deserted hill-tops that plunge down to

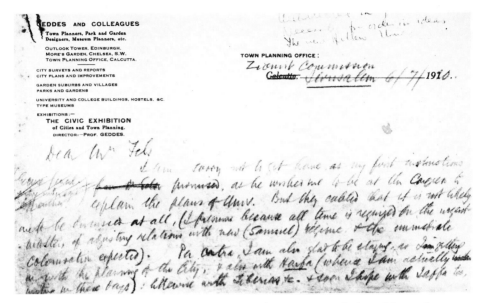

Beginning of P.G.'s lengthy letter to 'Dear Mrs Fels', widow of
Joseph Fels regarding his Jerusalem plans. The letterheading gives
more than a hint as to his habit of putting his 'best professional
foot forward'

This snapshot of Geddes on a mule during his 'diagnostic survey' of
Jerusalem is first-hand evidence of how he used all kinds of transportation in his studies

the Jordan Valley and the Dead Sea, behind which rise again the
mountains of Moab.

After weeks of tramping in and around Jerusalem, of quiet meditation
in his study (which had been temporarily set up in Dr Eder's home),
Geddes also discovered exactly the buildings to crown Mount Scopus
most fittingly.   A great Central Dome on a hexagonal base, the
historic six-sided Star of David, set the keynote simultaneously for
physical and spiritual harmony.   Its very design symbolised the
elements of unity in the Jewish, Moslem, and Christian religions,
for the dome is one architectural form common to them all.   The
underlying hexagonal construction, said Geddes, was biologically
sound, witness the bees and their six-sided honeycombs but, most
important, it permitted a materially convenient and philosophically
satisfactory plan for laboratories, classrooms, studies, and lecture
halls.   He wanted this University to be 'the first in the new order
of Universities', and worked out careful relationships among its
many compartments and subdivisions of knowledge.

An examination of the ground plan shows sciences on one side of the
Great Dome, arts and literature on the other; a simple arrangement
and one well adapted to the terrain.   But the genius of Geddes lies
in making the five buildings which almost form a hexagon around the
dome serve both as gateways to and as links between the schools of
art and science.   The sixth side is left open for the main approach
to the university, facing squarely south-west towards the centre of
old Jerusalem.   In a culminating stroke, he designated the three
buildings of the hexagon behind the dome to be the combined material
and intellectual bond between mathematics and science on one hand
and music and art on the other.   As link and passageway between
conventionally isolated schools, the middle building was given over
to philosophy which is, or ought to be, concerned with finding
unity in knowledge, of reconciling and relating all specialisms to
human life.   In this structure Geddes also put psychology, ethics,
and sociology.
    For though it is the latest comer among the sciences, Sociology
    is the most comprehensive in that it regards all studies, all
    activities as social products.

There was a place for every part of a university on his plan and
provision for future growth of these parts.   Throughout the whole
scheme were carried the principles of organising the divisions of
knowledge in relation to each other and of applying science and art
to human needs.   Thus fine arts, architecture, engineering, and
town planning were grouped on four sides of a common courtyard.   He
insisted that a regular part of the programme of these students, and
of chemists, biologists, and physicists as well, be actual work in
the replanning and rebuilding of Palestine.   He compared the university to a 'great electric battery of the spirit' in which each
department and institute is a separate generating cell, and reasoned
that if these cells could only be linked together, the resulting
energy would far exceed the individual yield of isolated cells and
could then be far more effectively applied to the outside world.

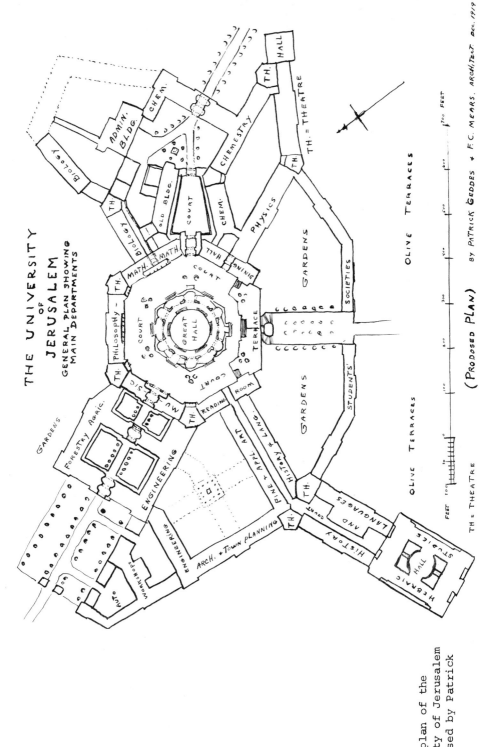

THE UNIVERSITY
OF
JERUSALEM
GENERAL PLAN SHOWING
MAIN DEPARTMENTS

(PROPOSED PLAN)

BY PATRICK GEDDES + F.C. MEARS. ARCHITECT. DEC. 1919

TH = THEATRE

General plan of the
University of Jerusalem
as proposed by Patrick
Geddes

But has not the designer overlooked one important matter?   What of
the Administration?   Scrutiny of the central plan reveals that the
two remaining buildings of the hexagon (left and right in front of
the central dome) are destined for reading and eating, not adminis-
tering.   However, a further search shows that a small building at
the back extremity of the science wing has been reserved for president and deans, registrar and treasurer.   Geddes explained this
location with a challenge:

> Universities do not exist to be 'administered'.   The Administra-
> tion exists only to serve Universities.   Though records are in-
> dispensable and regulations may be useful, even necessary;   the
> true regulation of the University comes from the mind, consci-
> ence, and character of those who make it up.   Hence I have seg-
> regated the administrators where they may be good servants, for
> when they usurp the central position of a university, as so often
> in France or Britain or America, they become the very worst of
> masters.

When the moment in November came for P.G. to take the boat-train
for Port Said and move on to his new professorial duties at Bombay,
he was still deep in ideas and projects for Jerusalem.   Even with
his car waiting at the door, he kept on expounding them to his
hosts.   Dr Eder relates dramatically:

> Geddes had been arguing with my wife and myself and demonstrat-
> ing to me beyond the last moment;   the driver was bidding us
> hurry up and as we ran down the steps with the luggage there
> burst open a bag stuffed with papers, plans and books - Geddes's
> luggage consisted mostly of this kind of clothes;   whilst I
> bundled the papers into the case my wife bundled Geddes into the
> car lest another idea should bubble up and lose him his train
> and steamer. (13)

The driver did make the train, so P.G. could write to his town
planning colleague Raymond Unwin from aboard the S.S. 'Etna' some
days later.   He reported optimistically that:

> The Jerusalem adventure has turned out satisfactorily so far:
> both the plans for the government of Palestine and the Governor
> of Jerusalem, and for the Zionists' University....   And all
> alike are pleased.
>   In this of course I'm greatly indebted to Frank Mears - who
> has e.g. materialised my long-dreamed Dome of Synthesis (for Aula
> Academica) in a way which will I'm sure interest you, & whose
> convincingly pretty perspectives have delighted our clients, who
> don't make much of mere plans!
>   They have kept him to go on, both with such pictures and with
> the needful elaborations of plans in detail until Xmas, when he
> has to go with the leaders of this Commission (Drs Weismann,
> Eder etc.) to the general assembly of Zionists at London or
> Geneva after New Year - when they are hopeful approval will be
> given.   They do not seem afraid of finding the funds thereafter.
> In that case they'll want us back in spring. (14)

NEW CHAIR ... NEW COLLEAGUE

The story of how P.G. got his Chair at Bombay has been told by the
then Vice-Chancellor, Sir Chimanlal Setalvad:

> I had the good fortune of coming across him in India.   I had
> vaguely heard of him as a botanist and a town-planner, and he
> was represented to me as a quixotical personality who dabbled in
> almost everything under the sun.
>
> We wanted, in the University of Bombay, to found a School of
> Sociology; and we were looking about for a man who would infuse
> into the students the real spirit of research and originality.
> It is always difficult to find such a man.   It was suggested to
> me it would be an excellent thing if we could induce Professor
> Geddes to come and make a beginning for us.
>
> When I mentioned this to the Governing Body of the University,
> some of my colleagues were amazed at my suggestion.   I, however,
> succeeded in persuading them to invite Professor Geddes to under-
> take the organizing of the School of Sociology.
>
> I never expected, when I got him for the University of Bombay,
> that he would do what an ordinary professor of Sociology might
> have done.   I only looked forward to the possibility of Profes-
> sor Geddes being able to inspire a given half-a-dozen students
> with his lofty spirit, of self-effacement and quiet working for
> the advancement of human knowledge and happiness without any
> recognition.   And, I can say, that when I came in closer contact
> with him, I congratulated myself on having done the right thing
> for the University. (15)

What the new professor taught at Bombay was, so to speak, predes-
tined by his extra-mural lectures in Edinburgh and London on Social
Evolution and by first-hand observations of Indian Place-Work-Folk.
One can take as a main clue to his curriculum 'The Essentials of
Sociology in Relation to Economics', a hundred-page article published in the 'Indian Journal of Economics' in two instalments in
1920 and 1922.   The first up-dates his 'Economics' (1881) and
'Evolution of Sex' (1889), emphasising the influence of physics,
biology and psychology on economics.

Turning to the use of graphics in social science, he groups the
three main interests of the everyday world as people, affairs, and
places and converts them into his 'thinking machine' of Place,
Work, and Folk.   These objective factors are equated with Geography, Economics and Anthropology, respectively, after which he adds
the corresponding triad of basic psychological concepts Sense, Experience and Feeling.   The resulting double set of nine plus nine
squares is his key to the simple objective and subjective aspects
of the outside world.*

---

* These first two triads of the 'Chart of Life' appeared in the
'Indian Journal of Economics', Allahabad, July 1920, p. 42 and
October 1922, p. 262.

PLACE (Geography)	place-WORK	place-FOLK
work-PLACE	WORK (Economics)	work-FOLK
folk-PLACE	folk-WORK	FOLK (Anthropology)

feeling-SENSE	feeling-EXPERIENCE	FEELING
experienced-SENSE	EXPERIENCE	experienced-FEELING
SENSE	sensed-EXPERIENCE	sensed-FEELING

Figure 9.1

Two more sets of triads (number three: Emotion-Ideation-Imagination, and number four: Ethopolity-Syngergy-Achievement) complete
P.G.'s 'Chart of Life'.*   Although the triads were to be understood and applied in their graphic form, he once used the fourth
in the prose statement that the ideal of studies of sociology 'and
of its indispensable sub-science of economics should be 'Ethopolity
Synergising Achievement'.

We cannot leave the 'Indian Journal' articles without citing his
vast and scathing charge that 'pre-scientific thinking' among economists has had the result that
     the concept of the Divine, and most of its attributes - unity
     and justice, power, creativeness and more - were transferred to
     money.
          Are we then suggesting that what most still call 'the sci-
     ence' of Political Economy has been to no small extent the theo-
     logy of the great god Mammon?   Frankly, Yes; Mammonology and
     mammonosophy of which the economists have been the teachers and
     preachers, with mammonolatry for their world-wide congregations.

Still he predicts that mammonosophy will yield to 'what we should
have to call biosophy'.   Eventually
     the popular faith, in Money more abundant, will have to give
     place to the ideal at once more ancient and more recent, of 'Life
     more abundantly', and even to that of Love as 'Creation's final
     Law'.

* An early version of Triads Three and Four is given on an inser-
ted diagram in the 'Indian Journal of Economics' October 1922, p.
304, while the full, thirty-six-squared 'Chart of Life' is contained here in the Appendix, together with an explanation of its
derived words.

Among the numerous correspondents of Geddes a new name begins to
occupy a more than casual place at the end of 1919.   A twenty-
year-old American student in New York had come across 'Cities in
Evolution' in 1915 and later written to the Outlook Tower for more
information about its author.   The two exchanged some letters in
1917 and 1918, but in December 1919 P.G. wrote to him: 'Your
letter is the most gratifying of all my Christmas morning budget,
& so I answer it first.'   The American's name was Lewis Mumford,
and this reply reveals that Geddes was already interested in him as
a potential disciple.

Thanking Mumford for his offer to help with reviews of the 'Making
of the Future' series, P.G. tells of his plans for 1920:   'Here
until the end of term, 10 March: sailing if possible 13th....
Then if all's well, back to Jerusalem for the summer; & due here
once more for 10 Nov., thus leaving Palestine by 15 Oct.'   About
his work, he comments:

> Of course the new Jm [Jerusalem] *may* fall through, as too many
> of my fine schemes have!   But for the first time I have had
> clients, in the Zionists, who were ready for all I could offer &
> not reluctant to leave their old & easy-going habits, as with
> all towns I have had to deal with elsewhere.   The Z. Comn [Zion-
> ist Commission] in Jerusalem were delighted - the Xns [Chris-
> tians] too - with our version of Rev. xxxi-2* ... for the Uni-
> versity on Mount Scopas.

In fact, Geddes was so optimistic as to the success of his Palestine
projects as to given up 'much more remunerative work e.g. Colombo
City etc which I am handing over to my admirable friend H.V. Lanchester, who is on his way here at present'.   P.G. wants to offer
employment to Mumford but explains that while his income 'is better
than most professors', its surplus is swallowed up by the deficits
& overdrafts of past life's adventures, plus the peculiar disasters
of the war years'.   He suggests nevertheless that Mumford might run
his Town Planning Exhibition in America 'after a term on it here',
or help him 'towards overtaking the unusually disproportionate pile
of materials for books beyond the small shelf of printed ones'.

Geddes says he always tried to find collaborators and points to
Thomson and Branford 'as the especial cases of this ... but as you
know, I lost my son, while the other is (& may too long be) semi-
invalided: so I must find others!   P.G. makes an offer of £200
as a 'small scholarship of research', plus more 'if you can help me
to earn it!'   However, he adds that this 'alas, is unlikely;   for
all my writing, throughout life, despite occasional trifling pay,
has but in aggregate added to the above-mentioned deficits, & even
this latest series 'Making of the Future' substantially so!'

The plans predicted for 1920 did not work out.   Although Mumford,
at Victor Branford's invitation, went to London and served as acting

* 'And I John saw the holy city, new Jerusalem, coming down from
God out of heaven, prepared as a bride adorned for her husband.'

editor of the 'Sociological Review' from May to October, Geddes remained in the East.   Planning in Colombo and Palestine occupied him
from April to November, so contact with the potential follower was
still by letter.   Their correspondence spanned a great range of
subjects and plans, P.G.'s continual apprehension about Ireland
being communicated to Mumford, as in these hard words concerning
events in the autumn of 1920: (16)

Ghastly business in Ireland: full of evil omen.   Empire can't
stand long with Dyer, Carson, Churchill & Co. working their will
while we are all powerless to prevent them!   And the folly of
it!   Is not *Delecta est Britannia* getting written up in flame,
in minds alike in America & Continent?   Are not even Canada &
Australia too etc. getting pretty sick of us, let alone Egypt &
India?   I feel the Lord Mayor of Cork our Dreyfus Case...

On returning from his second summer in Palestine the new Professor
sent a description of conditions and projects in his Department of
Sociology and Civics to the 'new colleague'. (17)   His teaching
quarters consisted of

a vast room 200ft x 30 + verandah-gallery outside, and plenty of
tables to lay out papers towards order....   But what disorder
from last year's accumulations moved about once & again by un-
skilled & careless hands!   No trained ass't though some willing
& more or less capable students - but all deficient in practical
comprehension of material & mental order as needing interrela-
tion anew.

This is a remarkable statement by the prolific thinker whose chief
method of work was to cover sheet after sheet of paper with notes
and diagrams and spread these out day by day on a flat surface so
that, ideally, all would be visible at once!   Yet he complains
that his students do not readily see

that tidy papers on desk, and new Jerusalem, are thoroughly parallel & cognate tasks, each complemental & integral to the
other!   And I too alas in practice falling away from this ideal,
as well as short of it!

Yet this idea of work is clear - towards an orderly presentment of sociological ideas in this gallery: & an orderly Town
Planning Exhibition in the Museum across the street; this latter
towards creatively aiding - by its expression of the progress of
cities - the Bombay Dev't scheme, now maturing under Gov't, and
the former towards better 'Making of the Future' more generally,
& not merely by books etc alone.

Geddes refers to this as an outline of what Mumford would have
helped him with could he have come to Bombay.   Even so, P.G. asks,
'why should we not be cooperating as it is, though materially far
apart?'   He suggests that their

conjoint presentment of sociology in general, & of cities in the
concrete - may be worked towards a more orderly one, & alike in
Bombay & New York as in Edin'g or London, or in Jerusalem etc:
each of course with its local perspective, yet thereby all the
more truly in harmony.

BIOGRAPHY OF J.C. BOSE ... PLANNING IN COLOMBO AND PATIALA ...
CONVALESCENT VERSE

The years 1920 to 1923 were fruitful ones in terms of publications
and reprints as well as in practical studies of cities, even though
the globe-spanning collaboration outlined by P.G. did not materialise.   Lewis Mumford did not return to London until 1922 when he
and his wife came for a two months' visit, and though Geddes was in
Great Britain in the summer of 1921, he had to spend July and August
of 1922 recuperating at Simla in the cool western approaches to the
Himalayas.   Thus the actual meeting of P.G. and Mumford was again
postponed.

Of P.G.'s publications, 'An Indian Pioneer: the Life and Work of
Sir J.C. Bose' was the most immediately successful, appearing in
1920 in both Britain and America.   Besides giving a very readable
and interesting account of Bose's struggle for recognition in
psycho-physics, the book is another of Geddes's tributes to India
as a nation with not only a great past but a promising future.   In
a chapter called 'Holidays and Pilgrimages', Geddes describes the
ancient and world-wide contacts of religions as well as of commerce
through pilgrimages, and documents how the Boses kept up this millennial tradition of Buddhism.

> To understand modern India we need better guidance than any of
> our modern writers, so often strident, even to harshness, when
> not more or less narrowly specialised....   For it is as a
> spiritual unity, underlying all the innumerable but more super-
> ficial differences, that India has primarily to be realised.
>
> It rests on sacred and epic literature and legend for the
> people, and on great and ancient philosophies, which are not
> merely cultivated by the classically educated, but deeply dif-
> fused, for good and evil, throughout the people as well.   All
> this variety of cultural influences, in essential harmony and
> (to us strangely) free from intolerance, has from unnumbered
> ages been steeping into the Indian villages with their old eco-
> nomic self-sufficiency and moral solidarity: Hence the apparent
> heterogeneity, of languages and castes and of mingled and
> changing Hindu, Mohammedan and European rule, has mattered far
> less than we are wont to suppose.
>
> India then, though not a nation in a European sense, is some-
> thing not merely less, but more.   It is rather the analogue of
> Europe: and though even vaster in population, and more varied
> in climates and peoples, has a more diffused and an often deeper
> community of spirit.   Not simply then through any mere political
> changes can this unity be more adequately realised - though on
> the modern spiral some may think so - but also, and more deeply
> and surely, through her cultural spirit.   That spirit not even
> the conquests of Islam have broken, nor yet the modern rule and
> other influences of the West.   This it is which is stirring
> towards its renaissance, as the religious groups of the past
> generation, or the political groups of the present, alike show:
> and this it is which will more fully revive its old values, and
> adjust them anew with those of the Western world.

Before going to Jerusalem in the summer of 1920 P.G. stopped in
Ceylon long enough to finish his Preliminary Report on 'Town Planning in Colombo'.   In its pages crowded with small print he covers
his usual general subjects like the need for survey and diagnosis
before treatment, of better housing for 'Working People', of the
need for civic bodies like the Pro-Jerusalem Society made up of
inter-faith and inter-racial groups.   He also makes numerous
detailed comments on this park and that museum as well as on roads,
railways and parkways.   But what characterises the Colombo study
is the amount of space given to the highly technical problem of
controlling river floods which steadily threaten Colombo.   After
studying all previous reports on floods he makes his own analysis
on the grounds that 'town planning is Applied Geography'.   He suggests observation of the meandering river on the plain as it cuts
the concave bank and adds to the convex one, 'thus tending to ex-
aggerate these meanders'.   When engineers protest that 'every
schoolboy knows all this', P.G. retorts typically, 'Why not investigate it more fully?   And why not act upon it also?'

Other concrete proposals are to make river section models with flowing water and sand, mapping all windings and obstacles upstream for
at least eighteen miles, and to consider all known flood-relief
devices: reservoirs, irrigation projects, dams with hydro-electric
power plants, and so on.   Tossing in swamp reclamation for good
measure, he sums up: 'In short, then, let us gradually model our
way upstream, contrasting as clearly as may be the stream as it is
with that after the suggested improvements.'

As in all Geddes's publications, there are tempting quotations on
nearly every page.   On slum-clearance, he states that
    The law at present claims impartially to defend the life and
    property of all men;   but it is not adequately doing either,
    until it protects the poorest citizen from eviction from his
    home ... until some reasonably adequate accommodation can be
    offered him elsewhere.

Another passage concerns 'the great sign of hope, which Jerusalem
at present shows':   the Pro-Jerusalem Society.
    For this has representative membership, and regular meeting, of
    both the temporal and spiritual leaders of each and all its com-
    munities - Moslems and Christians (Catholics and Protestants
    alike), with old Jews and new Zionists, all in active co-opera-
    tion towards the betterment of their city, in any and every
    practicable way.
Finally, P.G. asserts that
    every religious body in existence, or which has ever existed,
    knows the arts of government better than do our modern temporal
    powers.   Not that they forget their economic needs, or lack
    vivid conceptions of trial and punishment, but they also under-
    stand how to associate themselves with their people, in far more
    direct ways because human and humane, and this individually
    throughout all periods of life, and collectively throughout the
    whole year and its seasons, its weeks and days. (18)

Having 'given up Palestine this season' and arriving in Bordeaux
early in April 1921, P.G. sends congratulations on the birth of
Norah's third son.   'I *am* pleased and proud & feel quite a reflected glory!'   (He had previously written of wanting to visit
her and 'cultivate what I may be able to of "l'art d'être grand-
père"'.)

He is 'going north by stages, so as to see cities & Univ's not previously visited, partly with fresh eye from Indian conditions, &
towards Palestine etc.'   A letter two weeks later from Brussels,
where he is 'busy with old friends Otlet & Lafontaine on the vast
Exhibition Palace into which their "Tower" has grown', informs
Norah of the three-day trip which he and Marcel Hardy made from
Château-Thierry through part of the war zone.

> through the extraordinarily kind & efficient offices of the
> British Army Graves Bureau ... I found Alasdair's grave.   As
> you know, it was at first alone, but 30 or 40 more now surround
> it, in a little inclosure.   The cross stands all right, the
> inscription from his comrades though weathered is still read-
> able, & the box plant growing too.
>
>   Need I tell you how I sobbed over it, as the day of news four
> years ago.   Hardy too could not but join me: & our good chauf-
> feur broke down too when we came back to the road, & saw our
> faces: & he too had had his sorrows.   (Do not think me so ab-
> sorbed as to have lost feeling, or for any of you all!) (19)

From July to September Geddes was engaged in his old-time routine
of lecturing in London, Oxford and Edinburgh; and of trying to
write with J. Arthur Thomson, this time staying at his home in
Aberdeen.   He attended the September meeting of the British Association in Edinburgh, and in mid-October was back in London giving a
talk on 'Women's Work, Actual and Possible'.   Later that month he
wrote to a woman friend that he was 'Off Port Said', again en route
to teaching and planning jobs in India.   Though 'dull & tired
after strenuous times, of various kinds' he expected that 'brain
will clear up as voyage goes on: only the first days one is down,
despite good weather etc'. (20)

In December 1921 Arthur came to Bombay and began a difficult apprenticeship in his father's sociology and town planning.   Contrary to
what had been agreed upon previously, the younger son found on
arrival that he had to share lodgings with his strong-willed father,
and in later years he would quote his brother Alasdair as once
having remarked that 'No human being could both work and live with
P.G.'   Even so, Arthur found the Geddesian study of cities reward-
ing as well as strenuous when he accompanied his father to Patiala
after the University term had ended.

'Town Planning in Patiala State and City', appearing in 1922, consists of mingled practical suggestions for, and generalist comments
on, this capital in North India.   As in P.G.'s other Far Eastern
reports, sampling from the Table of Contents yields topics as varied
as 'Silk Industry for Patiala' and 'A Greek Interpretation of the
Garden', 'Future Garage Accommodation', 'The Current Revival of
Education', and 'Essential Condition of City Development'.

The mention of garages brings up once more Geddes's views on motor vehicles.   He was fully aware of their usefulness and of the need to plan both for their accommodation, as in this report, and for special motor roads not burdened with functions of lanes - and vice versa - as we saw in one of his earliest studies in South India in 1915.   Further, in the Colombo Report he proposed motor buses as a more economical investment and as more adaptable in traffic than tramcars in new built-up areas.   Yet even his imaginative foresight did not reach far enough to predict their coming share in the burden of pollution.

In other areas, however, he foresaw planning methods of broad val- idity.   His experience in Patiala
> has compelled wider and deeper surveys, more cautious yet more thorough diagnoses, and thus treatment more comprehensive; yet also more moderate, even gentler, than is customarily applied. [The beginner in] would-be civic surgery soon amputates a dam- aged limb; but with more experience, he applies himself to mend and restore it to usefulness. (21)

P.G. dwells on themes of the spiritual and the ideal, saying:
> Through the past fixation of these, or the present lapse, there have come about many of the evils from which the City suffers; and of which material decay, disease, poverty and more, are out- ward symptoms.   Hence these evils are not really curable by material methods only: witness the many disappointments of would-be 'Improvement Schemes'.

The summer of 1922 brought Geddes an enforced change from his varied tasks in the form of a convalescent vacation.   As in 1918 in Dar- jeeling, it was a mountain setting in north India, but at Simla, where he had friends in the regional Department of Archeology. What he did this time was so unique that not even his closest friends could have predicted it: the writing of verse for several hours each day, and for six or seven weeks!   Here is P.G.'s own account as, with suddenly easy-flowing pen, he corresponds in blank verse, first with Norah, then with many friends.

'Best of life is Convalescence!'   With this keynote we pick up the verse-letter of 1922, first quoted in Chapter 2 to tell the inner story of his illnesses in London and Mexico.   It goes on, saying that he might tell of other such crises in his life:
> Earlier, later - but come to last month's.   After near year on plains,
> And that's burning plain - Punjab, April May June - to hottest,
> Town-planning Patiala, and other towns; contriving to renew
> The last great Moghal Garden, terraced, streamed but greatly lapsed,
> Much now ev'n forest, jungle; then roasted at Amristsar's Temple Golden.
> Barefoot, days long, on sun-hot marble pavements by its sacred Tanks
> I got fresh fever, so came to this hilltop
> Of chilly mists and rains torrential...

> But change too sudden; in one night to pass from level plain to height -
> Like Snowdon or Ben Nevis, seven thousand feet - is over-strain...

The result was exhaustion and depression, and 'Worse still, my mind a blank'.   With all interests extinguished, nothing was left but

> To consider if I should not now give Arthur his directions
> For final pyre, and ashes with his mother's.   Thus experience full
> Of sad Old Age, towards its approaching end. (22)

Yet after some days as a complete invalid his body slowly adjusted to the altitude.   'Blood was renewing; growing, as it does on heights.'   At the end of the second week he found that a 'Small walk uphill no longer tired' and that 'mind came to life anew'.   He thought of 'Planning Reports to finish, send to press...', strange flowers woke his interest, and then:

> Great panoramas of dawn, and sunset, dispelled my inward mist:
>
> -Till, suddenly - I realise anew! — Not old, near dying -
> But Alive, well again! Young once more! Mind awake, a-dream!
> These states often mingled, pressing, striving! Old thoughts, no longer
> quietly speculative; — came new thoughts — came, surging, full-emotioned,
> Freshly imaged! I, who all my life -- you know -- have hated writing.
> Delayed it, shirked it, — with writer's cramp, expressing mind's
> Took my pen to release this tension; this raced into verse!

The same story of change from months of burning heat to 'high, cold damp, thin air' is told to the Scottish singer, Margaret Kennedy Fraser, but without emphasising his utter debility.   Instead he tells of reading 'voraciously' even before he could walk and, 'just a few days ago' of himself discovering truth in the theory that 'speech came to man, and grew to language - not as we speak now, in plain prose' but as 'rhythmic cry, then call ...'

> So I - after a life of thinking - always in plain prose
> Or technical, oftenest graphic (thus so far mathetic) - yet
> Of working too, and only by rarest impulse scribbling a rhyme -
> Suddenly found myself aroused anew to write, as if by Caldmon's call.

> Rugged, uneven rhythms like this - yet rhythm so far - came sudden, flowing
> In spate, So I - who've so rarely written at all, and then
>   With utmost difficulty - alteration, correction, recorrection,
> Making my page all but illegible, even to myself, my print
> Unreadable to all save patient few - (then fatigue, writer's cramp -)

        - I suddenly find myself writing - all day long, straight off
          as now,
    In this style or some other - with no more trouble, pain, or
        weariness.

P.G. roams at length from anthropology and archaeology to her
father's and her own careers in singing and recording Scottish folk
music; from the revival of folk-lore and culture in Denmark and
Norway to Ireland's problems and to her duty to re-awake Scotland
by song.   Thinking of her and her father had inspired him to
'yesterday's long screed, on Anthropology' of which he sends her a
page or two.   True anthropologists 'compel dry bones to live anew'
and voices to return, 'Though oft inhibited - like me so long ... '
He spurs her on to renewed efforts:
    Search on, Song-gatherer.   Toil on, Transcriber: Sing out,
        Singer.
    We both wax old together: strength ebbs, through shortening
        years;
    Yet Life's Rhythm, to the last, has vital flows.   Even upsurges
        ...
    ...
    I see my letter, meant only as a page or two ...
    Has run on for whole hours.   Forgive its length.
    - Out of the abundance of the heart the mouth speaks,
    The pen runs.   You'll believe me, Yours,

Verse-letters were written to Victor Branford, J.C. Bose, and possibly to others like J. Arthur Thomson, who did not keep everything
he received.   None, however, was addressed to Lewis Mumford according to internal evidence in a letter to him in mid-November in which
Geddes deprecates both his illness and his verse in the same parenthesis:
    (68 nearly two months ago, though not yet feeling it, save for a
    few days at Simla in rains, & that followed by convalescent
    bardic yells! (which V.B. may have shown you sample of)).

In addition, two fairly long poems survive, entitled respectively,
'Proteus' and 'NAMES'.   The latter is really a self-review epistle
addressed to Branford, opening
    Say, Victor - Victor Verasis - if for these last years, you and
        I - Victor and Patrick
    Could more live up to these fine names of ours, what might we
        not do?...

P.G. suggests that some of the nicknames applied to him, 'but suit-
ing you as well!', should also have been lived up to.   Such as
    'Intellectual Whore' - for our varied interests, studies, would
    be all-embracing! [and] 'High Explosive' for our criticisms,
    intensive - detonant, shattering....   [But above all they
    should] live up to 'Merlin'! - Now arousing Youth, guiding to
    seize the Sword Excalibur; now counselling it to right use...

They should 'be Victors!   Victors one by one, in all the "Battles
Twelve" ... ' and in reconstruction: 'The captives freed, the

wounded sained - all hands to replowing, building, weaving ... '
Still another reference to Celtic folklore concerns Vivien, the
scheming courtesan who finally seduced Merlin into revealing the
spell which she promptly used to render him powerless.   The Vivien
theme will return in Geddes's life, hence this quotation in full
from 'NAMES':

> So too we fail of Merlin.   For though 'the spell of woven paces
>   and of waving arms'
> Which too much haunts all men, ev'n through life, ay, age, be
>   least for us to fear -
> - Since I can ne'er forget - and you still keep - companionship
>   as far from Vivien's
> As Una's from Duessa's, Sita's from Circe's - we fall short, by
>   far, of him.

Late that August P.G. wrote again to Branford from Simla.   'Here-
with more rants and rhymes!   The pot keeps boiling.'   He comments
in verse on the latest issue of the 'Sociological Review' just received, and from his 'Macbeth witch-cauldron' pour out informative
items mingled with exhortation.   He hopes to visit Ireland the
following summer and is glad Branford gets on well with A.E. (George
Russell), 'since unfortunately A.E. has always fought shy of me'.
He speaks again of his 'long-planned books' on Olympus and Parnas-
us, announcing 'Now I dream of doing these in verse'.   And he calls
Victor and Patrick to action:

> Time now for war-paint, tomahawk, and trail!
> Battle on battle - not forgetting scalping!

Compared with the conversational flow of the letters to friends, the
two pages of verse called 'Proteus' are of introvert nature and contain highly original and forceful imagery.   Part I relates how all
the grapes and dry raisins he has gathered 'o'er half the world'
have come together 'thus yielding juices varied' and how on some
days

> two, three, more, different streams
> Try to force their way at once through this one single tap, my
>   pen!...
>   my temples swell and throb, my eyes perplex
> With images too num'rous, too swift changing.   Inward ear
> Can catch but fragmented expression, fit, or failed;
> Tongue murmurs rhythms, soon interrupted, rimes soon jangled,
> As needs must be 'mong diverse striving thought-streams tangled.
>
> Ideals clashing, even akin - dashing like Cain on Abel:
> Moods merry, grave, grim, sable - words, ev'n languages, in
>   Babel;
> Tunes thrumming, strumming, drumming.   How expel this eery hum?
> - Images coming, mumming!   Opium? - would it dumb this babble -
>   Babel in Delirium?

Part II is very short and describes the weariness that comes over
him, so 'No opiate needed'.   Geddes employs more end-rhymes as well
as occasional echoes within the lines.

> Tired, passive, I lie in chair;   Outside the darkening room

Comes down the heavy night-mist; grey monotony of gloom
Like silent doom enshrouding ere the long sleep entomb.

Quiet gazing, dulled, indifferent, I rest me, nothing thinking,
Unshrinking Lethe drinking - floating, sinking
Within its darkening fume towards utter Night.
What matters Life!...

The last section of 'Proteus', also rhymed, is a series of mytholo-
gically flavoured word-pictures of the storm cloud formations he
sees through rifts in the gloomy mist.
   In slow succession, the cloud-walls - confronting pylons
      battered,
   Give way, fall back, inward explosion-shattered;
   Roll into mounded ruins.   Yet from these arise shapes new;
   On right, slowly a mighty form emerges - vast to view -

   Behold the Temple's God! - weary of throned slumber
   With droning hierophants, burst forth to disencumber
   His weight of offerings!   High raising head, colossal as vast
      shrine,
   To tow'ring view - terrible, then benign.   Yet melts again,
      supine;...

Two more stanzas of imaginative description end Part III, while IV
concludes the poem:
   There Proteus' world: here Proteus' dreams within!
   - Let Proteus have his way!   Life's Change!   Ev'n passing
      madness,
   Moods wild to melancholic - ay, pain, disease, ev'n sin -
   To fuller life may sublimate: - Life's change is beauty,
   gladness!

THE POET'S UNIVERSITY AT SANTINIKETAN

Unlike the brief encounter with Gandhi, Geddes achieved lasting
friendship and cooperation with the poet Rabindranath Tagore, dating
from the Darjeeling Summer Meeting in 1917.   Their closest contact,
however, was in 1922-3 and concerned the latter's plans for an 'International University in India'.   Its purpose was to pave 'the
path to a future when both the East and West will work together for
the general cause of human welfare', and its official opening set
for January 1923.   'I need not say', the poet wrote already in May
1921, 'that it would help me greatly if you could personally take
part in organising it.'

The first reply extant, dated 15 April 1922 is an abridgment marked
'From letter to R.N. Tagore from P.G. 15/4/22', and written in the
hand of a third person (probably Arthur Geddes).   In the six pages
copied Geddes explains how his Cities Exhibition presents the past
and present of cities, 'their possible improvement too, as from
Edinburgh to Jerusalem, and with something of Indian cities also'.
He also describes his new Department of Sociology and Civics as a

miniature outline of the University's resources, applied towards
clearer social thought, & better civic practice.   For social
science needs all that the preliminary sciences can teach it, &
civics needs all the corresponding & independent arts.
     We need to be logical in our statistics and graphics, physical
in our construction, biological in our agriculture, horticulture
& hygiene, economic in our general undertakings: yet all the
sciences & arts, as Ruskin saw before us ... are ineffective,
when not calamitous, while expressing only the sciences and arts
of the material and mechanical order, still so predominant, & so
characteristic of the West.

P.G. outlined thereafter a coordination of arts and sciences which
he claimed would satisfy both conventional academics and poets.
Though he progressed from logic, with which 'the traditional University began', through mathematics and natural sciences to those of
men and society, Geddes did not box them into thinking machines.
Instead, he used 'Conduct', 'Behaviour' and 'Activity' as three
simple terms which revealed without 'academic jargon, the world-old
simplicity, since unity, of Life';   and even explained them in
linear prose, partly aided by arrows and parentheses:

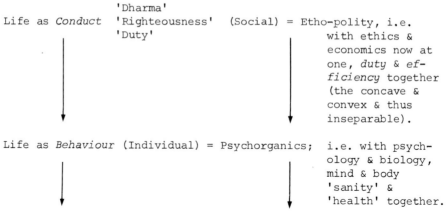

                    'Dharma'
Life as *Conduct* 'Righteousness' (Social) = Etho-polity, i.e.
                    'Duty'   with ethics &
                                                economics now at
                                                one, *duty* & *ef-*
                                                ficiency together
                                                (the concave &
                                                convex & thus
                                                inseparable).

Life as *Behaviour* (Individual) = Psychorganics; i.e. with psych-
                                                    ology & biology,
                                                    mind & body
                                                    'sanity' &
                                                    'health' together.

Life as *Activity (Practical & applied in)* = Eutechnics; i.e.
                                               with esthetics &
                                               physics, arts &
                                               industries at
                                               one, 'gesture' &
                                               'grasp' together.

As a further concession to the poet Geddes wrote:
     If the preceding be clear, (uncongenial though may be the dia-
     grammatic method & presentment, since this suspends any attempt
     at literary expression, - as mere foundation plans lack architec-
     ture, yet I trust prepare for it) it will, I hope, be agreed that
     this is not the conventional & 'hard-shell' presentment of Sci-
     ence, but at least contains a form of the life we are all seeking
     in however different ways.

Answering a few weeks later, Tagore found it difficult to comment on
P.G.'s plans for a university since his 'Santiniketan Institution'
had developed in the same way as he wrote: without a distinct plot
or outline.

> I merely started with this one simple idea that education should
> never be dissociated from life. I had no experience of teach-
> ing, no special gift for organisation....
>
>   I began anyhow. All that I could do was to offer to the five
> little boys who were my first students my company. I talked and
> sang to them, played with them, recited to them our epics, impro-
> vised stories serially given to them from evening to evening,
> took them on excursions to neighbouring villages.... (23)

Tagore's intuitive method of developing his school was completely
different from P.G.'s, yet there was a strong affinity between these
two utterly different minds and personalities. The Indian poet
declared:

> I have often wished for my mission the help of men like yourself
> who not only have a most comprehensive sympathy and imagination
> but a wide range of knowledge and critical acumen. It was with
> a bewilderment of admiration that I have so often followed the
> architectural immensity of your vision. But at the same moment
> I had to acknowledge that it was beyond my power to make a prac-
> tical use of the background of perspective which your vision pro-
> vides us with.
>
>   The temperamental characteristics of my own nature require the
> most part of my work to remain in the subsoil obscurity of mind.
> All my activities have the character of play in them - they are
> more or less like writing poems only in different mediums of ex-
> pression. Your own schemes also in a great measure have the
> same element which strongly attracts me, but they have a dif-
> ferent idiom which I have not the power to use.
>
>   You will understand from this, my dear friend, that though I
> always enjoy listening to you when you formulate your ideas and
> my mind is stimulated by the vastness of their unity I cannot
> criticise them. I suppose they are being stored in my uncon-
> scious memory waiting for living assimilation with my own
> thoughts.
>
>   Cordially yours
>   Rabindranath Tagore

P.G.'s answering letter, if any, is not available, but according to
notes made in his peculiar abbreviation-shorthand, he had intended
to say that while all plans are dry, they do express the foundations
of the University's 'special completeness - not for knowledge only
but for Good, True & Beautiful'.

> So think of us architectural workers & students as planning out
> the foundations of your & others' ideal Universities & of locat-
> ing more clearly, & more spaciously too, the gardens of the Muses
> upon their sacred hill.

Geddes was then in the midst of his spell of overwork at Patiala
which led to convalescence and verse-making at Simla, and did not
write to Tagore until November 1922. He could then report from

Bombay that he and Arthur had spent 'two active days at Shantiniketan & Sherul' in addition to discussing plans with Mr Mahalonobis, and now needed to know what the poet envisioned: 'give me your ideas as clearly as you can *boldly* for the future.... For as the essence of all planning is *foresight*, it is your vision & ideal which must guide the whole scheme.' P.G. envisages Santiniketan as an 'International University' with many possibilities for expansion, although 'you cannot compete with Universities on the great world scale - at least for many years to come - (such as I have been planning at Jerusalem - on a scale surpassing Oxford & Cambridge, Harvard & Chicago).' He finishes by reminding Tagore that if he is to plan

> in such a way as to meet growing & future requirements, I cannot be too fully 'briefed', or too speedily.
>   With congratulations and good wishes - great hopes also, believe me always

Yours faithfully & cordially
P. Geddes

Arthur was also greatly interested in Santiniketan, and at the end of December Tagore told P.G. that

> It would be delightful to have him [Arthur] here to advise on the carrying out of your schemes which we will gladly follow within the limit of our resources.... We can offer him Rs 150/ per month for his expenses. Lodging is free, board will come to about Rs 30-40, and servant Rs 30-40.

But the 'briefing' was far from speedy, for it was late in February 1923 before Geddes received any plans from Santiniketan. His response to Mr Mahalonobis is a masterpiece from a frustrated planner. The long-awaited letter arrived just as P.G. was leaving on an excursion with students but he would open it next day, 'hoping it may be found all right for working on'.

> But alas, *there is now no time* for this. When it was promised me and by all concerned in the beginning of November, and *in a few days - and without fail* - I was at a rare period of freedom for it. Also I had my mind full of clear mental photographs of Shanteniketan, with which I was ready and free to work, (even without the concrete photographs for which I asked, and which were also promised me with the same amiable assurances, but which also never arrived & - (presumably) - forgotten.
>   Still I might recall my memories, and work now.... But last November I was then free of other plannings, and until Xmas - a very rare opportunity for work on your problems, and on which I was then fresh, as well as keen.
>   But I had in the Xmas vacation (of less than a fortnight) to go and tackle 1. the Lucknow Zoo, and also the Osmania University at Hyderabad; each, and especially the latter, on large scale and needing much work. They thus pledged me to my remaining free time - (after term here closes 10th. to sailing for home and U.S. A. on 31st.)
>   Next came in the demand for criticism of Bombay City Improvements: each of the three is largest of its kind in the cities of the world at present - and the *worst* in execution - with corresponding urgency.

Next this University has gone into eruption - and I have its
future planning on my hands - with regular meetings of Committee
concerned accordingly.

Finally the new Non-Co-Operative University College [Gandhi's]
at Ahmedabad.   Again with plans, visits from Principal and
active correspondence.

And now the electricians are wiring in this department - with
confusion accordingly.   And I have ten days to wind up my (thus
disordered) exhibition, and do what I can to plans of all preceding, before leaving Bombay for Lucknow and Hyderabad, before
sailing.

Then P.G.'s blunt summary: 'So instead of having your plans ready,
and your case clear to plead in America as I hoped last November, I
have just nothing - save disappointments all round'.   Nevertheless,
Geddes does not want this letter to be mistaken 'for a mere grumble'
since it is 'the needed explanation' of why he can't work on the
plan, 'but shall have to send it back to my son now at Sherul, with
such notes - too brief and few, as I can find time for - so that he
may be doing what he can this summer.'

Having delivered himself of all this scolding, P.G. promises to go
over the plans 'with any of your Committee who may come to Bombay -
from next November (10th onwards).   But I can't come to Shantiniketan till next Xmas and perhaps not even then.'   Reconciliation
and optimism return: 'I shall also do my best to go over what he
[Arthur] can send me to U.S.A. meantime ... we'll surely manage next
winter instead of this one - (if the Poet, and Andrews & you can
then spare any time).'

At the end of March Arthur writes from Santiniketan to 'My Dear
Daddy', then en route to Scotland, with similar hopefulness.   He
looks
　　back on our 16 months together & our winter to come, & who knows
　　what after that?   I look back with pleasure to our work for a
　　year past.   In Patiala especially I was finding my feet, & in
　　Sociology too my old feeling & belief that your thought was what
　　was needed for re-interpretation has been confirmed.   What are
　　you going to tell us about next winter?   Give us warning some
　　months before, & then we can think things out beforehand and be
　　ready with questions in our heads, & tuned for it; so that I
　　trust you may find us not so stale, more responsive or suggestive
　　than heretofore.   And when you come back I hope you'll find me
　　better, both as student-disciple & assistant, & as son too.
　　　I've been asking myself again how I can train for effective
　　co-operation with you, whether nearer, or further, as here, &
　　certainly this Santiniketan work seems excellent in every way,
　　all round the Life Diagram, as seldom possible.

Following his summer's recuperation at Simla, Geddes had returned to
Bombay for the terms of 1922-3, during which he wrote frequently
about future plans as well as current doings.   A mid-November
letter to Lewis Mumford tells about visiting 'Tagore's School & incipient "International University" - to plan for developments', and

about a student of drama in his sociology class in Bombay who is 'better than all the 1500 Edin'h & London Masquers' whom he hopes to persuade Tagore to take over.   Then a suggestion to Mumford:
> (Such Masques ought also to be done at one of your film-producing centres.   It is a great pity the Masques of 1912-13 were not filmed.   But matters were not then so dev'd - & the idea never materialised.)

P.G. says he has to go 'at Xmas vac'n to Hyderabad (Deccan) where the Nizam's "Osmania Univ." has a hilly site of 1200 acres, thus promising for arch'l effect and grouping (though how far modifiable educationally remains of course to be seen)'.   After this fairly hopeful bit of news he reports on two utter fiascos in higher education:
> I have never been more disapp'd [disappointed] with Univ. dev'ts than lately - 1. at Benares (which I lost through an officially minded enemy, the Principal of Allahabad) & now with 20 miles of roads - ie. impossible distances & useless outlay & vast buildings - an abominable failure between European & Indian, without good qualities of either, but 25 lakhs debt & heavy yearly deficit!   All conventional univ. ideas too - despite Indian aim! Then in contrast 2. 'Lutyens' plans for Lucknow Univ. - superextravagant monuments to himself, in coldest refinement of Georgian architecture indiff't to Indian & European alike, and of fabulous expense - with, so far as I could make out, *no* useful accommodation for *any* dept - & expansion unprovided, & indeed made impossible as cold façading everywhere can do.

Much of this letter deals with the prospective collaboration between its sender and recipient and even suggests four books for Mumford to write on Geddesian lines: Cities, University Developments, Palestine & Jerusalem, and Culture Institutes.
> Here I see is our long-dreamed* collab'n beginning in very effective ways, & with promise of work, indeed for my very effective colleagues like F.C. Mears & I trust also my son Arthur, some of whose simple but effective drawings of Patiala actual & cleansed of rubbish might enliven your pub'n [publication] ...

P.G. mentions the possibility of getting the 'Times of India', the leading Bombay paper, to reproduce such illustrations and 'possibly also bring out your whole pub'n here as a special number'.   This would be
> helpful to our work & practice here, which despite recent engagements (all from native states etc) is now much limited by the opposition created in official circles everywhere by my frank criticism of their too generally *Haussmannic* spirit & methods -
>   Must close today -
>   Yours cordially
>   P. Geddes

---

* Observe that 'long-dreamed' is now a recurrent, almost compulsive, adjective in P.G.'s vocabulary.

Despite haste, a P.S. was added offering money to help Mumford face
'such unremunerative writing'.   He could keep the sum as his 'first
commission as a colleague of this firm - or if you prefer, realise
that it will be in my will as a legacy to asspiritual kinsman'.
(In the margin of the letter, lent to this biographer, Mumford has
written 'not accepted'.)

Letters to Mumford from January 1923 on deal with possible showings
of the Cities Exhibition in America, and with the differences
between American surveys and P.G.'s.   The former, 'although more
highly elaborated than ours, are still in our earlier phase so far
as principles, methods and scope are concerned'.   They are still
handled, 'it seems to me, sporadically, without any correspondingly
adequate & exact technique - whether mine, as of the 36 ('Chart of
Life' of 36 squares), etc, or any other?   Is this so or not?'   So
detailed are the early-type surveys that their makers do not 'see
the trees for the leaves or forest for trees', nor what sort of
city they are disentangling from 'the medley of cities (city types)
which make "the city" as we see it'.   Whereupon follows Geddesian
nomenclature at its wildest:

> More generally of course, the American city is *more frankly Mech-*
> *anopolis* and *Mammonopolis* than even our own - Its 'West End' more
> unashamedly - and so more joyously - *Scholopolis* (*Schole -*
> *leisure*) or Thelema of leisure class than ours, and so on.   Less
> obviously & less really - *Strategopolis* than our old war cities,
> less of *Tyrannopolis* developed (than Berlin, less too of *Eupolis*
> than Paris, Oxford, Edinburgh etc.   Less of *Biopolis* than Bour-
> neville or Garden City etc.;   less of *Geopolis and Regionopolis*
> (Diocesopolis) than some, save in lower forms e.g. coalfields,
> towns etc. (where we run each other hard):   and less too of *Etho-*
> *polis* than the old sacred cities, despite their deteriorations.
> In short, too much huge larval cities (Larvalopolis) for
> future. (24)

P.G. AND MUMFORD MEET ... 'ROMAN EMPIRE, USA'

As the time drew near for P.G. to sail for Britain and the USA,
matters of practical urgency were reflected in correspondence.   He
had made a selection of plans and diagrams from the quarter mile of
Cities exhibits and from an unmeasurable number of notes and thinking machines, but even this was too much to carry as luggage.   His
solution is revealed in a letter to the Secretary, Russell Sage
Foundation, New York, after first invoking 'Our mutual friend, Mr
Raymond Unwin':

> As I am closing my winter's work here today I have bundled up a
> mass of manuscripts & of plans, diagrams etc... I am advised that
> it is safest & simplest to send all by post & in separate par-
> cels.   But I have as yet *no address!*
> So it occurs to me, greatly daring, to take the liberty of
> addressing the whole lot of parcels & plans to your care!   I
> take it you have a spacious office, & that you will forgive me
> for thus burdening you?   (They will look alarming - numerous,
> perhaps 12 packets: but may be fitted on top of a bureau, until

I arrive - about May 5th or 6th - & then remove them to such
working den as I may have discovered. (25)

Another practical problem involved the distribution and sale in
America of 1,000 copies of a neat little volume bound in green paper
covers, 'Dramatisations of History'.   Except for the preface
written in Bombay and dated April 1923, it consisted of integral
reprints of the 'Masques of Ancient, Medieval, and Modern Learning'
performed in Great Britain in 1912 and 1913.   Addressed to Messrs
Boni & Liveright, the opening-wedge letter this time was a reference
to their request, a year or two ago, to have a book of his for consideration.   But he has 'always been too busy - planning towns,
colleges, universities (six on hand this year), bot. gardens &
"zoos" ... ' to compile a book of general interest.   The second
paragraph relates how the Masques in Edinburgh and London resulted
in descriptive booklets which 'went to 12,000 or so (my only large
circulation at any time) which got out of print before the war...
But these helped to stimulate demand for Wells's "Outlines of
History", & now this reacts in re-opening interest in my Dramatisations'.

Consequently, one of P.G.'s 'masterful young asst's has made me send
off my last surviving copy' to a Madras printer who is making 1,000
copies for use in India.
     & as there may be also some demand at home, & some even in U.S.A.
     I am getting another 1000 for each.   But now, on my way home &
     to U.S ... there is no time to correspond with London, let alone
     N.Y.   (I have to correct proofs before sailing.)
          So I take a liberty, & with each, as I never did before!   I
     put down for London pub'rs 'Sociol'gl Pub'rs L'd'...   But what
     to do for U.S. edition?   With an audacity you can never have
     experienced, I put down your name on title-page also!   No time
     to ask permission!
          If you resent this, (as you are quite entitled to!) I can
     paste your name over, with a strip, when copies arrive in
     America: but meantime the thing is being done, & you are too
     late to stop it, even by cable! (26)

The letter continues more humbly with Geddes saying he will accept
any terms Boni & Liveright 'see fit to define... (Or I can give it
away if you don't take it.)'   He tells of another paper of his
which is being reprinted, 'Essentials of Sociology in Relation to
Economics', saying it
     expresses some of the views which, as a wandering student, I am
     coming over to your side, to maintain as best I may.   I am out
     for the watery blood of political economists, (Orthodox or
     Marxian matters little) and so again can give this away, as
     challenges, if you don't take it!
          So I leave you as free as I can! despite my audacity as a
     total stranger to you.   This is at any rate a very distinct
     overture towards acquaintance, & not without hopes of this becom-
     ing a friendly one.   I trust you will see that as mitigating
     circumstance, & so remain

                                        Yours cordially
                                        P. Geddes

But what to do for N.A. edition? With an audacity you can never have experienced, I put down your name on title — happily — also! No time to ask permission!

to maintain as best I may. I am out for the watery blood of political economists, (orthodox or Marxian matters little) and so again can give this away, as

P.G.'s 'audacious proposal' to his hoped-for American publisher, Boni & Liveright

Geddes and James Mavor at Wood's Hole in Summer of 1923

On second thoughts, I send this through Mumford, as he can perhaps help to explain, although despite long acquaintance, we
have also never yet met! (He can perhaps show you 'Masques'
etc.)   P.G.

To complete this part of the story one may quote the note which Mumford, many years later, wrote on the back of the envelope: 'I was
shocked & horrified by this letter & never gave it to Liveright -
nor did I introduce P.G. to him'.

April and May 1923 found both Patrick Geddes and a considerable
sampling of his works converging upon New York City. To Norah, on
board the S.S. 'Adriatic' out of Liverpool, he wrote nostalgically
of his recent visit to Edinburgh:

here on the voyage I have with me your songs - and even hum them
on deck or in my den. I am very glad to take away with me that
image of home - (though I missed again my chance of winning my
wee grandsons: alas!) (27)

He urged her to sing constantly to her children as her mother had.
'Don't be taken up too much as Martha-housewife; be Mary-mother
too! (She must have sung all her life.)'

Though your mother couldn't educate me to music, much less to
song, & though you don't succeed with Frank either, that is not
exactly our defect, our deficiency educational (and, or) congen-
ital, as still commonly believed. It is - as now commonly
understood - our *inhibitions* which impede us. The shaking off
of mine, as by versing last summer, would now make it possible
for me (could your mother - again now take me in hand!) to join
a chorus, & even to sing - (to myself!).

P.G. follows up this very rare personal confession with other unusually emotional insights.

To crack the crusts of inhibitions & let the life come through,
released, is thus the secret for us all. Genius is not external! not 'gift', but burgeoning versus bud-blighting.
    Here in this vast ship ... all sorts of obviously human people
are sitting alone & apart, as I do - & without my excuse of constant work or thought. And so on all such voyages - as of life
itself - all depends on individuals who have sympathy and use its
releasing powers.
    There opposite me the genial Irish doctor of the ship was
thawing a group, & now has moved on to the next.

The 'Adriatic' docked in New York on 7 May, and the historic occasion was at hand for both imperious master and hesitant disciple.
For close on five years they had exchanged ideas, made plans for
collaboration in Palestine and India, and almost met in London in
1920. Forty-three years later this account would appear in Mumford's autobiographical article, 'The Disciple's Rebellion':

My first glimpse of Geddes was at the White Star pier near 23rd
Street, on the other side of the customs' barrier: a little,
narrow-shouldered man, frail but wiry, with a flowing, gesticu-
lating beard and a head of flaring reddish-grey hair, parted in

> the middle: hot and impatient that warm morning, vexed that I
> had not got a ticket to take me past the customs' barrier, talk-
> ing in a rapid stream whose key sounds were muffled by the grey
> thicket of moustache and beard. (28)

The customs' barrier incident proved to be symbolic of their relations that summer.   P.G. had paid $200 in advance for secretarial
services, so that all of Mumford's time would be available: 'but
neither of us knew how to make use of our opportunity'.   'Somehow,
our companionship got off on the wrong foot; and we never managed
to fall in step afterwards.'

Three days after disembarking Geddes appeared in Cambridge, Massachusetts to deliver a lecture on town planning to the students of
the Harvard Schools of Architecture and Landscape Gardening, which,
according to Professor Hubbard, was 'very fine and stimulating'.   A
more lasting result of this visit is the excellent collection of
Geddesiana which Harvard possesses.   Indeed, in many respects Harvard has, along with the New York Public Library, a better Geddes
collection than the British Museum.

P.G. spent practically the whole summer of 1923 in New York, except
for occasional travels.   He had a reunion with his old friend G.
Stanley Hall, then living in retirement at Worcester, Massachusetts,
and again spent some days at Woods Hole at the marine biological
station for old times' sake.   Ever since student days at Roscoff he
felt particularly at home in these seaside stations.   While at
Woods Hole he met another old friend, James Mavor, who came from
Toronto to meet him.

As agent-secretary, Mumford had arranged for a few lectures in the
hinterland, but the main engagement was at the New School for Social
Research.   (Victor Branford had long ago warned him that P.G. had
neither the 'mediocrity nor the vocal power' to be a successful popular lecturer in the USA.)   Despite proximity, the personal contacts between P.G. and Mumford continued to have many ups and downs.
For one thing the master did not take time to get really acquainted
with his new disciple, as Branford had done in London,   Instead,
> Geddes started out by making a direct demand on me I was unpre-
> pared emotionally to fill, so that I put up my guard and never
> thereafter fully lowered it.   On the day after his arrival, in
> the basement lounge of the New School, which gave out on the
> garden, he took me squarely by the shoulders and gazed at me
> intently.   'You are the image of my poor dead lad,' he said to
> me with tears welling in his eyes, 'and almost the same age he
> was when he was killed in France.   You must be another son to
> me, Lewis, and we will get on with our work together.'

Reminiscing, Mumford makes a sharp judgment on Geddes, first for
letting his 'grief and desperation' lead him to overwhelm a young
stranger and find a 'wholly spurious physical likeness' between him
and Alasdair.   And second, for assuming that Alasdair would, if
spared, have become the father's 'docile junior partner, who would
carry through his hundred unfulfilled projects and tasks'.   'Those

who knew both father and son', says Mumford, 'realised that in this respect the imperious old man was wilfully dreaming.' Yet whatever the disciple's inner disappointments, the master carried on his accustomed routine quite unconscious, for the most part, of any difficulties.

His course of lectures at the New School lasted from 25 June to 4 August and covered the broad field of Geddesian City and Regional Planning. Even before the opening lecture P.G. was firmly established in the School's building on 24th Street, where a room had been provided 'for a few days'. Week after week passed; yet he not only did not move elsewhere but spread out his charts and maps, his manuscripts and diagrams until he, like the camel in the Arab's tent, literally had possession of the entire study building.

The lectures were rambling mixtures of telling stories, drawing blackboard diagrams, and expounding ideas. From experience acquired through almost fifty years of mature reading, travel and work, Geddes could illustrate whatever subject he happened to touch on with 'sociological anecdotes'. We learn from Mumford that the audience consisted 'mainly of young architects and the usual vague sprinkling of females', and that Geddes touched on all his customary themes. There was the valley-plan of civilisation, whereby he traced the evolution of fundamental occupations from mountains to sea and on into their complex offshoots in modern town and city. There were graphic outlines of human history and thinking-machines that made short work of biology, sociology, and psychology; and interwoven with all this ran the theme of cities as developing from natural conditions and the work of men, and of regional survey as the necessary first step towards controlling city development.

A social workers' weekly, the 'Survey', had the idea of making a series of articles out of these lectures in its monthly 'Survey Graphic' and sent a stenotypist to take them down and a department editor to check up on the steno. 'This turned out a terrible botch', says Mumford, 'the beard got in the way of the words, and he was far too discursive to be followed, all the more because he so constantly used the blackboard.' When the notes were finally handed to P.G., he could scarcely follow them himself. It took him the best part of a year of filling in and revision before there was anything resembling magazine articles, and nearly two years elapsed before they were published as 'Talks from My Outlook Tower', in six issues of the 'Survey Graphic' from February to September 1925.

Meanwhile both parties were dissatisfied: the writer because his thought had not been adequately presented; and the editor because of the inordinate expense. At one time even epistolary relations between the two were broken off, though not for long on P.G.'s part. (Yet by 1932 the 'Survey' put irritation aside to pay a tribute to Geddes in which he was described as a sociological counterpart to Francis Bacon.) (29) Nevertheless, the six existing articles, whose total wordage would make a small book, provide a mine of source material for anyone wishing to delve into didactic anecdotes,

ideas and interpretations which, however scattered at first reading,
are related in the full range of his conception of life and civilisation.

Despite the dust and noise of the neighbourhood and the almost complete lack of growing things, Geddes stayed on at the New School.
He hated these inhuman attributes of the modern unplanned city;   yet
had to accept them if he were to fight them.   His mission there as
a city-planner required him to be able to exist under adverse conditions just as he had fought the slums and fevers of India.   So P.G.
remained in New York throughout the heat of the summer when he might
have been enjoying a vacation in many a delightful rural spot with
old friends.

Discovering that his former right-hand man of the American branch of
the Paris Exposition school, Robert E. Ely, was now director of the
League for Political Education, Geddes tackled him with a project
for setting up an Outlook Tower on the top of Town Hall in West 43rd
Street.   Although even P.G. had to admit that unless Town Hall were
made into a skyscraper there would not be much to survey from its
top, the idea still had exciting possibilities in his optimistic
mouth.   What better means of educating the city's voters and officials than by making a complete study of their region, of its burden
of evil and its heritage of good?

About this time the Regional Planning Commission of New York completed the first year of its preliminary studies.   Thomas Adams,
British town-planner and general director of these surveys, was also
a friend of P.G.'s and the latter was invited to address the Commission's governors and staff.   He of course gave them his staple
advice about 'diagnosis before treatment' and 'constructive surgery', and worked out the valley plan of civilisation.   The commission was directing its main attention to the Place and Work factors
of the New York region, whereupon Geddes warned them not to neglect
the vital one of Folk.   To understand the social heritage of a city
was quite as important as to know its topography and economics, and
he left this final word: 'You must plan the city as though you were
working for a Labour Government!'

The results of P.G.'s third visit to the USA are, like those of his
two others, hard to measure objectively.   There were men such as
Benton MacKaye, author of 'The New Exploration' (1928), and Waldemar
Kaempffert, former director of the Chicago Museum of Science and industry and science editor of the New York 'Times', on both of whom
he made a lasting impression.   As an engineer, Kaempffert was particularly impressed by P.G.'s paleotechnic and neotechnic subdivisions of the industrial age.   MacKaye's book is an excellent though
anonymous brief for applying Geddesian geotechnics - including his
all-important biotechnics - to the rehabilitation of American
regions.   Yet regrettably, P.G.'s message of 1923 did not bear
clearly indentifiable published fruit until 1950-2 when MacKaye
wrote the series of articles 'From Geography to Geotechnics'.   He
there disclosed how his own many-sided interests as forester, wilderness conserver, regional planner and - a decade later - advisor

to the Tennessee Valley Authority had been coordinated and synergized
by meeting Geddes.   He also told how the mistaken advice of friends
and his own 'dictionary-inhibitions' had, for twenty years, kept him
from using 'the proper Geddesian term' - geotechnics (see p. 441).

(Conversely, the Russell Sage Foundation's group for the Regional
Survey of New York, to judge from their eight-volume report pub-
lsihed between 1927 and 1931, did not take P.G. seriously enough.
In any case, despite competent studies of communications, economic
problems, park areas, etc they did not produce an all-sided diagnosis and treatment of the human beings involved, in relation to
their heritages and burdens such as the Scot had shown was possible
- from Edinburgh to Indore, from Dunfermline to Jerusalem.)

Geddes spoke at meetings of the League for Industrial Democracy in
its summer camp in Pennsylvania and, according to Norman Thomas,
made a favourable if not startling impression.   Mr Thomas himself
first met Geddes through a friend of both men, Walter Fuller, who
long had been an ardent admirer of The Professor.   If he did not
convert the Russell Sage planners, he was effective in his individual contacts with the leading planners and architects of the
Regional Planning Association of America, an organisation that included Clarence S. Stein and Henry Wright, the future planners of
Radburn, one of America's most original contributions to town
planning.

'Geddes made a marvellous impression', Mumford reports, 'one memorable weekend when we met at the Hudson Guild Farm, near Netcong, New
Jersey.   I remember him sitting under a big tree in the woods,
cross-legged, telling about his Indian experiences, and looking himself like a true wise man from the East.'

As with Jane Addams of Hull House, P.G. had a friendship of many
years' standing with Lillian Wald of the Henry Street Settlement.
Miss Wald looked on him as a 'prophet and a great man' and has told
of 'never-to-be-forgotten visits with him - in New York, Connecti-
cut, and Washington'.

During P.G.'s many weeks in his 24th Street home base, Lewis Mumford
had frequent contact with him.
      But the collaboration that we were both hoping for didn't mater-
      ialize.   I was overwhelmed by him; our rhythms of work and
      thought were entirely different, and I couldn't bear to be talked
      at for hours at a time.   Consequently we didn't get along well
      together, and I disappointed him.   Even my secretaryship was
      carried on with a sense of frustration, for he would often
      absent-mindedly make two appointments for the same hour - in
      addition to the one I had made! (30)

Even more aggravating was the curious trait that led Geddes to
spend much time with casual strangers, neglecting opportunities with
Mumford, and on one occasion to forget completely an invitation to
his home.
      Somehow, it is symptomatic of the strain and tension that existed

between us that, after promising to spend a whole Sunday with my
wife and me in our little apartment on Brooklyn Heights, visiting our home for the first time, he entirely forgot the engagement and never even phoned. (31)

Though no direct collaboration like that with J. Arthur Thomson and
with Victor Branford was possible, something lastingly valuable did
result.   'In general', Mumford has explained, 'Geddes gave me the
frame for my thinking: my task has been to put flesh on his abstract skeleton.'   Among the acknowledgments in 'The Culture of
Cities' (1938) he states:

> even more than in 'Technics and Civilization', my chief intellec-
> tual debt is to my master, Patrick Geddes.   To take over
> Geddes's contributions in block, however, would be to betray
> their organic nature.   Not mimicry and automatic acceptance, but
> a vital assimilation, was what Geddes sought; for to him think-
> ing was a function of living, not a sequestered sort of play.
> While I have sometimes utilized Geddes's bold summaries and short
> cuts, I have never felt bound to respect the mere letter of his
> teaching, nor to give its details the same emphasis that they had
> in his own schemata.   Many disciples slay or betray their mas-
> ters while they are still alive, perhaps *because* they are still
> alive.   By waiting till Geddes's death before embarking on these
> systematic works, I perhaps avoided that sad necessity.

After his first foray to Harvard and to Clark University early in
May 1923, P.G. realised that on this visit, unlike 1900, 'I must not
lay myself out for lecturing (despite desirability of boiling pot!)
but rather learn & reconnoitre'.   Letters to Norah (mid-June to
mid-August, 1923) reflect this theme as well as his encounters with
well-known Americans.

> In this place, at once so magnificent & so frightful, I feel more
> a student than ever, yet with ideas getting clearer towards
> books....
>
> I have no doubt much to learn of the devt's of Behaviourism,
> and am looking forward to meeting Prof John B. Watson, who is to
> give a course on this at same time as my own in this School.
>
> (I have been reading John Dewey's 'Reconstruction in Philo-
> sophy' & 'Human Nature & Conduct' - & with cordial agreement: in
> fact he has quite a lot of the text for my diagrams, & converse-
> ly.   We have had one brief talk, but agreed to meet again after
> his holiday.)

In another letter Geddes reports having 'friendly chats, often with
keen people'.   One of these was Dr Cassius Kayser,

> Prof. Math. here whose 'Human Worth of Rigorous Thinking' you
> should get from Library, for you & Frank to whet your wits on!
> He thinks my thinking machines wd be 'epoch-making', & presses
> getting them out.

Again he tells Norah that the opportunity of being free in 'this
vast gridiron town *bigton* of America' may turn out 'like the first
months of freedom in India which were so helpful to subsequent
work'.

> And just as I am 'hustling the East' in India, so here I am an
> Indian in America - a quiet old Oriental, taking in impressions,
> & considering the ideas which they call up from day to day, one
> quiet morning after another.

Typical of Geddes's planning foresight is the comment made in a
letter to Mumford months before coming to New York.   He reviewed
his 'historic formula of City Development' whereby the ever-expand-
ing Metropolis becomes in turn Mega-polis, Parisito-polis, Patholo-
polis, and finally Necro-polis.   For those who dreamed of 'New York
at 47,000,000 and the whole East coast conurbation at 500 millions',
he urged reflection upon the final stage of 'City of Death'.

In addition to what he saw at first hand during this summer, twenty-
three years after his last visit in 1900, P.G. found confirmation of
his prophecy in the writings of Guglielmo Ferrero.   'What a Roman
Empire this is!' he exclaimed to Norah:
> Get Ferrero's book....   Not his History of *Rome* (as an American)
> but his discussion of *America* (32) (as new Caesaristic etc.
> Rome).   Still, if so, there are spiritualising elements scat-
> tered in catacombs, & this School is one of these.)

He made another trip to Harvard before his return sailing to Liverpool in August.   Stanley Hall was away, but he had further discussions with George Sarton, Editor of 'Isis', (partly to prepare for
impending talks with Henri Bergson in Paris) and he stayed for two
nights in Cambridge with 'Prof Dana ... who is Longfellow's grandson ... in his interesting ancestral home'.   He also visited Emerson's home at Concord.

Meanwhile, the master-disciple relationship was still far from satisfactory.   In a letter of early July the disciple protested that
they 'had never met' and that Geddes's images of him were not correct.   He was neither P.G.'s earlier hoped-for 'vigorous young
apprentice who might work at the same bench with you' nor the
'clever young hack writer, rather sullen in temperament' whom a
disappointed P.G. seemed to find when they finally met.   The
master, in his reply, 'rose to the occasion ... with overwhelming
insight and magnanimity: not angry, but sorry over his own apparent failure to take me in;   realising "only too sadly" the gap
between our generations.'

There was a brief reconciliation and meeting of personalities, but
then P.G. 'fell back into the old soliloquy ... '
> As the moment for his departure came nearer, our relations got
> even worse: for he felt obliged to use these last weeks in
> drilling me, yes, drilling me, in the elements of his systematic
> graphs and diagrams.   That, from the fierce opponent of
> drill! (33)

Despite his resentment at having to cram P.G.'s thinking machines
and be examined in them, Mumford secretly looked forward, as reward
for submission, 'to at least one day of his undivided attention;
but it never came'.   Instead, their parting was a complete fiasco.

On his last evening before sailing at midnight, the master went out
to dinner and left the disciple with the 'dreary task of packing his
bags and papers - those heaps of clothes, those middens of notes and
charts, those shelves of new books!'

> By the time eleven o'clock came, I was tired, and too sick at
> heart to retain the reproachful fury I had felt earlier in the
> evening.   When Geddes came back, I found a taxi and put his bags
> into it, but I refused to accompany him the few blocks to the
> pier.   For a moment he began to protest and urge me; but he
> must have sensed my bitter disappointment; for he let me go.
> We shook hands hastily on the sidewalk and the taxi rolled off.

RETURN TO EUROPE

In November 1923 Geddes and his son Arthur turned up in Bombay as
professor and assistant, respectively.   Arthur had spent the summer
at Santiniketan working at Tagore's embryonic university and gathering material for a socio-geographical doctoral thesis.   He had also
helped Leonard Elmhirst, an English agricultural expert from Cornell
University, with his projects for renewing this rural area of
Bengal.   Elmhirst wanted Arthur to stay on, whereas P.G. encouraged
him to continue in sociology with him.   'Much to be said on both
sides', the father had written to Norah in August, 'so I am leaving
him to decide'.

Regarding the American disciple, there is a strange lag in correspondence after Geddes's departure from New York.   It was the end
of November before Mumford addressed a letter to 'Dear Master' to
say that Mabel Barker had told him 'what good form you were in when
you passed through London'.   Significantly, he added, 'and from
your silence I conjecture that you have had few vacant moments on
any part of the trip'.   He told of offering 'Dramatisations' to
Boni & Liveright 'on any terms they might care to handle it for, and
they refused altogether', and of then starting it on the rounds to
minor publishers 'with the faint hope that something may finally be
done with it'.

In early February 1924 P.G. replied to 'Dear Lewis' with these lines
of apology and information:
> Is it possible I haven't written since I returned?   I thought I
> had!   However I sometimes think letters - & then by and by come
> to imagine them written - so if you have not heard, that is a
> likely alternative hypothesis to blaming the P.O. system.
>   I stayed only a week end with Branford on returning, & a day
> or two also at Edinburgh: went on to Brussels, to old friend
> Otlet.   Then to Paris for discussions with Bergson over Inter-
> national Intellectual Relations - & with Paul Desjardins on
> things in general: cheered up too by seeing old friend Schrader
> - the grand old man of Geography who has completed his great
> atlas at last....
>   Then Geneva for a week - looking into L. of N. - & Labour
> Office.   On the whole favourably impressed - as per summary of
> lectures I am sending you.   What do you think of them as the

outline of a book?   Give me your impressions - why should reviewers always wait till they're too late to be of any use! (34)

Patrick Geddes was then teaching his last term at the University of
Bombay, both because of the terms of his contract, and because of
illness.   He had arrived from Europe at the beginning of November,
being met at the ship by Arthur and an Indian friend, and at his
lodgings by masses of letters.   But the climate of India was now
definitely a threat to his health:
   Very busy here when I got back - then attack of colitis neglected
   until very serious - packed off to Nursing Home for 3 weeks, then
   near fortnight in hills.   Getting on all right till chill the
   other day - now on my back with touch of fever (malaria) which
   makes one very weak ... ' (35)

Later that same month he is:
   about all right again getting the last germs of fever (now quite
   over) dislodged from their last lurking places in spleen & spinal
   cord by a new drug....   Also being massaged daily by the powerful barber of the Nursing Home ... an Indian expert answering
   curiously to your osteopaths, & who unstiffens the old back etc -
   & has made me with a month's treatment quite keen for exercise....
   So there's life in the old dog yet!

He informs Mumford that Arthur will wind up the Exhibition in Bombay
as well as the planning for Lucknow and Tagore's University.
   He has meantime shaped into a keen writer - & after these 3 win-
   ters with me, has got hold of main ideas, & is convinced he can
   put them better than I do - into less unreadable form than mine
   - in which view he seems to be right: So it looks as if I were
   getting my long-needed collaborator... (36)

'I am a little concerned about LSD [£.s.d]', Geddes writes, 'as both
my sources of income now come to an end shortly (Chair, & Indian
Town Planning), so may have to sell my Exhib'n.'   He wonders
whether Mumford can find a buyer, saying the price would have to be
$15,000 '(or at least $12,500)'.   Other possibilities would be to
arrange for an itinerant showing at several cities.   Again Arthur
is brought into the picture, for such an exhibition would require
an expert guide-lecturer.   'I don't know that I should face this
now - but my son can now explain it as well as I, & more popularly.'

Concern about his future work is expressed in many of Geddes's
letters ever since his return to India in November 1923.   In a
lengthy epistle to Branford marked 'urgently practical', he proposes Geneva as
   may be the likeliest centre for one's remaining activities,
   though of course from there I should hope to come, and at least
   yearly, to Paris & Brussels, London & Edin'h: & perhaps again to
   U.S.A. sometimes.
      The weakness of the L. of N., and Labour Office too, is that
   those have no sociology, nor civics either to speak of!   Why
   not try to focus on supplying both?
      But how is this to be done?...   How about forming a contact

with Univ. of Geneva? and on other side with L. of N. organisa-
tions?   Brit. & U.S. especially?...
     In short an Institute of 'Sociology, Etho-Politics and
Civics', in connection with Univ., yet near L. of N. & new Labour
Office. (37)

As for 'What popular name?', he proposes: 'Univ. of Geneva Peace
Institute, or Peace Research Institute?'   The only difficulty
Geddes could see in the way of this vast plan was the attitude and
aims of 'F.O.'s', the Foreign Offices of League members.   His and
Branford's peace organisation would not exclude the Germans but be
open to 'all men of good will';   hence there might be 'a danger of
knife from F.O.'s etc'.   Nevertheless, he concludes his sixth page
of enthusiastic plans by reassuring himself and Branford that they
would not be abandoning any of their past endeavours but rather
'forming the central ganglion for better innervation of these'.

Geddes sent three letters to Branford before departing from Bombay,
one of which concerned the latter's 'Science and Sanctity' and
another lamented the poor sales of that book and of his own best
works, on Dunfermline and Indore.   The former is now, '20 years
after ... lying as unsold remainder stock with John Grant, George
IV Bridge, though himself a leading specialist in getting rid of
such!'
     Yet the book has not been ineffective - in educating Town Plan-
     ning Movement from John Burns (who therefore put me up for Delhi)
     to Unwin, Abercrombie, etc.:   i.e. it helped them to see a city
     in cultural aspects, - and you and others too.
     So 'Indore' volumes also unsold, and unwanted (?).   Yet it
     got me the Jerusalem job, - besides continuing the above educa-
     tional process. (38)

For nine pages more P.G. speculates about how to get good reviews,
reach such 'live men' as are open to ideas and how find able
women.   '... though I know "Cherchez la femme"!   I can't find
her!'   He also asks why there is such opposition to their ideas,
and whether,
     you can focus and define the general dislike of me you record:
     e.g. of editors of Discovery, (of whom I know nothing mostly.)
     And why, exactly, that outburst of Seth's to Mackenzie? etc,
     And so on.
     Of course I've been all my life accustomed to it in Edinburgh,
     in Dundee too, in St. Andrews, etc, etc. but I'd like to under-
     stand it a little!
     You see I'm not asking because it worries me - for it really
     doesn't!   I'm not a bit interested in public opinion or reputa-
     tion, and rather take disapproval, all my life, as a compliment,
     and as confirmation of problems and theories, schemes and tasks.
     But now that I am coming home (sailing I hope in March) and
     coming out more into the open, it would be useful to understand a
     little better and more concretely than I do - who are one's en-
     emies? and why?   What personal grounds sometimes - what general
     ones, e.g. a disturber of the peace?

P.G. as an Indian Guru
(Bombay 1923)

Farewell gathering for Patrick Geddes, Bombay's first Professor of
Civics and Sociology, March 1923. He is standing fifth from left.
Seated at left are Arthur Geddes and Gopal Advani (later secretary
of the Scots College, Montpellier)

The Indian students had a farewell gathering for their professor
with speeches and gifts, and when writing to Norah two days before
sailing, Geddes mentions a silver rose bowl which he has sent to
her.   'Perhaps I'll want it back if I ever have a little nest of my
own, but use it meanwhile.' (39)

On the back of the same sheet Arthur added on 15 March that he had
just 'seen Daddy off' and that he had no fever.   'He has sterilised
milk for the voyage ... and may really be well by Genoa.   He's not
allowed to eat solids, it's true, but he *can* rest & so the doctor
has no anxiety.   I'm so pleased.'

Thus did Patrick Geddes, almost nine-and-a-half years after his
first arrival, leave that vast Oriental sub-continent whose villages, cities and temples he had come to know in a way few, if any,
other Europeans did.   Not only had he spent months and years in
studying and re-planning the homes and cities of India's people as
his fellow human beings but had incessantly spoken out for their
liberation from Western and British mis-education and mis-culture.

At the same time he did not forget European problems or those of the
interlying countries like Palestine.

Nearly a decade ago, when turning sixty on his first outward sailing
through the Red Sea, he had had a virile and optimistic vision of
the years ahead.   Now he could look back on some of his best
achievements and challenges, yet those years had also taken away his
elder son and most promising colleague, and cruelly ended the love
and partnership of his and Anna's pioneering home in James Court and
of their 'Seven-towered Castle' on the High Street.

Chapter 10

'LATE-FLOWERING AGAVE', 1924-8

RECOVERY IN MONTPELLIER

When the Peninsula & Orient steamer from Bombay docked in Marseilles
early in April 1924, it was an utterly enfeebled Patrick Geddes who
had to be helped on to the train for Montpellier.   Despite his
Bombay doctor's optimism the voyage had not been one of that happy
convalescence which many times had been his lot.   Instead he was on
his back 'mostly all the 18 days to Genoa - only in last days up on
deck for a few hours but never at dinner in cabin.   Milk diet'.
Yet he claimed it was not illness, but 'utter weakness & lassitude -
a full experience of old age, such as never before!' (1)

In Montpellier he was taken to a 'pension of old folks & invalids'
which he found very melancholy, and not until 20 April (Easter
Sunday) could he write to Norah that he was 'really on the mend'.
He knew she was 'sorry for the poor old dad in this long & weary
breakdown', but assured her that it was relieved by reading '& even
by almost daily, though brief, progresses of thinking'.   Daily in-
jections of 'neurasthenic serum' were helping, appetite was returning and also 'desire of some daily exercise'.

In fact, he had 'been to Suzanne's church with her on Good Friday
afternoon ... and was sufficiently impressed ... to go back alone
yesterday morning, & again with her this afternoon!'   (Anna and
P.G. had hoped that Suzanne, née Charmont, would be Alasdair's
fiancée, but some years after his death she had, still sorrowing,
married a Dr Bousquet, himself a war invalid.)   Her church was that
of Abbé Prévost, well known for its music and boys' orphanage
school.   The Abbé was a 'Great fellow!   I must tell you about him
when I come.   The best school as to garden, & zoo!, I have ever
seen;   and singing too, so far as I can judge.'

A week later P.G. wrote a veritable epistle of melancholy to Lilian
Brown (a spinster acquaintance from the Edinburgh Summer Meetings
with whom he had begun a rather curious correspondence in 1921).
At the Montpellier 'pension' he wishes he could write to her as he
felt,

but the long stern discipline of science make us poor old students unable to write outside their pages & style! Shut out from music, seldom now seeing a picture that speaks to me, outside all the religious faiths, away from the few surviving friends, and with one's dearest dead, the world is saddened, and even the spring, opening here, is not what it was in happier days.

He is going out that afternoon 'for an hour or two on the "garrigue" (the heath of the south) with my one surviving friend [Charles Flahault] of forty years ago and more - our first ramble together - & perhaps our last.... Alas, I am letting myself go after all, & in melancholy! - which perhaps I'll escape when I go out.' He plans to leave soon for the Swiss cure place at Territet which Victor Branford and his wife recommend highly but hopes 'in June to come and see you in your home [in London] ... like a properly affectionate U P [Uncle Pat].'

Further evidence of P.G.'s beginning convalescence is found in a letter to Lewis Mumford of late April. Although complaining of 'no sustained energy even for correspondence', he manages to fill over three folio pages with closely written lines on many subjects in addition to his illness. He hopes 'the needed energy for writing may return ... since now I have neither chair nor practice!' On the other hand, he has 'more calls for unpaid work than ever - say four chairs if I could fill them! - at Paris, Brussels, London, Edin'h'.

Bad news from India of my remaining practice. E.g. court intrigue around Nizam [of Hyderabad] has (temporarily I trust) knocked out University & probably myself (& Mears too) permanently. Other worries & losses too - But as sign of convalescence, these troubles invigorate.

As if to prove this point he starts a defence of certain diagrams which Mumford has criticised.

Such highly condensed generality needs endless explanations for its appreciation & use: & it needs long talks beyond compass of a letter. Yet see (& say) if this does not help towards clearness:

The main point, I take it, for you & for others, is that all this sort of thing seems so personal to me - idiomatic, individual & so on.

But what was at first more personal than the notations of 'Mercator', at first the exclusive patent of that particular Chapman of ideas! - and so uninteresting and abstract to his contemporaries, fascinated by the concrete interest of new geographical discoveries!

At first sight his blank diagram of squares was mere dullness & emptiness & lacking in all the concrete knowledge of the old charts, let alone the vividness of the old pictures & descriptions of many lands. But by & by people understood how it showed all the world & for the first time with the relations, the respective positions, of such land & sea reasonably clear.

Yet even now, how few can really read a map? Not merely to

recognise places, but to *see*, & each place in its position - & with its regions & cities, thus evocable, to their detail.

At the end of this letter P.G. comments on his own conversation as being 'a run of footnotes & allusions and suggestions from personal to general, from concrete to philosophical'.   Much the same could be said of his correspondence, though he varied both subject matter and treatment according to the person written to.   For example, after his walk on the garrigue that afternoon in April he mentions to Norah that he has found 'an amusing ploy in planning' but with no details.   To Mumford he says nothing about the matter, yet not many days later, as he journeyed to his cure at Territet (where Branford was to join him), Geddes reveals to Lilian Brown that

> I have found a 'ploy' ... in an old cottage on the nearest garrigue to Montpellier - half an hour's walk from edge of town....   There are $2\frac{1}{2}$ acres of ground from heath to a few young olives & vines, 200 or so, & thus a sample of whole Mediterranean region for the botanist & farmer alike....   The great attractions are the fine views all round: northern to hills (Cevennes etc) & south, to the best possible view of the old city, projected against the Mediterranean. (2)

After telling that his old botanist friend Flahault, to whom he has long sent his best students 'as well as own young folks', had seen him off at the station, P.G. turns to general and philosophic implications.   It will be a place where old friends can gather - 'perhaps you will try a stay there?', and possibly the 'beginning of a centre for northern studies, & of international developments more extensive'.

> The purchase is not completed, & may still fall through, but I think not.   I am even enquiring about nearby heath but fear it may be quite beyond my little savings.   Anyway here is an example of how to convalesce, & how to lay the ghosts of the past, *by acting & planning towards the future*.   Any amount better than the self-centred thought & training of the psychoanalysts.

Later that summer Lewis Mumford wrote to Victor Branford about a package of P.G.'s manuscripts which he had just found and gone through.   Some of them were fragmentary, others were 'full of valuable reflections and diagrams', and Mumford was afraid that in twenty years they would become undecipherable because of the poor quality of the paper and because 'the key to some of the thoughts will have been lost'.

> Moreover, in their present form - little sheets of paper, big sheets, empty sheets, huge charts, and repetitions - Geddes's notes are too complicated for even his own mind to grasp easily. No room could hold them; no merely human brain could wade through them or knit them together.   Thus there is a huge physical obstacle in the way of the Opus.
>   On the other hand, even without systematic elucidation, the notes tell a great story by themselves: I never read them without a fresh illumination, without a fresh influx of power and an ability to seize my own life and my own intellectual problems

more vigilantly.   Is it not high time that something was done
with these vast accumulations: FIRST, to preserve them; SECOND,
to make them accessible.   How could this be done? (3)

What Branford replied is not known, but back in Montpellier some
three months later, P.G. himself tells Mumford that it was very kind
of him to suggest 'the writing up of my old notes'.

> it is true there must be a good many thousands of pages! most of
> which will/may [sic] never get written.   Yet these are mostly
> jottings by the way - products of sleep on waking & though I
> don't re-read them, & fail to arrange, their writing fixes a
> good many ideas for further incorporation into the ever-growing
> web.   To get that written is the main problem - & largely why I
> am making a winter home here. (4)

This last statement was, it would turn out, one more of the self-
delusions which are found in many of Geddes's letters from the
Indian period on.   Moreover, the same letter contains enough evidence of his real intentions - and also of his state of health - to
make anyone reading it sceptical.

> I fancy my varied restaurant life, in N.Y., was not very good
> for me - and early in winter in Bombay I got run down - then
> dangerously ill - with colitis, but so severe that good specia-
> list told me afterwards he thought he might lose me.   However,
> 3 weeks of his nursing home & several in country brought me
> round - but soon with relapse & fever - touch of malaria - 3
> weeks more - after which he turned me out of Bombay for Europe.
> Very weak on voyage - long rest, 2 months, here at Montpellier -
> then month in Switzerland with V.B. at sanatorium - thus again
> seeming OK - but after spurt of writing a book ('Biology', with
> J.A. Thomson - Home University Series, January issue) I had a
> minor relapse in September.   Then better - Congress of Reli-
> gions in London - & busy time with Otlet re his Geneva schemes.
> Then here.

After a few words on what he is doing 'here', P.G. has to turn to
other correspondence, for 'there is trouble at Jerusalem University' and he is again enlisting the help of Mrs Joseph Fels.*   The
letter closes on an unusually personal note:

> Cordial remembrances to Mrs Mumford - (whom I have seen so little
> - & I think of often with regret & even shame for failing her
> hospitality that time!)   Always yours, P. Geddes.

'THE MAPPING OF LIFE' ... 'A WHOLE RESEARCH COLLEGE'

The two months between Switzerland and P.G.'s return to Montpellier
were, as noted in his brief summary, well filled with activities.
While his quick recovery from colitis, malaria, debility and long

---

* In July 1920 Geddes had written her a long, informative letter
from Jerusalem, quoted in Mairet's biography (pp. 186-9) as a revelation of the spirit of his planning in Palestine.

over-work is something of a medical mystery, his thoughts and doings followed a by-now very predictable pattern.   The successful completion of 'Biology' with Thomson was mainly due to the latter's tenacity and sacrifice of much free time.   But the lecture on 'Dream and the Deed - Religion on the Map of Life' at the Congress of Religions in London in late September was his own doing, though inspired by Branford's preoccupation with this subject.   In fact, the Congress itself was arranged jointly by the Sociological Society and the School of Oriental Studies.   The July 1924 issue of the 'Sociological Review' had carried a preview of this lecture, entitled 'The Mapping of Life', in which Geddes not only propagandised for the use of graphics in general but also demonstrated how, in his extended chart, the spiritual aspects of life could be expressed as well as the physical.

The two basic triads of Place-Work-Folk and of Sense-Experience-Feeling are completed by two more nine-squared diagrams.*   One is the triple 'Chord of the Inner Life', Emotion-Ideation-Imagination, and the other the expression of these longings, thoughts and dreams by the corresponding triad of deeds: Etho-Polity, Synergy and Achievement.   (The resulting diagram of thirty-six squares is shown in the Appendix.)   The third triad is compared to a cloister of religion, thought and art:

> To whoever has fully entered the religious cloister ... there is no returning to the simple everyday life of place and work and folk, of sense, experience and feeling alone....   For whether we be men of today or of old, if once at home in any of the retreats of living religion, in the studies or laboratories of the sciences, or in a studio of the artistic dream, we are henceforth content to abide.   This was the Limbo where Dante saw the sages, the thinkers, the poets of the pre-Christian past.   And here, too, we are beginning to build the University of the Future.

But P.G. is not content with placing all sorts of emotionals, intellectuals and religious in 'this varied cloister of the Inner Life'. He finds doors that open out 'once more into the objective world', and these make the fourth triad of Etho-Polity, Synergy and Achievement.

In his September lecture in London he gives examples of how usual norms of behaviour may even be put aside. (5)   The natural 'folk-feeling' of an infant's love for its mother can be negated, or superseded, by a 'newly developed yet maturer range of feeling. In this the old ties are strained, well nigh to breaking.'

> One day, the gentlest of sons says to his gentlest and most loving of mothers the most terrible thing son can ever say to mother: 'Woman! what have I to do with thee?'   Why does he say this? - 'I must be about my father's business!'   Here, typically presented, is the great life-crisis of feeling.
>   Thus too Buddha forsakes his wife and child, his father and

* See illustration from the 'Indian Journal of Economics', used on p. 321.

his kingdom.   Thus also Moses breaks his Egyptian ties, though strong and great and full of promise from earliest infancy;   thus Muhammad separates from his kindred.

Geddes shows how deterioration tends to set in in all religions when agreement upon doctrine becomes 'more important than their emotive guidance towards a common and intensifying love.   Doctrines thus fix to dogmas.   Correspondingly, Symbols crystallize'.   Each religion 'is ever menaced from within', even though its own faithful are not aware of its deterioration.

> But this becomes increasingly manifest to external faiths, since it is always easy to discern the errors and faults of others; while we may 'rationalize', and thus justify, our own.   The mutual intolerance of historic religions is thus intelligible; the rarity of their mutual conversions also.   And hence the study of comparative religion too often readily gives an impression of coldness, as if it were but the latest form of palaeontography and palaeography.   For each and every religion can only be studied from within.   However strange to us, we must enter into it, heartily, that is, not only intelligently and respectfully, but even lovingly.

While much of P.G.'s mapping of life involves old diagrams and concepts, he also calls for a psycho-social diagnosis of both 'neurasthenic' rural areas and 'hysteric' urban ones to supplement the psycho-analysis of certain of their inhabitants.   The latter are, after all, 'but extreme cases of a mental disharmony from which we all are suffering more or less'.   His goal is a World-Eutopia in which the 'vague Utopias of the past and present' will be replaced by 'definite and realisable Eutopias, regional and civic'.   To illustrate his own approach to one element of Eutopia, the Temple, he asserts that even

> without definite confessional adhesion, the designer may work by turns for many faiths;   since so far entering into the spirit of each as the supreme creation of its time, and still of vital appeal;   and realizing, with each new experience, the lesson given to Peter from his vision of the net;   that 'in every nation, he that feareth God and doeth righteousness, is accepted of Him.'

Regarding his work in Dublin, Geddes writes 'that it was a gratifying surprise to the planner of this cathedral - since not of its historic and dogmatic faith - to find its design congenial to, and even cordially accepted by, the responsible hierarchy'.   He credits the validity and completeness of his Chart of Life for this acceptance.   Another example of the 'many-sided renewal of the religious life, and along with the advance of intellectual harmony' is 'the design for the central temple of the Bahai faith for India'.

> For here my able colleague, Mr. Frank Mears, has peculiarly succeeded in giving lucid form and expression to its essential doctrine of peculiarly sympathetic (not simply tolerant) appreciation of other faiths of which it is not necessary to abandon membership.   Hence nine entrances for these, each with its domed chapel, and symbolic pool of pure water, as appreciative symbol

of the enduring values recognized in older faiths.   These all
have entrances to the central dome; of which the inner roof is
supported by a central pillar - symbol of unity - and enclosing
a stairway, open to all to ascend to the ambulatory above.   The
emotional life of brotherhood, and in intellectual unity, thus
here finds a fresh symbolic expression in architectural form:
the full chord of inner life is thus presented fully in this new
cloister, even cathedral, of the ever-renewing spirit.

P.G. defines 'Etho-Polity' as the vitalised social group which
arises when some great initiator emerges from his retreat and in-
spires disciples 'with a new and full intensity of emotional
appeal'.
    A new type of community is thus born: no mere folk-group, but
    of it matters not what folk-origins: the essential bond being
    'not according to the flesh but to the spirit'.   This new type
    of group thus needs a type-name; and as fundamentally of ethic
    bond, yet social purpose, let us call this an Etho-Polity.   Its
    inspiring moral purpose unites it around its leader, indeed often
    all the more strongly when his bodily presence passes away;
    since his influence remains, and even grows.   The Etho-Polity
    thus increases, and acts upon the social world, bringing over new
    members from the folk into its fold.

Then he asks what happened when there were true Etho-Polities in
Athens and Jerusalem.
    When Solomon in his wisdom rules, what is then the Achievement?
    The building of the Temple.   And in the Etho-Polity of Athens,
    headed by Pericles the wise?   The building of the Parthenon.
    In brief, then, Sacred Art!...   Yet the greatest Temple is,
    after all, but the culminant folk-Place; as so conspicuously
    for Jews and Greeks throughout their history, as for simpler
    people too; in fact, for every village of East or West.

Geddes promises, 'if circumstances permit', to attempt a more specific charting of 'the particular religions' at the next Conference
of Living Religions.   Meanwhile, he ends his paper with a highly
condensed subjunctive phrase reminiscent of the final lines of his
'Classification of Statistics' over forty years earlier:
    Enough, then, for the present here, if the above-outlined ele-
    mental concept of religion be clear, in its most general and
    fundamental psychological and ethico-social terms as the bringing
    and binding together of men, by bonds of sympathy, and of syn-
    thesis, into a community of fellowship and of doctrine, appro-
    priately imaged.

After this conference Geddes has a 'busy time with Otlet re his
Geneva schemes', and in mid-October he writes to Branford, an
'Active time here in Paris'.   That morning P.G. awoke 'at 4 a.m.
with an answer to Mumford's proposal' of the previous July for
preserving his notes, which he hadn't had time to think about
before, 'since a little choked off by idea of mere conservation v.
clarification'.
    As you know I'm egoistic enough at thinking about problems &

tasks in my own way without reference to opinions or proprieties
of others - but not I think as to my own pot or pocket or status
or the like - which I've practically never thought about at all.
   But here is a fearfully ambitious scheme come to light - and
curiously like Tagore's!
   needed
   wanted   'A whole Research College of Collaborators!'
   Possible!

Whereupon Geddes set up on paper a team of colleagues like the original one at the Outlook Tower, and with many of the same names.
Rachel Annand Taylor could take over his 'History accumulations ...
& continue "Dramatisations"....   Paul Reclus might still be willing
to renew the "historic Chart" ... Lewis Mumford might do something,
could he but be paid something....'

In short, he outlined a super-partnership, with a rosy future for
all concerned: providing Mears with a part-time fellowship 'would
produce his amazing dreams - Parnass-olympus etc. (greatest design
in history of architecture!)'; Paul Reclus would 'pass on his dull
pot boiling as a technical translator - & renew his youth with us';
and so on for old and new collaborators, though J. Arthur Thomson
was not mentioned.   Geddes also named 'two distinct allies' recently gained in the publishing field: Gordon and Minchin of
Williams & Norgate, 'and similarly Paul Kellogg, Editor of "Survey".
Again he vows to get down to doing books himself.
   Between writing for 'Survey' & with J.A.T., I am stirred up for
   writing much more than ever.   It was not good enough to be so
   isolated from you, & only doing my part in Making of Future books
   away in India, between or among town-plannings - & with these
   necessarily in the foreground!   But now you must slack off in
   business - & so realise more fully the cooperation & collaboration we so long ago began - & are largely made for, though never
   able properly to adjust in our driven conditions....   These are
   now abating for me - & so I trust they are becoming for you.
The Paris letter ends here with no conclusion or signature, so it
may have been, like others, never finished or posted.

SCOTS COLLEGE, 1924

Not many days later P.G. was back in Montpellier, out on his favourite bit of heath northwest of the city.   His new address is
given to Lilian Brown early in November as *Collège des Ecossais,
Garrigue des Brusses,* Montpellier (Hérault) France', along with
the gist of his new project.
   Very busy here - this will be the most interesting & varied of
   all my houses & gardens - a very minor Ramsay Garden as yet, but
   with possibilities even larger - & my three acres here will correspondingly make the most varied of gardens....   Yesterday I
   bought a little house fully half a mile away, behind next hilltop, so out of sight - four, sufficient annexes, & $\frac{7}{8}$ acre of
   meadow-park around, suitable for tree-planting etc, and by
   auction for exactly £50!   I am now offered the better house on

the hilltop just above that one, with 6 or 8 acres (not yet
measured) for about £400.

At present only Arthur & myself - but besides him two other
candidates for D.Sc. degree may come in after Xmas, & I expect
my niece Mary, & old friends with her also on visit here next
week, rough though things are.   If you come after New Year's
with Miss Ida [Lilian's sister], I'll be pleased to put you up -
until your new house is ready. (6)

P.G. thought the £400 house might be suitable for the sister to buy
and repair and that 'she might become a great recruit to our group,
& take over our agricultural side, milk, eggs, rabbits etc, as well
as gardening for my probably growing family!'   He also suggested
that Lilian ought to escape from her present 'medical & medico-psy-
chological environment into that here'.   The interest of getting
things done and being in the open air as much as possible 'will do
far more for your health & peace of mind than London ever can!'

A letter of early December 1924 is P.G.'s classic description and
justification of the Montpellier scheme.   It was quoted nearly in
full in 'The Interpreter Geddes' as having been written especially
to its author, but 'Dear Lewis & Missus' in New York received an
identical copy on which 'Dear' was typed and their names filled in
by hand.   Internal evidence suggests that it was originally intended for Mabel Barker.   'So when you personally conduct Banabhard to
Italy, pause ye here awhile.'   (Mabel was a friend of 'Banabhard',
Rachel Annand Taylor.)   Copies were apparently sent to others. (7)
In any case, its writer was then in top form.

  Here now these seven weeks, hard at work building and gardening,
  and with constant supervision of both: half a dozen gardeners
  at it - not to speak of masons, joiners, tilers etc.   I've not
  had such a time since making D'ee [Dundee] garden, and building
  Ramsay Garden - for though of course this is a much smaller
  affair, it is more complex.

He describes the setting of his *Collège des Ecossais:* the garrigue,
old quarry, terraces being reclaimed, the 'indispensable Bois de
Pins' or pine grove which has to be planted, the olive orchard and
the vineyard to be cared for, and so on.

  So you see I'm greatly pleased with place, and with myself, as
  again happily at real *work* - open air all day long - and bed
  after bread and milk supper - say 8 p.m. - to begin next day with
  a spate of thinking, from 5.4.3. (or 2.) a.m. as the case may be,
  and before going up to work, at 7 or 7.30 or 8.   I am only writing today - and the first non-business letter for long - because
  it is pouring, and no one can work!   (We have had the edge of
  the great N.W. European storm here - and beyond local memory they
  say).   In short, I am again realising *vivendo discimus!* - and
  even *Creando pensamus.*)

      Also I hope here to illustrate and develop my theory of varia-
  tion   in planting out - indeed I dream anew of
          veg.   floral
getting at my long-laboured botanic *opus*, entombed since I left
Dundee and indeed never cleared up there.

So I might ramble on, for here are dreams emerging towards
deeds, and some of the high Gestes I've failed to do opening out
for a new try at each!   e.g. University Hall, Edinburgh and
Crosby (each in its way failure, though I hope towards new ava-
tars) improved on here;   and as experimental type for new Universities and old ones;   And *Collège des Ecossais* for renewed
siege of that at Paris.

Geddes also hopes to re-awaken the ancient University of Montpellier, 'La Belle au Bois Dormant', which like all others is too much
engaged in the 'rancidising, fossilising & dis-specialising' of
Religion, Learning and Science.   Then, reverting to his 'real
work', he tells of the extensions already made to his unfinished
Scots College.   Four students just 'over the first ridge', a
quaint ruined tower at Domme, and 'two or three cavern cottages at
Les Eyzies'.   The tower and cottages are located about 250 miles
west of Montpellier in the Dordogne département near where Paul
Reclus now lives.   Also at Domme is 'a massively built old wind-
mill' appropriate to 'my particular line of quixotism, that of re-
constructing after capture'.

These acquisitions cost him, all told, only about £200.   '(Of
course, I can't afford to do them up very much, or almost at all,
till ship does come in again - somehow!)'   Geddes was sufficiently
hopeful of this to say he would send Arthur, then busy decorating
the College's outer walls, to Domme during the Christmas vacation
'in study of possibilities and to draft plans'.

By January 1925 Geddes could report to Norah that his Tower on the
heath was nearly finished and that, as it became visible above the
neighbouring pine grove, its 'formidably feudal aspect' caused
passers-by to exclaim 'What does it mean.... *Qu'est-ce que cela
veut dire*?'   (Rumours spread: it was a 'mad Englishman - *un
anglais fou*' who thought he could make the 'garrigue' fertile;   or
was he an enemy spy in disguise?)   Arthur had done 'a good job of
the blazon-stone - & is now at another for over salon door'.   Meanwhile the first visitors found their way to this edge of Montpellier.   Mrs Fraser Davies and Miss Gladys Mayer, members of Le Play
House, in February; his niece Mary Geddes from New Zealand in
March; and then daugher Norah in May.

This period of happy work and of the arrival of guests from overseas
was also one of highly varied personal experiences.   On one hand he
was in the midst of a lively exchange of letters with a spinster
friend; while on the other his own daughter, for some reason,
broke off friendly relations with him after her visit.

'MERLIN & VIVIEN': LETTERS TO LILIAN

Besides giving a great deal of factual information, the correspondence between Patrick Geddes and Lilian Brown reveals a new aspect
of his life.   It consists of forty-three extant letters from him,
but only one from her.   In this very personal exchange of letters

P.G.'s 'Mediterranean
Outlook Tower', the
first part of his
Scots College dating
from 1924-5

Vivendo Discimus, blazon of the Scots College as done by Arthur
Geddes in bas relief on the front of the original tower building

the main theme was her health problems and a minor but persistent
one, her interest in him.   The first letter (of June 1921, from
London) is to 'My dear Lassie' and contains advice 'about the intellectual task - which to my mind should take you out of yourself'.
She should write to him her ideas, 'Remember I know very little of
your interests....   You were not at college were you (not that
that is very important) - But what do you care for?   Can you
sketch?   If so, that will help.'   He knows, however, that she
plays the violin and urges her to take it along on an impending
trip to Norway

> & play when asked.   Play too to children etc - to servants,
> anybody - & you'll find yourself rewarded by the pleasure you
> give....   Realise what Ole Bull, the old violinist, did for
> Norway!   No man more!

P.G.'s next letters, in July and August, are short ones about emotional problems which Lilian has confided to him.   She thinks she
is now in love with an old flame she once rejected and asks Uncle
Pat to be a go-between, since the two men happen to know each other
slightly.   Geddes was on the point of doing this but decided it
was better to wait until she was more sure of herself.

> Don't think me unsympathetic.   With all my scientific life &
> interests, I have been reading the novels of a good many lives
> too.   And I have had my own - & been - & twice in my life -
> nearer madness, & suicide, than I ever told anyone before.   But
> I have found my anodyne in work - work til sleep compels, and
> then the same each day.

What she replies is, as mentioned earlier, not known; but in mid-
August, in a note from Aberdeen where he is staying with J. Arthur
Thomson, P.G. says consolingly: 'it is well that you can both weep
& play: it would be worse if like so many women you had only the
first outlet, or like so many artists only the second!   Then a new
paragraph: 'What can I say!   I cannot give you what you would
wish of me - there is the undying dead between me and all living!'

A few days later he writes at greater length suggesting that she
contact a Miss Bess Loch of the Sociological Society, and Mabel
Barker who is also in London.   He has asked Mabel

> to take you to Mrs. (Rachel Annand) Taylor, to play to her.
> She is a genius, & has her troubles, only too many of them.
> (But don't tell her I suggest this, as we have long fallen
> apart.)
>   But certainly write to me as friend, & confessor!   I won't
> leave your letters lying about (as I do some) so you may write
> without restraint, whenever it relieves you.   I wish I could
> answer better: but write anyhow.

He discourages her from coming to Aberdeen, for she would have '0 to
do' since he and Thomson are so busy 'at what will likely be our
last book together (if we can even manage that - which seems very
difficult!)   It is a hard world for us all!'   Again his advice is
to 'Play, play, play!   Is not there your real psycho-analysis? -
and your best anodyne too?'

A note from Port Said tells of his return journey to India in late
October, while these words from Bombay on 2 December offer a clue as
to her highly personal response to his concern over her problems:
Dear Lilian,
I am not a little perplexed over your letter in my pocket ... I
cannot but thank you warmly - but the old love is always with me
- unforgotten & unforgettable ... no other woman in the world
for me....   (Think of me simply as a passing 'transference' as
the Freudians call it.)

A year later the same psychological theme: 'Yes, tell your Daddy
all your troubles & griefs, and have a good cry in his arms: you
need not fear lack of sympathy, and it will be a relief.   In fact,
the main use of the psycho-analyst is as a "father (confessor")!'
Along with personal consolation, he tells of his own work: planning universities for Tagore and the Nizam of Hyderabad, and a zoo
for Lucknow.
And in the midst of all this, I am reluctantly getting let in for
a fight! - for the 'improvements' of this great city [Bombay] ...
turn out to be *the worst on human record* - & I have the hateful
task of saying so, and proving it....   Still, work is life:
self-concentration & self pity only lead the other way, to life
not worth living.
                         Always your affectionate Uncle Pat (8)

(Significant to mention here is that when Arthur came in 1922 to
Bombay P.G. one day showed him an envelope, telling him, 'You can
open any letters you like to me *except* letters from Lilian Brown
whose handwriting you see'.   Over forty years later the son would
remark, 'So I never opened them which was perhaps a pity'.)

In mid-January 1923 P.G. wrote again about university plans, mainly
describing the 1,000-acre site at Hyderabad given by the Nizam:
'the biggest & finest in the world, & though with less magnificent
& historic views than from Jerusalem, wonderfully akin too'.   But
his first three lines are an enigmatic reference to a tale from
King Arthur's Court:
Alas, no I *cannot* say *come*.   (You too would be no happier here,
for in the 'Merlin & Vivien' story (see Tennyson) which *this*
would come to, Vivien did not find happiness, after all).

According to Tennyson, 'the wily Vivien' had tried to seduce King
Arthur and on being rebuffed, she set herself to gain Merlin.
Though The Wizard saw through her tricks and refused to tell her a
fateful charm which she begged to know merely 'as proof of trust',
Vivien kept on following him around until, after many hundreds of
lines of verse, they sought shelter from a storm in an old hollow
oak, and finally
... what should not have been had been,
For Merlin, overtalk'd and overworn,
Had yielded, told her all the charm and slept.

Then in one moment, she put forth the charm
Of woven paces and of waving hands,

> And in the hollow oak he lay as dead,
> And lost to life and use and name and fame ...

In February 1923 P.G. gave Lilian more advice on health.   'In
plainest phrase, the condition of mental steadiness and of bodily
health are one and the same - to know your *Work*, & *do it!*'   He
reproves his patient for wandering from flower to flower, 'to this
cure or that friend, or that concert or lecture, or that instrument, or that beautiful place, & so on - all self-centred - and
with never a sign of useful working *Service* for which Life made you,
as she made all of us!'

> Don't think I'm not a flower-seeker too - a wanderer - through
> life & cities of all lands, seeking the things I value & which
> interest me.   Nor that I have not - once, & again, & again -
> known the difficulties & indecisions of life - ay, & been
> crushed down by some of its very bitterest possible experiences -
> & in youth, in middle life too, before the latest ones - of age,
> and often with badly shaken health - to death's doors.
>
>   It is because I so much share your qualities of many-sided
> interests - your defects of difficulty of choosing among them -
> that I write as I do.   Because I have learned that *the one
> thing* which can restore sane mind & sound body together is -
> *facing your work and doing it* - day by day - until you can do it
> *well* - & then go on, doing it *better*.
>
>   ... the first word of Socrates - & the last of Philosophy, I
> am sure - is 'Labour & make Music'!   It *isn't* 'Think about your-
> self!' - as you have essentially done, and still do....
>
>   I know these remedies because I have practised them - & so
> survive in Sanity & Health - Do you the same as your old U.P.

As we have already seen, Geddes's letters to Arthur were an unending
series of guidance and uplift, in great contrast to those written to
Alasdair which treated him as a colleague even when in his early
twenties.   P.G.'s relationship with his two sons is well summarised
in that letter of reconciliation to Mumford in early July 1923 after
the latter's eloquent protest that they had 'yet to meet'.   Speaking of the difficulties of the war generation as compared with the
pre-war one, Geddes invokes his own experience with students and at
home:

> e.g. my full partnership with the joyous Alasdair - my anxious
> years during & since the war about Arthur - who is only now gain-
> ing something of equilibrium, of joy in life, of vigour towards
> tasks with reviving hope ... but he has had & is having to re-
> construct a shattered youth.

While nothing was said in this letter about the younger son's lack
of opportunities to get university training, P.G. did once write to
Norah suggesting that Arthur spend a summer with J. Arthur Thomson
'to abate his loss of university experience in general & biology in
particular'.   At that same time Geddes also admitted that Arthur
was 'sub-consciously bothered with a "father-complex", despite conscious affection', and hoped that he would go to their Zionist
friend, Dr M.D. Eder, for relief. (9)

With this background of unequal treatment of the two sons, even
though partly due to outside circumstance, it seems likely that the
sister took up the issue during her visit to the new Scots College
in the spring of 1925.   In any case, the one standing subject for
her disapproval was that P.G. kept Arthur too close to him at Montpellier just as he had done in Bombay.   How could the son concentrate on a doctoral thesis when his father constantly made demands
on his time?

Whatever the immediate cause, Norah broke off filial relations for
a time.   However long it lasted, there was a reconciliation near
the end of May 1925, for the father then wrote to his daughter from
Tel Aviv.
> It is such a relief to have one of your old letters again - for I
> have been really suffering - more than I can tell you, since I
> felt your anger - (however justified! - though I submit enquiry
> would have mitigated this - since again you can little know how I
> have thought & tried - as well as sometimes blundered!)

After this partial admission of error, Geddes shakes off repressions
and composes these remarkably sentimental lines, written in a close
hand less than half the size of his usual script.
> For look you - here is the essential life-history, & main fact of
> a man's life!   We too live on love - & that of women above all
> - from cradle to grave.   My life history - for all its masculine
> doings, strivings, thinkings, is, *fundamentally*, summed thus
> 1. *Mother* - and *Sister* (too soon lost - while you were babe).
> 2. *Your mother* - whose photo is beside me as ever, & while I
> write - then 3. *You* - with 4. Ethel, Mabel, & other 'nieces' -
> not forgetting 5. your dear old Granny Burton (my second mother)
> & dear old Auntie Jeannie, still with us, (& to whom take my
> love!)
>   I do not forget brothers either - not only 6. Robert (& to a
> much less degree, John), but JAT & VB. especially, with others
> you have known less - now also many & valued friends - but, after
> all, these feminine attachments go deepest - and affect us most!
> Even not forgetting my father - & my much-loved sons.
>   So in short *write me*, & often, as so kindly so long, & as of
> old!   I know you are busy, & your life is full - while mine is
> far away - & inevitably fading, as it must!   Yet with all symp-
> toms of breaking up - in the past year & half, many - my Opus
> sustains me - and the strife for you & yours, & Arthur as well.
> But you too have to sustain me - and with your love: even more
> than all your kindly care of my troublesome affairs, for which I
> *am* grateful.
>   '(*Aqui est* [*está?*] *encerrado el alma del licenciado P.G.*', an
> old Spanish epitaph I have never forgotten!)

CRISIS IN JERUSALEM

After the first winter and spring of work on his southern *Collège
des Ecossais*, Geddes turned up in Palestine.   His purpose is
briefly told to Lewis Mumford in late April 1925.   'I have now been

here [Jerusalem] a month for the opening of the University & in the endeavour to retrieve an imperilled situation.   For in my $4\frac{1}{2}$ years absence our planning of '19 & '20 had too much fallen into obliv- vion.'

Fortunately however they [the Zionist Organisation] had used our plans for world-wide advertisement of Univ. scheme, & thus came to realise how they were committed to it.   As also I think to some extent at least, that our 'sublimation' of Old Jerusalem was more appropriate & pleasing than the last Baroquerie of Berlin etc.   That block is happily out of sight behind ours.

Dr Chaim Weizmann, the Zionists' President, has devoted two pages of his autobiography to the Inauguration Ceremony which took place on 1 April 1925 at the University's site on Mount Scopus.   While his lifelong task was the establishment of the Jewish National Home, he fully recognised the importance of developing a seat of higher learning and ascribed great importance to Lord Balfour's interest in both causes.   Looking back on the development of the University, he wrote that this

would not have come to pass without the great impetus given to the idea in April 1925, when Balfour stood, like a prophet of old, on Mount Scopus, and proclaimed to the world that here a great seat of learning was being created - seeing far beyond the few small buildings which then formed the skeleton of the uni- versity of the future. (10)

A detail of the Ceremony is that Geddes was present in an official double capacity, both as Designer and as Sociologist.   The Presi- dent of the Sociological Society of London, not being able to accept his invitation to Jerusalem, appointed P.G. to represent him and the Society.   Consequently it was Geddes who addressed the University's Governing Board to welcome the 'rise of your new centre of research and study in the most venerable of historic cities' 'and express the Society's confidence that

your work will be inspired by the lofty idealism, and the dis- tinguished intellectual grasp and originality, which have so often and well characterised your people through its chequered past, and which are again so conspicuously eminent throughout the world of science and philosophy to-day. (11)

Two days after the inauguration P.G. told Branford of his grievous disappointment 'to find £40,000 had been spent in extending small laboratories I planned (for a fraction of this) in 1920, and in spoiling Gray Hill House..., so it seemed all up with our designs, and for which all the needed land not yet purchased, despite 5 years of our advice!'   However, he could also relate that because of the shock these buildings 'have given Dr. Weizmann and others' and their feeling that they 'could hardly go on collecting money and support on the beauty of our scheme while carrying out so far an inferior and more costly one, the tide has suddenly changed'.

Yesterday afternoon, I fell in with Dr. Weizmann, whom I have not met, nor got answer from, since 1919!   He said, to my great sur- prise - 'I hope to announcé in a few days the definite expansion of University on Geddes-Mears plans, and to send the new prin-

cipal Dr. Magnus' (who is a *very fine* and able fellow!) 'to
U.S.A. for funds.'

Another part of the changing tide was that, earlier the same day,
Geddes was 'startled by a letter from the Prime Minister's Secretary ... saying Prime Minister and King had awarded me a Civil List
Pension of £100!'   He asked Branford whether he was the 'villain of
the piece' working behind the scenes or whether it was
> consolation for refusal of Board of Trade (Reparations Committee)
> - on technical grounds - of the £2000 claimed for Emden loss of
> Exhibitions? ... (R.S.V.P.!)   Anyway it comes at a time when
> badly needed - for between Montpellier and expenses here (beyond
> mere seafare) etc. etc. I was feeling anxious.

In sharp contrast to the sudden hopefulness of 1925 are exchanges
arising from P.G.'s working sojourns in Palestine in 1919 and 1920.
His long letter to the Chief Secretary of the Palestine Administration, in February 1923, states that: (12)
> I have long postponed reply to yours of 6th Sept., repudiating
> responsibility in the matter of my account for Town Planning of
> Haifa, and in Jerusalem etc. etc....   This delay is partly from
> sheer shock & depression, over so unexpected and so unparalleled
> an experience;   partly also in expectation of being able to pay a
> short visit to Jerusalem on my way home this season.

P.G. admits there was no written agreement;   'Hence your official
misunderstanding is not unnatural', but refers to many other unwritten contracts in his long practice, as 'under Lord Aberdeen for
Irish Government' and in both Provincial and Native States in India.
'Thus my last summer's planning in Patiala towns, was simply on
strength of oral instructions from its Maharaja.'   Nearly half of
his undertakings were of this nature:
> The reasons for this are two fold.   First one is called in often
> urgently, or on impulse, as when people send for a Doctor.   The
> other is, that it is not possible to forecast the time required;
> & one is thus like many other workers - left simply to honour -
> not to charge falsely, or to exceed the ordinary professional
> time-rate.   In all professions are not such arrangements made?

Coming to 'the Palestinian facts', he explains at length how Colonel
Storrs had discussed with him the defects of the Plan of Jerusalem
exhibited in London in 1919 and how, later on in Jerusalem, he and
Dr Eder had called on General Watson: '*whereupon he expressly in-
structed me to prepare, for him, a Report on Jerusalem.*   The first
portion of this was written out on my return here [Bombay] and sent
him in course of the following winter.'   P.G. had also gone to
Haifa for the Zionists, and there the Governor of Phonecia, Colonel
Stanton, had asked him to 'undertake the *Town Planning of Haifa;*
which I accepted accordingly'.   They had even agreed in advance on
a fee of £250.   Geddes had then written to 'Gen. Lord Allenby in
Egypt', at the latter's request through a third party, 'explaining
the whole situation as above'.
> You will thus better understand my surprise over your letter, not
> to speak of the financial disaster, of this falling through

between two stools, & with nothing coming in of what I legitimately expected from your Government, to make up for a part of
the Indian earnings I sacrificed by coming to Palestine in 1920,
& without fee from Zionist Organisation at all.

Concluding, P.G. asks for further investigation of the matter and
makes this offer of compromise:
1. That you recognise for your part the justice of my claim for
   the Town Planning of Haifa, (which can in no wise have been
   confused with planning for Zionist Organisation) and pay me
   my fee of £250 accordingly.
2. As to the other elements of my report and account for Jerusalem etc., reduced in account to £200, that you and I agree
   that this amount be paid by you to aid the funds of the *Pro-
   Jerusalem Society*.

This in evidence of my goodwill to Jerusalem, and sincere desire
to be of service.

Nearly nine months passed before an answer came from Government
House, Jerusalem.   The Chief Secretary agreed that Geddes had 'a
fair claim for payment for services against the Haifa Municipality',
but stated bluntly regarding the Jerusalem town plan that the Palestine Administration 'is unable to admit that it has incurred any
liability for your remuneration therefor....

Major General Watson, who was the Chief Administrator, states
that he has no recollection of having given any orders to you to
report upon the planning of Jerusalem; and Mr. Ronald Storrs
has stated that at no moment was any contract between you and
the Pro-Jerusalem Society or the Municipality of Jerusalem suggested either verbally or in writing. (13)

To uncover all the facts in P.G.'s disputes with either municipal or
military offices is a challenge to coming students of Geddesiana.
(That is, if such records are still available, and have not disappeared like the journals of the Lord Provost of Glasgow for 1902-
6, or like the quantities of letters and documents from the Geddes
Collection at Strathclyde in 1966, see p. 431.)   However, on the
basis of the letters cited here and earlier, it appears that not
only was he unable to keep accounts but half the time did not even
get around to having a contract for his town planning jobs.   Another Herculean task would be to audit and report on P.G.'s financial
transactions year by year, though the results would probably not be
worth the effort.

His attitude towards money seems to be that of the boy who, when
helping his father in their garden, treated it as merely a notation, like notches on a stick to represent how many real potatoes
they had planted.   So why not turn over some of these 'notches' to
a friend?   Furthermore, the real thing for him was work, not pay.

Clear evidence of this is given in a letter of late May 1925 to
Lilian, telling how fortunate he is to have the planning of Jaffa
and Tel Aviv and how
glad to say I'm making a good job of it - more use to the town

than any other before in proportion to size - & with savings (of
waste) on an Indian scale: hundreds of thousands in return for
my modest fee!
      Difficult to tell you more of myself, since neither town plan-
ning details nor sociological theory can contribute much to
letters!   And I see nobody - read 0: just work, & sleep!
Great thing of course that my 'work' is & has been *play* - doing
what amuses me, just as I gardened, & built, & dreamed as a
child.   And so I get the fun of it whether I get paid or not!

DISCIPLE'S REBELLION ... HOPEFUL INTERLUDE

En route from Palestine to Marseilles in the first week of July 1925
Geddes writes optimistically to James Mavor about both past and proposed projects.   The Jerusalem University is starting, he has been
planning 'Culture Institutes on great scale' in Jaffa and Tel Aviv,
and he is now on his way to help with the 'planning of the Bergson
Committee's "International Institute of Intellectual Cooperation" to
be fixed in Paris'.   In southern France his Scots College 'is now
built - and my School of Archaeology at Les Ezies and of Regional
Survey at Domme (Reclus) had its first session last April, and will
have its next in September'.   Finally, after meeting J. Arthur
Thomson in Cambridge in mid-July, he is to lecture at the International Education Congress in Edinburgh and to try to revive 'Town
and Gown ... by renewed educational life of enhanced intensity -
extensity too!'

He also answers a suggestion which Mavor had made about P.G. himself
making more accurate financial arrangements for his undertakings.
      Alas, your proposed economy is impossible for me.   I should need
      a business office all the same!   For I can't and won't keep
      accounts (the minister must *not collect* the seat-accounts!)
            As Mary needed Martha, so in all things social - the spiritual
      side needs the temporal, as the temporal need the spiritual.   In
      isolation, each fails! - in converse ways - (or in both, as we go
      on doing!)
            But now my life's work has been ripening, and with the short
      time before me, I must make the *best* of it, and on the largest
      scale -

Early September found P.G. living in his original Outlook Tower and
again making efforts to tidy up the middens of notes and manuscripts.   Though some of his old assistants like Mrs Galloway, the
faithful housekeeper, must have helped him, he worked like a con-
script himself.   At his invitation Lewis Mumford also came to the
Tower after lecturing in Geneva and spent a memorable five days
which would later be fully described in the 'Disciple's Rebellion'.
It was the American's first visit to Edinburgh, yet like his first
encounter with Geddes in 1923, he found it one of frustration and
disappointment.
      I slept on an improvised cot amid bookcases and boxes of notes in
      the library ... alone with the Master himself!   My adolescent
      dream had come true, but with the fingermarks of reality, as
      usual, smudging the shining surface.

Mumford had plenty of time to explore Edinburgh alone, for after
breakfast P.G. was daily occupied with letters and memoranda 'on
his difficult relations with the Zionist organization'.
>That was a vivid week; but it was only at meals, or over a drop
of neat whisky before turning in for the night, that I got anything out of Geddes, except for a single ramble we took to
Calton Hill on the last afternoon - as if he wished to make belated amends for bidding me visit him without providing any time
for our meeting.

'The Interpreter' did take time, however, to show him the Outlook
Tower from top to bottom, as he had done for neophytes ever since
the 1890s.   On first reading about the terrace outlooks and the
storey-by-storey representations of city, region, Europe, world,
Mumford had been filled with excitement.   'But now, as if to jeer
at Geddes's actual presence, everything had crumbled and fallen
apart.'   There were
>dusty piles of manuscripts, the records of his lectures, too
rapid and unexpected in content to be taken down accurately by
even the swiftest of court stenographers, lectures that never
more than hinted at the living essence; bins of teasing notes,
mostly on folded paper, that pointed to ideas, often brilliant,
that had never been transformed into more communicable discourse
once the original voice had vanished.

P.G. begged for help to sort out this lifetime's accumulation,
asking Mumford to bring his wife and child to Montpellier the coming
winter and work with him in 'tidying up these idea-middens'.   It
was something like that first appeal the day after Geddes's arrival
in New York when
>he took me squarely by the shoulders and gazed at me intently ...
with tears welling in his eyes....   You must be another son to
me, Lewis.

The wording is curiously reminiscent of an incident which occurred
thirty years earlier in Edinburgh.   The hero of Riccardo Stephens's
satirical novel is explaining to 'The Professor' why he must leave
town for a while.   Whereupon,
>He took me by the shoulders, and, looking at me pathetically,
sighed in a touching way.
>'One after another you desert me.' (14)

Returning to the American rebellious disciple in Edinburgh in 1925,
we quote him saying that when Geddes appealed for help 'there was a
soft womanly pathos ... that contrasted with the almost ferocious
virility of his usual self'.
>At such moments he would shrug his shoulders, fling out his arms
with a gesture of utter despair, and sometimes a film would cover
his haunted sorrow-laden eyes, bringing him close to tears.
>Tears of frustration? of self pity? of desperation?   Loving him
despite the distance between us, grateful to him for all he had
given me, I could not help being moved by his plight; and as the
years went on, these calls and these appeals, alas!, became more
urgent, for his hope of mastering the job himself ebbed from him
with increasing symptoms of senescence.

By this time, fortunately, I had steeled myself to resist Geddes's blandishments. I realised that 'helping Geddes' would be a career in itself: a career that would need the patience of a saint, the single-mindedness of Browning's Grammarian, the physical stamina of an athlete; and even then would be so full of frustrations and humiliations that it might come abruptly to an end before anything was accomplished.

Lewis Mumford asserted that forty years earlier P.G. 'might have used someone as devoted as Boswell - and far more self-effacing - to wing his flying words', but now it was too late for anyone to help him.   He related an incident on the top of the Tower which illustrated how unable he himself was to satisfy P.G.'s demands.   They had viewed scenes of Edinburgh from inside the Camera Obscura and then gone out onto the observation terrace.

Instead of letting me take in the landscape in my own way, he insisted on my seeing it through his eyes, standing back of me and holding me by the shoulders, almost savagely demanding that I pick out of the panorama what he was seeing, and respond to it in the same way.

That settled it.   Much as I admired Geddes, much though I valued his help, I would not see Edinburgh or aught else through his eyes.   If any single moment marked the ultimate parting of our ways, this was the moment, and that rooftop the place.

At the end of September 1925 on the train from Paris to Montpellier, Geddes penned another of his enigmatic replies to Lilian Brown. 'Alas, what can I say!' he began.   'You don't know my hard driven life, early to late: & no getting out of it, but only deeper in!'

This is almost the first (certainly not more than the second) of letters got to since you were at Tower!   Arrears so many.   You can only say, 'Don't work so hard' (as others do) but yet that is my relief too: and I could not now change, but must just go on till I drop.

Fifty years of work & thought *now* to be made something of, & not just left as waste paper.   And very little of it would really ever interest you, though it possesses me!

I wish I *could* help you, but your interests are other than mine.

He is relieved that her eyes were not in such danger as he feared (she had symptoms of glaucoma) and that she was 'looking so well generally'.

You are of a good long-lived family, (and nothing tends to be more hereditary than that!) so take courage & make the most of the long time before you.   I'll try to do the same, & we'll be friends a long while yet!

Always your old
U.P.

Several letters to Norah from the *Collège des Ecossais* between October and December describe its first session.   Amongst the residents that arrived was his god-daughter Mabel Barker, others were Indian students from Bombay.   Mabel had left the school in Cumberland where she was teaching, partly to do a thesis at the University of

Montpellier and partly because her headmistress's conversion 'to "Anthroposophy" (Dr. Steiner's combination of Theosophy, Sociology, etc.) is too much for her'.   Anthroposophy was a concept of which Geddes had a completely negative opinion until one of his female 'disciples' partially defected to Rudolf Steiner. (She was Gladys Mayer who, with Mrs Fraser Davies, had visited Montpellier earlier in 1925.   Both went on to Steiner's headquarters at Dornach, partly seeking an answer to P.G.'s annoyed: 'What's he got that I don't have?'   Yet after returning, Miss Mayer says Geddes agreed to add Steiner to his private list of 'synthetic thinkers', kept somewhere among heaps of papers. (15)   She later wrote a booklet which presented Goethe, Steiner and Geddes as three kindred spirits, the latter in spite of himself.   See   Bibliography.)

Two distinguished guests who signed the Scots College guestbook in October were Sir Thomas and Lady Barclay, friends and colleagues since P.G.'s earliest campaign in 1889 for a revival of the medieval *Collège des Ecossais* in Paris.   Being widely known in both France and Britain for his book, 'L'Entente Cordiale - By One of Its Artisans' or 'Thirty Years of Anglo-French Reminiscences', Sir Thomas's coming from Paris to Montpellier created a stir in official circles.   'How different his way of doing things!' Geddes writes to Norah late that month.

    Before leaving [Paris] he wrote Prime Minister (Painlévé) to introduce us to Prefect. He wrote such a letter that Prefect sent out officer at 6.30. a.m. next morning to make appointment, & so we went in, & he telephoned Mayor, Rector, etc to receive us in turn, & stir up Deans of Faculties etc.   Imagine the like in Edinburgh!

The Barclay's ten-day visit coincided with the first anniversary of the start of P.G.'s Mediterranean *Cité Universitaire*, as he liked to call his Tower on the heath.   It also marked a real opportunity for gaining official recognition and support for the project. Mabel Barker, who was both writing a thesis and acting as housekeeper, tried to hurry up furnishing the house, while Geddes urged on his masons and gardeners.   Sir Thomas insisted that there be a public opening and said he would place articles in both the 'Manchester Guardian' and the 'Fortnightly Review'.   Thus P.G. could truthfully tell Norah about great educational schemes that were developing, and never were his inveterate hopes more flourishing.

An American professor and former college president (Dr F.A. McKenzie of Fisk University) who had been living at Ramsay Lodge, Edinburgh, came to Montpellier, and Geddes soon had him marked out for raising funds to build the *Collège des Américains*.   Its cost was estimated at $20-25,000, 'which did not alarm him, "Wal, I raised a million dollars for my University last year."   So this *may* come off - though of course I have had so many delays and disappointments in life that I must not be too sanguine over this.'   Two additional projects are on plan: an extension of the tower building;   and houses for French staff, 'as in Ramsay Garden'.

He is also pleased that a former secretary from Edinburgh, Miss Ker, is coming to help him,

Lewis Mumford, the American 'dissident disciple' of Patrick Geddes, in 1922 when in London as acting editor of the 'Sociological Review'. From a charcoal portrait by Gladys Mayer

Arthur Geddes, Mrs Fraser Davies, Gladys Mayer and Patrick Geddes at the Scots College, February 1925

though I'll often have to play truant from her too.   Again
planting - shrubberies, fruit trees, & formal garden of box
varieties, but shall have to leave my long-dreamed type botanic
garden - development from Dundee - till next winter.   Still in
a year or two some results will be coming on.   Large (& costly
reclamation of garrigue behind house, knocking out rocks & getting deep soil trenches for asparagus etc - still a great satisfaction to have such dramatic change, & better investment of
real life & work than towns offer, with all their mammonisms.

Other news is that 'Arthur seems very well, & is sticking in to his
thesis'.   Frank has come on a short visit, and drawn plans for the
American and the Indian Colleges, before going on to the university
project in Jerusalem, which 'is now essentially Frank's affair'.
But nothing permanent resulted from the Paris-directed 'shake-up'
and recognition in Montpellier.   Sir Thomas was over 70 and blind
and could not engage in follow-up activities, and P.G. soon lapsed
into old routines.

FAMILY POLEMICS

After the Barclays returned to Paris correspondence with Norah
turned to accounts of early dawn thinking, outdoor activities and
what can best be termed family 'psycho-educational polemics'.   True
to the pattern, the father sends on 24 December:
   Just a line of Christmas hopes - & though these may be late in
   reaching you, it is not too late for New Year wishes; & for
   whatever virtue there may be in an old daddy's & grand-daddy's
   blessing!

He again mentions Frank's help with drawings and hopes that Norah
will come to visit him with her boys '- and in happier circumstances
for us all.   For I am trying to make you & them a little Paradise
to complement your own.   And if my ship comes in ... there must be
a cottage in Scotland too.'

Geddes once described truth as 'diamond-shaped' with so many facets
that, taken individually, the various surfaces seem unrelated to or
incompatible with other parts of the whole.   This simile applies
to P.G.'s character with equal accuracy.   The Christmas letter
ends in a typical sally of self-vindication combined with pleas for
affection.
   And, oh dear lassie, do try to credit me with more understanding,
   of the educational ideal of my life, of teaching men of high
   ability to find *their own* ways & work, (though I *can* add some
   charts & thought-instruments to their outfit - and some experience and insight of the stars by which to steer).
   (I am sorry to have run on into this - I had no idea of writing so till now - but it is the deepest pain of my sub-conscious,
   normally so happily dormant, irised or serene - that you two whom
   I most love & care for, should so gravely & readily - as I think
   - misunderstand me - as the spiritual tyrant I am *not*.)
   So to finish with this matter, I hope - for good & all - &

towards the better understanding I hope for, & would be relieved
by having some day assurance of its re-establishment.

Meanwhile Arthur was struggling between the nether millstone of
finishing his doctoral thesis and the upper one of having at the
same time to work on some building or decorating task for his
father.   Indeed, the double pressure was so great in 1926 that he
had to take refuge in the home of his thesis adviser, Jules Sion,
Professor of Geography at the University.   An infuriated P.G., to
whom Indian students had not for nothing given the nickname of 'Old
High Explosive', included Dr Sion in his wrath: whereupon the
latter told the father straight out what an unreasonable and harmful parent he was in this matter.*

As mentioned earlier, Arthur attended P.G.'s Bombay lectures on
'Contemporary Civilisation' in 1922-3.   Recalling this many years
later, Arthur said in a recorded statement: 'Well, he begged me to
write these lectures up, so I took them down in a kind of shorthand
of my own and wrote them out in bits when he wasn't pulling me out
to do something else.'   While Geddes was in the USA in 1923 the son
'was then free without his constant interruption and I got this book
written....   It took me most of my time during those six
months'. (16)

Yet when Arthur showed him the results saying, 'What about publication now that you've got the book you wanted?', P.G. said '"No, No"
and put it off'.   Later, in Montpellier, when unable to locate it
again, he told Norah that 'Arthur never wrote the book'.   However,
Gopal Advani, the Indian student who had typed Arthur's manuscript,
was then at the Scots College as secretary, and the typescript was
found.   Even so, many months passed before Geddes admitted to
Norah that Arthur
    has shown me from the actual papers, ms & typescripts, 1. that
    he *had* written out the greater part of them from his notes, & 2.
    also *other* lectures of my final teaching in Bombay to which I
    attached importance....   Yet as I saw them unfinished, I was
    discouraged too, and so came to forget how much he *had* done.
    No doubt therefore had I been more encouraging, (as I see it is
    a great pity I was not) he *would* have finished up that
    course. (17)

P.G. goes on to say that he is taking over the remaining notes from
Arthur for dictation to his own typist, 'and so release him from
any further work in this matter - or with other Ms. either'.
Nevertheless, they both hope 'that our *indirect* cooperation in kindred work in the future may be successful: and so perhaps something
even direct may arise in time'.
    Oh dear lassie - I do not want to lose touch with any of you -
    and I see our dreadful Scottish & other repression in *myself* as
    well as in others - and how that grows with all manner of separa-

* This incident was told to author by Sion's step-daughter, Suzanne
Tandy.

tions & estrangements, over all manner of things & lives!   And
old age, besides fatigue, forgetfulness etc. has increasing
solitude!

Love P.G.

CHÂTEAU WHITE ELEPHANT

In the spring of 1926 one of Geddes's ships did come in, and quite
unexpectedly.   Nearly twelve years after the 'Emden''s exploit a
governmental war damage agency decided that the loss of the original
Cities Exhibition was worth £2,054, and this sum was paid to him.
The kindly disposed reader will immediately wonder into which of
his deficit undertakings this money was placed: the struggling
Tower in Edinburgh; the cataloguing of its precious contents; or
the repayment of overdrafts; or perhaps another college to be
founded on more acres of dry heath, with the blasting out of more
rocks to create more deficit vegetable gardens.   But P.G. did none
of these things with this windfall.

On one excursion or an other, he had seen the tiny village of Assas
a few miles north of Montpellier where there was an uninhabited
'château' or country mansion of a former aristocrat.   What happened
was, according to Geddes, the best of all possible solutions.   To
Lilian he simply announced that
> My last ploy is the Château d'Assas, a fine old Louis XV château,
> five miles inland from here with medieval survivals too - for
> which I have to find the various possible uses!   One as a holi-
> day centre of course for our Montpellier world; but perhaps also
> for the studious, artistic & musical connection from further
> away....   So I hope you'll come & see it some day! (18)

To Norah, though, he gave advance notice of his plans.   In fact,
when first telling her of the windfall in March, his words were as
sensible as any advice she could have offered: 'So that clears off
Bank & liabilities here & leaves something over'.   But not many
weeks later came two closely-written pages of rationalised proof
that acquiring the château was the only justified course of action.
He thanks her for common sense advice but explains that he has
'taken weeks to consider, & with hundreds of notes accordingly -
gone over too, more than is my wont!'   The result:
> Broadly speaking, I'm in for it --and for much more - a culmina-
> tion so far of all my schemes of University design ... since not
> only now from here to Montpellier - or even from Assas; but from
> Aigoual [a hilltop in the Cevennes] to Cette zoological station
> [on the Mediterranean coast].   And with contacts by & by with
> the cities of the University's province, from Arles, Nîmes,
> Avignon & Tarascon on one side to Béziers, Narbonne etc on
> other. (19)

He would also propose to Spanish or Italian universities that the
Scots College and Assas be used as holiday centres.   'And as for
business prudence, if you could get the best mansion house within
seven miles of Edinburgh for the value of ... two or three Roseburn

cottages, you need not be too alarmed for your investment.'*   He
assures Norah that he hasn't forgotten thought and books, being
'only too painfully aware of slowness'.   However, his study rooms
in the Tower 'are coming to order & with notes for Biology & Sociology getting laid out' on the many tables.

It has been a long - a life-long - delay no doubt, this of
writing - but my late-flowering *Agave* symbol *is*, I trust being
so far justified: if even a very few years remain.

And I just have to go on with *Vivendo Discimus*!   My whole
life is strengthened & thought freshened & deepened & broadened
too, by action.   I've learned a lot by all this return to gardening & building & repairing.

So while it is very kind of all one's friends to want to take
care of the old man, it's no use for 'Old-and-Bold' as Nevinson
[an old journalist friend] & I call each other!   We're still out
for adventure, for all risks; & did not need Nietzsche to teach
us to 'live dangerously'!

Geddes marshalls all possible support for his project: his four
Indian students 'are bucked up to push on their *Collège des
Indiens*'; he has found a French 'regionalist & forestry enthus-
iast' to live at the Château and supervise the 'carrying out of
Flahault's plan of 40,000 pines on my ten hectares available at
Assas'; and can thus realise his 'long-delayed dream of coopera-
tion with Old & Bold Flahault' and of 'further Forestry schemes of
wide bearing'.

So I might go on - but enough to show I'm *meditating* my many
moves; & if there have to be sacrifices, as may be, (as in a
measure must be) that too is the way of life best worth choosing.   And after all, don't I survive - somehow? - though it
must be now some 60 years [i.e. at age 12] since I formed the
rule for & in my ramblings & excursions at each fork of the unknown road - *choose the more adventurous*!

Despite all these arguments, Norah apparently was not convinced,
for P.G. continues defensive explanations.   'The château is
bought', he confesses in mid-May; however 'the vendor has also
given me the bulk of the furniture, some of it fine old things,
electric fittings, carpets, etc. at very moderate price - under
£250'.   He has found the medieval part of more 'interest & variety
than I knew, so my dream of presenting both culture periods very
simply, clearly, vividly, can be realised here better than in any
other house I can remember having seen'.

Even so, enthusiasm for Assas is tinged with anxiety for practical

---

* The point has been raised as to how much Patrick's apprenticeship
in the Perth bank was responsible for 'his extraordinarily fecund
manner of property-buying and company-starting later on' (Kitchen,
pp. 43-4).   Bank Manager Jolly might have had some grounds for comment on this matter in the 1870s, but about all one can say now is
that neither young nor old Geddes ever showed any zest for ledger-
balancing.

problems at the Scots College.   Mabel Barker will be leaving soon,
her thesis (20) being finished and published.   Can Norah find someone 'of intellectual type as far as may be' to replace her?   'I
wish the good Suzanne [Charmont] would take me in hand, for one
house or other!'   Then, either unaware of, or ignoring the irony
of the situation, he invokes the 'need of paying off overdraft for
Bank etc' and suggests that his Town Planning Exhibition might be
sold for this purpose.   The Department of Urbanism at the Sorbonne
is already trying to get funds to bring it from India for showing
in Paris.

Late in June P.G. is still engaged in self-justification.   He
deplores Norah's explanation 'last year' of his delay in getting
down to writing, for that hurt him 'more than any ordinary criticism, though I have mostly in life had these'.   Combining reproach
and conciliation, he goes on:

> But if you stick to it, I'll say no more - save that it's also a
> wee bit hard that you see no more in new schemes like Assas than
> excitement, loss of quietness, & so on.   I'm *not* neglecting
> older ones; but doing much more for them, & with detailed atten-
> tion, than you know - & my recuperative philosophic calm, of
> reflection etc seldom fails me, even for a day, save when hurt
> by those I love most, & when (I think) unjustly judged.   How-
> ever, I now will say no more.

The rest of this letter mainly concerns happenings in Scotland.   He
congratulates Norah on her success with a Viennese Exhibition at the
Outlook Tower 'which must have made some impression beyond its immediate circle' and adds

> All I am doing is *Tower*, indeed all I have done since it started,
> & though I can hardly expect that to be very intelligible to most
> people in Edinburgh, I trust some do, more or less.

He closes with the news that Mrs Branford 'died a fortnight ago - &
now I fear for Victor - who can but overwork to drown sorrow.   Sad
world!   But work is the best anodyne for us all.'

ABBEY OF THELEMA?

Given the documents now available and the resulting hindsight, one
can easily pronounce judgment.   P.G. should have contented himself
with creating, in this appropriate setting, something of the Abbey
of Thelema of Rabelais, his predecessor at Montpellier.   His
friends and colleagues should have taken turns in residing there
and systematically following J. Arthur Thomson's example in getting
Geddes organised and into print.   They could have again privately
campaigned for a fund, this time to make secure his Mediterranean
Outlook Tower.   Ample grounds and argumentation for such action
were contained in P.G.'s own letters.

In January 1925, for instance, he urged both Victor Branford and
John Ross to leave their London tasks for a half-year or more and
recuperate health with him in southern France.   To Ross he said:

It's an illusion which keeps all you business men at the City!
Here am I with no visible means of support & using up not only
all cash - but up to overdraft!   Yet, when urgent, I'll boil
pot again somehow - between planning & writing! (21)

Another time he prefaced a plea to Branford with the significant
remark:

My letter-writing is largely of *answers* to others - though of
questions to you.   I wish you would return the ball.   Question
me.   Criticise me (get Mumford & others to help).   What do *you*
want *me* to work at? to work up etc.?   Very difficult to be always so much alone - as you feel too.

According to signatures in the Guest Book of the *Collège des Ecossais,* several well-known friends did pay short visits during the
years 1925 to 1927, when only the new tower and its engulfed cottage
existed.   J.C. Bose and his wife Ahala spent three days there,
apparently at the same time as Branford made his one brief visit,
March 1927.   (Dorothy Harbert, who had helped an invalid P.G. from
the boat in Marseilles, came for a week.)   Apart from Sir Thomas
and Lady Barclay, other names include Geddes's staunch supporter
Martin White, and his botanical assistant Marcel Hardy who as tutor
to the young Maharajah of Indore brought his pupil to the College
for one day in June 1926.   Yet the signatures of John Ross, J.
Arthur Thomson and Lewis Mumford do not appear.   On the other
hand, Mabel Barker turned up in October 1925, faithful disciple as
always, taking charge of household affairs and working for her
French doctorate at the same time.   An Indian student from Bombay,
Gopal Advani, also came to his professor's aid in February 1926,
serving as secretary for over six years.*

Thomson did plan to make the journey to Montpellier and though it
was never realised, he supported the Scots College actively by recruiting residents as best he could.   Above all, he was the one
colleague who had patience, guile and skill enough to collaborate
with P.G. and see that biological results got published.   The two
men spent part of nearly every summer together at Thomson's home in
Old Aberdeen, whereas Geddes once confessed that he and Branford had
but rarely spent an entire week-end together working on sociology.
They were constant correspondents, but as P.G. mildly complained to
Branford: 'I write more to you than you to me'.   And as was pointed out by reviewers of their 'Making of the Future' series, neither
one's style could serve as a corrective for the other's.

Lewis Mumford not only never accepted any of P.G.'s repeated invitations to come to the College but, as he confessed years later, did
not intend ever to do so.   He states in 'The Disciple's Rebellion'
that he failed 'to be captured even for a moment by Geddes' plan
for creating a series of residential "colleges" at Montpellier.
From the first, that project seemed to me a folly.'

* Mabel Barker has written to author 30 December 1945 that 'Dr
Gopal Advani was a most faithful friend to P.G. & one of the most
reliable people I have ever met.'

Regarding the Château d'Assas, a 'weekend retreat from a college
that was itself a rural retreat from Montpellier', Mumford calls
the whole enterprise 'a white elephant, and it produced in Geddes'
fertile mind a whole herd of little white elephants'.

In that final phase Geddes was not so much a scientist or a
philosopher as an imperious master builder, or perhaps I should
say a too-long frustrated architect. This was his last opportunity to turn his dreams, his plans, his graphs, into firm
stone structures, in his hope that they would testify by their
solid presence to his ideas when he was no longer there to explain them.

In 1931 Mumford told Geddes frankly that he wished he had been five
years older when they met in 1923, and had had fewer unsolved problems of his own.

For I should have either aided you at the beginning of the Montpellier scheme, or have diverted you completely away from it
toward something of greater immediate urgency and prospect of
accomplishment - namely, the various books that you have still
to write.

In the same letter Mumford also confessed, half-humourously, that:

For the sake of the ideas that both you and Branford had to give
to the world, I could wish that you both had either gone into a
lay monastery in 1920 or been imprisoned by the civil authorities, with nothing other than pen and ink and a library to keep
you company! (22)

Idle though it is to speculate about what might have been, it can
not be unreasonable to suggest that had Branford followed up Mumford's plan of July 1924 for salvaging the Outlook Tower's notes
and manuscripts, this action would later have helped similar problems at the Scots College. It is also fair to recall P.G.'s belated response (partly quoted on pp. 358-9) to the plan in which
he outlined 'A whole Research College of Collaborators' with roles
assigned to specific persons. In that letter of 14 October 1924
and again on 11 January 1925 he appealed to Branford. 'Is it too
much to say that you too, old friend, would be encouraged also to
feel we were again a growing group of collaborators? Come to
Montpellier for a month or two this winter.'

Branford and John Ross were active for years in appropriate war
damage commissions, in pressing Geddes's claim for the loss of his
Cities Exhibition in 1914. Though they obviously could not have
had its payment marked as valid for 'Research College' purposes
only, they would have had a fighting chance, on the spot in Montpellier, to pressure the beneficiary to invest heavily in resident
colleagues when that draft for two-thousand-odd pounds sterling
finally came into his unpredictable hands.

Collegial visits, however, remained sporadic and ineffectual, and
there developed no Abbey of Thelema. P.G. continued in his ways
of life, unhelped with writing and unimpeded in financial vagaries,
though still confident of creating a *Cité Universitaire Meditér-*

ranéenne and at the same time finishing the opuses worthy of a
'Late-Flowering Agave'.   He kept on hoping to find the perfect
secretary, this time in the long-awaited Miss Ker.   Yet a while
after her arrival he laments to Norah:

> ... oh dear, it's a pity that so seldom one finds collaboration
> ... and my brain & paper middens just full & the latter increas-
> ing daily from the former - while I still find it so hard to
> write them up.   Miss Ker helped me splendidly with the dictat-
> ing of the Evolution of Cities - but this time she told me when
> she came frankly she had no more interest in any of my ideas, as
> she was now in another world altogether - so her work was merely
> business letters & ordinary mechanical typing.   My next typist
> however is more keen, but just a lassie fresh from school.
>
> If you come across a bright typist - *interested* in social
> science & advance, & not merely a fanatic of socialism or Cook-
> Lenin*, I believe I could talk out my books to her - at times
> very clearly & easily. (23)

Perfect secretary and colleagues-at-hand or not, the 'imperious
master-builder' filled each day with continuous activity from pre-
dawn notations of thought to evening forays in gardens and countryside.   On the very last day of 1926 he informs Norah that they
'are having fine weather' and that all are 'off in an omnibus
immediately to Château d'Assas for afternoon.   Now practically
furnished in the main, & beginning to look quite itself of old.'
There, thanks to a contemporary snapshot, we can see him surrounded
by residents at the College and friends from Montpellier, looking
pleased with himself and as unaware of any financial problems as if
he were young Patrick setting out for a ramble in Perthshire.

---

* Perhaps a reference to C.J. Cook, leader of the Miners' Union,
suggests the National Library of Scotland.

Omnibus to Assas, P.G.'s 'Chateau White Elephant'! The happy pur-
chaser on roof in middle, while Arthur Geddes holds the horses, and
Mabel Barker stands beside the vehicle

Group of visitors on a conducted tour of Assas. *Back row left:* Ahala
Bose, wife of the Indian bio-physicist, *second row,* third from
right, P.G., then Tagore's active man, Mr Mahanalobis then Victor
Branford; *front row*, second from right: Sir J.C. Bose (May 1927)

Chapter 11

REMARRIAGE AND DÉNOUEMENT, 1928-32

STORY OF A 'LONG-PLANNED OPUS'

The year of 1927 passed much like 1926 with Geddes carrying on his combination of 'real work' outdoors and neglect of the real problems spread around inside his tower studies.   Letters to Norah tell of various Indian visitors and his always increasing hopes for a *Collège des Indiens*, of buying more land on which to place the school which a new colleague-of-great-expectations was to start, and of a hoped-for visit from 'the great Einstein'.   In February there is good, conciliatory family news.

> You will be pleased to hear ... that Arthur's thesis has been sustained with high distinction, and *mention très honorable*, given with regrets that no higher terms available!...   The Sions and other examiners came to supper last night & though Flahault never breaks his rule of not going out in evenings, he wrote very nicely - a note passed on for Arthur to keep....
>
> We have each tried to clear up our too frequent strains of separations - very sad these should be with such fundamental affection!   Yet so that while he found later I'd liked to go to 'soutenance' [doctoral disputation] yesterday, & I found later he'd liked to ask me - neither of us realised that - & so I stayed home!...   That's an example of how we miss your Mother! (1)

At the end of March 'Uncle Pat' can write to Lilian about 'an interesting succession of visitors' to the College, 'all in past fortnight or so!'   Besides the Bose's and Branford there arrived Miss Josephine Macleod (Anna's and his friend from New York and Paris in 1900, and later in India), 'Tagore's active man' Mahanalobis, Professor Cecil Desch of Sheffield, and Miss Moya Jowitt, 'the active "Kibbo Kift" girl who runs our Dordogne Tours'.   'Very interesting', he repeats, 'but very embarrassing too!', undoubtedly referring to the lack of adequate sanitary facilities.   No reference was made, though, to the war-damage windfall which could have been partly used to relieve this embarrassment.   Instead he reports that things are progressing, especially the gardens, 'but a heavy weight of anxieties & cares ... have been depressing me more than they used to do, & can't be shaken off so easily.   Still I am fairly well.'

P.G.'s summer visit to Aberdeen for a bout with J. Arthur Thomson
on their long-planned 'Essentials of Biology' was to take place in
1927 as usual, but a series of mishaps intervened.   From an exchange of letters in February it appears that although Thomson had
produced over 200,000 words and Geddes was to write 50,000, they
still needed to revise each other's work and to fill in many gaps.
However, the latter was feeling low at that time, having just
learned that he had symptoms of 'heart wearing down'.

Thomson, on hearing that his old teacher had been forbidden the use
of coffee and tea by Dr Galen, who also imposed the 'misery' of
trying to stop smoking, relates that he himself had had so many
months 'of miserable discomfort in giving up tobacco that I am pre-
judiced against drastic reform'.   He also tells of a mutual friend,
a doctor, who

> was talking in a friendly way about you, and said in a burst of
> frankness that you had a *remarkably* tough constitution, and would
> see many a year if you would take less out of yourself.   So
> cheer up old friend. (2)

Thomson had hoped they could deliver their finished manuscript by
March, but the publisher preferred an October release 'with delivery
of copy by the beginning of July'.   J. Arthur sanguinely calculates
their new schedule as of 2 February:

> Now if I send you my whole stuff at ... the end of March, can you
> give April to revising it; and I should do the same for your
> 50,000 words....
>
>   I have got about 60 figures done, and if you will indicate
> what you wish, and especially the end-papers, I shall get Smith
> [Thomson's assistant] to do them.   I thought 30 about your
> share.
>
> Yours ever   J.A.T.

A postscript adds that 'I am quite willing to pay you £200, your
half of the advance (due on publication), when you send me your
"copy"... '   But only a fortnight later, and without mentioning
the receipt of any manuscript or making any comment on what must
have been a call for help from P.G., Thomson writes: 'I enclose
the advance with pleasure, but as we are both precarious, will you
send me the receipt or something like it.'

For reasons not now known, since Thomson did not preserve old
letters even from his revered teacher, Geddes must have suggested
delaying the book.   In any case, the pupil confesses on 2 May
that, because of illness,

> I have not, till yesterday, been able to touch the book for two
> months; and it will have to be as you suggest, I fear.   I don't
> think we need to meet this summer over the book; if it were
> something fresh, it would be different.   But we have been at
> *this* too long.

Just how displeased the publisher, Williams and Norgate, was is not
known either, but Mrs Thomson certainly welcomed a summer without
the disturbance which the annual work-visits of Geddes entailed.

J.A.T.'s son, Sir Landsborough Thomson, has told the writer that
his mother, while very fond of Anna and Patrick, 'used to dread
P.G.'s coming in the 1920s.   He would talk, talk, talk, then leave
all the work behind for her husband to rewrite and send to P.G. for
"revision";   which later resulted in even more work for the
sender.' (3)

During the 45 years since J. Arthur had first struggled with
Geddes's writings and been 'rendered desperate by the sentences', he
displayed a patience and a faithfulness that usually are attained
only by saints.   In spite of forfeited deadlines and chores of rewriting which impaired his own work, this first disciple remained
consistently faithful to his master and friend, besides being his
most doggedly helpful co-author.   As modest as he was loyal, Thomson never publicised the fact that, though Geddes had given him his
start in science, it was he who salvaged his own teacher's reputation in biology through their joint publications.

Mid-August 1927 found P.G. in Edinburgh at the Outlook Tower instead
of in Aberdeen and, according to a long letter to Lilian, engaged in
activities far from creative.   She must have just told him about
many personal problems, for he begins:
> I should indeed be a harder old uncle than I am, not to be
> touched ... & sorry to write so little!   But I'm more hard-
> driven & care-worn that you can imagine: & just peg on at work -
> (clearing up literally hundred weights of old books & papers here
> in these days - & glad of the drudgery, since keeping graver
> worries out of mind!)
>   (Less thinking accordingly (though that's the main use of me,
> rather than all my working -) and no longer the old poetic im-
> pulse - though it isn't really dead, I think, but only choked
> down.)

At this time the first book about Patrick Geddes and his ideas had
appeared: 'The Interpreter Geddes' by Amelia Defries. (4)   Its
main title was very good, expressing one of his chief traits and
activities, but the sub-title heading every other page, 'The Man
and His Gospel', was ill-chosen.   A first glance gave the impression that here was just another 'prophet' being over-praised by an
uncritical disciple.   In reality the book represented P.G. exactly
as he was in many situations, and it is now more than ever a valuable source of faithfully recorded conversations and lectures.   Yet
the jumbled presentment of his seemingly haphazard day-by-day ideas
and doings probably confirmed the opinion of many contemporaries
that here was a brilliant meddler in everything but not a recognised
achiever in any field.   Before it was published Geddes wrote to
Norah:
> I've not meddled with Miss Defries' book beyond necessary proof
> corrections....   A sad breaking into one's peace - but inevit-
> able....   Of course it will work both ways - probably more hos-
> tile criticism than other.   However, I have never felt much
> moved by either. (5)

After its appearance he commented in the August letter to Lilian:

I'm glad you liked Miss D's book: she took no end of trouble &
has put a lot of my ideas & endeavours very clearly, it seems;
but will even that make anybody *understand*? (much less join hands
and help? -) no signs!   (Yet who knows?)

P.G.'s fears of having his peace broken into by the public attention
brought upon him by that first book about him proved groundless.
That 'The Interpreter Geddes' received favourable attention from
many reviewers is attested by a selection of quotations made by its
author and printed as a fly-leaf.   On it one finds such phrases as:
'Patrick Geddes ... among the great thinkers... ' 'Manchester Guardian'; 'No other man of our time has so correlated the arts and
sciences of life ... ' 'New York Times'; and, significantly, from
the 'Scotsman' 'The Outlook Tower may become a future place of pil-
grimage'.

Despite such favourable appreciations in leading newspapers, P.G.'s
pessimistic predictions to Lilian were more realistic.
  Few are really interested - hardly so far as helping ... especially as the real help has to be personal & human, of effort &
  thought - and not simply of money!   So though you are very kind
  to think of it, & now even suggest it, I have always shrunk from
  asking you! or even now hesitate about accepting! - in crisis
  though I am.

He refers to a Workers Educational Association scheme which she is
backing, saying that his 'Montpellier beginnings' and his 'old
struggle of forty years' in Edinburgh mean much more to him than she
can see.   For the WEA
  (and you too I suppose) assume the existing university and educational scheme is all right - so merely want more of it.
  Whereas I see it all has got to be *put right* before it can justify these hopes; and so spend my life & all in trying to do
  that.

Geddes suggests they try to meet in London after his lectures in
Edinburgh and a trip to Stratford-on-Avon, but before he goes on to
France the day after.   'If & when you come to Montpellier', he
promises, 'you'll find a less driven wretch I hope'.   The letter
also contains this spontaneous summary of purpose:
  You see I'm *possessed by the urge* to get something going on, of
  all I've thought & tried towards City betterment, and rural too -
  & towards getting some *life* into the dull education-machines they
  call schools & Universities.   In short, *something* of 'Kingdom of
  Heaven' - of 'Eutopia' - or what you will!....
    And if you, and others too, see I don't succeed much after
  all, I can only take comfort from knowing that there's always a
  little mustard-seed growing, a bit of leaven spreading - (perhaps? - or surely! which is it?) (6)

ST MARTIN'S SUMMER

The turning point of relations between Lilian and P.G. can be dated
22 August 1927.   Immediately on his return to Montpellier three
documents were dispatched to her, the first of which was a typed
business letter, addressed to 'Dear Miss Brown'.   In it Geddes
thanks her for a remittance of £200 which had arrived 'just in time
to meet the cares' of two months.   (Specifically, these were his
losses on a blue-eyed Franco-British School project.)   He confirms
that, 'as explained to you in conversation', this sum is to be considered neither as a one-time subscription to the College nor as a
personal loan, but rather as

> *an investment* in these present endeavours and comparable to my
> own investment, the main one so far - and to T.R. Marr's, and to
> Mrs. Branford's i.e. each and all ranking alike towards interest,
> and at rate not exceeding 5% per annum - as soon as the College
> is able to pay this!   As yet, you understand, in these 2 pre-
> liminary years now ended - (and I fear in this one now or soon
> opening, though not without increasing encouragement), these ad-
> vances are *not* yielding dividend: but I do not despair of reach-
> ing this stage in the next two or three years, if I live or am
> well replaced.
>
> I have been considering some substantial gift - though not of
> my whole capital involved (say £7000 cash, not to speak of three
> years main work so far) since that would be too severely disin-
> heriting my family, but of a substantial part, say one half of
> above sum.   This may possibly be arranged e.g. with trustees for
> and by the representatives of the S.R.C.S.U. (i.e. the Represen-
> tative Councils of the Students of the Scottish Universities);
> and if they can (possibly) find the means to pay off the remain-
> ing half of my capital to my family.
>
> If and when some such scheme can be arranged, it will be open
> to you, as to Mr Marr etc. to consider some similar arrangement
> as to their own investment.

Exactly how P.G. figured he somewhere and sometime could get '£7000
cash' out of past ventures is part of the continuous financial mystery of his life.   A likely explanation is that it was wishful
speculation with his shares in the old Town & Gown Association.   In
the second document, a hand-written note to 'Dear Lilian', he emphasises the need to keep business affairs in order, 'else troubles
might arise between our respective representatives some day', and
also says he is glad

> we have not accepted your help sooner, though so kindly & repeat-
> edly offered - for it is best not to complicate friendships with
> business relations, which other friends are apt to misunderstand!
> It is only as real colleagues - i.e. of common interest in common
> endeavour, & this of social or educational progress, or both,
> that I have been willing to accept advances from any friends.
> Yet thus indeed frequently - as for Edinburgh Halls of Residence,
> & other Old Edinburgh improvements - or as now again here....
>
> I believe it is quite right, and quite fair, to accept such
> help as we are now accepting from you; & the more since put off
> year after year - so that you should have full time to consider

at leisure - so *not* acting on the simple impulse of generosity
you have once & again expressed in these years.
    So I attach this to business letter; & remain with best
thanks, always your very cordially
                                        Pat Geddes

Yet it is the third letter of 22 August which discloses something
of new feelings that are stirring in Uncle Pat's repressed Scottish
soul.
Dear Lilian,
Now your letter itself! (apart from business matter ...) I've re-
read your recent letters ... & I could not but feel (when they
came - & also when we met - and now still) deeply grateful for
the feeling they express; for despite all these past years (five
or more, is it not) I have not been insensible as I must have
seemed: - and so it *was* right to express this, as I did the other
morning! (Yet - quite right! - & not a bit silly!)   And yet I
go away! & because I *must* go my way - & do my work - and as a man
goes off to war.
    You see you hesitate to face that world of ideas & activities
- and continue your own past, & as habits so strongly compel ...
but the other way is to face what life can offer apart from them.
Why not seek just that?
    In these years past you have often spoken of coming here.
Well, *come*, & see for yourself - how far some co-operations &
understanding may be possible?   I can't really say.   No one
knows the future - but some way may appear.
    Here beside us is a strange story: like Abelard's & Hel-
oise's, but happier.   A hopeful young couple were parted by
their hostile families here a good few years ago: so both entered the order of St Francis, as nun & monk (friar) [i.e. the Abbé
Prévost].   And now they carry on a great orphanage together,
with much else - the best music & ritual the Church has seen for
long - & an inspiration throughout city & university, region &
land - more than either could have done separately!
    Neither you nor I would carry religion as far: yet there is
something in their story, is there not?
    Come then for a visit, yet be free - and consider if you can
make me of *more* effectiveness, not less - & so yourself also!...
                            R.S.V.P. to yours as ever PG

During the autumn his moods and activities wavered between wanting
Lilian to come to the College and his routine as thinker, gardener,
and planner.   There are five more letters to her before Christmas.
One in September urges her to start on her journey south before students arrive and make demands on his time.   In the next, in October, he thanks her for a birthday card (he was 73 on the 2nd), and
is glad she is better now.
But I dread all this psycho-analysis of yours.   While I don't
regret expressing my feeling (- only as it should be, in view of
yours! -) alas, what further is possible?...   What more can I
say! - only what you repeat: come on visit - stay nearby - ...
and see how far you may find interests & possibilities for expression - musical etc.

No letters exist from November, but that of 1 December begins
'Sorry you go on with your psycho-analytic worries instead of *real
life* - real music - real activities & interests outside yourself
instead of inside! that's really all I can say!'   There have been
many visitors, and P.G. is in arrears with correspondence and books.
(Thomson had written in October that their new deadline for 'Biology' was Christmas 1927, but Geddes still couldn't get on with his
part of the job.)   He informs Lilian that the 'tiresome school ...
is now happily let to City at $7\frac{1}{2}$% on cost of production', reports
that her £200 have been thus invested, and asks whether she would
be willing to put £500 more into it.   If so, he could undertake
'the sanitation of the Château, & other urgent repairs ... which
I've no spare capital for'.   A Riviera agency is interested in
hiring it but 'won't look at it until I get in baths, etc.'

On 6 December P.G. warns Lilian that a Le Play House excursion will
be occupying all available rooms after Christmas but that 'we can
take you earlier as you suggest, and welcome!'   After two pages of
letter comes a financial 'NB' in which he repeats:

> *I want no subscription* from you!...   I only suggested a *change
> of investment* - (& to one of peculiar solidity, since with the
> City as tenant who can't fail us....)
>   That's the difference I'm trying to work out, from orthodox
> finance, which tries to *keep* what's profitable, & hand on what
> is not!   Whereas by handing on what becomes profitable, I get a
> little capital for the non-paying part of the concern, & its
> needed extension: e.g. more rooms for desirable students & con-
> genial guests ... I hope you understand: for I should hate to
> have you think me begging aid in the usual way, & making myself
> a nuisance to my friends.
>   Bring your violin of course!
>
>   Always yours PG

As a down-to-earth afterthought he adds this unusually realistic
description of existing 'conveniences':

> Only one metal bath, to which hot water is carried (& a shower-
> bath, for summer mostly, on ground floor).   Future sanitation
> in new wing.
>   But a saucer-bath in each room, for sponging down.
>
>   PG

The New Year did bring a flowering of the old Agave but not the kind
he had so long been promising to Norah and his colleagues.   For
some reason neither December 1927 nor January 1928 is represented by
any letters from him to either family or friends, although Branford
did write on 22 January thanking him for much material written for
the January 'Sociological Review', and about a possible visit of the
young Maharajah of Indore and his tutor Marcel Hardy to the College
at Easter time.   Finally, on 5 February, Geddes broke his epistolary silence with three small pages to Branford, headed 'Montpellier, Sunday early'.   The first merely asked for some reprints of
a 'Review' article, but the other two dropped this bomb-shell:

> Now news which I hope won't too much pain you - nor make you
> think harshly of me - for I am less forgetful of past life & love

& their fruits & friends than I may seem! But - there are matters we can't discuss - and you will not grudge me such St Martin's summer as may be.

So, in short, I am to be *married* (at British Consulate Marseilles, this Thursday) to my old friend - Lilian Brown. We go for a few days to her sister's vacant cottage *Clos du Plan, Cassis,* near Marseilles & then return here to such further work still as may be done.

Is this rejuvenescence? You may ask? I trust so far - but time will soon show!

To make best of such time, I wish the Mumfords would come next summer! Also that I could find some effective *sec.* (Let me hear of any - not easy!) But above all, believe me, Dear old Brother,

always yours - Pat -

Two days later P.G. wrote another unusual letter, marked 'Tues. noon' and addressed to Lilian herself:

Dearest,

Very busy here, & making progress in the tidying up of my study, so as to get over the accountings which have so long overpowered & discouraged me, and be in better order to come back to.

But there's so much to do that I am going to take the *afternoon express* ... & so have a clear forenoon's work here tomorrow to get things forward for our return. But I shall thus only arrive at Marseilles at 7.5 p.m. in time to dress for dinner with you all three. At 7.30 if all's well. (I'm sure you'll forgive me, since it is for a better return here after our stay at Cassis.)

Then too today & tomorrow I've an important visitor here & staying - M. Garnier, the French Vice-Pres. of Franco-Socttish Society who may help to arrange an excursion of them here, & thus some stirring up of Scots Universities, etc.

This will still leave us time to get the ring on Thursday morning (and I'm not forgetting my promised New Year present, the more since needed for the *real* ceremony, in the evening at Cassis!)

Don't forget your *passport* - indispensable for Consul!)

Yours - and always more & more disciplined towards abating my faults & developing such qualities as I may, so as really to be your 'Dear Beast', my Beauty!...

With the letter, on a separate sheet of *Collège* paper, this bit of verse was quoted without comment or signature:

An' sae, t' preserve the puir bodie in life,
I think I maun wed him tomorrow, tomorrow!
I think I maun wed him tomorrow!

The wedding, however, took a most unexpected course. A former resident at the College, John Tandy, (7) recalls on that Wednesday of forty-odd years ago, seeing Geddes leave 'to get married, dressed in grey and looking very spruce and handsome and remarkably young for his age. We said goodbye and thought we wouldn't see him for some little time since he was going off on a honeymoon.' But the very next day they were 'shocked and surprised to get a telegram saying that he and Lilian were returning because she had gone blind'.

Lilian Brown had been suffering from glaucoma in one eye especially but was getting better until, on the day of the wedding, she suddenly lost the use of both eyes.   She suggested postponing the ceremony, but

> he wouldn't have anything of the sort and went through with it, thus marrying a blind woman, which was extremely courageous because he could so easily have postponed everything as she was suggesting....   They got married in the morning and were back in Montpellier that same night.
>
> The annex building was cleared for Lilian and her sister Ida, and P.G. stayed with the rest of us in the main building.   The next day somebody, a great pontiff as it were, arrived from the Faculty of Medicine at Montpellier.   He prescribed remedies for Lilian, and every day we'd get good reports of her recovery. Her eyesight was improving daily, dramatically.
>
> Everybody was very pleased, and nobody more than P.G. - until one night some time after dinner, we suddenly heard loud and extraordinary noises from the annex.   It was P.G. who came out bellowing like a bull.   I shall never forget it - I have never heard any human being uttering those sorts of noises - just like a bull bellowing in the night.

The reason for this outburst, unusual even for 'Old High Explosive', was his accidental discovery that Lilian had *not* been following the treatment prescribed by the professor of medicine.   Instead, his medicaments had been poured down the sink while she took some herbal remedies provided by her 'fanatical vegetarian' sister Ida. The students at the College were greatly puzzled by P.G.'s reaction, for he was always anti-establishment, and yet now suddenly supported the establishment against an apparently successful though unorthodox treatment.   The non-conformist sister responded to P.G.'s fury in kind.

> Ida Brown, who was a woman of great temperament, said she would never set foot in the place again and she didn't.   Ida left forthwith in the middle of the night, never to be seen again in Montpellier.

Interestingly enough, Geddes wrote his version of the incident to Branford, complaining that his wife's sisters, 'both able and strong-willed women - devoted to their sister's well-being', had persuaded Lilian to follow the Cure-all of 'one Arnaldi of Genoa'. Indeed, Ida had gone

> so far as to propose & even insist to one of the greatest of occulists the abandonment of the perfectly standardized treatment for arresting glaucoma, & in its galloping form (without which she would have been blind in three more days instead of recovering) - & this in favour of the Arnaldi regime which she had begun, & which authorises no rivals - like the cult of other jealous gods! (8)

Exactly how much the rhythm of Geddes's life was changed by his
second marriage is not easy to show.   His correspondence pattern
was greatly altered, especially in 1928.   Naturally the letters to
Lilian ceased, although two notes to her in London from 1932 have
been preserved, plus an undated third, perhaps written in 1929 or
1930.   What is certain is that no letters exist to or from Norah in
1928 and only one in 1929.   The daughter disapproved, to put it
mildly, of her father's re-marriage, and it seems likely that she
not only did not write him for a long while afterwards but destroyed
the letters of explanation he surely must have sent her.   There are
none from Arthur either, and from his comment many years later about
it being a pity that the family had not discovered Lilian's early
letters, one can deduce that he did not approve either. (9)   But he
did say that Lilian was warm-hearted and spontaneous, and ventured
the explanation that his father could never get over his madness of
over-expenditure.

>He wanted to go on spending and a very simple way was to accept
>her offer of warm cooperation ... you know he was apt to rather
>imagine her as an ideal hostess: warm, welcoming, understanding,
>etc.

Arthur said further that this trait of idealising was of long standing, and that 'it had annoyed my mother ... he would waste time on
adoring women ... who would sit at his feet with rapt eyes and
stimulate him to talk, and the talk was wasted on the air'.*   But
the enticement, if any, of these women on P.G. was likewise completely wasted.   He once told Arthur that 'he never had sexual
relations with any woman except your Mother.   He said this voluntarily; it was not in answer to any question and I have no doubt
that it was true.'

In the same reminiscence Arthur also states: 'There was a terrific
sense and awareness of sex as if he enjoyed sex.'   This appears to
be confirmed by the undated note mentioned above, of which the opening and closing lines are:

>Dear wee witch-Mistress!
>I was hoping you might come today....
>
>Again love from your starving solitary!   Prepare for a warm
>reception!...

To the outside world the most tangible result of the new state of
matrimony was the rapid progress of the large extension to the *Collège des Ecossais*, thanks to Lilian's payment of bills.   In Novem-

---

* Norah once commented that her father 'was more of a faun (as Mrs
Annand Taylor called him) than a human being in human relations.
Fauns ... are good-natured, playful, inquisitive, but not remarkable
for their consideration, considerateness.   I mean he would habit-
ually talk 16 to the dozen when feeling himself: when flat, he
would say out of the blue to wife or daughter "Now talk to me".   No
result to speak of: disappointment on his part.'   (This continues
quote on p. 41 from letter to author 18 May 1945.)

ber that year was laid the cornerstone of the new dining hall and
library which would link an enlarged kitchen section with single
study-chambers for twenty more residents.   The Rector of the University, aided by the workmen essential at such ceremonies, put the
stone in place with its inscription RECTOR ME POSUIT ('The Rector
placed me') facing towards Montpellier.   After polite phrases
about the value his University placed on the Scottish savant's project, the Rector let the Mayor take over to promise that the city
council would shortly decide upon the bringing of water to this
suburb and the surfacing of the dusty road into town.   The ceremony was conducted in front of a mingled gathering of Indians in
robes, Frenchmen in striped trousers, barefoot children from a
neighbourhood school and university students from Britain and America.   They heard P.G. explain why he had settled in this part of
southern France and tell of his plans for a Mediterranean *Cité
Universitaire*.

> There, I am glad to announce, ground will soon be broken for a
> *Collège des Indiens*; while up yonder is the location for a pro-
> posed *Collège des Américains*.   In sum, what brought me here four
> years ago is the ideal of once more grouping the 'colleges of the
> nations' around a French university just as in medieval times in
> Paris, though now attuned to modern conditions and here in this
> incomparable region of Languedoc.   For in this way may we not be
> able again to make it a cross-roads, a strategic point of learn-
> ing and culture?

About a year later many of the same French guests, along with a different crop of residents, attended the ceremony which opened the new
part of the Scots College and afterwards inspected such novelties in
outlying Montpellier as central heating, showers, and three complete
bathrooms.   During 1929-30 the normal complement of the College
was about twenty-five students from India, England, Scotland, the
USA, Switzerland, and Germany, plus head-cook and husband, head-
gardener and wife, and Professor and the second Mrs Geddes.

To keep this number of people in drinking and washing water proved a
constant headache.   Though kitchen, baths and study-chambers were
equipped with hot and cold water taps and hot-water radiators, and
piping, storage tanks and automatic pumps were properly installed,
a steady supply of water was lacking.   So when cisterns got low
after the autumn rainy season, old François the assistant gardener,
and his mule frequently spent whole days carting water from a hy-
drant a half-mile away.   Judged by efficiency standards P.G. was
highly unqualified to have such managerial responsibility, while
Lilian soon revealed herself most inept at guiding French servants.

Anna Geddes would have established a smooth-running hostel and won
cooperation from university and city officials even in spite of
themselves.   Together, she and Sir Thomas Barclay and Monsieur le
Maire could have had politicians and workmen laying new water mains
already in 1926 (instead of, as it turned out, in the 1940s).   But
unfortunately the new Mrs Geddes became known in Montpellier chiefly
for her eccentric English ways, such as riding a bicycle, attending
university lectures only to fall asleep during them, and not understanding the niceties of the French social code.

In justice to Lilian, her generosity and good-heartedness must be recorded.   She wanted to help P.G. in other ways than financial but simply did not have the background or experience to know how or where to start.   She tried to understand the ideas he was working out in buildings, gardens and thinking-machines, and on occasion her puzzled queries punctuated his talks or explanations of diagrams.   'What does that mean, Pat?' or 'But I don't understand this!'   No one else may have understood these points either, but her questions irritated P.G. exceedingly, and the ensuing glare or brief staccato reply did not help anyone's comprehension.

With Arthur's testimony in mind, this writer (whose first residence at the College was in the spring of 1929) can now appreciate the disillusion and perhaps embarrassment that Geddes felt when his idealised picture of Lilian-helpmate was publicly shattered, both in household and intellectual matters.   Another idealisation of his concerned her violin-playing which he had urged her to cultivate both for herself and others in almost every letter he wrote. But in this field P.G. was admittedly not a judge nor, happily, did his ear distinguish much in the way of musical sounds.   However well Lilian may have performed in younger days, those who heard her at the College could only agree that her intonation was incredibly inadequate.   But poor Lilian's musical hearing must have been impaired as well as her eyesight, and since no one made such comments openly, Geddes was mercifully spared this disillusionment.

'COMPULSIVE REPETITION', RE-EDUCATION, AND RESIDENTS' REVOLT

A typical Geddesian day in 1929-30 ran something like this.   At breakfast, where Scots porridge and Balkan yoghurt were staples, P.G. took some item of current news or from the morning's post as pertinent to his recent articles in the 'Sociological Review', expounding and questioning as long as any students were at table.   In good weather he afterwards stalked individuals or small groups outdoors until they disappeared, invoking lectures in town or work in their rooms.   Only then did he go to his tower study where a fresh heap of morning thought-notations partly hid yesterday's and today's urgent tasks.   These varied from overdue printer's proofs of the biology book to new articles for Branford and drafts of 'Parnasso-Olympus'.   Also partly visible were several months of pleading reminders from J. Arthur Thomson:

Williams & Norgate refuses further grace for the completion of 'Essentials of Biology'....   It must be now or *never*, so send me all you have....   This is desperate [11 October].

Unwin said you were reported to be the costliest author in Britain, because you made so many proof-corrections; and he wished you to allow me to do all the proof-reading [22 December].

I send the rest of the proofs with this....   I have written about the title.   As a compromise, 'Life: Outlines of General Biology' might pass for America....   I must return all proofs by June 10th at latest, and that in the midst of a crowded and strenuous session [30 May]. (10)

P.G. started to work with the best of intentions but within the
hour a workman knocked apologetically at the door to say his foreman needed *Monsieur* immediately at the newly begun Indian College.
So the delinquent co-author picked up a battered felt hat and a
cane and spent the rest of the morning trying to effect synthesis
out of the differing views of architect and foreman over the location of certain windows.

After lunch, served outdoors on the main terrace, Geddes felt more
of an urge to talk than return to his study and called for volun-
teers to make a tour of the garden.   Having cut a dozen cigarettes
in two, his way of carrying out Dr Galen's orders against excessive
smoking, and stowing them in a pocket of his old corduroy jacket,
he began in this vein:
  Now I know some of you are saying to yourselves, 'Oh hang! we've
  heard all about these gardens before'.   You may think you know
  what Candide meant by *Il faut cultiver son jardin*, or what I
  read into it in the way of doing constructive physical work instead of merely reading books or dirtying pieces of paper, but
  that's not all.   A garden can have intellectual and spiritual
  qualities as well.
     The humblest gardener is a steward of Mother Nature, a stage-
  hand - or even a minor director - in her never-ending pageant of
  the seasons.   He can also be a thinker, writing his thoughts in
  living forms and colours instead of mere printed words.   So come
  and see for yourselves a few of the intellectual fruits I have
  been cultivating, and which in return also cultivate me - and you
  too, if you will but give them a fair chance.

Today's tour featured philosophy and mythology, with minor digres-
sions.   Hegel's concept of *synthesis* was materialised in the form
of a seat halfway along a path leading from a white stone table to
a black one.   The guide placed two students, 'Black' and 'White',
to suit his words:
  Black, you come half-way along the path, and White, you do likewise.   Behold!   You meet at the middle where you can sit down
  together and discover that truth is a mixture of black and white.
  But just as there are a hundred kinds of grey, so are there as
  many possible syntheses;   an effective 'meeting of minds' is
  therefore no simple task.

The afternoon passed with one demonstration of the 'gardens of
thought' following another and no respite except when The Professor
had to reload his smoking apparatus.   Thinking-machines lurked in
flower beds, and hidden meanings in the most innocent objects.   A
huge earthenware jar, quite empty save for dead leaves and a snail
or two, turned out to be metaphysical economics.   The snails, said
P.G., admirably represented most politicians!   A small level space
near the entrance gate contained a square made up of nine cement
blocks, and two opposing semi-circles of seven blocks each.   No one
asked what these signified, but the guide voluntarily explained at
length.   The first blocks, though still waiting for statues of the
nine Muses, represented the nine squares of the fourth quarter of
his 36-squared Chart of Life.   The other fourteen blocks were intended for the Greek Gods and Goddesses of Olympus.

In lieu of statuary, P.G. selected various students to personify the
Olympians and had them stand on the pedestals while he interpreted
the inner meaning of Greek mythology.   Briefly, he claimed that the
seven gods, from Cupid to Zeus, represented the seven ages of man in
his normal development, and correspondingly that the goddesses, from
Artemis to Demeter, symbolised the seven phases of womanhood.   (He
had recently contracted to write a volume for the Yale University
Press on this subject, but like so many other 'long-dreamed' opuses,
'Olympus' was never completed for publication.)

The insistent ringing of a bell brought the weary gods and goddesses
quickly down from their stands, for it meant that tea was being
served on the main terrace.   P.G. grudgingly followed the Olympians
but once in the shade of his favourite holm oak he too enjoyed the
break.   However, no Briton would have recognised the light amber
liquid, which he mixed for himself, as tea.   'The drinking of tea',
he insisted as a biologist, 'should be a means of getting needed
water into the system, not of tanning one's innards!'

Tea-time almost always yielded a visitor, and today it was a retired
British army man, a distant relative of Lilian's en route to the
Riviera.   'I say', he exclaimed to Geddes, 'what a curious place
this is!   And why all these tiled squares and symbols on the terrace?'   Most willingly P.G. explained his staircase Classification
of the Sciences, (see ch. 2 and Appendix) using such students as
were still around as pawns.

At six the two men were pacing the salon of the old tower exchanging
a barrage over the political situation in Britain.   Delighted to
have an ultra conservative in his clutches, Old High Explosive let
loose one broadside after the other.
    'You think I am a Revolutionary?   Well, among other things,
    yes.   But I claim to be an Imperialist, a Home Ruler, a Nation-
    alist, a Conservative, a Sinn Feiner, a Tory, a Socialist, a Co-
    operator, and a Liberal as well!   If you want to pin one label
    on me you must pin them all! (11)   People are always asking me
    whether I'm this or that, an Aristotelian or a Platonist, a
    Hindu or a Theosophist, a Roman Catholic or a Protestant, a
    Deist or an Atheist, a Freudian or a Jungian, and so on, and I
    always tell them: "Of course I am!"   For there is some truth
    in all these doctrines, some good in all specialisms, and I
    accept the truth wherever I find it.   But the trouble with most
    Britons is that they can only be one thing or the other.   Look
    here... '
    'Really, it's getting late, don't you think?   Almost time to
dress for dinner.'

Geddes was fully wound up and like the Ancient Mariner to whom he
compared himself in his letter to Gandhi, he could withhold neither
words nor thinking machines.   Paying no attention to the guest's
anxiety, he went on:
    'Look here, I shall diagram the whole field of politics for you.
    It's very simple: take a sheet of paper, fold it in four quar-
    ters, write the appropriate label for each system of collective

(above) The *Collège des Ecossais* as completed in 1930 with the financial support of Lilian Geddes whom P.G. married in 1928 after eleven years as a widower

(left) P.G. in one of the gardens with residents of the Scots College, Spring 1930. Indian College under construction in background

Tea on the terrace under the Mediterranean live oak (often mistaken by visitors for an olive tree to P.G.'s immense disgust as biologist and educator). Geddes third from right

College residents and Le Play House visitors on Classification of Sciences Terrace, *Collège des Ecossais*, Easter 1930

(below left) P.G. and Paul Reclus
(below right) P.G. seated in front of the tower of the Scots College, 1929, making a diagram while smoking one of the half cigarettes ordained by his doctor

human error, of which there are four; and there you have the
world today, in which men bearing one tag are ready to kill men
with a different one.'

Following his own words, he noted down the systems which, 'despite
their few grains of truth, together exhaust all possible political
fallacies', and showed his result.

Conser- vative Tory Anarchy	Socialism
Commun- ism	Fascism

Figure 11.1

Ground between P.G.'s shocking political views and his own fear of
not having time to dress, the Major was writhing inwardly, and when
his watch marked seven o'clock, he broke out.
    'But damn it! I've simply got to go and change!'
    'Why of course, my dear man', [said Geddes with soothing sar-
casm]. 'By all means go put on your stuffed shirt, or your
pyjamas if you like. As for myself, I shall enjoy my dinner
immensely in this old corduroy suit!'

A bright moon was shining that night, and Geddes slipped away after
dinner to walk alone through the gardens and on the *garrigue* as a
perfect fresh-air conclusion to his day. He liked to study the
shapes of terrace walls and shrubs and trees by moonlight, for
ideas often thus came to him for new designs. At nine o'clock he
paused in the salon to say good night and went up to the little bedroom adjoining his neglected study. Perhaps, before falling
asleep, he vowed that tomorrow he *would* get at those proofs for
Thomson.

As Senior Resident of the Scots College and as a self-styled re-
educator, P.G. was decidedly a mixed blessing. John Tandy has described life during the months before remarriage as a kind of daily
game of wits between the omnipresent Professor-of-All-Things and
students trying to escape his didactic efforts. Though exaggera-
ted, Tandy's account does bring out one of Geddes's weaknesses as a
teacher in his later years:
    I remember being there when professors from various parts of the
    world came; they had the misfortune sometimes of correcting
    him, and this would spoil the whole day.... You had to let him
    go on until he got to the end. If you listened to him the
    whole way you ought to be able to get something that was very
    valuable, but he would be infuriated and become mad with rage if
    you corrected him. (12)

In spite of this trait and his love of long monologues, students
were impressed by his total personality. For example, when the

actor Sir Nigel Playfair sent his son Giles to the Scots College
thinking it would help prepare him for a conventional English university, the son reported that even though 'my chances of a successful Oxford career were not materially advanced during my two months'
stay in Montpellier, I could not have had a happier, a more interesting and a more enjoyable time.   I did not regret one moment of
it.'   Even so, Giles admitted frankly that he tried to avoid being
left alone with Geddes.   'For we knew that "to be caught" would
mean a three hours' minimum session of walking and being talked
at.' (13)

Another trait of P.G. that has been mentioned earlier was his 'oppo-
sitional compulsion'.   When someone's person or opinion was
attacked, he would take the defence, as when Huxley scoffed at
Comte's Positivism or Spencer's Sociology.   Conversely, if a view
or dogma was strongly or officially proclaimed, Geddes turned challenger or prosecutor.   Thus when Andrew H. Drummond, a Scottish
theological student and relative of the noted evangelist Henry
Drummond, came to the College at the end of 1927 'to get his ideas
widened on comparative religions', P.G. seems to have played the
Devil himself.   A young woman student, Moya Jowitt, has given the
writer this account:
    I remember P.G. trying, as it seemed to me, to destroy Drummond's
    faith in Christ.   He went on & on, ridiculing everything & pro-
    ducing all the 'scientific' attacks - also relating Christianity
    to all old fables & legends.   Until I remember Drummond saying,
    rather desperately, 'No matter what you disprove, I will still
    believe...'
    I clearly remember P.G.'s waspish attacks.   As I myself was
    at that time an atheist, it did not shock me.   But now I see
    clearly how P.G. seemed to rage against a faith he could not
    accept: I think so much because of his loss of Alasdair. (14)

The enlarged capacity of the Scots College from 1929 on resulted in
a larger yearly total of residents, though not necessarily a pro-
portionately increase in successful 'Re-education'.   In fact, among
the known items of published testimony there are none which can
match the earlier enthusiasms of Mabel Barker, or Indian students
like Pheroz Bharucha, or Dorothea Price who captured the thrill of
one of P.G.'s Sunday 'at-homes' in these words:
    Who can forget it?   Brilliant sunshine, a crowd of sixty or more
    folk, French, Indian, British, gathered on the terrace.   Before
    them on a low stone parapet, a slight, frail figure with leonine
    head silhouetted against the blue of a Mediterranean sky.   By
    the vibrant beat of the voice he seemed to be chanting prophetic-
    ally, ecstatically.   It was the story of his College; its in-
    tention, difficult birth, promising childhood, tremendous future.
    We looked up at the grey stone building before us, read its sym-
    bols, noted its turret chamber, felt some of its mysterious sig-
    nificance, and wondered the more. (15)

Mabel Barker had known Geddes in his many moods far longer than any
other resident at Montpellier, for she had also 'served time' in
Edinburgh, receiving her share of apparent ingratitude.   Yet she
remembered him only at his best. (16)

... as an example of how much may be accomplished by one virile
mind in a frail but active body, of how full a life may be when
every hour is precious for what may be done in it, Patrick Geddes
is an inspiration.   There was something Caesar-like in the
quality of his activity, in the driving force which made his
milieu exhausting at times to those of lesser fibre who strove to
keep pace with him.   This was partly because, with his complete
absence of pride in his own power and his belief in the high po-
tentiality of all men and women, he would not admit that they
were of lesser fibre!*

From personal experience the writer knows that many who came to the
College in its later years had little grasp of what P.G. really
stood for and had accomplished.   This was inevitable, given his
sporadic and redundant talks from and about his southern Outlook
Tower.   Yet no alert person could spend even a day there without
feeling the presence of an unusual personality.   To be caught by
him and taken up the high ground back of the College for a first
view of his incomparable region was a re-education in itself.   P.G.
would wave his walking-stick out over the early spring countryside
already verdant and sprinkled with white almond blossoms.
  Look!   There are the books you now must read: the realities of
  nature which enslavement to printed pages has kept you from
  seeing and understanding.   There, in all that beauty lying
  between mountains and sea, is salvation from the evils of our
  too-bookish civilization.   Don't you know that nature intended
  young men first of all to be active animals: fishing in yonder
  Mediterranean, hunting across these heaths, or at least fighting
  with one another?   Yet what are most of you nowadays but sedentary, eye-strained students cramming for damnfool examinations?

But the real personal shock came when P.G. seized one's hands and
continued half-kindly, half-ferociously:
  Aha!   Look at them - how clean and white and useless: the hands
  of a paper-gentleman!   My young friend, I shall turn you over to
  Malépine the head-gardener, this very afternoon.   From him and
  blisters, perspiration and honest fatigue you will discover that
  the only way to learn anything is to take part in life.   Daily
  labour is the basic, age-old path to both health and intelligence
  simply because it is a basic part of life in this world.

Although more or less appreciative of Geddesian 're-education', the
majority of residents became dissatisfied with practical arrangements at P.G.'s college.   What should have remained just a small
'tower-nest of his own' with gardens of health and philosophy, and

* The writer can testify that Geddes at 75 would sit working com-
fortably in his unheated tower study in winter with inside temperatures around 10-15° C. (50-60° F.) wearing just his corduroy suit.
When a student invited to talk with him, clad in sweater and overcoat, began to shiver visibly P.G. would take the other's icy hands
in his own warm ones saying 'Poor fellow!   But it's not really cold
here!'   His metabolic adaptation was indeed remarkable.

with a rotating staff of proven colleagues to transmute those idea
middens into usuable books, became overgrown and nondescript, no
thanks to Lilian's money. The non-appearance of his real colleagues also contributed to our sense of frustration and resentment.
Lewis Mumford was expectantly considered as the main possibility of
salvation, both for P.G.'s wasted days and the students' own un-
organised opportunities, but we could not know of his inner difficulties with Geddes which would be revealed in 'The Disciple's Rebellion'. All we knew then was that the young, vital American continuator so often invoked by P.G. never arrived, much to our disappointment and dismay.

When the Easter invasion of Le Play House excursionists had receded
from the College in 1930, an event occurred which took the old and
hardy critic of universities himself by surprise: a student revolt.
Causes were partly trivial, such as the presence of uncongenial non-
student residents. More serious was the demand to know how the
place was financed and exactly what happened to the fees paid by
bona fide students. Two spokesmen presented their ultimatum: co-
responsibility in choice of residents and in accounting, or else all
would leave the College immediately. The writer, chosen as one
delegate partly for his vague duties as secretary of the 'incipient
American College' and partly as a student, will venture this personal account.

While some aspects are hazy after forty-odd years, I can still
see the bearded P.G. sitting at his study in the midst of docu-
ment-strewn tables as we read the list of grievances and its conclusion. He jumped up, his hair and beard bristling even more
than usual. With eyes like an angry Jove he discharged the
vocabulary lightnings of his master mind in full force against
two trembling up-starts. His exact words I do not remember,
nor could they have been remembered, for such an eloquent condemnation of our unjustified suspicions and our 'infamous un-
friendliness' towards certain 'guest residents' could only have
been captured by a tape recorder, not then invented.

After ten or more endless minutes of such vituperation I found
to my surprise that we were still alive and heard my companion
declare that we had done our duty, and that he and others would
leave the College in protest. He departed and suited action to
the word. Then, suddenly, I realised that the violent words
were somehow passing harmlessly over my head as I stood there
alone with Old High Explosive. His thundering seemed to be a
review, a diatribe against previous challenges to his judgment
or authority.*

* After writing the above account, I was intrigued to locate the
passage in 'The Cruciform Mark' of 1896 (p. 192) where the hero (and
hoped-for disciple) describes what happened when he told 'Professor
Grosvenor' that he was leaving Edinburgh next day instead of heeding
the former's plea to attend his epoch-making lecture. 'At this he
broke out into vehement and contemptuous reproach.... He spoke to
me as I would not have spoken to a dog. He abused me as a slug-
gard, a turncoat, a poltroon, and followed me to the door with
sarcasms.'

Again, suddenly, I was surprised to hear myself contradicting the super-opponent and saying that the students were justified in moving out.   I too would move out.   Imitating some of his force, I repeated what I had once timidly tried to tell him as 'secretary': that he misrepresented facts in his brochures. It was not 'a College at the University of Montpellier'; it was a residence way out on the garrigue with no official connection as yet.

A quarter-hour later P.G.'s denunciation had become explanation and justification.   I brought up other weak points in his public-relations methods, and he began talking in an ordinary voice with conciliatory words.   Yes, it would perhaps be a good thing for the protesters to leave.   But why not go out and enjoy the Château d'Assas and think things over again, while he considered what could be done.   But above all, let us not quarrel uselessly, let us try to find a solution for our problems and his.   We shook hands, and the long verbal encounter ended. P.G. went back to his writing desk, and a much less shaky go-between left to report his peace-offer to the others.

To his credit, during our interesting but apprehensive days at the château, he took measures that ought to have been arranged years before.   He turned over more fully the business management to Mr T.R. Marr, who for many years was warden of a residential hall in Manchester.   To Paul Reclus he gave the responsibility of directing and co-ordinating the studies undertaken by College residents at the University of Montpellier.   Meanwhile the disputed guests moved voluntarily to another habitat, and most of the rebels returned to the fold.   Accordingly, by the summer of 1930, the Scots College appeared to be on the way to succeeding as a student hostel.

'THE VILLAGE WORLD' ... 'RURAL AND URBAN THOUGHT'

Certain aspects of life in P.G.'s Montpellier could have been satirised just as in Old Edinburgh, yet his real thought and work went on, though in varying amounts, during both epochs.   Did he accomplish any new thinking and writing during the years at his Scots College?   Or does Lewis Mumford make the final judgment when he says that the Scots College was an evasion, 'an excuse for not completing the task too long postponed, that of ordering his ideas into some final form'? (17)

Part of the answer lies in articles written during 1926-30 for the 'Sociological Review' as well as in the one opus actually completed, 'Life: Outlines of General Biology' (1931), with Thomson as co-author.   Even more of it is hidden, or lost, in letters still scattered around the world, and in countless irretrievable conversations.   Still, we may begin by examining two articles which treat rural problems and values, the topics basic to all of P.G.'s thinking and doing.   These are 'The Village World: Actual and Possible' (April 1927) and 'Rural and Urban Thought: A Contribution to the Theory of Progress and Decay' (January 1929).   The content of 'The Village World ...' falls into two sections:

Part I, a 'Comparative Rural Survey', brings to light how neglected and depressed the villages of France and Great Britain are,
and how little they share even in the scientific advances of
public health.   But it also describes how individuals like A.E.
(George Russell) in Ireland and, in particular, Tagore in Bengal
are turning the tide towards renewal, both material and cultural.
Arthur Geddes's thesis on rural civilisation in Bengal is praised
as indicating 'with care and fullness the conditions of past decline, and those of the needed and incipient reconstruction and
renewal'.

Part II is called 'A Village Eutopia Envisioned', and hails a
new development in rural sociology which is learning to 'see the
village as the essential unit, and this alike for general study
and for a careful survey, for specific treatment and for social
renewal'.   Yet how can migration to the town with its many
attractions be slowed down, let alone reversed?   P.G. answers
with three examples: 'the most distinguished dramatic performance of the whole world' at Ober-Ammergau;   the return of a
world-famed singer, Madame Calvé, to teach music in her native
French village;   and his own current project near Montpellier.

He expands the last example by urging that Assas, 'and many
other châteaux, should begin making amends to its village ... as
village centre of a new kind'.   He envisions a tennis court and
dancing green in the 'neglected old park', University courses
'extended' to Assas, and re-afforestation as a local example of
what is needed all the way from Mediterranean lands to Asia.
'Our village is thus no mere Sleepy Hollow, but our latent
Eutopia ...'

In 'Rural and Urban Thought ...' (originally given as a lecture for
a meeting of the International Association for the Improvement of
Industrial Relations, at Girton College, Cambridge) Geddes again
documents the failure of advances in natural science to improve the
world either morally or socially, but as a mitigating circumstance
points out that 'biological and evolutionary sciences' have not been
given their chance.   Nor has his own 'scientific and educational
method' of 'Survey, of the Region and City' been applied on a large
enough scale to prove its value to society.   As in other writings
P.G. emphasises that the green leaf is the foundation of all life,
that the essentials of civilisation and origins of urban institutions all go back to workers in the nature occupations and their
villages.   He insists, further, that such deteriorations in
present-day society as war-lords, greedy politicians and slothful
bureaucrats are results of the loss of rural ideals and work-ways.
He returns to George Perkins Marsh as not only a pioneer ecologist
but as the necessary complement to Gibbon in explaining the 'Decline
and Fall of the Roman Empire', for Marsh 'was able to see with new
clearness the far more terrible ruin of old Italy, as indeed of all
Mediterranean lands ... through the destruction of the forests'.

New thought emerges as P.G. uses modern socialism as his next example of 'the blindness of urban thought to rural reality'.   He names
Marx, 'with his precursors and successors', the Fabians and their
administrative endeavours, and the Shavians with income-equalisa-

tions, asserting that even though all their proposed changes could be accomplished, these would still be 'essentially in the urban thought-circle, mechanistic and pecuniary by turns'.

> Were this not so, how could any Socialist have gone on for the past two generations preaching socialism or trying to practise it, without seeing that beyond his familiar illustration of the ancient and undeniable socialism of the public highway, is the forest, to and from which it should lead, instead of to desolated moorland.   Surely it is a commonplace to every social geographer, that of all forms of rural development over Europe, it is the forest which most definitely thrives and prospers under collective ownership, that of the village, the town and city, the province or State also....
>
> So, for Marx and his successors to have thrown away this magnificent argument for collective ownership, is to our rural minds an amazing illustration of the limitation of urban thought.

Turning to 'British India', Geddes points out how knowledge of the value of forests in conserving downpour is but slowly spreading. The full economic and social significance 'has still to be grasped, both by our utmost imperialists and their severest Indian critics'.

> Witness even Mr Gandhi, with so much of spinning wheel, but as yet nothing of spade.   The countless Indian intellectuals who now qualify as lawyers and politicians, both at home and in England, have as yet shown no policy in which forestry, irrigation or drainage appreciably figure;   these seem to have no more existence in their minds, than in those of our own innumerable urban sufferers from barristeria.

An additional attack is made on Britain and deals with the continuing crisis of coal production.   An indignant P.G. quotes from what he calls the 'open letter to the Government' which he, Victor Branford, Patrick Abercrombie (President of the Town-Planning Institute), Cecil H. Desch (later head of the National Physical Laboratory), and others had published in book form in 1926. (18)   It was a 'specific challenge' to the public, to the Royal Coal Commission, and to mine owners and workers 'before the coal crisis lapsed into its persisting catastrophe'.   Their argument was 'briefly this: Try Regional Planning.   Give us our hearing, and our chance, as an evolutionary group, and not a party'.   The open letter also strongly reproached those concerned for not accepting previous offers of help:

> If either central or local governments had had the wisdom to employ us, and give us our chance, as captains of reconstructive industry, to utilise even a fraction of their doles, we should by this time have cleared up many a squalid village and town, both industrial and rural.   We should have applied their waste to use, providing building materials here, and cheap fuel there, or turning it to fertility.   We should have drained marshy places, and sometimes irrigated meadows.   Our forestry-plantations would already be growing;   and so on;   and all with labour so manly, so healthy, and even joyous as to attract youth to a period of such service.

Now, three years after this challenge and early plan for 'civilian
service', P.G. has to tell his audience at Cambridge that still
nothing had happened. Neither the 'Coal Crisis' book nor his later
article, 'Coal: ways to reconstruction', 'Sociological Review',
July 1926, reprinted as a pamphlet, had accomplished anything,
'since, so far as we could ascertain, they were left practically
unread' by the five groups concerned: 'i.e. the public, the
masters, the workers, the Government, or even the Royal Commission.'
The one extenuating circumstance is that, 'had time and powers
allowed', these publications 'might have been better and more fully
done, and more convincingly presented'. On the other hand, he
claims that 'it is not their limitations which explain their failure, but their qualities!'

P.G. next admits the symposium authors' error of rashly going
beyond speaking of planning and engineering, and even of hygiene,
in ordinary readable technical terms - to refer to the real
social issues....
   We dared to affirm that the coal situation is far more than a
money squabble; we have treated it as a collapse of the paleotechnic order of industry, yet with opening for the neo-technic
one....
   We challenge criticism; and we invite fuller verification by
such members of the Cambridge Congress as will grant it consideration, if they do not know it already. And if granted, we
again challenge and invite consideration of the necessary revolution in thought which this material transition carries with it.

In spite of partly 'weird' illustrations and a style that could
either be diffuse or over-condensed, it is possible, in these
'Review' articles, to find new interpretations and applications of
Geddesian thought, sometimes even in brief, readable passages. For
instance, after belabouring Marx and successors for not understanding the forest as a 'magnificent argument for collective ownership',
Geddes continues:
   No wonder the peasant, from Ireland to France, or thence to
   Russia, is little moved by the urban socialist, be he simple
   orator, or metropolitan dictator; and this is why the 'red' revolution is now plainly evoking against it the green banner of
   the peasant, as now rising at various points of Eastern Europe,
   and destined to spread, and come to power.

Again upbraiding government agencies and capitalists for not giving
his colleagues and him an opportunity to survey and reconstruct, he
says ironically that the so-called 'practical man' will object that
this would cost money: 'and where and how is that to be got?'
Whereupon the parenthetical, piercing remark: '(Always money,
observe - never money's worth; never a word of real energy-saving,
or industry-improving!)'

In considering P.G.'s new interpretations one may safely affirm that
everything of social nature he wrote after reading Huxley, Ruskin,
Spencer, Kropotkin and Comte from 1874 on was originally their
thought: Workers' education; the blunders of industrialism;

Mutual Aid vs. Darwinism; the place of sociology.   Yet P.G.'s
fifty years of lecturing, writing, planning and building are there
to show how he cross-fertilised, combined, extended *and applied* the
ideas of others until the results bore unmistakable Geddesian ear-
marks.   The same can be said of his borrowings and fabrications of
the Comte-Le Play interpretations of history, occupations and
society.   The only difference is that the older he got the more he
added himself as a third partner and continuator of the two Frenchmen.

The idea of up-dating Comte had already possessed Geddes in London.
Early evidence is the classification of the sciences which, when
made into a 'thinking machine', was perhaps the most often demons-
trated of all graphics in P.G.'s repertory, along with Place-Work-
Folk, of course.   The latest example is his attempt to continue
Comte's analysis of human history as consisting of 'Three States'
(Theological-Military, Statist-Individualistic, and Industrial-
Scientific) by adding three more to interpret the future in terms of
'Biotechnics', 'Synergy in Geotechnics', and 'Etho-Polity/Eu-
Psychics'.

This plan was mentioned as early as 1922 in a letter to Norah, lectured upon at Cornell University in the summer of 1923 and put into
final form in two articles in 1929 and 1930.   These are, respectively, 'An Interpretation of Current Events - a Sociological
Approach to the General Election' and 'Ways of Transition - Towards
Constructive Peace'.   Both lead up to, and are summarised in, the
double graph of 'Transition IX to 9', as Geddes steadily referred to
it ever after (see Appendix).

'Transition IX to 9', as might be guessed, was expressed by placing
Comte's Three States in one interacting, nine-squared diagram ('IX')
and Geddes's three in the other as the goal ('9') to be attained.
In his words, future societies must somehow progress from today's
'predominantly militant and statist, mechanistic and pecuniary
civilisation ... so essentially urban, and towards a vital and initially rural order ... of more hopefully evolutionary character'.
Most of the practical examples for accomplishing this are taken from
his past six years of developing the Scots College, 'albeit on the
small initial scale of leaven and mustard seed'.   But he also insists that to attain peace, there must be widespread preparations
for peace: *Si vis pacem, para pacem.*
> Not as War-peace interregnum, after all mere Truce, but as Peace-
> war, not only utilising this period, but indefinitely prolonging
> and ameliorating it, by demonstration of its fresh advantages.
>   ... when constructive pacifists really get to work, they will
> survey and report, with schemes and plans and estimates, each for
> his country's development throughout its regions, cities and
> villages, and these for place, work and people.

As one ploughs through the often complicated sentences of P.G.'s
writings of 1926-30, a striking simile of his comes to mind.   It
was used when, as a young biologist tackling his own 'Principles of
Economics', he described the chores of background reading involved.

Often he had to crush 'a whole stony volume for a few grains of
genuine gold'.   A pity that so many readers of the 'Sociological
Review' in the 1920s shunned the labour of crushing when they saw
a Geddesian contribution, for there were and are nuggets in those
pages.   Speaking of small examples of 'Transition' like affores-
tation of the neglected *garrigue*, he explains clearly that:

> In course of this, we use all we can of physical and chemical
> knowledge and of mechanistic powers, so far as applicable to our
> biotechnic purposes.   There is here not abandonment of the
> mechanistic order, but direct utilisation of its resources and
> appliances, as from microscope to motor;   and even active desire
> and hope of more, so far as applicable to the service and advan-
> cement of life.

P.G. can also wax eloquent as well as wise, witness this final
sample from 'Ways of Transition':

> If our syllabus of economic studies - as Neo-Physiocratic - gets
> written, its frontispiece should be made from a photograph of
> 'Real Investment' - a line of sturdy labourers working at the
> reclamation of our hard-beaten and stony soil, for the first
> time in its geologic history being tilled, but now thoroughly and
> deeply, so as to yield crops for indefinite time to come with
> only ordinary care, without re-trenching....
>
> ... even this hardest of toil is no curse submitted to from
> mere poverty, but a strenuous task of victory over wild nature.
> As each howks deep, and levers out the big stone, or smashes the
> obtruding rock with heavy steel mallet, he is rejoicing in his
> strength, as plainly as the strong man in scripture.

In the same vein it can be stated that Geddes summed up in the 'IX
to 9' diagrams nothing less than his lifelong campaign to replace
Wardom by equally exciting Peacedom, to remake the 'bad-places' of
every region into Eu-topias.   Optimally, his every word and deed
was, in one way or another, in furtherance of the Biblical 'Thy
Kingdom Come!'

FAREWELL TO BROTHER VICTOR

Early on New Year's Day 1930 P.G. writes another 'self-review' to
Branford, starting with 'All good wishes!   Good year to you - &
more of them!   *Make* them more', and going on:

> My year has begun hopefully!   After rest yesterday from fatigue
> a little increased of course by Le Play House Visit (& too long
> final talk!) I woke fresh this morning, & in the last two hours
> have come to comparative clearness of decision & resolution -
> essentially of making the long delayed step beyond my student
> life & constructive endeavours towards its fundamentals, mate-
> rial, intellectual etc - *the step of leadership*.

Despite the confident beginning, Geddes does not arrive at any new
plan of action.   What he proposes boils down to getting more and
better groups of visitors at the College.   'Or, in more ambitious
terms - something of our old Summer Meetings at Edinburgh - some-

thing of Pontigny discussions.'   (Summer gatherings at Pontigny in
Burgundy arranged by his French friend, Paul Desjardins.)   Yet as
always, interesting comments and ideas crop up amid P.G.'s lamenta-
tions and hopeful thinking.

> My long endeavours, since beginning of Edinburgh Halls, have of
> course been as fisher of men, and - despite encouraging cases! -
> there has not been much % of result.   I don't (to any signifi-
> cant extent) catch the fish & know I must not too simply blame
> them!   (From fishy cold to terrestial life of anon sun and sha-
> dow is surely the hardest of evolutionary transitions!)
>
> *Tres fascient collegi* - but I've never yet fully found the
> other two in same year - though always some approach to this -
> which I have not made the best of!   Still too simply a student
> myself!

Geddes finishes at the crowded bottom of page three, only to continue on another page two days later, saying 'Alas!   Snowed under
instead of posted!'   The equally crammed fourth page informs Branford that T.R. Marr has settled in a house not far away and, as new
staff member, 'has already got on with students farther than I could
do'.   It also admits that P.G. is 'in disgrace with Yale Press re
"Olympus"', so that promised articles for the 'Review' will have to
wait.   Finally, Branford is asked to use his influence at the London School of Economics to get their man Farquharson in as one of
the successors to Professors Hobhouse and Westermarck.

Other letters to Branford during the spring of 1930 follow the same
pattern of reminiscence, planning and health exhortations.   On 20
May the sociology book is mentioned, mainly in connection with
P.G.'s disagreements with Farquharson over his part in it, especially his lack of vitalisation.   Attached to the same letter is a
sheet headed 'More Ambitions Still' on which, recalling their joint
activities, P.G. says Branford has had 'the large political vision.'

> And I too, i.e. Paris in 1900 especially, with J. de Bloch on
> War & Peace - with International Association and Rue des Nations,
> as prefiguring even the League of Nations let alone its Inter-
> national Intellectual Relations, & with Le Play School the Labour
> Office as well....
>
> (What of lecturing again on Contemporary Social Evolution from
> the newspapers as I used to do sometimes of old, at Essex Hall,
> there reaching some of the Press.)

In early June P.G. sends an anxious letter to 'Cher Frère Victor':

> I am very much concerned about your painful illness....   Yet,
> painful though arthritis be, it is *not so dangerous as many
> others*: and you will pull through this, and find your way into
> a port of convalescence and repairs!

After informing Branford that he now has diabetes 'in first stage',
though not doubting but that this attack will be cured, he concludes:

> But with other deterioration, & age so far, I have to mobilise my
> mental control & stabilise sub-conscious too - & am convinced I
> can for a while yet.   So can you!   So can Thomson!   We all

need each other.... Let us take hands & help each other to be
men, & not mere patients. Said Frederick before the battle -
'The King has no time for fever', so turned out his physicians,
won the battle, & was all right after it! Can't we play up?
Yes, of course shall!

Salut et fraternité
PG

A P.S. said that he and Lilian would be in London by 22 June, but
they apparently had not got beyond Paris when news was forwarded
from Montpellier of Branford's own worsening illness. To Norah he
described how he had rushed to Folkestone

from which I motored to Hastings, & spent night & next day beside
him, but his coma prevented any sign of recognition before he
passed away....

Went back to Hastings for funeral in beautiful hilltop of
churchyard beside his wife - then two days tiring work arranging
his papers, & so back here London very tired. But after rest in
bed for a day or more I'm at work again - and with much to do to
make the best of our long collaborations. (19)

In the 'Sociological Review' for January 1931 Geddes paid a double
tribute to his colleague: first a factual and almost impersonal
account of his education, experience in newspaper work, accounting
and banking; and of his long career as a founder-benefactor of the
Sociological Society, and long-time editor of its 'Review'. Then
he wrote well over a page of blank verse, signed *Confrère*, in which
feeling was mingled with intellectual praise as in these opening
and closing lines:

VICTOR BRANFORD

Victor in many struggles - not yet all! -
Toiling and thinking in so many fields
Of generous ideal, ever aspirant
Towards others' weal, through willing sacrifice -
Life-time, life-strength, and hard-earned wage as well ...
- So touching us towards like, and ev'n in fellowship -
How can we carry on those many tasks you leave?
- Your soul-deep strenuous strivings shall not die!
....
Thinker of vital deeds, deedsman of vital thoughts,
You leave us much of each to carry on!
Here tangled dossiers, Teufelsdröckhian bags
Of papers to unravel; each a student's task
'Mid which he'll find his wings, much as you did
With elders long ago. Among your schemes
Many are well begun, yet need firm hands
To bring them to fruition. Many more await
Thinker and leavener, sower, realiser.

So we your friends, the old, the younger too,
Will strive to carry on, and out, your aims,
Winning some victories for you in these coming days,
Thus Victors we in turn!

It was to his daughter, however, that Geddes most freely expressed
something of what he felt.   'Yes, this is the great sorrow since in
India 1917 - my true brother & comrade: and now I can't but be
anxious about the other - J.A.T., also much overstrained'. (20)

'OUTLINES OF GENERAL BIOLOGY' FULFILLED

After the sad farewell to Victor Branford, Geddes settled at his
wife Lilian's house in Netherton Grove, SW 10.   Summer plans, as he
told Norah, began with an address as President of the Sociological
Society, after which he had to stay on in London 'for many reasons'.
One of these was his comparatively recent connection with an organisation of London Adlerians, The New Europe Group, of which he was
made president.   Another was over old business in Palestine, for he
had written to Dr Eder for an appointment, and now asks Frank Mears
to send him a line 'to say if any development of Jerusalem affairs,
& what he advises me to do?   I hear Dr Weizmann is also in town, so
there is no time to be lost, as he is very migratory.'

P.G. also gave some lectures at the newly founded Le Play Society
which had finally split off from The Institute of Sociology and Le
Play House due to personal clashes between two key workers: Alexander Farquharson and Margaret Tatton.   This break was most unfortunate for the continuance of Geddesian sociology, and added one
more dispersion of time and energy to P.G.'s already too numerous
burdens.   All in all, his residence in London brought more distrac-
tions and threats to both health and writing than did Montpellier.
According to various letters, he did not return to the Scots College
until early in 1931 after spending the entire autumn, and more, lecturing and writing.

In spite of outside disturbances and his own generalist activities,
Patrick Geddes finally managed, thanks to the gentle persistence of
J. Arthur Thomson, also to finish his share of the final proofs for
Williams & Norgate.   Accordingly, at least two years after Thomson's first hopeful prediction, came the June 1931 publication of
their long-laboured 'Life: Outlines of General Biology'.   It was a
two-volume, 750,000-word distillation of two long lifetimes of
study, experiment and teaching.   'How shall one summarize this
book, or convey an adequate sense of its importance?' asked the 'New
Republic''s reviewer, on 16 September.
    On the surface, it is a comprehensive treatise on biology.   In
    the course of fifteen hundred closely written pages, the authors
    have systematically covered the entire world of living organisms
    ....   But whoever goes to this book merely for biological know-
    ledge will get more than he has bargained for.   LIFE is more
    than a textbook on biology: it is a summary of the life experi-
    ence of two eminent scientists and scholars, and it is an outline
    of their biological philosophy....   He who touches this book
    touches a man, in this case, two men; one shrewd, gentle, kind-
    ly, humorous, with a real talent for literary expression and
    lucid exposition; the other vigorous, incisive, systematic, sat-
    irical, who, like the teachers of Greece, communicates more fully
    in his conversations and diagrams and brilliant impromptus than

he has ever done before within the covers of a book.   The men
themselves are lifelong friends; Thomson is seventy years old,
Geddes seventy-seven: like Ulysses they feel that old age hath
yet its honour and its toil, and this prolonged essay is a final
account of their voyage in the realms of life.

Appearing only a few months after another comprehensive work on biology, 'The Science of Life' by Wells, Huxley and Wells, the Geddes-
Thomson work was promptly compared with its predecessor.   Although
'The Science of Life' arrived first in print and captured much of
the popular market, many reviewers were of the opinion that the
long-delayed work of the two Scots deserved the widest possible sale
as a book 'written for popular understanding without pandering to
popular prejudice'.   The 'Nation' wrote:
> Without detracting from the merits of Messrs. Wells and Huxley's
> 'Science of Life', it may be said that this work ['Life'] is far
> superior to it.   Indeed, as far as the reviewer is concerned, he
> frankly confesses that he finds it difficult to overpraise the
> book, so ideal are both its conception and its execution.

A critique by Julian Huxley, grandson of P.G.'s teacher, Thomas
Huxley, was in the main favourable to 'Life':
> The layman will at once realise that he is enjoying the results
> of great erudition and long reflection, expressed in a pictures-
> que and on the whole easy style; the professional biologist will
> continually be finding some unfamiliar item of fact, some inter-
> esting interpretation, some reminder in the shape of all-round
> discussion, of the dangers of one-sided or hurried theorising.
> Whatever criticism one may make, the work is a monumental one.

But while unhesitatingly admiring Thomson as a biologist, Julian
Huxley could not refrain from sniping at P.G. for the 'dispropor-
tionately large amount of space given to "Geddesian generalisation"', meaning the final chapters which treated such things as education, essentials of sociology, classification of arts and sciences, and the charting of life.   One can well understand the per-
plexity of a specialist when confronted with the almost limitless
range of P.G.'s mental processes.   Yet what stands out clearly in
the tangle of Geddes's relations with other men is that a condemnation of either his ideas or his projects was often based on inability or unwillingness to understand them.

As S.K. Ratcliffe has already been quoted as saying, London intellectuals in general looked on P.G. with amused condescension, as a
scientist gone rather daft, since interested in all knowledge, all
art.   But not one of them ever mastered his categories and methods
of thought sufficiently to be able to criticise them on his grounds.
When H.G. Wells, for example, chanced to meet a mutual friend of his
and Geddes's he flippantly queried, 'Well, how is old P.G.?   Still
hatching out colleges all over the world, I suppose?'   On the surface this is a harmless, even witty remark, yet it covers up tragic
depths of misunderstanding and intellectual neglect.

Returning to 'Life', one should emphasise that nothing can give a

satisfactory idea of its scope and worth except reading it at first
hand.   Geddes and Thomson insist on the 'apartness and uniqueness'
of life as well as on its interrelations with the physical world,
and assert that the fact of beauty in animate nature

> is as real in its own way as the force of gravity....   We main-
> tain that all living things are beautiful;   save those which do
> not live a free life, those that are diseased or parasitised,
> those that are half-made, and those which bear the marks of man's
> meddling fingers.

To these biologists the seventh wonder of life is the process of
Evolution.   'It is not merely that all things flow;   it is that
life flows up hill.   Amid the ceaseless flux there is not only conservation, there is advancement.   The changes are not those of a
kaleidoscope, but of an "onward advancing melody."'

In the preface, its writers list for fellow-workers some of their
more personal contributions to biology.   A few of these follow:

> 1. A radical revision of the concept of *Parasitism* (Chapter II).
> 2. A restatement of their physiological (metabolic) Theory of
> *Sex* - first advanced in 1889 - supported by much additional and
> experimental evidence (Chapter IV).
> 3. Readvancement of their concept of the *Cell-Cycle* as of vital
> significance to pathology and to *Cytology* (Chapters VI, XII, es-
> pecially pages 1229-31).
> 4. A remarshalling of evidence to support their interpretation of
> *Evolution* as working out, not in unlimited *indefinite* variations,
> but instead through variations of *definite* nature: i.e., floral
> or vegetative;   self-maintaining or species-maintaining, anabolic
> or katabolic, etc. (Chapter IX).

Geddes and Thomson call themselves Neo-Vitalists in mood and method
of study.   They look on the old conflict between mechanists and
vitalists, Darwinians and Lamarckians, as being solved by a new synthetic point of view which accepts and harmonises both views of
life.   The organism to them is simultaneously a Body-Mind and a
Mind-Body, just as a curved line is at once concave and convex.
They admit the great importance of bio-chemistry and bio-physics,
yet insist that biology proper is something apart and requires its
own special concepts.

> The living being enregisters its past, both individual and
> racial;   it exhibits purposive behaviour in its interaction with
> environment, and with increasing complexity.   It grows and mul-
> tiplies, it develops, it varies and it evolves, as no mere phy-
> sical mechanism can do, nor simply chemical process either.
> While there is a mechanics, chemistry and physics of the living
> body, and while these are invaluably progressive alike for
> thought and in applications, they do not as a matter of fact
> suffice for an adequate description of Life as we know it or live
> it.   Organic life is based on mechanism, but transcends it.

As for P.G.'s possibly over-senescent thought, there is no hint in
the reviews of 'Life' that he was not at his height in completing
this great opus.   On the contrary, one appreciator asks the French

poet's well-known question: 'What is a great life?'   His opinion
is that both Alfred de Vigny's query and answer, 'It is a thought of
youth wrought out in maturity', apply to P.G., since the 'Outlines
of General Biology' consisted of many such thoughts.   What again
must be regretted is that colleagues in other fields were not as
faithfully insistent as Thomson, and so did not or could not help
Geddes to record those interpretations in like manner.

As a young instructor at Edinburgh University Geddes had set two intellectual goals before himself: 'to weld more compactly the biological sciences in theory and mode of teaching and to organise upon
these a system of economics'.   If we substitute all-inclusive
social science for economics, then both goals were squarely aimed
at, and largely attained in the 'Outlines'.   Chapter X, 'Biology
among the Sciences', is P.G.'s final answer to what biology includes, what its sub-sciences are, and how it fits into the whole
pattern of human science, art, and philosophy.

The last two chapters, 'Biology in its wider Aspects' and 'Towards
a Theory of Life', together sketch out the foundation of what one
reviewer called the 'sociology of the future'.   Geddes's development of Le Play's 'Famille, Travail, Lieu' into a valley-section
reading of civilisation, graphically expressed by thinking-machines
all starting out from the simple triad of Place, Work and Folk has
evoked this panegyric:

> Orientating the vast and multifarious data of sociology: ethno-
> logy, history, archaeology, economics, geography and more, with
> reference to these three co-ordinates, is a task for genius, but
> it discloses relationships which enable the biologically-trained
> evolutionist to construct an outline of the evolution of human-
> ity, of man as a social organism.   A theory of social evolution,
> integrated with organic evolution into a unified 'Theory of Life
> in Evolution' constitutes a remarkable chapter of 'Life'.   It is
> a *tour de force*, rich in luminous ideas; capable too of some
> clarification in presentment.   It is safe to say, however, that
> it or something like it will form the framework of the sociology
> of the future. (21)

Praise of this sociology also comes from Lewis Mumford who fully
agreed that 'Life' was indeed thought fulfilled in maturity.

> The relations between organic life and social life, between bio-
> logy and sociology, have never been put so clearly as in the
> final chapters, where Professor Geddes marshals together his
> systematic thought in both departments.   For Geddes a sociology
> that remains at the level of statistics is no more sociology than
> a biology that remains at the level of bio-chemistry or bio-
> metrics....   Geddes's correlation of the fundamental sciences of
> biology with the parallel sciences of sociology is an essential
> contribution to orderly thought.

After referring to the two Scots as 'among the best educated men in
Western civilization' and as being themselves the best illustrations
of their book, Mumford concludes:

> What, finally, is their outlook on the world?   They see the

forces of life today, human life above all, subjected to the
vandalism, the debasement, the murderous competitions and wars
that mark what we optimistically call the Machine Age.   They
behold an education chained to routine, an industrial system
bent upon pecuniary success, and a social life in which the
vital values - those of health, racial improvement, reproduction, education - are subjected to foreign pecuniary and mechanical demands.

The authors have no simple formula for reviving the values and
activities of life: they believe in a new orientation in science, with increasing emphasis upon the biological and sociological disciplines, they believe in the renewal of education, with
the acquisition of a richer experience through regional survey
and the practice of the arts and experimental intercourse with
the natural and social environment, an education that faces the
future as well as the past; they believe in the stabilization
of the family relations through intelligent control of births and
through permanent mating; they are against war, as a destructive
and mis-selective process, and they are against mammonism and
mechanolatry, in their many forms and phases.   Above all, they
are filled with the wonder and awe of Life: they exhibit, in
their own right, a sense of its highest potentialities.   These
two volumes are a comprehensive answer ... to all the dreary mis-
education and discouragement that have arisen out of our venal
and mechanical civilization with its brutal wars and its aimless
and bewildered states of peace. (22)

JEANNE D'ARC ... PAUL ROBESON ... MORE BOOKS PLANNED

Apart from 'Life' and a German translation of his biography of Sir
J.C. Bose, (23) P.G.'s publications in 1930 and 1931 consisted of
'Ways of Transition ...' and short reviews and notices in the
'Sociological Review'.   Privately, however, he printed four addi-
tional, miscellaneous items.   Three of these were small leaflets of
verse by him and others: 'Centenaire de Mistral' and 'Centenaire de
Jeanne d'Arc' dated 13 and 15 June 1930, respectively, as of the
Collège des Ecossais, Montpellier; and 'Song-Sheet and Welcomes'
in honour of the 'Visit of French Branch' of the Franco-Scottish
Society, 22-27 September 1930, issued by 'Patrick Geddes and Col-
leagues, Outlook Tower'.   The centenary pamphlets are a final expression of P.G.'s love of France and pride in Scotland's 'Auld
Alliance' with her.   The first and last of his five stanzas to
Jeanne d'Arc et sa Garde Ecossaise read:
    To this day, our Scottish Banner's
    Ruddy Lion, ramped on gold;
    Still around him flames his tressure,
    Fleur-de-Lys from times of old...

    Still of all our memories proudest,
    - History's trumpet sounding loudest -
    We, your Kings' Guard, man by man
    Stout we fought, and died, for Jeanne!

The 'Song-Sheet and Welcomes' for the French visitors to Scotland
consists mainly of reprints from the two 'Centenaires'. In addition to 'Jeanne d'Arc ...', Geddes was represented by a new poem,
'Pinel', commemorating Philippe Pinel (1745-1826) the French doctor
who became a courageous pioneer reforming the inhuman treatment of
mental patients. Four of its five stanzas are quoted as evidence
not only of his use of emotional and religious images, but also of
his ability to narrate clearly and briefly when deeply personally
involved:

PINEL

Since Christ - and Dante - passed through Hell,
No place on Earth so grim to tell -
Sad tale of minds, weak, shaken, lost;
Poor souls interred alive, at cost
Of all that made life bright and free,
With only miseries to dree!

In earlier age the hapless witch
Was drowned, or burned in flaming pitch;
Worse still their lifelong cruel fate,
With shaken minds, 'mid harshest hate!

In darkness deep, in cell left foul,
Scarce for companion bat or owl,
With fettered hands, feet chained to wall,
Scourged, starved, mocked, jibed - harsh warders all!

Yet to their help came good Pinel:
- Ring out, sweet bells, as for Noël!
For these entombed, their Resurrection morn;
Life free - wounds healed - and Love reborn!

The fourth item, edited and printed by P.G., was a 64-page collection of tributes to Marjory Kennedy-Fraser entitled 'Our Singer and
Her Songs'. Viewing it now as one of his last efforts, both of
writing and of trying to achieve a practical result, one feels mingled pity and admiration. Geddes hoped that Scotsmen all over the
world would appreciate these tributes to their great musician and
contribute generously to the memorial proposed for her. But
neither hope was realised, and his work of love and loyalty for
Anna's and his old friend turned out to be the ultimate deficit venture of 'P.G. & Colleagues'.

A partly new element which appears in letters and some articles
after Geddes's return from India is that of reminiscence. While
the 'verse-letters' from his convalescence at Simla in 1922 contained certain recollections, it was in 1925 that he published many
incidents from boyhood and youth in 'The Young Barbarian' (Perth
Academy's magazine); in 'Nature' as his contribution to Thomas
Huxley's centenary, and in the 'Survey Graphic' as part of 'The Education of Two Boys'. However, at 76 or 77 (i.e. in 1930 or 1931)
he wrote a letter (24) of combined reminiscence and exhortation to a
famous singer then in London. Geddes had been invited to meet him

in person but to his great regret could not accept.   Later, he went
'to hear and see him' and wrote: 'Paul Robeson - A Letter to a
Mutual Friend':
> What a man!   What a Singer!   What an Actor!   What an Artist!
> Simple feeling to deep emotion, simple joy of life to pathos, to
> humour, homeliness to spirituality!   Never have I seen or heard
> anyone so able to give the culminating expression of his
> people. (25)

It is here that P.G. tells his childhood memories of the 'American
war' and how the
> old Kentucky and Virginia songs were sung in every gathering....
> I remember too the Christy Minstrels, both real and sham ones,
> and finer groups since them; up to the Yale Singers.   But never
> before have I seen such a full personality as Robeson's, plainly
> culminant in all my seventy years of memory.

Thereafter The Interpreter explains and derides the custom of musicians having to appear only in evening dress, condemns the 'London
managers' foolish notions' of arranging concerts, and exclaims:
'poor Mr Robeson - still enslaved to our conventions.'   He deplores
'that wholly irrelevant comediette of modern degeneracy' which pre-
ceded the 'vigourous scene of Emperor Jones at opening of his
tragedy'.
> What a far more effective performance had the curtain risen on a
> simple old scene of plantation labour and life, and with Robeson,
> as its protagonist, thence emerging, from manly leadership in all
> these to his own splendid powers, rising into fullest range and
> passion of song!   And with not only his Company in chorus, but
> communicating this to the audience; thus at the close of each
> Act bringing them to their feet in full-voiced unison, themselves
> stirred into liberated souls.

Two more pages suggest that the great singer's own artistic 'liberation' could come through study of dramatic performances 'from Bengal
plain and village' led by their 'foremost song-master, Rabindranath
Tagore'; and of 'Folk-expression at best and highest ... as from
Welsh Eisteddfod as oldest, to our Scottish Village Players today.
Let Mr Robeson take note of these, and soon he will be leading
them.'

Then comes a final exhortation in verse, both typed and handwritten,
to rise above the 'poor surroundings, London's dull common-place!'
and 'Make you that worthy setting befits your face and Race!'   One
stanza is given here in both versions as an example of P.G. at work
in verse:
> Well done, your falling Emperor's part;
> Othello, matched to Shakespeare's art:
> Next show your people's vivid heart:
> Play Toussaint L'Ouverture,
> 'Tween pale and dark, too long apart.

Well done, your falling Emperor's part;
~~You've shown Othello's tortured heart.~~
Othello, matched to Shakspere's art
Next ~~show you~~ your Paply's vivid heart:
~~play the wide literature~~
Play Toussaint L'Ouverture!

'Tween pale and dark, too ~~wide~~ long apart,

Another trait that appears in correspondence in these last years is P.G.'s search for new colleagues among well-known contemporaries. In October 1929 he wrote to H.G. Wells from Montpellier: 'Many years since we met! - as at Sociological Society, etc...'   With a quick review of his and Branford's approach to sociology via Comte and Le Play, Geddes makes this advance:

> You seem to me doing the like implicitly, alike in tales and in social thought: so is there not beginning to appear some field for cooperations, as of your Open Conspirators with such practical workers as may be....
>
> We have each worked mainly alone, but it now seems to me that we have come so definitely to kindred results & methods that it would be of real interest & use if we could now talk this over. You come largely to these parts - will you not think of giving us a visit here?...
>
> Anyway, pray consider the above ... & believe me, with renewed appreciation, Your cordially
>
> P. Geddes (26)

After the publication of 'Life' in 1931, and while still in London, he appeals to a competitor in biology, Sir Julian Huxley, for suggestions concerning a new book.   (Though how Geddes reconciled this project with the non-completion of two books already under contract, 'Sociology' and 'Olympus', is quite a mystery.)   The letter opens tactfully:

> I've been much interested in your book with Wells, and realise its real excellence in so many ways, its freshness & vividness, its excellent illustrations & so on.   All in so many ways *better* than our big one; (though I hope you may have seen something in it too?).
>
> So let us have a talk, over how we may not only respectively but even so far as may be collectively - & with others - advance the movement we are working in - and towards - of biologic & psycho-biologic vision, & synthesis, and education.
>
> (& soon - before I leave for Montpellier at end of this

month).   Say first at tea some of these days? & say with
Ruggles-Gates? - with Arthur Thomson when he comes up to town? -
and so to a (why not extending) Symposium?

Yours faithfully,
Patrick Geddes

As many times previously, the faithful and practical Thomson provides useful biographical facts and clues in his letters to P.G.
He relates in June 1931 that he is trying to recruit Scots College
students and of course wishes 'to visit Montpellier some day, when
it is practicable' and that 'The clever *Hogben* has been making male-
volently merry over our book ['Life'] in 'Time and Tide' this week
end.   He is a bit devilish with his pen and vanity' and, finally,
a 'pleasant letter' is enclosed from Langdon-Davies 'about your suggestions in regard to "The Science of Sex"'.   In September Thomson's words are likewise revealing:

Editorially, I am hoping you can give me 'Sociology' *very soon*,
else it will miss publication in the beginning of the year.
    I wish to raise the question now of *giving up* the 'Sex' book
which seems as if it would be a burden to us both....   The home
opinion here is that I am not a bit fit for such a big swot.
But I am in your hands - willing to go on, if you so decide.

That Geddes of course went on is shown by brief letters from Thomson
regarding their meetings in London for discussions, and by a six-
page draft to Mr Unwin, the Director of Williams & Norgate, marked:
'J.A.T. - please return with notes, comments, etc.'   P.G. had just
met Unwin at a luncheon, which started him 'furiously to think' of
Thomson's and his book 'in preparation for you - the coming one you
want, of Life's fullest fire - of "Sex"!'   The letter is a masterpiece of Geddesian enthusiasm and self-confidence when facing a new
challenge.   He reminds the publisher that he and Thomson have been
in this field since before 1889, and 'have advantage over the Freudian movement so long specialised among sex-evils and perversions',
because they are

naturalists - and yet idealists - ranging over sea and land life
in their beauty and perfection - to peacock and skylark and to
poet - and from Mammals - Mothering Creatures - to Madonna.   We
are thus in this book getting beyond Freud - and even his successors, though these have been escaping his pessimisms, and
coming into Life again - as with Jung, Adler, and yet later
ones....
    (By Jove, this time we should deserve, and doubly, considera-
tion for a Nobel Prize! - since uniting two of their lines - the
medical, as psychiatric - and the *idealist* as well - practicable
too - as towards Sex Re-Moralisation - and all that socially
implies!)

P.G. suggests publishing 'not only an English edition - but a French
one too - and why not simultaneously?' and exclaims: 'I'd go to
Vienna etc, and learn all I can - to "steal their thunder" and surpass its light(e)ning!'   He also proposes printing the book serial-
ly in 'monthly - (2/6d) - parts', since it 'is plain we *can't*'
deliver the whole at the date of our contract!'   Naturally there

must be more and better illustrations than in 'Life', so he and
Thomson
> were planning quite a lot of these yesterday evening, and see our
> way to more.   These would make the book of far wider possible
> appeal!   And if you & *we* don't do it, the *Cinema* will!... Pray
> then be considering the above, & let us discuss it with you.
>
>   Yours cordially, PG

J. Arthur Thomson's comment, in late January 1932, was in part: 'If
your letter does not move Unwin, what will?   It seems to me ...
just a little too exuberant with its "By Joves" and so on.   But I
do not know how well you know the man... '   He finds the general
idea a good one but lists objections 'which a cautious pre-occupied
Director will be likely to trot out to save adventure, bother, and
departure from routine methods'.   Among these: 'our dual bad reputation among young biologists (and many contemporaries too) and
among publishers for delays and costs'.   His conclusion is: 'I
think a less discursive letter would be more effective.   Yours
ever, J.A.T.'

P.G.'s boasted motto of 'living dangerously' was followed even more
thoroughly in 1931 than earlier.   He and Lilian resided in her flat
in Netherton Grove within a mile of scenes of his student days at
the Royal School of Mines, and a shorter distance from the Embankment where he used to meet Carlyle walking by the Thames at sunset.
Like many dwellings in this section it had kitchen and dining room
in a dank basement, living rooms above, and bath and bedrooms another storey up.   Heat was provided by gas fires in each room.   But
London in winter time, as his doctors told him, was health-wise
about the worst place he could have chosen.   Compared with his
accustomed outdoor life on the *garrigue* in southern France, to remain beyond October in this Megapolis of polluted air, available
lecture halls and partly willing publishers was sheer folly.

He had flouted fate in this manner in 1930-1 with results confessed
in a letter of mid-February to the author:
> The hard winter and severe over-pressure have landed me in ten
> days breakdown ... and though the cure for diabetes at Montpel-
> lier for which I am leaving tomorrow is probable, I have much
> doubt if I can ever now face my hoped-for tour to America.

Yet he did recover from this breakdown and in April, apparently
having learnt his lesson, wrote wisely.
> I am resolved not to risk another illness from either British
> winter climate or American, but to stay here at Scots College for
> next autumn and winter - the Mediterranean winter being less de-
> pressing than ours, less cold outside and warm within than yours.
> But I might come to the States next summer - 1932 - if there be
> any real prospect of starting a Tower somewhere, and a Tower
> (regional survey) movement. (27)

One morning on a folded sheet of notepaper Geddes jotted down in
mixed diagram and abbreviations what was in his mind:
    U.S.A. - 1932?

Plans for American College at Montpellier...
Lectures - reorganization of Universities; development of
surveys; interpretation of social changes...
Go on to California for winter...
Return by way of India?...   Then to Jerusalem?...
Clearly, P.G. was still the insatiable planner.

PILGRIM'S BURDEN ... BELATED KNIGHTHOOD

On 2 October 1931 Geddes marked his 77th birthday by recording his
pre-dawn thought-stream as on several other such occasions.   This
time they filled only two pages, in great contrast to the lengthy
Red Sea epistle of his 60th anniversary, yet what he noted down was
also related to Mount Sinai.

                                                         4 a.m.
Dear Norah,
Here's my birthday - & good early start - & vivid waking - with
jottings of great vision of History - the Masque of Mammon -
already clear!
    First birthday of so many that I've so clearly identified in
waking thought what remains of my own life with that of Social
Progress, & IX-9! through main idea since it came clear at Cornell in '23.

He explains the background: his current exhibition of cities and
civics 'at French Institute' had suddenly to be closed down on
account of demolitions, '(with fatigue which made me rest in bed
yesterday)' while an assistant was getting a new room ready 'to hang
it today at *School of Economics*!   London's great College Temple of
University Faculty of Divinity - next the City - where Mammon is
God!'
    So I've seen Moses coming down from Sinai with his Tables* of the
Law - to find his Brother Aaron - High Priest! of Golden Calf! &
leading his ritual dance.
    I've seen inside Pilgrim's Burden, in 'Progress' - & how
stupid never to have realised its weight of Sins was weighted
essentially in *Gold*!   (Yet this turned to lead - yet remaining
twice as heavy.)
    Seen Uncle Sam, & Jacques Bonhomme & John Bull too - in his
better days - all in their characteristic Dances - in their City
of Destruction - & next as Pilgrims - weighted down.
    How disburden each!...   And what a quaint coincidence for my
own Life Comedy - to be going today to the very place & type I
have most abominated since I began economics with Ruskin nearly
60 years ago.
    Yet in School of Economics there are Modernists - Rolls

* P.G. makes an interesting personal variation of this image in his
birthday letter to Arthur of the same date, at 4.30 a.m.: 'Great
event for me to bring the Tables of the Social Law to the very heart
of the Temple - the essential University Faculty of Divinity of the
City where God is Mammon.'   (Quoted in Kitchen, p. 317.)

Tawney - Malinovski & doubtless others. And I bring impact of British Association as type organisation for Sciences. Gen. Smuts is coming next week, & others.

Interesting time, to demonstrate Exhibition for next week (perhaps longer) for it's worth doing in the very heart of the enemy, is it not! (So I'll learn something whether they do or not!)

In mid-December P.G. asks Norah to tell Frank that he has 'at last fixed talk with Weizmann for tomorrow'; then brings up a problem he has not had since 1912!

Now advise me. As you may know, my old friend Lord Pentland sounded me 20 years ago or so, as to acceptance of Knighthood - but I declined, on grounds of lifelong policy and views of life.

But now Ramsay Macdonald repeats this, for Xmas or New Year honours. Should I *accept* - as this time I am tempted to do on business grounds, though *not* for pleasure. It did not stir a touch my pulse (nor *Lilian's* either, rather to my surprise) but it *might* do both for my purse - (though I fear making shop, hotel & other expenses more?)

He lists 16 factors to be considered as to whether they weigh for or against acceptance, and asks Norah 'after sleeping over this, & talking it over with Frank - & Arthur too', to mark them '+ or -'. Here is a sampling:

1. *as to helping Frank...*
5. Even *Publishing*? Help to find Partner of business value?...
12. *Opinion abroad*. e.g. would it help with wretched Scots & Highland Societies over Empire & U.S.A. which have done 0 for Marjory Kennedy Fraser Memorial practically!...
16. In short, if I must take it - *what uses can be made of it?* as to above or in other ways?... (But if you feel strongly NO *wire me that*, tomorrow Saturday)

Love to all - Daddy

Norah's reply is not now available, but his favourable decision was revealed to Amelia Defries shortly before Christmas, as 'strictly private and confidential'. The reasons given to her, however, were quite different from those submitted to Norah. Twenty years ago he was in his

hermitage, thinking out theories, so shrinking from 'Society' - not ready to act in it or on it, as fully as needed. But now I'm more ready, my thought has come clearer, enough for applications, now also clear-seen, & for the Crisis. (28)

Geddes is ready for publicity as well, and asks her to 'be considering how to reach such Press as may be open to you in these few days when Honours List is being discussed'. He also tells of the split in Le Play Society.

At first Farquharson etc. furious, threatening even the Law - but I adjusted & reconciled them - at solicitors' yesterday - and hope for *doubling* Sociological action accordingly - since each now free to spread Surveys & Tours at home & abroad.

In fact, such was P.G.'s habitual optimism that this squabble also
led him to make a
> *Three Years Plan* of many features ... as enough for Exposition &
> Initiatives (when I'll be 80! so no time to lose) - then leaving
> the years of Development to others - say a dozen more!   [A post-
> script suggests their meeting after New Year] but don't come here
> before that - as too busy finishing 'Sociology' book....   I must
> hurry off to Montpellier as soon as King's Ceremony is over -
> about 10-12 January probably - so must devolve all I can on
> others - partly on *you* - we'll see & discuss what.

After publication of the New Year's Honours List telegrams and
letters came pouring in to Sir Patrick Geddes with congratulations
upon his Knighthood 'for services to education'.   Not only did his
friends wish him well, but many persons also whose contacts with him
had been of casual nature when not, indeed, hostile; for the moment
the insurgent professor-of-all-things bore the title of 'Sir', he
was generally accepted as one of the faithful.   Conversely, a few
old acquaintances considered it a doubtful honour, a fellow Scot
even going so far as to assert that Geddes had been 'belittled by
the knighthood that is available to any pushful politician or Provost'. (29)   Not Thomson, however, for on 1 January he wrote:
> My dear Sir Patrick (I must be allowed this once),
> Let me re-express to Lady Geddes and yourself our felicitations -
> for it *does* mean a widespread social approval and encouragement
> ....   May it help your causes and please you both for many a
> year to come.

To Lewis Mumford P.G. tells the story of earlier refusal and present
acceptance, adding that Thomson had influenced his decision by admitting that being 'Sir Arthur' had increased his 'usefulness and
influence with a wider public'.
> So I already find it!   What shoals of congratulatory letters -
> what photographers! next interviewers.   There is no doubt that
> the public *are* more impressed by honours than I knew.

Much the same account was sent to another American, Charles Ferguson, author of 'The University Militant':
> I have accepted this time: as an aid to carry out schemes
> against the Philistines who have long hindered me, but whom it
> now bluffs and silences amazingly - and even turns around to
> quite an extent!   Hence forgive me!

The knighthood ceremony in 1932 had to be postponed a number of
times because of the illness of King George V.   Consequently P.G.
was obliged to spend another winter in the depressive, damp climate
of London.   Not until 25 February was the King able to hold the
investiture of the new knights, and for some reason Sir Patrick
stayed on into March before returning to Montpellier, accompanied by
Philip Mairet and Norah's son Kenneth.

On the 16th he wrote to Lilian, still in Chelsea, that the journey
had gone all right for him and Mairet but that his grandson was
tired '& off his feed'.   'I am feeling already better, on going

over my dear old garden, & with its threefold welcome from the three
gardeners ...'   In his biography Mairet relates:
> P.G. supported the twenty-four hour journey well, as keenly ob-
> servant as ever of the country, pointing out the effects of the
> drought as the train passed through Normandy and, in the early
> hours of the next morning, commenting upon various features of
> the Provençal landscape which the genius of Van Gogh has made
> familiar to millions who have never seen it.   During the ten
> days that followed, his conversation, his teaching, and his dis-
> cussion and direction of work in progress with gardeners and
> others, showed much of his accustomed brightness and humour, if
> much less of his old energy.   Only by contrast with the Geddes
> one had known in the past did one feel that he was under a
> cloud. (30)

One of the last letters P.G. wrote, dated 16 April 1932, is a reply
to an American student who had been in contact with Mumford and who
was interested in coming to the Scots College.   Its three hand-
written pages give no hint of illness or decreasing vitality; on
the contrary they sketch his very active plans for the rest of the
year.
> I return to London about mid-June: after a visit if possible to
> Geneva & Brussels ... it would help you to meet me there, to
> make acquaintance with the 'Palais Mondial' of my old friend,
> Paul Otlet, an amazing Museum of Museums, and World-Centre of
> Bibliography.

The perpetual seeker of disciples proposes in addition not only
visiting London but says: 'I'd like to take you with me for a fortnight or so to Edinburgh'.   Afterwards they could return to France
for 'the New Education Congress at Nice - July 28-Aug. 12, which
will bring together many live people'; and then proceed to Montpellier where the student could prepare a doctoral thesis.   Geddes
then makes criticisms of education which, while not brand-new, reveal him as thinking and writing clearly.
> ... though I have little use for the usual over-memorising for
> the ordinary University degrees, the preparation of a *thesis* is
> really educative; since depending on the elaboration of such
> personal ideas as come to the active mind, and thus often leading
> to its later productive career.

Speaking of the 'progress of integration' in primary schools 'from
Rousseau up to Madame Montessori and the Dalton Plan etc', he finds
there 'have been few *secondary* schools as progressive, & still less
the Universities'.
> This is disguised by the enormous multiplication of their spe-
> cialised Institutes and Departments: but the problem of their
> *harmonisation & orchestration* is *what we are after here*.

Of the many letters from Lilian to 'Uncle Pat' between 1921 and
their marriage in 1928, not one, as has been mentioned earlier, is
in existence.   From the next four years there exist three of P.G.'s
to her, but only a single one from Lilian, dated 30 March 1932.   On
a letterhead of the Lyceum Club in Piccadilly she writes that a
woman friend of hers is leaving for the Scots College in a few days,

but I don't think I shall.   At least I am not ready yet.   But
good news for you!   Cure for diabetes I've been reading about
in the 'Heidelberger Freundenblatt' I found here.   Wish I could
find a copy for you & send it.

Lilian suggests that they go to this place in the Harz Mountains
some time for his sake, though she is sure his doctors are treating
him along the same lines.
> ... but then you don't give yourself the chance here for good
> results.   There are too many distractions in London for you to
> concentrate on 'cure'.   What about going there in June & simply
> giving up all engagements here, or postponing them....   Of
> course now out there & getting on fairly well you may feel ob-
> liged to stick a bit as long as there are students who need you.

After telling that Banabhard (Rachel Annand Taylor) had come for
dinner, she asks whether he ever got 'the velvet waistcoat?' and
what is to be done 'with the case of books & the other big packet
of books?...   Lovingly Lilian.'

P.G. replies on 9 April, referring first to Arthur's engagement to
Jeannie Colin, daughter of old family friends in Montpellier and a
descendant of Elisée Reclus.
> Dear Wifie - Very glad you are pleased with Arthur & Jeannie - an
> excellent Franco-Scottish mating! - & I pass on your note as
> Jeannie is of course taking round Arthur on the leash to show to
> her friends - this week-end at Avignon.   But I fear he'll be
> gone north again before you get here.   So I won't invite for
> Saturday or Sunday next, but let you rest after travelling, & be
> at your best the week following & for a crowd.

He asks that the books be sent as soon as possible, since 'Kenneth
has taken keenly to helping Librarian here' and then speaks of
Lilian's dinner guest.   In view of the chequered friendship between
the latter and P.G. since Dundee times, these lines are of interest.
> Alas, Banabhard!   Yes, her death-wish is sadly manifest - yet
> three weeks here would revive her.   What beauty of spring - what
> sunshine - what flowers!   Lose no time of coming!
>   I'm convalescing (with return to insulin):   & still taking it
> easy - reading a bit but not yet writing.   That I trust will
> come before too long now, for there is much to do - even to over-
> take arrears.
>   Yours - with Love, & xxx.
>   PG

PYRE OF HERCULES

On 18 April 1932 the newspapers of the world again carried the name
of Professor Sir Patrick Geddes, but this time to announce his
sudden death at Montpellier.   Obituaries of from two paragraphs to
whole columns attempted to tell who this Scot was and what he had
done in seventy-seven-and-a-half years of life.   To friends and
former students scattered in many lands, the news came without

warning; and was a shock the mind refused to grasp.   P.G. had
always been the very symbol of life and energy.   No one ever
thought of him as really growing old.

In the absence of any published eye-witness account, there were
various stories in Montpellier about his last hours.   One said a
severe choking spell had caused his death; another that it was
heart failure.   A third suggested that had it been possible to get
medical care from Montpellier sooner, he might have pulled through
the crisis and recovered.   Still another version told of his asking
for his secretary to come and take down his final thoughts.   Norah,
however, has given the following definitive information to the
author.*

Lilian had returned to Montpellier the week before, and Geddes had
been on one or two excursions by car and on foot to the Château
d'Assas and to the seashore but 'was unusually tired during and
after these expeditions'.
    The night of his death, i.e. just before 17th April, he looked
    into the salon at 10 as usual with a cheerful goodnight & a smile
    for everybody.   At 12 he called Lilian, at 3 a.m. 17-4-25 he
    died.   There is no foundation in the tale of a secretary by his
    bedside.   Lilian was there & heard him talking rapidly & quietly
    to my mother.**   Lilian took this with a very good grace.   The
    choking was a diabetic manifestation....   There was a doctor in
    the *Collège* at the time as well as the doctor called in.

A former resident at the Scots College, the Indian lawyer Pheroze
Bharucha, has made this comment on the swift dénouement of P.G.'s
life:
    He achieved the death he deserved - that of the good worker and
    the good fighter.   When the hour struck he went, without having
    time for suffering, unseemly struggle or regret. (31)

The funeral services at the College were just as Geddes would have
wished.   On the terrace in front of the battlemented tower, in the
warm sunshine of a Languedoc spring, a group of townspeople and
students reverently paid tribute to the man who had transformed the
garrigue into a wealth of gardens and built the nucleus of a *Cité
Universitaire Méditerranéenne*.   Indian students in colourful costume chanted a farewell dirge, the European students sang in French
and English, and then everyone joined in Geddes's favourite songs
like *Gaudeamus Igitur* and *Auld Lang Syne*.   There were brief tributes from students and neighbours, while Professor Charles Flahault
spoke of his long friendship with the young Scot he had first met at

* In her letter of 2 April 1945, *after* the publication of 'Patrick
Geddes: Maker of the Future' which contained these hearsay
versions.

** Did he perhaps recall the words which concluded Anna's very first
love letter to him: 'Good night, sweet friend; thy love ne'er
alter till thy sweet life end'?   (Cf. chapter 3.)

Roscoff over a half-century ago, and of his long years of service in
many parts of the world.   Then, borne on the shoulders of these
friends, Patrick Geddes made his final trip down through garden
paths lined with irises in full bloom and filled with the fragrance
of early roses.

Just as Anna had been carried, flower-garlanded, to an Indian pyre
so now Patrick was covered with flowers of his own planting, though
his coffin had to be shipped anti-climactically by train to the
crematorium at Marseilles.   Only four persons were present there:
Lilian, her sister Ida, and the young English student John Tandy and
his French wife Suzanne (who were then living at Aix-en-Provence).
Tandy has described the final scene. (32)

The attendants asked Lady Geddes in French whether she and her
friends wished to witness the cremation, and whether the body should
be removed from the coffin.   To both questions the answer was 'Yes'
   and in the state poor Lilian was in I don't think she understood
   the questions or the answer she gave.   Quite unprepared therefor we found ourselves being taken 'behind the scene' ... and saw
   the body lifted onto a bed of iron rollers which advanced the
   body shortly into the opening oven.   As ... the feet entered,
   the whole body glowed from the intense heat of the white hot oven
   and his beard and flowing hair on his head burst into flames before the body completely entered the oven and the doors finally
   closed all from view.
      A most dramatic spectacle and one that P.G. would have appre-
   ciated to the full - of that I have no doubt - even if it left us
   very shaken.

When Arthur Geddes heard the story he called it an 'extraordinarily
fitting end' and was sure that his father would have approved of
this dénouement, for it re-enacted a scene in one of his favourite
poems: 'Le bûcher d'Hercule' by Henri de Regnier. (33)   Hercules
is lying on his funeral pyre, and as the flames shoot up and consume
the hero, the poet sees all the monsters that Hercules had slain,
revive like so many evil Phoenixes.   The moral of the poem, as
Patrick Geddes used to interpret it, is that if humanity is to survive, each generation must produce its own heroes who will again
fight the new evils.   Human beings must themselves always take an
active, courageous part in the great 'ethical process' of Evolution.

Chapter 12

PATRICK GEDDES TODAY

'MAGNIFICENT FAILURES'

A review of the present state of Patrick Geddes's ideas and deeds
may well begin with his material creations.   While not seeking to
build as massive worldly memorials as his rival Lutyens in India,
he did try to express his thought permanently in buildings, gardens
and city plans.   Dozens of places on earth: Edinburgh, Cyprus and
Dunfermline; Paris, Ghent, London and Dublin; Darjeeling and
Indore; Jerusalem, Tel Aviv, Montpellier and many others have received impulses from P.G. Unlimited.   Each still bears faint or
strong traces of that remarkable presence, for each has both rejected and received him in some measure.

Our inquiry logically starts in Edinburgh with the Outlook Tower,
which looks almost the same externally as in its hey-day of Summer
Meetings, and of autumn and spring lectures by The Professor.   Yet
the crenellated Observation Gallery and turreted Camera Obscura are
now mere attractions for the casual visitor.   The Geddesian exhibits which were to teach the citizen to survey his city and region
from many viewpoints, and to perform vital civic duties, slowly
dwindled to 'but a shadow of past ones' and today have all vanished. (1)   Of what once was a sociological laboratory, index museum, and cradle of Cities Exhibitions which aroused planners in West
and East, only the empty shell remains.

Briefly, the sad story is that by 1948 the Outlook Tower Association, founded by Geddes before 1900, was no longer able to keep its
heirloom in repair.   A limited liability company, Castlehill Properties (Edinburgh), was then organised to take over and physically
restore the Tower.   By letting out the lower floors to artists and
operating the new Camera Obscura installed in 1946 for the paying
public, the company succeeded in making ends meet for a number of
years.   An Edinburgh Room and a Scotland Room were set up, thanks
to a grant from the Carnegie Trust, and Castlehill Properties 'continued to manage the Tower in a manner sympathetic to the spirit of
Patrick Geddes'. (2)

But in the late 1950s membership in the original Association diminished steadily, and in the 1960s a new and serious problem arose. Building inspectors pronounced the upper part of the Tower unsafe for public use, and the Camera Obscura had to be closed down until an emergency stairway was installed and drastic structural reinforcements made.   The company could not face the expense involved and sold the Tower to the University of Edinburgh under an arrangement whereby the latter carried out the repairs and leased back the top storeys to Castlehill Properties.   Adversity continued, however, and increased operating costs forced the company to wind up its affairs in March 1972 after paying a first and final dividend to shareholders.*

The Outlook Tower Association held a final, publicly advertised meeting in December 1972 which was attended by only *six* persons, and filed a petition in court for dissolution and the transfer of its funds of some £3,000 to a 'Geddes Memorial Trust'.   The purpose of this Trust was stated in part as to promote
> the study of living society in its environment and the principles
> of regional survey, Town and country planning, environmental con-
> servation, and the preservation of open spaces. (3)

In this connection one ventures to suggest that just as Sir Walter Scott has his commemorative tower in the 'Athens of the North', so also should Patrick Geddes be honoured as her greatest all-round *citizen*.   For him what could be a more fitting memorial than the permanent re-establishment on Castlehill of not merely a 'Geddes room' but of the entire Outlook Tower as an inter-disciplinary, even inter-university, institute for the study of civic and regional problems in all their interrelations?   Such a commemoration should include the Joint Department of Town and Country Planning of Edinburgh's College of Art and of Heriot-Watt University, for was not P.G. himself - ninety-five years ago - a teacher in both the University's Medical School and in the then Heriot-Watt College?

Pending such a rebirth, however, the jinx which so often beset his best work in Scotland has reappeared.   A staff member of the Town and Country Planning Association, visiting the Tower in July 1974, was so depressed by its decay that he bluntly stated that this
> has been accelerated by vandalism: original Geddes papers were
> taken to the corporation dump some years ago;   and ... some
> books, relief models and a globe built by Elisée Reclus had only
> recently been retrieved by lecturers from the same corporation
> tip.   A bronze model of the Royal Mile and other exhibits used

---

* As for other failing associations, the settlement of P.G.'s estate in July 1933 listed his 1000 Town & Gown shares of £5 each and 866 Eastern & Colonial shares of £1, as 'of no value'.   Further, the sum of £1500 lent by him to Town and Gown for repayment 'Should future profits render it possible to do so', was appraised at 'say, £50'.   Of his liquid assets (mainly life insurance of £3700) bank overdrafts claimed c. £2400, repayment of loans from friends c. £900, and sundry bills c. £300, leaving net cash residue of £205.15s. and personal effects valued at £474.

by Geddes ... have gone missing, and Edinburgh today spurns
Geddes as much as it did in his lifetime. (4)

On the other hand, partly favourable news has come in 1976 from
LANDMARK (Visitor Centres Ltd) which has taken over the needed restoration of the Tower and its future running as a combined commercial and academic landmark in Edinburgh.   A coffee house, offices
and storage will vie for space with the Camera Obscura and the one
floor given over to 'Patrick Geddes Archives and Research' under
Edinburgh University auspices.   Yet a proposed P.G. Exhibition in
the building was abandoned because the new directors felt 'on reflection that this would be ... totally at odds with Geddes's own
concept of the Outlook Tower'. (5)

Another manifestation of the jinx occurred in Glasgow several years
earlier when newspaper headlines proclaimed: 'WE'VE LOST RESEARCH
PAPERS' and 'LOST PAPERS MAY HAVE BEEN BURNED'. (6)   Curiously
enough, there were no follow-up stories in the press, and no official account of what happened to these documents, which Arthur
Geddes donated to the University of Strathclyde in 1954, has ever
appeared, to this writer's knowledge.   (From his own sources,
though, he has heard that from one-third to one-half of the letters
and reports concerning Geddes's work in the Near East perished in
the holocaust.*)

Looking next at the University Halls of Residence started by Geddes
in 1887, one finds another story of financial difficulties and
forced liquidation of assets instead of the support which now would
be expected from the University in its own self-interest.   When
taken over by the Town & Gown Association in 1896, the first accom-
modations for seven students had grown to include four buildings
with 120 residents, and these survived First World War difficulties
and on into the 1930s.   Thereafter, most unfortunately for Edinburgh's students, the Association had to dispose of its historic
Halls until the last survivor, Ramsay Lodge, was sold in 1945 to the
Commercial Bank of Scotland as a residential hostel and training
centre.   Even so, the Bank organised its trainees into a 'Ramsay
Lodge Association' and adopted the motto *Vivendo Discimus* ('By
living we learn') as a link with the Lodge's founder.   'The fine
set of mural paintings, conceived by Geddes and painted by the late
John Duncan, R.S.A. ... are still in the Common Room and will

* A 'Register of the Papers of Professor Sir Patrick Geddes', published in June 1970 by the Department of Urban and Regional Planning, University of Strathclyde, makes no reference at all to the
loss of documents;   while the author's letter of 4 April 1971 to
that department, asking for a statement to include in this biography, has never been officially answered.   Conversely, Strathclyde's Andersonian Librarian, informed the writer in October 1976
that the Library had very recently taken over full responsibility
for the Geddes Collection.   Unfortunately, no statement could be
made as to when it would be rehoused and completely indexed because
of acute lack of space and professional help.   Under these adverse
circumstances one wonders whether the National Library of Scotland
might not be a more appropriate custodian.

always be there, as this is one of the conditions of sale'.*

Speaking in October 1954 at the Edinburgh Centenary Celebration of
P.G.'s birth, the Vice-Chancellor of Edinburgh University, Sir
Edward V. Appleton, cautiously touched on Geddes's career in Edinburgh with a veiled admission of academic if not municipal sins.
'Sir Patrick' (as he was meticulously referred to) was given credit
for 'the institutions of self-governing University Halls of residence for men students' and for revealing a real need which 'has
certainly been one of the factors influencing our subsequent
policy'.   In the matter of such housing, Sir Edward said,
> We can claim that the University has followed his lead, although
> to my mind in much too leisurely a fashion....   At present ...
> it is definitely University policy to extend our residential
> accommodation quite considerably, and I hope that when our plans
> are completed they will be worthy of the man who influenced the
> development of the former University Hall, to which so many of
> our graduates look back with feelings of gratitude and nostalgic
> regard.

The Vice-Chancellor should also have quoted P.G.'s prediction of
1906 that if the same rate of expansion of University Halls as from
1887 on could be kept up 'for another half generation', Edinburgh
University would 'thus have been adequately supplied with residential facilities within a single generation'.   Had the speaker done
so, the pioneer action of Patrick and Anna would have appeared even
more strikingly effective in contrast to the slow pace of official
action for two whole generations.   Their nineteenth-century record
in both repairing and new construction is only now being surpassed
by architects and builders fully backed by municipal and university
resources.

The year 1973 saw still another recognition of the value of Geddes's
non-botanical ventures, delayed though this gesture was by many
decades.   The University acquired the premises of No. 6 James Court
with the intent 'to conserve this building and re-condition the
accommodation to provide acceptable flats for students or other
suitable occupiers'.   May one also suggest that a plaque, at least,
ought to mark this strategic spot where the young botanist and his
bride first practised 'conservative surgery' in the slums of the
Royal Mile?   Conservation and 'renewal from within' not only became
famous trademarks in his plans for dozens of Indian cities from 1915
on, but have recently been re-discovered as strokes of genius and
sheer common sense by planners who, under the name of 'rehabilitation', utilise them instead of the wholesale demolition which Geddes
showed often to be completely futile.

Another successful hall of residence founded by Geddes was Crosby

* Booklet of the Ramsay Lodge Association, 1948, and letter from
its Lady Superintendant, Miss Agnes Newton, of 1 April 1973 which
also stated that the Lodge had been bought in 1972 'by the Lloyds &
Scottish Finance Co. and is run as a residential Training College'.

Hall in Chelsea, London.   It too changed hands, temporarily during
two World Wars as well as permanently in 1922 when the British Federation of University Women acquired it as their national headquarters and as a residence for members.   Today the new wings of
Crosby Hall can house 90, a great increase in capacity over More's
Garden hostel in 1907.   Yet despite its being a well-known landmark on the Chelsea Embankment neither casual visitor nor resident
has any inkling of its Geddesian past unless she or he notices the
commemorative plaque in a corridor.   The embattled days of P.G. and
the Earl of Sandwich when saving Sir Thomas More's town house in
1908 are nearly forgotten history.   So, too, are stirring civic
events like the opening of Geddes's Cities Exhibition by Cabinet
Minister John Burns in 1910 and the rehearsals for the great Masque
of Learning staged in London in 1913.

On the other hand, the 400-year history of the Hall is available to
Federation members in an illustrated pamphlet. (7)   It is a tale of
pomp and splendour, hospitality, neglect and rebuilding which includes the housing of refugees and near-destruction by bombs as well
as present use as 'a collegiate home centred in a living community'.
The one mention of Geddes's name in the pamphlet gives only a hint
of his part in the rebuilding and of his services to education, and
is thus a typical example of his 'Impact Anonymous'.   Yet he would
be the last to complain, since all that mattered to him was that a
good idea should succeed.   In reality, therefore, Crosby Hall
stands today not only as an architectural gem and a vital institution but even more, in Philip Mairet's words, 'as London's memorial
to Patrick Geddes'.

Passing over the plans worked out or outlined for universities in
Indore, Hyderabad, Bombay and elsewhere, one pauses at the truly
great one for Jerusalem.   The Indian projects never got beyond the
paper stage, except at Santiniketan, though such influence as P.G.
had there was adapted and expressed in Tagore's own educational
idiom.   But in the Palestine of the 1920s Geddes did make a real
impact even though only the Library was built according to his and
Mears's plans.   As Dr E.M. Eder tersely says:
> It was not wholly due to want of money, for Geddes was an econo-
> mical builder and planner....   Suffice it to say that there are
> few who could rise to the lofty heights of Geddes's imagination
> or **of** his practical knowledge. (8)

Chaim Weizmann, President of the Zionist Organisation, was likewise
enthusiastic about P.G.'s designs and regretted in his autobiography
that 'none of them has been actually carried out, though the general
plan has been followed'.   He does not explain why but adds optimistically: 'And for myself I still hope before I die to see the great
assembly hall which Geddes designed rising on the slopes of
Scopus.' (9)

What came about was quite different, for although Dr Weizmann became
the first president of Israel in 1949, P.G.'s domed hall was never
built.   Mt Scopus remained in Israeli hands only as an isolated
outpost when Arab forces took over parts of Jerusalem after the

British mandate ended in 1948, and the university had to be started again from scratch.   It was scattered in 50 buildings in the 1950s, reports a grand-daughter of Geddes (10) who settled in Israel, while a new campus was created at Givat-Ram.   When Mt Scopus again came into the Hebrew University's hands in 1967 it housed the Arts Faculty while Science stayed at Givat-Ram and Medicine moved to the new Hadassa hospital;   a separation of faculties both by *force majeure* and because of 'the large numbers of students and their crowded timetables'.

Similar dispersion has occurred at other institutions of higher learning in Israel with the result that 'there is nothing of P.G.'s synthetic vision in the structure or the physical layout of the universities here'.

The years 1903-4 saw the creation of both the Dunfermline report, 'City Development', and the Sociological Society in London.   The latter had a long, though chequered, existence from its founding in 1904 by Branford and Geddes until its dissolution in 1955.*   Two World Wars played havoc with the plans of these optimistic 'makers of the future', and their 'Review' as well as the two Le Play offspring of the Society finally had to give up.   The last number of the original 'Sociological Review' appeared in October 1954 after it had been taken over by Keele University in North Staffordshire in 1953.   It is now published under the same title as a 'New Series' but with a wider public than the old 'Review', although without P.G.'s all-embracing approach to social science.

Keele University's Library received most of the Sociological Society's library and all of the Victor Branford papers.   A catalogue of the books has been made, but the indexing of the Branford papers is not yet complete although Lewis Mumford made a start in sorting out the collection during a visit to England in 1957.

The two pragmatic branches of the Sociological Society had likewise a difficult time after Geddes's death.   Le Play Society, organised in 1932 by Margaret Tatton as a split off from Le Play House, had to cease its activity of making regional surveys (by volunteer groups from Britain in various parts of Europe) by the 1950s.   Both it and Le Play House were bombed out of London in 1941, but the latter was carried on from Ledbury by Alexander Farquharson and, after 1954, by his widow.   The Farquharsons were instrumental, along with members of the academic staff, in getting Keele University to carry on the 'Sociological Review' in its new form and to take charge of the Branford documents.

Our survey of material projects now comes to the *Collège des Ecossais* which, like the Outlook Tower, went through many trials after the death of its founder.   From 1933 to 1939 it served as a resi-

---

* It was then called the Institute of Sociology, having changed its name in 1930 when its headquarters were moved from Westminster to Gordon Square, Bloomsbury.

dence for a small international group of students, with T.R. Marr as
manager and Paul Reclus as an adviser of studies, while Lilian (Lady
Geddes) continued her generous financial support until her death in
1936.   The session 1938-9 was the last one, with but few students
in residence.   As the second year of the Second World War began,
the future of the Scots College became even more uncertain.

Paul Reclus, as agent for Norah and Arthur who inherited the place
from Lilian's estate, wrote in January 1940 of his efforts to make
use of the buildings.   He was in contact with organisations trying
to place Polish and Czechoslovak women refugees, and German and
Austrian scientists who were interned.   Reclus preferred the second
project, 'as it would put the Indian College in the bargain and
offer other advantages....'   At the beginning of March, he sent a
postcard to 'My dear Norah' saying 'The College is off your hands'.
The Ministry of National Education had telegraphed him to advise
that 'utilisation of *Collège des Ecossais* arranged ... let us agree
immediately on arrangements'.   Reclus had also written to Arthur
and promised a letter with full details, but this has since disappeared.

From 1941 on there was a complete blackout of the original aims of
the *Collège* as it changed from Vichy to German and to liberated
French hands.   A post-war use that P.G. would have approved of,
however, was as a school-home for handicapped children.   The first
sign of potential restoration came in October 1967: the founding in
Montpellier of 'L'Association Patrick Geddes' by architects, geographers, physicians and sociologists.   Dr Paul Marres, Emeritus
Professor of Geography, presided over the meeting, recalling his
long years of friendship with the founder of the *Collège des Ecossais* and the highlights of the latter's work, for the benefit of
younger scholars.   Once formally constituted, the Association
adopted as its double aim to make the Geddesian kind of planning
better known in France, and to help revive the *Collège* as an international centre for students at the University of Montpellier in the
spirit of Geddes.

Since then this aim has been expanded to include the establishment,
in cooperation with the University as main partner, of an *Institut
d'Environnement* which would provide facilities for graduate research
of an inter-disciplinary nature.   Along with the new School of
Architecture, this *Institut* would utilise the old *Collège* with the
former erecting new buildings on part of P.G.'s *garrigue*.   Despite
much good-will on the part of some local authorities, the project
exists only on paper.   The Ministries concerned in Paris have not
agreed upon necessary priorities, and as of 1976 the Scots College
was being utilised as a training centre for French educational
administrators.

IMPACT ANONYMOUS

The present state of Geddesian thought is much stronger than that of
his material creations, for vital ideas can outlive even the insti-

tutions founded to propagate them.   Yet any attempt to measure the
impact of Geddes on the contemporary world is rendered almost hopeless by the anonymity which has always marked the results of his
ideas and examples.   He consistently disclaimed priority or originality for his contributions in either the natural or social spheres.
'Nobody has ideas of his own - we scientists do not take out patents
in ideas', he said.   Or, 'One should as soon sell one's children as
one's ideas!   In science, if you have an idea worth anything, you
give it to the world.'

Here is one instance of how widespread yet anonymous the influence
of P.G. can be.   In the 1890s a physician-politician named John
Cockburn read the 'Evolution of Sex' and was deeply impressed by
the biological case there made for equality between (though not
identity of) the sexes.   As a Cabinet Minister of South Australia,
he introduced a Bill giving the franchise to women, which became
the first equal rights act of many to follow in England and the
USA.   Presiding at a dinner given in honour of Geddes at Le Play
House in September 1923, Sir John publicly acknowledged his indebtedness to the biologist for his own pioneer achievement of suffrage
for women in Australia. (11)

In rural and urban planning Geddesian words and examples have, since
Dunfermline in 1904, been affecting more and more cities and
countrysides in both West and East.   S.K. Ratcliffe has written
that when Geddes came back from India and Palestine,
    he could look around Britain and see on all hands the fruit of
    his sowing in the widespread civic revival, the multiplying
    groups of student enthusiasts, and the general acceptance of his
    idea of the organic community, however imperfectly it was being
    realised.   For thirty years he had talked to a seemingly un-
    heeding world of the regional survey and what it could be made
    to mean.   He lived to hear the phrase on the lips of county
    councillors and borough surveyors. (12)

One can now extend this comment, saying that wherever the present
and future needs of village or city are being studied in terms of
its place and people and the work they do, and of the relationships
of all with the environment, there is the influence of Patrick
Geddes.   Revisiting Coimbatore in India as long ago as 1939, Arthur
Geddes was greatly pleased to find city officials carrying out concretely and in a 'thoroughly economical, intelligent, and artistic
way', the plans with which his father had inspired these men in
their youth. (13)   On the other hand, in this Scottish town or that
English city, neither inhabitants nor their leaders may realise who
planted the mustard seed which, generations later, is inspiring
civic renewal.   But, as P.G. again would quickly say, 'Ideas are
what count.   The important thing is not who has them, but what is
done with them!'

In present-day India, however, it unfortunately appears that not
much has been done with his ideas in some places where he worked
from five to six decades ago.   After a two months' study tour in
his wake in 1973, Dr Helen Meller has commented:

> P.G. is well known by reputation still, but there is total ignorance about his planning ideas and his work.... For the first few years after he made them, some plans were implemented to a certain extent, especially Indore; but the vagueness of some of P.G.'s outlines plus the pressures of economic incentives soon obscured the direction which the plan was to take. I found no evidence of follow up by others at a later date on a P.G. plan. (14)

In his lifetime Geddes was far from being an honoured prophet in Great Britain. For example, when he gave his public Farewell Lecture at University College, Dundee after 30 years of service, it was his students and not colleagues who came to hear him. But after his death, fellow-academics were able to appraise him more objectively and, in consequence, more generously. A good case in point is the discussion which arose after the biography of D'Arcy W. Thompson, Professor of Zoology at Dundee, appeared in 1958. One reviewer declared, in the 'Times Literary Supplement' of 4 July, that 'A biography of Thompson which makes only four perfunctory references to Geddes can therefore, hardly be considered adequate.' A reader commented to the 'Supplement''s Editor that though colleagues at UCD for almost thirty years, P.G. and D'Arcy were not intimate friends, and hinted that the latter was being confused with P.G.'s former pupil J. Arthur Thomson. Whereupon another reader quoted Professor W.J. Tulloch of Dundee as informing him that Geddes and Thompson 'did see a good deal of each other ... and that their conversation was lively, entertaining and friendly.'

The most significant tributes to Geddes, however, were these. Nearly half of 'The Times' review of Thompson's biography was devoted to his colleague P.G., including this assertion: 'Geddes was one of the greatest and most obscure influences on our times. Europe and Asia are equally in his debt.' And on 15 August 1958 the biographer herself (D'Arcy's daughter, Ruth Thompson) wrote to 'The Times' explaining that she had been too young, at the time her father was in Dundee with P.G., to be interested in his opinions of colleagues. However, she wished to relate the following story* which she had 'heard for the first time last week':

> After Patrick Geddes's funeral my father and a few friends talked together of his life and work. My father spoke at length and when he ceased one of his colleagues said, 'But, D'Arcy, you speak as if Geddes had been the best man of all of us.' To which my father replied, 'Well, wasn't he?'**

* Lewis Mumford has told the author how, in justice to P.G., he took care to end his 'Disciple's Rebellion' with this same 'stunning quotation' from D'Arcy Thompson.

** A similar comment was made by D'Arcy Thompson on 27 April 1938 in an address on the Dundee Social Union, 'Fifty Years Ago and Now'. Describing the 'remarkable band' of young professors at UCD, he said: 'Lastly came Sir Patrick Geddes, as great a man as any there'.

In this context one may also quote a tribute by the dissident American disciple who nevertheless has done even more to make P.G.'s name and ideas known in the English-speaking world than faithful Victor Branford and practical, loyal Arthur Thomson.   In a review of the second edition of 'Cities in Evolution' many years before his rebellion-memoir, Mumford wrote:

> Geddes had greatness of soul as well as of mind; and though I
> never achieved any real degree of intimacy with him, that first
> sense of his greatness was not dulled by successive contacts.
> He could be wilful; he could be self-absorbed; he could even be
> tyrannical, with the ruthlessness of a man wholly intent on his
> own ideas, to the exclusion of any other human considerations
> that stood in their way.   But behind such petty phenomena was a
> noble understanding.   Perhaps what makes his writing so pregnant
> with thoughts beyond anything he actually expressed are the per-
> petual hints he gave of that magnanimity and amplitude of
> spirit. (15)

The great talent Geddes had for detailed planning as well as finding and stating basic principles should also be emphasised.   His own accounts of criss-crossing on foot an entire slum quarter that was threatened with drawing-board 'relief of congestion' until he could show by his map of the neighbourhood how conservative surgery would achieve the desired result without wholesale demolition and at a fraction of the cost, are given in 'Patrick Geddes in India'.   This is still an essential 'pocket P.G.' which ought to be in the working kits of planners in every part of the world, not to forget administrators of rural and urban affairs.   Members of both professions could, for example, reflect upon this bit of wisdom from its page 70:

> We men are hypnotized by money but have lost sight of economics -
> the real functioning of life, in real and energetic health,
> creating real and material wealth.   Real wealth can only be
> created in a life-efficient environment.

The rediscovery of P.G.'s house-by-house and block-by-block analyses by today's town planners, who in turn apply them to the preservative 'rehabilitation' of depressed urban areas, is a very hopeful sign. But he has still more to offer, for as the late Arthur Glikson* has stated:

> Geddes had a peculiar talent of relating his comprehensive intel-
> lectual syntheses to a specific reality, and to illustrate them
> by concrete cases in concrete locations.   He could also give a
> meaning to the general visual view of a town, a river valley or
> region by giving it stimulating, surprising and convincing inter-
> pretations.   His synthetic theoretic insight complemented his
> empirical impressions and vice versa.   This synoptic method of
> his had a strong influence on his pupils and successors.   On one

* Lewis Mumford has told the author that he counts Glikson as
P.G.'s most understanding critic and interpreter - and active follower - in this generation.   'He would have been closer to P.G.'s
heart than I was - though just as independent!'

Sir J. Arthur Thompson
(1861-1933), P.G.'s pupil,
friend and colleague of
longest standing

Victor V. Branford
(1864-1930), P.G.'s lifetime
friend and sociological colleague of the Edinburgh
Summer Meetings and the
'Sociological Review'

hand this method was an expression of a most vital personality
and on the other it brought his ideas ever closer to the most
important problems of our time... (16)

Of the important areas where P.G.'s cumulative impact can be discerned if not measured, there is no more striking example than that
of the Tennessee Valley Authority in North America.   In 1933, one
year after his death, the Congress of the United States voted to
establish a decentralised governmental agency to reconstruct an
entire region for the benefit of all its inhabitants.   TVA's first
director, David Lilienthal, has written:
> For the first time in the history of a nation the resources of a
> river were not only to be envisioned in their entirety;   they
> were to be developed in that unity with which nature herself re-
> gards her resources - the waters, the land, and the forests
> together - a seamless web... (17)

That the TVA's political sponsors like Franklin D. Roosevelt and
Senator George Norris saw the need for multi-disciplinary regional
surveys before drawing up plans is obvious.   Likewise certain is
that much of this 'valley section' influence can be traced to
Geddes through colleagues such as Walter Glikson, Benton MacKaye
and Lewis Mumford.   The following lines from Lilienthal could,
accordingly, just as well have appeared in one of P.G.'s Indian
reports:
> The people must be in on the planning, their existing institu-
> tions must be made part of it;   self-education of the citizenry
> is more important than specific projects or physical changes.

Not until 1950 did Benton MacKaye publish the story (18) of his
meeting P.G. in the spring of 1923, writing in part that he would
never 'forget my first walk with Patrick Geddes ... the sandy-
bearded Scot ... with the whole epic of civilization visioned from
his famed Outlook Tower in Edinburgh'.   MacKaye had been telling
about his own adventures
> in conservation under Gifford Pinchot and in regional planning
> ... when Geddes rounded on me in the path.   'None of those!' he
> caught me up - 'Not conservation, not planning, not even geo-
> graphy.   Your subject is geotechnics.'
>   And then with a lunge he resumed speed, but only for a few
> strides.   'Geography,' said he, 'is descriptive science; ... it
> tells what *is*.   Geotechnics is applied science; ... it shows
> what *ought to be*.'   And on he bounded.
>   *Geotechnics*!   I wanted to use it right away, and like a pre-
> cious nugget found in the path, I carried it hidden in the deep-
> est pocket of my brain...

However, MacKaye could not find this word in American dictionaries,
and when colleagues suggested that the time was not ripe for its
use, he settled for 'habitability', which one of them proposed
instead.
> Forthwith, in the 1920's, I proceeded to write about 'habita-
> bility'.   Later, in the 1930's, when with the Tennessee Valley
> Authority, I gave birth to a long memorandum ('Opus One' they

called it) on how to achieve greater habitability for that water-
shed.   But never did I dare mention out loud the proper Geddesian term though I grew ever more impatient.

The climax came in the 1940s.   MacKaye was 'about to use the real
name, anyhow, baptized or not ...' when, in a St Louis library, he
turned to *G* in Webster's International Dictionary.
    There I found it:
    '*Geotechnics - the applied science of making the earth more
    habitable*'.   I swallowed a howl lest I should break the library
    edict of 'silence'.   My inhibitions over the years evaporated
    ....   And so, at long last, the *name*.

But the story is not complete without Lewis Mumford's confession in
his introduction to the 1962 edition of 'The New Exploration'.
After telling about MacKaye's and Geddes's mutual discovery of each
other and of the former's delight in the new word, 'geotechnics', he
writes:
    In the original manuscript of 'The New Exploration', he [MacKaye]
    had used this term, and wanted to put it in the subtitle as well.
    As an intermediary with the publisher, I foolishly thought that
    the book would have enough difficulty in getting accepted with-
    out the instrusion of this new term;   and I persuaded him to
    change it to ... 'regional planning'.   Long after, MacKaye dis-
    covered, to his delight, that 'geotechnics' had officially
    entered the dictionary;   but by that time he had completely for-
    gotten my officious interference with his early use of it.   Let
    the reader correct my error by taking this book as a study in
    geotechnics!

Also traceable are indirect links between Geddes and the Greek
planner, the late Constantinos A. Doxiadis.   Not to be outdone by
his Scottish forerunner's thinking machines and Hellenic neologisms
like 'Eutopia', 'Necropolis' and so on, Doxiadis worked out a
graphic representation of the possible admixtures of elements in
human settlements as they range from extreme badness ('Dystopia',
bad-place) to ideal goodness ('Utopia', no-place or the unattainable
ideal).   Desirable reality or the attainable ideal is included as
'Entopia' (here-place), whereas P.G. calls it 'Eutopia' (the good-
place jointly achievable by citizens and planners).

Likewise a multi-disciplinarian, Doxiadis made a synthesis of the
branches of science dealing with man's work and habitations which he
called 'Ekistics - the Science of Human Settlements'.   A human link
between the two planners is the writer Jaqueline Tyrwhitt who,
after editing 'Patrick Geddes in India' (1947), has become Consult-
ing Editor of the periodical, 'Ekistics'.   She herself has stated
that P.G. '... was perhaps the most important formative influence in
my life' and that 'Doxiadis never actually read Geddes as far as I
know, but he imbibed some of his ideas via me and came up with his
grids on his own.' (19)

The American sociologist, Buckminster Fuller, is sometimes described
as also being akin to Geddes, though the indexes of the former's

main books reveal no mention of P.G. Paddy Kitchen, for example, writes that Abraham Maslow's

'high-synergy society' is a concept Geddes would have applauded; and it is also reminiscent of ideas developed by Buckminster Fuller. There are indeed many parallels between Geddes and Fuller - not least their ability to talk out their all-embracing theories at prodigious length. (20)

Recent evidence of P.G.'s wide and continuing impact is the interest shown in the 'Patrick Geddes Proposals' to the Habitat gatherings at Vancouver, BC in June 1976.   Initiated by the 'Association P.G.' of Montpellier and seconded by an International Committee based in Oslo, Norway, these proposals asked the United Nations Conference on Human Settlements, and the concurrent Forum of Non-Governmental Organizations, to:

1. Recall Geddes's pioneer work in sound rehabilitation of slums as a better alternative than wholesale destruction and urge the general adoption of this humane treatment of people and their environment;
2. repeat his 'early ecological warning' as even more needed today than when first sounded in 1884; and
3. consider plans for giving a new dimension to the three institutions founded by Geddes: the Outlook Tower, the Department of Sociology at Bombay University, and the *Collège des Ecossais*.   Namely, by having all three serve as regional centres where planners and citizens may meet and help promote Habitat's goals of world-wide exchange of plans and interpretive information concerning human settlements.

Although no official UN recommendations resulted, the International Committee's two 'men in Vancouver'* could report that besides general distribution to individuals, the Proposals were well received at one P.G. Workshop in English and at another in Spanish, and that their text was printed in the Forum Handbook for sale to all delegates.   Jaqueline Tyrwhitt of 'Ekistics' and Percy Johnson-Marshall of Edinburgh University were also present at Habitat, and both took public occasion to emphasise the present validity of much of Geddes. There was general agreement that his ideas and examples would have an even better chance of being heeded during the follow-up activities of Habitat as each country sought to implement such widely accepted aims as creating a world-wide chain of centres where professionals and laymen could interact, encouraging citizen participation in planning processes, and furthering education as a main key to improving human settlements everywhere.

Turning to Geddes's work in biology, we find the same mingling of acknowledged and anonymous traces as in city planning.   Many of Sir J. Arthur Thomson's widely known works are as he himself freely

* David Lock, Planning Officer of the Town & Country Planning Association of London (founded by P.G.'s contemporary, Ebenezer Howard), and Salvador Jury, a graduate student of planning from Mexico.

admitted, extensions and applications of ideas, theories, or keen
guesses thrown out to him by his teacher and colleague.   Yet conversely, perhaps due in part to P.G.'s habitual largesse as a
scientist, some biologists have borrowed theories and experiments
from him without so much as acknowledging their source.   Even when
Geddes was in the midst of his 'escape activities' in southern
France, Thomson maintained that if he had only published the botanical interpretations

> which he scatters generously among pupils and friends, his repu-
> tation and value would have been much greater.   Had he followed
> up these interpretations by research, he might have been the
> greatest of botanists.   But then he had other things to do. (21)

In a memorial article in 'The Times' (19 April 1932) Sir Arthur
filled almost two columns with partly sober, partly superlative
praise.   The same day he wrote to Arthur and Norah:

> To me your father meant more than any other influence, and I have
> never concealed my gratitude.   I could not get more than four
> hours for my appreciation in to-day's 'Times', but I have tried
> to indicate my conviction that he was even bigger intellectually
> than his best friends knew.

Thomson recalled the four main fields - or worlds - in which Geddes
had laboured.   He was well known 'as a biologist fertile in original ideas', 'as a pioneer sociologist'; 'as a conservative town-
planner ... offering wise counsel that has made for the saving of
life and beauty and sacred tradition'; and finally 'as fearless
educationist always involved in some experiment'.

> But few of those who knew him well in one or other of these
> roles, or in yet another, had more than glimpses of his extra-
> ordinarily complex synergy of activities, unified in his main
> motive - the service of man.   We remember at Dundee William
> James's incredulity at Geddes being a Professor of Botany; and
> how Stanley Hall,* another visitor, exclaimed, 'But I am looking
> for Geddes, the psychologist!'

The former pupil described, in phrases often quoted since, three
gifts which P.G. had 'at an unusually high potential'.   When lecturing he had 'an almost bewildering celerity of thought, with more
new ideas to the quarter of an hour than any three men together'.
From precise observations in boyhood:

---

*   It now appears that 'Impact Anonymous' is the main traceable
effect of Geddes on Hall.   As stated in the Introduction, the
latter's early dream of becoming P.G.'s Boswell vanished so completely that by 1923 Hall's 'Life and Confessions of a Psychologist'
does not even mention Geddes's name.   Nevertheless, clues like the
phrase, 're-education ... of the heart as well as of the intellect',
and the condemnation of Prussian distortion of Darwinism into 'Might
is Right', on pages 21 and 565, respectively, are plausible reflections of P.G.   One unquestionable trace, furthermore, is a sub-
title on page 355 reading 'Some Outlook Tower views of present-day
psychology'.   Yet again, in the text which presents these views
there is no reference whatsoever to the Tower.

he developed remarkable visualizing power, picturing the pageant
of history as if he had been an eyewitness, discussing the aeonic
process of organic evolution as a drama in which he had personally shared.   And finally, he had a great 'gift in discerning, almost instantaneously it often seemed, how things might be bettered - a garden, a village street, an exhibition, a university, a
painting, a poem.'

Of Geddes's 'brilliant power of evolutionary diagnosis', Thomson
wrote:
He saw everything always, his own theories included, as part of
an endless process of 'Becoming, Being and Having Been', as Hegel
phrased it....   Geddes's special gift was to see a plant, an
animal, a human type, a social organization, a historic crisis,
not merely as something which had evolved, but as something that
had evolved in a particular way and was still evolving....
   Always discerning, he thought, the 'inner impulse', Geddes was
more Lamarckian in the deepest sense than Darwinian;   and while
appreciating the rapid advances in our knowledge of the chemistry
and physics of the body, he always saw a Dryad in the tree and
was always ready to champion the autonomy of biology or the vi-
talistic view of life.   Biologically he was closely akin to
Goethe.

Thomson continued with an evaluation of his master's mental powers
in old age which contradicts Mumford's in 'The Disciple's Rebellion'.
It was Geddes's meat and drink to interpret plants and animals,
men and their organizations, as phases in evolution, and the outcome of trends which he discerned more and more clearly as the
years passed.   He seemed abler and more illuminating at 77 than
at 27;   and it is an intellectual tragedy that so much of his
interpretative speculation has never been published.
   ... his output of books was cramped by a strange fastidiousness which led him, like many an artist, to throw away one brilliant sketch after another till the opportunity passed altogether, or else to over-elaborate the canvas till intelligibility
was obscured.   And yet, as many passages and short essays show,
he had a remarkably felicitious style.

The long tribute ended simply and fittingly: Patrick Geddes 'was
very rich in distinguished friends, yet richer still in a multitude
of humble students who are mourning to-day with a great pride in
their hearts'.

COMPRENDRE, C'EST PARDONNER ... CENTENARY APPRAISAL

After such praise by the man who knew Geddes longest, something
should be said about family relationships in keeping with Thomson's
spirit of understanding and goodwill.   P.G.'s sporadic disputes
with Norah and Arthur have been documented enough in earlier pages
so that readers can make their own diagnosis.   In the son's case,
however, there are some later bits of evidence which are both en-

lightening and conciliatory.   In the tape recording made in 1968
Arthur did give vent to certain resentments and regret over the
many opportunities for real co-operation which had been neglected.
He even confessed what his first reaction was on receiving the news
from Montpellier in April 1932 about his father: 'I remember how
sad I was to open this telegram announcing his death, how sad I was
to feel nothing but sheer relief.'

On the other hand, he spent far more time and energy in carrying on
some of P.G.'s unfinished work than was compatible with his own
career as a geographer.   The renewal of the Outlook Tower in the
late 1940s owed much to Arthur, likewise the publication of three
books (22) almost within the decade following the Second World
War.

The first was 'Patrick Geddes in India', 1947, for which the sel-
ections from P.G.'s Indian reports were edited 'in co-operation
with H.V. Lanchester and Arthur Geddes'.   Next, a re-edition of
the 1915 classic 'Cities in Evolution', 1949, with 30 pages of illustrations from the Cities Exhibition partly chosen by Arthur.
The third book was Philip Mairet's 'Pioneer of Sociology', 1957,
for which Arthur wrote the Introduction in addition to making
P.G.'s private letters available to its author.   There Arthur
praises his mother for her great part in his father's achievements.
    Without Anna ... Patrick's flashes of discovery might have
    lacked the fire which sustained thought and civic action.
    Without her he could not have dwelt so continuously nor with
    such understanding in the sick core of the Old Town.   A great-
    hearted man with many faults, he could not have attained his
    moral stature without her ardour of love, faith and clear-eyed
    critique.

Further evidence exists of mutual reconciliation between father
and son.   There is Geddes's last letter to Norah, 9 April 1932,
which contains optimistic words about his grandchildren and their
futures, and ends:
    Don't worry about Arthur either!   [Professor] Sion is much
    pleased with plan of his India book, and so am I with his
    various projects & outlooks - which marriage will now strengthen.
    We have had one or two good talks.

As for Arthur, he not only assisted with the publication of the
books described above but tried to get two of P.G.'s manuscripts
into print.   One was the long ill-fated 'Civilisation - a Challenge', which would have appeared in 1938 but for Munich and resulting uncertainties.   The other project, likewise unsuccessful, was
to have P.G.'s interpretation of 'Olympus' published as 'one of the
most important among a half-dozen works ... to be edited'.   Though
'unwilling to take up the job myself ...' because of having 'spent
so much time in vain for P.G.', Arthur did write a sonnet, 'A Servant of the Gods', and a prose introduction for the book which de-
pict Geddes's life in terms of Olympian phases of development.

Particularly appropriate are his descriptions of the final stages.
'The long, dour struggle for completion and mastery of one's task

was symbolised for him by Ephestos (Vulcan), supremely skilled yet
already lamed at his forge.' Had the World War not come, wrote
Arthur, had Anna and Alasdair survived and the value of P.G.'s initiatives been earlier recognised, he 'might have handed on the
hammer and anvil to another, to enter into the final patriarchal
phase symbolised by Father Zeus or the Roman Jove.' Instead came
sorrows, frenzied work and illnesses from which his return to
southern France brought only partial recovery. Being of a long-
lived family he might not have died in his 78th year,

> yet restless and ill he could not complete the tasks he under-
> took nor resist the temptation to begin one new errand before
> the preceding one had been completed. In this sense his end
> was a tragic breakdown rather than the serene attainment which
> happier years, health and above all the survival of his wife and
> son would surely have brought.

The above, and the last lines of the sonnet which follow are authentic testimony from the younger son that 'to understand is to forgive':

> Age found him worn, widowed and desolate,
>> Torn to the entrails: Though Mercurial still -
>> Eager to speed on errands of Jove's will -
> He, who would die too soon, lived on too late.
>> Yet, though he sank ere Zeus' phase arose,
>> His life shall find fulfilment since its close. (23)

Centenary Celebrations of P.G.'s birth took place in several parts
of the world in October 1954. In his own 'City Beautiful' a Symposium was held in the Andrew Grant Gallery of the Edinburgh College
of Art in cooperation with the University of Edinburgh, 'the Forbes
Trust and other organisations and societies in Edinburgh' while 'A
selection of Sir Patrick Geddes's own material was on exhibition in
the Gallery', to quote from the 37-page Report afterwards published. (24) In moving a vote of thanks to speakers at the morning session, Arthur Geddes urged the participants to remember the
celebration 'as the opening of a new century' and not only to look
'back to 1854 but also forward to 2054'.

Indeed, as one now reads the tributes and addresses by distinguished
officials and professors one may well wonder, even after discounting
some of the praise as obligatory, why more of the big words were not
long ago turned into deeds in England and Scotland.* The Earl of
Home:

> I am glad to have the opportunity of sending a message of greet-
> ing on behalf of Her Majesty's Government. It is only in this
> generation when we are experiencing at first hand the effects of
> the unplanned growth of our industrial belt, that we realise the
> full extent of Geddes's insight and foresight.... I hope that
> as a result of his pioneering work in social planning and the

---

* Had he heard these comments, P.G. would undoubtedly have explained them as 'pious homage' or even 'expiatory verbiage'. (See Mumford's remark on p. 449.)

inspiration he handed down to those he taught we are gradually
working towards a solution of our problems of which he would have
approved.   It seems to me that this is a fitting time to acknowledge our indebtedness to this great Scotsman.

The Lord Provost of the City of Edinburgh, the Rt Hon. John G.
Banks, was chairman of the morning session.   After welcoming the
participants and mentioning the wide range of Geddes's interests and
activities, he said:
> I am glad to learn that much of his life was spent in this city
> of Edinburgh, where the centre of many of his activities was the
> Outlook Tower....   There was very little if any planning one
> hundred years ago as we know it now, and to men of vision and
> courage such as Geddes, who opened up a new vista, we must ex-
> press our indebtedness....

The veteran town planner, Professor Sir Patrick Abercrombie, opened
a symposium by reviewing the most important phases of P.G.'s work,
one of which was the study of Dunfermline in 1903 which he described as a fundamental book
> for the teaching of civic design.   As you all know Geddes ex-
> panded a commission to write about the proposed park into what
> is really the first comprehensive Town Planning Report....   It
> was a pregnant volume; I have read it over and over again, and
> used it as a basis for other reports which I have been engaged
> on myself ... He proposed a financial scheme for ... investment
> and realisation by stages, that in itself was an early attempt to
> practise period planning.   Nothing indeed could be finer and
> broader and more inspiring than his outlook, ideas and proposals
> in that Dunfermline report....

Professor Abercrombie gave many personal recollections of Geddes's
methods of working in India and Palestine and concluded with these
anecdotes typical of the impulsive and, to conventional Britons, unsettling ways of the renegade botanist.   One day he received a
phone call at Liverpool University from P.G. asking him to get hold
of two or three persons and meet him in Chester.   They sat in an
architect's office there
> while he harangued us... it was a wonderful experience; three-
> quarters of an hour of intellectual exhortation which did us all
> good....   As soon as he had finished he folded up his diagram,
> walked off, jumped onto a tramcar bound for the station and dis-
> appeared.   On the other occasion I received a telephone call,
> this time at my house in the evening, asking me if I would meet
> him at Lime Street Station, bringing a pair of pyjamas and £5....
> I found him on the platform ... without any luggage except a
> double-bass fiddle.   He was on his way to Belgium.   I got the
> £5 returned, for he was meticulous about such matters: but not
> the pyjamas....

Another noted planner, Sir William (later Lord) Holford, explained
to the Centenary gathering that he was there as President of the
Town Planning Institute,
> and for the simple reason that the Institute, without Geddes,

would hardly have existed.   As a trade union it might, perhaps,
have come into existence; but as a voluntary association, a
learned society, it would have had an insecure foundation without
the work that Geddes did.   Then I am here as a teacher, to acknowledge him as the great educator and interpreter of the function of environmental planning in modern life.   Without Geddes
the pioneer departments of Town Planning (or Civic Design) in the
Universities of Liverpool and London would not have come into
existence.

Sir William added that he was also present because he did *not* know
P.G. in person, because he 'was never directly stimulated nor exasperated by his prescriptions for civic survey, his proposals for
"conservative surgery", his plans for regional development'.
    On the other hand, I cannot escape his influence.   The Greek
    epigram on Plato is applicable to him: 'Wherever I go in my mind
    I meet Geddes coming back!'   No teacher, no practitioner, no
    amateur of cities can fail to absorb some of his lessons when
    first he studies his subject....

After pointing out the similarity between Robert Owen and Geddes as
visionaries who combined 'common sense and common feeling' with
idealism and as pioneers 'constantly stepping ahead of their contemporaries and calling to them to catch up', Holford traced the progress of some Geddesian ideas.   One was his concept of a true university which was only partially expressed in the unfulfilled plans
for that of Jerusalem.   He was sure that Geddes would have thoroughly approved of the multi-racial Central African University College which was just then being organised, and that other seeds were
coming to fruition in other institutions.   P.G.
    was never one for examinations or curricula or degrees, and he
    never took degrees himself; but nevertheless some of the new
    universities are founded on some of his educational principles,
    and I even wonder whether we shall not get something like adult
    education or a university extension system which might be called
    a Geddes Extension System connected with the older universi-
    ties....
        Another idea was that of the mixed community ... Geddes was
    always conscious of the infinite variation in patterns, species,
    types, groups, places and jobs which really go to make a mixed
    community, whether of plants or humans.   His very carefully
    planned neighbourhood units are really not just simply a mixture
    of incomes and different types of building.   He realised that
    there had to be a cross-fertilisation of ideas, and that a mixed
    community was based on incentive and example....   Unless the new
    community produced incentive and example and imagination, it
    would not really be mixed but would even out into an extremely
    monotonous pattern....

Concluding, Sir William emphasised that Geddes's designs and buildings which were completed were
    mere casual records or mementoes of the really important thing,
    ... [his] view of life as a whole.   He had the ability to link
    up specialisms with a general philosophy of life so that you

could understand the flow between the past and the future....
To one who like myself is teaching and practising in a minor way
it is extraordinary, as one goes along making and meeting small
failure after small failure, how inspiring it is to go back to
Geddes's magnificent failures and to see how much success there
really was in them.   In catching up with our own future we shall
be continually overtaking Geddes's past.

The afternoon session was presided over by the Vice-Chancellor of
the University of Edinburgh, Sir Edward V. Appleton, whose tribute
to P.G.'s work in starting residential halls for students has been
quoted earlier in this chapter, together with his statement that the
University was now following his lead, 'although to my mind in much
too leisurely a fashion'.   Sir Edward also confessed that while
Geddes was a prophet not without honour in his own country as a
planner,

> I am afraid I must qualify that so far as the University of Edin-
> burgh is concerned.   He was a student here at the University,
> but he did not somehow find what he wanted and he betook himself
> to London....   Later we tried to make amends ... by appointing
> him to our teaching staff in the Botany Department.   But here
> again we failed him for, although he was a candidate for the
> Regius Chair of Botany, his candidature was unsuccessful and we
> did not appoint him.

But the chairman did not explain why earlier proposals to award P.G.
an honorary degree had been turned down,* nor did he mention the
dilemma of the Outlook Tower.   The latter point, however, was taken
up by the first afternoon speaker, Professor F.A.E. Crew, who deplored that

> its scope and progress are hampered by a lack of interest and a
> lack of funds.   Those who on this day are gathered to salute the
> memory of Patrick Geddes might, I would submit, look to the Tower
> and all those who work in it and consider the desirability of
> making this a permanent memorial to a famous man.   For unlike
> many of such tokens of grateful respect it has the great advan-
> tage of being filled with activities of a scientific kind, and
> out of these new knowledge will certainly emerge, and it may well
> be that this knowledge in application will help mankind to find
> its way in this bewildering world.

Professor H.J. Fleure, an old friend and geographer-colleague of
P.G., devoted most of his address to the latter's Place-Work-Folk

* Lewis Mumford received an LLD at Edinburgh in July 1965, and in
the presentation remarks was described as coming early 'under the
influence of Patrick Geddes, the Scottish Pioneer of Regional Planning, and has repeatedly acknowledged that influence in his own
thinking'.   Afterwards Mumford wrote the author (22 November 1968)
that he felt his LLD 'was a kind of belated vicarious atonement for
the shabby way in which the University had treated P.G., the man who
singlehanded had conceived and built the residence halls they so
badly needed.   A shocking neglect.'

approach to, and combination of, Geography, Economics and Anthropology as the triple basis of Sociology.   He also praised Geddes's
Regional Survey techniques as valuable to the study of history as
well as essential to any rural and urban planning worthy of the
name.

As the final speaker of the day, Professor Fleure summed up with
these words:
> The papers read at this centenary celebration have given a sketch
> of a very active imaginative observer with so many facets to his
> mind that we can hardly visualise the whole, an idealist full of
> practical and practicable schemes generally to be implemented by
> others.   He thought passionately, and yet kept a certain objec-
> tivity of mind in many fields.   In a period of increasing spe-
> cialism he tried hard to the end to see the whole.   How far he
> succeeded one may discuss without end, but he was one who felt
> that to journey usefully was more than to arrive, that a loyal
> and sincere struggle for a great ideal was perhaps more than a
> victory for a lesser aim ... when we talk of Geddes we may think
> that if at times he seemed almost to fail, yet his work is going
> on and going on most nobly.

AGNOSTIC BELIEVER

Though Patrick Geddes professed an intellectual denial of belief in
a divine power or being on many occasions, he was at times ambivalent, perhaps in spite of himself.   A frank statement occurs in a
letter of 14 March 1926 to 'Dear old Friend' (Harry Barker), thanking him for 'Maeterlinck's able and beautiful book' which the former
had sent him.   P.G. is sorry for having delayed so long in writing,
> but I suppose it is because anything I can say must be dis-
> appointing to you.   For I have never had any feeling of immor-
> tality for myself or my dear lost ones, any more than for autumn
> leaves like myself, or those already gone.   I just work away to
> do what I can with such days as may remain, and think of death as
> sleep - I hope not with too painful a getting-to-sleep, but in
> any case without hopes, fears or dreams of any hereafter for
> myself, apart from such bits of work as may usefully endure, and
> be of use for others.
>   In the doctrine of reincarnation too, I see only an antique
> dream of the evolution process of ordinary life.   So, in a word,
> the only 'continuance of personality' I can imagine is in the
> limited measure of such work, and influence, as may have been put
> into the continuing life of our successors.

Geddes praises his old friend for having done his bit 'in the prime
task of man, the tilling of Mother Earth.'
> You enjoy the beauty of the world, and the daily kindly relations
> with all around you: you leave posterity, already as to be of
> service and in joy of life in their turn; so why trouble because
> at the end of life, just as at the close of each day, there will
> be sleep?   That's really all I have ever had to say on the
> matter, for the ancient and modern teachings leave me cold, the

latter especially; and even Maeterlinck's philosophic poetising
and speculation gets me no further.   Some day we shall 'sleep
with our fathers' - but let us work away meanwhile.*

Briefly, P.G. tells of his making 'a ruinous wee cottage on a rough
heathside' into a 'Joyous Gard' or '*Abbaye de Thélème*'
> with its gardens conquered from rocky heath into varied beauty to
> go on increasing after I am gone, and be of suggestiveness and
> encouragement to others - and while the University lasts!   And
> in helping to alter these old mixtures of good seed with bad,
> which we call universities, into purer cultures, - *Studia Synthe-
> tica* instead of dispersive details - and even *Agenda Synthetica*
> too instead of petty competition.
>   I am in short, too busy trying to utilise life to trouble
> about death, though I naturally do what I can to postpone it!
> > Yours ever,
> > Pat Geddes

A complement to these lines is this positive statement of belief
which Amelia Defries has transcribed in 'The Interpreter Geddes'
(1927):
> 'All the gospels are various views of life, and *all true* - as far
> as they go.   All the myths are true too.   It is pitiful non-
> sense that one has heard, ever since Darwin frightened the cur-
> ates: "Do you mean to say you believe in the Bible?" spoken in a
> fearful voice by would-be scientific folk.'   'Of course I
> believe in the Bible,' went on Geddes, with passion, 'and in the
> Koran, and in all the bibles of all people, whether savages or
> Buddhists, Celts or Christians.   To those vast storehouses of
> past wisdom, one makes one's contribution.   I make mine by see-
> ing that Life is bigger and more wonderful than has been thought;
> and that all the gospels put together cannot encompass it.   The
> ecstasy of the highest Mystics is one with the elemental life-
> emotion of the Biosphere....' (25)

At the end of April 1930, in partial answer to questions 'too vast
in scope for any letter', P.G. wrote to Amelia Defries that 'Theo-
logies, Theosophies and Philosophies have more and more to become
Biosophy: and not go on neglecting this life in quest of complete
and transcendent *Theo*-sophy, as too commonly....'
> Instead of writing J.H.V.H. or I.H.S. or other sacred names of
> other faiths, I think of G.T.B. (Good, True, Beautiful) in the
> old Platonic way and see this Unity (of Trinity) as having been
> variously so far personalised, and socialised also, throughout
> history, and so far in our very imperfect present; so why not
> yet more in the future?
>   To me the finest passage of the New Testament is the vision of
> St. Peter correcting his first refusal to go to the Roman (cf.
> Acts of the Apostles).

---

* Mabel Barker has written to author (30 December 1945) that
'though father made no pretence of keeping up with P.G.'s career,
the friendship was never broken ... when dying (at 80) one of the
last things he said was "Where's Geddes?   He can't be far behind."'

> Thus like Dante, and many more, we see Hell, Purgatory and
> Paradise all in the world around us and much the like in his
> Protestant analogue, Bunyan's Pilgrim's Progress; so why not
> more and more lovingly, faithfully, hopefully, continue our
> journey in the high resolve it requires?

As a planner in India Geddes was as much concerned with temples and
shrines as with homes and gardens.   Not only did he assume and
accept that these people, whom he wanted to be cared for at least as
well as plants, should have their faiths and sacred buildings;   but
he also experienced the cultural and spiritual forces in their
lives.   Having earlier cited his praise of the beauty and organic
development of south Indian temples, we add here his comment that
the rhythmic interplay of outer contact with nature and inner contemplation

> which has been for so many ages pulsing in the soul of India, is
> the origin and explanation of her varied temples and their
> styles;   each the stage and scene-work for some new canto of the
> unending epic of her religious evolution.   In all lands reli-
> gions have grown, and lived;   but commonly also died: here
> beyond all other lands, religion is ever rising anew, in fresh
> metempsychoses, recurrent avatars. (26)

Even in practical matters of public hygiene and health he called for
'stimulants of a deeper psychological nature' than the mere 'diffu-
sion of scientific knowledge'.   He cited the Diwali Procession at
Indore in 1918 as his best example of

> using images of ancient symbolism which expressed the difficul-
> ties and hopes of life, its besetting evils and the means of
> ultimate victory.   Thus science, which at first sight appeared
> to destroy old faiths, was seen to renew and fulfil them.   Every
> ancient discernment of the facts and possibilities of life is
> still as true as ever and it only needs a vital re-statement,
> adapted to present conditions, to regain its ancient dynamic
> power....   If this connection between material and moral purifi-
> cation could again be made manifest, health and religion might
> once more become one, as with every priesthood of the past. (27)

In sum, P.G. was at the same time a sceptical Western scientist *and*
an Indian mystic.   Witness again his comment when he and Alasdair
first visited Benares in 1914 and saw how floods of the Sacred
Ganges had destroyed riverside temples: 'Contrast of cosmic indifference and human religions can go no further!   Yet the religions
too are right;   and in the main they hold back the cosmic stream,
and make it the human one it is.'

Still another aspect of P.G.'s concern with religion is his use of
well-nigh parson terminology. (28)   We have seen, in a letter to
Branford in 1902, that he had asked how they could effect 'the Conversion of sinners' and pointed out that 'we have the Temple, but
what of the Mysteries?   What of the Initiation?'   A later example
occurs in the two pages of verse, 'All the World's a Stage', at the
end of his 1923 reprint of 'Dramatisations of History':
> Within our common garments, are all forms divine...

Divine?   Ay, surely!
Have you forgotten man was made in God's own image?
- But his face - today?   Ay, even his face: Has God not
    suffered too?

Geddes also made his own 'sociological' version of the Lord's
Prayer:
    Our ideal past which art in
    The Ideal future be kept to heart by thy presentments.
    May Thy complete realization of inward life
    And its direction of outward life and fruitions
    Come to pass.
    Thy directive impulse be obeyed in all life in every
        life and in the life-ideal.

This text was given in 1923 to Lewis Mumford who has commented fifty
years later, 'Why he thought this Comtean farrago an improvement I
can't guess!' (29)   Improvement or not, the wording is quite in
line with P.G.'s interpretation of evolution as a vast 'ethical
process'; and the concept of full inward life directing 'outward
life and fruition' is likewise the essence of his Chart of Life.
Of interest to psychologists and theologians might be the omission
of 'Our Father' as petitionee while still applying the familiar
possessive 'Thy' to the being or power whose 'directive impulse' is
to be obeyed.

Our final instance of 'agnostic belief' - or was it 'wish-belief'? -
consists of a poem which Geddes copied, around 1917 on the back of
a letterhead sheet from the Deputy Commissioner's Office, Lucknow.
The front is covered with notations and squares, mostly illegible,
but with a reference to Cobb: 'Mysticism and the Creed'.   'Salvation (At-one-ment)' can be read, also 'miraculous mediation' but not
much more.   Yet the poem is clear, even though in P.G.'s hand.
Why did he, with his writer's cramp, take the trouble to write out
four verses of 'The Mystic Catholic'? (30)   The first and last
read:

The Mystic Catholic.

Lo, in the silent night a child to God is born,
And all is brought again that are was lost or torn;
Could but thy soul, o man, became a silent night,
God would once more be born in thee, and set all things right.

Lo, in the silent night a child to God is born,
And all is bought again that ere was lost or torn;
Could but thy soul, O man, become a silent night,
God would once more be born in thee and set all things right...

Christ rose not from the dead, Christ still is in his grave,
If thou for whom he died art still of sin the slave.
Hold there!   Where runnest thou?   Know Heaven is in thee;
Seek'st thou for God elsewhere, His face thou'lt never see.

'MEMO TO SUCCESSORS' ... CAMPAIGNS UNENDING

What is the essence of what Patrick Geddes wanted so desperately to
give during the last years to his colleagues and still unreached
public?   He touched upon many subjects in the 'Sociological Review'
and he told wishfully in letters about the many 'long-dreamed
opuses' that were about to be written, or even actually under contract with publishers.   Yet the two documents from this period
which fairly well bring together the dispersive parts of his message
are the 'Memo to Successors ...' (31) of VII sections, and the two-
part article 'Ways of Transition - Towards Constructive Peace'
('Soc. Review', January and April 1930) which was mentioned in
Chapter 11.

Like much of his writing, the 'Memo' reviews many previous arguments
or interpretations in the subject at hand, in this case education.
But despite redundancy there are some good sentences and many vital
ideas, for example this opening:
 I am deeply impressed, through life, by the formalisation of the
 spirit of all good beginnings.   Function forms structure, but
 these soon inhibit further developments, through fixation of the
 freedom of the spirit.   As Emerson put this long ago - 'Every
 spirit makes its house; but afterwards the House confines the
 spirit.'   I search History for exceptions to this, and they are
 hard to find.

P.G. states that 'The best bit of my work, if any will look into it,
is the clear psychological and educational explanation of the mental

arrest to commonplace so general throughout the world.'   He has
found the cause in the unwitting fossilisation of schooling in past
and present.   It is the basic predicament of most teaching that
while the greatest minds of the past created treasures of imagination, emotion and ideation,
> the would-be educationalist ... (coldly and dully, hence stupid-
> ly) [tries] to impress these high products ... upon his pupils'
> everyday feelings.   [Consequently,] Education is turned to in-
> struction, and this tested by memory-examination, so with result
> of all these - as COPY, as CRAM, as JAW.

Section V of the 'Memo' raises the central question of 'understanding *how good beginnings, and even great developments go wrong*?'
> Recall from histories, and from biographies too (Say to St
> Peter's more than triple failure - yet recovery - even to vision
> on house-top) *how* such lapses have taken place? [consider] the
> heroic Templars, yet brought to ruin by their wealth....   So too
> for Friars, soon down to contempt, as per Chaucer, and fiercer
> satirists - ('Lift up thy tayle, O Sathanas') yet revivance too,
> in at and from Assisi.

The Benedictines likewise declined, for after having renewed and
improved the Roman tradition of agriculture,
> they waxed rich and left this to lay brothers and to serfs or
> tenants, - so hence the surrounding rulers and nobles - though
> themselves worse landlords and ruder men - said - 'Lazy monks,
> you have gone corrupt, (much as we): so we take your land and
> spoil your churches' - the so-called 'Reformation' for the most
> part; for though the people got something of the Bible, their
> master got the land: - as so readily happens after missionary
> enterprise to this day.

The answer to 'What went wrong?', says Geddes, is 'Routine - in
prosperity'.
> The danger lies, not in living dangerously ... but in the re-
> verse: in living cautiously, prudently, 'practically' - and thus
> sleeping comfortably like each wooden university and torpid col-
> lege upon past laurels.

P.G. concludes with this advice to his successors at the College:
> Let those who see further than we as yet do ... waste no time in
> mere criticism unaccompanied by suggestion and endeavour; but do
> what they can to move forward their comrades and colleagues,
> their teachers also....   If they then fail in this, after due
> patience and example, let them start a new swarm, to set better
> example....   Here let there be no rigid and inflexible monastic
> or temporal rule, but a growing consensus of sympathetic and
> reasonable order in and towards progress.

As for the 'Ways of Transition ...', one may usefully recall here
that Geddes regarded its two nine-squared thinking machines and
accompanying text (see Appendix) as a summary of his whole life's
experience in civics, sociology, planning and peace-making.   Both
in word and deed he still has basic remedies to offer whether it

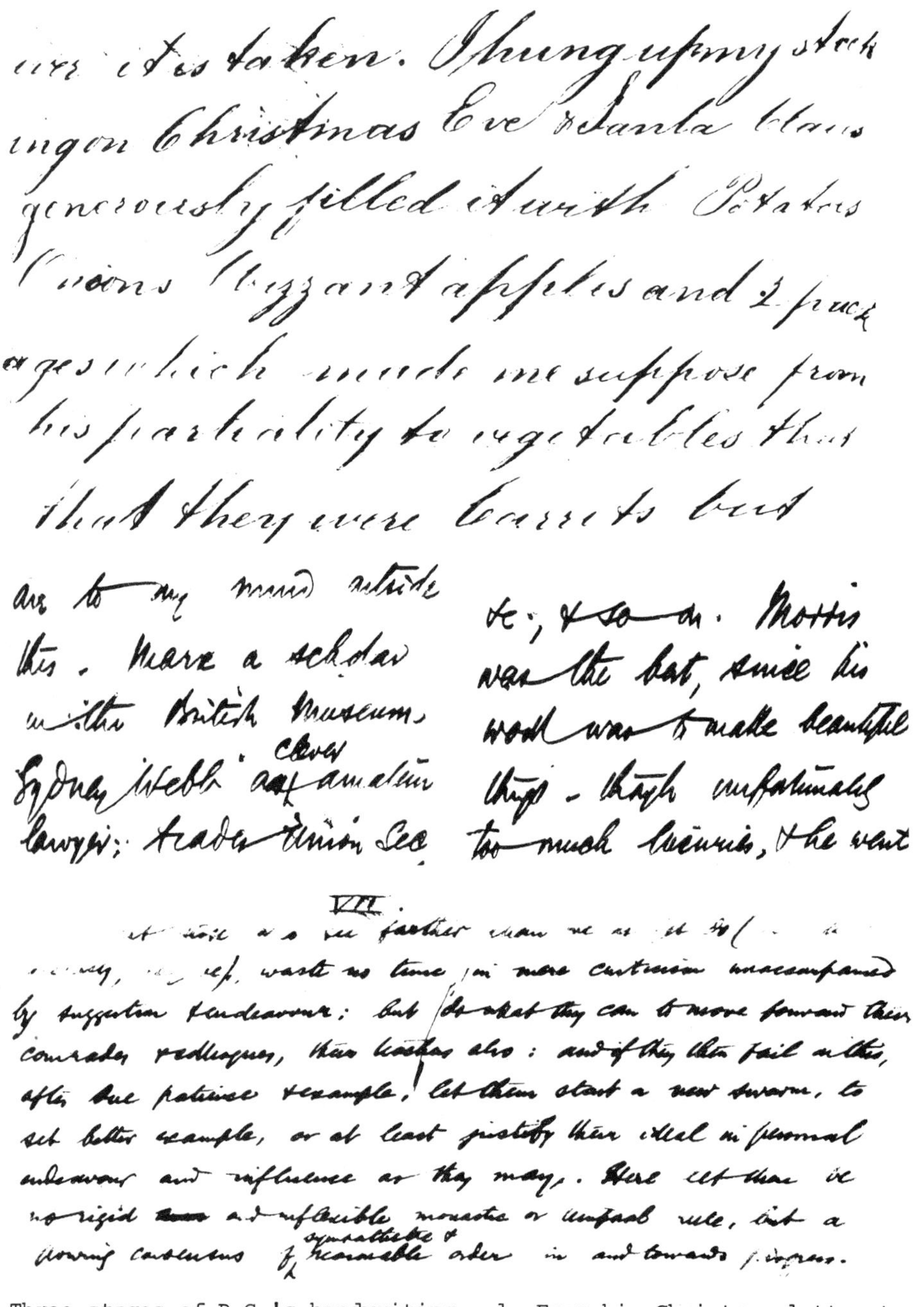

was it is taken. I hung up my stocking on Christmas Eve & Santa Claus generously filled it with Potatoes Onions [illegible] apples and 2 oranges which made me suppose from his partiality to vegetables that that they were carrots but

are to my mind outside this. Marx a scholar in the British Museum. Sydney Webb a clever amateur lawyer: trades union sec &c., & so on. Morris was the best, since his work was to make beautiful things - though unfortunately too much luxuries, & he went

VII.

[illegible] farther than we [illegible] waste no time in mere criticism unaccompanied by suggestion & endeavour: but do what they can to move forward their comrades & colleagues, their leaders also: and if they then fail in this, after due patience & example, let them start a new swarm, to set better example, or at least justify their ideal in personal endeavour and influence as they may. Here let there be no rigid and inflexible monastic or unequal rule, but a growing consensus of sympathetic & reasonable order in and towards progress.

Three stages of P.G.'s handwriting: 1. From his Christmas letter to brother Jack (18 January 1864); 2. Writing to Mr Sawat, Indore (2 May 1918), Geddes belabours socialists for being 'unrelated ... to *Real place - real work - real people*' and characterises Marx, Webb and Morris thus; 3. Item VII of his 'Memo to Successors ...', written at the Scots College in Montpellier c. 1930, is a relatively legible sample of the rapid, crowded hand of his later years.

concerns political (i.e. agricultural, economic, ethnic and religious) impasses like Cyprus, Israel and the United Arab Republic,
and Ireland; or the world-wide flouting of the laws of ecology
(interrelations of Place, Work and Folk). He also reminds us of
fundamental, unsolved problems:

> How are we to get from Wardom to Peacedom? and from the exciting
> Nationalism and Imperialisms of the first to peaceful Regional
> and Civic developments in the second?...
>
> With Business ever expanding ... what can be thought of, or
> devised, much less applied, to abate the ever-increasing world-
> domination of Finance, with its accepted faith in *Money*, as
> supreme and quint-essential Power, to and by which the essential
> prayers (i.e., of aspiration) of civilised men seem ever more
> convincedly directed?

Constructive solutions were proposed by Geddes in the scores of lectures at Summer Meetings, the Outlook Tower, and in various forums
in London where he used to interpret 'Contemporary Social Evolution'
in terms of his own Place-Work-Folk theory and practice. Before
1900, for example, he analysed the perennial conflicts in Cyprus
partly as age-old clashes between relígions and basic occupations of
Greeks, Turks, and Armenians, and more recently as the blunders of
British colonial administrators whose main qualifications were those
of 'urban mis-education'. The combination of London lawyers and
politicians without any experience of valley-section life and work,
either at home or in Mediterranean areas, and of their 'Oxbridge-
handicapped' agents in Cyprus was a guarantee that no real solution
would be found for Cypriot problems. But probably not even Geddes
suspected that the unhappy island would still be suffering from
these problems, compounded, eighty years later.

'Solve the agricultural problem and you solve the Near-East Question!' P.G. not only said and wrote this in 1897; he and Anna
proved it in farm after farm, village after village in Cyprus.
'There is no permanent reason for men to kill each other.... Give
them hope of better land, of enough food for their families, and you
remove a main cause of bloodshed.'

Although the twentieth century was ushered in amid 'the clash of
steel and the howling verses of vengeance', to use Tagore's words,
there were other and more hopeful circumstances. The International
Exposition of 1900 in Paris provided the background for the two
campaigns of Peacedom which Patrick and Anna Geddes waged between
1899 and 1901. First, the multi-lingual Summer Meetings arranged
for scientists, citizens and men of affairs from many countries, and
then the dramatic battle to save the *Rue des Nations* and create what
could have been the beginning of a UNESCO almost half a century in
advance of history. Although the latter ended as a 'Magnificent
Failure', the peace-warriors continued the fight as long as they
lived. Their last joint drive was also in Paris, at the *Exposition
de la cité reconstituée* in 1916, but from 1917 Patrick had to carry
on the struggle alone.

In town planning reports in India during and after the First World

War, and in lectures in France and Great Britain he proclaimed the
unpleasant truth that Berlin was not the only 'Prussian war-
capital'.   London and Paris, Rome, New York and Washington were
equally guilty of mistreating their own provinces and exploiting
their natural and human resources as though they were conquered
'enemy' territory.   He saw the 'bureaucratic and financial octopuses' of capitals in all supposedly civilised countries as creating
policies and conditions of latent war while always preparing, by
their very nature, for open warfare against like-minded competitors.

In the years 1919-25 Geddes made three working visits to Palestine
and afterwards maintained contact with Zionist officials in London
himself or through his son-in-law, F.C. Mears.   While disappoint-
ingly little came out of either his plans or Dr Weizmann's great
hopes, there still remains much of current interest in the reports
on Jerusalem and the proposed Hebrew University.   P.G. also fought
the old fight against blunders of the bureaucratic (including the
military) mind when trying to administer civic affairs.

Occasionally he aired his views on certain professional soldiers in
private letters, such as this remark to Lewis Mumford in 1920:
'Empire can't stand long with Dyer, Carson, Churchill & Co. working
their will while we are powerless to prevent them!'   Or again, to
Norah early in 1921:   'Good sign for India that they are sending
out decent men like Reading ... and not poisonous firebrands like
Churchill.   Gen Dyer etc have created the worst situation since the
Mutiny two generations ago.'   But when in actual contact with military men Geddes always tried to win them over by superior arguments
just as he did with other officials.

Writing to Dr Eder in mid-November 1920, P.G. describes his clash in
Jerusalem at the Governor's office with a general and staff over
their plans to build a camp on ground proposed for the University or
to appropriate the Zionist housing project of Talpioth.   The result
would be to raise land values and rentals and so inflict on the city
'what could only be accurately called *the evils of a permanent state
of siege*'.

> The soldiers were very polite of course, but pretty obstinate.
> But having only fallacious arguments, they were obliged to con-
> sent to look into the alternatives I offered ... nearer Railway.
> But I since hear 'they won't look at this', but did not tell us
> so....
>
>   Again, 'the distance from the existing shooting-range would be
> too great!'   'How much?'   'Oh, a kilometre!'   'Well,' said I,
> 'I am older than any of you - and 4 Klm. (1 Klm back and forward
> twice a day) more or less is still nothing to me!'   'Oh.' said
> they, 'in summer! some of our men would be in doctors' hands.'
>   (More Bosh.)   I pointed out advantage of Railway and Railway
> siding possible.   Said the Colonel of Engineers - 'Siding impos-
> sible;   slope too steep' - But he soon admitted it could be
> brought from Station.   Then, five minutes later, said the Gen-
> eral: 'I fear that site may not be healthy.   Possibly difficult
> for drainage - I must get medical report!'   I had just suffi-
> cient self-control not to irritate him by comparing this view of

the ground, as *too level*, with that just given, as *too steep*.
Of course neither corresponds to facts.

Geddes then takes up the political angle, asking Eder to mobilise
friends in London.   The soldiers 'have the War Office to back their
reports and Plans and are only too likely to manage this'.   On the
other hand, P.G. points out, one could make the Zionist plans known
to the press, 'so leading to questions in Parliament etc. which War
Office of course hates.'

While this little skirmish ended successfully, not so his main
battle.   When he learned about plans the Mufti had for utilising
certain buildings 'for collegiate use - in fact Moslem University
use', and about Christian colleges buying up building sites, Geddes
quickly reported this information as a challenge useful in Dr.
Weizmann's campaign for funds.

'In short then, you see the other faiths are not to be behind
Israel, and Jerusalem wil] be a threefold University City....
Better rivalry on higher planes than on lower ones - and sublimating
these perhaps accordingly.'   But P.G.'s University scheme was
finally lost, as Dr Eder hinted, by the hesitant and short-sighted
among the Zionists, and only the library and a few minor buildings
were erected.

As early as 1929, however, there was a foretaste of the disaster to
come which Geddes had perceived.   Riots broke out in Jerusalem that
he claimed could mostly have been prevented by his plan of the city
made for the Military Governor in 1919, a plan both neglected and
never paid for!   In letters to Branford of August and September
1929 P.G. expressed great indignation over this unnecessary tragedy.
    Very concerned about Jerusalem, & Palestine Government. eg.   In
    1919 I planned for Wailing Wall's entire protection with gain to
    Arabs too!   But Government & Zionists alike pigeon-holed it in
    their foolish wooden conceit that each could do all things well!
       (If they had sense, they'd alike send me out, to help to
    pacify!)
       Another folly was dropping Pro-Jerusalem Society, the best
    ever was!   For problem is not merely police-order - but Peace-
    War of Helpwill & Hope!   The peace of Jerusalem always fell
    through for want of that.

Over a year later (9 November 1930) he wrote in similar vein to Lady
Aberdeen, sending her his Jerusalem report.   'Old though the enclosed is, is it not more concrete and definite than the recent discussions show?'   It 'would have made that particular trouble henceforth impossible, and at insignificant expense!'

While P.G.'s scathing comments on the Palestine situation in 1929-30
were those of a far-seeing interpreter of men and their cities,
there was also a bit of piqued 'I told you so!'   The generalist had
so dispersed his talents that when age reduced his ability to fight
on many fronts, he could not help beco ing something of a frustrated
prophet crying in the wilderness.   In 1919, however, his 'Prelimi-

nary Report' on the University showed not a trace of pessimism: he
simply expected that every one else would understand his suggestions
and even surpass them.   For example, when he conceived the Great
Hall with its 'Dome of Unity' as the natural dominating centre of
the campus he also, with deep educational insight, placed the administrators in a minor building where they could 'be servants, not
masters'.   Yet when the Hebrew University had to be started again
at Givat-Ram in 1954 P.G.'s philosophy seems likewise to have been
left behind.   The new site has buildings which generally 'have been
kept low'.   Yet, 'the tallest structure is the seven-storey Administration Building which dominates the entrance of the campus'. (32)

Returning to P.G.'s well-documented work in Ireland in 1914 and his
wise counselling in 1916 and 1921, one can only wish that those now
involved with her fate could share all of his intelligent concern
and love for this other 'unhappy island'.   But where are the politicians, men of religion or planners who can match his talent and
faith in winning over the James Larkins, the governors and the
clergy to mutual conciliation followed by deeds of synergy?   Who
can 'abate the evil centuries' and inspire men to turn the 'City of
Destruction' into something of the Kingdom of Heaven on earth?

Where may one read today such words of faith and idealism as these
to Norah of 10 December 1921?
     Among my notes of this morning's vigil are a few on Ireland - the
     sub-conscious mobilisation of past experience & thought stirred
     by the great news of the Irish Free State in yesterday's paper.
         There for instance will be the garden as well as pasture of
     Britain against the coming *Vienn*ification of London; there too
     the next development of the common civilisation from 'Anglo-
     Saxon' in its debased imperial sense, and even from 'Anglo-
     Celtic' to *Celto-Anglian*, for the isle which civilised us of old
     has now to do it again.   She will return good for our evil more
     than ever, & by far!
         Perhaps a model of rejuvenescence surpassing Israel's, which
     so sadly lags; (through its urban vulgarisation, I suppose)....
         Rising now to the world of ideas - education, literature,
     arts, sciences - what possibilities!   Education no longer stink-
     ing of Whitehall in its primary, of public schools in secondary,
     of London & Oxford in higher!   The recovery of Trinity will only
     be a beginning the renewal of Catholic education may also be in
     Ireland.   And think of the old faith recovering the cathedrals
     for centuries polluted by State worship!

Yet the best summary of Geddes's many-sided campaign for active,
exciting peacedom is what he wrote about replacing Middle Eastern
quarrels and bloodshed with friendly and literally fruitful co-
operation.   His words and deeds of eighty years ago in Cyprus could
be usefully adapted today to apply to other storm centres of the
world.

P.G. also had experience bearing on the problems of pollution.   He
used this word in its local and regional sense, but not merely because it applied to this industrial centre or that river.   Its

remedies had likewise to be local and regional, then as now. He
was aware of the interdependence of man and nature ever since exploring Perthshire as a boy, and of the retribution that follows
one's breaking of this 'web of life' ever since he discovered Darwin
the naturalist and George P. Marsh the geographer-ecologist in the
1870s. Later, he expressed not only the interrelations of Organ-
ism-Function-Environment and Place-Work-Folk in his algebraic-juxta-
position graphs, but also the wrath to come which followed neglect
of these 'trinities'.

Geddes often repeated Marsh's early warning about drought and famine
in the Mediterranean region being caused by de-forestation practised
since the dawn of its civilisation. On his solitary 'wedding trip'
to Greece in 1886 Patrick first saw for himself what Marsh had discovered, and again in 1897 when he and Anna journeyed together to
Cyprus. Lewis Mumford has stated that it was Geddes who first
brought Marsh to his attention, adding that 'it was in all probabil-
ity the little memoir I had written on Marsh in "The Brown Decades"
that helped draw the attention of American geographers back to the
pioneer they had neglected'. (33)

Likewise of current importance is P.G.'s lecture of 1886 on '... the
Capitalist and the Labourer' in which, after treating at length
'such criticism of modern life and industry as we owe to Carlyle,
Ruskin and Morris', he urged his public to invest capital in 'progressive ways, evolutionary ways'.
> Not in more smoke and nuisance, more percussion and corrosion,
> nor in more factories, and more back streets full of workers in
> them ... but in nobler dwellings, in giving the higher industries
> their long-delayed turn.

Two years earlier, before the Royal Society, the young botanic economist had, as told in Chapter 3, applied a law of biology to the
processes of industry and production, which was both a warning
against today's pollution and the only adequate remedy for it in
all its forms. Speaking of the 'modification of the organism by
its material environment', he insisted that all factors in such
modification 'be observed and appreciated' and that their own modifiability 'be discussed and acted upon'. Consequently,
> when any given environment or function, however apparently pro-
> ductive, is really fraught with disastrous influence to the or-
> ganism, its modification must be attempted or, failing that, its
> abandonment faced.

The above two themes were reiterated with varying applications at
Summer Meetings and University Extension courses; in the Dunfermline Report, in 'Cities in Evolution' and Indian town planning
studies, and in correspondence. Writing to Norah, for instance,
en route to Dublin, in the summer of 1921, P.G. analyses and describes the dual pollution of chemicals and of 'octopus' government
by over-grown capitals.
> Patriotism of Highlanders in all lands ... has, as its (largely
> unconscious) but vital economic base, the struggle for bare ex-
> istence on the very margin of fertility - ruined by exactions of

metropolis for its (*food*) *taxes* in return for sham government, &
further exactions whenever possible for its rents, paid to absentees, there.

The ruin of our Highlands is thus as definitely by London,
helped by Edinburgh 'law & administration', as the blight of
trees at Newcastle by the chemical fumes - & this is but the
extreme case of process at work everywhere - eg. our frontier
wars in India.   (The satanic ingenuity with which said Highlanders are then described as robbers, is also admirable - more
even than any parasitic devilry in nature.) (34)

Indeed, so penetrating was his analysis of human happenings that he
not only talked biologically like 'an eye-witness to Evolution', as
Thomson said; he could also describe the 'Making of the Future'
like a modern Merlin let loose in sociology.   As he once wrote to
Norah,

My grip of things - which, frankly, exceeds that of the politicians - has largely come from reading of current events, & in
light of thought & of *constructive action*.

When others found it difficult to follow the methods of explanations
so clear to him, he might say, 'Remember it is not my fault that
history has been so complex, and that social life still is so!' (35)

George Sarton's 'History of Science' (36) gives an excellent illustration of how universal and unending are the tasks which Geddes set
out to accomplish.   Naming the Greek architect Hippodamos of the
fifth century BC as the first planner on record to suggest combining
urban and rural ways of life,   Sarton relates that Aristotle considered Hippodamos as simply a Pythagorian dreamer.

Yet some of his dreams were more practical than Aristotle realized, [Sarton insists.   Hippodamos] was a dreamer indeed, but a
good dreamer, the distant ancestor of such men as Patrick Geddes
of our own time, who tried to harmonize the physical requirements
of town planning with the moral and social aspects.

REBIRTH AND HEAVEN - FOR OTHERS ... 'THE CHILD WONDERFUL' ...
'SING US PEACE!'

The worlds of Patrick Geddes will not be complete without a reminder
of his inspiring influence on others at his best and of the intensity of his poetic feelings when he let himself go.   One need only
recall J. Arthur Thomson's enthusiastic, even worshipful letter in
his early student days, saying to Geddes: 'More than a brother are
you to me'.   He confided to his teacher the story of three re-
births: first in faith, and later 'By your help, I was slowly led,
not without pain, to a wider synthesis and a surer knowledge.   I
was born again of hope....   For this I thank you.'   The third
occasion was on meeting his future wife: 'I have been born again
of love.'

A young student of history at Edinburgh, Victor Branford, also came
under P.G.'s spell and soon began a career as combined disciple and

promulgator.   His words of thanks to the master in 1902 for being
'allowed the privilege of the glimpse into the working of your mind'
have already been quoted.   Likewise his earliest tribute to Geddes
on reading 'A Synthetic Outline of the History of Biology' in 1885,
which 'struck me as being one of the most interesting documents in
the history of science'.   It was the 'birth of a new master science' as sharply defined in outline as 'the birth of modern mechanics with Newton'.

Since Branford died before Geddes, we cannot know what the sociological colleague would have written in eulogy.   It was Thomson more
than any other friend who always emphasised the 'essential Geddes'
and raised him above all his foibles, and who also brought out the
best aspects of family relations.   He wrote, for example, these
words to the younger son after his father's death:
> I am glad that you were over at Montpellier for a little and that
> he gave you and your fiancée his blessing.   Please accept feli-
> citations - both of you - from an old couple who have been very
> happy for many years now.

A propos P.G. at his best, one immediately thinks of his closeness
and faithfulness to Anna, and of this incident.   When his own tiny
bedroom in the Mediterranean tower was cleared out after his death,
they found, carefully hung away in his closet, one of Anna's dresses
which he had kept for over twenty years!   There also comes to mind
a letter to their friend Jo MacLeod (in India) written from Montpellier in May 1924 when P.G. was starting to regain his health and
spirit.   He has just heard from her and is
> Very glad you are so well, busy, and at peace.   A great thing to
> find one's heaven!   I shall never be so fortunate.
> Quite true, you did give Anna a share of your Paradise, & I
> doubt not it helped her in her long last illness!   Yet you are
> quite right too in saying that it is not the heaven for me -
> though I have visited it, & not unappreciatively, once & again.

Patrick and Anna wrote many fine letters to each other from their
engagement in 1886 up to the last ones received during her illness
in 1917, but none is as long or as much worked over as the joint
Christmas Letter of 1898 to 'Dear Children over sea', referred to in
Chapter 6.   A few lines here will remind us of the Geddes family of
five at one of its happiest periods.   They have watched the lighted
tree symbolise the universe and, when the candles burned out, seen
the stable underneath with the 'kindly human glow' of its lantern,
the 'Mother and Child, Joseph tending the weary ass, the kingly
shepherds ...'   After the 'glories of the world-tree', they are
glad
> to shelter under the homely roof and see here the birth of human,
> as there the cosmic religion of nature.   Around us the infinite
> and omnipresent, the unchangeable yet protean energy of the Uni-
> verse;   within, the Divine humanity, the hope of the human world.

Geddes speaks of the unique individuality of every child born, and
the 'vast range of human possibility'.   What is greatest, he asks,
energy, intellect or emotion?   His answer is put in these words of

high faith and purpose which, had he himself been able to heed them,
might have reconciled him to the loss of Anna and their Alasdair:

> We must unite action and knowledge and sympathy, are we to reach
> wisdom.   We must widen wisdom till she live not for herself
> alone but for others;   then and then only our world evolution is
> complete: the Child Wonderful is born - to live and to die for
> men.

For a farewell glimpse of Patrick Geddes, one turns to his Mediterranean Scots College as he sought relaxation in the open air before
going to bed.   Occasionally a student accompanied him, for in his
gardens of an evening he could be the most friendly and fatherly of
comrades.   But more often he walked by himself, since 'old age and
thought must ever be alone', as he said of the solitary Carlyle.

Whether strolling along the intricate paths of evolution and philosophy by bright moonlight or wandering over the heath on moonless
nights when this second Outlook Tower would stand in dark outline
against a heaven of brilliant stars, old P.G.'s erect, corduroy-clad
figure was one to command respect and affection.   The explosive
critic, the overwhelming thinker, and the maker of diagrams had all
given place to a man at peace with his fellow humans and with
nature.

Pheroze Bharucha has described how this western man of science was
received by many Indians as a Guru.

> He inspired you; he brought the best out of you; he re-kindled
> the creative spark in you.   It is as a Teacher that he will live
> in our hearts and memories....
>
> Assuredly there have been very few like him - they hardly come
> once in a century.   He just set you on fire with love of this
> earth and with desire to cleanse it, to beautify and re-beautify
> it, to build and re-build it....
>
> What was the secret of Geddes's amazing activity?   What was
> *his* inspiration?   It was, we believe, an unbounded love for the
> human kind with all its faults.   No poet, prophet or theologian
> has regarded man as verily created in the image of God with a
> clearer perception, with more absolute certainty of conviction
> than Patrick Geddes. (37)

After such eloquent testimony from the East, the only words that
will not be anti-climactic are these lines from a review in verse of
'The Georgian Poets' around 1918.   While appreciating their poems
devoted to war-time sacrifices and idealism, Patrick Geddes - as
biologist, re-educator, planner and Peace-Warrior - took them to
task for not confronting the realities of coming Reconstruction:

> ... sing us Peace!   Not her of dove and olive;
> But after-war Peace, full of strange perplexities,
> And social stress, dilemmas inescapable ...
>
> Not Dante driven from Florence had such themes
> As call today you singers.   Dark and stern
> Again must be your showings of Hell's gape,
> And Purgatory's fire before us all:
> Yet point us ways towards Heaven's high-gated Hall!

THE THINKING MACHINES OF PATRICK GEDDES

The diagrams presented here are to supplement and tie up those used
in and after 'Self-Review in Mexico' (ch. 2, pp. 47-9).   The oldest
is the Classification of the Sciences, the origins of which go back
to Patrick's near-blindness in 1879-80.   He certainly made hundreds
of Classifications on folded sheets of paper, explaining them to
watcher-listeners over the years, yet none was published until 1931
- as an end-paper in 'LIFE: Outlines of General Biology'.   It is
reproduced as Figure A.1.

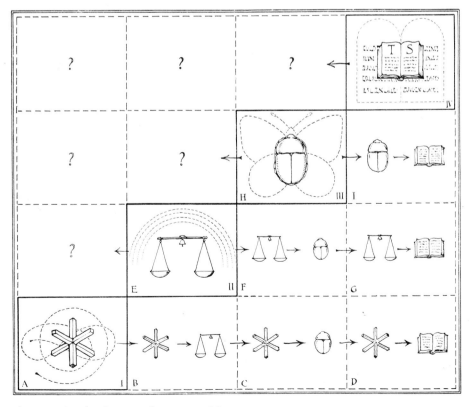

Figure A1   'Sciences in General'

Geddes's own 'Explanation of "Sciences in General" End-Paper' follows, but with the word-diagram of Figure A.2 as an additional aid.
  Lowest on the left, the field of pure Mathematics, is marked by
  axes in three dimensions.
    The space or step above this, towards the right, indicates
  the field of the Physical Sciences, symbolised by the Balance.
    In the next space (above to right) the field of Biology, in-
  dicated by the Scarabaeus.
    And in the last space (above to right) the field of Sociology
  - indicated by the Book; and marked 'T' and 'S' for its 'Temporal and Spiritual' elements, more or less conspicuous in each
  and every form of Social Life, and in its Heritage (and Burden).
    Descending in reverse order, note, behind the Book, for Socio-
  logy, Moses' Tables of Commandments, as old symbol for Ethics.
  Beyond the Scarab of Biology spreads the Butterfly (Psyche) of
  Psychology. Above the Balance for Physical Science, the Rain-
  bow (Iris) of Esthetics: and around the Mathematical Axes the
  swirl of Logic, as most universal of all sciences. This des-
  cending series of subjective sciences is in Plato's order; of
  'Good, True, and Beautiful'; and is thus complemental to the
  previous ascending series - that from Aristotle to Bacon, Comte
  to Spencer, and modern scientific workers generally.
    Again in ascending order, note that each main science, shown
  on its step, is preliminary to the succeeding one - and also ex-
  tends on its own level below it. Thus Mathematics primarily
  subserves the Physical Sciences; yet also Biology, as Biomet-
  rics; and Social Science, as Statistics. The Physical Sciences
  similarly underlie Biology (as Bio-Mechanics, Bio-Physics, and
  Bio-Chemistry); and even the Social Sciences also, since all in
  physical environments. Biology underlies Social Science; since
  the Social life of Region and State, City and Citizen, are all
  biologically conditioned (as by Physiology and Hygiene, with
  Heredity, Eugenics, etc.).
    Yet each succeeding science retains its own distinctiveness -
  as fresh 'Emergence'. Hence with the clear foundation of Sociology, on 'the preliminary sciences', their respective underlying
  contributions were defined as so many 'legitimate Materialisms'.
  Only when the needed preliminary contribution - to each main
  field or fields above - is mistakenly assumed sufficient to
  supersede it or them (as too often by their most active cultivators, and thus their readers) do 'illegitimate Materialisms'
  arise. Bio-Physicists and Bio-Chemists for Biology, and Hygien-
  ists and Eugenists for Sociology, are alike often liable to such
  errors.
    The interrogation-marks in the six spaces otherwise vacant (to
  the left of the diagonally ascending stair of the main sciences)
  indicate the fields for inquiry into the suggestive contributions
  of each higher science to its so far 'preliminary sciences'.
  Hence then for the evocations from Social Life and Science to
  Biology and Psychology. Biology has similarly aided Physical
  Science; and Psychology Esthetics; and similarly Physical
  problems evoke Mathematical methods, and even advance Logic.
    Such inquiries ... have been termed 'legitimate transcenden-
  talisms' - and are to be distinguished from 'illegitimate' ones;

- as of some philosophers, with inadequate knowledge of the sciences, and sometimes by their specialists as well.   Thus each and every one of the sixteen fields of this Graphic needs and rewards full investigation, alike for its own sake, and for its services to others.   The Unity of Science has thus to be realised.

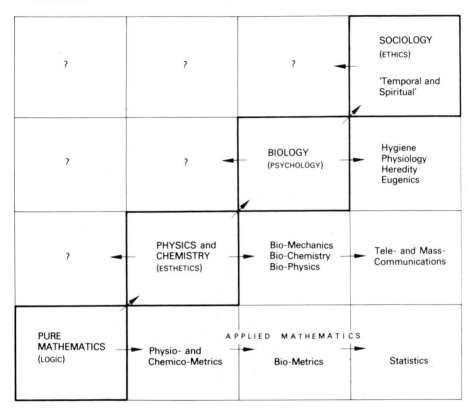

Figure A2 Classification of the Sciences

Figure A.3 the 'Notation or Chart of Life', is P.G.'s basic and most complex thinking machine.   It too developed over many years but appeared in print in 1927, four years earlier than 'Sciences in General', in 'The Interpreter Geddes'.   That book and the 1949 edition of 'Cities in Evolution' also published his description of the 'Notation', based partly on his 'The Mapping of Life' ('Sociological Review', July 1924;   Cf. ch. 10, pp. 356ff.) and partly on an account he wrote for Amelia Defries.   In 'Life' (1931) Geddes devoted 40 pages to this diagram and to a summary of his life-long argumentation for the graphic representation of thought.   We have, however, made a composite condensation of the explanations in the first two books as more suitable here than the 1931 account.   To start off, here is his statement of the logic involved, quoted from A Proposed Co-ordination of the Social Sciences ('Sociological Review', January 1924):

In general terms, ANY TWO FACTORS IN SOCIAL LIFE HAVE TWO SUB-RELATIONS.

GRAPHICALLY this may be expressed:-

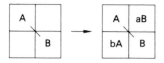

SIMILARLY, in general terms, ANY THREE FACTORS IN SOCIAL LIFE
HAVE SIX SUB-RELATIONS.
THUS, graphically on the foregoing model:-

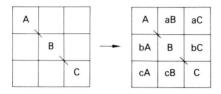

Figure A3(i)

The next step is obviously to substitute triads of social factors
for A B C, which leads to the 3 x 3 = 9 squares as above and then
to 9 x 4 sets of such triads = 'The 36-Chart'.   But the reader is
urged not to puzzle over the final diagram of 36 squares until he
has followed its gradual building up in these pages.   He would also
do well to heed P.G.'s suggestion of folding his own thinking
machine out of a double sheet of note paper and of marking it as he
goes along.   We now turn to Geddes who explains that this sheet is
'our ledger of life'.
    The left side is for the more passive aspects, or man shaped by
    place and his work, while the right side is for action;   man
    guiding his daily life and remaking place.   Now fold this ledger
    in half horizontally;   we thus get four quarters, one for each
    of the main chambers of human life;   the out-world both active
    and passive, and the in-world both passive and active.   In each
    of these quarters belongs a nine-squared thinking machine, but
    before introducing them let us make clear the general structure
    and relationships of the chart.   Here it is:

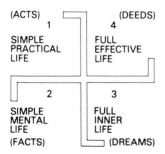

Figure A3(ii)
    The movement from one quarter to another corresponds to facts
easily verifiable, for everyone in some degree goes through
these four steps of life.   How full and rich each step might be

and ought to be will become apparent as we fill in the subdivisions of the main squares.   But one further general observation. Where does the fourth quarter lead?   To the first again, or a fifth if you prefer.   That is, the world as remade by effective men of action becomes in turn the environment that shapes other men, stimulates their mental life, which in turn leads them on to change the world still further.   Thus we may diagram* the

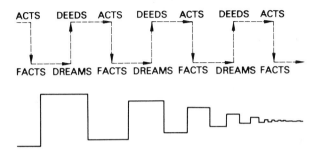

Figure A3(iii)
whole process of history, the succession of human generations by means of lines symbolising this unending interplay of the four parts of life.   Thus also is it vividly shown how history both ever and never repeats itself.

Taking the triad PLACE WORK FOLK, both alone and with its six correlations, P.G. fills in the upper left corner which depicts
1. SIMPLE PRACTICAL LIFE

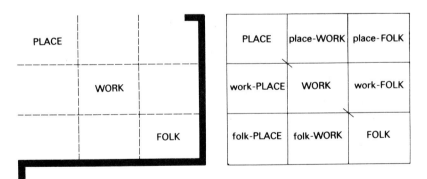

Figure A3(iv)
   Here the study of Place grows into Geography;   that of Work into Economics;   that of Folk into Anthropology.   But these are commonly studied apart, or in separate squares, touching only at a point.   Witness the separate Chairs and Institutes and Learned Societies of each name.   But here we have to bring them into a living unison.   Place studied without Work or Folk is a matter

* These diagrams elongated into space are P.G.'s answer to those who claim that the time-factor is not included in his thinking machines.

of atlases and maps.   Folk without Place and Work are dead -
hence anthropological collections and books contain too much of
mere skulls and weapons.   So too for economics, the study of
Work, when apart from definite Place and definite Folk, comes
down to mere abstractions.

But what do these side squares mean?   Below our maps of Place
we can now add pictures of the human Work-places, i.e., of field
or factory: next of Folk-places of all kinds, from farm-house or
cottage in the country to homes or slums in the modern manufacturing town.   Our geography is now fuller and our town planning
of better Work-places, better Folk-places, can begin.

So again for Folk.   Place-folk are natives or neighbours;
and Work-folk are too familiar at all levels to need explanation.

Our anthropology thus becomes living and humanised and surveys
the living town.

Work too becomes clearer.   For Place-work is a name for the
'natural advantages' which determine work of each kind at the
right place for it;   and Folk-work is our occupation, often tending to accumulate into a caste, not only in India.

Our geography, economics and anthropology are thus not simply
enlarged and vivified;   they are now united into a compact outline of Sociology.

From these three separate notes of life we thus get a central
unified Chord of Life, with its minor chords as well.

At this point the demonstrator turns to the lower left quarter saying that it is not enough even to unify geography, economics and
anthropology.   'Social life has its mental side, so we must here
call in the psychologist.'

2. SIMPLE MENTAL LIFE

Sense, Experience, Feeling.   Can we not relate these to Place,
Work and Folk?   Plainly enough.   It is with our Senses that we
come to know our environment, perceiving it and observing it.
Our feelings are obviously developed from our folk in earliest
infancy by our mother's love and care.   And our Experiences are
primarily from our activities, of which our work is the predominant one.

Thus to the Chord of Elemental and Objective Life in village
and town, there now also exactly corresponds the Elemental Chord
of Subjective Life, and with this chord we must evidently play
the same game of making nine squares as before.

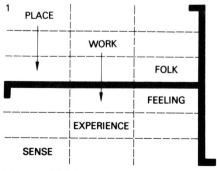

Figure A3(v)

Here we borrow P.G.'s parallel presentation of these triads and their inter-connections from 'Life' (vol. II: 1408) and thereafter quote him on 'things' and 'thoughts' (1418).

To understand things in the world without or thoughts in the world within, we must thus take them together. Yet no longer merely in the too abstract terms of 'Subject' and 'Object', but as Subject-object and Object-subject in perpetual interaction, as Psycho-biosis and Bio-psychosis, Mind-body and Body-mind; and these as expressed and observed in actual life, and interpreted from it. And all this as concretely and clearly as may be, throughout each and all Life's levels, lower to higher, past to present, and with due evolutionary forelook towards further possibilities.

The above words will also serve to introduce the third quarter, lower right.

3. FULL INNER LIFE

How can we go further? Can we penetrate into the world of imagination in which the simple natural sense impressions and activities, which all observers can agree on, are transmuted in each separate mind into its own imagining?

How indeed has it come, as it so often has done, through individual (and even social) history, to seek for the transcendant and divine, to reach all manner of mystic ecstasy? Without asking why, or even here considering exactly how, we must agree that all these three transmutations are desirable. From the present viewpoint, let us call them the three conversions, or, in more recent phrase, three sublimations: Emotion, Ideation, Imagination - the essential Chord of the Inner Life.

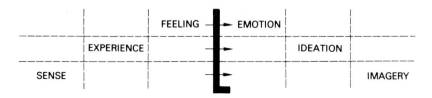

2   3

Figure A3(vi)

Ideation of Emotion - thought applied to the mystic ecstasy, to the deepest and the most fully human emotions - from that process comes the Doctrine of each Faith, its Theology, its Idealism. But Ideation calls for Imagery, and this in every science, from geometry onwards. Mathematics, Physics, Chemistry have long had these notations and the historian condenses his annals into graphic 'rivers of time'. Thought of all kinds was first written in pictorial hieroglyphics, and it is from these that have come even the printed letters of this modern page.

Completed, the nine squares of FULL INNER LIFE look like Figure A3(vii) with common words for the resulting correlations given in parentheses:

EMOTION (Religion) (Mysticism)	emotioned Ideation (Philosophy) (Pro-Synthesis	emotioned Imagery (Poesy)
ideated Emotion (Doctrine)	IDEATION (Science) (Pro-Synthesis)	ideated Imagery (Design)
imaged Emotion (Symbol)	imaged Ideation (Graphic Notations) (Mathematics)	IMAGERY (Imagination)

Figure A3(vii)

So far then this cloister of thought with its ninefold quad-
rangles: and here for many, indeed most who enter it, the possibilities of human life seem to end.   Yet from this varied
cloister there are further doors; and these open out once more
into the objective world; though not back into the too simple
everyday town-life we have long left.   For though we have out-
lived these everyday Acts and Facts, and shaped our lives according to our highest Dreams, there comes at times the impulse to
realise them in the world anew, as Deeds.

With these words Geddes arrives at the upper right quarter of his
Chart of Life, in which thoughts and dreams are expressed in deeds.
4. FULL EFFECTIVE LIFE
Not every thought takes a form in action; but the psychologist
is ever more assured that it at least points thither.   With increasing clearness and interests, with increasing syntheses with
other thoughts, ideas become emotionalised towards action.   Synthesis in thought thus tends to collective action - to Synergy in
deed: and Imagination concentrates itself to pre-figure, for
this Etho-Polity in Synergy, the corresponding Achievement which
it may realise.

Here then is a new Chord of Life - that in which the subjective creates its objective counterpart.   We thus leave the
cloister.   We are now out to re-shape the world anew, more near
the heart's desire.   Here then is the supreme Chord of Life and
its resultant in Deed - that is in fullest Life.

This is no small conclusion; that from the simplest chord of
the Acts of everyday life, from the Facts of its ordinary experience, there may develop not only the deep chord of the inward
life and Thought, but that also of life in Deed....

achieved Polity and Life	achieved Synergy	ACHIEVE-MENT
synergised Polity and Life	SYNERGY	synergised Achievement
ETHO-POLITY	politised Synergy	etho-politised Achievement

4

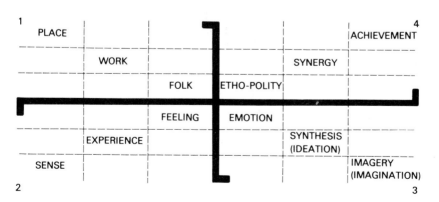

Figure A3(viii)

It is now time to put the four quarters of the 'Notation' together, first showing only the triads (Figure A3(ix)) and then the correlations (Figure A3(x)) with some of their synonyms in parentheses. Finally, after quoting part of P.G.'s summary in 'Life', we will venture a reproduction of the 36-squared diagram complete with his superimpositions of chords, arrows and brackets.

Figure A3(ix) The Four Triads

1					4
PLACE	place-Work (Natural Conditions)	place-Folk	achieved Polity and Life	achieved Synergy	ACHIEVE-MENT
work-Place	WORK	work-Folk	Synergised Polity and Life	SYNERGY	synergised Achieve-ment
folk-Place	folk-Work (Occupation)	FOLK	ETHO-POLITY	politised Synergy	etho-politised Achieve-ment
feeling Sense (Home)	feeling Experience (Mastery)	FEELING	EMOTION (Religion) (Mysticism)	emotioned Ideation (Philosophy) (Pro-Synthesis)	emotioned Imagery (Poesy)
experienced Sense	EXPERIENCE	experienced feeling (Folk-ways)	ideated Emotion (Doctrine)	IDEATION (Science) (Pro-Synthesis)	ideated Imagery (Design)
SENSE	sensed Experience	sensed Feeling	imaged Emotion (Symbol)	imaged ideation (Graphic notations) (Mathe-matics)	IMAGERY (Imagin-ation)
2					3

Figure A3(x)   The triads and their correlations

In his 'Summary and Applications' ('Life': 1439-40) Geddes recalls his coordination of geography, economics and anthropology as 'unified into social science and in full harmony with evolutionary biology'. He emphasises that this correlation does not 'end with these three concrete sub-sciences of sociology', for 'First the elements of psychology have been integrated with these, and they with it...'.

Next from this elementary psychology, we have passed to its deeper and wider fields; and these have been more clearly outlined accordingly. For in this cloister of the inward life, folk-feelings are seen and felt as transmuted to social emotions and ideals. Empiric work-experiences are clarified into ideas, and these organised into the rational sciences. These are advanced towards synthesis; and next our external sense- and place-impressions yield materials for creation of individual and collective imagery. In this complex world of inward life, these three main elements, too often separate, there as idealistic, here as scientific, or in others as imaginative - are seen as normally uniting into a single chord of inner life, and this harmonious to that simplest material life-activity with which we started.

Nor does this synthetic presentment end in the cloistered

world of thought.   On the contrary, it becomes plain how we may
and do return from it, to the objective world;   yet no longer
simply acceptant of the place, work, and folk with which we set
out;   but now modifying, or even reshaping, these, as far as may
be;   and that in terms of our inwardly emotional discernment and
vision.

Our ideals thus attain outward form and expression;   they re-
group and re-associate all who share our ideal, whatever that be,
into some fresh form of social organisation, great or small.   So
our initial work-experience, now ideated and theorised as science, impels to application, even upon some fresh line;   yet this
no longer so externally conditioned, as mere act, but inwardly
clarified towards realisation, and thus in collective or individual energy of deed.   Our sense-acquired, yet thence transmuted,
mental imagery thus finds outward embodiment, be this in victory,
in art, or other achievement.   But only in the measure and harmony between these three inward elements and impulses can be
their effective realisation.   This fresh chord of life thus
attains its intensest and highest expression - and hence passes
beyond individual effort;   it rises to Etho-polity, with its Synergy, and its Achievement.

As a further clue to the cumulative complexity of P.G.'s graph it
may be added that, in developing the fourth quarter of FULL EFFEC-
TIVE LIFE, he claimed 'the Greeks of old knew all this before, and
had thought it out to the same conclusions ...'   His diagram had
turned out to be 'that of Parnassus, the home of the nine Muses';
whereupon their names in brackets were duly added to section four!
And having warned of this latest surcharge of symbols, we present on
the following pages the complete Geddesian 'Notation of Life'.

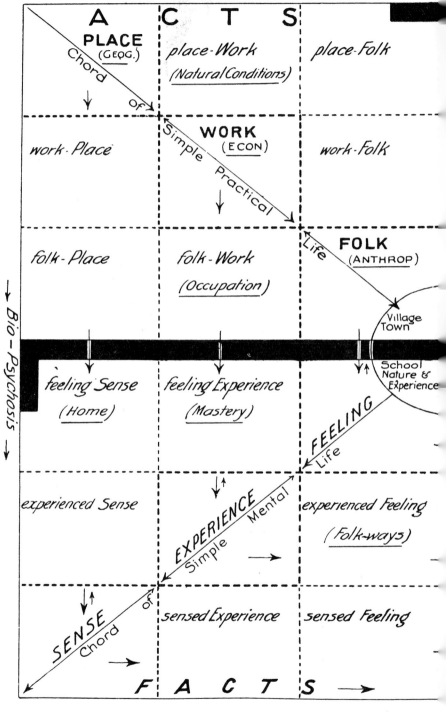

Figure A3 The Notation, or Chart of Life, of Patrick Geddes
(This version of 'The 36' was first published in Amelia Defries's

D E E D S

achieved Polity & Life
(Death, Tragedy)

[MELPOMENE]

achieved Synergy
(Rhythm)

[TERPSICHORE]

ACHIEVEMENT

Effective / Life
(Nature & Architecture)

↑[URANIA]

synergised Polity & Life
(Career)

[CALLIOPE]

SYNERGY

Expression in (History)

↑[CLIO]

synergised Achievement
(Success)
(Comedy)

[THALIA]

ETHO-POLITY

Chord of

Love

City in deed

[ERATO]

politised Synergy
(Wisdom)

[POLYMNIA]↑

etho-pol.ᵈ Achievement
(Sacred Art)

[EUTERPE]↑

Psycho – Biosis ↑

Hermitage
Cloister
University
Studio

EMOTION Chord

(Religion)
(Mysticism)

emotioned Ideation
(Philosophy)
(Pro-Synthesis)

emotioned Imagery
(Poesy)

ideated Emotion
(Doctrine)

of

IDEATION full
(Science)
(Pro-Synthesis) Inner

ideated Imagery
(Design)

imaged Emotion
(Symbol)

imaged Ideation
(Graphic Notations)
(Mathematics)

Life

(Imagination)

IMAGERY

→ **THOUGHTS** ("DREAMS")

'The Interpreter Geddes' (1927) and later used as an end-paper in
Philip Mairet's 'Pioneer of Sociology' (1957).)

The 36-squared 'Chart of Life' is indeed the complicated climax of
all published Geddesian thinking machines.   There exists, however,
a rough notation of the negative aspects of Place/Work/Folk: Sense/
Experience/Feeling which was apparently intended for expansion into
18   times 36 compartments, or a total of 648!   Labelled 'City of
Destruction' and dated 17.2.07, it documents both his fascination by
'Pilgrim's Progress' and what J. Arthur Thomson described as his
having 'more new ideas to the quarter of an hour than any three men
together'.   P.G. has written down only the key words for the four
quarters of a potential eighteen Celtic-Cross diagrams, but the note
'(Miss Home)' under the date would indicate that he dictated a
fuller prose version to his secretary.   (Another draft chart called
'HELL', with twelve crosses partly worked out, also bears the same
date and note.)   Here are four examples of the many sets of labels
he used to illustrate the destructive sides of country and city
life:

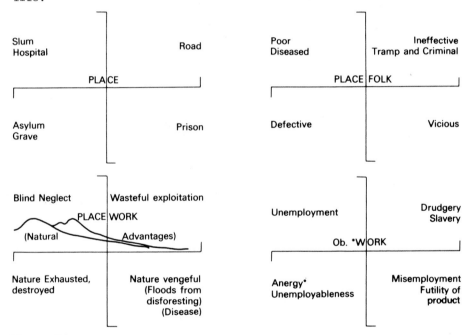

Figure A4
* 'Ob. Work' = negative corollary of work.   'Anergy' = P.G.'s neo-
logism for 'no-energy'?

A much later thinking machine which follows up these themes on an
even broader basis, and of which the detailed argument is available
in published form, appeared in articles in the 'Sociological Review'
by Geddes in 1929-30.   (The main one, 'Ways of Transition - Towards
Constructive Peace', is briefly treated in ch. 11, pp. 408-9.)
The transition from Wardom to Peacedom is a steadily recurring concern in both his prose and diagrams, and after 1923 he consistently
abbreviated this vast complex of problems as 'IX to 9' or just 'IX-
9' (see Figures A6(i) and (ii).   'IX' is the heading of the nine-
squared diagram which reflects the present, basically, evil, Wardom

state of society, while '9' depicts a possible future state of goodness and Peacedom in nine squares corresponding symmetrically to
those of 'IX'.   Yet though each diagram is built on a triad of
factors with six interacting compounds, P.G. did not include the
resulting compound terms as in the 'Chart of Life' - despite the
fact that No. 4 ('Full Effective Life') of that chart is nearly
identical with '9'.   Nevertheless, and in the interests of clarity,
we venture to list here first, the basic triads with Geddesian explanations and second, an algebraic set-up of their letter symbols:

		Element or Stage	Characteristic	Triad Symbol
A	Based on the Comte-Geddes analysis of history = Wardom	1 MILITARISM	(Despotic & Destructive)	M
		2 STATISM	(Individualistic & Nationalistic)	S
		3 INDUSTRIALISM	(Mechanotechnic & Profit-centred)	I
B	Based on Geddes's analysis of Peacedom	1 ETHO-POLITY	(Communal & National Good Feelings/Ideals)	E
		2 CO-OPERATION	(Communal & National Synergy)	C
		3 BIOTECHNICS	(Industries Serving Life)	B

Figure A5

To prepare further for viewing the charts in their authentic* but
somewhat cluttered form, we also quote Geddes on their significance
to him (letter to Lewis Mumford, 20 October 1929):

I hope [soon to work on] that diagram of IX-9 ... which has grown
to many more sheets than I have time to look at, and yet which
are worth deciphering.   Tell me what you make of its outlines in
recent paper in Sociol. Review and think that dual diagram over!
For either I am quite mad, or have got main Keys towards opening
the 9 (or 18!) doors from the present Industrial-Political-Mili-
tant age and towards the *Revivance*.   What say you?   *Critically!*

* Figures A6(i) and A6(ii) are facsimiles of P.G.'s 'IX to 9' diagram, 'Sociological Review', January 1930, pp. 2, 3.

WAYS OF TRANSITION—TOWARDS CONSTRUCTIVE PEACE

(a). *"Three States" (as IX.)* **IX.**

ARMAMENTS | **WAR** *FEAR* | *HATE*	**POLITICS** **(MECHANISTIC)** *POLITICS (OP--PORTUNIST)*	**INDUSTRY** **(MECHANOTECHNIC)** *SCIENCE (MECHANISTIC)*
NATIONS, EMPIRES *NATIONALISM* *" Dieu et mon Droit!"* *"Gott mit Uns!"* *"America! America!"* *etc.*	**STATE** **&** **INDIVIDUAL** *STATISM & INDIVIDUALISM* *LAW (Rights) &c.*	**BUSINESS** *POLITICAL ECONOMY* *Individualist* | *Bolshevik* *Fascist* | *Socialist*
MILITANCY *(Rapine)* *THEOLOGICAL INTER-PRETATION*	**BUREAUCRACY** *(Taxation)* *PUBLIC INSTRUCTION*	**FINANCE** *(Profits)* *MONEY ACCOUNTANCY* *$, £, fr., mk.*

Figure A6(i)

WAYS OF TRANSITION——TOWARDS CONSTRUCTIVE PEACE

9.

(b). Three further States (as 9).

{ Forestry, Agriculture, Horticulture, &c. Medicine & Public Health, &c. } **BIOTECHNICS** *SCIENCE (BIO- LOGICAL & PSYCHOLOGICAL)*	**TRANSITION (SOCIAL)** *INTERPRETATION (SOCIAL)*	**PEACE-WAR & EQUIP- MENT** *HELPWILL & HOPE*
SOCIAL SERVICE *SOCIAL ECONOMY { Place, Work, Folk. } { Folk, Work, Place. }*	**SYNERGY IN GEOTECHNICS** *COSMOGENY (Evolution) in (Place, Work, Folk)*	**REGION & CITY** *REGIONALISM & CIVICS in (Folk, Work, Place)*
DIRECTION (SOCIAL) *LIFE- ACCOUNTANCY (Days, Years, Lives)*	**SOCIANS (SOCIALLY EFFICIENT** *RE-EDUCATION (Occupational, Synthetic, &c.)*	*(Folk, Work, Place) in* **ETHO-POLITY** *EU-PSYCHICS in (Good, True, Beautiful)*

Figure A6(ii)

As we turn over the pages bearing Geddes's compact analysis of War-
and Peace-dom, it is, in one of his phrases, 'peculiarly appropriate' to hear him explain further to Mumford that
> the entire inability of V.B. and me alike to make any appreciable
> impression on our public ... is not so entirely due to our defi-
> ciencies of style and presentment ..., but to the solid and well-
> integrated character of the whole *IX* world-system.... More and
> more we have to realise how schools and universities - press etc.
> of course too - are definitely arresting and congealing their
> victims into the moulds of IX, and that to change then is often
> as impossible as to dissolve cast metal in our social tea-cup ...
> is it not a pity that *no one* who can really help us with the
> Transition - IX-9 - has ever turned up, since yourself long ago!

Mumford's final answer to 'What say you?' (about thinking machines)
was ambivalent ('Encounter', September 1966, p. 19). First, a categorical assertion that the Scots College scheme at Montpellier was
an evasion of the task
> of ordering his ideas into some final form that would both ex-
> plain and justify the endless hours and days he had spent ...
> hunting wild truths within the well-fenced zoo of his graphs....

Yet later in the same 'A Disciple's Rebellion' Mumford softens his
judgment and thinks
> more charitably of those last years, for they did not prevent him
> after all from finishing with Thomson his long-contemplated opus
> on biology, and it is there the reader will find some of the best
> of his graphs, outlined and explained: magnificently audacious
> and original, and yet inadequate because of their assumed
> finality.

The mathematician, Professor Cassius Kayser, has earlier been quoted
(ch. 9, p. 345) as having called P.G.'s diagrams 'epoch-making' and
as urging him to publish them. Likewise, Arthur Geddes who was far
from uncritical of his father's thought, has consistently pointed
out that his technique of using Valley Section, Place-Work-Folk and
similar diagrams accounted for much of his skill in quickly diag-
nosing the problems of Indian cities and in prescribing detailed as
well as general remedies. He did not bring thinking machines into
planning reports directly, but these provided him with the background and framework upon which to coordinate all aspects of civic
and regional life and work, history and culture.

An argument that has been used against the value of Geddesian graphics is that none of his colleagues* ever convincingly adopted them

* William W. Mann, former Editorial Secretary of the International
Federation for Housing and Planning (The Hague) and long a 'thinking machine' follower of P.G., did use many of his diagrams in a
lecture on 'Education in Citizenship' (Eldon Lodge, Kensington,
London, 18 July 1946) but appears not to have published anything on
them. Jacqueline Tyrwhitt, on the other hand, has made a study (see
Bibliography) of both Geddes's and Le Corbusier's grids but concludes that the 'ekistic grid' of C.A. Doxiadis is 'a more powerful
tool fur urban analysis'.

himself or persuaded others to do so.   Yet it would be rash to
assume that no one ever will find some way of perfecting his scheme
of interrelating triads and of applying it successfully to the ever-
increasing areas of generalist and inter-disciplinary studies.
Preparatory to such an outcome, one might suggest that clues to
future applications may well be found in this or that file of fools-
cap pages or typescripts in one of the Scottish collections.   Meanwhile, some concluding sentences about the biographical possibilities of the 'Chart of Life'.

The four chambers of the 'World Without and the World Within' of
1905 not only symbolise the completeness of P.G.'s life pattern
since early childhood, but in their more complex expression as
quarters of 'The 36' of the 1920s they provide landmarks against
which to check personal lacks and fulfilments.   Thus the contrast
between his daily preoccupation with square no. 20, 'imaged Ideation' including graphics, and his outward avoidance of no. 25,
'Emotion' including mysticism, is strikingly obvious.   Even so,
there is probably not one square of the 'Chart ' - including nos 28
to 36, each with its Muse from Erato (Love) to Urania (Nature and
Architecture) - in which pages if not a chapter could be written
about his own activities therein.   Not to mention the host of
appropriate quotations to illustrate ideas and deeds.   When he,
under stress, admits 'Emotion' into daily routine there is a letter
like that of May 1925 to daughter Norah, responding to her reconciliation:
    It is such a relief to have one of your old letters again - for I
    have been really suffering....   For look you - here is the
    essential life-history, & main fact of a man's life!   We too
    live on love - & that of women above all - from cradle to
    grave.... (Ch. 10, pp. 366 and 376)
Or that of late February 1927:
    Oh dear lassie - I do not want to lose touch with any of you -
    and I see our dreadful Scottish & other repression in *myself* as
    well as in others....

Again, from the period of happy fulfilment in his own early married
life, we find these lines of wisdom and rare mysticism in 'Every Man
His Own Art Critic' of 1888:
    And thus the fairy tale *is* science ... no spot on earth but is
    the Enchanted Palace where one-half of being waits its awakening
    with the other's kiss ...

    ... shall we listen as he [Darwin] did, to the complex piping of
    old woodland Pan....   Or shall our souls ever be lifted from the
    hurrying stream of vicissitude into the presence of the All?
    (Ch. 4, p. 99)

As a final example of 'emotional evidence', these stanzas from the
autobiographical poem, 'Preface', also recall that period of temporary blindness and despair in Mexico which was the origin of his
discovery of thinking machines.   Indeed, may not much of his long
attachment to folded and symboled diagrams be accounted for as the
compulsory ritual of a modern Merlin?

From tropic rides and quests and finds
- Prisoned in night-dark room!
Long weeks, then months, its boding binds
Hope between gloom and doom!

Yet youth is Hope, and searches far,
Seeks Life, though maimed, ev'n blinded;
Thus, touching darkened window's bar,
Hope woke afresh - new-minded!

The fingers see! oh wonders rare!
The window bars turn graphic!
Dark panes now each their vision bear!
Thus mind wins power seraphic!

It must be recognised that the devising and steady use of diagrams
was only one manifestation of the many 'powers seraphic' of Patrick
Geddes.   Yet though most people will appreciate him for other
qualities, and other achievements than that of charting basic triads
and their compounds, the fact remains that his sketch 'Maps of Life'
did help him to attain an astonishingly complete understanding of
the many worlds in which he was active.   For not only did he exhort
the Georgian Poets to sing of 'after-war Peace, full of strange per-
plexities';   it was he himself who interpreted 'social stress, di-
lemmas inescapable', who showed 'Hell's gape, And Purgatory's fire
before us all', and who consistently and hopefully pointed the 'ways
to Heaven's high-gated Hall!'

NOTES

485

Mumford	Lewis Mumford.
NLS ms.	National Library of Scotland manuscript in the Patrick Geddes Collection.
Norah, 'Letters'	'The Letters of Patrick Geddes, edited by Norah G. Mears', NLS ms. 10508, ff. 1-159 and 160-92.
Norah, 'Reminiscences'	A typescript of 212 pages lent to author by Jeannie Geddes: also fragments in NLS: MS ACC. 5796, no. 17.
RSE	Royal Society of Edinburgh.
'Soc. Rev.'	The 'Sociological Review', London.
Tagore	Rabindranath Tagore.
UCD	University College, Dundee.

INTRODUCTION

1 See pp. 253, 369, 431, 435 regarding losses: 'Emden', 1914, Montpellier, 1940-5, and Strathclyde, 1968.
2 P.G., 'The Life and Work of Sir J.C. Bose - An Indian Pioneer', London and New York, Longmans, 1920.
3 P.G., 'An Analysis of the Principles of Economics', Edinburgh, 1884, p. 31.
4 P.G., 'Cyprus, actual and possible: A study in the Eastern question', 'Contemporary Review', London, June 1897, p. 897. See also chapter 6, pp. 154ff., of this book.
5 Mumford, 'The disciple's rebellion', 'Encounter', September 1966.
6 G. Stanley Hall to Anna, 23 March 1909. Kindly made available by the Clark University Library.
7 P.G., 'Education in Return to Life', New Education Library, no. 3, Bombay, 1924, p. 24.
8 Cf. David Shillan in 'Biotechnics', New Atlantis Foundation Lecture, Richmond Hill, Surrey, 1973, p. 2.

CHAPTER 1   CHILDHOOD AND YOUTH, 1854-74

1 P.G., 'Our delightful uphill road, ...', 'C. des E.' typescript, 1930. (Quoted from notes by Edward McGegan, Curator of the Outlook Tower, pp. 91-6.)
2 P.G., 'Happy childhood ...', 'C. des E.' typescript 1930-1 and Norah to author, undated but summer or autumn 1938.
3 Norah to author, c. September 1938.
4 P.G., 'Earliest recollections ...', undated, NLS.
5 Paddy Kitchen, p. 39.
6 P.G., 'Education in Return to Life', New Education Library, no. 3, Bombay, 1924, p. 20.
7 P.G. to 'Paul Robeson: A Letter to a Mutual Friend', undated, c. 1929-30, NLS.
8 P.G., 'Memories and reflections', 'The Young Barbarian', March 1929, Perth Academy, reprint, p. 2.
9 P.G., 'Earliest recollections ...'.
10 'Testimonials in favour of Mr. Alexander Geddes, Late Sergeant-Major, Reserve Battalion, 42nd Highlanders', printed sheet.

11   P.G., 'Happy childhood ...'.
12   Norah, 'Letters', P.G. to his father, 16 April 1898, NLS.
     Also cited by Mairet, 'Pioneer', pp. 87-8.
13   P.G. to Professor H.J. Fleure, 11 April 1917, NLS.
14   P.G., 'The education of two boys', 'The Survey Graphic',
     New York, September 1925, p. 573.
15   P.G., 'Memories and reflections', p. 1.
16   P.G., 'The education of two boys', p. 574.
17   Mairet, 'Pioneer', p. 8.
18   P.G., 'Memories and reflections', p. 2.
19   P.G., 'The education of two boys', p. 573.
20   Norah, 'Letters', pp. 9-10, NLS.
21   P.G., 'Huxley as Teacher', Supplement to 'Nature', no. 2897,
     London, 9 May 1925, p. 741.

CHAPTER 2   THE WANDERING STUDENT, 1874-88

 1   P.G., 'Huxley as Teacher', Supplement to 'Nature', no. 2897,
     London, 9 May 1925, pp. 740-3.
 2   Mairet, 'Pioneer', p. 2.
 3   Ibid.
 4   P.G., 'Homes and haunts of famous authors, no. 8, Carlyle',
     'Weekly Leader', London, 28 August 1902, p. 341.
 5   P.G., 'Huxley as Teacher', p. 741.
 6   Ibid., p. 742.
 7   P.G., 'Homes and haunts of famous authors', p. 341.
 8   Ibid.
 9   Ibid., p. 342.
10   Mairet, 'Pioneer', p. 23.
11   P.G.'s Introduction to Susan Liveing, 'A Nineteenth Century
     Teacher: J.H. Bridges', London, Paul-Trench-Trubner, 1926,
     pp. 1-2.
12   J.H. Bridges, 'Five Discourses on Positive Religion', London,
     Reeves & Turner, 1882, preface.
13   John P. Reilly, 'Early Social Thought of Patrick Geddes',
     PhD thesis, Columbia University, 1972, ch. 1.
14   P.G.'s Introduction to Susan Liveing, pp. 13-14.
15   P.G. and J.A.T., 'Life: Outlines of General Biology',
     London, Williams & Norgate, 1931, vol. II, p. 1454.
16   P.G., 'Huxley as Teacher', p. 742.
17   Mabel Barker to author, 30 December 1945.
18   Norah, 'Letters', p. 15, NLS.
19   Mairet, 'Pioneer', pp. 22-3.
20   Ibid., p. 23.
21   P.G. and J.A.T., 'Life: Outlines of General Biology', p. 1457.
22   Norah, 'Letters', p. 18, NLS.
23   P.G., unpublished typescript on student days in Paris, copied
     by me at Outlook Tower, Edinburgh, 1935.
24   Interview with Arthur by author, Tape Transcript 'C', p. 5.
25   Mairet, 'Pioneer', p. 30.
26   P.G., 'On paleontological and zoological researches in Mexico',
     'Report of the Fifteenth Meeting of the British Association for
     the Advancement of Science', London, August and September 1880,
     p. 255.

27 'Verse-letter' from P.G. to Marie Bonnet, July 1922, NLS.
28 'Sur la chlorophylle animale et la physiologie des planaires
    vertes', 'Archives de Zoologie Expérimentale et Générale',
    Paris, 1879, vol. 8, pp. 51-8.   Also in 'Proceedings',
    Royal Society, London, 1879.
29 Hubrecht (Director of the Dutch Museum of Natural History)
    to P.G., 12 June 1879, NLS.
30 The Week's Message,'Woman Teacher's World', London, 5 March
    1913.

CHAPTER 3 WHICH IDENTITY, WHAT MESSAGE? 1880-6

1 'Letter of 1888', pp. 5-6.
2 Paddy Kitchen, p. 70.
3 Ibid.
4 Letters to author from Keeper of Manuscripts, Edinburgh University Library, 8 Nov. 1971 and 6 Jan. 1972.
5 Paddy Kitchen, p. 79.
6 P.G., 'Nearly fifty years ago...', typescript from Outlook
   Tower or 'C. des E.', 1935; undated but presumed to be
   1927-8.
7 Ibid.
8 'Letter of 1888', p. 13.
9 Ibid., p. 18.
10 Ibid., p. 26.
11 Ibid., p. 25.
12 Ibid., p. 83.
13 P.G., 'Sur la chlorophylle animale et la physiologie des
    planaires vertes', 'Archives de Zoologie Expérimentale et
    Générale', Paris, 1879, vol. 8, pp. 51-8.
14 A.D. Peacock, 'Patrick Geddes: biologist', 'Alumnus Chron-
    icle', St Andrews University (Commemorative Address given on
    22 October 1954), reprint, p. 3.
15 Mairet, 'Pioneer', p. 46.
16 P.G., 'On the phenomena of variegation and cell-multiplica-
    tion in a species of enteromorpha', 'Transactions RSE', XXIX,
    1880, pp. 550-9.
17 P.G., 'On the classification of statistics and its results',
    'Proceedings RSE', XI, 1881, pp. 295-322.
18 P.G., 'An analysis of the principles of economics', 'Proceed-
    ings RSE', XII, 1884, p. 943 ff.
19 P.G., 'On the classification of statistics ...', p. 304.
20 Ibid., p. 312.
21 Ibid., p. 315.
22 Ibid., p. 322.
23 Further condensed into 2½ columns of 'Nature', 29 September
    1881.
24 P.G., 'Histologie des pédicellaires et des muscles de l'oursin'
    and 'Nouvelle sous-classe d'infusoires', 'Comptes rendus de
    l'Académie des Sciences', Paris, 1881; vol. 92, pp. 308-10
    and vol. 93, pp. 1085-7.
25 P.G., 'On the nature and functions of the "Yellow Cells" of
    radiolarians and coelenterates', 'Proceedings RSE', vol. XI,
    pp. 377-96, read January 1882.

26   'Letter of 1888', p. 57.
27   Ibid., p. 58.
28   A.D. Peacock, 'Patrick Geddes: biologist', pp. 5-6.
29   'Letter of 1888', p. 58.
30   'Viri Illustres' (P.G., editor), Edinburgh, Pentland, 1884
     (Directory of famous graduates of Edinburgh University).
31   P.G., 'An analysis of the principles of economics', 'Proceed-
     ings RSE', XI, 1834, pp. 947-78.
32   Mumford, 'Who is Patrick Geddes?', 'Survey Graphic', New
     York, February, 1925, p. 523.
33   P.G., 'An analysis of the principles of economics', p. 961 ff.
34   Ibid., p. 965 ff.
35   Ibid., p. 971 ff.
36   Ibid., p. 973 ff.
37   Ibid., pp. 975-8.
38   P.G., 'Evolution', 'Chambers's Encyclopaedia', vol. IV, 1888,
     1895, 1901 and 1923.
39   'Letter of 1888', p. 18.
40   J.A.T. to P.G., 10 November 1883, NLS.
41   Mairet, 'Pioneer', p. 46.
42   Ibid., p. 47.
43   P.G., 'Nearly fifty years ago...'
44   Mairet, 'Pioneer', pp. 44-5.
45   The Edinburgh Social Union, 'Sixth Annual Report', Edinburgh,
     November 1890, Darien Press, p. 3.
46   Mairet, 'Pioneer', p. 46.
47   J.A.T. to P.G., undated, c. 1886, NLS.
48   P.G., 'John Ruskin, Economist', Edinburgh, William Brown, 1884.
49   Ibid., pp. 3-7.
50   Ibid., pp. 16-17.
51   Ibid., p. 35 ff.
52   Mairet, 'Pioneer', p. 48.

CHAPTER 4   MARRIAGE, AND THE CIVIC CRUSADE, 1886-8

1   Anna to P.G., 14 February 1886, NLS.
2   Anna to P.G., 3 March 1886, NLS.
3   Anna to P.G., 14 February 1886, NLS.
4   Mairet, 'Pioneer', p. 48.
5   J.A.T. to P.G., 10 August 1886, NLS.
6   J.A.T. to Arthur, 26 April 1932, NLS.
7   P.G., 'Nearly fifty years ago...', typescript from Outlook
    Tower or 'C. des E.', 1935; undated but presumed to be 1927-8.
8   Norah, 'Reminiscences', p. 1.
9   Mairet, 'Pioneer', p. 52.
10 Norah to author, 9 January 1938.
11 James Mavor, 'My Windows on the Street of the World', vol. I,
    London and Toronto, Dent; New York, Dutton, 1923, p. 215.
12 Norah to author, 24 March 1939.
13 Norah to author, 23 June 1947.
14 Ibid.
15 J.A.T. to Arthur, 26 April 1932, NLS.
16 Ibid.

17 P.G., 'A synthetic outline of the history of biology', 'Proceedings RSE', vol. XII, pp. 904-11, 1886.
18 Defries, 'Interpreter', p. 321.
19 P.G., 'Conditions of Progress of the Capitalist and of the Labourer', Edinburgh, Co-Operative Printing Company, 1886.
20 A testimonial signed by twenty-two participants in this course is printed in 'Letter of 1888', p. 27.
21 Norah, 'Reminiscences', p. 11.
22 P.G., 'Every Man his own Art Critic - Manchester Exhibition', Manchester, John Heywood, 1887, p. 15.
23 P.G., 'Every Man his own Art Critic (Glasgow Exhibition, 1888)', Edinburgh, William Brown, 1888, p. 13.
24 'Letter of 1888'.
25 James Mavor, op. cit., vol. I, p. 213.
26 George Eyre-Todd, 'The genius of the Outlook Tower', 'Scots Observer', Edinburgh, 20 July 1931.
27 James Mavor, op. cit., vol. II, pp. 91-8.

CHAPTER 5   PART-TIME PROFESSOR, FULL-TIME GENERALIST, 1888-97

1   Interview with Arthur by author, 1 March 1968, Tape transcript 'D', p. 1.
2   Keeper of Manuscripts of Edinburgh University Library to author, 8 November 1971 and 6 January 1972.
3   J.B. Salmond to G. Dundas Craig, 28 November 1938, given by the latter to author.
4   H.R. Fletcher, 'Royal Botanic Garden, Edinburgh, 1670-1970', London, HMSO, 1970, ch. 16
5   Ibid.
6   G.R. Tudhope, 'Presidential Address', 'Universities Review', London, vol. 27, no. 1, October 1954, reprint, p. 2.
7   Defries, 'Interpreter', p. 147.
8   Mairet, 'Pioneer', p. 111.
9   Miss B.D. Craig to author, 18 October 1938.
10 G.R. Tudhope, 'Presidential Address', p. 1.
11 University Extension Manuals Series, ed. Professor Knight, St Andrews University.
12 Norah to author, 9 January 1938.
13 P.G., 'Evolution', 'Chambers's Encyclopaedia', vol. IV, 1888, 1895, 1901 and 1923.
14 P.G. and J.A.T., 'The Evolution of Sex', London, Scott, 1889, p. 127.
15 Ibid., p. 271.
16 P.G. and J.A.T., 'The Evolution of Sex', pp. 293-4.
17 S.A. Robertson, 'A Scottish tribute', 'Soc. Rev.', London, October 1932, p. 395.
18 P.G. and J.A.T., 'The Evolution of Sex', pp. 280-1.
19 P.G., 'Chapters in Modern Botany', London, John Murray, 1893, p. 188.
20 P.G. and J.A.T., 'Life: Outlines of General Biology', London, Williams & Norgate, 1931, vol. II, p. 1455.
21 P.G., 'Chapters in Modern Botany', pp. 24-5.
22 Defries, 'Interpreter', pp. 320-1.

23 Norah, 'Reminiscences', pp. 27-30, NLS.
24 Dunfermline 'Journal', 16 February 1887.
25 P.G., 'Scottish university reform', 'Scottish Review', Edinburgh, January 1888, p. 176.
26 'Daily Free Press', Aberdeen, 17 October 1891.
27 P.G., 'Scottish university needs and aims', 'Scots Magazine', Perth, August 1890, pp. 184-92.
28 Ibid.
29 P.G., 'Abstract of Evidence to be.Presented to the Scottish Universities Commission', 16 July 1891 (author's copy).
30 'The Edinburgh Summer Meeting', Prospectus, 1895.
31 P.G., 'Tribute to Victor Branford', 'Nature', London, 19 July 1930, reprint p. 2.
32 Abbé Félix Klein to author, 17 March 1936.
33 Norah, 'Reminiscences', pp. 30-1, NLS.
34 R.M. Wenley, 'The University Extension Movement in Scotland', Glasgow University Press, 1895, p. 37.
35 S.A. Robertson, 'A Scottish Tribute', p. 396.
36 Riccardo Stephens, 'The Cruciform Mark', London, Chatto & Windus, 1895.
37 James Mavor, 'My Windows on the Street of the World', vol. I, London and Toronto, Dent; New York, Dutton, 1923, p. 216.
38 P.G. to T.H. Marr, 24 October 1895, NLS.
39 Professor Charles Zueblin, Chicago University, in 'Am. J. of Soc.', March 1899.
40 John Kelman, Jr, 'The Interpreter's House: The Ideals Embodied in the Outlook Tower', Edinburgh, Oliphant, Anderson & Ferrier, 1905, p. 9.
41 Ibid., p. 27.
42 P.G., 'A First Visit to the Outlook Tower', Edinburgh, P.G. & Colleagues, 1906, p. 26.
43 Quoted in 'Patrick Geddes, Maker of the Future', p. 192.
44 Norah to author, 24 March 1939.
45 Reproduced in 'Interpretation of the Pictures in the Common Room of Ramsay Lodge', Edinburgh, Leighton, 1928, 16 pp.

CHAPTER 6   FROM NEAR-EAST PEACEMAKER TO INTERNATIONAL EDUCATOR, 1897-1901

1 Mr and Mrs Patrick Geddes, 'Cyprus, and its Power to Help the East', reprinted with illustrations from the 'Report of the International Conference on Armenian Aid', London, May 1897, p. 6.
2 P.G., 'Cyprus, actual and possible: a study in the Eastern question', 'Contemporary Review', London, June 1897, p. 896.
3 Mr and Mrs Patrick Geddes, op. cit., p. 13.
4 P.G. to 'Dear Mr. and Mrs. Bunting', 13 March 1897, NLS.
5 P.G., 'Cyprus, actual and possible ...', pp. 897-907.
6 Mr and Mrs Patrick Geddes, op. cit., pp. 5, 14.
7 Mairet, 'Pioneer', pp. 85-6.
8 P.G., 'Cyprus, actual and possible ...', p. 908.
9 Norah, 'Reminiscences', pp. 58-64, NLS.
10 Anna to P.G., 2 February 1898, NLS.

11 P.G. to 'My dear Father', 16 April 1898, reproduced in Norah's 'Letters' and in Mairet, 'Pioneer', pp. 87-8.
12 Mairet, 'Pioneer', p. 97.
13 John Ross to P.G., 10 March 1898, NLS.
14 P.G. to the Rev. Dr James Stalker, 17 November 1898. It is quoted almost in full in Kitchen, pp. 171-3.
15 Mairet, 'Pioneer', p. 92.
16 P.G. to 'Dear Sir', 12 January 1899, NLS.
17 Mairet, 'Pioneer', p. 93.
18 Ibid., pp. 93-4.
19 Ibid., pp. 94-5.
20 Ibid., p. 98.
21 P.G., 'A schoolboy's bag and a city's pageant', 'Survey Graphic', New York, vol. VI, no. V, February 1925, p. 525.
22 Anna to her children, 16 January 1900, NLS.
23 Anna to her children, 23 January 1900, NLS.
24 Flora Cooke to author, c. 1938. Quoted in 'Maker of the Future', p. 219.
25 Anna to her children, 2 February 1900, NLS.
26 Josephine MacLeod to author, 8 November 1937.
27 First quoted in 'Maker of the Future', pp. 221-2. Original source, letter to author from Josephine MacLeod.
28 Anna to her children (cf. note 22).
29 Georges Bizet, 'Professor Patrick Geddes', 'Scottish Life', Edinburgh, 1 April 1899, pp. 957-8.
30 Norah, 'Reminiscences', pp. 78-9, NLS.
31 Ibid., pp. 85-6.
32 Firmin Roz in 'Une réunion d'été', 'Revue Bleue', Paris, 1903.
33 P.G., 'Closing exhibition - Paris 1900', 'Contemporary Review', London, November 1900, pp. 664-5.
34 Mairet, 'Pioneer', p. 106.
35 Miss MacLeod to author, quoted in 'Maker of the Future', pp. 228-9.
36 Le Swâmi Vivekananda, 'Conquête de la nature intérieure', Paris, Publications Théosophiques, 1910.
37 P.G., 'Closing exhibition - Paris 1900', pp. 665-6.

CHAPTER 7 LIFE PROJECTS DISCOVERED: TOWN PLANNING AND SOCIOLOGY, 1901-14

1 P.G. to Mavor, 4 May 1902 and 8 July 1902, NLS.
2 'Defences', William Cuthbertson vs. P.G., prepared by James F. MacDonald, SSC, Edinburgh, 1902, NLS.
3 P.G. to Mavor, 3 July 1925, NLS.
4 Mrs C. Kelly, archivist, Royal Geographical Society, London, to author, 9 January 1972.
5 'Sociological Papers', London, 1905, vol. 1, pp. 119-20.
6 P.G. to Mumford, 5 May 1922, NLS.
7 P.G., 'City Development, A Report to the Carnegie Dunfermline Trust', The Saint George Press, Bournville, Birmingham, 1904, p. 57.
8 Edward McGegan, 'Geddes as a man of action', 'Soc. Rev.', London, October 1932, p. 355.

9   P.G., 'City Development ...', pp. 221-2.
10 Mairet, 'Pioneer', p. 121.
11 'Dunfermline & West of Fife Advertiser', 23 April 1932.
12 P.G., 'City Development ...', p. 227.
13 S.K. Ratcliffe to author, c. 1938, quoted in 'Maker of the Future', pp. 240-1.
14 Interview with Philip Mairet by author, 9 October 1969, Tape Transcript 'A', p. 2.
15 This anecdote was related in a letter from Professor Brooks of the University of North Carolina, to the author, c. 1940. This document, unfortunately, cannot be located at present.
16 'The Twentieth Century Moliere: Bernard Shaw', London, 1915, p. 97 (translated by Eden and Cedar Paul).
17 James F. MacDonald, SSC, to P.G., 21 May 1903, NLS.
18 Kindly provided by Clark University Library from the papers of President Hall.
19 John Ross to P.G., 28 March 1907, NLS.
20 Earl of Sandwich, 'The saving of Crosby Hall', 'Soc. Rev.', October 1932, pp. 362-4.
21 S.K. Ratcliffe, 'A light that lighted other minds', 'Soc. Rev.', October 1932, pp. 366-7.
22 Earl of Sandwich, op. cit., pp. 362-4.
23 Anna to P.G., 2 July 1897, NLS.
24 Ibid., 10 December 1905, NLS.
25 'Town planning exhibition', 'Evening Standard', London, 10 October 1910.
26 Defries, 'Interpreter', pp. 322-3.
27 P.G., 'The Civic Survey of Edinburgh', reprinted from 'Transactions of Town Planning Conference', London, October 1910, p. 538.
28 Ibid., pp. 551-62.
29 Ibid., p. 574.
30 P.G., 'A Symposium on Town-Planning', supplement to 'The New Age', London, 3 November 1910, p. 5.
31 S.K. Ratcliffe to author, c. 1938, quoted in 'Maker of the Future', p. 254.
32 P.G., 'An educational Approach', 'Ideals of Science and Faith', edited by J.E. Hand, London, George Allen, 1904, pp. 207-9.
33 Branford, 'A Citizen Soldier: His Education for War and Peace - Being a Memoir of Alasdair Geddes', London, Headley, 1917, p. 6.
34 P.G., 'An educational approach', pp. 193-216.
35 Ibid.
36 Jeannie to author, 25 May 1971.
37 Quoted in 'Maker of the Future', pp. 301-2.
38 P.G. and J.A.T., 'Sex', London, Williams & Norgate, 1914, pp. 168-9.
39 Also reprinted in 'Sex', p. 193, but without the reference, as below, to the philosopher's books and the curate's sermons!
40 Mairet, 'Pioneer', p. 128.
41 Interview with Arthur by author, 1 March 1968, Tape Transcript 'B', p. 12.
42 R.J. Halliday, 'The sociological movement, the Sociological Society and the genesis of academic sociology in Britain', 'Soc. Rev.', University of Keele, November 1968, p. 394 (new series).

43 Mairet, 'Pioneer', pp. 129-31.
44 Interview with Arthur by author, 1 March 1968, Tape Transcript 'B', pp. 1-2.
45 Mairet, 'Pioneer', pp. 132-5.
46 P.G., 'Dramatisations of History', London, Sociological Publications Ltd, Edinburgh, Patrick Geddes & Colleagues, Bombay & Karachi, The Modern Publishing Co., sixth edition, 1923, p. i.
47 Defries, 'Interpreter', pp. 44-5.
48 P.G., 'Dramatisations of History', pp. 1-3.
49 J.A.T., 'A life of service', 'The Times', 19 April 1932.
50 Defries, 'Interpreter', p. 70.
51 Ibid., pp. 75-6.
52 Ibid., p. 76.
53 J.M. Hone, 'James Larkin and the Nationalist Party', 'Contemporary Review', London, December 1913, p. 786.
54 Mairet, 'Pioneer', p. 150.
55 Mabel Barker to author, 30 December 1945.
56 Defries, 'Interpreter', p. 180.

CHAPTER 8 FIRST YEARS IN INDIA, 1914-19

1 P.G. to Alasdair, 5 August 1914, NLS.
2 P.G., to 'Dear Folk', 1 to 4 October 1914, NLS.
3 P.G. refers to Vincent A. Smith's 'Asoka - the Buddhist Emperor of India' in the series Rulers of India (Oxford, 1909).
4 P.G. to 'Your Excellencies' (Lord and Lady Aberdeen), 30 October 1914, NLS.
5 Mairet, 'Pioneer', p. 157.
6 P.G. to Frank Mears, 3 December 1914, NLS.
7 P.G. to Anna, 2 December 1914, NLS.
8 Mairet, 'Pioneer', p. 159.
9 'Reports on Towns in the Madras Presidency', Madras, 1915.
10 P.G. to Anna, 21 December 1914, NLS.
11 P.G. to 'Dear Folk', 7 January 1915, NLS.
12 'Patrick Geddes in India', edited by Jaqueline Tyrwhitt, London, Lund Humphries, 1947, p. 22.
13 Ibid., pp. 57-8.
14 Branford, 'A Citizen Soldier: His Education for War and Peace ...', London, Headley, 1917, p. 3.
15 P.G., 'Wardom and peacedom: suggestions towards an interpretation', 'Soc. Rev.', January 1915, p. 20ff.
16 J.A.T., 'A life of service', 'The Times', 19 April 1932.
17 P.G. and Gilbert Slater, 'Maker of the Future', London, Williams & Norgate, 1917, p. 337.
18 P.G. to Alasdair, 14 January 1916, NLS.
19 'The life and work of Sir J.C. Bose: An Indian pioneer', London and New York, Longmans, 1920.
20 Anna to P.G., 10 June 1916, NLS.
21 Mairet, 'Pioneer', p. 174.
22 P.G. to Norah, 2 January 1917, NLS.
23 P.G. to Alasdair, 25 December 1916, NLS.
24 P.G. to H.J. Fleure, 11 April 1917, NLS.
25 P.G. to J.C. Bose, 28 April 1917, NLS.

26   Mairet, 'Pioneer', p. 175.
27   P.G. to Amelia Defries, 3 July 1917, NLS.
28   'Maker of the Future', p. 347.
29   P.G. to Norah, 10 October 1917, NLS.
30   P.G. to Norah, 12 September 1917, NLS.
31   P.G. to Norah, 2 June 1918, NLS.
32   P.G. to Arthur, 27 July 1918, NLS.
33   P.G. to Mahatma Gandhi, 5 April 1918, NLS.
34   Gandhi to P.G., 11 April 1918, NLS.
35   P.G. to Gandhi, 30 March 1918, NLS.
36   P.G. to Arthur, 4 March 1919, NLS.
37   P.G., 'Town Planning ...', vol. II, pp. 57-8.
38   Charles Ferguson, 'The University Militant', New York, 1911.
39   P.G. and V.B., 'The Coming Polity', London, Williams & Norgate, 1917, revised edition, 1919, p. 229.
40   P.G., 'A schoolboy's bag and a city's pageant', 'Survey Graphic', New York, vol. 54, February 1925, p. 525ff.

CHAPTER 9   THE MAKING OF THE FUTURE, 1919-24

1   P.G. to 'Dear Dreoline', (Mrs Podmore), 24 April 1919, NLS.
2   P.G. to Branford, 9 January 1919, NLS.
3   Ibid., 5 April 1919, NLS.
4   Defries, 'Interpreter', pp. 172-90.
5   P.G. to Rachel Annand Taylor, undated, written on University College, Dundee letterhead, summer 1919, NLS.
6   P.G. and Branford, 'The Coming Polity', London, Williams & Norgate, 1917, rev. ed. 1919, p. 224.
7   Ibid., pp. 311-12.
8   Mairet, 'Pioneer', p. 183.
9   M.D. Eder, 'In Palestine', 'Soc. Rev.', October 1932, p. 376.
10   Defries, 'Interpreter', p. 260.
11   Ibid., p. 262.
12   Ibid., p. 260.
13   M.D. Eder, 'In Palestine', p. 376 (cf. note 9).
14   P.G. to Raymond Unwin, 14 November 1919, NLS.
15   Defries, 'Interpreter', p. 328.
16   P.G. to Mumford, 25 September-2 October 1920, NLS.
17   P.G. to Mumford, November 1921, NLS.
18   P.G., 'Town Planning in Colombo', Ceylon, H.R. Cottle, Government Printer, 1921, pp. 38-9.
19   P.G. to Norah, 22 April 1921, NLS.
20   P.G. to Lilian, 26 October 1921, NLS.
21   P.G., 'Town Planning in Patiala State and City', Lucknow, Perry's, 1922, p. vii.
22   P.G. to Marie Bonnet, July 1922, NLS.
23   Tagore to P.G., 9 May 1922, pp. 1-2, NLS.
24   P.G. to Mumford, 25 January 1923, NLS.
25   P.G. to 'Dear Mr Keppel', 10 March 1923, NLS.
26   P.G. to Boni & Liveright, 1 March 1923, NLS.
27   P.G. to Norah, 1 May 1923, NLS.
28   Mumford, 'Disciple's rebellion, a memoir of Patrick Geddes', 'Encounter', London, September 1966, p. 12.

29   Staff and Board of Survey Associates, 'From New York', 'Soc. Rev.', October 1932, p. 380.
30   Mumford to author, originally written in 1937, reconfirmed 5 November 1974.
31   Mumford, 'Disciple's rebellion', p. 14.
32   G. Ferrero, 'Ancient Rome and Modern America', New York and London, Putnam, 1914.
33   Mumford, op. cit., pp. 14-16.
34   P.G. to Mumford, 3 February 1924, NLS.
35   Ibid.
36   P.G. to Mumford, 18 February 1924, NLS.
37   P.G. to Branford, 16 November 1923, NLS.
38   P.G. to Branford, 1 February 1924, NLS.
39   P.G. to Norah, 13 March 1924, NLS.

CHAPTER 10   'LATE-FLOWERING AGAVE', 1924-8

1   P.G. to Mumford, 26 April 1924, NLS.
2   P.G. to Lilian, 16 May 1924, NLS.
3   Mumford to Branford, 19 July 1924, NLS.
4   P.G. to Mumford, 14 November 1924, NLS.
5   P.G., 'The mapping of life', 'Soc. Rev.', July 1924, vol. 16, pp. 193-203.
6   P.G. to Lilian, 4 November 1924, NLS.
7   P.G. to 'Dear   ', the original presumably addressed to Mabel Barker.   A carbon copy was sent to Mumford with 'Lewis & Missus' filled in by hand, 3 December 1924, NLS.
8   P.G. to Lilian, 11 December 1922, NLS.
9   P.G. to Norah, 17 January 1921, NLS.
10   'Trial and Error, The Autobiography of Chaim Weizmann', London, Hamish Hamilton, 1949, pp. 395-6, 401.
11   'Soc. Rev.', July 1925, vol. 17, pp. 223-4.
12   P.G. to Sir Wyndham Deedes, 24 February 1923, NLS.
13   Chief Secretary, Government House, Jerusalem to P.G., 4 November 1923, NLS.
14   Riccardo Stephens, 'The Cruciform Mark', London, Chatto & Windus, 1895, p. 191.
15   Gladys Mayer to author, 9 January 1969.
16   Interview with Arthur by author, 1 March 1969, Tape Transcript 'B', p. 5.
17   P.G. to Norah, 23 February 1927, NLS.
18   P.G. to Lilian, 26 June 1926, NLS.
19   P.G. to Norah, 3 May 1926, NLS.
20   Mabel Barker, 'L'Utilisation du milieu géographique dans l'education', Montpellier, 1926; republished by Flammarion, Paris, 1931.
21   P.G. to John Ross, 25 January 1925, NLS.
22   Mumford to P.G., 3 May 1931, NLS.
23   P.G. to Norah, August or September 1926, NLS.

CHAPTER 11   REMARRIAGE AND DÉNOUEMENT, 1928-32

1   P.G. to Norah, 23 February 1927, NLS.
2   J.A.T. to P.G., 18 February 1927, NLS.
3   Interview with Sir Landsborough Thomson by author, 16 September 1971.
4   London, Routledge, 1927; New York, Boni & Liveright (with Mumford's help).
5   P.G. to Norah, 14 February 1927, NLS.
6   P.G. to Lilian, 11 August 1927, NLS.
7   Now a director of THM Design Consultants Ltd, London. His comments are from a taped recording of October 1969.
8   P.G. to Branford, 17 February 1928, NLS.
9   Interview with Arthur by author, 1 March 1968, Tape Transcript 'C', pp. 5, 8.
10 J.A.T. to P.G., 11 October 1929, NLS 22 December 1929, NLS 30 May 1930, NLS.
11 For a fuller transcription of a Geddesian 'label-diatribe' see 'Interpreter', p. 167.
12 Interview with John Tandy by author, 8 October, Tape Transcript 'A', p. 9.
13 Giles Playfair, 'My Father's Son', London, Geoffrey Bles, 1937, pp. 146-7.
14 Moya Jowitt to author, 16 April 1969.
15 Dorothea Price, 'At Montpellier', 'Soc. Rev.', October 1932, p. 379.
16 Mabel M. Barker, 'The better by his having lived', 'Soc. Rev.', October 1932, p. 390.
17 Mumford, 'The Disciple's Rebellion', op. cit., p. 19.
18 'The Coal Crisis and the Future: a study of social disorders and their treatment', London, Williams & Norgate, 1926.
19 P.G. to Norah, 30 June 1930, NLS.
20 Ibid.
21 R.M. Neill, 'Seeing life whole', 'Contemporary Review', 1932, p. 724.
22 Mumford, 'Vivendo discimus', 'New Republic', New York, 16 September 1931, p. 130.
23 'Leben und Werk von Sir J.C. Bose', Erlenbach-Zürich, 1930.
24 Undated, but refers to 'The Spirit of the Tartan' which was performed at the Outlook Tower in 1931.
25 P.G. to 'a mutual friend of' Paul Robeson, undated, c. 1930-1, NLS.
26 P.G. to H.G. Wells, 22 October 1929, H.G. Wells Archive, University of Illinois. There is, however, no record of any reply by Wells to this offer, either in Illinois or at the National Library of Scotland.
27 P.G. to author, April 1931.
28 P.G. to Amelia Defries, 22 December 1931, NLS.
29 Stewart Robertson, 'A Scottish tribute', 'Soc. Rev.', October 1932, p. 395.
30 Mairet, 'Pioneer', p. 211.
31 John Tandy to author, 22 August 1973.
32 Interview with Arthur by author, 1 March 1968, Tape Transcript 'A', p. 6.
33 Ibid.

CHAPTER 12 PATRICK GEDDES TODAY

1 Professor A.S. Travis to author, 6 March 1973.
2 A.C. Frazer, Secretary, Outlook Tower Association, to author, 9 February 1973.
3 'Petition of Alexander Trevor McIndoe and others, for Approval of a Cy-pres Scheme', 'Court of Session, Scotland', Revised Draft, 31 January 1973, Hagart & Burn-Murdoch, W.S., Edinburgh, pp. 5-6.
4 'Patrick Geddes: planner and reformer', 'Planning', 29 August 1975.
5 Letter to author, 4 February 1976 from David Hayes, LANDMARK.
6 'Scottish Daily Express', 2 December 1966.
7 'Crosby Hall', Summer 1966, 23 pp.
8 M.D. Eder, 'In Palestine', 'Soc. Rev.', October 1932, p. 377.
9 'Trial and Error, The Autobiography of Chaim Weizmann', London, Hamish Hamilton, 1949, p. 391.
10 Mrs Anne Geddes Shalit, in a letter to the author, 25 May 1970.
11 Defries, 'Interpreter', p. 271.
12 S.K. Ratcliffe, 'A light that lighted other minds', 'Soc. Rev.', October 1932, p. 367.
13 Arthur Geddes, 'His (P.G.'s) Indian reports and their influence', 'Journal of the Town Planning Institute', London, November 1939 to October 1940, vol. XXVI, p. 193.
14 Letter to author, 5 April 1973. Dr Meller intends to elaborate this statement in a forthcoming work on P.G.
15 Mumford, 'Mumford on Geddes', reprinted from 'Architectural Review', London, 1949, in 'News Sheet of the International Federation for Housing and Town Planning', Amsterdam, February 1951, p. 8.
16 Arthur Glikson, 'The planner Geddes?', 'News Sheet of the International Federation for Housing and Town Planning', The Hague, May 1955, reprint p. 2.
17 'TVA-Democracy of the March', Harper, New York, 1944.
18 'From Geography to Geotechnics', University of Illinois Press, 1968, pp. 22-4.
19 Letters to author of 22 March and 2 July 1976. See Bibliography for her article on the grids of Geddes, Le Corbusier and Doxiadis.
20 Kitchen, 'A Most Unsettling Person - An Introduction to the Ideas and Life of Patrick Geddes', Gollancz, 1975.
21 Defries, 'Interpreter', pp. 240-1.
22 A fourth book planned was 'Olympus: An Interpretation of Phases and Sex in Human Life', but never published. See pp. 445-6.
23 Arthur Geddes, introduction to 'Olympus' (typescript) by P.G., April 1946, p. 3.
24 'Sir Patrick Geddes Centenary Celebrations', Edinburgh College of Art, 1 October 1954, pp. 3-5.
25 Defries, 'Interpreter', pp. 320-1.
26 P.G., 'The temple cities', 'Modern Review', Calcutta, March 1919, reprint, p. 6.
27 'Patrick Geddes in India', pp. 71-2.
28 Wendy Lesser has made an interesting study of his mystic and religious terminology in 'Patrick Geddes: the practical visionary', 'Town Planning Review', July 1974, vol. 45.

29 Mumford to author, 10 October 1973.
30 P.G.'s reference: 'Scheffler, quoted in Cobb, 'Mysticism and the Creed', London, Macmillan, 1914.
31 'Memo from Prof. P.G. to Successors in continuing and conducting this Collège des Ecossais in its developments and co-operation, and its relations to circumstances as they arise.' Undated, but c. 1930-1.
32 'The Hebrew University of Jerusalem', The Jerusalem Post Fress, 1958, p. 23.
33 Mumford, 'Disciple's Rebellion', p. 20.
34 P.G. to Norah, undated, 1921, NLS.
35 P.G. to Amelia Defries, 30 April 1930, NLS.
36 George Sarton, 'History of Science', London, Oxford University Press, 1953, vol. 1, pp. 295-6.
37 Pheroze Bharucha, 'Professor Sir Patrick Geddes', 'Bombay University Journal', vol. 1, no. 1, 1932, pp. 224-8.

SELECT BIBLIOGRAPHY

A 'P.G.'S PROGRESS'

(A short chronological list of Patrick Geddes's writings which reflect the development of his widening interests between 1879 and 1931. See alphabetical list (B) for bibliographical references.)

1879	'Chlorophylle animale et la physiologie des planaires vertes'
1881	'The Classification of Statistics and Its Results'
1883	'A Re-statement of the Cell-Theory'
1884	'An Analysis of the Principles of Economics'
1884	'John Ruskin, Economist'
1885	'Synthetic Outline of the History of Biology'
1886	'Conditions of the Progress of the Capitalist and of the Labourer'
1887	'Industrial Exhibitions and Modern Progress'
1888	'Co-operation vs. Socialism'
1888	*Every Man His Own Art Critic* (Glasgow Exhibition)
1889	*The Evolution of Sex* (with J. Arthur Thomson)
1890	'Scottish University Needs and Aims'
1893	*Chapters in Modern Botany*
1894	'University Systems, Past and Present'
1895	'Education for Economics and Citizenship'
1896	'Contemporary Social Evolution' (ten lectures at the Edinburgh Summer Meeting)
1897	'Cyprus, Actual and Possible, A Study in the Eastern Question'
1900	'Man and the Environment, A Study from the Paris Exposition'
1900	*'Projet de conservation de la Rue des Nations, Paris'*
1902	'Edinburgh and Its Region, Geographic and Historical'
1903	'Universities in Europe and in India'
1904	*City Development: A Study of Parks, Gardens and Culture Institutes*
1905	*The World Without and the World Within - Sunday Talks With My Children*
1905	'Civics As Applied Sociology'
1907	'Town Planning in Theory and Practice'
1908	'The Town-Planning Bill and Its Needed Schedule of Local Inquiry'
1910	'The Civic Survey of Edinburgh'

1911 *Evolution* (with J. Arthur Thomson)
1911 'Cities and Town-Planning Exhibition' (at Belfast, Chelsea, Dublin and Edinburgh)
1912 *Masque of Learning and Its Many Meanings: A Pageant of Education Through the Ages*
1913 *'L'Exposition internationale comparée des villes'* (Ghent)
1914 'Problems of the War'
1914 *Sex* (with J. Arthur Thomson)
1915 *Cities in Evolution - An Introduction to the Town Planning Movement and to the Study of Civics*
1915-17 Town Planning Reports on Cities in the Madras Presidency; also Balrampur, Baroda, Dacca, Kanchrapara, Jubbulpore, Karputhala, Lahore, Lucknow, Nagpur
1917 'Making of the Future Series': *The Coming Polity* (with Victor Branford), *Ideas at War* (with Gilbert Slater)
1918 *Town Planning Towards City Development* (two-volume Indore Report)
1919 'Jerusalem Actual and Possible' (Report to the Military Governor)
1919 *Our Social Inheritance* (with Victor Branford)
1920 *An Indian Pioneer: The Life and Work of J.C. Bose*
1921 'Palestine in Renewal'
1922 *Town Planning in Patiala State and City*
1923 *Dramatisations of History* (reprints of *Masques of Learning*)
1924 'The Mapping of Life'
1925 *Biology* (with J. Arthur Thomson) - 'Talks from My Outlook Tower'
1926 *The Making of Our Coal Future* (i.e. Great Britain's)
1927 'The Village World: Actual and Possible'
1929 'Rural and Urban Thought'
1930 'Ways of Transition - Towards Constructive Peace'
1931 *Life: Outlines of General Biology* (with J. Arthur Thomson)

B PUBLICATIONS OF PATRICK GEDDES

'Analysis of the Principles of Economics, An', *Proceedings of the Royal Society of Edinburgh*, XII (1884), pp. 943-80; reprint, London, Williams & Norgate, 1885.
'Biological Approach, A' (with J.A. Thomson), in *Ideals of Science and Faith*, ed. J.E. Hand. London, George Allen, 1904.
Biology (with J.A. Thomson). London, Williams & Norgate; New York, Henry Holt, 1925 (Home University Library, No. 111).
'Burns, The Homes of', *The Living Age*, 18 October 1913, pp. 166-72.
'Carlyle' ('The Homes and Haunts of Famous Authors, No. 8'), *The Weekly Leader*, 28 August 1902, pp. 341-2. See also 'Early Homes and Haunts of Carlyle'.
Chambers's Encyclopaedia. London and Edinburgh, W. & R. Chambers, rev. edn, 1888-92. Articles by Patrick Geddes on agave, algae, aloe, aquatic plants, aquatic animals, bark, bast, biology, botany, branch, bud, cycads, Darwinian theory, evolution, ferns, flower, fruit, fungi, leaf, etc.
Chapters in Modern Botany. London, John Murray; New York, Charles Scribner, 1893 (University Extension *Manuals*, ed. Professor Knight).

'Charting of Life, The', *Sociological Review*, XIX (January 1927),
   pp. 40-63.
'Chelsea, Past and Possible', *Sociological Review* (1 October 1908).
   pp. 357-63;   reprint, London, Sherratt & Hughes, 7 pp.   See also
   in Hollins, Dorothea, *Utopian Papers*.   London, Masters, 1908,
   pp. 6-16.
'Chlorophylle animale et la physiologie des planaires vertes',
   Archives de Zoologie expérimentale et générale (Paris, 1879),
   vol. 8, pp. 51-8.
'Cities and the Soils They Grow From', see 'Talks from My Outlook
   Tower'.
Cities and Town-planning Exhibition, 1911.   Edinburgh, 13 March-
   1 April, Hutchinson, 76 pp. (guide book & catalogue);   also
   Dublin, 24 May-7 June, Browne & Nolan, 61 pp. and Belfast, 23
   July-2 August.
*Cities in Evolution: An Introduction to the Town Planning Movement
   and to the Study of Civics*.   London, Williams & Norgate, 1915.
   Reprinted: 1949, Williams & Norgate, London, Intro. by Jaqueline
   Tyrwhitt & Arthur Geddes;   1968, Ernest Benn, London, Intro. by
   Percy Johnson-Marshall;   1969, Fertig, Harrow, NY;   1971, Torch-
   book Edition, Harper & Row, NY, Intro by Pierre Clavel;   1972,
   Rutgers University Press;   Italian translation *Città in Evolu-
   zione*, Il Saggiatore, Milan, 1970, Intro. by Carlo Carozzi.
'City Deterioration and the Need of City Survey', *The Annals of the
   American Academy of Political and Social Science*,   XXXIV (July
   1909), pp. 54-67.
*City Development: A Study of Parks, Gardens, and Culture Insti-
   tutes: A Report to the Carnegie Dunfermline Trust*.   Edinburgh,
   P.G. & Colleagues, 1904.   Reprinted by the Irish University Press,
   Shannon, 1973, Intro. by Peter Green with detailed account of Car-
   negie Trustee's reaction to P.G.'s plans;   also Rutgers University
   Press, 1973.   (Has good account of Trustees' reactions.)
City Surveys for Town Planning.   London, *J. of Royal Institute
   Public Health*, 19 February, pp. 79-90;   reprint, Edinburgh, 1911,
   P.G. & Colleagues, 12 pp.
'Civic Education and City Development', *Contemporary Review*
   (London), LXXXVII (March 1905), pp. 413-26.
'Civics: as Applied Sociology', *Sociological Papers* (London), I
   (1905), pp. 103-38.
'Civics: as Concrete and Applied Sociology, Part II' (continuation
   of preceding article), *Sociological Papers* (London), II (1906),
   pp. 57-119.
'Civic Survey of Edinburgh, The', *Transactions of the Town Planning
   Conference, October, 1910*, pp. 537-74;   reprint, Edinburgh, The
   Outlook Tower, 1911.
'Classification of Statistics and Its Results, The', *Proceedings of
   the Royal Society of Edinburgh*, XI (1881), pp. 295-322;   reprint,
   Edinburgh, A. & C. Black, 1881.   In condensed form in *Nature*
   (London), XXIV, 29 September 1881.
Coal Crisis and the Future, The (with Victor Branford and others).
   'Introduction: A National Transition', by P.G.   London, Williams
   & Norgate, 1926 ('The Making of the Future' series).
Coming Polity, The (with Victor Branford).   London, Williams & Nor-
   gate, 1917.   New edition, Le Play House Press, 1919 ('The Making
   of the Future' series).

Conditions of Progress of the Capitalist and of the Labourer.
'Claims of Labour' Lectures, no. 3.   Edinburgh, Co-operative
Printing Company, 1886.
Co-operation versus Socialism.   Manchester, Co-operative Printing
Society, 1888.
'Cyprus, Actual and Possible: A Study in the Eastern Question',
Contemporary Review (London), LXXII (June 1897), pp. 892-908.
Dramatisations of History.   Bombay, Modern Publishing Company,
1923.   Edinburgh, P.G. & Colleagues, 1923 (reprints of Masques
of Ancient, Mediaeval, and Modern Learning).
'Early Homes and Haunts of Carlyle', *Oxford and Cambridge Review*,
No. 8 (Michaelmas Term, 1909), pp. 11-17.
'Edinburgh and Its Region, Geographic and Historical', *Scottish
Geographical Magazine*, XVIII (June 1902), pp. 302-12.
'Educational Approach, An', in *Ideals of Science and Faith*, ed.
J.E. Hand.   London, George Allen, 1904.
Education in Return to Life.   Bombay, Govind, 1924, 31 pp.
'Education for Economics and Citizenship', Manchester, Co-operative
Printing Society, 1895.
'Education of Two Boys, The'.   See 'Talks from My Outlook Tower'.
Encyclopaedia Britannica, 9th ed.   Edinburgh, A. & C. Black, 1875-
89.   Articles by Patrick Geddes on insectivorous plants, man-
grove, manioc, mimosa, millet, morphology, parasitism, proto-
plasm, reproduction, sex, variation and selection, etc.
'Essentials of Sociology in Relation to Economics', *Indian Journal
of Economics* (Allahabad), III (July 1920; October 1922), pp. 1-
56, 257-305.
Evergreen, The: A Northern Seasonal.   Edited and contributed to by
P.G.   Vol. I (1895), *Spring*; Vol. II (1895), *Autumn*; Vol. III
(1896), *Summer*; Vol. IV (1896), *Winter*.   Edinburgh, P.G. &
Associates.
Every Man His Own Art Critic at the Manchester Exhibition.   Man-
chester, Heywood, 1887.
Every Man His Own Art Critic (Glasgow Exhibition).   Edinburgh,
Brown (1888), 58 pp.
Evolution (with J.A. Thomson), London, Williams & Norgate; New
York, Holt, & London, Butterworth (1912), 256 pp.
Evolution of Sex, The (with J.A. Thomson).   London, Scott, 1889.
New York, Humboldt, 1890; reprint of 1901 edn by AMS Press, New
York, forthcoming.
First Visit to the Outlook Tower, A.   Edinburgh, P.G. & Associates,
1906.
'Graphic Methods, Ancient and Modern, A Note on', *Sociological Re-
view* (London), XV (July 1923), pp. 227-35.
'Huxley as Teacher', *Nature* (London), CXV (9 May 1925), pp. 740-3
(special supplement on Huxley's centenary).
Ideas at War (with G. Slater).   London, Williams & Norgate, 1917;
reprint by Kelley, Clifton, NJ, forthcoming.
'In an Old Scots City', *Contemporary Review* (London), LXXXIII
(April 1903), pp. 559-68.
Indian Pioneer, An: The Life and Work of Sir J.C. Bose.   London
and New York, Longmans, Green, 1920.   (German translation, *Leben
und Werk von Sir J.C. Bose*, Erlenbach, Zurich, 1930.)   Well organised and clearly written, this biography is still giving

impetus to the tardy world recognition of Bose's achievements in
psycho-physics - ranging from publication of Bose's work in the
USSR to inclusion of a credible section on Bose, closely parallel-
ing Geddes's book, in the 'biology-thriller' by Peter Tompkins and
Christopher Bird, *The Secret Life of Plants*, Penguin, 1975.

Industrial Exhibitions and Modern Progress.   Reprinted from 'Industries', Edinburgh, David Douglas, 1887.

'John Ruskin, as Economist', *International Quarterly*, I (March
1900), pp. 280-308 (a shortened version of the 1884 article,
listed immediately below).

John Ruskin Economist.   Edinburgh, W. Brown, 1884; also published
in the 'Round Table Series', as no. 3.   Edinburgh, W. Brown,
1887.

Life: Outlines of General Biology (with J.A. Thomson), 2 vols.
London, Williams & Norgate; New York, Harper, 1931.

'Making of the Future' Series, ed. Patrick Geddes and Victor Branford.   London, Williams & Norgate and Le Play House Press.   See
individual titles, such as *The Coming Polity, Ideas at War, Our
Social Inheritance.*

'Making of Our Coal Future, The', *Sociological Review* (London),
XVIII (July 1926), pp. 178-85; reprint, *Coal: Ways to Reconstruction*, London, Le Play House Press, 1926.

'Man and His Environment - A Study from the Paris Exposition',
International Monthly, II (August 1900), pp. 169-95.

'Mapping of Life, The', *Sociological Review*, XVI (July 1924), pp.
193-203.

*Masque of Learning and Its Many Meanings, The: A Pageant of Educa-
tion through the Ages.*   Edinburgh, P.G. & Colleagues, 1912.

'Nature Study and Geographical Education', *Scottish Geographical
Magazine*, XVIII (October 1902), pp. 525-35.

'On the Classification of Statistics and Its Results', *Proceedings
of the Royal Society of Edinburgh*, IX (1881); reprint, Edinburgh,
A. & C. Black, 1881.

'Our City of Thought'.   See 'Talks from My Outlook Tower'.

Our Social Inheritance (with Victor Branford).   London, Williams &
Norgate, 1919.   Le Play House Press, 1919.   ('The Making of the
Future' series.)

Outlines of General Biology.   See *Life: Outlines of General Biology.*

'Palestine in Renewal', *Contemporary Review* (London), CXX (October
1921), pp. 475-84.

'Projet de conservation de la Rue des Nations', Paris, *Bulletin
Universel des Congres* I (December 1901), pp. 31-7.

'Proposed Co-ordination of the Social Sciences, ', *Sociological
Review*, 16 January, pp. 54-65.

'Re-statement of the Cell Theory, a', *Proc. Royal Soc. Edinburgh*,
1883, vol. 12, pp. 266-92; reprint, Edinburgh, Neill, 1884, 27
pp.

'Rural and Urban Thought: A Contribution to the Theory of Progress
and Decay', *Sociological Review* (London), XXI (January 1929),
pp. 1-19.

Ruskin, John.   See 'John Ruskin, as Economist'.

'School at Abbotsholme, Conducted by Dr. Cecil Reddie', *Elementary
School Teacher* (Chicago), V (February, March 1905), pp. 321-33,
396-407.

'Schoolboy's Bag and a City's Pageant, A'.   See 'Talks from My Out-
    look Tower'.
'Scottish University Needs and Aims', *Scots Magazine* (Dundee), Aug-
    ust 1890; reprint, Perth, Cowan, 1890.
Sex (with J.A. Thomson).   London, Williams & Norgate, 1914;   New
    York, Henry Holt (Home University Library, No. 85).
'Suggested Plan for a Civic Museum, A', *Sociological Papers*
    (London), III (1906), pp. 197-249.
'Summer in an Old Scots Garden', *Living Age* (Boston), CCLIV (Septem-
    ber 1907), pp. 620-6.
'Talks from My Outlook Tower', *Survey Graphic* (New York):
    'Schoolboy's Bag and a City's Pageant, A', LIII (February 1925),
    pp. 525-9, 553-4.
    'Cities and the Soils They Grow From', LIV (April 1925), pp.
    40-4.
    'Valley Plan of Civilization, The', LIV (June 1925), pp. 288-90,
    322.
    'Valley in the Town, The', LIV (July 1925), pp. 396-400, 415-16.
    (The June and July 'Talks' are reprinted, somewhat abridged, in
    the *Architect's Yearbook*, No. 12 (1968), pp. 65-71.)
    'Our City of Thought', LIV (August 1925), pp. 487-90, 504-7.
    'Education of Two Boys',The', LIV (September 1925), pp. 571-5,
    587-91.
'Temple Cities, The; a town planning lecture'.   Calcutta, *Modern
    Rev.*, 25 (1919), pp. 213-22.
Town Planning Reports (India):
    'Aden, a report to the government of Bombay'.   Bombay, Gov't
    Central Press, 15 pp., 1919.
    'Balrampur, a report to the Maharajah Bahadur'.   Lucknow,
    Murray's, fol., 80 pp.. + 6 plans, 1917.
    'Dacca, report on'.   Calcutta, Bengal Secretariat Book Depôt,
    fol., 21 pp. + 1 plan, 1917.
    'Jubbulpore, a report to the Municipal Committee' (with H.V.
    Lanchester), Jubbulpore, Hitkarini Press, fol., 10 pp., 1917.
    'Karpurthala'.   Lucknow, Murray's, fol., 38 pp. (report to the
    Maharajah), 1917.
    'Lahore, a report to the Municipal Council'.   Lahore, Commercial
    Ptg Works, fol., 44 pp., 1917.
    'Lucknow: A Report to the Municipal Council'.   Lucknow,
    Murray's, 1916.
    'Model Colony at Kanchrapara, report on'.   Eastern Bengal Rail-
    way Press, fol., 14 pp., 1917.
    'Nagpur, a report to the Municipal Council'.   Nagpur, Municipal
    Press, fol., 17 pp., 1917.
*Town Planning toward City Development: A Report to the Durbar of
    Indore*, 2 vols.   Indore, Holkar State Press, 1918.
Universities in Europe and in India.   Madras, National Press, 40
    pp. (5 letters to an Indian friend, reprinted from *Pioneer*, 14
    August 1901 & *East and West*, September 1903.)
'Valley in the Town, The'.   See 'Talks from My Outlook Tower'.
'Valley Plan of Civilization, The'.   See 'Talks from My Outlook
    Tower'.
'Wardom and Peacedom: Suggestions towards an Interpretation', *Soc-
    iological Review* (London), VIII (January 1915), pp. 15-25.

'Ways of Transition - Towards Constructive Peace', *Sociological Review* (London), XXII (January, April 1930), pp. 1-31, 136-41.
World Without and the World Within, The (Sunday Talks with My Children). London, George Allen, 1905.

C BOOKS AND ARTICLES ON PATRICK GEDDES OR HIS WORK

ABERCROMBIE, PATRICK, see Defries, Amelia.
ABERCROMBIE, PATRICK, *Town and Country Planning*. London, Butterworth, 1933, 225 pp. (22-3, 103, 128-9).
ASHBEE, C.R., *Jerusalem, 1918-20 and 1920-22*. London, Murray, 1921, 87 pp.; 1924, 109 pp. (records of Pro-Jerusalem Council; re: P.G., I: 12-23, II: 15-16).
BARKER, MABEL, *L'Utilisation du milieu géographique pour l'éducation*. Montpellier, Librairie Nouvelle, 1926. Réédition, Paris, Flammarion, 1931.
BOARDMAN, PHILIP, 'Esquisse de l'Oeuvre éducatrice de Patrick Geddes', Montpellier, Imprimerie de la Charité, 1936 (doctoral thesis).
BOARDMAN, PHILIP, *Patrick Geddes: Maker of the Future,* Chapel Hill, University of North Carolina Press, 1944. (First systematic biography of P.G., but weakened by a semi-fictional chapter 4.)
BRANFORD, VICTOR, *Interpretations and Forecasts,* London, Duckworth, 1914.
BRANFORD, VICTOR, *Citizen Soldier, A: His Education for War and Peace - Being a Memoir of Alasdair Geddes*. London, Headley Brothers, 1917.
BRANFORD, VICTOR, *Whitherward? Hell or Eutopia*. London, Williams & Norgate, 1921.
BRANFORD, VICTOR, *Living Religions*. London, Williams & Norgate, 1924.
CAROZZI, CARLO, Introduction to *Città in Evolzione*, 1970 (see p. 3).
CARTER, HUNTLY, 'The Garden of Geddes', *The Forum,* LIV (October, November 1915), pp. 455-71, 588-95.
CLAVEL, PIERRE, Introduction to reprint of *Cities in Evolution* (see p. 3).
DEFRIES, AMELIA, *The Interpreter Geddes: The Man and His Gospel*. London, Routledge, 1927; New York, Boni & Liveright, 1928. (Contains a Foreword by Rabindranath Tagore, an Introduction by Israel Zangwell, and appreciations by Lewis Mumford, J. Arthur Thomson, Patrick Abercrombie, H.V. Lanchester, and C. Setalvad. A valuable source-book of authentic conversations with Geddes, despite partly jumbled sequences.)
FERREIRA, J.V. and JHA, S.S. (eds), *The Outlook Tower - Essays on Urbanization in memory of Patrick Geddes*, Bombay, Popular Prakashan, 1976. (Includes reprint of 'The Temple Cities.')
FLEURE, H.J., 'Patrick Geddes (1854-1932)', *Sociological Review*, ns, vol. 1 (December 1953), pp. 5-13.
GARDINER, A.G., 'Patrick Geddes', in *Pillars of Society*. London, J.M. Dent, 1913, pp. 128-34.
GLIKSON, ARTUR, 'The Planner Geddes', *News Sheet,* International Federation for Housing and Town Planning, The Hague, May 1955.

GOIST, PARK DIXON, 'Patrick Geddes and the City', *American Institute of Planners Journal,* vol. 40, no. 1 (January 1974), pp. 31-7.

GREEN, PETER, Introduction to reprint of *City Development* ... .

JHA, S.S., see Ferreira.

JOHNSON-MARSHALL, PERCY, Introduction to reprint of *Cities in Evolution* (see p. 3).

KELMAN, JOHN, *The Interpreter's House: The Ideals Embodied in the Outlook Tower.* Edinburgh, Oliphant, Anderson & Ferrier, 1905, 35 pp.

KITCHEN, PADDY, *A Most Unsettling Person - An Introduction to the Ideas and Life of Patrick Geddes,* Gollancz, London, 1975. (Very good factual account of P.G.'s unsettled life and unsettling effect on various establishments for general readers. Scholars would have appreciated fuller references to certain sources.)

LESSER, WENDY, 'Patrick Geddes: The Practical Visionary', *Town Planning Review,* Liverpool University, vol. 45, no. 3 (July 1974), pp. 311-27.

MAIRET, PHILIP, *Pioneer of Sociology - The Life and Letters of Patrick Geddes,* Lund Humphries, London, 1957. (Excellent short biography emphasising P.G.'s work in sociology.)

MCGEGAN, EDWARD, 'Geddes as a Man of Action', *Sociological Review* (London), XXIV (October 1932), pp. 355-7.

MCGEGAN, EDWARD, 'Sir Patrick Geddes', *Scottish Bookman* (Edinburgh), I (December 1935), pp. 99-106.

MCGEGAN, EDWARD, GEDDES, ARTHUR and MEARS, F.C., 'The Life and Work of Sir Patrick Geddes', *Journal of the Town-Planning Institute* (London), XXVI (September, October 1940), pp. 189-95.

MACKAYE, BENTON, *The New Exploration.* New York, Harcourt, Brace, 1928.

MACKAYE, BENTON, *From Geography to Geotechnics,* University of Illinois Press, 1968.

MACKRELL, ALICE, 'Register of the Papers of Professor Sir Patrick Geddes', University of Strathclyde, Dept of Urban and Regional Planning, June 1970.

MANN, WILLIAM W., 'Ave et Vale: A Geddesian Odyssey', *News Sheet,* International Federation for Housing and Town Planning, The Hague, February 1956.

MAVOR, JAMES, 'My Windows on the Street of the World', London & Toronto, J.M. Dent; New York, E.P. Dutton, 1923.

MAYER, GLADYS, 'New Ways of Thinking About Social Problems', Threefold Commonwealth Research Group, 35 Park Road, London, NW1 (c. 1936). (Comparison of Goethe, Geddes and Rudolf Steiner.)

MELLER, HELEN E., 'Patrick Geddes: An Analysis of His Theory of Civics, 1880-1904', *Victorian Studies,* Indiana University, vol. 16, no. 3 (March 1973), pp. 291-315.

MUKERJEE, R., *Foundations of Indian Economics.* London, Longmans, Green, 1916 (Introduction by Patrick Geddes).

MUMFORD, LEWIS, see Defries, Amelia.

MUMFORD, LEWIS, 'Patrick Geddes, Insurgent', *New Republic,* LX (30 October 1929), pp. 295-6.

MUMFORD, LEWIS, *Technics and Civilization.* New York, Harcourt, Brace, 1934.

MUMFORD, LEWIS, *The Culture of Cities.* New York, Harcourt, Brace, 1938.

MUMFORD, LEWIS, *The Condition of Man*.   New York, Harcourt, Brace,
   1944.
MUMFORD, LEWIS, 'Patrick Geddes', *Architectural Review*, August 1950;
   reprinted in *The Human Prospect*, ed. H.T. Moore and K.W. Deutsch,
   Southern Illinois University Press, 1965, pp. 99-114.
MUMFORD, LEWIS, 'The Disciple's Rebellion', *Encounter*, London, Sep-
   tember 1966, pp. 11-21.
NEILL, R.M., 'Seeing Life Whole', *Contemporary Review*, vol. 141
   (June 1932), pp. 715-24.
PEACOCK, A.D., 'Patrick Geddes: Biologist', *Alumnus Chronicle*, St
   Andrews University, October 1954.
PEPLER, SIR GEORGE L., 'The Regional Planner' (Tribute to Geddes),
   Sociological Review, October 1932, p. 382.
REILLY, JOHN P., 'The Early Social Thought of Patrick Geddes' (doc-
   toral thesis), Columbia University, New York, 1972.
SETALVAD, SIR CHIMANLAL, see Defries, Amelia.
STALLEY, MARSHALL (ed.), *Patrick Geddes: Spokesman for Man and the
   Environment* (includes reprint of *Cities in Evolution*), New Bruns-
   wick, NJ, Rutgers University Press, 1973.
STEVENSON, W.I., 'Patrick Geddes and Geography: Bibliographical
   Study', University College, London, Occasional Paper no. 27,
   March 1975.   (A valuable account of P.G.'s influence on geo-
   graphers C.B. Fawcett, H.J. Fleure, Marcel Hardy, A.J. Herbertson,
   and his own son Arthur.)
TAGORE, RABINDRANATH, see Defries, Amelia.
THOMSON, J. ARTHUR, see Defries, Amelia.
'Tributes to the Late Sir Patrick Geddes, A Sheaf of', *Sociological
   Review* (London), XXIV (October 1932), pp. 349-400.
TYRWHITT, JAQUELINE, Introduction to reprint of *Cities in Evolution*
   (see p. 3).
TYRWHITT, JAQUELINE, *Patrick Geddes in India*, Lund Humphries,
   London, 1947.
TYRWHITT, JAQUELINE and BELL, GWEN (eds), *Human Identity in the
   Urban Environment*, Penguin Books, 1972.   (See Introduction, pp.
   15-37, for comparison of grids of Geddes, Le Corbusier and
   Doxiadis.)
WARD, COLIN, 'The Outlook Tower, Edinburgh: prototype for an Urban
   Studies Centre', *Bulletin of Environmental Education*, London,
   December 1973.
WEIZMANN, CHAIM, *Trial and Error*, autobiography, London, Hamish
   Hamilton, 1949.
WHEELER, KEITH, 'Note on the Valley Section of Patrick Geddes',
   Bulletin of Environmental Education, London, January 1974.
ZANGWILL, ISRAEL, see Defries, Amelia.
ZUEBLIN, CHARLES, 'The World's First Sociological Laboratory', *Amer-
   ican Journal of Sociology* (Chicago), IV (March 1899), pp. 577-92.

INDEX

509